GENDER-BASED

VIOLENCE

IN THE

CARIBBEAN

GENDER-BASED VIOLENCE IN THE CARIBBEAN

HISTORICAL ROOTS, CONTEMPORARY CONTINUITIES

EDITED BY

DALEA BEAN AND **VERENE A. SHEPHERD**

UWI PRESS
The University of the West Indies Press
Mona • St Augustine • Cave Hill • Global • Five Islands

The University of the West Indies Press
7A Gibraltar Hall Road, Mona
Kingston 7, Jamaica
www.uwipress.com

A catalogue record of this book is available from the
National Library of Jamaica.

ISBN: 978-976-658-028-5 (paperback)
978-976-658-029-2 (ePUB)

Cover image: "Strive" by Evadey Kerr; photographed by Aston Spaulding
Cover and book design by Robert Harris
Set in Scala 10.5/15 x 24.

This book acknowledges funding from UKRI Project AH/T006951/1.

Printed in the United States of America

TO THOSE WHO STRIVE

Contents

Section 6: Activism for Change: Reflections and Perspectives

List of Tables and Figures

LIST OF TABLES

LIST OF FIGURES

Abbreviations and Acronyms

AWID	Association for Women's Rights in Development
BCC	Bahamas Christian Council
BET	Black Entertainment Television
BPW	Business and Professional Women's Club
BWIR	British West Indies Regiment
CADV	Coalition Against Domestic Violence
CAFRA	Caribbean Association for Feminist Research and Action
CariMAN	Caribbean Male Action Network
CAPRI	Caribbean Policy Research Institute
CARICOM	Caribbean Community
CATT	Children's Authority of Trinidad and Tobago
CBC	Canadian Broadcasting Corporation
CCPG	Coalition for Community Participation in Governance
CDW	Committee for the Development of Women
CEDAW	Convention on the Elimination of All Forms of Discrimination Against Women
CGDS	Centre for Gender and Development Studies
CPDC	Caribbean Policy Development Centre
CSO	civil society organization
CWP	Committee of Women for Progress [Jamaica]
CWP	Concerned Women for Progress [Trinidad and Tobago]
DAWN	Development Alternatives with Women for a New Era
DV	domestic violence
DVSSHSG	Domestic Violence Survivors Self-Help Support Group
ECLAC	Economic Commission for Latin America and the Caribbean
EIGE	European Institute for Gender Equality
FBO	faith-based organization

FEB	Friedrich Ebert Stiftung (Friedrich Ebert Foundation)
FGD	focus group discussion
FPATT	Family Planning Association of Trinidad and Tobago
GBV	gender-based violence
GD	gender discrimination
GDI	Gender Development Index
GNC	gender non-conforming
GSHS	Global School-Based Student Health Survey
GTU	Guyana Trans United
GWAR	Grassroots Women Across Race
HATT	Housewives Association of Trinidad and Tobago
HDI	Human Development Index
HFLE	Health and Family Life Education
IDB	Inter-American Development Bank
IGDS	Institute for Gender and Development Studies
ILO	International Labour Organization
IWY	International Women's Year
J-FLAG	Jamaica Forum for Lesbians, All Sexuals and Gays
JWA	Jamaica Women's Assembly
LGBTQ	lesbian, gay, bisexual, transgender and queer
MAP	Men Against Patriarchy
MOP	Men Opposing Patriarchy
NGO	non-governmental organization
NOW	National Organisation of Women
NRSV	New Revised Standard Version
OECS	Organisation of Eastern Caribbean States
ONS	Office for National Statistics
OWP	Organisation of Women for Progress
PAHO	Pan American Health Organization
PIOJ	Planning Institute of Jamaica
PPP	People's Political Party

SASOD	Society Against all Forms of Sexual Orientation Discrimination
SID	Small island developing states
SRHR	sexual and reproductive health and rights
STATIN	Statistical Institute of Jamaica
STI	sexually transmitted infection
SV	sexual violence
TPP	Ten Point Plan for Reparatory Justice
TTPS	Trinidad and Tobago Police Service
UNFPA	United Nations Population Fund
UNIA	Universal Negro Improvement Association
UNIFEM	United Nations Development Fund for Women
UNODC	United Nations Office on Drugs and Crime
VAW	violence against women (and girls)
WAB	Women's Affairs Bureau
WAND	Women and Development Unit
WE	Women's Empowerment Group
WHO	World Health Organization
WID	Women in Development
WLC	Women's Liberal Club
WLL	Workers Liberation League
WMW	Women's Media Watch
WPA	Working People's Alliance
WPJ	Workers Party of Jamaica
WROC	Women's Resource and Outreach Centre

Foreword

Diana J. Fox

AS A FEMINIST SCHOLAR-ACTIVIST OF GLOBAL MOVEMENTS FOR gender justice, I was deeply moved when the editors of this volume, Dr Dalea Bean and Professor Verene Shepherd, two icons of Caribbean feminist history, invited me to write the foreword to this much-needed contribution to the historical underpinnings of contemporary violence in the Caribbean. I grew up in a family of historians, and although I alone majored in anthropology and became an anthropologist, I was imbued with the critical perspective that history offers. In 1991, when I first came to Jamaica as a graduate student and lived in upper Clarendon parish in a rural community, one to which I have returned to over the decades, this lens opened me to the living history before me. On arrival at the Mona campus of The University of the West Indies (UWI) in 2004 on a Fulbright with the then Centre (now Institute) for Gender and Development Studies (CGDS), I became more deeply exposed to pioneering feminist research – much of it excavating the past through the lens of women's and gender histories – that was transforming the region's understanding of itself. This edited collection continues that pathbreaking scholarship, including works from both the trailblazers of Caribbean feminisms and subsequent generations. We must continually engage the present with the past, as this text reminds us. How we do that – the theoretical lens we invoke – unearths new ways of understanding that shape our everyday perspectives and equip us with the tools for transformation. *Gender-Based Violence in the Caribbean: Historical Roots, Contemporary Continuities* is a collection that fully appreciates and undertakes this work.

Well-researched narratives of the past and scholarly insights into the present draw readers into them, enlivening, challenging and provoking their own perceptions. For me, living in rural Jamaica throughout the 1990s, infused with my socialization into the feminist historical gaze, the space seemed to me fully entangled in stories of times gone by. These were not just of the recent past of the turbulent 1970s and 1980s, but a deeper past rendered into the present. Of course, the violence of the 1980s impacted people's perceptions of me – was I CIA? But I honed in especially on the frequent references to "Bible times" and "slavery times" in daily conversation, as if they were just around the temporal corner. And they were, in living consciousness, harnessed in various ways, often as warnings – threats, even; morality tales exhorting the avoidance of wickedness. From elders came also more recent nostalgic remembrances of times gone by: of children travelling on donkeys to school or in donkey-pulled carts to market; time spent with siblings, cousins; folk remedies for the sick. Childhood stories often turned to sanctions exerted, and, as I listened, having grown up in a liberal, children's rights-oriented home, I was often shocked by the descriptions of corporeal punishments meted out to youngsters in matter-of-fact tones that belied their psychological ramifications. I often thought about how centuries of violence – through enslavement, resistance to enslavement, post-emancipation coloniality, independence struggles, and the contemporary imposition of neo-colonial corporate labor and wealth disparities – found their way into modes of disciplining children.

The past was, and is, inscribed in the Caribbean landscape – from the daily close presence of gravesites in yards, physical markers of living ancestors, enlivened in the stories that people told, sitting on porches in the evenings in the days before cell phones and televisions. The ruins of both tortured and resilient pasts are built into visual consciousness, in the crumbling, vine-ridden aqueducts and water wheels scattered throughout the countryside – the infrastructure of enslavement panoramically alive. This living visual and oral history became a bridge for me, from the past to the present, as I perceived contemporary violence and also witnessed it. I saw parents and grandparents beating children in public, unsure, at the time, how to intervene; I sometimes heard screams from domestic disputes filtering through the rural nighttime music of cicadas and frogs through shuttered windows – the absence of glass exposing the lives of neighbours – melding into the echoes of glorious church hymns, hand clapping, and gospel wafting from transistor radios, mixing with the bleating of goats and crowing of roosters. Sounds of violence mingled with those of worship, love, laughter, nature.

When the all-night dancehalls from the town square drowned out everything else, tired ladies on Sunday mornings, baffled by the phenomenon, gritted their teeth and went to church. In the 2010s, other forms of violence arrived in this rural community via gangs, contributing to the mélange. Once, returning home from the town, I witnessed a stabbing in front of a rum bar. Peace was recently restored to the community, I learned, through vigilante violence. Those gang members are no more. These ethnographic reflections spanning three decades underscore a key insight of this volume: scholarship has a responsibility to disentangle the past from the present, harnessing the feminist insight that social location and positionality are ever important in conditioning perspective and shaping experience.

Other crucial contributions of this text are the implications of these perspectives – how can they empower and exert influence? The volume brings together an enormous range of writers, many of whom have been formative in the creation of Caribbean feminist and gendered scholarship, advocacy, and policy initiatives from The UWI and the Institute for Gender and Development Studies (IGDS), and beyond. In this way, the text follows the tradition of edited collections emerging from the IGDS and other UWI institutes and faculties, underscoring the community of gender scholars birthed by Caribbean feminisms. Intellectually, the collection also demonstrates how the gender lens is one of relationality; that is, lives are constructed and lived in relationship to other lives. In turn, they are imbued by power dynamics built through ideologies concretized in law and in social, religious, economic, political and educational institutions; and meted out in social norms, beliefs and value systems. As these are explicated in the volume, we come to a deeper understanding of the violence, in its many forms, which has become endemic to Caribbean life, and how these webs of relationships became systematized. Yet, critically, they also embody contradictions, opening cracks both for daily negotiations and multiple forms of refusals.

The volume also highlights the complex diversity of the region through social class, ethnicity, race, religion, nationality, disability, sexuality and culture – demonstrating how such heterogeneity is implicated in gendered violence, whether between white upper-class British and black women; white women and white men; or white and black men; LGBTQ experiences of precarity set against normative heterosexuality, and so many more examples.

Both Dalea Bean and Verene Shepherd – and the many distinguished authors whose chapters fill this volume – have built a *his*story/*her*story/*their*story of the Caribbean region by mining the archives and contemporary sources through a gendered historiography. They have culled details to construe narratives from court records, literature, newspapers, film, music of the region, and other sources, analyzing and directing our attention to new readings of the past that explode any attempt to simplify, homogenize or reduce.

In doing so, Bean and Shepherd respond to a pressing need, filling a lacuna in this landmark collection, a rich bricolage of the region. The editors mobilize the chapters toward a larger cause: transforming the present crisis of gender-based violence. Shepherd's opening chapter, "Gender-Based Violence in the Caribbean: Historical Roots", addresses the central and timely question framing the volume: what circumstances in Caribbean history created the conditions for gender-based violence (GBV), such that it has long been an endemic part of everyday life in the region?

We must be able to respond to this question not with uncertain references to a vague past, but with the kind of concreteness afforded by historical specificity. There is a contemporary crisis, exacerbated by the COVID-19 pandemic, rising inequalities, climate emergencies and species extinction – all forms of violence that influence human behaviour. The crisis persists, despite many changing conditions, including robust legislative agendas and national plans that seek to arrest the phenomenon of GBV; interventions from multilateral lending institutions, various UN agencies and a panoply of civil society organizations (CSOs) and non-governmental organizations (NGOs) conducting studies and implementing projects. What are the continuities that Caribbean societies have sustained and how have they become so embedded in cultural norms, beliefs and value systems? This text tackles these questions, yet offers hope that, despite the prevalence and persistence of GBV regionally, the efforts of changemakers will be enhanced through this collection. It is precisely this kind of archaeology of knowledge – a re-reading of the archive through a gendered lens – that engenders a more sophisticated understanding.

We learn of the distinct strategies deployed to shape variously women's and men's lived experiences of coloniality across both gender and its intersectional dimensions. This includes the lives of the region's First Peoples – a decolonial theoretical framework accompanies the text and helps to constitute this volume. Many of the stories are painful: reading about cruel and unjust acts fuelled by power, hatred and twisted ideas is agonizing. Other narratives detail acts of bravery and resistance. Just as Black Power movements across the region – in alliance with the black radical intellectual tradition – have sought to reverse deeply entrenched ideologies of racism that stymie psyches in self-doubt and self-hatred, so, too, do movements toward women's and gender equality, powered by Caribbean feminist scholarship, build on legacies found across the region. Caribbean gendered histories tell us newly illuminated stories of the past that are also records of survival and legacies of agency that can help to reconfigure a sense of dignity and identity in the present.

INTRODUCTION

"Decolonization Never Takes Place Unnoticed"[1]

An Introduction to the Past and Future Project of Understanding and Ending Gender-Based Violence

DALEA BEAN AND VERENE A. SHEPHERD

IN JAMAICA IN 1971, AS PART OF HER RADIO MONOLOGUE "Miss Lou's Views", Louise Bennett, Jamaican cultural matriarch, delivered commentary on the fictional Wife-Beating Assessment Bill. We are told that on All Fool's Day, the radio programme "Man in the Street" canvassed the views of regular Jamaicans on the Bill and to Miss Lou's surprise, women in particular, shouted their disapproval of wife beating and longing for harsh sentences for perpetrators. The mere existence of the monologue, aired on public radio as part of Miss Lou's social commentary, indicates the normalization of wife beating in the immediate post-independence era.

With no legislative framework yet in place for addressing gendered violence, the people used voices and bodies to oppose oppressions and to fill gaps left by colonial blind eyes. The roots of decolonial stances on gendered violence were to be found in the colloquial and the ordinary: "Prison dem yes! Lock up the advantage tecker-dem! . . . no man shouldn be able fi lik him wife at all widout Authority lock dem eena prison!" (Bennett 1993, 76–77). ["Put them in prison, yes! Lock up the advantage takers! . . . no man should be able to lick his wife at all without the authorities putting them in prison!"]

What sweet Miss Lou was "fi see how dem tek it serious" (Bennett 1993, 76) when little serious governmental thought was given to the perennial problem of violence against women and girls. Since the 1970s the region has treated the issue of gender-based violence (GBV) with more seriousness, with anti-violence conventions and legislative frameworks, policy development, community interventions, donor-funded research and rich scholarship.

Globally, the manifestations of GBV are many. Undergirded by deeply entrenched, harmful gender norms and asymmetries of power, GBV is directed against a person because of these culturally informed mores (CEDAW 2017). Traditionally understood as violence against women and girls perpetrated by men, nuanced research has implored us to think of GBV in intersecting ways, rather than in a binary mode. Violence against women and girls is often central to such intersections (Trotz 2004; Biholar 2013; Robinson 2004; DeShong 2018), but GBV also includes state and interpersonal violence against men and boys, LGBTQ+ and non-binary persons (Gayle 2018; Robinson 2011; Haynes and DeShong 2017; Alexander 1994). As Biholar (2022, 1) reminds us, these include actions as well as omissions that are intended or likely to cause death, physical, sexual, psychological, economic or social harm. Recent perspectives of Caribbean men and boys, both as perpetrators of violence and as key allies in the fight for permanent solutions, have also been refreshing additions to the scholarship (see Casey et al. 2017; Joseph and Jones 2023).

While it is difficult to distinguish between different types of violence, GBV includes domestic violence; sexual harassment; rape; sexual conflict and harmful customary or traditional practices; trafficking in women; forced prostitution; violations of human rights in armed conflict; forced sterilization; forced abortion; coercive use of contraceptives; female infanticide; and prenatal sex selection.

Despite attracting large and consistent funding from regional and international agencies for research and interventions,[2] an abysmal lack of amendments to the region's laws remain (particularly in addressing violence against persons with disabilities, gay, lesbian and transgender persons). UN Women Caribbean also indicates that globally at least one in three women is beaten, coerced into sex or otherwise abused by an intimate partner in the course of her lifetime.[3] On average, 46 per cent of women in five CARICOM countries – Suriname, Jamaica, Grenada, Guyana, and Trinidad and Tobago – have experienced at least one form of violence in her lifetime.[4] The United Nations Office on Drugs and Crime (UNODC) 2016 report indicates that the Caribbean has among the highest rates of total female homicide and intimate partner homicide compared to global trends (UNODC 2019). Complicating the matter further is that many intimate relationships continue during and after violence. In modern society, love is not inconsistent with violence; persons experience love and violence in the same body and in the same space (DeShong 2014, 104).

One is tempted to agree that violence against women and girls, in particular, is part of Caribbean men's "responsibility", as revealed by stories of lionheart women's lives compiled by Sistren and Honour Ford Smith (2005, xx). However, GBV is not as simple as a uni-directional power imbalance, where men dominate women, and the phenomenon did not appear in the contemporary period. The historiography of the region is replete with the grandiose scale of physical, psychological, sexual, economic, emotional and discursive violence. More than this, the dichotomous hierarchy between the human (white) and non-human (non-white) was central to the creation of violent colonial modernity in service of Wynter's (2003) man that is colonial, white, rational, human. As Lugones (2010, 743–44) explains her concept of the coloniality of gender, "Under the imposed gender framework, the bourgeois white Europeans were civilised; they were fully human (and) judging the colonised for their deficiencies from the point of view of the civilising mission justified enormous cruelty." The imperial/colonial disclaimer would read: *no humans were harmed in the making of this slavery*; allowing for unimaginable violence to be unleashed in service of humans. But the process to resist such dehumanization also required violence. In true Fanon (1963, 39) style, we celebrate those who reclaimed violence in a decided attempt to embody history in their own person, surging into forbidden quarters. Violence, therefore, is neither uncomplicated nor linear; not only colonial, but also decolonial. While gender is not the only factor to be studied in unpacking histories and continuities of violence, Bean (2022, 10) presses us to consider that the history of the region presents an important locus for the study of the inherently gendered nature of imperialism, colonization, the planation economy, forced systems of labour, and anti-colonial/decolonial movements.

The evidence is clear. Scholars like Mair (1974), Higman (1976), Bush (1990), Beckles (1999), Brodber (2004), Shepherd (2011), Morrisey (2021) and Patterson (2022) have spent entire careers wading through the region's history to ascertain the overlapping and intersecting ways in which gender served to buttress race as twin pillars of a rugged Caribbean identity. The more than fifteen million enslaved Africans trafficked to the Americas (Inikori and Engerman, 1992)[5] were not de-gendered bodies; within them existed gender norms and they contended with new and often conflicting gendered and racialized realities, which facilitated perverse punishments and fetishized violence. Hilary Beckles (2016, 29) perhaps said it best: "The violent sexual extraction of services from enslaved African women especially was first and foremost an attack upon them as humans and as females."

As is well known, the system of production in slave societies depended upon the successful subjugation of the enslaved body, largely through the use or threat of macabre punishment (Mair 2011, 223 and 225). Women and men were punished with similar implements or torture, but the gendered underpinnings were clear; men were often punished in ways to emasculate, undermine any notion of male authority, while women, as Bush (1993) confirms, were perceived as persistent offenders and as such, were punished on average more frequently than men. White women also punished with impunity and their treatment of black women was often indistinguishable from that of white men, as was recounted by Mary Prince (1831). While the entire plantation economy relied on violent coercion for its survival, strong traditions of wife-beating, women's inferiority and acceptable family violence accompanied European colonizers wherever they went. Amussen (1994, 71) indicates, for instance, that English law and custom held that man, as head of the household was expected to correct and guide his wife. Many African pre-colonial traditions accorded women high status and were less focused on family violence, but they also included examples of acceptable chastisement of wives (Rotimi 2007).

Political discourse around violence against women and girls was also nuanced by gender. Stipendiary magistrates' and abolitionists' discourse was often related to the female body since they regarded physical violence against women as a particularly insidious crime against humanity. The sight of naked, pregnant women being lashed within inches of their lives, while men were "flogged with the cat on their bare backs and shoulders only" (British and Foreign Anti-Slavery Society 1866) was much too much to bear for stipendiary magistrate H. Pringle. These gender-based punishments were also a convenient tool to undermine the masculinity of black men, who were often powerless to mitigate punishments and vile sexual access to black women. Patriarchal heteronormativity predominated the slave society, even to the extent that evidence of white men's sexual abuse of black men is merely a whisper in the archives. The site of anti-slavery discourse as well, black women's bodies were pulled and tugged in various political directions, as abolitionists told stories about the volitation of women's bodies when they wanted to convey the horrors of slavery.

The post-slavery era was perhaps even more fraught with gender-based contestations, as newly freed people, new bonded labourers and colonial structures grappled for power and etched out gendered identities under the umbrella of multiple patriarchies. As Patricia Mohammed (2011, 156) insists, for instance, at the end of the Indian indentureship period in the early twentieth century, three competing patriarchies bestraddled Trinidad and Tobago's social structure: that of the dominant whites, who controlled the state; creole/Afro and mixed patriarchy; and Indian patriarchy, with its own mix of Indian and creole understandings. Undoubtedly, various factors contributed to upholding and challenging these overlapping systems of dominance, but it is clear that women and subordinated masculinities suffered violence at the hands of each type of patriarchy. Indian women, for instance, were imported to the Anglophone Caribbean in smaller numbers than Indian men. Shepherd (2011, 554) estimates a ratio of forty women for every hundred men for the major importers, including British Guiana, now Guyana, Trinidad, Suriname, Guadeloupe and Jamaica. The women at times faced sexual exploitation on ships by crew members and deadly domestic abuse at the hand of jealous partners (Shepherd 2002; 2018). In Trinidad and Tobago, between 1872 and 1900, eighty-seven wives were murdered, with forty occurring in British Guiana between 1885 and 1890 (Reddock 2011). As Indian men vented their frustration on Indian women, they also took it out on themselves. Suicide rates were high among Indian men in all immigration territories (Kondpai, quoted in Reddock 2011).

Complicating matters were the messages around ideal femininities in the nineteenth and twentieth centuries. Class-based in orientation, European ideals that served to uphold male privilege and racial hierarchies were espoused by the colonial state, while the working class wrestled with such ideals by engaging in acceptance and rejection of norms as they saw fit, and as material conditions of the era allowed. Modest deportment, sexual purity, motherhood within the confines of wedlock, marital and moral dependence on a stable male breadwinner were some of the European ideals for the nineteenth-century Caribbean woman. The extent to which working-class Caribbean women accepted/rejected/negotiated these ideals for themselves has been thoroughly investigated by Bush (1996), Altink (2011), Reddock (2007), Shepherd (2018), Bryan (2002), Dunkley (2021), Moore and Johnson (2004) and Mahase (2018), among others. However, as Moore and Johnson (2004, 159) indicate, in the nineteenth century male leadership over women was never in question: "Whether marriage was legal or not, the idea prevailed that the man was the boss of the domestic unit and the woman was his property. Those women who married legally were perhaps in a worse situation since they were bound by the vow to 'honour and obey' their husbands, many of whom took it as their duty to enforce that pledge by physical force."

Race-based imperialism and dehumanizing projects consistently engaged in stripping men of powers they believed to be inalienable within the wider framework of "ranking", which Shepherd (2007b, 214–15) explains as a metaphor for social ordering that offers respect and respectability in direct proportion to such hierarchization. But masculinity is resilient. As Lewis (2004, 238) asserts, "One of the important real strengths of masculinity is its ability to bounce back; to face tremendous obstacles yet survive." Positive Caribbean masculinity is evidenced throughout history, and the pride and dignity of Caribbean men has been instrumental in the building of the region in the post-slavery era. However, masculinity has also co-opted negative traits to secure privilege in colonial societies, and colonial gender structures – in creating a "politics of envy" of white hegemonic masculinity (hooks 1995, 99) – ensured that non-white/non-human masculinities were kept in competition for white male validation, which would never fully be received, but would be dangled as the proverbial carrot on a measuring stick. By not granting newly freed people rights to full citizenship though restricted franchise; limited access to land and resources; little to no social services; criminalization of autochthonous beliefs; the colonial gender machinery contributed to interpersonal and gender-based violence as frustrations bubbled between and among subaltern peoples.

With the aim of paying greater attention to the colonial project and its spawning of GBV, we journeyed to the Cayman Islands in 2016 to do a joint presentation on historical roots and contemporary continuities of GBV.[6] This collection does not claim novelty in the critical link between colonial processes and violence against women and men in intersecting and overlapping ways, but it emerged out of that lecture series and specifically the co-editors' joint lecture in the Cayman Islands. This collection proffers a historical feminist framework for the understanding of contemporary GBV as being hinged on past evidence of *deliberately* curated violence, which was neither gender-free nor ad hoc. It is decolonial as it borrows from (Lugones 2010; 2016) and historicizes the creation of the colonial gender logic/system and offers an account for how one set of bodies (sometimes male, but not always) have come to epitomize the human and powerful abuser, while others (sometimes female, but not always) have been portrayed as degenerate and abuseable. Finally, it aims at exposing colonial relations of power and colonial ways of thinking about violence that continue to persist in our present (Méndez 2015, 49).

As Barriteau (2003, 67) insists, Caribbean gender systems exist in all socially and historically constructed systems of identity: "Gender is within race, within class, within economic activity, within sexualities and sexual orientation, within language." Plantation economies in the Caribbean profited from state-sanctioned, gender-based violence, facilitated interpersonal GBV, and left the contemporary Caribbean with continuing legacies of violence. Dismantling the creation must, therefore, be decolonial and deliberate, and it is within this framework that this critical collection is presented.

This volume engages in very necessary revisiting of the past, which is presented as a living breathing entity, rather than a static, unchanging relic. Few contemporary works on GBV in the Caribbean have employed detailed historical analysis as part of the deconstruction of the problem (with DeShong, Lacy et al. (2019), and Biholar and Leslie (2022) being notable exceptions). This work proposes historical gender analysis as a missing link to deeper unpacking and more fruitful solutions to GBV in the region. Our history is both a risk factor and a panacea for many of our current social ills. As Shepherd (2007c, 43) has argued, especially in her lobbying for compulsory history education at the secondary level across the region, "History, of course, possesses one of the greatest possibilities for anchoring people emerging from a colonial past to a more positive beginning, helping us to deal with the epistemic violence of the imperial project."

Following in the strong tradition of work undergirded by Caribbean feminist theory and praxis, this work critiques what we think we know of the historical roots of GBV; creates new knowledge about the range of strategies employed to combat it to the present day; and presents a call to action for greater emphasis on retrospectives to solve current issues. In six sections, authors bravely unearth personal stories of violence, while others rage against systemic GBV. These memories are part of a powerful "process of politicisation . . . that politicized not just the telling, but the tale" (hooks 1988, 110). Others have had to disturb dormant evidence of violence against women and girls, asking new questions of the historical record. Yet others have reckoned with beloved culture – poetry, literature, film and music – and offer critique of relics once held dear. Some have spoken out against the silence towards violence within and towards the LBT community, and persons living with disabilities, while others chose to discard colonial decorum and indelicately shout "bad" words across pages to continue to upset (maybe even your own) "delicate sensibilities, because the time for being polite in our proceedings have passed" (Stephens 2020, xi). In reality, the "bad" words are any attempts to silence survivors and present GBV as normal, inevitable or acceptable.

The chapters in section one, "Enslavement as Gender-Based Violence", unpack colonial gender hierarchies and the system of slavery. Verene Shepherd's "Gender-Based Violence in the Caribbean: Historical Roots, Contemporary Redress" acts as a contextual foundation for the volume as it historicizes the phenomenon of GBV towards answering the question: what circumstances in Caribbean history created this phenomenon? Hilde Neus offers a critical perspective on "Violence against Enslaved Women in Eighteenth-Century Suriname", where GBV was particularly brutal. Closing out the section, Hilary Beckles' unique perspective on "Black Masculinity in Caribbean Slavery" offers an important commentary on how black masculinity was constructed and how it interacted with the hegemonic structures of white masculinity.

Section two, "Unfree Societies, Unfree Bodies", grapples with GBV in the period of so-called freedom, problematizing the very notion of bodily autonomy in the face of well-entrenched colonial gender schema. Bridget Brereton's "The Historical Background to the Culture of Violence in Trinidad and Tobago" traces the violent creation of the modern twin-island republic. Anne Ulentin offers commentary on "Gender-Based Violence in The Bahamas in the Late Nineteenth to the Early Twentieth Centuries" and importantly "reads against the grain" to uncover previously unheard voices of Afro-Bahamian women. Jonathan Dalby's "The Brutal Passions of the Licentious: The Prosecution of Rape and Sexual Abuse in Nineteenth-Century Jamaica" offers a critical excavation of court records to present evidence of and motives for the rampant GBV in Jamaica. Victoria V. Chang offers an important perspective in "Indo-Trinidadian Narratives of Violence: Histories, Trauma and Representations", which considers fictional narratives surrounding rape and highlights the imposed silence – another form of violence – imposed upon victims.

Section three, "Private Violence, Public Secrets", addresses GBV across the region in the nineteenth and twentieth centuries. Dalea Bean's "At the Intersection of Noise and Silence: Intimate Partner Violence in Jamaica, 1900–1938" is concerned with how IPV was able to hide in plain sight, having been publicly revealed in *The Daily Gleaner,* while being largely ignored by social activists. Halimah A.F. DeShong's "Mock Trials and Effigy Hangings as a Community Response to Sexual Violence against Girls in Vincentian Communities" offers insights into community mock trials and ritualistic hanging of life-like images representing guilty parties. O'Neil Joseph's "Rage and Regret: Narratives of Violence and Resolve Among Couples in Trinidad and Tobago, 1940–1960" gives an unprecedented account of the retrospectives of two couples on years of intimate partner abuse. In "Paying It Forward: Discrimination and Stigma as a Causal Factor of IPV in LBTQ Relationships in the Caribbean", Jennan Paige Andrew zones in on acts of IPV among lesbian, bisexual, trans and queer women, and the extent to which much of this violence is triggered by homophobic and transphobic societal norms.

Section four, "Violent Facts, Violent Fiction", allows for interdisciplinary focus with historic analyses of Caribbean cultural literary relics through poetry, literature/stories and film. Kelsi Delaney and Lucy Evans use poetry as their literary medium. In "'Here are the Stories Underneath': Representing Gender-Based Violence in Contemporary Jamaican Poetry", they argue that poetry can offer an important contribution to ongoing conversations around GBV, while Paula Morgan's "The White Woman's Burden: Empire Embodiment and Trauma in Caribbean Fictions" contends that white women were not removed from the "messy fray of gendered and racial politics" (Sterling 2002, 34). Lisa Tomlinson argues that black male filmmakers have significantly reproduced the sexual violation against enslaved African women in cinema in "Violence, Black women, and Slave Films: Revisiting *Sankofa* and *12 Years a Slave*". Sonjah Stanley Niaah and Nicole Plummer offer a deeply critical reading of the intersections between Jamaican cultural patterns and reinforcements of GBV in "Public 'Dis-chord': Popular Music and Gender-Based Violence in Jamaica", while Patricia Mohammed interrogates Trinidad and Tobago's most beloved art form in "Gender-Based Violence in Calypso: Grappling with Shifting Paradigms".

Section 5, "Contemporary Continuities: Breaking the Chains", offers fresh perspectives on contemporary considerations of GBV. In "Heteropatriarchy, Intersectional Structural Violence and Adolescent Girls' Sexualities in Trinidad and Tobago", Gabrielle Jamela Hosein presents a case for the ways in which young girls' bodily autonomy is challenged by lack of sex education and inconsistent attention to their sexual health. Present-day Bahamas is the locus for Jennifer Munnings' "Smile for Me, Sweetie!": An Analysis of Contemporary Gender-Based Violence and Discrimination in The Bahamas". Natasha Mortley and Carol Watson Williams address typically marginal topics of GBV research in "Intersecting Vulnerabilities and Experiences of GBV: Voices and Experiences of Jamaican Women". Knotty issues surrounding male efforts against GBV are tackled by Amílcar Sanatan in "Reflections on Men's Organising to End Gender-Based Violence in the Anglophone Caribbean", while Kendra Pitt sifts through various activist avenues to similar end results in "Historicizing 'The Domestic' in Domestic Violence: Solidarity and Struggle in the Domestic Violence Lobby in Trinidad and Tobago".

Section six, "Activism for Change: Reflections and Perspectives", borrows from Mair's (2006, 235) assertion that "the woman was always central to the preservation of the community" and celebrates some of the region's sheroes in the fight against GBV and creates a space for their own reflections of decolonial struggles. Susan Collymore, Karen de Souza, Halima Khan, Joy Marcus, Vanessa Ross and Wintress White (with Alissa Trotz) collaborated on "Everybody's Business: Reflecting on Red Thread's Anti-Violence Advocacy in Guyana", which signals the importance of this NGO's ground-breaking work with grassroots women on the mainland. Taitu Heron's photo essay, "Standing with Survivors: A Reflective Essay on Disruption, Testimony, Performance and Ritual in Jamaica's Survivor Empowerment March", offers a provocative portrayal of a recent, under-reported mass protest in Jamaica against GBV. In "A Personal Reflection on the Influence of Gender-based Violence on Activist Women", Grenada-born scholar/activist Peggy Antrobus shares how femicide in her family shaped her work life and focus on women's economic freedom. "Diligent, Enterprising and Painstaking: Reflections on a life of Activism" tells the story of Linnette Vassell and her journey from childhood in a peasant village in Jamaica to a becoming a lifelong activist and student of women's history. Judith Wedderburn (with Helen Atkins) shares "Silver Learnings: Reflections on Feminist Advocacy to Prevent Gender-Based Violence in Jamaica", which gives insights into Wedderburn's life and journey, juxtaposed with the younger generation of activists embodied by Atkins.

Today, sexism, power and hegemonic masculinity – combined with notions of a gender, class and race hierarchy, religious orthodoxy, lack of education about gender relations and the economic situation in which many men and women find themselves – continue to feed the problem of GBV. Understanding, on a basic level, the fact that violence follows power in a social context is a building block to being able to adequately address it. There are no sides to this debate; only the move to halt the protracted violence that sears the souls of all those involved. This, then, is our history. It is time to leave this violence in the past, learning from it, so that we do not repeat it. We are thankful to these authors who answered our call and led to the production of this important volume. Like Miss Lou, it "sweet" us "fi see how dem tek it serious" (Bennett 1993, 76). We all take GBV serious. We hope you take it serious too.

NOTES

1. Frantz Fannon, *The Wretched of the Earth* (New York: Grove Weidenfeld, 1963), 35.
2. Agencies include the United Nations, World Bank, Caribbean Development Bank (CDB), European Union, Inter-American Development Bank (IDB), CARICOM (Caribbean Community), Organisation of Eastern Caribbean States (OECS), Organization of American States (OAS) and many others. The Global Spotlight Initiative among the UN, EU and partner agencies alone has invested no less than US$12 million in the region since 2020 to combat violence against women and girls. See https://www.spotlightinitiative.org/press/regional-spotlight-initiative-programme-launched-reduce-family-violence-across-eastern.
3. https://caribbean.unwomen.org/en/caribbean-gender-portal/caribbean-gbv-law-portal/gbv-in-the-caribbean.
4. https://caribbeanwomencount.unwomen.org/#:~:text=On%20average%2046%25%20women%20have,of%20violence%20in%20her%20lifetime.&text=Lifetime%20prevalence%20rates%20among%20women,cent%20in%20Grenada%20and%20Jamaica.
5. The debate continues over the quantitative dimension of the transatlantic trafficking in enslaved peoples to the Americas. There is still no accurate figure, though many use Inikori's fifteen million. Others use 15–200 million.
6. This lecture was part of a regional series on a variety of Caribbean issues hosted by the Regional Coordinating Office of the Institute for Gender and Development Studies at The University of the West Indies.

REFERENCES

Altink, Henrice. 2002. "An Outrage on All Decency": Abolitionist Reactions to Flogging Jamaican Slave Women, 1780–1834." *Slavery and Abolition* 23 (2): 107–22.

———. 2011. *Destined for a Life of Service: Defining African-Jamaican Womanhood, 1865–1938*. Manchester: Manchester University Press.

Alexander, Jacqui. 1994. "Not Just (Any) Body Can Be a Citizen: The Politics of Law, Sexuality and Postcoloniality in Trinidad and Tobago and the Bahamas." *Feminist Review* 48 (1): 5–23.

Amussen, Susan Dwyer. 1994. "'Being Stirred to Much Unquietness: Violence and Domestic Violence in Early Modern England." *Journal of Women's History* 6 (2): 70–89.

Bean, Dalea. 2022. "Looking Back to Move Forward: A Historical Reflection of Gender-Based Violence and Intimate Partner Violence in Jamaica During Slavery." In *Critical Caribbean Perspectives on Preventing Gender-Based Violence*, edited by Ramona Biholar and Dacia L. Leslie. London: Routledge.

Beckles, Hilary. 1999. *Centering Woman: Gender Discourses in Caribbean Slave Society*. Kingston: Ian Randle Publishers.

———. 2016. *The First Black Slave Society: Britain's "Barbarity Time" in Barbados, 1636–1876*. Kingston: University of the West Indies Press.

Bennett, Louise. 1993. *Aunty Roachy Seh*. Edited by Mervyn Morris. Kingston: Sangster's Book Stores.

Biholar, Ramona. 2013. *Transforming Discriminatory Sex Roles and Gender Stereotyping: The Implementation of Article 5a CEDAW for the Realisation of Women's Right to be Free from Gender-Based Violence in Jamaica*. School of Human Rights Research Series Vol. 62. Cambridge, Antwerp: Intersentia.

Barriteau, Eudine. 2003. "Confronting Power and Politics: A Feminist Theorising of Gender in Commonwealth Caribbean Societies." *Meridians: Feminism, Race, Transnationalism* 3 (2): 57–92.

Brodber, Erna. 2004. *The Second Generation of Freemen in Jamaica, 1907–1944*. Gainesville: University Press of Florida.

Bryon, Jessica. 2012. "Regional Integration and Caribbean Civilisation: Continuing the Debate." In *Love and Power: Caribbean Discourses on Gender*, edited by V. Eudine Barriteau, 151–82. Kingston: University of the West Indies Press.

Bryan, Patrick. 2002. *The Jamaican People, 1880–1902: Race, Class and Social Control*. Kingston: University of the West Indies Press.

Bush, Barbara. 1990. *Slave Women in Caribbean Society, 1650–1838*. Kingston: Heinemann.

———. 1996. "History, Memory, Myth? Reconstructing the History (or Histories) of Black Women in the African Diaspora." *Nature, Society and Thought* 9 (4): 419–46.

Casey, E.A., R.M. Tolman, J. Carlson, C.T. Allen, and H.L. Storer. 2017. "What Motivates Men's Involvement in Gender-Based Violence Prevention? Latent Class Profiles and Correlates in an International Sample of Men." *Men and Masculinities* 20 (3): 294–316.

DeShong, Halima. 2014. "Gendered Discourse of Romantic Love/ing and Violence." In *Doing Gender, Doing Love: Interdisciplinary Voices*, edited by Serena Petrella. Freeland: Inter-Disciplinary Press.

———. 2018. "The Language of Partner Violence in the Caribbean: A Decolonial Feminist Analysis." In *Caribbean Crime and Criminal Justice: Impacts of Post-Colonialism and Gender,* edited by Katharina Joosen and Corin A. Bailey, 123–38. Abingdon and New York: Routledge.

Dunkley, Dave. 2021. *Women and Resistance in the Early Rastafari Movement.* Baton Rouge: Louisiana State University Press.

Fannon, Frantz. 1963. *The Wretched of the Earth.* New York: Grove Weidenfeld.

Gayle, Herbert. 2018. "The Torture of Inner-City Boys and Its Contribution to the Construction of Repeat Killers in Jamaica." In *Crime, Violence and Security in the Caribbean,* edited by M. Raymond Izarali. New York: Routledge.

Hall, Douglas. 1999. *In Miserable Slavery: Thomas Thistlewood in Jamaica 1750–86.* Kingston: University of the West Indies Press.

Haynes, Tonya, and Halima DeShong. 2017. "Queering Feminist Approaches to Gender Based Violence in the Anglophone Caribbean." *Social and Economic Studies* 66 (1&2): 105–31.

Higman, Barry. 1976. *Slave Population and Economy in Jamaica, 1807–1834.* Cambridge: Cambridge University Press.

hooks, bell. 1988. *Talking Back: Thinking Feminist, Thinking Black.* Toronto: Between the Lines.

———. 1995. "Doing it for Daddy." In *Constructing Masculinity,* edited by M. Berger, B. Wallis, and S. Watson. New York: Routledge.

Inikori, Joseph, and Stanley Engerman. 1992. *The Atlantic Slave Trave: Effects on Economies, Societies and Peoples in Africa, the Americas and Europe.* Durham, NC: Duke University Press.

Jean-Baptiste, Polovna. 2000. "To Have and To Own Until Death Do Us Part: Slave Relationships." Slave Resistance: A Caribbean Study, website created by History Department, University of Miami. https://scholar.library.miami.edu/slaves/womens_resistance/individual_essays/polovna.html.

Joseph, Debra, and Adele Jones. 2023. "Understanding Violence Against Women in the Caribbean Though an Exploration of Men's Perspectives." *Violence Against Women* 9 (5): 1005–23.

Lacey, Krim K., Rohan D. Jeremiah, and Carolyn M. West. 2019. "Domestic Violence Through a Caribbean Lens: Historical Context, Theories, Risks and Consequences." *Journal of Aggression, Maltreatment & Trauma* 30 (6): 761–80.

Le Franc, E., M. Samms-Vaughan, I. Hambleton, K. Fox, and D. Brown. 2008. "Interpersonal Violence in Three Caribbean Countries: Barbados, Jamaica, and Trinidad and Tobago." *Revista Panamericana Salud Publica*24 (6): 409–21.

Lewis, Linden. 2004. "Masculinity, the Political Economy of the Body, and Patriarchal Power in the Caribbean." In *Gender in the 21st Century: Caribbean Perspectives, Visions and Possibilities*, edited by Barbara Bailey and Elsa Leo-Rhynie, 236–61. Kingston: Ian Randle Publishers.

Lugones, M. 2010. "Toward a Decolonial Feminism." *Hypatia* 25 (4): 742–59.

———. 2016. "The Coloniality of Gender." In *The Palgrave Handbook of Gender and Development*, edited by W. Harcourt 13–33. Houndmills: Palgrave Macmillan.

Mahase, R. 2018. "The Men who Controlled Indian Women": Indentureship, Patriarchy and Women's liberation in Trinidad." In *Women in the Indian Diaspora*, edited by A. Pande. Singapore: Springer.

Mathurin Mair, Lucille. 2006. *Historical Study of Women in Jamaica, 1655–1844*. Edited by Hilary Beckles and Verene Shepherd. Kingston: University of the West Indies Press.

Méndez, X. 2015. "Notes Toward a Decolonial Feminist Methodology: Revisiting the Race/Gender Matrix." *Trans-Scripts* 5: 41–59.

Mohammed, Patricia. 2011. "Writing Gender into History: The Negotiation of Gender Relations Among Indian Men and Women in Post-Indenture Trinidad Society, 1917–1947." In *Engendering Caribbean History: Cross Cultural Perspectives*, edited by Verene Shepherd, 146–64. Kingston: Ian Randle Publishers.

Moore, Brian L., and Michele A. Johnson. 2004. *Neither Led nor Driven: Contesting British Cultural Imperialism in Jamaica, 1865–1920*. Kingston: University of the West Indies Press.

Morrissey, Marietta. 2021. *Sex, Punishment and Protest in Slave Women in the New World: Gender Stratification in the Caribbean*. Lawrence, KS: University Press of Kansas.

Nurse, Keith. 2004. "Masculinities in Transition: Gender and the Global Problematique." In *Interrogating Caribbean Masculinities: Theoretical and Empirical Analyses*, edited by Rhoda Reddock, 3–37. Kingston: University of the West Indies Press.

Patterson, Orlando. 2022. *The Sociology of Slavery: Black Society in Jamaica, 1655–1838*. Cambridge and Medford, MA: Polity Press.

Reddock, Rhoda. 2007. "Diversity, Difference and Caribbean Feminism: The Challenge of Anti-Racism." *Caribbean Review of Gender Studies* 1: 1–24.

———. 2011. "The Indentureship Experience: Indian Women in Trinidad and Tobago 1845–1917." In *Engendering Caribbean History: Cross Cultural Perspectives*, edited by Verene Shepherd, 574–86. Kingston: Ian Randle Publishers.

Robinson, Tracy. 2004. "An Analysis of Legal Change: Law and Gender-Based

Violence in the Caribbean." Presentation at the Caribbean Judicial Colloquium on the Application of International Human Rights Law at the Domestic Level, Nassau, Bahamas, 17–19 May.

———. 2011. "Our Imagined Lives." In *Sex and the Citizen: Interrogating the Caribbean*, edited by Faith Smith, 201–13. Charlottesville and London: University of Virginia Press.

Rotimi, Adewale. 2007. "Violence in the Family: A Preliminary investigation and Overview of Wife Battering in Africa." *Journal of International Women's Studies* 9 (1): 234–52.

Shepherd, Verene. 2002. *Maharani's Misery: Narratives of a Passage from India to the Caribbean.* Kingston: University of the West Indies Press.

———. 2007a. "Petticoat Rebellion: Women and Emancipation in Colonial Jamaica." In *I Want to Disturb my Neighbour: Lectures on Slavery, Emancipation and Post-Colonial Jamaica*, edited by Verene Shepherd, 95–121. Kingston: Ian Randle Publishers.

———. 2007b. "The Ranking Game: Discourses of Belonging in Jamaican History." In *I Want to Disturb my Neighbour: Lectures on Slavery, Emancipation and Post-Colonial Jamaica*, edited by Verene Shepherd, 212–90. Kingston: Ian Randle Publishers.

———. 2007c. "The University of the West Indies and the Decolonisation Project." In *I Want to Disturb my Neighbour: Lectures on Slavery, Emancipation and Post-Colonial Jamaica*, edited by Verene Shepherd, 44–49. Kingston: Ian Randle Publishers.

———, ed. 2011. *Engendering Caribbean History: Cross-Cultural Perspectives.* Kingston: Ian Randle Publishers.

———. 2018. "Constructing Visibility: Indian Women in the Jamaican Segment of the Indian Diaspora." In *The Subaltern Indian Woman*: Domination and Social Degradation, edited by Prem Misir, 195–214. Singapore: Palgrave Macmillan.

Sistren with Honor Ford-Smith. 2005. *Lionheart Gal: Life Stories of Jamaican Women.* Kingston: University of the West Indies Press.

Sterling, Marvin D. 2002. "Gendering 'Smadditisation': Labour and Violence in the (De)Colonisation of Afro-Jamaica Consciousness." In *Critical Caribbean Perspectives on Preventing Gender-Based Violence*, edited by Ramona Biholar and Dacia L. Leslie, 27–43. Abingdon and New York: Routledge.

Trotz, A. 2004. "Between Despair and Hope: Women and Violence in Contemporary Guyana." *Small Axe* 8 (1): 1–20.

United Nations Office on Drugs and Crime. 2019. *Global Study on Homicide: Gender-related Killing of Women and Girls.* Vienna: UNODC.

Vassell, Linnette. 2004. "Feminisms, Gender Studies, Activism: The Elusive Triad." In *Gender in the 21st Century: Caribbean Perspectives, Visions and Possibilities*, edited by Barbara Bailey and Elsa Leo-Rhynie, 236–61. Kingston: Ian Randle Publishers.

Wynter, Sylvia. 2003. "Unsettling the Coloniality of Being/Power/Truth/Freedom: Towards the Human, After Man, Its Overrepresentation – An Argument." *CR: The New Centennial Review* 3 (3): 257–337.

SECTION 1

ENSLAVEMENT AS GENDER-BASED VIOLENCE

chapter 1

Gender-Based Violence in the Caribbean

Historical Roots, Contemporary Redress

VERENE A. SHEPHERD

THE AIM OF THIS CHAPTER IS TO HISTORICIZE the phenomenon of gender-based violence (GBV), which is widespread in the Caribbean and elsewhere, and to answer this question: what circumstances in our history has brought us to this place? For the past is connected to the present, and only a long, historical view of the scourge of domestic and GBV can explain that connection. I am quite aware that GBV is not the only form of violence that has dogged our past. The late historian Michael Craton (2004, 53) writes about the Cayman Islands, for example, in 1773:

> Whatever differences arise among them are generally submitted to the arbitration of neighbours; but if the parties do not choose to stand by the Award, as there is no legal method of compelling them, they finally determine the matter by coming to blows and the victor gains the cause.

The violence towards enslaved and free Africans in the region is also well-known. It is not enough to know the historical roots of the phenomenon, however. There must be concern in the contemporary with redressing the persistent legacies of the past, so this paper will also suggest ways in which reparatory justice can be a way of addressing the problem today.

To provide historical context, I start with two quotations: the first from an 1824 publication titled *The Horrors of Slavery* by Robert Wedderburn, whose father owned several plantations in Jamaica; and the other from the

1831 publication, *The History of Mary Prince,* and is from Prince herself, who was enslaved in Bermuda and Antigua before being taken to England, and whose experience of enslavement was used to fuel the anti-slavery cause. "My father's house was full of female slaves, all objects of his lust; amongst whom he Strutted like Solomon in his grand seraglio, or like a bantam cock upon his own dunghill. . . . By him my mother [Rossanna] was made the object of his brutal lust . . ." (Wedderburn 1824, xx).

> After abusing me with every ill name he could think of, and giving me several hard blows with his hand, he said, "I shall come around tomorrow morning at twelve on purpose and give you a round hundred." He kept his word . . . He tied me up upon a ladder; Benjy stood by to count them for him. When he got weary, he rested, then beat me again. An earthquake interrupted, and in the confusion, I crawled away, my body all blood and bruises" (Prince 1831, 847).

These flashbacks from the nineteenth century, references to the totality of the exercise of male power over women – to rape, sexual exploitation, verbal abuse, physical violence, threats, cruel and inhumane treatment, and general female unfreedom, seemingly unrelieved, except when interrupted by external forces, an earthquake in this case – illustrate that GBV has a long genealogy in the region. In the historical period, it may not have taken all the forms it does today, but some were present. According to the European Institute for Gender Equity, while it is difficult to distinguish between different types of violence, since they are not always mutually exclusive, GBV includes:

- domestic violence
- sexual harassment
- rape
- sexual conflict and harmful customary or traditional practices (for example, forced marriage and honour crimes)
- trafficking in women
- forced prostitution
- violations of human rights in armed conflict (murder, systematic rape, sexual slavery, forced pregnancy)
- forced sterilization
- forced abortion
- coercive use of contraceptives

- female infanticide
- pre-natal sex selection

No historical antecedents existed for pre-natal sex selection, forced sterilization, forced marriage and honour crimes, and coercive use of contraceptives, since they were not common. During slavery, GBV more normally encompassed three sets of acts:

a) Physical, sexual and psychological violence occurring as part of the human trafficking and perpetrated by crew against women and girls on the Middle Passage;
b) Physical, sexual and psychological violence, including battering, sexual exploitation, sexual abuse of females in the household, and violence related to exploitation on the plantation and other spaces of exploitation during the slavery period;
c) Physical, sexual and psychological violence perpetrated in the home against men, women and children in the post-colonial period and at times condoned by law enforcement officials.

Undergirding such practices in the early period was unequal power – typically white, male power over the enslaved and colonized. From the fifteenth to the nineteenth century, such power was manifested in various forms of violence over indigenous, enslaved, and later, indentured labourers. From the late nineteenth through the twentieth century, the Victorian gender order – along with the male as breadwinner ideology, which was so clearly articulated after the 1930s labour protests and the report of the Moyne Commission, as Joan French (1988) has shown – clashed with women's claims to socio-economic and political power to act as justification for violence. This link between violence and power has been highlighted by the UN Declaration on the Elimination of Violence against Women (1993), which states: "Violence against women is a manifestation of historically unequal power relations between men and women, which has led to domination over and discrimination against women by men and to the prevention of the full advancement of women, and that violence against women is one of the crucial social mechanisms by which women are forced into a subordinate position compared with men."

Today, sexism, power and hegemonic masculinity – combined with notions of a gender, class and race hierarchy; religious orthodoxy; the lack of education around gender relations; and the economic situation in which many men and women find themselves – continue to feed the problem. In most places, men possess more economic, political, domestic, and overall decision-making power than women. Research has shown that violence is instrumental in maintaining control of that power. More than 90 per cent of "systematic, persistent, and injurious" violence is perpetrated by men. Understanding, on a basic level, the fact that violence follows power in a social context is a building block to being able to adequately address it.

Feminist theory holds that it is impossible to sever gender from power and hegemonic masculinity; that gender is implicated in the conception and construction of power. Joan Wallach Scott (1988) states clearly that: "Gender is a primary way of signifying relationships of power." In other words, gender is a primary field within which or by means of which power is articulated. Power is a relationship of dominant and subordinate, and men have traditionally held the reins of power. Women have not traditionally had the same access to the resources that are associated with power. For example, inheritance law used to favour male heirs, thus denying women access to economic resources of power. Women have struggled to destabilize the male dominance in power (whether resource- or authority-based), and to seek access to the means of power; mostly power "to", rather than power "over".

This belief of what masculinity should be rested on the power of the acceptability of the heterosexual discourse, strengthened by evangelical/biblical ideas/teachings. Within this discourse, masculinity is a social construct based on male/female power relations. Hegemonic masculinity also rests on a public/private dichotomy that renders women in the private sphere in the division of labour. Therefore, men should be the head of their family and as such, entitled to their roles as fathers and providers. But when economic and social factors are not aligned with these embraced roles, the result is conflict, at times leading to GBV.

But to return to my initial question: what fed this violence in the past and propelled it into our present? In general, GBV has its roots firmly embedded in the history of colonialism, more specifically, the conquest of the Indigenous Peoples who inhabited some Caribbean countries, the transatlantic trafficking in Africans and African enslavement; in a slave society that was characterized by racism, ethnocentrism, classism and discrimination against women in the field and the home; in Asian indentureship; in a post-slavery Victorian gender order manifested in the exercise of male power; and in patriarchal ideologies that continue to have contemporary meanings and manifestations.

CONQUEST AND COLONIZATION

Violence linked to power relations was gendered from as far back as the development of civilizations. Colonialism in the region did not begin the global practice, but it provides a useful starting point for its introduction in the Caribbean. Jürgen Osterhammel (2009) defines colonialism as: "A relationship of domination between an indigenous (or forcibly imported) majority and a minority of foreign invaders. The fundamental decisions affecting the lives of the colonized people are made and implemented by the colonial rulers in pursuit of interests that are often defined in a distant metropolis. Rejecting cultural compromises with the colonized population, the colonizers are convinced of their own superiority and of their ordained mandate to rule."

Gender discrimination also operated in indigenous societies, where roles were distributed according to gender, not sex. In the islands called the Greater Antilles, which included Jamaica, Taino men believed that, unless in emergency situations, men should be the rulers – the power holders and the warriors. Europeans perfected this system, but added racism and ethnocentrism to it, exploiting indigenous women in gender-specific ways, including trafficking and rape.

CHATTEL ENSLAVEMENT

Under chattel enslavement, women's bodies became the site of power contestation. Indeed, any honour or esteem attached to being an enslaver arose only from the power that one could exercise over the bodies of their chattel enslaved; and this was sanctioned by laws which allowed white men and women to exercise intimate power through punishment, torture and control. In drawing up and enforcing such laws, the enslavers in the Caribbean, like those in the rest of the Americas, created their own version of slavery. They invented from scratch all the ideological and legal underpinnings of a totally new slave system.

This violence was manifested in:

- The invasion and capture (of lands and peoples) in the Caribbean;
- The forced kidnapping and trafficking of indigenous Caribbean peoples and Africans;
- The shackling and shipment of Africans in inhumane conditions;
- The throwing of live African male and female captives overboard (as in the case of the ship *Zong* heading to Jamaica in 1781, in which one hundred and thirty-four live Africans were thrown overboard;
- The sale and branding of Africans on the plantations;
- The sexual harassment of women;
- Rape and other forms of violence on the Middle Passage, and later on, the ships with indentured Indians;
- Flogging and degrading punishment of enslaved field workers and enslaved domestics, like Long Celia in the Cayman Islands, who was tried for inciting rebellion in 1820, found guilty by two magistrates and a jury of twelve white enslaver men and sentenced to fifty lashes on her bare body "in some public place at Georgetown" (Craton 2004);
- Murder (including during and after armed conflicts).

To expand on some of these, I will emphasize that the capture and shipment of Africans testified to the racially motivated violence that occurred on the Middle Passage, manifested in the experiences of those on the voyage of the ship *Thomas* from Liverpool to Africa to Jamaica, as captured in the writings of one known as Dicky Sam:

> The sickly slaves were scarcely attended to at all; sometimes the captain of the ship would inspect them, and if he found they were likely to give any trouble, he would call two or three of his crew, saying, "I think these niggers had better go overboard, they will leave us more room and help to feed the sharks; I see they are in our track." Her lading bill consisted of 630 slaves, of which 100 have died in the horrible middle passage; the ship was soon emptied of her living cargo, they were much worse in condition on landing than when they embarked. (A Genuine Dicky Sam 1884)

Once located in the Americas, women were enslaved in large numbers and subjected to various forms of exploitation and control, not least those of being categorized as property and unfree labourers, and forced to work without wages. Indeed, women served an essential ideological function: enslavers appropriated their reproductive lives by claiming their children as property to eventually perform unwaged labour; and used their blackness as justification for making them reproduce the status of enslavement, unlike white women who could only reproduce free status, even if black men fathered their children. On sugar plantations, women weeded, planted, harvested, worked in the factories (where many lost fingers while feeding cane into the mill), and generally contributed to the productive processes. They laboured in enslavers' residences as domestics and nursed the sick in the hot houses. They worked in coffee, cotton and sugar industries and supplied food, especially to the urban areas. Men had a wider range of tasks, as evidenced from plantations like the Romney estate in St Kitts, with men distributed over ten occupations and women two – field and domestic. Men were dominant in the supervisory and plantation management fields.[1] In Guyana, weeding and moulding young canes (described as a dangerous and tedious task) was usually assigned to women. They were expected to go over one-eighth or one-ninth of an acre per day. Females were expected by their managers to gin thirty pounds of cotton (DaCosta 1997).

As field labourers (and as domestics and concubines), women's bodies became the site of power contestation. Plantation labour placed great physical strain on enslaved women; and any infraction of the "slave codes" or the instructions of the slave-driver was followed by severe beating and other forms of physical abuse of her body. Gracy, of Success plantation in Demerara, was locked in the stocks and then sent to work in the task gang. Rachel was flogged for taking a sick child to the fields after the estate manager had told her to leave the child with the field nanny (DaCosta 1997, 59). Jacuba, Julia, Dorothea, Una and Effa, who belonged to Le Repentir, but were working on La Pénitence, complained against the manager when they were unfairly assigned the most difficult tasks on the plantation – carrying megass (bagasse) from the mill (DaCosta 1997, 67–68). Children were not exempt from the brutality. The most horrifying punishment was that of a seven-year-old girl who had committed acts which Governor van Hoogenheim considered only "trifles and childishness deserving only a child's punishment". However, Gerlach, her manager, had ordered that she be given two hundred and fifty lashes and placed in the stocks, where she remained without any food, except what was given to her by sympathetic enslaved people. When van Hoogenheim saw her on a visit to her plantation three weeks later, her body had been "cruelly torn to pieces". He ordered her release, to the displeasure of Gerlach (Thompson 2009).

In fact, the history of slavery in Guyana and elsewhere demonstrates that many confrontations between enslaved females and managers arose from contradictions between "women's roles as mothers and as workers – which were intensified by growing labour exploitation after the abolition of the slave trade" (DaCosta 1997, 59).

In addition to the abuse of their bodies through arduous physical field regimes, and severe whipping, enslaved women were open to sexploitation – to a far greater degree than enslaved men, as far as the records go. For neither colonial statutes nor slave codes invested enslaved women with any rights over their own bodies, but rather, transferred and consolidated such rights within the legal person of the enslavers (Bailey 2006, 23). Beckles (2011) argues that male enslavers thus claimed violent access to enslaved women's bodies, and male and female enslavers to the sale of enslaved women's bodies for money upon the sex market. Novelist Marlon James' Night Women in his historical novel *The Book of Night Women,* set on a Jamaican plantation, had their usual comment on this phenomenon of sexploitaiton: ". . . It was enough to make a nigger wonder if white men didn't know they born with cocky until they come to the colony". [But] negro get to understand that white men body in bondage in the mother country and when they come to the West Indies, the cocky be the first thing they set free. As for the white woman, she can only turn her eye and sip tea" (James 2009, 43–44).

Thomas Thistlewood, who owned and managed properties in western Jamaica and left daily journals of his activities, is perhaps the most documented example of what today we would call a sexual predator (Hall 1987). His violence was expressed in sexploitation, and in verbal and physical abuse; such as the collaring and branding to which one enslaved woman, Sally, was routinely subjected. He used sexual violence as a weapon of control over practically every girl or woman on properties he owned or supervised.

The stories of rape also come from Guyana. DaCosta tells us that Betsy was raped by the manager, and Jemmet and Susannah had been coerced into sexual relationships Even children were raped. A case of rape of a ten-year-old slave girl by her master has come to light. She died a few weeks later (DaCosta 1997, 204 and 65).

I should point out that much of the evidence of violence against women resides in the documents generated by men; but a few narratives generated by women, such as the enslaved woman Mary Prince, survive. Prince recounted the physical violence that she and her fellow enslaved, Hetty, endured. Here is what she recounts of what Hetty went through: "While pregnant, she was tied to a tree, flogged till she went into labour, later delivering a dead child, after recovering briefly she was flogged by both master and mistress, her body and limbs swelling to great size till the water burst out of her and she died" (Prince 1831, 847).

Lucille Mathurin Mair reinforced the way in which law and custom facilitated acts of violence against the black woman, writing that, until 1826, the enslaved female had no legal protection from sexual attack: "Neither age nor pregnancy exempted women from corporal punishment; [rather] they were laid down in the filthiest place the driver could find for floggings" (Mair 2011, 223 and 225). Such drivers were overwhelmingly male. Of course, enslaved men were also brutalized, especially for their acts of resistance – their audacity in seeking liberation. After major wars, they were murdered or shipped out of the region. During slavery, their roles as husbands and heads of households were diminished by white men, who appropriated the bodies of their women. But they also they took out their frustration on black women in the domestic arena; and as floggers and drivers, they were commanded to violate women in unspeakable ways in the public arena.

The violence of enslavers should not, however, be hidden beneath our condemnation of black men. White men committed most of the murder and mayhem in the Caribbean – right up to the end of colonialism. The following table extracted from the punishment list after the 1831/32 Emancipation war in Jamaica, led by Samuel Sharpe, illustrates:

Table 1.1: Punishment List Emancipation War

Name	Property/Enslaver	Parish	Sentence
Catherine Brown	Cascade Pen – Mrs. Griffiths	Hanover	Death – commuted to 50 lashes and 6 weeks imprisonment
Catherine Clarke	Dr W Skirving	Hanover	50 lashes and 3 months in prison at hard labour
Anne James	Free	Hanover	Death/executed
Christina James	Cascade Pen – Mrs. Griffiths	Hanover	50 lashes and 3 months in prison at hard labour
Mary Fowler	Dromilly	Trelawny	6 months in prison
Elizabeth Samuels	Bunkershill	Trelawny	100 lashes and 6 months in prison
Rosanna alias Annie Steele	Orange Valley	Trelawny	3 months in prison
Charlotte Reid	Lambs River	Westmoreland	6 months in prison
Eliza Whittingham	Cowpark	Westmoreland	Death
Jane Whittingham	Cowpark	Westmoreland	Death/hanged

Source: CO 137/185 – Accounts of the 1831/32 Emancipation War – UK National Archives

THE POST-SLAVERY PERIOD

Violence against women would continue in the post-slavery period. The main reasons were the ruling classes' attempts to recreate the actions and mentalities of slavery. Colonization cemented British and African gender systems, which became even worse after emancipation when jobs became gendered, along with wages, rewards and positions in the workplace. The male as breadwinner ideology was promoted by the elite and the church, and this was accompanied by ideas about the woman's place being in the house. Women have had to struggle against this domestication ideology for a long time, and despite the advances, hegemonic masculinity is proving hard to dislodge; and so, the struggle for gender equality in all spheres of life continues.

Violence against women in the century from 1838 to 1938 would manifest itself:

- in the sexual abuse of subaltern women on the ships from India to the Caribbean, the most famous case being that of Maharani on the *Allanshaw* to Guyana in 1885;
- in uxoricide or wife murder, and in other forms of spousal abuse during and after the indentureship system;
- in the murder, flogging, sexual abuse and imprisonment of women after protest movements, such as in the case of the Morant Bay War in Jamaica and labour protests of the 1930s all over the Caribbean;
- in domestic violence as a result of women's refusal to cooperate with the gender-discriminatory policies in economic, political and social life in the post-modern period.

The case of Indian women in the Caribbean deserves elaboration, not because of any attempt to hierarchize oppression, but because these stories are rarely told in the Caribbean. One case that I have written about in *Maharani's Misery: Narratives of a Passage from India to the Caribbean* is that of the young Maharani. Most of the documentary evidence used in the book comes from the more than four hundred pages of correspondence generated by the investigation into the journey of the ship *Allanshaw*. Briefly, during the early morning hours of 24 July 1885, Maharani, along with six hundred and sixty other contract labourers, embarked at Calcutta on this James Nourse-owned ship bound for colonial Guyana. Maharani did not complete her passage to the southern Caribbean; she was among the seventeen who died before the ship reached colonial Guyana. While the causes of death of sixteen were ascertained and recorded unproblematically, Maharani's death was the subject of intense controversy, uncertainty and speculation. The surgeon-superintendent of the ship vacillated between "shock to the nervous system", "inflammation near the womb", "shock from shame" and "peritonitis" as the cause of death; a few fellow female emigrants attributed her death to "criminal assault", based on what Maharani allegedly told them before she died; both Inspector Wright of the Guyana Police Force and Dr Robert Grieve, acting medical officer with the Immigration Department and later surgeon-general, and a member of the commission of enquiry ordered by the governor of colonial Guyana, believed that rape was the cause of her death. His fellow commissioners disagreed with him, arguing that the evidence presented was contradictory and inconclusive. The mystery was never solved, despite four commissions of enquiry into the case and no one was convicted. But her voice was heard through the testimonies of others.

There were other aspects of the social experience of Asian migrant workers, however, which demonstrated the convergence of class, ethnic and gender considerations. For example, patriarchal notions of the role and status of women, and gender ideology grounded in ethnic culture, were clearly at work in social relations between Indian men and women. The sexual disparity gave rise to a competition for women and an accompanying new independence among women in their choice of sexual partners. Where such social behaviour conflicted with working-class Indian men's racial prejudices, manifested in their resentment of the liaisons between Indian women and black or Chinese men, and notions about the "proper gender order" in Hindu and Muslim culture, violence against women, especially uxoricide, was the consequence.

The phenomenon of spouse murders was found in Guyana, Grenada, Jamaica, Suriname and Trinidad. There were twenty-seven cases in Trinidad between 1859 and 1863. Between 1879 and 1898, out of one hundred and nine murders committed by Indians in Trinidad, sixty-three were murders of females by their Indian male partners. From 1872 to 1900, eighty-seven Indian women were killed (sixty-five by husbands/lovers) in Trinidad. In Guyana, between 1886 and 1890, there were thirty-one such murders of women, of which twenty-five were committed by Indian men. From 1894 to 1905, there were twenty-nine. In Suriname, forty Indian women were killed in crimes of passion from 1885 to 1890. Where female spouse murder was treated as a crime of passion, the men were not hanged, but imprisoned; but if there were no mitigating circumstances, they were hanged. For example, Gopaul of Grenada was hanged "within the walls of the common gaol" for murdering his wife "under circumstances of great cruelty". The witnesses reported that Gopaul used a cutlass to chop his wife on the head, neck and hands. In fact, he chopped off three of her fingers completely. When the police constable who came upon the murder scene instructed another Indian, Joseph, to ". . . tell Gopaul in coolie that what he had done was not right", Gopaul is reported to have replied in French, ". . . I do not care for what I have done."[2] He claimed that his wife was living with another man. Similarly, in Jamaica in 1915, Chedda of Tremolesworth was hanged for killing Basharan, his wife, as well as a male immigrant called Chrooni. The motive, as in the case of Gopaul of Guyana, was jealousy.[3]

Class, race and gender also intersected and determined white plantation officials' attitude to Asian women. Notions of white superiority, of elite dominance over working-class people and of female inferiority created the ideological landscape on which overseers and managers carried out their physical and sexual abuse of Asian women, as indeed some had done under slavery. Official regulations were passed to stop the sexual abuse of female immigrants by white estate personnel, but the practice never stopped. The attempts to dichotomize work and family, public and private, and place women in the domestic sphere and to encourage the male as breadwinner ideology were all resisted by women, who used education and smart economic planning to rise above their circumstances. In the meantime, hegemonic masculinity still rules and the inability of men to match their belief in their right to power over women with the economic status that would support such a belief continues to cause havoc in gender relations in the world, and to manifest itself in violence against women.

Tonya Haynes, who is also a founding member of CODE RED for Gender Justice and CatchAFyah Caribbean Feminist Network, in one of her articles on violence against women highlighted the misogynistic views that still persist in the annals of power in reference to the violence which claims the lives ofwomen. Statements such as "Women who are murdered by their intimate partners have provoked such violence against them by failing to 'act appropriately' after men have 'invested' in the relationship" and "Some men reacted badly i.e. murder, when they felt mistreated by women after 'investing' in relationships" in many ways reflected a broader problem. Women are seemingly perceived as accomplices in the violence meted out to them – agitators – as if to justify the cruel and depraved acts meted out daily. According to Haynes (2014): "Women are losing their lives. And activists are being told that they should work with groups whose public statements suggest they see women as less human than they are. Women are losing their lives. And we are being offered justifications for the violence against them. Women are losing their lives. And Bureau of Gender Affairs staff are being publicly 'warned' for refusing to support sexist rhetoric."

CONCLUSION

There should be no partisan sides to this debate, only the collective move to halt the protracted violence that sears the souls of all those involved. This, then, is our history. It is time to leave this violence in the past, learning from it, so that we do not repeat it. The fight against domestic and gender-based violence cannot be tackled if we do not understand the past. Domestic violence is a pattern of behaviour used to establish power and control over another person through fear and intimidation, often including the threat or use of violence. That definition was applicable to the past; and it is still applicable now. Our ancestors fought against it then; and we must fight against it now. Violence directed at persons on the basis of their gender constitutes a breach of their fundamental right to life, liberty, security, dignity, non-discrimination, equality, and physical and mental integrity. It reinforces inequalities between men and women, boys and girls, and while it is mostly manifested in physical violence (mostly by men against women and girls), it is also evident in sexual, psychological or economic harm or suffering done to women – in deprivation of liberty, and threats of violence in public or private life.

The availability of data on violence against women and girls has improved considerably in recent years and data on the prevalence of intimate partner violence by UN Women are now available for at least 161 countries. Statistics are also available in academic publications and police reports. The persistence of this scourge on our landscape makes its elimination urgent. We need to interrupt the current trend and the unacceptable statistics. It is unacceptable that, according to UN Women 2024, approximately 736 million girls would have been traumatized by sexual or physical assault, by an intimate partner, a non-sexual partner or both; that 30 per cent of these women are aged 15 years and older; that over 640 million women have experienced intimate partner violence.[4] It is unacceptable that according to the Cayman Islands police report in 2023, there were 399 physical domestic violence crimes and 89 reported sexual crimes (both increased from 2022 figures, 377 and 88); that 17 of the 89 sexual crimes were domestically related. Out of the 2001 domestic referrals, the most frequent crime with 268 cases was physical domestic violence crimes.

It is unacceptable that, according to Sameena Mulla, "in the US, sexual assault is normalized in early adolescence, intimate partner violence is experienced by nearly a quarter of all women and accounts for about half of women's homicides".[5] It is also unacceptable that in the United Kingdom, according to statistics issued by the Office of National Statistics (ONS), the Crime Survey for England and Wales year ending March 2024 estimated that 4.8 per cent of people aged 16 years and over (2.3 million) experienced domestic abuse in the year before. Data from the British Association of Social Workers also reveal a hidden link between poverty and domestic abuse, with women living in the poorest households more than three times more likely to be victims of domestic abuse, including stalking, than those in higher income families. It is unacceptable that the National Police Chiefs' Council reported that, in 2022–23, 20 per cent of all police-recorded crime in the UK, was related to violence against women and girls.

It is unacceptable that currently high levels of domestic violence exist in Jamaica, Guyana, and Trinidad and Tobago. A 2023 World Bank Report indicated that 39 per cent of women in Jamaica have experienced some form of intimate partner violence; and UN Women reported that in Guyana 55 per cent of women between 15–64 years old have experienced a form of intimate partner violence, and 4 in 10 have experienced physical and/or sexual violence from a partner in their lifetime. At the time the study was conducted, one in 10 women had experienced physical and/or sexual violence from an intimate partner in the past 12 months.[6]

It is unacceptable that, according to the *Daily Express*, in 2022 in Trinidad and Tobago, 57 women were killed, 15 of them being as a result of domestic violence while 10 were as a result of gang-related activities. These figures push the number of women killed to 307 between 2017 and 2022.[7]

It is also unacceptable that lesbian, bisexual and transgender women are at risk of sexual violence due to their real or perceived sexual orientation and gender expression.

It is unacceptable that, according to the World Health Organization (WHO), recent global prevalence figures indicate that 35 per cent of women worldwide have experienced either intimate partner violence or non-partner sexual violence in their lifetime; on average, 30 per cent of women who have been in a relationship report that they have experienced some form of physical or sexual violence by their partner, and globally, as many as 38 per cent of murders of women are committed by an intimate partner.

It does not have to be the norm, but while contemporary societies are called upon to find strategies to eliminate GBV, those who laid the foundations in the period of colonization must not get away scot-free. That is the reason for the gender dimension of the reparation movement. While chattel enslavement, now universally recognized as a crime against humanity, affected both men and women, sexual violence and domestic abuse were experienced disproportionately by enslaved women. Indian indentureship, a post-slavery project, also saw the disproportionate abuse of Indian women on the journey from India and on the plantations.[8] The demand for redress for historic wrongs, which is the raison d'*être* of the reparation movement, must therefore embrace a gender dimension in the narrative that accompanies the Caribbean Community's (CARICOM) Ten Point Plan (TPP) for reparations. A quick review of the TPP reveals that CARICOM demands from former colonial powers, on behalf of the men and women of African descent in the Caribbean, a full formal apology, as opposed to statements of regret for the trafficking and enslavement of their African ancestors; an Indigenous Peoples' development programme to rehabilitate survivors of genocide; repatriation and resettlement in Africa as the descendants of more than fifteen million Africans, who were abducted from their homes and forcefully transported to the Caribbean, have a right to return to their ancestors' homeland; the establishment of cultural institutions; the return of looted cultural heritage; the alleviation of the public health crisis in the Caribbean; illiteracy eradication and support for educational infrastructure; an African knowledge programme; measures to promote psychological rehabilitation because of the trauma of capture, sale, storage in barracoons and chattel enslavement; technology transfer for greater access to the world's science and technology culture; and debt cancellation to address the fiscal entrapment with which Caribbean governments are struggling; as well as the return, in modern-day value, of the twenty million pounds sterling paid to the planters at emancipation. The revised TPP (2025) also includes a specific demand for reparations for the violence against women and the disruption of families under chattel enslavement.

Members of the CARICOM Reparation Commission has also insisted that this rehabilitative and development plan must apply to indentured labourers, aspects of whose contractual arrangements were not honoured by the importing nations and who suffered from exploitation/sexploitation, racism and other harms in the period after 1838. All points in the TPP implicates Indigenous, African and Indian women: the impact of the conquest and the ways in which gender roles changed; the brutality of the trafficking and chattel enslavement, including violent punishment (see table 1), and physical and psychological harm; the racism inherent in the landless and cashless emancipation; and the colonialist ideologies, policies and acts in the post-colonial period which intensified sexism, and which led to more resistance and more violence against protestors of all ethnic groups.

Reparation is a just call. Sir Ellis Clarke, the Trinidadian government's United Nations representative to a sub-committee of the Committee on Colonialism in 1964, stated clearly, "An administering power . . . is not entitled to extract for centuries all that can be got out of a colony and when that has been done to relieve itself of its obligations . . . Justice requires that reparation be made to the country that has suffered the ravages of colonialism . . ."[9]

Clarke was fervent in his belief that Britain could not just fob off Caribbean people with independence on the cheap. He and people of his generation may not have all used the word reparation, but they left us in no doubt that Britain was responsible for the current mess and had a responsibility to return to the scene of her crime and clean it up.

Of course, the call for reparations and reparatory justice in whatever language used by Clarke and those of his generation, and by more modern scholars like Hilary Beckles, had long been supported by enslaved Africans through their resistance activities, including anti-slavery wars and by freed people who struggled for social justice in the aftermath of the unjust Emancipation Act. These previous waves of articulation and activism inspired the entry into the movement of the committed Rastafari, civil society actors, scholar activists, individual politicians, and since 2013, by CARICOM heads of government as a collective. Together, they have brought us where we have reached.

NOTES

1. Romney Estate, Manuscripts and Special Collections (MSS), St Kitts and Nevis Archives.
2. CO 384/118, Enclosure in Despatch #62, Governor-in-Chief of Barbados to the Secretary of State for the Colonies, 30 June 1878.
3. CO 571/3, Protector of Immigrants' Report, 1915.
4. https://www.unwomen.org/en/articles/facts-and-figures/facts-and-figures-ending-violence-against-women Global Estimates 2024
5. Mulla, Sameena. 2018. "Gender-Based Violence in the US." *American Anthropologist* website, April 3.
6. UN Women. 2019. *Womens Health and life experiences: A Qualitative Research Report on Violence Against Women in Guyana*. GUYANA WOMEN'S HEALTH AND LIFE EXPERIENCES SURVEY REPORT, 9. https://caribbean.unwomen.org/sites/default/files/Field%20Office%20Caribbean/Attachments/Publications/2019/Guyana-Womens-Health-and-Life-Experiences-Survey-Report-2019.pdf
7. https://trinidadexpress.com/news/local/57-women-killed-in-2022/article_9fdaacf8-8971-11ed-9bc6-43ff2398d4a8.html-T&T statistics
8. See Verene A. Shepherd, *Maharani's Misery: Narratives of a Passage from India to the Caribbean* (Kingston: The University of the West Indies Press, 2002); and Shepherd, *Transients to Settlers: The Experience of Indians in Jamaica, 1845–1945* (Leeds: Peepal Tree Press, 1993).
9. Sir Ellis Clarke was the Trinidadian Government's United Nations representative to a sub-committee of the Committee on Colonialism in 1964, see quote in Gordon K. Lewis, *The Growth of the Modern West Indies* (New York: Monthly review Press, 1968), 385.

REFERENCES

Anonymous [A Genuine Dicky Sam]. 1884. *Liverpool and Slavery: An Historical Account of the Liverpool-African Slave Trade*. Liverpool: A. Bowker and Son.

Bailey, Anne. 2006. *African Voices of the Atlantic Slave Trade: Beyond the Silence and the Shame*. Boston: Beacon Press.

Beckles, Hilary. 1989. *Natural Rebels: A Social History of Enslaved Black Women in Barbados*. New Brunswick: Rutgers University Press.

———. 2011. "Sex and Gender in the Historiography of Caribbean Slavery." In *Engendering Caribbean History: Cross-Cultural Perspectives*, edited by Verene Shepherd. Kingston: Ian Randle Publishers.

———. 2013. *Britain's Black Debt: Reparations for Caribbean Slavery and Native Genocide*. Kingston: University of the West Indies Press.

———. 2021. *How Britain Underdeveloped the Caribbean: A Reparation Response to Europe's Legacy of Plunder and Poverty*. Kingston: University of the West Indies Press.

Clarke, Ellis. 1964. Speech delivered at the conference of the UN Committee on Colonialism. New York: United Nations. https://ibw21.org/reparations/capitalism-slavery-handbook-for-reparation-advocates-in-post-colonial-caribbean/.

Craton, Michael. 2004. *Founded Upon the Seas: A History of the Cayman Islands and Their People*. Kingston: Ian Randle Publishers.

da Costa, Emilia. 1997. *Crowns of Glory, Tears of Blood: The Demerara Slave Rebellion of 1823*. New York and Oxford: Oxford University Press.

French, Joan. 1988. "Colonial Policy Towards Women after the 1938 Uprising: The Case of Jamaica." *Caribbean Quarterly* 34 (3/4): 38–61.

Hall, Douglas. 1987. *In Miserable Slavery: Thomas Thistlewood in Jamaica, 1750–1786*. Kingston: University of the West Indies Press.

Haynes, Tonya. 2014. "Bajan Reporter letter to Editor Gains Steam: 'An activist walks out of a meeting'." *Bajan Reporter*, 23 March. https://www.bajanreporter.com/2014/03/bajan-reporter-letter-to-editor-gains-steam-an-activist-walks-out-of-a-meeting-by-dr-tonya-haynes/.

James, Marlon. 2009. *The Book of Night Women*. New York: Riverhead Books.

Mathurin Mair, Lucille. 2006. *Historical Study of Women in Jamaica, 1655–1844*, edited by Hilary Beckles and Verene Shepherd. Kingston: University of the West Indies Press.

Osterhammel, Jürgen. 1997. *Colonialism: A Theoretical Overview*. Translated from German by Shelley L. Frisch. Princeton, NJ: Markus Wiener and Kingston: Ian Randle Publishers.

Prince, Mary. [1831] 1987. *The History of Mary Prince: A West Indian Slave, Related by Herself*. Edited by Moira Ferguson. Ann Arbor: University of Michigan Press.

Scott, Joan Wallach. 1988. *Gender and the Politics of History*. New York: Columbia University Press.

Shepherd, Verene. 2002. *Maharani's Misery: Narratives of a Passage from India to the Caribbean*. Kingston: University of the West Indies Press.

Thompson, Alvin. 2002. *Unprofitable Servants: Crown Slaves in Berbice, Guyana, 1803–1831*. Kingston: University of the West Indies Press.

Wedderburn, Robert. [1824] 1991. "The Horrors of Slavery." In *The Horrors of Slavery and Other Writings*. Edited and introduced by Iain McCalman. New York and Princeton: Markus Wiener Publishing.

Williams, Eric. 1944. *Capitalism and Slavery*. Chapel Hill: University of North Carolina Press.

chapter 2

Violence Against Enslaved Women in Eighteenth-Century Suriname

Hilde Neus

IN THE DUTCH COLONY OF SURINAME, GENDER-BASED VIOLENCE (GBV) was a given fact during slavery, but has hardly been researched. General assumptions are readily made if the topic is discussed as part of the violent history of the region. Abuse was executed in all domains: physical, verbal, sexual, emotional and financial. By reading against the grain (Stoler 2010) and focusing on the subaltern (Spivak 1994), it is possible to distil information from the archives and other sources, and thus unearth this untold story.

In this chapter, GBV in Suriname between 1730 and 1830 is explored. A general frame will be described, and a number of concrete cases examined, within the particular geographical and historical context of the Dutch colony. Double standards were dominant. On the one hand, white women were seen as vulnerable and in need of protection; on the other, black women were treated as property. This was expressed in domestic violence, intimate partner violence and rape. Violence was executed in a very private manner, or extremely public ways. Some in the urban environment, others on plantations, as Zemon-Davis (2011) described.

An intersectional approach of these issues – focusing on gender, race and class – will show that many women fell victim to GBV. In spite of the severe oppression, however, they were able – within the limitations of the law – to claim agency and act against the barriers of legislation. At times they circumvented explicit violence and found ways of resistance, individually or in groups. By describing concrete cases, it is possible to step away from generalizations of the category of 'women' and create different continuums on which they moved through daily life.

Most of the women in colonial Suriname were exported from Africa and spent their lives as forced labour. The transatlantic voyage was extremely disruptive, their family lines broken off by natal alienation (Patterson 1982). The legislation regarding slavery was a local product, steeped in violent power.[1] The government imposed publicly executed punishments to keep the great slave might under control. Regulations, however, were not all-determining. Everyday life was marked by the arbitrary practices of owners, but also by different acts of resistance. These issues have been presented in studies before. The canonical coverage of slavery has left women underexposed, thus shaping the narrative. Here, the focus lies specifically on women, which can bring about a counter-narrative.

VIOLENCE DURING THE VOYAGE

The Dutch institutionalized slave trade was executed by the West India Company from 1621 on, and in private hands from 1791 (den Heijer 2013). A shortage of enslaved people was constantly felt because of negative birth rates. Within the transatlantic triangular trade, ships departed from Middelburg or Terschelling for the West African coast. Factories were frequented (such as Elmina) to take in the human cargo. Not every location could supply enough enslaved in one turn to fill the ship's hold. The Dutch were responsible for 5 per cent of the transatlantic trade, mainly to transit ports in Curaçao and St Eustatius. Suriname was a final destination, where a total of two hundred and thirteen thousand slaves were shipped to between 1668 and 1830 (van Stipriaan 1993, 57).

The accounts of the Middle Passage lean heavily on the manual for the treatment of enslaved during the crossing by surgeon David Gallandat (1769). On the ships, women were kept separate from men on steerage deck. Sporadically, there were reports in journals of women's abuse such as rape, which is not surprising since the charters of the Middelburg Company ordered crew not to mistreat the enslaved. Much abuse remained unrecorded because once known to the shipowners, the captain would forego subsequent appointments. In 1751, however, crew members of the *Elisabeth* testified to notary Phaff in Amsterdam. Already off the coast of Africa, some enslaved girls were maltreated. They served as companions during the captain's dinner, "showing off their pretty paantjes".[2] Supercargo Duijff lay in the hammock with Marij and Griet, in the presence of the captain. Once done, they sent the girls below deck, allowing the crew to do with them as they pleased. Catharina also stayed in the cabin and was later exchanged for two enslaved males.[3]

The ship's journal tells of the journey of *De Eenheidt* (1761–1763). This vessel visited Liberia, Ivory Coast and Ghana. The merchandise comprised of textiles (47 per cent), guns (33 per cent), drinks (4 per cent), beads (3 per cent), and so on. The ship was 22.5 metres long and carried 350 people on board, including 319 enslaved. Women and girls were locked up at night in the stern. During the day they stayed in a wooden hut, built for the journey. Unhealthy food, poor quality drinking water and abominable hygiene on board were the causes of death. On average, 16 per cent of the human cargo did not survive the crossing. Surgeon Couperus determined the cause of death of four deceased women and three girls. Upon arrival, another three women died on the coast of Suriname. On 30 May, Couperus noted: "A female slave from the Upper Coast died, always seemed to mourn, sat looking desperate, barely spoke, ate and drank little. I believe that her melancholy must have arisen from the fact that she had a child, that the negroes kept for themselves." She must have languished in grief over her lost child. He visited a woman who had been beaten and was left with bleeding from her ear and severe headaches. He gave a detailed description of "the situation under her skull". Two babies died shortly after birth. In total, ten enslaved females were written off on this journey, and twenty-two males.[4] Many images, as published in *The Slave Trade*, speak volumes about the horrors of the crossing (Walvin 2011).

VIOLENCE BY TRADE

The government painstakingly recorded arriving ships.[5] The enslaved were fed, bathed and oiled in quarantine until their auction. The purchase prices for "saltwater Negroes" supplied from West Africa rose from *f*82 per person in 1740 to *f*486 in the record year of 1754 (Bakker 1993, 42).[6] The buying owner had the initials of his name or plantation branded on the new possessions. Identification was important, especially when runaways were caught. Given the content and number of placards issued on the sales, payment often went awry.[7]

A list of the *Vriendschap* shows that figures on the male-female ratio are not always represented correctly.[8] In 1777, at the request of Captain Müller, arriving from Guinea, a *vendue* (public auction) was held. It concerned "40 slaves according to conditions in the slave trade book".

In total this group consisted of (values included): eleven men (*f*1258.10), eighteen women (*f*2665), zero boys and eleven girls (*f*1480), with total proceeds of *f*5403.10.[9] A few were listed as "sound", most qualified "as is" and were sold without their health being checked. This list shows that men did not necessarily fetch higher prices than women; for girls, equal amounts were paid.[10] The highest price for a man was *f*205, the (only) pregnant woman fetched the most. The most expensive girl cost *f*190, the cheapest *f*51.

The majority of the enslaved on most vessels were male; this ship carried more women, and the number of girls equalled the men. It is unknown why the *Friendship* only transported forty enslaved.[11] No generalizing statements can be made from these figures. Normally, a human cargo of as many as one hundred to five hundred were stowed in ship holds. The most tragic journey was of the *Leusden*, which, in 1738, shipwrecked in the Marowijneriver. Consequently, 664 people drowned since the hold was boarded up (Balai 2013).

After the slave trade abolition in 1814, supply figures from Africa declined sharply, despite smuggling. In Suriname, resale took place for various reasons. On 2 July 1759, Barend de Jong was banned from the colony and his Negress

Table 2.1: Excerpt of Enslaved Persons on *De Vriendschap*

No.	description	man	woman	boys	girls	price
38	as is	1				*f*100
39	as is				1	*f*170
40	sound and pregnant		1			*f*250

Source: NA 1.05.03-362-0030

sold publicly.[12] Departure or the owner's death was often the reason why the enslaved were put on the auction block. Sijfke wanted to sell the enslaved from the estate of the late widow Talbot and received permission in December 1768.[13] As soon as the first newspaper was published in 1774,[14] public auctions of the enslaved were advertised regularly (among other goods like furniture), sometimes entire families.

If Maroons were caught after running away, they regularly ended up in sales, such as the Negress Bessie, who was captured in January 1769 at the runaway village called Tesfissie. Or the "Bush criolin Affiba with her child".[15] The sale of children was seldom registered. And while they weren't legally allowed to be sold separately from their mother, archival sources show a different practice.[16] Heartbreaking is the public auction on 8 December 1768 of an eight-month-old infant who was among the runaways.[17]

PUNISHMENT LAWS

The legal framework for slavery in Suriname was designed by the government, and proposals for placards were sent to the Society in Amsterdam for approval.[18] A strict legal system for a regulated society was necessary because of the huge demographic imbalance between the enslaved and freemen. Severe penalties were imposed to set an example for others; *oderunt peccare mali fomidine poenae* [*The wicked hate to sin because of the fear of punishment*], aimed at deterrence rather than amelioration. The extent to which this was adhered to is apparent from public sentencing.[19] Disciplinary law was subdivided into domestic jurisdiction, based on Roman law, which the owners imposed, and criminal law, executed by the government. This division undoubtedly led to arbitrariness. Mutilation and death sentences were pronounced by the court. These took place at a public location.[20] Inventories were regularly drawn up to list detainees in Fort Zeelandia, where interrogations took place. For example, on 2 December 1793, the list included five men and two women; "a new negress from plantation Waterswijk, and a new negress, name unknown".[21]

Interrogations – of any detainee – could be executed through pressure and coercion. Zemon Davis (2011) indicates that enslaved, free Negroes and mulattoes were not allowed to testify against whites. However, many

Figure 2.1: Selling of mother and children in Suriname

witness statements show that their vote was of influence. In the Netherlands, corporal punishment and death penalties were also imposed, though abolished at an earlier date (Steensma 1982, 37). Tying up to a tree with rope was banned in 1784, but Boekhoudt (1874) provides an eyewitness account. Staying on a plantation he awoke to a frightening noise. "A youthful Negress, suspended from a tree, whimpered under screeching lashes that carved her loins, administered to her by two Bastians (Negro officers). The host raved, urging them on to greater severity. Later in the day he acted as if nothing had happened" (van Lier 1977, 15). The Spanish buck[22] was the most feared corporal punishment. After 1828 its administration was forbidden, but still mentioned in the Picket list (1843), according to Bosch van Suchtelen (2018). This beating was performed in Fort Zeelandia, or on corners of four, sometimes even seven streets within Paramaribo.

Legislation regarding slavery was enacted and adjusted locally, but due to leniency towards the actions of the owners, arbitrariness and mistreatment remained the order of the day. Enslaved women also fell victim to this.

FORMS OF PUNISHMENT

In his 1757 diary, American traveller Greenwood described that Mrs D., a lady of the first character, brought her slave girl (with a baby at her breast) to the fort for:

> . . . what they call a Spanish buck, because she couldn't appease her child. I heard her say in the negro house: "*Gib him den onderds.*"[23] One day I left a plantation I was visiting, because I could not bring myself to witness a beating, carried out for the smallest offence. Slaves were taken to the Citadel [the Fortress] to execute the punishment. Other slaves carried out these cruel punishments in order to avoid revenge among their fellow slaves. After the punishment, the parts were washed with water and salt to prevent inflammation, but it was common for maggots to develop in the wound. Every day I have come across many who have undergone this correction, it leaves terrible scars. (Greenwood 1757)

Canfijn and Fatah Black (2022, 42) looked into seven hundred lawsuits to obtain a balanced overview of the functioning of the criminal justice system. From 1820 onwards, they note a decrease in corporal punishment and death penalties, as well as more regulation of the privileges of the owners. Sentences were increasingly imposed by the government and appeals handled by the lower courts. Due to the establishment of the Picket in Paramaribo – and district bailiffs who supervised the execution of sentences on plantations – fewer enslaved were brought before the High Court.[24]

As far as gender-related research is concerned, Bosch van Suchtelen (2018) looked into types of crimes and punishment for the years 1843–1845. Including figures for both the enslaved and owners, it appears that female private mistresses owned more women. They (126 men and sixty-six women) paid for the punishment. Private masters (women in particular) imposed less harsh penalties and awarded the Spanish buck less. The maximum punishment for men was twenty-five lashes, fifteen for women. However, reports show that many more lashes were administered. Frequent conflicts with the colonial government over the implementation of domestic jurisdiction are recorded, as owners felt it was their prerogative and responsibility. In the *Picketboek* the Spanish buck was recorded twenty-one more times. When registered, personal data, types of crime, penalties and owners were included.

Table 2.2: Excerpt of Punishments

Gender	Desertion	Rudeness	Others
Male	46%	33%	21%
Female	43%	37%	20%

Source: Bosch-van Suchtelen, 2018

A calculation shows that, in 1844, there were 43,129 persons living in slavery, of whom 678 were punished – about 1.6 per cent. Of these, 537 sentences were analysed: 354 imposed on men, and 171 on women. Most crimes were committed between the ages of twenty-five and thirty-four. In general, the offences consisted of desertion or bad behaviour.

Other offences included laziness (lowest penalty), theft, fighting, dereliction of duty, drunkenness or complex offences (highest penalty). Of the total number of enslaved, 15 per cent lived in Paramaribo, 85 per cent on plantations. However, 50 per cent of those punished were registered as plantation slaves and 23 per cent were privately owned by a man, 12 per cent by a woman. Various crimes occurred in the city, while marronage happened more from the plantations.

In addition to corporal punishment, some sentences consisted of banishment from the colony. The Fiscal filed a criminal claim against the Negress Seraphina and the Negro Bootsman of Mon Plaisir for administering poison. They were sold away from the country.[25] The number of poison cases rose from seventeen in the early 1730s to forty-two in 1745, and these were increasingly carried out by women. In 1742, Baron confessed to poisoning his mistress with herbs, in order to "cool her down" and avoid further punishment. She didn't survive (Berry 2019).

Figures from 1843 show the punishment of 2 per cent of the enslaved population, but this number should not be generalized in creating the impression that punishment was not severe or often administered. Undoubtedly, much was left unrecorded, especially on the plantations where everyday government supervision was lacking. Punishments were carried out to control violation of restrictive measures. At times offences indicate forms of agency.

COMPLAINTS BY THE ENSLAVED

Enslaved people were not completely disenfranchised. They could lodge a complaint with the court. In the archives, the voices of the enslaved can be heard, and their rights become apparent. On 9 December 1767, a petition from Biertempels Negress about her master's conduct was filed, and the commissioner interrogated her.[26] In May 1774, the Fiscal was authorized to question De Courval for cruel treatment of a Negress.[27] On 1 August 1778, the Fiscal investigated the complaints deposited by the Negress Julia.[28] In September 1775, the Fiscal heard Siefaart for mistreatment of Fontane's slave girl.[29] Women – both the enslaved and the manumitted, as well as owners – filed complaints.

Detainees were interrogated within twenty-four hours of detention, and trials followed within days. Severe corporal punishment was executed by the court. Enslaved sentenced to death were compensated by the government for half their value, except in the case of murder. On 18 June 1750, the governor remarked on a negro of Miss Hertsbergen who was supposedly hanged without due process.[30] This case shows that at times the court was divided over proper procedure.[31]

The killing of the enslaved was discouraged, but if a white man killed an enslaved person, the punishment was quite different from when an enslaved killed a white person. On 11 August 1768, a case was filed against Ditmar for stabbing a Negress to death with a knife. He was banned from the colony for his offence.[32] This shows that gender-based violence was judged arbitrarily, and the system was designed to punish people according to their status of being free, or not. The same judgment befell Croesius on 8 December. He had shot and killed a Negress "by accident".[33] Despite various exhortations by the Fiscal not to mistreat the enslaved, this remained regular practice. In May 1771, it was determined that in a case of serious abuse, the director should be replaced.[34] In 1775, however, there were two additional cases of a director convicted of maltreatment of the enslaved. An enslaved girl from Rust tot Lust was whipped so immoderately by Salsman, that she died the same day. He received a fine of *f*300 plus legal costs, and was not allowed to visit the plantation again.[35] For whipping an enslaved girl on Clemensburg plantation, J.H. Borchard received the same verdict.[36]

In researching criminal cases in Berbice (1819–1832), Burnard (2010) argued that the voice of the enslaved can be heard pre-eminently.[37] This also applies to Suriname. The archives do not reproduce exactly what the slaves discussed with each other, but the dissatisfaction with their situation shows in the interrogations, mediated by scribe and context. The secretary adapted the language, but it is likely that the testimonials were accurately recorded. Of course, both the slaves and the overseers told the story from their perspective in order to create a positive base. There were complaints about hard work, unjust punishment and ill-treatment of relatives.

A wide variety of cases indicate that the enslaved were very aware of what was minimally expected of them, but also where the extreme limits lay. Burnard posits that the defence discourse of the owners shows the human and individual sides of the enslaved and, ironically, their idiosyncratic behaviour. The owners' arguments, he posits, were curtailed by an obligation of mutual solidarity imposed by their numerical minority, more or less forcing them to unite against the collective power of the enslaved. In Berbice, twenty-eight cases of fornication or adultery (against eleven men) were recorded (Burnard 2010). In Suriname this category was not judged. Under Dutch law, the enslaved were not allowed to marry.

A CASE OF SUICIDE

In the Netherlands one cannot feign ignorance over the mistreatment of the enslaved – including torture and capital punishment. Before 1800, Stedman's publication, especially because of the images, produced a shock effect. In the run-up to the abolition of slavery, the works of Teenstra (1842) and Van Hoevell (1854) were also known for their many descriptions of distressing cases, including punishments imposed on women by women.

Teenstra (1842, 148) refers to a lawsuit against Anna Elizabeth Lindsay, who was openly flogged on a scaffold in Paramaribo in 1822 and banned for life because of the "far-reaching and horrific abuses in the punishment of a Negro woman named Henriette", who had succumbed to her injuries on 14 August 1821. Lindsay thought Henriette had died of the torture and had her body thrown in a ditch. The next morning, however, she was found more dead than alive. The torture was repeated, whereupon Henriette collapsed, unconscious. Lindsay wanted to bury her alive, but the involved Fiscal was able to prevent this act. The year before, Lindsay had supposedly tortured Henriette's eleven-year-old daughter, Fanny, in the same way. Lindsay was a free-born, coloured woman of English descent who lived in the Danish island of St Cruz around 1777 who was known for "her cruelty in punishing her slaves with whips, bull-ropes, buckles, chains and shackles, wooden collars, hanging from trees, burning under the feet, as well as internal punishment by abstaining from eating and drinking". Teenstra generally stated, "If the Whites are cruel and stern in punishing guilty slaves, they are no less harsh and negligent in tending to the innocence of Negroes in their care."

Suicide was not an unknown phenomenon among the enslaved. In Van Dyk's play dialogue (1765), the director demanded the enslaved girl Filida to come to him at night. She begged him: "Lord Master, I cannot do this, because if my husband gets wind of it – he is a Kormantynsze Neeger – he would kill himself . . . " This fictitious story was based on truth, as recorded suicide cases show. On 11 August 1767, Surgeon May submitted a report of a "self-murder" committed by a Negress of Mr G. Schilling. Earlier, on 6 August, her owner explained the incident with Cato to the court.

The case of Sara shows – in spite of the fact that she was enslaved – that she possessed some level of agency. Sara had died on the Leyden plantation. Pichot, the Fiscal, investigated a suspected murder and the culprit, Jan Cruffel, was detained on 1 May 1751 in Fort Zeelandia. On Pichot's report, the court discussed whether the accused had beaten a Negress to death on 25 April in the evening, and furthermore had abandoned the Leyden plantation "at the discretion of the slaves". Cruffel never denied knocking Sarah over the head with a bag-stick, after which she entered her room and died later that night. The question remained whether she fell victim to the beating, or possibly had "put it upon herself by desperation or wickedness". According to the court, Cruffel never should have hit Sara like that, knowing the result could be fatal. This carelessness would not have happened if he had just whipped her – as usual.

Sara's owner was inconsistent in his report. He claimed he left for the city immediately on Monday, 26 April. Later, he stated he had slept through the night on the path next to Leyden, in the *wi'wiri*.[38] The next day, he travelled to Paramaribo, accompanied by Mr Gutz, director of the neighbouring plantation L'Union. Despite his fear of the enslaved – since he had violently killed Sara – he visited Leyden unobtrusively, to fetch his belongings. The court deemed this suspicious behaviour and judged his negligence more important than Sara's death. As the person responsible, he left "a huge capital" unattended. In fleeing to Paramaribo, he could have boarded the first ship leaving for Holland. The question of whether Sara had committed suicide remained. Cruffel insisted he had no intention of killing her, as she was his concubine and the reason for beating was insufficient for murder; she had refused to chase the dog from the room. There were no additional signs of abuse on her body, according to several witnesses. So, Sarah might have choked herself out of desperation after Cruffel hit her. He also nearly lost his thumb because she'd bitten him when he "wanted to wrench her mouth open".[39]

Legally, as a slave, Sarah had few opportunities for agency. It remains unclear whether she was coerced into a relationship with Cruffel. At some point she chose to refuse to carry out his orders, after which he hit her on the head. This violent behaviour was the way for Cruffel to keep her under control. He claimed that he had tried to save her from suffocation, but this looks – given his other statements – more like an attempt to excuse himself. Sara died as a result of the assault – her agency crushed.[40]

LIMITING MOBILITY

Good behaviour was rewarded, bad behaviour punished, and randomness played a major part. The way in which the enslaved were able to move about the city was – in relation to general safety – a constant point of discussion, which resulted in tightening the rules. This becomes evident in the story of Fortuna. This Negro girl, belonging to Samuel Townshend, had gone out into the street at 9:30 on a Sunday night to pick up her mistress, Johanna. Townshend submitted a memorandum to Governor Jan Nepveu on 8 May 1774.[41] Fortuna had been captured by the Civil Guards and Townshend visited officer Leijsner to unsuccessfully urge him to release the girl. The officer demanded he pay six guilders and he could have his maid. Townshend got angry and told Leijsner off. As Fortuna's master, he could have easily punished her himself, and this was not the time to throw away six guilders.

The next morning, he received a message that the civilian patrol had turned Fortuna over to be jailed in the fort. If he didn't pay, she would be handed over to the provost, who was entitled to give her a Spanish buck.

Townshend claimed that he would vow for his slaves if they behaved wrongly. But he doubted this, as the patrol had picked Fortuna up right outside his door. Meanwhile he had been informed by various witnesses, and expected to be exempt from the fine. On Monday morning he reported to the provost in Fort Zeelandia to pay. The provost, however, was allowed to take anybody into custody, but could not punish or release without permission of the Fiscal. This prosecutor, I.G. Wichers, then presented the owner with a large bill. Townshend felt troubled because the Fiscal had disadvantaged him in the eyes of his enslaved and fellow citizens. This way, he argued, justice could ruin anybody. He was advised to write to the governor.

Neighbour Daandels declared that Fortuna was arrested in front of Mr Walraven's house, together with the Negro Tranquil and Katarina, while heading out with two lit lanterns to fetch her mistress. Nevertheless, she was taken by the patrol. Corporal Hiene testified that he saw an enslaved person walking near the inn, not knowing whether it was a man or a woman. The person jumped into the ditch, "wanting to hide", but was caught. It turned out to be a girl, and that she "was not provided with a lantern or a letter". Three guards supported this testimony. The arrest and dismissal cost a total of 18.18 Surinamese guilders. In the end Townshend paid three times the original amount to have Fortuna released.

Her internment shows that the government was committed to curbing the freedom of movement in town. This was to prevent gathering – with the possible intent to rebel or run away. Fortuna was on the street at the behest of her master, but nevertheless arrested for not carrying a permission slip or lamp, as prescribed.[42] The reason why the sex of the suspect was not recognized initially might have been caused by the darkness, or by the fact that Fortuna did not yet have a pronounced female figure due to her young age. Frequent arresting of slaves on public roads was to prevent this behaviour from leading to freer movement of the enslaved throughout the city.

A MOST GRUESOME CASE *(*TRIGGER WARNING: CONTAINS GRAPHIC DESCRIPTIONS)*

The vilest atrocity under the system of slavery that I found in the archives is a lawsuit against the wife of a Jewish planter, Oliviera. De Vriendt and Maur issued a report to the Fiscal on 17 April 1773.[43] Oliveira had just moved fourteen days prior to live opposite the doctor's house, and ever since, his wife had not ceased to treat the Negress Premiere belonging to her barbarously and inhumanly, so much so that she passed away miserably the night before. According to his duty, the Fiscal examined the case to the utmost and sent several witnesses to the Jewess to look into the horrific details of the torture.[44] The *chirurg major* Neitsen produced a medical *actum*, in which his examination was captured.[45]

Fiscal Wichers issued a request to the governor for further investigation into "these atrocities which seem to be increasing day by day, and are to the utmost contrary to humanity and to the good order of the bourgeoisie". The court discussed the case, since an enslaved person had allegedly died as a result of abuse.[46] The head of the Civil Guard, Vriendt, testified to support the doctor's report, with councils of the court present as witnesses. Widow Agnetta Krak, the free mulattress Cicilia, the Negresses Beya (belonging to Maur) and Trina (from Rouleau) also testified. Agnetta Krak declared that she lived right across from the Oliviera house and heard the Negress' suppressed moaning. A friend's maid came to her and said, "Oh my God, come and see, this negress is being beaten to death." With difficulty, they listened to the moaning and the maid's outburst that Oliveira's housewife was holding ". . . a piece of burning wood, burning that '*meit*' in her female parts". The free mulattress Cicilia declared that at eight o'clock in the morning she went across to Maur's maid to buy a duck. Next door, she saw a woman punishing a Negress to such a degree that the victim could hardly speak, and exclaimed, "Missie, you will kill me". She consequently fell to the ground and her 'foundation' came out. Her owner took a piece of hot wood and stuck it in her 'foundation'. She beat the maid with continuation and put a piece of wood in her mouth to break open her teeth. This went on until midnight three o'clock. Cicilia heard this until a silence fell at 9 a.m., at around which time she certainly believed the girl was dead. Her daughter, Mitie, was behind her, and witnessed the scene.

Beya added some more details to the statements already issued. She was living next door to the Oliveira house. On the previous Thursday, Mrs Oliveira had fetched the Negress from the Jew Josua Aria, where she had stayed to be healed. The next day at 6 a.m., Premiere was told to split a piece of bolletrie wood, whereupon she replied: "Missie, I have no power to split that wood."[47] Again, Mrs Oliveira had her beaten while naked. Then she kept her in the house for a few days, not wanting others to see her. In the meantime, Premiere had weakened, and Oliveira brought her outside again, where Beya heard her screaming day and night, "Missie, I can't take it any longer" and also heard the blows over and over. That lasted for five days. At nine o'clock on Friday morning, she saw how Oliveira's wife put the Negress to stand against the fence. Premiere had to take off her clothes, and Beya saw through the cracks in the fence that "the foundation of the girl was hanging from the body". She saw Mrs Oliveira take a piece of hot wood and put it in the maid's 'foundation' and throw her to the ground. Beya called the Negress Trina (who belonged to Rouleau) to witness it all. Premiere was dragged back into the house, where they heard her screaming until she died that same night. Trina testified that she knew nothing of the matter other than what she saw after Beya had called her over. She explained that she was not able to continue watching, so horrific was the torture. These witness statements were recorded on 20 April.[48]

The Negress Eva van Oliveira was examined separately by councils Bedloo and Kennedy. She was a new Negro slave who did not speak the language, so her statement was translated by the Negro Schrik van't Land.[49] Eva declared that Premiere was ill but that Missie Oliveira wanted her to work anyway, even though she didn't have the strength to do so. Missie then beat her to death saying: "You don't want to work. I'll make you work." During the torture Premiere did not want to eat. Mrs Oliveira then violently forced a piece of wood into her mouth, breaking two front teeth. 'Missie' sent Eva to fetch water, but the girl was afraid to return since Mrs Oliviera had threatened to kill her as well the next day. Out of fright, Eva turned to the bailiff and told him what had happened. Mr Oliveira was absent during the entire ordeal.

On 12 May the court decided to question Mrs Oliveira and her husband separately.[50] Maur declared that Jacob Oliveira had asked him to look after Premiere because she needed healing from sores and *crabbejas*. She stayed for eight days.[51] During this time she complained that when she was in distress her bowels came out, which Maur reported to her master. He planned to cure her of this evil and only send her back after she had healed.[52] Mr Oliveira was a native of Amsterdam, sixty-two and of Portuguese Jewish heritage. He was the owner of the Negresses Premiere and Eva. According to him, Premiere died of the discomforts of her intestinal problem, as indicated by the surgeon Josua Arias, in the presence of Gratia Patheels. When asked how burns came to be on her body, he answered that her abdomen was swollen, and denied any knowledge of the burns. His wife had indeed ordered Premiere to split a piece of bolletrie, and she had done so willingly. He denied that his wife ordered Eva to beat Premiere. He did not see a need to stop his wife because she had not mistreated anybody, knowing the severe penalty for such actions. Asked about Eva, he explained that his wife took her and a large copper kettle to the Moodj at the Jewish church to fetch water to throw on the clothes on the bleaching meadow. Eva came back late and his wife prevented her from going a second time because it was already evening and she might fall into the well. Eva went anyway and did not return. Apparently, she left for town, saying, "The Jews beat all the girls to death. They are crazy." The kettle remained with the lady at the well and Eva stayed at the fort with Van Veen.

Fiscal Wichers confronted Judig Aron with the subsequent statements of Miss Agneta Krak and the free mulattress Cicilia. Judig denied knowing them, or her wrongdoings, even though the witnesses persisted in their testimonies. During the interrogation, Judig Avon denied all accusations and declared that Premiere had died from her indisposition. The swollen belly had not healed, and she had not been able to speak for several days. She was not burned; the marks were from the *jas*. The owner claimed she did not act contrary to the law.[53] In the marriage book of the Jewish community, the wedding between widower Jacob Oliviera and Judicq Aron Pollak (born thirty-two years prior as a member of the German Jewish nation in Frederiksstad, Holsteijn, Germany) was recorded. Even though she had four children, they were not properly married, though cohabiting was against the edicts of the country.[54] This case is testimony of the violence of a woman against women, owner against the enslaved. But also, that diverse women were called as witnesses.

CONCLUSION

It can be argued that as far as women are concerned, gender-based violence played a prominent role throughout their lives. The supply of enslaved persons from Africa has not yet been sufficiently researched. Women may have played a more important role on the West African coast than has hitherto been assumed. The transatlantic crossing gave them little say over their own bodies. Conditions on the ships were fatal for some. The trafficking of women across the ocean and the selling in slave markets was a crime in itself, and the conditions for women were not very different from the ones men faced. Once in the colony, slave prices varied. General supply figures in Suriname are extensively recorded, but detailed analysed data – about age or sex – are lacking. More in-depth research needs to be undertaken to determine whether the perception that men produced more coffee and sugar – and the hardship of the labour – needs to be adjusted.

Everyday life in the colony was laced with violence, and much of the personal zest for life stemmed from the behaviour of the slave owner. There was a great deal of arbitrariness in the frequency and degree of punishment of the enslaved. Peer pressure on the actions of the planters undoubtedly played a role. According to Oostindie (1993), the image of Suriname as one of the cruellest slave societies was created mainly by the publication of Voltaire's *Candide* (1761) and Stedman's *Reize through Suriname . . .* (1796). Van Stipriaan's *Surinaams contrast* (1993) highlights incorrect figures that give wrong impressions of punishment. However, due to the absence of comparative research, these statements are hard to debunk.

Contrary to existing notions, the enslaved, including women, filed petitions with the court and did have rights. In a case of great dissatisfaction with the actions of fellow enslaved, people higher up in the plantation hierarchy – masters or mistresses in Paramaribo – filed complaints which were investigated, whereby the testimony of other enslaved people was honoured. It is presumed that the enslaved could not raise their voice, but in the archives a number of requests by women are recorded. In witness statements, drawn up during interrogations, the voices of enslaved women can be heard. One way of going against the system was marronage. However, in this area as well the role of women is still underexposed.

Within the limits of the law women had possibilities to practise agency, at times even limit or completely ban certain actions by the owner. This could be through testifying, filing requests, fighting back or – as a last, tragic resort – suicide. These actions can be seen as resistance to the oppressive system. At times, well aware of the consequences, enslaved women chose to act, knowing the outcome might be a gruesome death. Women in slavery had the least opportunities and possibilities to go against the system. The colonial government raised all kinds of restrictions to prevent agency and acted, as much as possible, to curtail any expression of freedom. And when it came to violence, women were not exempt.

NOTES

1. Placards, laws and regulations from 1669 to 1816 in: Schiltkamp, J.A. en J.Th. De Smidt 1973, mentioned as Placard.
2. *Paantje* is a piece of cloth that is wrapped around the loins. In Sranan: panji.
3. https://archief.amsterdam/inventarissen/scans/5075/341.1.59/start/1580/limit/10/highlight/9 https://www.amsterdam.nl/stadsarchief/themasites/amsterdam-slavernij/1751-opgepronkt-mooije-paantjes/
4. https://eenigheid.slavenhandelmcc.nl/
5. National Archives, The Hague. NAHa 1.05.03-28-006, fol. 141.
6. People recently transported from Africa were called *zoutwaternegers* ("salt water negroes").
7. Placard: 31.
8. It is suggested that of the enslaved, 60 per cent were male, and 40 per cent were female. These figures changed over time, depending on circumstances.
9. According to accountant Pater, *f* stands for *florijn*, the Dutch currency.
10. Prices fluctuated, men fetched higher prices than women, especially pro slave trade abolition. This list shows there are exceptions.
11. NAHa 1.05.03-362-0030.
12. NAHa 1.05.03-183-0329.
13. NAHa 1.05.03-183-0272.
14. As in *Surinaamsche Nieuws Vertelder* (Surinamese news narrator), 1788.
15. NAHa 1.05.03-183-0013.
16. Placard 862.
17. NAHa 1.05.03-183-0272.

18. There was no institutionalized slavery in the Netherlands.
19. See Placard book, under Strafrecht, from 1669 onwards.
20. NAHa 1.05.03-182-0279.
21. Museumstof nr. 40.
22. The 'Spanish buck' consisted of bending a slave's arms to his knees, then fastening them together with a stick underneath in preparation for a beating on the backside until no skin was left.
23. Meaning a beating on the lower parts.
24. These lawsuits date back to 1722, 1750, 1775 en 1799, a report from 1854 was added for completion.
25. NAHa 1.05.03-167-0551.
26. NAHa 1.05.03-183-0114.
27. NAHa 1.05.03-182-0234
28. NAHa 1.05.03-182-0261.
29. NAHa 1.05.03-182-0250.
30. NAHa 1.05.03-182-0197.
31. NAHa 1.05.03-182-0162.
32. NAHa 1.05.03-182-0162.
33. NAHa 1.05.03-182-0223.
34. NAHa 1.05.03-183-0362.
35. NAHa 1.05.03-166-0548.
36. NAHa 1.05.03-166-0549.
37. Berbice was British territory by then.
38. *Wi'wiri* are low bushes in wetland.
39. NAHa 1.05.10.02-550-0333.
40. Cruffel was banned from Suriname.
41. NAHa 1.05.10.02-558-0111 to 0121.
42. Placard 185, the earliest in 1698. Often repeated.
43. NAHa 1.05.10.02-824-0133.
44. NAHa 1.05.10.02-824-0149.
45. NAHa 1.05.10.02-824-0135.
46. NAHa 1.05.10.02-824-0161.
47. Bolletrie is a very hard type of wood.
48. NAHa 1.05.10.02-824-0149.
49. People recently transported from Africa were called *zoutwaternegers* (saltwater Negroes).
50. NAHa 1.05.10.02-824-0177.

51. *Crabbejas* or *jas*, referring to yaws, an infection of the skin, bones and joints caused by a spirochete bacterium that causes hard swellings under the skin, the centres of which may form ulcers.
52. Statement of J. Maur, 6 May 1773. NAHa 1.05.10.02-824-0163.
53. NAHa 1.05.10.02-824-0159.
54. NAHa 1.05.10.02-824-0199. 18 December 1772, extract from the wedding books of the Jews as asked by the court.

REFERENCES

Bakker, E., L. Dalhuisen, M. Hassankhan, and F. Steegh. 1993. *Geschiedenis van Suriname: Van stam tot staat [History of Suriname: From Tribe to State]*. Zutphen: Walburg Pers.

Balai, Leo. 2013. *Slavenschip Leusden [Slave ship Leusden]*. Zutphen: Walburg Pers.

Boekhoudt, W. 1874. *Uit mijn verleden: Bijdrage tot de kennis van Suriname [From My Past: Contribution to the Knowledge of Suriname]*. Winschoten: Van der Veen.

Bosch van Suchtelen, R. 2018. "'Met eenige vaderlijke tucht'. De bestraffing van mensen in slavernij in 'het wekelijksch rapport der afgestrafte slaven op het piket der justitie'." ["'With some paternal discipline': The punishment of people in slavery in the weekly report of punished slaves on the picket line of justice."] Thesis, Radboud University Nijmegen.

Burton, Trevor. 2010. *Hearing Slaves Speak*. Georgetown: Caribbean Press.

Canfijn, I., and K. Fatah Black. 2022. "The Power of Procedure. Punishment of Slaves and the Administration of Justice in Suriname, 1669–1869." *Journal of Global Slavery* 7: 19–47.

den Heijer, Henk. 2013. *Geschiedenis van de WIC. Opkomst, bloei en ondergang [History of the WIC. Rise, Prosperity and Fall]*.Zutphen: Walburg Pers.

Gallandat, David. 1769. *Noodige onderrichtingen voor de slaafhandelaaren [Necessary Instructions for the Slave Traders]*. Middelburg: Pieter Gillissen.

Greenwood, John. 1758. *Diaries 1752–1758, 1763–1765*. https://researchworks.oclc.org/archivegrid/collection/data/58665250.

Oostindie, G. 1993. "Voltaire, Stedman and Suriname Slavery." In *Slavery & Abolition* 14 (2): 1–34.

Patterson, Orlando. 1982. *Slavery and Social Death*. Cambridge, MA: Harvard University Press.

Schiltkamp, J.A.. 1973. *West-Indisch plakaatboek: Plakaten, ordonnantiën en andere wetten, uitgevaardigd in Suriname 1667–1816 [Dl. I en II] [West Indian Placard*

Book: Placards, ordinances and other laws, issued in Suriname 1667–1816 (Vol. I and II)]. Edited by J. Th. De Smidt. Amsterdam: Emmering.

Spivak, Gayatri C. 1993. *Outside in the Teaching Machine*. London: Routledge.

Steensma, H. 1982. *Straffen door de eeuwen heen. De beul, het tuchthuis en de gevangenis [Punishments Through the Ages: The Executioner, the House of Correction and the Prison]*. Den Haag: Omniboek.

Stoler, Laura Ann. 2009. *Along the Archival Grain: Epistemic Anxieties and Colonial Common Sense*. Princeton, NJ: Princeton University Press.

Teenstra, M.D. 1844. *De negerslaven in de kolonie Suriname [The Negro Slaves in the Colony of Suriname]*. Dordrecht: Lagerweij.

van Dyk, Pieter. 1765. *Nieuwe en nooit bevoorens geziene onderwyzinge in het bastert Engels of Neeger Engels [. . .] Alles, na veel jaarige beproeving en Ondervinding, Opgesteld en in het Ligt gebragt [New and Never Before Seen Instruction in Basterd English or Neger English [. . .] All, After Many Years of Trial and Experience, Compiled and Brought into the Light]*. Amsterdam: De Erven de Weduwe Jacobus van Egmont.

van Hoevell, W. 1854. *Slaven en vrijen onder de Nederlandse wet [Slaves and Free Persons Under Dutch Law]*. Zaltbommel: Noman en zn.

van Lier, R. 1977. *Samenleving in een grensgebied: Een sociaalhistorische studie van Suriname [Borderland Society: A Socio-historical Study of Suriname]*. Amsterdam: Emmering.

van Stipriaan, Alex. 1993. *Surinaams contrast: Roofbouw en overleven in een Caraïbische Plantagekolonie 1750–1863 [Surinamese Contrast: Overexploitation and Survival in a Caribbean Plantation Colony, 1750–1863]*. Leiden: KITLV.

Walvin, James. 2011. *The Slave Trade*. London: Thames and Hudson.

Zemon Davies, Nathalie. 2011. "Judges, Masters, Diviners: Slaves' experience of Criminal Justice in Colonial Suriname." *American Society for Legal History: Law and History Review* 29 (4): 925–84.

chapter 3

Black Masculinity in Caribbean Slavery[1]

Hilary McD. Beckles

CARIBBEAN ACADEMICS AND PUBLIC POLICY PLANNERS ARE ENGAGED in several interactive discourses that concern the ideological constructions, and social effects, of historicized black masculinities. The social representations of these masculinities, and their relationships to the meanings of everyday life, have produced discernible cultural results over time. One of these results is endemic imbalances between males and females in public institutions and social processes. In areas of political power and domestic authority, other results are seen, as manifested in the problematized popular behaviours of young black males, now perceived as labyrinths, or laboratories, for detecting the origins of dysfunctional deviance in cultural life (see Bond and Peery 1970; Brod 1987; Brittan 1989; Connell 1987, 1995; Easthope 1986).

One recommendation of the discourse calls for the detection of the historical origins of what is a starling "discovery"; that the postcolonial black male is psychically defeated and socially at risk. It is said, furthermore, that the very notion of "nation" is at risk, subverted, if you will, by socially dysfunctional masculine attitudes and cultural tendencies. Analytical subtleties apart, the idea is aggressively promoted that historically shaped and validated masculinities within the region have been parked by postmodernity in a derelict cul-de-sac as far as the ideologies of community and development are concerned.

All too often in these conversations, seminal moments and critical ideas within the historical contexts, and the perspectives they should yield, are ignored, missed or understated. Critical historical evidence is often set aside, condemned and discredited as an apologetic voice for particular antisocial types of masculinities. Linked to this posture is a suspicion of the traditional historian's craft as a politically supportive ideological activity of patriarchy within the gender order. With keen awareness of these positions, what is proposed here is not an attempt to confront these postures nor to suggest an escape route through historicism. Rather, this intervention is intended to fully open the historical narrative at the primordial juncture of the slave society.

The search is for a perspective that may illuminate the historical nature of relations and structures within Caribbean civilization and allow one to comment on the process of social and ideological continuities (see Baker and Chapman 1962). Definitional specification requires that since our concern is with black masculinities, analytic attention should focus on the terms "black" and "male". The proposal here is that we adopt them both at the general level of popular understanding, and take on board the view of Hare and Hare (1984) that recognizes masculinity in terms of a culturally determined tendency to act as a provider and protector. It is important to recognize that the ideology of masculinity is largely "a socially produced script" on which historical notions of role fulfilment have been coded. This feature of the process dictates that the script is under constant revision; it is therefore unstable, even though the continuity of certain fundamental elements can be discerned. These elements, collectively, constitute the rollers on which masculinities evolve as sites of cultural power within changing social realities. As male role fulfilment changes over time, ideological representations of masculinities are revised, an indication of the interactive nature of ideology and institutional power.

The intention here, then, is to discuss how the masculinity of enslaved blacks was constructed and how it interacted with the hegemonic structures of white masculinity. The principal site of this interaction was property rights cultures (including blacks as capital assets) and the public governance of colonial society. The focus is on differentiated, marginalized, subordinated and stigmatized black masculinity that struggled by violent and non-violent means to develop what Messner describes as an "autonomous positional identity". This dialectical process was driven largely by an intense concern for personal and collective survival, and a general quest for independent power and privileges (Messner 1991). During slavery the right to life and social liberty was denied blacks not on the basis of gender, but by the race inequities of colonial culture. Gender differences, however, and inequalities among males and females served to demonstrate how considerations of race differentiated black and white masculinities. At the same time, gender difference provides a lens through which to view attempts by all men to construct and legitimize their domination and control of all women in private and public social relations (see Beckles 1993).

Connell's concept of the "gender order" is relevant and useful. The "gender order" is presented as a turbulent, dynamic process that moves the analysis beyond static gender-role theory and reductionist concepts of patriarchy. It demonstrates, furthermore, how competing masculinities – some hegemonic, some marginalized – interact, particularly with respect to the shared project of the domination of social culture, material resources and women. Not all men, however, consumed equally the produce of this ideological investment – hence endemic contests between masculinities across class, ethnic and cultural lines (Connell 1995).

The enterprise of Caribbean colonization was essentially a white male – owned and managed – project. The construction of agrarian and mercantile systems called into existence the institution of chattel slavery as the mechanism to exploit the labour services of Africans. For most of the slavery period Caribbean businesses displayed a preference for male labour. Establishing infrastructure for large-scale production (land clearance, communications networks and so forth) in formative periods generated a greater demand for muscle power.

The slave trade, responsive to this preference, delivered a 65 per cent male "cargo" to the region. Colonial societies were constructed, therefore, upon the demographic basis of a dominant white-black male encounter. Over time the process of maintaining and reproducing businesses focused on female labour, and despite limited natural growth performance in a few places, failed to equalize sex ratios. In 1800, some 55 per cent of the slaves in the English colonies were situated in Jamaica. There, 70 per cent of them were male. Only Barbados, of all the major sugar economies, achieved a balanced sex ratio. Most territories were never normalized, and males within all so-called races predominated in the populations of rural and urban communities.

In this respect, then, the origins of the institution of slavery can usefully be discussed in terms of the military defeat and subsequent violent subordination of black males by white men. While it is true that the slave trade flourished, in part, as a result of some voluntary commercial exchange between European and African male business elites, the fact of European military conquest and ultimate superiority in most parts of West Africa provides a compelling explanatory context. In most West African societies, during the period of the slave trade, states were constructed and defended by armies drawn mostly from among men. The enslavement in the Caribbean of defeated male warriors, now required to labour on estates, symbolized the achievement of white male triumphalism. While women also participated in the political and military rule of some West African societies, the prevalence of dominant patriarchal formations reinforced the significance of this development (see Law 1977; 1991; Hilton 1985).

Black men, therefore, embarked on a Caribbean experience within the context of institutional environments that reflected the conquistadorial ideologies and interests of white patriarchy. Empowered white men ideologically represented their masculinity by reference to the dominant imperatives of their imperial project. Central to these representations was the quest for monopolistic control, ownership and possession of all properties and power in these societies. The monopoly possession of power, profits, glory and pleasure was specified as a core element in the social translation of white masculine ideologies in which enslaved black men were relegated to otherness.

Outnumbered by black men in West Africa and the Caribbean, colonial white men, though armed to the teeth with guns, cannons and battleships, privileged the apparatus of mind power over body and appropriated for themselves an iconography of the former, while projecting an imagery which associated the latter with black men. The conquest and control of the black male body, and the denial of a mind to it, reside at the centre of the dichotomized masculine Caribbean contest. The managerial culture of empire, established as a function of white patriarchy, fuelled forces that produced a complex apparatus for the ideological representation of black men. The control of the enslaved required it. The survival of colonialism mandated it. Enslaved black men, as the Caribbean social majority, had to be "kept", and kept down, in order to ensure the success of the dominant socioeconomic project (Tiffin 1987; Low 1990; Markus 1990; Fanon 1986).

Imported Africans, and their creole progeny, however culturally understood, shared and actively supported the important tenets of the ideology of masculinity as represented by white men within the colonial encounter. Notions of political authority, economic power and domestic dominance, as publicly presented by white elite masculinity, were culturally sanctioned by enslaved black men. Similarly, white men's denial of these states of consciousness and experience to disenfranchised and dispossessed white women within colonialism set in place conditions for enslaved black men to assert their physical and social subjugation of black womanhood. But unlike white women, many of the African-born enslaved black males were denied much of the power and status that were personally familiar.

In social relations, the enslaved black male and his offspring were fed, clothed and sheltered by white men whose hegemonic masculinities determined that being "kept" and "kept down" were symbolic of submissive inferiority, and gendered as feminine. The enslaved black male received as "gifts" a number of social concessions, in addition to his subsistence rations and allocations of leisure time. He was denied consumer access to the night by strict regulatory systems and could neither claim nor assert any right beyond or outside those of his owner, in public or private social spheres.

According to Patterson (1967), he was natally alienated, his masculinity dishonoured, and his being rendered "socially dead". The condition of being "kept" and "kept down", then, located enslaved black masculinity within white patriarchy as a sub- form starved of role nourishment, and ideologically "feminized" (see also Patterson 1982; 1993). Chattel slavery, therefore, an institution built upon private property rights in persons, was thoroughly gendered in its design and functions. Throughout the Americas, European enslavers decreed, for example, that the status of an infant at birth should not be derived from that of the father. Slaveholders had neither social nor economic interest in black fatherhood. Black children at birth entered into a social relation that was predetermined by the status of their mothers. Legally, it had absolutely nothing to do with the status of the father. Children fathered by free black men or white men were born into slavery if their mothers were enslaved. Since white women, by virtue of their race, were not enslaved, their children – under all paternal circumstances –were born into freedom.

Throughout the West Indies, white women produced free-born children with enslaved, free black, and free coloured men. Slavery, as a socio-legal status, completely marginalized and alienated black fatherhood, and focused its attention upon black motherhood. Estate managers generally had no policy interests in the identity of the fathers of children. The documents on families, for example, are rich and detailed on the maternal dimensions of kinship, but silent on paternity. An excellent way to demonstrate this characteristic is to examine the records of plantations that were known for meticulous documentation. The Newton and Seawell plantations in Barbados were such properties. They were perhaps the best documented eighteenth-century slave plantations in the Caribbean. Both were owned by the absentee Lane family, and the records for Newton, in particular from the 1720s to the 1830s, are a rich source of literature on the black domestic experience. In the 1776 annual report of manager Sampson Wood, for example, he lists all the "matriarchs" on the two estates, and sets out a schedule of their children, grandchildren and great grandchildren.

Evidence of paternity is almost completely missing from these records. Take Great Occoo, for example. She had six children and great-grandchildren. Her first daughter, Violet, had four children. Nothing is said of fathers, grandfathers or great-grandfathers. The same is true for Great Phebe. She had five children and five grandchildren. Her spouse is not recorded, nor is Statira's, her only daughter who had a child. Great Sarcy's family can be shown in figure 2.

She had six children: four daughters and two sons. All her daughters had children –a total of eight grandchildren. Great Sarcy's spouse is not recorded, nor are the spouses of her four daughters. The records are silent on the fathers of these children. Sampson Wood did not think it important or necessary to list these fathers, husbands and lovers; they remain invisible, outside of history (see Newton Plantation Papers). Fatherhood, as an aspect of masculinity, then, is non-existent within the archival literatures of the estates. Such an issue raises the question of men's greater "invisibility" within historical records, a matter that has been considerably ignored and underestimated. Describing the enslaved woman as essentially a "submerged mother", Edward Brathwaite locates her "invisibility" within the "archival

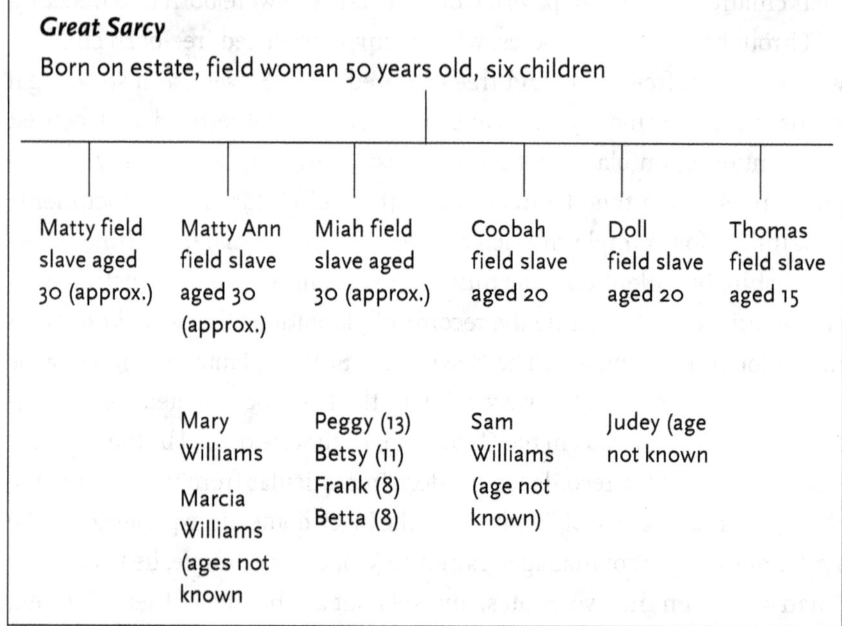

Figure 3.1: Family tree of Great Sarcy

material" and suggests that it is but an "aspect of that general invisibility which haunts [black history]".

For him, the enslaved woman, being black and female, suffered a "double invisibility", which in turn promoted an historiography of neglect (Brathwaite 1975; 1984). There is, therefore, a significant conceptual and empirical problem to be tackled with respect to the "invisibility thesis". It has to do with the fact that the archival evidence that historians have (over!) used as baselines for social history narratives – deeds, wills, manumission lists, diaries, plantation accounts, managers' reports and so forth – says considerably more about enslaved women than it does about enslaved men. The latter, in fact, is the one who was rendered largely invisible (Beckles 1995; Brathwaite 1975; 1984).

This characteristic of the evidence has to do with the female-centred nature of the slave system. Its principal concern was with maternity, fertility, the management of white households, and the sociosexual expression of patriarchal power and ideology. More is recorded about enslaved mothers than enslaved fathers; more was said about female enslaved lovers of white men than about male enslaved lovers of white women. Certainly, in this last regard, enslaved men have been rendered almost completely invisible – though partly, it should be said, for their own safety. The general intimacy of enslaved women with the empowered agents of the colonial world – white male and female – placed them at the top of the documentary queue (Beckles 1998, 34–38).

This condition, in turn, raises the question of whether modern historians of slavery – mostly male – have contaminated historiographic discourse with the women's "invisibility" thesis, which is really a conceptual borrowing from European historical discourse. Slave owners' fictional literature, where representations of black masculinities were constructed and ventilated, however, used a vocabulary which made reference to the term "infantilization" rather than "feminization". Infantilization was also a central concept used in slave owners' representation and "imaging" of women. The enslaved black male, by virtue of being denied dominant masculine roles and access to recognized institutional support systems on which to construct counter concepts, and kept in a childlike welfare-subsistence relation, was conceived to have degenerated into a pre-gender consciousness – a condition of nothingness associated with innocence and femininity.

In this literature, furthermore, slave owners coined the terms "Quashee" to represent their ideological characterization of enslaved black men. Quashee was "gay, happy-go-lucky, frivolous, and cheerful". In his 1808 account of Jamaican slave society, John Stewart described Quashee as "patient, cheerful, and commonly submissive, capable at times of grateful attachments where uniformly well treated". He was also "possessed of passions not only strong but ungovernable; a temper extremely irascible; a disposition indolent, selfish, and deceitful; fond of joyous sociality; riotous mirth and extravagant show". Stewart, in addition, was keen on informing his reader that "creole" white women exhibited many of the personality traits of "Quasheba" – the feminine of Quashee (Stewart 1808; see also Long 1774; Nugent 1939).

Quashee, then, was ideologically constructed and fixed within pre-slavery texts as the "typical" black male in a state of enslavement. Furthermore, he was, says Stewart, "docile but irresponsible, loyal but lazy, humble but chronically given to lying and stealing; his behaviour was full of infantile silliness and his talk inflated by childish exaggeration". In addition, his relationship with his master was one of dependence and childlike attachment; it was indeed this childlike quality that was the very key to his being. Slave owners' archives assure us that black males as "a group of atomized, childlike individuals had no means by which to relate themselves to others save the integrative framework provided by the owner's authority. The self-(slave) they allegedly related to was a direct function of the other (owner)" (Patterson 1967).

Congruity in the concepts of infantilization and feminization, as systems of representation of the black male, indicates clearly the direct nature of slave owners' political and ideological intention. As distortions of the relations of everyday life, these representations operated as important weapons, with measurable political effects, in that they helped to shape understandings of the encounter between whites and blacks. By fixing reality through language and fantasy, slave owners denied that enslaved black men were "men" in the sense of their ascribed normative characterization of manhood. This discourse, as an apparatus of power, provided slave owners with several privileges – particularly the psychic courage to manage the colonial enterprise.

The slave-owning community, considerably outnumbered by subordinated groups, devised systems of governance by which it could reproduce its dominance. Military might was important, but insufficient. The slave owner had to walk among the enslaved, eat what they cooked, and sleep within their physical reach. To function within this environment, it was necessary to psychologically "read", "write" and "imagine" subordinated black masculinities as inversions, represented within popularized gender ideology as timid, passive and submissive.

The systems of violent terror used to suppress and punish insubordination – the burning alive, dismemberment, castration, lynching and so forth – were conceived to offer the slave owner a functional degree of comfort in the assumption of success. When we enter the world of Thomas Thistlewood, for example, an English slave manager/planter in Jamaica (1750–86), the language and political effect of this violent power is immediately encountered. Thistlewood records in his diary:

> Wednesday, 28th January, 1756 – Had Derby well whipped, and made Egypt shit in his mouth.
>
> Friday, 30th July, 1756: Punch catched at Salt River and brought home.
>
> Flogged him and Quacoo well, and then washed and rubbed in salt pickle,

> lime juice and bird pepper; also whipped Hector for losing his hoe; made New Negro Joe piss in his eyes and mouth.
>
> End of October 1766 – A Stout Negro man of Dr Lock's is now gibbitted alive in the Square . . . a resolute rebel.

Actions such as these highlight the contradictory and ambivalent nature of stereotyped representations as major discursive strategies. The physical violence directed persistently against enslaved black men by white men indicates the fact of their recognition of an irrepressible black masculinity, and their inability to fix everyday patterns of behaviour to fantastic ideological constructions (see Hall 1989).

This disarticulation between social reality and imagination, however, provided the instability needed to constantly reconceive the constituent elements of representations in order to express changing forms of domination. In addition, it contributed to the evolution of complex language forms and perceptions that tracked and targeted the multiple forms and expressions of black masculinities. The thought-leader (sage, priest, obeah man), for example, was stripped conceptually of power within a representation that projected him as childlike, incapable of rational thought and devoid of scientific method. The Ashanti- Mandingo warrior groups were represented as easily tamed and subdued by caring friendship and compassion. Subordinate white males, whose dependent social existence openly subverted from within the ideological texts of white hegemonic masculinity, were driven into colonial outbacks, and their condition accounted for in terms of the degenerative impact of tropical climates and intimate exposure to black culture.

Black men, furthermore, were expected to offer non-violent responses to the social effects of white men's unrestricted sexuality. Colonial mastery, it was understood, demanded as a property right access to the sexuality of the enslaved. Both male and female among the enslaved were sexually exploited by whites who understood their "racial" authority in terms of its power over the life, body and mind of the enslaved. Patterson (1967, 42) asserts: "The sexual exploitation of female slaves by white men was the most disgraceful aspect of Jamaica slave society. Rape and the seduction of infant slaves; the ravishing of the common law wives of the male slaves under the threat of punishment, and outright sadism often involving the most heinous forms of sexual torture were the order of the day."

An English traveller, during his three-month tour of Jamaica in 1832, was told by a white bookkeeper that he had twelve "negro wives" in six months, and that this was expected of him by his peers. Black husbands or partners who protested, noted Henry Coor, speaking in 1791 before a parliamentary commission on the slave trade, were flogged "under the name of some other misdemeanour" (Evidence of Henry Coor, House of Commons Select Committee on the Slave Trade, 1790–91, vol. XXXLV, 42).

Non-slave-owning observers of slavery paid particular attention to the impact of white men's sexual culture upon black masculinity. The denial to enslaved black men of the right to family and patriarchal status, and its occasional conferment as a concession for "good" behaviour, meant that they could not expect to assert domestic "authority as a husband and a father". Thomas Cooper noted in 1824 that his wife was the property of another, and her commitment to the owner took privilege over any duty to husband or family. "The net result of all this," Patterson states, "was the complete demoralisation of the Negro male." He concludes:

> Incapable of asserting his authority either as husband or father ... the object of whatever affection he may possess, beaten, abused and often raped before his very eyes, and with his female partner often in closer link with the source of all power in the society, it is no wonder that the male slave eventually came to lose all pretensions to masculine pride and develop the irresponsible parental and sexual attitudes that are to be found even today (Patterson 1967, 167–68).

The anonymous author of an abolitionist pamphlet was explicit on the point: "Patent submission to the lash and manly feelings are incongruous." The pamphlet asked whether slavery had not destroyed any masculine feelings that enslaved men might possess, and intimated that white men pursued this objective in several ways – particularly in the sphere of competition with black men for sexual access to black women. Another visit to the diary of Thomas Thistlewood reveals three issues:

1. Thistlewood's claim of a right to sexual access to all enslaved black women on the estate, and the right to punish enslaved black men who confronted or in any way questioned this right;
2. His right to allocate enslaved black women for the sexual pleasure of his friends, whatever their domestic relations with black men;

3. His right to punish enslaved black men for physically abusing their "wives" or "partners", since this constituted a violation of his property rights on the female.

With respect to the first of these, Thistlewood documents some of his sexual encounters with enslaved estate women during 1751:

> 8th January,"cum Phibbah"
>
> 9th January,"Pro. Temp. A nocte. Sup. lect. *Cum* Marina"
>
> 10th September, "About 2 am *Cum* Negrue girl, super floor"
>
> 21st November,"About 1 am. *Cum* Ellin, an Ebo, by the morass
>
> side, Sup. Terr. Toward the tittle plaintain walk"
>
> 1st October,"Last night *cum* Dido"
>
> 11th October,"Paid Dr Joseph Horlock, for curing me of the clap, £2.75s. 6d – yet am in some doubt if perfect. Was 44 days curing."
>
> 3rd December,"Last night cum Jenny. Jenny continue with me *as noctibus*"
>
> 21st December,"In the evening *cum* Susanah (a Congo negro) Stans, in curinghouse"

In the early part of 1752, he added Sabina, Phoebe, Little Mimber, Warsoe, Little Lydde and Daphne to the list (Hall 1989).

Many of Thistlewood's enslaved females lived with "husbands", whose protests were occasionally recorded in his diary. Dido's "husband", for example, beat her when he discovered that she slept with Thistlewood. For this he received a flogging from Thistlewood. When Jenny courted a Negro man from a neighbouring property, Thistlewood took away a necklace and fine clothing he had given her. When she promised not to see her new lover, he returned the gifts. On 6 March 1754, Thistlewood whipped Quacoo for severely beating his wife, Yara, and on the sixteenth he advised Sancho not to beat his wife, Quasheba, but to separate from her, when he found her sleeping with Morris, the estate cooper.

On 2 April, however, Thistlewood did not punish Cobenna for giving London "a good thumping" when he was caught having sex with his (Cobenna's) wife, Rossanna. Lincoln, however, was less fortunate; he was severely dealt with by Thistlewood for twice beating his wife, Violet, after a domestic dispute. When Thistlewood hired Robert Gibbs, a Barbadian, as overseer, he allowed him "use" of Nanny as a "wife" and "matched" Susanah with the Irish overseer, Christopher White, for the same purpose (Hall 1989).

That enslaved black men shared some basic patriarchal values with white men, expressed in terms of an assertion of masculine authority and power over women, seems evident from Thistlewood's and other accounts. Their inability, however, to "live" this ideology outside the jurisdiction of dominant white authority confirmed the subordinated status of their masculinity. There were areas, nonetheless, where enslaved black men were allowed by white men to exercise male power in relation to black women. Moitt tells us that in the French slave colonies, especially Saint Domingue, *courrir les filles* (girl-hunting) was a popular pastime among enslaved males. They were given leave from estates by overseers and owners to wander through the countryside in search of sex (Moitt 1995).

The rape and kidnapping of enslaved black women was a common enough expression of this activity. When the Barbados Council debated in 1823 a dispatch from the Colonial Office which called for an end to the unsupervised flogging of enslaved women by black drivers, Councillor Hamden invoked the interest of black husbands in his opposition to the proposed policy. He told the council, "Unfortunately our black ladies have rather a tendency to the Amazonian cast of character; and I believe that their husbands would be very sorry to hear that they were placed beyond the reach of chastisement" (Beckles 1989, 40).

With respect to Jamaican slave society, more needs to be known about the role of kidnapping and sexual exploitation of enslaved women in the formation of Maroon communities. Maroon men did kidnap plantation women in order to secure wives and forced labour; this much also figures prominently in the social history of all colonies that harboured Maroon communities. Little is known, however, of the life experiences of enslaved women who were integrated into the polygynous households of Maroon males. It is entirely possible that some Maroon women experienced at the hands of black men a continuation of the kinds of occupational and resource discrimination, and sexual domination, that typified enslavement on the plantations. Esteban Montejo, the Cuban runaway slave, for example, expressed views of women and sexual relations in his autobiography that corresponded to the ideological expression of his owner's masculinity, and that of other men within the slave-owning community. Slave owners, of course, knew this, and developed an obsessive interest in the sexual aspects of black masculinity. Terrified in their fantasies about the power implicit in perception of the black male sexual culture, white men developed a range of social attitudes and policies concerning relations between white women and black men. Castration and lynching were placed before black men as a likely response by white males to their sexual access to the white woman (see Craton 1982).

The hostility of colonial power, and the fetishization of black masculine sexuality, were but aspects of a wider discourse that involved the violent responses of enslaved black men in the projection of their own perceptions of masculine values. Violence was the principal social action by which enslaved black men could subvert the security and stability of the slave owner's project. Only violence by the enslaved could terminate the colonial mission and liberate their community. Enslaved black men could take away white men's lives and property through violence, and this reality became endemic to the relationship. It was not that enslaved black men needed violence to assert or secure their masculinities, but that the right to take life, which white men held as a constitutional privilege, could also be grasped by black men – hence the function of the subaltern's violence as an ultimate and intimate equalizer.

There was, therefore, nothing surprising about the manner in which enslaved black men in the Haitian Revolution took hold of the instruments of the independent state in 1804 and effectively marginalized women as second-class citizens, despite women's popular involvement at the leadership and rank-and-file levels. The significance of this political development is widened by the fact that Haiti was the first society in the Caribbean to experiment with the concepts of citizenship and nationhood. Mimi Sheller (1997, 20) has shown how, after the violent defeat of slave owners and their imperial allies, "building black masculinity became a central task in the construction of Haitian national identity". The effect of this project, she argued, was the "exclusion of women from the wholly masculine realms of state politics and citizenship".

The "highly symbolic" images of the state emerged from the functions of the military and the organs of national governance – areas that white men had monopolized and defined as masculine space. The feminine space was considered to be agricultural labour, domesticity and petty commerce.

Masculinity was associated with national strength and security. The nation was defined in the first constitution of 1805 as a "family", headed by the president and his generals, all of whom became rich landlords employing masses of female subsistence workers.

In fact, Article 9 of the constitution was explicit on the matter of gender and citizenship: "No one is worthy of being a Haitian if he is not a good father, a good son, a good husband, and above all a good soldier." The iconography of the black male warrior, the liberator and protector, was enshrined within the discourse of nation building, and the woman, despite her revolutionary experience, was set aside as the "nurturer" of the hegemonic masculinity that emerged with the new nation. Haiti's freedom, then – achieved through the struggle of both men and women – resulted in a nation-state that was designed to suit masculinist interests. Haitian women protested these realities, and much of the anti-state struggles of peasants and urban workers that destabilized both President Dessalines and King Christophe originated in women's opposition to exclusion from equal citizenship. This struggle was also violent, and served to illustrate that oppositional militarism underpinned the politics of men as well as women within colonialism (Sheller 1997).

Colonial masculinities, then, took social form within the context of a culture of violence that embraced all relations of social living and consciousness. Violence was the principal instrument of all contending parties; it held them together and tore them apart. It assumed a quasi-religious character as groups sought constantly to control the balance of power and terror. Creole black males were socialized as infants within this crucible of death, blood and suffering. They learned to use it as it was used against them. This explains, in part, the enormous loss of life that this region experienced in more than one hundred slave revolts, indicating how relations between the enslaved and the enslavers were characterized by ongoing psychological warfare and bloody battles.

Within the black community other emancipations provided grand opportunities for reconstruction, particularly with respect to the perceptions of masculinity outside of warfare and power conflict over life and liberty. At the same time, they reduced the intensity of the struggle for political determination, economic power and cultural self-definition. In most parts of the region white hegemony within economic life, social institutions and ideological discourse persisted. The majority of black men remained marginalized and subordinated; today, the cultural values of these subordinate masculinities seem at odds with new social imperatives, many of which have emerged from the regenerative forces within women's and feminist movements. Implosive community violence remains an expression of subordinate black masculinities. The seemingly rudderless quest for an inversion of the dominant agenda has left the streets of communities, the language of social discourse, sexual relations, political dialogue and the lyrics of popular music shot through with violence – both virtual and real. That it is socially destructive is evident; that it is new or phenomenal is less obvious. New representations of subordinate black masculinities are taking shape in much the same way today that they were during the slavery period. Now, as then, these constructions are part of a process of subjectification necessary for the perpetuation of forms of discursive and discriminatory power.

NOTE

1. Reprinted with permission from *Interrogating Caribbean Masculinities Theoretical and Empirical Analyses*, edited by Rhoda E. Reddock. Kingston: University of the West Indies Press, 2004.

REFERENCES

Baker, George W., and Dwight W. Chapman. 1962. *Man and Society in Disaster.* New York: Basic Books.

Beckles, Hilary. 1989. *Natural Rebels: A History of Enslaved Black Women in Barbados.* New Brunswick, NJ: Rutgers University Press.

———. 1993. "White Women and Slavery in the Caribbean". *History Workshop Journal* 36 (1): 66–82.

———. 1995. "Sex and Gender in the Historiography of Caribbean Slavery." In *Engendering History: Caribbean Women in Historical Perspective,* edited by Verene Shepherd, Bridget Brereton, and Barbara Bailey. Kingston: Ian Randle Publishers.

———. 1998. "Historicizing Slavery in West Indian Feminism." *Feminist Review* no. 59: 34–56.

Bond, Carey, and P. Peery. 1970. "Is the Black Male Castrated?" In *The Black Woman Anthology*, edited by T. Cade. New York: New American Library.

Brathwaite, Edward. 1975. "Submerged Mothers." *Jamaica Journal* 9 (2/3): 48–49.

———. 1984. "Caribbean Woman during the Period of Slavery". Elsa Goveia Memorial Lecture, University of the West Indies, Cave Hill.

Brittan, Arthur. 1989. *Masculinity and Power.* Oxford: Basil Blackwell.

Brod, Harry, ed. 1987. *The Making of Masculinities: The New Men's Studies.* Winchester, MA: Allen University.

Connell, R.W. 1987. *Gender and Power: Society, the Person, and Sexual Politics.* Stanford: Stanford University Press.

———. 1995. *Masculinities.* Oxford: Polity Press.

Cooper, Thomas. 1824. *Facts Illustrative of the Condition of the Negro Slaves in Jamaica.* London: Phillips.

Craton, Michael. 1982. *Testing the Chains: Resistance to Slavery in the British Caribbean.* London: Cornell University Press.

Easthope, Anthony. 1986. *What a Man's Gotta Do: The Masculine Myth in Popular Culture.* Boston: Unwin Hyman.

Fanon, Frantz. 1986. *Black Skins, White Masks,* with foreword by Homi Bhabha. London: Pluto Press.

Hall, Douglas. 1989. *In Miserable Slavery: Thomas Thistlewood in Jamaica, 1750–1786.* Warwick University Caribbean Studies series. Basingstoke: Macmillan.

Hare, Nathan, and Julia Hare. 1984. *The Endangered Black Family: Coping with the Unisexualization and Coming Extinction of the Black Race.* San Francisco: Black Think Tank.

Hilton, Anne. 1985. *The Kingdom of the Congo.* Oxford: Oxford University Press.

Law, Robin. 1977. *The Oyo Empire.* Oxford: Oxford University Press.

———. 1991. *The Slave Coast of West Africa.* Oxford: Oxford University Press.

Long, Edward. 1774. *The History of Jamaica.* London: T. Lowdes

Low, G.C. 1990. "His Stories? Narratives and Images of Imperialism." *New Formations* no. 12: 97–123.

Markus, A. 1990. *Governing Savages.* Sydney: Allen and Unwin.

Messner, Michael. 1991. "Masculinity and Athletic Careers." In *The Social Construction of Gender,* edited by Judith Lorber and Susan Farrell. New York: Sage.

Newton Plantation Papers, M.523 Series. Senate House Library, University of London.

Nugent, Maria. 1939. *Lady Nugent's Journal of Her Residence in Jamaica from 1801 to 1805.* Kingston: Institute of Jamaica.

Patterson, Orlando. 1967. *The Sociology of Slavery.* London: Macgibbon and Kee.

Moitt, Bernard. 1995. "Women, Work and Resistance in the French Caribbean during Slavery, 1700–1848." In *Engendering History: Caribbean Women in Historical Perspective,* edited by Verene Shepherd, Bridget Brereton, and Barbara Bailey. Kingston: Ian Randle Publishers.

———. 1982. *Slavery and Social Death: A Comparative Study.* Cambridge, MA: Harvard University Press.

———. 1993. "Slavery, Alienation and Female Discovery of Personal Freedom." In *Home: A Place in the World,* edited by A. Mack. New York: New York University Press.

Sheller, Mimi. 1997. "Sword-Bearing Citizens: Militarism and Manhood in Nineteenth-Century Haiti." *Plantation Society in the Americas* 4 (2/3): 233–78.

Stewart, John. 1808. *An Account of Jamaica and Its Inhabitants.* London: Longman.

Tiffin, Helen. 1987. "Post-Colonial Literatures and Counter-Discourse." *Kunapipi* 9 (3): 17–34.

SECTION 2

UNFREE SOCIETIES, UNFREE BODIES

chapter 4

The Historical Background to the Culture of Violence in Trinidad and Tobago[1]

Bridget Brereton

THIS CHAPTER WILL ANALYSE THE HISTORICAL EVOLUTION OF a 'culture of violence' in Trinidad and Tobago, from the first contact between Europeans and Indigenous peoples, to the mid-twentieth century. Clearly, developments in the post-Independence period after 1962 –which this chapter does not examine – constitute a fundamental part of the reasons for the country's current situation with respect to crime and violence. But the foundations for it had, tragically, been extensively laid in the preceding centuries.

The recorded history of the Caribbean began in sustained violence against the Indigenous peoples of the region, the first great genocide of modern history. The enslavement of Africans, which followed the extermination or displacement of most of the indigenes, was a peculiarly violent system of coerced labour and social control. Post-slavery contract or indentured labour schemes, though less overtly violent than African slavery, still rested on coercion and the actual use or threat of force. By the end of the nineteenth century, a culture of violence certainly had been established in the Caribbean colonies, and Trinidad and Tobago was no exception. While this culture was pervasive and, in some respects, 'gender neutral', there is no doubt that women of all ethnicities were prominent among its victims – as well as being, in some situations, its active agents.

GENOCIDE AND THE INDIGENOUS PEOPLES

Almost from the moment of first contact between Spaniards and the indigenous Lokono and Kalina settled in Trinidad, these people were attacked and enslaved. Most were seized for slave labour in the Greater Antilles (depleted of their own Taino population within just a few years of Columbus' first settlements) or in the pearl fishing grounds of Cubagua, near Margarita. In the early part of the sixteenth century, long before the Spaniards had established any permanent presence in Trinidad, the Indigenous population was being steadily depleted by frequent raids (Boomert 1984, 141–55; Boomert 2016, 83–96).

Bartolomé de Las Casas, the famous defender of the Indians in the New World, described a raid in Trinidad carried out by one Juan Bono. He tricked the friendly Indians into entering a large house they had built for the Spaniards, then tied them all up and whenever any tried to escape:

> . . . he was cut to pieces. Some of the Indians managed to escape, either wounded or unharmed, and they, with the villagers who had not entered the house, seized another house and with bows and arrows defended themselves against the Spaniards until the Christians set fire to the house, burning to death all the Indians inside it. Then, with their captives numbering 180 or 200, the Spaniards went down to their ships, hoisted sail and voyaged to San Juan [Puerto Rico], where half the number of Indians were sold as slaves, after which they voyaged to Hispaniola where the remainder of the captives were sold. (Johnson 1997, 28–29)

Others went to the infamous pearl fisheries of Cubagua, where the enslaved were forced to dive for pearls under conditions that guaranteed a short, miserable existence. It is Las Casas again who describes their work:

> They put them under water some four or five ells deep, where they are forced without any liberty of respiration, to gather up the shells . . . sometimes they come up again with nets full of shells to take breath, but if they stay any while to rest themselves, immediately comes a hangman rowed in a little boat, who as soon as he hath well beaten them, drags them again to their labour . . . they lie upon the ground in fetters, lest they should run away; and many times they are drowned in this labour, and are never seen again . . . oftentimes they

> are also devoured by certain sea monsters . . . or succumb to a death so much more painful, by reason that by the coarctation of the breast, while the lungs strive to do their office, the vital parts are so afflicted that they die vomiting the blood out of their mouths. Their hair also, which is by nature black, is hereby changed and made of the same colour with that of the sea wolves; their bodies are also so besprinkled with the froth of the sea, that they appear rather like monsters than men. (Johnson 1997, 26)

By 1592, when a permanent Spanish settlement was established at St Joseph, the local population had already been drastically reduced by aggressive raiding. This continued and perhaps intensified after 1592, with Indians enslaved and sold to settlers in Margarita, and their lands seized and given to Spaniards, provoking significant rebellions by 1593–95. Spanish slave raiding was the main reason for the flight of Indians from Trinidad to the mainland in the 1590s and early 1600s. With frequent slave raids, losses from disease and the disruption of traditional subsistence activities, and flight to the mainland, depopulation accelerated in the first part of the seventeenth century. Probably fewer than four thousand survived to the 1630s, as compared with some forty thousand a century before (Boomert 1984, 155–62; Boomert 2016, 97–119; Naipaul 1973, 25–69).

Insurrections against the Spaniards were frequent in the seventeenth century, followed by 'pacifications' – executions and destruction of huts and gardens. Some Indians were herded into *encomiendas*, villages where they were effectively enslaved by Spanish landowners. Others lived precariously in the forests. The last Indian rebellion in Trinidad was in 1699, when some under the charge of the Capuchin missionary order killed friars, the governor and a few other Spanish notables at Arena. The reprisals were predictably brutal; many who survived the final conflict at Punta Galera drowned themselves, but sixty-one were captured, tortured and executed, their bodies quartered and the pieces displayed on spikes on the St Joseph public road. This was the final 'pacification'. The Indian population dwindled in the eighteenth century to about two thousand, and by the next century a distinct Amerindian group no longer existed (Naipaul 1973, 117–21; Boomert 2016, 115–46). Trinidad's modern history had been inaugurated with violence on a scale that amounted to genocide.

THE VIOLENCE OF ENSLAVEMENT

It is well known that the enslavement of Africans for labour in the New World was accompanied by massive violence and huge levels of mortality. The Middle Passage was a veritable 'way of death', and loss of life, from the initial capture of victims in Africa to the enormous mortality of the 'seasoning' process during the first two years after arrival in the Americas, was so unthinkably great as to constitute a genuine holocaust. The great principle of New World slavery was that the owner should have absolute power to coerce and punish their chattel.

In Trinidad and Tobago (which were separate colonies up to 1889) as everywhere else, corporal punishment (usually flogging) was a routine aspect of plantation discipline, and – short of actual murder – no effective restrictions existed on the right of an owner or manager of enslaved people to punish at his discretion. Trinidad Governor Picton's Slave Ordinance of 1800 put the limit at thirty-nine lashes at any one time, but no serious attempts were made to enforce this, and it was only in the last decade of slavery (1824–34) that half-hearted efforts were made to restrict corporal punishment. Moreover, quite apart from floggings administered as punishment for 'offences', a heavy cartwhip was routinely carried by the slave drivers in the field, to be casually applied to the bodies of the workers (male and female) as a spur to labour. This was considered to be indispensable for exacting sufficient amounts of work from the field gangs, just as the right to punish by flogging was considered to be necessary for maintaining discipline and control over the enslaved population as a whole. And it was not only field workers who were flogged; domestics (men and women, but especially women) were also flogged or otherwise assaulted, sometimes by the mistress of the house personally. Corporal punishment was a norm of the domestic routine during slavery as much as it was in the plantation fields and factories.

The centrality of corporal punishment to plantation discipline and to the slave system as a whole was illustrated by the hysterical reaction of the Trinidad slave owners to the announcement, in 1823, that the British government had decided to embark on some modest reforms: the abolition of the use of the whip in the fields; a complete ban on the flogging of women; and restrictions on the flogging of men. Reports from indignation meetings held all over the island poured in to the governor (himself very doubtful about the proposed reforms). "To deprive the master of inflicting corporal punishment on any slave, male or female, would subvert the discipline of his estate," declared the Arima slave owners. The abolition of whipping would be "virtually a deprivation of property" in slaves, said their counterparts in north Naparima. "Flogging is the most *humane*, prompt and efficacious mode to crush disorderly behaviour," stated the planters of Pointe-a-Pierre; while W.H. Burnley, the island's largest slave owner, felt that the idea of prohibiting the flogging of women was "so monstrous and extraordinary that I hardly know how to approach the subject", while ending the use of the whip in the field was "a fatal error" in view of the "habits and morals" of the enslaved (CO 295/60 and 295/65; Brereton 1989, 58–60).

The traditions and accepted usages of slave control in Trinidad were largely dictated by the French settlers who came to the island after 1777 from the French colonies and Grenada, including a few influential refugees from the great rebellion in St Domingue (Haiti). With support from the early British governors, especially Picton and Hislop in the years between 1797 and 1811, the brutal methods of controlling enslaved people which were the norm in the French colonies, above all in Martinique, were introduced here. Of course, the British were not exactly backward in such methods, and it is noteworthy that the infamous British tradition of excessive flogging of soldiers was carried on in Trinidad. Every Sunday morning, it seems, soldiers (black and white) were ceremoniously flogged on the parade grounds outside the main military barracks at St Joseph, Port of Spain and St James. Such spectacles no doubt made the even greater brutality meted out to the enslaved more acceptable (Naipaul 1973, 185).

While whipping and flogging were routine aspects of the slave system in Trinidad and in Tobago, with both women and men the victims at least up to 1824, even more horrific punishments were devised for enslaved people accused of crimes. They were the main victims of the refined cruelties devised to terrorize the whole population. In the Port of Spain jail, the keeper received fees for each flogging and mutilation carried out (runaways had their ears cut off). In 1801–2, men and women 'convicted' of poisoning livestock and workers were sentenced to horrific punishments by special 'poisoning tribunals' organized by the powerful Martinique-born planter, St Hilaire

Begorrat. Torture was used to exact 'confessions'. One man, Pierre François, was burnt alive, along with the headless corpse of another, Bouqui, who had been hanged and then decapitated (his head was spiked for public display on the St Joseph Road). Besides Bouqui, four others, including a woman (Thisbe), were hanged, decapitated, their bodies publicly burnt and their heads displayed on spikes; those sentenced to lesser punishments were forced to watch the grisly proceedings. Others were branded, flogged, had their ears cut off, and were sold out of the island. That was how they did it in Martinique, where they knew how to keep the enslaved under control. When an apparent plot to rebel was discovered in the Diego Martin valley at Christmas 1805, the reprisals were similarly brutal. Four men were hanged, decapitated, their bodies displayed hanging in chains and their heads spiked at the entrance to their plantations. Many were flogged (up to a hundred lashes), mutilated, sold off the island, or forced to wear heavy iron collars or chains for long periods. All this was approved by London (Naipaul 1973, 196–201, 209–14, 291–99; de Verteuil 1987, 51–54, 63–64, 71–72 and The Plates 111; Brereton 1989, 35–40, 47–48).

Of course, these spectacular punishments, intended to terrorize the enslaved people, were not an everyday affair. But violence in the form of regular, routine whippings and floggings was a normal part of the slave system, sanctioned by both law and custom (except during the last ten years of slavery when corporal punishment of women was prohibited and that of men was restricted). So was sexual abuse of enslaved women. It was normative for white men, and indeed for some black men in positions of authority, such as the drivers and headmen, to coerce sex from enslaved women, regardless of their age or involvement in sexual relationships. A few such women might gain privileges from unions with white men, especially if they were based on some mutual affection, and if the men were well-to-do and possessed of some sense of decency. But for the majority, coerced sex and outright rape were part of the violence endemic to slavery.

It seems clear, too, that the conditions of enslavement encouraged 'black on black' violence: fighting and assaults between enslaved people, wife beating, and excessive punishment of children. Mrs A.C. Carmichael, the wife of a British planter who lived in Trinidad in the 1820s, claimed that enslaved *parents* objected when the 1824 Order prohibited the owners from flogging women. They objected because they preferred the master to punish their 'girls', knowing that they themselves would flog them far more severely! Though this is a dubious assertion, especially granted that Carmichael's polemical book was mainly an attempt to discredit the British reform programme, there is little reason to doubt that severe child-beating was a normative feature of slave life. The beating of a child by a parent or relative, of course, was a very different thing from the overseer's whipping workers in the field or flogging people as a punishment for offences; but it seems very likely that such beatings were often quite severe, originating an African-Trinidadian tradition of excessive corporal punishment of children. As V.S. Naipaul put it, the "drama of the plantation whip" was transmuted into community and family rituals of punishment (Naipaul 1973, 373, 384–86; Carmichael 1834, Vol. II, 140–47).

THE VIOLENCE OF INDENTURE

Violence in the sense of outright kidnapping of persons for forced transportation and labour, and in the sense of a legally sanctioned right to inflict corporal punishment on indentured workers, was not as salient in the system of Indian indentured immigration to Trinidad (1845–1917) as it had been in African slavery. Employers of indentured labour had no legal right to flog or whip their workers; the main legal sanction for the enforcement of the indenture laws was prosecution in the courts, followed by fines or (more likely) jail sentences. Incarceration in jail as a criminal, for breaches of the indenture laws which were really civil offences, was the major form of *legal* 'violence' against the indentured Indians – the jail substituted for the whip. Nevertheless, physical violence against indentureds on the Trinidad plantations enjoyed customary, if not legal, sanction; and Indian workers, including some who had served out their contracts, were routinely beaten, cuffed and kicked by managers, overseers, *sirdars* (Indian foremen, the successors to slave drivers) and, at times, African labourers or policemen. In the towns, the few Indians who lived or worked there (usually as porters, gardeners or domestics) during the period of immigration were often the victims of casual brutality from Africans or others, including policemen.

As David Trotman has shown, a great deal of (extra-legal) violence was inflicted on the bodies of the "bound Coolies", and the perpetrators were rarely punished, even when death resulted. In 1867, Soudar Singh was severely beaten by the owner of his estate and seven African labourers; they were all acquitted. In 1871, an estate manager was fined six pounds for horse-whipping two Indian women, one of whom subsequently died. This woman, Labjadee, was whipped and kicked on three consecutive days. The manager was not even *charged* with manslaughter because of medical evidence that she was in poor health before the whippings. In 1899, a woman called Sahti died fourteen days after a beating by the son of the estate owner; he was charged with manslaughter, but the coroner's verdict was death from natural causes. "East Indians could be whipped, kicked and beaten to death with impunity," Trotman concludes. This was violence against Indian workers on the estates, sanctioned not by law, but by the brutal customs of plantation life and found all over the British Empire where indentured Indians were employed under white management. The most spectacular incident of violence against Indians in Trinidad, however, was the Muharran (Hosay) massacre in 1884, when at least sixteen people were killed and more than a hundred injured when the police fired on persons taking part in Hosay processions who were trying (as had become customary) to enter the town of San Fernando. (Trotman 1986, 139–42; Singh 1988, passim).

Some Indians retaliated against estate owners, plantation staff, and African or Indian foremen. In 1870, two indentureds were convicted of the murder of an African foreman on Macoya estate; they were sentenced to death, but the governor commuted the sentence. In 1911, on the Sainte Marie estate, eleven indentureds beat an Indian *sirdar* to death over a wage dispute. But the more common pattern was for the Indians to vent their aggression and frustration against the weaker members of their own community – above all, but not only, the women. As Kumar Mahabir has expressed it poetically (based on oral testimony from surviving immigrants): "Indian must fight/ if e play bad/e start to fight/ if e do wrong/ e start to cut e arse/dat time so/ no Indian cyan play bad/beat e arse/if e run away nex man daughter/e go beat e arse too/if you have to run way wid man wife/leave one time/dat man go kill e wife/kill two a dem" (Trotman 1986, 141–42; Mahabir 1985, 56).

Indians in Trinidad soon acquired a reputation for violence – including murder – against members of their own community. In the 1880s they committed 60 per cent of all murders in the colony, while constituting only about 30 per cent of the total population; in the 1890s the figure was 70 per cent. The great majority of their victims were fellow Indians, and most were women. Between 1872 and 1880, twenty-two Indians were murdered by Indians, and all the victims were women; between 1901 and 1910, sixty-two Indians were murdered by Indians, with twenty of the victims being women. Between 1872 and 1900, there were eighty-seven murders of Indian women, of which sixty-five were 'wife-murders'. The tragic 'Coolie wife-murders' reflected the skewed sex ratio on the plantations during the period of indentured immigration; the abnormal living conditions in the estate barracks; the disruption of traditional gender relations and patterns of marriage; and the concentration of young single males competing for the relatively small number of Indian girls and women of marriageable age. Women who left their mates for another man – or were believed to have done so – were often the victims of homicidal rage by jealous and frustrated men; these men were usually tried and convicted for murder and duly hanged. Inward-looking violence was also inflicted on Indian men, with the ubiquitous plantation tool – the cutlass – the weapon of choice. Disputes over dowry and marriage, over land and wages, could all lead to violence and murders. Moreover, suicide by male immigrants was quite common, suggesting again an inward-looking violence, and often apparently linked to marital disputes and jealousy (Trotman 1986, 169–75; Brereton 1979, 182–83; Reddock 1994, 34–35, 44–45; Mohammed 2002, 45–46, 155, 169, 180–81, 186–92, 202–5).

The plantation barracks during the period of indentured immigration were a fertile breeding ground for Indian-on-Indian violence; the incidence of such crimes, especially the wife-murders, declined significantly when large numbers of Indians moved off the estates to settle in independent villages and peasant communities. Declined, but certainly did not end. Violent crimes by Indian men against women continued to be a tragic feature of the post-indenture ethnic community, as Patricia Mohammed shows in her study of the community in the period 1917–47. A characteristic case occurred in 1919:

> On Sunday morning Palwan, immigrant on Exchange Estate, killed his wife Mukdeah with a cutlass. It is stated that the parties were not on good terms. Palwan was jealous of his wife who was about to leave him to live with some other women on the estate. This annoyed Palwan and it is alleged that he seized his cutlass in one hand and the woman by her hair with the other, and inflicted three fatal blows on the neck while severing the head from the body while he held her down . . . . (Mohammed 2002, xx)

Mohammed shows that the number of such cases reported after 1920, when all remaining indentures were terminated, consistently decreased; but this certainly does not indicate that there was a reduction in the actual numbers of violent assaults on Indian women by Indian men. Many such cases never reached the courts, or the newspapers. "Violence as a means of control and a male assurance of continued ownership of women as property persisted," Mohammed concludes, "and was manifested through murders, woundings, beatings and threats to Indian women" (Mohammed 2002, 103–4, 189–90, 192, 210–13).

A CULTURE OF VIOLENCE, 1840s–1950s

Nineteenth and twentieth-century Trinidad, states Trotman, was "a violent society", with a "high incidence of crimes against the person and other forms of violence". The legacy of history and the nature of the colony's society bred "a pattern of violence which was both impulsive and implosive: that is, it manifested itself as the violent actions of irrational men [and women] wreaking havoc on themselves rather than on the source of their frustrations and oppression". Slavery had been intensely violent; indenture only a degree less so. Colonialism rested on racism which meant "separate and unequal" treatment for the non-white majority, psychological violence against the 'inferior' groups, and disrespect for the culture of the people. This was a climate in which violence, physical and psychological, could thrive. Colonialism and racism made possible atrocious living conditions and a low quality of life, which in turn promoted a milieu in which violence and aggression were salient (Trotman 1986, 134–39).

Slavery ended in the 1830s, indentured immigration in 1917 (though a few remained under indenture until the end of 1919), but colonialism rested, in the final analysis, on force, on the infliction or threat of official violence against the people. Official violence was a reality in colonial Trinidad. Policemen, and at times troops, were ordered to fire on protestors and demonstrators, resulting in injuries and deaths; subsequent enquiries rarely apportioned blame to the men who did the shooting or gave the orders. In 1884, as we already noted, at least sixteen Indians were killed, and more than a hundred injured, in the Hosay massacre outside San Fernando. In 1903, sixteen men and women were killed and forty-three injured in the Water Riots in Port of Spain, when the police fired on, and in some cases bayoneted, rioters in the area of the Red House. These victims were urban blacks. And in 1937, during the island-wide strikes and riots associated with Tubal Uriah "Buzz" Butler, twelve civilians were killed and fifty injured (African and Indian) by police action (two policemen were killed, and nine policemen or volunteers injured, by the rioters) (Singh 1988, passim; Brereton 1989, 149–51, 180–81).

Though British troops or naval personnel could be summoned in a grave emergency, as in June 1937, it was of course the colonial police force that inflicted official violence as a rule. It is not surprising that the police were hated and despised by the ordinary people of all ethnic backgrounds during this period. The force was reorganized in the last third of the nineteenth century along the lines of the Royal Irish Constabulary (RIC), as a paramilitary force operating in a society where large segments of the population were opposed to the system of law and justice the police were defending, as – in effect – an alien occupying army. Non-commissioned officers (NCOs) – sergeants and corporals – from the RIC were imported into Trinidad and soon became the men who really ran the local police force and created its professional ethos. The officers were all white, English or Irish; the NCOs were mostly Irish, ex-RIC; and the rank-and-file men were nearly all from the smaller islands. In 1895, out of 537 "other ranks", 301 were Barbadians, only forty-seven had been born in Trinidad, and there were no Indians. Poor working conditions, low educational levels and minimal pay, along with the foreign origin of the great majority, all encouraged a tradition of brutality and abuse of power on the part of the local policemen, who earned a well-deserved reputation for being rough, unsavoury characters who had often "left their country for their country's good". On a day-to-day basis, Trinidadians of the working classes – African and Indian, men and women – were subjected to violence of different kinds from these agents of the colonial state. They often retaliated. In 1891, for instance, an Irish sergeant was critically wounded and other policemen injured when they tried to stop an illegal drum dance at Arouca (Trotman 1986, 95–102, 284; Brereton 1979, 127–28).

Official violence might include the infliction of corporal punishment, an immensely emotive issue in a society of ex-enslaved and their descendants, for fairly minor offences. Ordinance 6 of 1868 – just thirty years after the end of slavery – allowed it for praedial larceny and the practice of obeah. In 1882, a person was sentenced to four floggings of thirty-six lashes each by a Couva magistrate; it was the governor who remitted three of them. A petition organized by a Methodist minister in 1883 to abolish flogging ("the great and disgusting vice of slavery is the brutal practice of flogging to blood the labouring population for petty larceny and other crimes") failed completely; indeed, an 1893 ordinance actually extended the practice by making flogging mandatory for a second conviction for praedial larceny (Brereton 1979, 126–27).

Under these conditions, it is hardly surprising that the incidence of violence against the person was relatively high in this period, especially in Port of Spain and the other urban areas. Trotman shows, for instance, that over sixteen months in 1870–71, there were 445 court cases of assault against the person brought in Port of Spain alone, the vast majority by and between working-class individuals, and located in the barrack-yards and tenements where the urban poor crowded together. This was typical of what Trotman terms implosive violence, turned inward on the oppressed community. Guns were relatively widespread in Trinidad at this time, triggering an 1877 ordinance imposing registration and a licence fee on gun owners; but, for the most part, violent crime did not involve shooting. On the plantations the cutlass was the weapon of choice. Elsewhere, knives, razors, sticks and stones, as well as fists, feet and heads were generally used. Barbadian immigrants were blamed for introducing the razor to working-class creoles as a useful weapon, and "cutting and wounding" became a typical form of urban violence (Trotman 1986, 143–45; Brereton 1979, 126).

Almost certainly, the incidence of violence in the urban areas increased from the 1880s onwards, the result of increased population as people flocked in from the countryside to escape the effects of the sugar depression, and as immigrants from many places, but especially the eastern Caribbean islands (including Tobago), came to Trinidad. Overcrowding in the urban slums worsened, while conditions on the estates also deteriorated. Many of the urban poor were chronically unemployed, or at best found odd, irregular jobs. The cramped, unsanitary barracks in the towns, especially the colonial capital, with their tiny tenement rooms and teeming open yards, were notorious breeding grounds for crimes of violence and dangerous quarrels. Alcohol use was widespread and often precipitated violence. These brutal living conditions, which probably worsened between the 1880s and the 1930s, encouraged fights and violent quarrels. The period 1875 to 1899 saw an annual average of 240 *jail committals* for fighting (the number of *convictions* for this offence was much higher, for many paid fines rather than going to jail) (Trotman 1986, 146–69; Brereton 1979, 116–20; Cummings 2004, passim).

Many of the men and women habitually before the magistrates for crimes of violence belonged to the urban 'bands', or gangs, whose members were loosely described as *jamettes* and 'badjohns'. It was especially at Carnival time that clashes between rival bands caused an increase in crimes of violence, but they could occur all year round. The female *jamettes* were famous for violent quarrels with each other and for larger-scale clashes during Carnival. Stick-fighting, the favourite sport of the band members, was quite violent in this period, with serious injuries common. Canboulay or Kambule, the night-time procession of people armed with sticks and carrying flambeaux which opened the Carnival on the Sunday night – before its suppression in the early 1880s – was often the occasion for injuries and arrests. As is well known, the Canboulay men inflicted serious damage on Captain Baker's policemen when they tried to stop the procession during the 1881 Carnival. There is no doubt that the working-class districts of Port of Spain and (perhaps to a lesser extent) other towns were fairly violent places in the late nineteenth and the first half of the twentieth centuries (Brereton 1979, 124–25, 128–29; Trotman 1986, 167–69, 180–82).

It was out of this urban matrix that the steelband violence emerged in the 1940s to 1950s. The newly created steelbands clashed over territorial rivalries (just like the late nineteenth-century bands), women, musical disputes and unpopular decisions by the judges at pan competitions. As in the period of the *jamette* Carnival, the festival provided the main arena for these clashes, which could attain considerable proportions. The accounts of these fights indicate that it was supporters or followers, rather than the pannists, who usually initiated the violence, but once started, everyone joined in, using cutlasses, knives, razors, bottles and stones as the main weapons. Injuries were common, though fatalities were quite rare. Serious clashes began in the 1947 Carnival and worsened in the late 1940s, with long-running feuds like that between Invaders and Casablanca causing major affrays, many injuries and hundreds of arrests. Efforts by the pannists themselves, and by middle-class supporters, did manage to control the violence in the 1950s. But the special 'Coronation Carnival' in 1953 was marked by eight major clashes, about two hundred injuries, and the fatal beating of a car driver in the middle of a steelband fight. According to the newspaper accounts, the 'proletarian' bands deliberately targeted the 'social' bands – middle-class youths who were apparently getting the gigs at the clubs and dances at the expense of the grassroots bands – and attacked them with baseball bats, sticks, bottles, whips, razors and cutlasses. It was not until the late 1950s that steelband violence at Carnival was more or less contained (Stuemplfe 1995, 60–64, 86–94, 110–12).

It has been noted that the severe corporal punishment of children was, at least in part, probably a legacy of slavery traditions, as well as of exaggerated Christian notions of "sparing the rod and spoiling the child". It continued to be normative among all groups in the post-slavery period, but especially among African-Trinidadians. Severe and prolonged beatings of children by mothers, fathers and other relatives, often conducted in public (in the yard or on the street) with an admiring audience, sometimes with a ritualistic or even theatrical element, remained a feature of the culture. Indo-Trinidadian parents were also enthusiastic beaters of children, though perhaps with less of the public performance aspect. This routine brutalization of children (including the very young) by parents and relatives had other causes also. Men and women were, no doubt, venting their frustrations on small, defenceless, easily accessible victims. But it was also probably an unconscious or conscious process of initiating the child into a harsh world, teaching him or her to suppress individuality and aggression, to know his or her place. And certainly, there was an element of public performance and ritual. No doubt the violent norms of slavery and indenture lay behind this kind of 'performance', as well as the very 'public' lives of the barrack-yard dwellers (Brereton 1979, 121–22; Trotman 1986, 174–77; Cummings 2004, passim).

Of course, as Trotman reminds us, corporal punishment of children was also a staple of the colonial school system (as indeed it was in Britain in the nineteenth and twentieth centuries). Virtually all teachers, at all levels of the educational system, used the strap or whip, and were encouraged to do so by the pedagogical principles of the day. Many teachers saw themselves more or less as lion-tamers, struggling to keep little savages under control. Though the great majority of the teachers were black or mixed-race, with some Indians by the early 1900s, they had no doubt internalized the racism of the period and sincerely believed that African and Indian children had to have 'learning' beaten into them. And the whip was the teacher's badge of authority in a world where black or brown men and women enjoyed few other forms of prestige or privilege. Beaten at home, in the yard or on the street and in the schoolroom, it is hardly surprising that the young colonials grew up with a firm commitment to physical punishment as a mode of control.

These aspects of the society also help us to understand the ubiquity of violence against women, especially wife-beating, among all the social and ethnic groups. It went almost unchallenged and virtually uncriticized; it was often carried out in public (especially among Africans); and an element of ritual and performance might also be present. Calypsos of the first half of the twentieth century illustrate how pervasive, and how accepted, the culture of violence was in marital or common-law relationships among all sectors of the society. Not until the mid-1950s did a women's group – the Caribbean Women's National Assembly, led by Christina Lewis – campaign against attacks and assaults on women and girls (Reddock 1994, 251; Cummings 2009, 57–66).

Indian men, perhaps, outdid the Africans in wife beating, often precipitated by the consumption of alcohol on plantation pay days, so that Saturday night beatings became almost a domestic routine in many Indian households. Mohammed's oral testimonies reveal a kind of fatalism among the women who suffered from spousal abuse of this sort. "If your husband drinking rum in a shop you can't go," one such woman said. "You just have to stop home and till he come and if he come he quarrel or he eh quarrel, he beat you or he eh beat you, or he go and sleep . . ." Mohammed concludes that "Women were forced to undergo ritual beatings from their husbands as part of the marital contract"; male control was enforced by alcohol-fuelled violence. Moreover, marital rape – or at best, sex demanded by a drunk and violent husband – was also a routine feature of many Indian marriages. But whether perpetrated by Africans, Indians or others; whether carried out in the yard, on the street or in the domestic space; wife-beating was virtually a norm in the society, and intervention was frowned on – except when it seemed that the victim was in actual danger of death. The home was no refuge from violence in colonial Trinidad (Mohammed 2002, 169–70, 212–13).

VIOLENCE IN TOBAGO

Colonial Trinidad was, unquestionably, a violent society. Tobago, joined to Trinidad administratively in two stages between 1889 and 1899, was perhaps less violent – if only because of its stronger rural and peasant ethos, and its more cohesive village and church-based culture. Yet, slavery in Tobago was every bit as brutal as in Trinidad, perhaps more so, and lasted longer. In 1819, Tobago's slave population had the lowest rate of natural increase and the highest crude death rate in the whole of the British Caribbean, and its 39 per cent decline in the period 1807–34 was the greatest in the region. Physical violence against the enslaved was routine; a British eyewitness told a 1790 parliamentary committee that "the greater part of the plantation Negroes" whom he saw in Tobago "were marked with the whip". No wonder that when Emancipation finally came, Tobago ex-enslaved sang "No mo' driver's lash for me/ No mo', no mo'/ Many a t'ousan' gone" (Craig-James 2008, Vol. 1: 36, 55, 66).

Tobago also developed a tradition of violent resistance to enslavement which has no parallel in Trinidad. A major rising in 1770, led by an African known to us only by his enslaved name, Sandy, and taking place only six years after the real start of plantation development in the island, saw at least twenty whites killed. It raged for six weeks before it was crushed. There were uprisings in 1771, 1773 and 1774. Savage reprisals and brutal punishments followed the heroic but doomed rebellions. In 1774, seven of the captured rebels had their right arms amputated and were then burned alive – in public, of course; Sampson was hung alive in chains, taking seven days to die. Even after the last major uprising in 1801, by which time the British authorities were becoming more squeamish about savage public spectacles in their dominions, several rebels were decapitated and their heads mounted on poles in the centre of Scarborough as a gruesome deterrent (Craig-James 2008, Vol. 1: 56–57).

After Emancipation, the Tobago masses continued to protest injustices and oppression – violently at times. In 1853, prisoners in the Scarborough jail rioted, seizing cutlasses, stones and other weapons, forcing all the warders to flee; soldiers from the garrison had to be called in. In 1867, there was a riot at Mason Hall, close to Scarborough, against an oppressive and unreasonable tax on dog ownership. Some one hundred villagers, armed with cutlasses, sticks, stones and bludgeons, beat up the policemen who tried to enforce the law. The largest post-Emancipation protest, the Belmanna Riots of 1876 in the Roxborough area, involved the brutal murder of Corporal J.H. Belmanna by a mob of labourers enraged at an earlier firing on a hostile crowd, which had resulted in the death of a woman. The rioters described their actions as war – war against the planters and their agents – and it was known as the Belmanna War throughout Tobago (Craig-James 2008, Vol. 1: 140–41, 240–41, 243, 249–51).

Despite this robust tradition of resistance against slavery and post-Emancipation oppression, Tobago was a less violent society than Trinidad in the decades between the 1880s or 1890s, and the 1950s. Susan Craig-James notes that, in the first half of the twentieth century, "serious crime was rare". At this time, it was common that, when the chief justice came for the Scarborough session of the colonial Supreme Court, there were no cases for trial or appeal. This was "a homogenous society with strong social ties", Craig-James states; intra-village ties were pervasive and powerful, and in the small-scale, close-knit, "face-to-face" village societies, behavioural norms were strongly entrenched and effectively sanctioned. Those who flouted the accepted norms tended to leave Tobago for Trinidad, or further afield. This village society, based as it was on land ownership and own-account farming and marketing, was powerfully shaped both by African traditions of communal solidarity and respect for elders, and by the moral teachings of nineteenth-century Protestant Christianity. Both traditions inhibited criminality and social disorder. Moreover, Tobago remained essentially rural until after the 1950s, and Scarborough was hardly more than a village itself.

It was the absence of significant urban slums, the more homogenous society, the rural and village culture, the widespread land-holding though cash-poor peasantry from the 1890s to the 1950s that made Tobagonian culture, in general, less violent than that of Trinidad up to the mid-twentieth century (Craig-James 2008, Vol. 2: 40–41).

Sadly, in the second half of the last century, and especially since the 1980s, this picture has changed. As the cohesive village society based on peasant farming and independent own-account activity has largely collapsed, as the Christian and communal traditions of that society have weakened, Tobago has begun to approach Trinidad in terms of violent crime and other forms of social disorder. But this is largely a development of the period since 1990 (Craig-James 2008, Vol. 2: 235–37, 240–43). Up to the 1950s, though far from a wholly tranquil place, Tobago was clearly a more orderly, less violent society in comparison to the larger island to which she had been joined at the end of the nineteenth century.

CONCLUSION

This chapter has tried to demonstrate the historical foundations of a culture of violence in Trinidad and Tobago, including the endemic nature of violence against women and gender-based violence. Colonial society began in an orgy of violence against the Indigenous people, and was consolidated through the exceptional brutality of enslavement. Slavery was abolished in the 1830s, but it was replaced by indentured immigration, another system of coerced labour, though admittedly less violent than slavery. By the middle of the twentieth century, a culture of violence was clearly entrenched in the colony, even if it had not yet taken on all the characteristics of the contemporary period. While the culture of violence, in many respects, transcended both ethnicity and gender, there is no doubt that a gender dimension was salient. Violence against women, especially murderous attacks and marital abuse (wife beating) by men, was a pervasive feature of the society, and the latter at least was widely accepted, often by women as well as by men. Violence against children, meted out by men and women who were their parents or caregivers, and by teachers, was equally pervasive, and even more strongly supported and condoned. These tragic historical legacies helped to shape the current crisis of crime and violence in Trinidad and Tobago.

NOTE

1. Reprinted (slightly revised) with permission from *Caribbean Review of Gender Studies.*

REFERENCES

Boomert, A. 1984. "The Arawak Indians of Trinidad and coastal Guiana, ca. 1500–1650." *Journal of Caribbean History* 19 (2): 123–88.

———. 2016. *The Indigenous Peoples of Trinidad and Tobago.* Leiden: Sidestone Press.

Brereton, Bridget. 1979. *Race Relations in Colonial Trinidad, 1870–1900.* Cambridge: Cambridge University Press.

———.. 1989. *A History of Modern Trinidad, 1783–1962.* London: Heinemann.

Carmichael, A.C. 1834. *Domestic Manners and Social Condition of the White, Coloured and Negro Population of the West Indies,* in two volumes. London: Whittaker.

Craig-James, Susan E. 2008. *The Changing Society of Tobago, 1838–1938: A Fractured Whole, Volumes I and II.* Arima: Cornerstone Press.

Cummings, J. 2004. *Barrack-Yard Dwellers.* St Augustine: University of the West Indies, School of Continuing Studies.

———. 2009. *Christina Lewis: Her Life and Times.* St Augustine: University of the West Indies, Open Campus.

de Verteuil, A. 1987. *Begorrat Brunton: A History of Diego Martin, 1784–1884.* Port of Spain: Paria.

Johnson, K. 1997. *The Fragrance of Gold: Trinidad in the Age of Discovery.* St Augustine: University of the West Indies, School of Continuing Studies.

Mahabir, N.K. 1985. *The Still Cry.* Ithaca and Tacarigua: Calaloux Publications.

Mohammed, Patricia. 2002. *Gender Negotiations among Indians in Trinidad, 1917–1947.* New York: Palgrave.

Naipaul, V.S. 1973. *The Loss of El Dorado: A History.* Harmondsworth: Penguin.

Reddock, Rhoda. 1994. *Women, Labour & Politics in Trinidad & Tobago: A History.* Kingston: Ian Randle Publishers.

Singh, K. 1988. *Bloodstained Tombs: The Muharram Massacre 1884.* London and Basingstoke: Macmillan.

Stuempfle, S. 1995. *The Steelband Movement.* Philadelphia: University of Pennsylvania Press.

Trotman, D.V. 1986. *Crime in Trinidad.* Knoxville: University of Tennessee Press.

chapter 5

Gender-Based Violence in The Bahamas in the Late Nineteenth to the Early Twentieth Centuries

Anne Ulentin

WOMEN HAVE TRADITIONALLY BEEN ABSENT FROM THE NARRATIVE, their voices marginalized or silenced, with only fragments of discourse available in the official records. In recent historiography, scholars have explored ways to recover, reclaim or retell the histories and stories of peoples who were omitted. In *Dispossessed Lives: Enslaved Women, Violence, and the Archives,* Marisa Fuentes asks about the difficult task of narrating "the fleeting glimpses of enslaved subjects in the archives and meet[ing] the disciplinary demands of history" (Fuentes 2016, 1). To do so, she reconstructs and narrates the lives of individual enslaved women in a non-linear fashion, subverting traditional methodological constraints of the discipline of history. Fuentes thus places women at the centre of the narrative, exposing the archive as a kind of fiction and challenging the authority of white colonial records (Fuentes 2016). Furthermore, her work and that of other scholars, such as Saidiya Hartman, offer new ways of contending with the violence of the archive and attempt to redress it. In recounting and reclaiming the fate of Venus, a girl murdered on a slave ship, Hartman exposes the violence of the archive and endeavours to write a counter-history of the lives of the nameless and the forgotten, "without committing further violence in [her] own act of narration" (Hartman 2008, 2).

This chapter aims to explore state and interpersonal gender-based violence (GBV) in The Bahamas after Emancipation through the early twentieth century. Colonial records provide rare information about the lives of Bahamian women in the post-Emancipation period; however, such records, established by the powerful to protect or enhance their position in society, merely provide numbers and statistics, and fragments of discourse, which is as close as we come to a biography of the colonized. Certain stories were privileged, and others were marginalized. Direct testimonies of Afro-Bahamian women are absent in the colonial archive, as were those of individuals of African descent elsewhere in the Caribbean, "most often appear[ing] in these sources as an undistinguished mass" (Fryar 2018, 4). The colonial archive – in its linearity, incompleteness and inherent violence – thus presents its set of challenges. In order to recover this silence, we have to critically engage with such records and take part in what we refer to as reading against the grain.

In doing so, historians analyse the dominant reading of a text and engage in alternative or 'resistant' readings, which scrutinize the beliefs and attitudes that typically go unexamined in a text, drawing attention to the gaps, silences and contradictions within. Court records provide powerful, substantial information about the lives and concerns of colonial black subjects and describe behaviour not easily uncovered in other sources. As Stephen Robertson expresses, court proceedings "produce texts that 'generate little dramas about human conflicts and dilemmas, that resurrect the otherwise hidden life of the street, gaming hall, counterfeiter's workshop, priest's bedroom, and prison cell,' that record the voices of the illiterate, of workers, and of women" (Robertson 2005, 161). While such records prove compelling narratives as they record the voices of ordinary people and their efforts to use the legal system, they are also prone to distortion, "[f]or while the staple texts of imperial bureaucracy had the capacity to bring black voices to the attention of imperial officials, black testimony never emerged unfiltered or unmediated" (Fryar 2018, 3). Reading against the grain thus involves a careful process of dissection, while striving to learn as much about how imperial officials maintained their power, but also how the oppressed, the marginalized, resisted the system in which they lived or found ways to survive it, in order to create fuller narratives of society.

Furthermore, adopting an intersectional approach enables one to understand how women were perceived in The Bahamas during colonialism, as structural racism and sexism, and socio-economic inequality impacted them in distinctive ways. Historians of the colonial period have demonstrated that both race and gender informed the perception and treatment of non-white women, who were racialized as inferior and occupied a separate space, outside 'civilised' society (McClintock 1995; Loomba 2015). Concomitantly, as Victorian sexual fixations were directed at non-white imperial subjects, female sexuality came increasingly under scrutiny. In this context, black female sexuality came to be perceived as deviant and women were often stereotyped as loose and immoral. In the late nineteenth- and early twentieth-century Caribbean, non-white women were viewed as disreputable outsiders (Trotman 1984, 60; Green 2011, 152; Suárez Findlay 1999, 25).

In this context, the sexist and racist attitudes formed in the Victorian era affected Afro-Caribbean women in unique ways, and improving the 'moral tone' of the population centred on women, specifically, as a result. David V. Trotman, in his seminal work on crime in Trinidad in the post-slavery era, demonstrated that considerable numbers of black men and women were incarcerated, and that re-inscribing the importance of gender was key to ensuring men's and women's proper place in society (Trotman 1984; 1986). Diana Paton, Cecilia A. Green, Dawn P. Harris and Jacqueline Mercier Allain reveal that punishment was similarly racialized and gendered in the emerging disciplinary regime of Barbados, Jamaica, and other British colonies (Paton 2004; Green 2011; 2012; Harris 2017; Mercier Allain 2020). The racialized and gendered body was thus "an important site for the marking of socio-racial boundaries" (Harris 2017, 176) and for reinforcing the social and racial order in the British Caribbean.

Even though The Bahamas never entered the world of colonial plantation economy, nor did it experience intensive labour-importing schemes, similar historical practices of violence deeply affected men's and women's lives and experiences. Gail Saunders, Michael Craton, Howard Johnson and Whittington B. Johnson provide crucial insights into the experiences of the newly freed in a white-dominated and prejudicial society in The Bahamas (Craton and Saunders 2000; H. Johnson 1996; W. Johnson,2006). After Emancipation, the white elite sustained their economic dominance through various systems of exploitation, and both socio-economic and legal mechanisms of enforcement were utilized to control the non-white population (H. Johnson 1986; 1988; 1996; Saunders 1988; Craton and Saunders 2000). The colonial period was characterized by harsh punitive approaches in an attempt to subjugate the newly freed, preserve the existing social and racial hierarchy, and maintain law and order. As a result, the social and economic divide remained profound after Emancipation. The small white elite effectively controlled the political and economic life of the colony, while the black majority had few political rights or economic opportunities. The labouring classes generally remained poor – perceived as social inferiors.

A close examination of legal records in The Bahamas at that time shows that the colonial state used different mechanisms to exercise total control and inscribe inferiority into the psyche of the colonized people, while racialized and gendered understandings of violence and criminality affected men and women differently, and found expression in the types of punishments imposed on confined men and women. On one hand, women who did not conform to society's elite moral code were considered a threat to colonial respectability and castigated as criminals, which resulted in continuous efforts on the part of the colonial state to control and contain them, and relegate them to a subordinate position in society. They experienced harsh and discriminatory treatment as a result, from policing to imprisonment and corporal punishment. On the other hand, the record also shows that women and girls were victims of interpersonal violence, including verbal, physical and sexual violence. In this context, overlapping systems of oppression intersected with race, gender and class status. Legal records can help understand the significance of GBV in The Bahamas after Emancipation; further critique the ways in which cultural and social norms define Caribbean gendered relations; enable women's voices to be heard and to listen to them, and situate their agency.

STATE VIOLENCE

In the late nineteenth century, Jane Storr was arraigned as many as fifteen times in the course of two years, while hundreds of other 'troublesome' women were arraigned on one or multiple occasions.[1] As wide-ranging social and structural conditions drove the criminalization and incarceration of Afro-

Bahamian men and women, several thousands were reported to, or arraigned by, the police for various offences every year, resulting in new charges that criminally implicated more than 5 per cent of the total population on an annual basis. Minutes of the criminal courts, including the magistrates' courts and the General Court (later, Supreme Court), provide invaluable information about gendered criminality. A quantitative analysis of cases brought before the magistrates' court in Nassau between November 1878 and December 1881 indicates that women were almost as likely as men to be summoned before the magistrate, representing 43 per cent of the accused.[2] They were accused of a variety of offences, including "offences against the person", "offences against property" and "other offences". While men were more likely to be arraigned for "offences against the person" (65 per cent), women were prosecuted for similar offenses, and some were as likely as men to be prosecuted multiple times per year. Similarly, while women were less likely to be arraigned for "offences against property", totalling just 30 per cent of all the accused, they were prosecuted for the same types of offences as men, including larceny and destruction of, or injury to, property.

Most interestingly, the proportion of women in the "other" category of offences was larger than that of men (54 per cent). The great majority of these women were arrested and charged with "abuse", interchangeably referred to as "abusive language", "indecent language", "obscene language" or "profane language" – in other words, insulting someone and swearing at them in public. Men's behaviour was also heavily policed for the same types of petty offences. However, it is clear that the majority of crimes associated with abusive language were attributed to women and that they were twice as likely to be arraigned for this. Thus, the heavy criminalization of the use of swearing, offensive or abusive language in a public place tended to reflect a desire to regulate the public behaviour of women specifically. Up to the early twentieth century, these "disorderly" women were prosecuted for cursing, slandering neighbours and generally engaging in "loud" behaviour (Ulentin 2022).

Thousands of women were similarly targeted for indecent behaviour in the British Empire (Green 2011, 172–73; Mercier Allain 2020, 782–85; Trotman 1984, 71; Damousi 1995). In the colonial discourse, women clearly stood at the frontier of 'civilization' and backwardness, and such disorderly women had to be contained to ensure the civilizing mission of the imperial project. At Emancipation, in Jamaica, colonial officials made a direct correlation between women and their role in uplifting the "uncivilized native race". In this context, Paton specifically points to the gender conventions of Victorian domesticity and the resultant remapping of gender roles and conventions. She asserts that "it was repeatedly argued that the way to 'improve' the level of 'civilization' of former slaves was to raise the status of women, which effectively meant persuading them to adopt the gender conventions of Victorian domesticity" (Paton 2004, 202, n.19). The newly freed woman thus became "a participant in the circulating Victorian discourse of sexual virtue and morality" (Smith 2011, 228–29) that was to be tightly controlled and supervised through a variety of mechanisms and practices.

In the late nineteenth and early twentieth centuries, high numbers of women were committed to the Nassau prison. Between 1860 and 1925, women represented on average one third of all adults incarcerated. Their population remained steady over the years and the number of women only exceeded that of men in 1918. Over the course of more than five decades, the overwhelming majority of prisoners were committed for penal imprisonment, reaching almost 90 per cent of the total number of committals. Among the latter, women represented more than 35 per cent of the total number of penal prisoners, sometimes averaging 40 per cent and over. These women were more likely to be re-offenders committed to short prison sentences (Ulentin 2022).

Evidence shows that colonial authorities struggled to discipline and 'reform' incarcerated women. In 1850, Governor John Gregory exclaimed: "The difficulty of finding suitable labour for females throughout the colony is felt to a great degree. I have observed the same thing in Australia with white convicts, but an imprisoned negress is even more unmanageable."[3] Thus, both gender and race informed the perceptions and treatment of incarcerated women in The Bahamas. These "African women" were considered "more unruly than men"[4] and "more difficult to manage than the males",[5] and colonial officials frequently emphasized the disruptive character of the female side of the prison. Furthermore, prison administrators blamed increases in prison punishments specifically on the fact that women knew they could not be flogged, which made them uncontrollable as a result. The Colonial

Office noted in 1898: "The number of minor punishments is in excess of the previous year and is due to the conduct of some of the female prisoners who, knowing, as they themselves state, that they cannot be whipped, defy all authority."[6] Time and again, authorities highlighted the uncontrollable nature of these women "of worst character" overpowering every effort to subdue them.[7]

Colonial authorities reported that offences "of the tongue" were most common, and presumably attributable to the female sex only.[8] Their behaviour was reportedly so disruptive that it was necessary at times to "reprimand" the matron and assistant matron themselves for "laxity in maintaining discipline" in the female side of the prison.[9] By the beginning of the twentieth century, such actions remained an issue.[10] While it is unclear why these women defied authority, such behaviour may be interpreted as a form of resistance. Challenging the rules of the prison, using offensive language, and engaging in persistent insubordination may have been strategies to exercise agency.[11] Damousi, in her study of women sentenced to penal servitude in Australia in the nineteenth century, reveals similar acts of resistance on the part of female prisoners who "strove to be autonomous and create a space for themselves" (Damousi 1997, 3). In The Bahamas, by engaging in subversive behaviour, female prisoners overtly defied and undermined authority and state violence, transgressing the boundaries that confined them as they attempted to redefine the nature of their imprisonment.

To discipline these women "of worst character", officials resorted to different types of punishment, including hair cropping (or head shaving). The rules governing hair cropping were clear. First-time prisoners could not be subjected to such punishment while and it was a penalty for "serious offences against prison discipline" only.[12] The sole purpose of imposing hair cropping was for punishment (as opposed to hygienic reasons) and considered the most effective means of imposing discipline and reforming prisoners. The "more abandoned and disorderly" female prisoners were thus subjected to such punishment, which allegedly had "a most deterrent effect upon incorrigible offenders".[13] For instance, such treatment proved its efficacy when prisoner Julia Johnson, an "old and hardened offender", was subjected to hair cropping when, "reckoning on impunity, she set the authorities at defiance".14 According to prison officials, the benefits of head shaving were instantly felt, and Johnson "ha[d] not been seen or heard of since".[15] Cutting women's hair was thus a form of bodily and psychological violence that carried a badge of shame believed to be most effective in dealing with intractable female bodies. As a result, policing and punishing black women's bodies served to reinforce colonial violence and hegemony (Ulentin 2022).

Finally, hundreds of women were admitted to colonial asylums, which were infamous sites of imperialism where physical abuse and degrading treatment were rife, and where women were most vulnerable. As Sally Swartz reminds us, "Histories of colonial asylums have consistently raised the possibility that colonial regimes deployed psychiatry as a means of dealing either with social dissent, or with legitimate suffering caused by the yoke of colonialism" (Swartz 2010, 172). Therefore, aside from the prison, colonial asylums also functioned as disciplinary spaces for incarcerating men and women who posed a threat to the colonial order. Historians have exposed the relationship between race, psychiatry, and the classification and treatment of mental disorder in various colonial contexts. In addition to racial theories, the effect of gender on the causes and experience of mental illness in colonial spaces have also been exposed (Trotman 1986; Swartz 1999; Jones 2008; Fryar 2016). Colonial systems of governance established regulations and legal frameworks that were particularly damaging for women, and the confinement in lunatic asylums were as much about social control as it was about care and treatment of the sick.

Between 1870 and 1926, the number of men and women committed to the Nassau Lunatic Asylum remained even, with an average of thirty patients per year, who were classified into four categories: "maniacal and dangerous", "quiet, chronic", "melancholy and suicidal" and "idiotic, paralytic, epileptic".[16] One of these women, Lucy Smith, was committed to the lunatic asylum in 1910. suffering from "perceptual mania". Resident surgeon John James Culmer testified that Lucy was "violent and dangerous", leading to her confinement.[17] While archival sources are silent on Lucy's experience and that of other women, the annual editions of the *Bahamas Blue Book* provide key information. Their ages varied greatly, from ten to ninety years old, with the largest number of patients between twenty and fifty. Saunders describes the asylum as "'accommodation of the poorest class of negroes'", with "no accommodation for private patients, and [where] acute and mild cases were often not segregated" (Saunders 2016, 86). The death rate was high, with an average of seven deaths per year, representing one third of all patients. The cause of death varied greatly and included various diseases of the brain, heart, lungs, intestines or kidneys, or malnutrition.[18] Men and women were committed to the asylum for a few months to decades, their suffering hidden from history. Historians have shown that female patients received particularly cruel and abusive treatment in lunatic asylums in the Caribbean, as exemplified by the Kingston lunatic asylum scandal in Jamaica, which exposed the widespread physical and mental abuse of black women (Jones 2008; Fryar 2016; 2018; Smith 2014). Such evidence allows to suggest that women – young and old – were certainly victims of this particular kind of state violence.

INTER-PERSONAL VIOLENCE

Moreover, minutes of police and court records provide evidence of thousands of cases of inter-personal violence. While crucial information can be obtained from such records, the context in which they were produced must be taken into consideration as well. Racial stereotypes informed the perception and treatment of the local population, as colonial officials often conflated violence and crime with ideas about race. Furthermore, judicial statistics did not distinguish individual reports of violence and abuse from police apprehension (the capacity of policing forces to solve crimes and apprehend offenders), making it difficult to evaluate inter-personal violence within the Bahamian community and locate people's agency. Purportedly, offences reported to the police were low. In 1898, colonial authorities partly attributed the scarcity of individual reports of violence to alleged popular attitudes towards law. Yet again, the colonial record, laced with bias and prejudice, shows that the state constructed a powerful discourse that rested on deep societal assumptions of racial difference, which emphasized the naturally devious and violent nature of the local population.

Despite this limitation, legal records can allow to evaluate social and gender relations in The Bahamas post-Emancipation. Voluntary engagement with the law transpired as men and women used the courts to bring cases relating to various offences. In Jamaica, Paton demonstrates that the labouring classes engaged with the judicial system in an "instrumental" rather than "supportive" way. She explains: "People used the courts to achieve a particular goal rather than because they believed the state's claims to fairness or supported its desire to monopolize conflict resolution" (Paton 2004, 166). Their willingness to use the law in The Bahamas can thus be placed and understood within such a context and help define the contours of social and gender relationships in the society.

There is no documentation and interrogation of inter-personal violence in Bahamian literature from a historical vantage point, apart from a brief examination of the infamous 1887 Lightbourn case (Wilmot 1980, 15–18; Themistocleous 1997, 22; Saunders 2016, 41–42). While this case attracted notoriety mainly for heightening racial tensions in The Bahamas, it also exposed views on gender-based violence, specifically those of English stipendiary and circuit magistrate Lewis D. Powles. In his 1888 memoir, Powles exposed the widespread existence of inter-personal violence in the Bahamian community, white and black alike, and the lack of enforcement of and access to justice for women and girls. Soon after his arrival, he exclaimed: "It did not surprise me to find that assaults by men upon women were very common among them, knowing how common they are among our own lower classes at home, but I thought they were too leniently dealt within the Police Court at Nassau" (Powles 1996, 305–6).[19] Shortly thereafter, he declared that "for a time at any rate – I should send all persons convicted before me of striking women, to prison without the option of a fine, except under very extenuating circumstances" (Powles 1996, 307). He embraced his role as champion of women's rights and proceeded to sentence several men to imprisonment without a fine for assaults on women.[20]

Powles' career in The Bahamas came to an abrupt end after he sentenced a white man to imprisonment without a fine for assaulting his black servant, Susan Hopkins.[21] Lightbourn, in his appeal, claimed that Powles was biased, the evidence thin and, more importantly, the victim, Hopkins, had overtly defied Lightbourn and assaulted him first.[22] Lightbourn won his appeal and his conviction was quashed. While the case exposed racial and class cleavages and prejudice, the tone of the societal response to acts of violence against women and girls also emerged. According to Powles, whites displayed utter contempt for lower-class black women and did not shy away from using violence against them. He recounted exchanges with a local white man, who blatantly asserted that "coloured woman [sic] were only women in a limited sense", while others exclaimed:

> "I have twice kicked a coloured girl from the top of the house to the bottom myself!" "How could you have sentenced him [Lightbourn] to imprisonment? If you wanted to express disapproval of his conduct, you might have fined him 20l. Nobody would have minded that, and all the town would have subscribed to pay it!" "You have put us all in a most painful position. Only the other day my poor uncle beat their maidservant after giving her several warnings. In consequence of your action in the Lightbourn case he has had to pay her 3l. For fear he should be brought before you and sent to prison!" (Powles 1996, 310).

Such assertions reflected the general belief that violence against black women was not only pervasive, but warranted in Bahamian society.

The incidence of violence against the person was high in the late nineteenth- and early twentieth-century Caribbean. In The Bahamas, most of the cases heard by the courts were assault and abuse cases rather than any other crimes, based on the records examined thus far. Historians have shown similarly high rates of violence in other colonies where the legacy of slavery and colonialism produced "a climate in which violence (physical and psychological) could thrive" (Brereton 2010, 8). Poverty and overcrowding in urban centres exacerbated violent and aggressive behaviours. In The Bahamas, working-class individuals, who often knew each other, engaged in various forms of violence. On a yearly basis, more than two hundred individuals – men and women alike – were convicted in the magistrates' courts for "offences against the person", including hundreds of cases of assault.[23] A refined analysis of cases brought before the magistrates' court in Nassau between November 1878 and December 1881 shows that men were more likely to be arraigned for such offences.[24] Additionally, this sample shows that hundreds of women lodged complaints against neighbours and people from the community, friends and acquaintances, family members, and the policing forces. In general, the sample also shows that women were more likely to lodge complaints against any other individual.[25]

Court records allow one to discern patterns of domestic violence. "Quarrelling" and "fighting" between husbands and wives, sometimes involving "sweethearts", appear in the record. Defendants were acquitted, "bound over to keep the peace",[26] punished by a fine or imprisonment, or a term of imprisonment.[27] Sometimes, cases summarily dismissed reappeared in the record. For instance, on 29 November 1880, Lucy Kemp withdrew her "assault and battery" charge against her husband, Lewis Kemp; however, a month later, Lewis was arraigned once again for the same charge, for which he was then sentenced to pay twelve shillings or spend six days in jail, in conjunction with hard labour. Kemp was committed, in addition to being bound over to keep the peace for £25 for six months.[28] Furthermore, some cases exposed violence against children. On 23 October 1879, Nicolas Morrison was arraigned for assaulting and beating Sarah M. Curry's son, Samuel Morrison, resulting in a £2 fine or twenty days in jail, in conjunction with hard labour.[29]

The General Court only heard such cases if the assault occasioned "actual bodily harm" or showed evidence of attempted murder or murder, which were rare (single digits per year). Individuals found guilty of "common assault" usually did not incur a serious sentence, as exemplified by a 1902 case, which found James Perpall to be guilty of common assault against his wife, Ellen, resulting in her experiencing a miscarriage at six months. James was initially let out on bail and bound over to appear at the next session of the Supreme Court. When he appeared in court, his conduct was then deemed "very good" and he was sentenced to one day in jail, upon which he was discharged.[30] Those found guilty of "common assault" were usually given sentences of one to six months in jail, while those found guilty of manslaughter and murder incurred years of confinement, sometimes life sentences. It appears such cases did not generate public scrutiny, unless the actions of the accused directly tarnished the image of the colony. For instance, the case of George Hubert Johnson, arraigned for attempted murder of Isadora Bullard, probably made headlines in 1921 only because Johnson was a World War I veteran and served as a police constable.[31] His actions were a dishonour and a disgrace to both the uniform and the state, rather than evidence of a general propensity for misconduct or physical violence towards women in Bahamian society that required swift responses and remedies. While both the magistrates' courts and the General Court tried cases of domestic violence, cases of sexual violence were tried in the General

Court only, where serious cases were heard. The highest court heard crimes relating to sexual offences, including prosecutions for rape and attempted rape, indecent assault and attempted indecent assault, and carnal knowledge and attempted carnal knowledge of underaged girls (under twelve, thirteen and sixteen).[32] Such cases show that women and girls used the law to seek redress and obtain justice. They gave accounts of events, which sometimes took the form of a full narrative, where we can locate the voices of ordinary people. Their accounts were accompanied by witnesses for the prosecution and for the defence and, at times, a midwife's or physician's testimony. In general, if women's and girls' accounts could not be corroborated by multiple witnesses, or if witnesses' accounts differed in certain ways, defendants were released.

A girl's or a woman's alleged reputation for promiscuity could also be used to support the defence's case. Indeed, statements about women and girls allegedly found drunk or deemed 'bad' further affected the court's perception of whether they were entitled to the protection of the law, and the jury usually returned a verdict of not guilty.[33] As Michael Craton and Gail Saunders contend, black Bahamians "were not only open for sexual exploitation by those above them on the social scale but were, by the customary hegemonic inversion, regarded by them as naturally promiscuous" (Craton and Saunders 2000, 97). This particular context made it particularly difficult for women and girls to achieve justice for themselves and others. Generally speaking, cases involving adult women returned a not guilty verdict, while cases involving teen girls often led to the defendant being sentenced to imprisonment, in conjunction with hard labour, for up to two years.

Actual numbers of cases of inter-personal violence against women and girls carried out during this period are impossible to know. Since GBV did not generate commentary in the mainstream newspapers, nor did contemporary observers and officials seem to think of raising concerns over criminal behaviour of the sort, court proceedings remain some of the only records that can offer a glimpse into the extent of such violence in Bahamian society. Legal records thus remain critical pieces of evidence to revealing circumstances related to GBV, people's attitudes towards it, and responses to it.

CONCLUSION

Intersecting racial and economic identities subjected women to overlapping systems of oppression and discrimination, and working-class women and girls were frequently victims of both state and inter-personal violence. Both types involved the prioritization of hegemonic masculinities over the rights of women and girls, and the latter found themselves subject to multiple forms of violence. As noted earlier, judgement of women's behaviour required different sanctions and, as a result, those who failed to meet the white ideals of feminine domesticity were branded as deviant and immoral. Furthermore, courts often failed to fully protect women from crimes of violence. Gender prejudice and stereotyping reinforced and unleashed state violence against women, failing to transform social, economic and cultural conditions that sustained and reinforced GBV.

Finally, court records from The Bahamas in the nineteenth- and early twentieth-century reveal that women used the law, rather than simply being subject to it, and that they chose not to be silent or be silenced. Time and again, they asserted their rights and overtly defied or undermined authority, by being 'loud' and using the court system to settle disputes and hold accountable those who wronged them. The voices of Afro-Bahamian women, though filtered by white socio-cultural norms, could be heard clearly as they shared their circumstances and stories with the courts. Legal records can thus help demonstrate that women were relatively familiar with the intricacies of the legal system and that they exercised their agency in the broader fabric of society.

As historians unlock the potential of court records to describe behaviour not easily uncovered in other sources, paying attention to what was written and what was omitted remains crucial. Ann Laura Stoler notes that colonial historians "have wrestled with this formulation to capture that which renders colonial archives both as documents of exclusions and as monuments to particular configurations of power in themselves" (Stoler 2002, 89). As we contend with the power of the archival record and its limits, it is important to read both along the grain and against it to emphasize women's ability to find agency, and deconstruct and fill in silences of the past.

NOTES

1. MAG. 1/68, Police Complaints Book, 20 Nov. 1878–30 Dec. 1881; MAG. 1/20, Police Minutes, 16 July 1880–29 Jan. 1881; MAG. 2/4, Evidence, 9 Aug. 1881–Dec. 1881, Department of Archives, Nassau, The Bahamas (thereafter cited as Archives, The Bahamas).
2. MAG. 1/68; MAG. 1/20; and MAG. 2/4, Archives, The Bahamas.
3. CO 23/135/120, Governor Gregory's Report upon the Bahamas, Archives, The Bahamas.
4. CO 23/241/77, 24 June 1895, Archives, The Bahamas.
5. CO 23/243/23, 2 April 1896, Archives, The Bahamas.
6. *Bahamas Blue Book*, 1898; CO 23/252/12, 2 February 1899, Archives, The Bahamas.
7. *Bahamas Blue Book*, 1903–1905; CO 23/275/17, 20 February 1915, Archives, The Bahamas.
8. CO 23/241/77, 24 June 1895, Archives, The Bahamas.
9. CO 23/241/77, 24 June 1895; CO 23/249/36, 26 February 1898, Archives, The Bahamas.
10. *Bahamas Blue Book*, 1903–1905; CO 23/275/17, 20 February 1915, Archives, The Bahamas.
11. See, for example, CO 23/215/58, 17 June 1876; CO 23/224/10, 16 February 1884; CO 23/241/77, 24 June 1895, Archives, The Bahamas.
12. Such serious offences included "continued insubordination, escaping or attempting to escape from prison, assault upon officers of the prison or prisoners, persisting in riotous or disorderly conduct or the use of blasphemous, violent or obscene language, destruction of clothing or prison property, mutinous conduct, [and] any repetition of misconduct." CO 23/219/36, 22 August 1879; CO 23/226/26, 8 June 1885, Archives, The Bahamas.
13. ibid.
14. CO 23/224/10, 16 February 1884, Archives, The Bahamas.
15. ibid.
16. Lunatic Asylum, *Bahamas Blue Book*, 1870–1926, Archives, The Bahamas.
17. MAG. 7/23, Criminal Minutes, 27 Jan. 1920–20 June 1910, Archives, The Bahamas.
18. Lunatic Asylum, *Bahamas Blue Book*, 1870–1926, Archives, The Bahamas.
19. For lack of enforcement of and access to justice for women and girls, see Powles' recollection of the Rosa Poitier case, pp. 110–11. For changing attitudes towards domestic violence in England and the United States, see Martin J. Wiener, "Alice

Arden to Bill Sikes: Changing Nightmares of Intimate Violence in England, 1558–1869," *Journal of British Studies* 40 (2): 184–212, and Elizabeth Pleck, "Criminal Approaches to Family Violence, 1640–1980," *Crime and Justice* vol. 11 (1989): 19–57.

20. See, for instance, the case against Moses Wright, sentenced to six months imprisonment with hard labour, *Nassau Guardian*, 5 February 1887, https://dloc.com/AA00076890/02995/zoom/0.
21. Wilmot, "Race and Justice in the Bahamas," 16–17; Saunders, *Race and Class in the Colonial Bahamas*, 41–42.
22. *Nassau Times*, 7 May 1887. https://dloc.com/AA00079430/01468/zoom/1.
23. "Offences against the person" included assault, assault and battery, making threats, throwing stones. Annual Colonial Reports, The Bahamas, 1879–1911; CO 23/209-252, 1872–1899; MAG. 1/36, Police Minutes, 14 May 1890–12 Aug. 1890; MAG. 1/38, Police Minutes, 5 March 1891–26 May 1891; MAG. 1/39, Police Minutes, 27 May 1891–14 October 1891; MAG. 7/23; MAG. 7/48, Criminal Minutes, 14 March 1921–9 June 1921, Archives, The Bahamas.
24. MAG. 1/68; MAG. 1/20; and MAG. 2/4, Archives, The Bahamas.
25. ibid. For further analysis of this sample, see Ulentin, "She Has Not Been Seen or Heard of Since".
26. A bind-over to keep the peace is an order used to prevent certain behaviour from occurring in the future. It is not a conviction.
27. Fines were minimal, given the seriousness of such cases (between ten shillings to a dollar which represented several days' worth of working-class wages).
28. MAG. 1/68 and MAG. 1/20, Archives, The Bahamas.
29. MAG. 1/68, Archives, The Bahamas.
30. The Queen vs James Perpall, 22 January 1902, SC. 20/13, Criminal Minutes, 2 Aug. 1901–22 Jan. 1902, Archives, The Bahamas.
31. SC. 20/56, Criminal Minutes, 26 Jan. 1921–19 July 1923, Archives, The Bahamas. *Nassau Guardian*, 21 January 1922, https://dloc.com/AA00076890/06516/images/3 (accessed 18 September 2022).
32. SC. 1/53, General Court Minutes, 15 April 1879–20 Jan. 1881; SC. 1/54, General Court Minutes, 21 Jan. 1881–18 Oct. 1882; SC. 1/56, General Court Minutes, 19 Oct. 1882–26 April 1884; SC. 1/62, General Court Minutes, 15 July 1890–1 Feb. 1895. SC. 1/63, General Court Minutes, 21 Oct. 1891–29 Oct. 1892; SC. 1/64, General Court Minutes, 3 Jan. 1893–17 Jan. 1894; SC. 20/1, Criminal Minutes, 15 July 1890–21 Oct. 1891; SC. 20/10, Criminal Minutes, 20 July 1900–4 Feb. 1903; SC. 20/11, Criminal Minutes, 25 July 1900–25 April 1901;

SC. 20/13; SC. 20/14, Criminal Minutes, 23 Jan. 1902–4 June 1902; SC. 20/56, Criminal Minutes, 26 Jan. 1921–19 July 1923, Archives, The Bahamas.

33. See, for instance, The Queen vs Wayman D. Rattray, 17 Jan. 1883, SC. 1/56; The Queen vs John Dorsett, 2 February 1921, SC. 20/56; The Queen vs Bruce Driggs, 9 February 1921, SC. 20/56, Archives, The Bahamas.

REFERENCES

PRIMARY SOURCES

Department of Archives, Nassau, The Bahamas:
Records of the Colonial Office, CO 23/135–275.
Colonial Office, *Bahamas Blue Book,* 1870–1926.
Annual Colonial Reports, The Bahamas, 1879–1911.

Magistrates' court, Nassau:
MAG. 1/20, Police Minutes, 16 July 1880–29 Jan. 1881.
MAG. 1/36, Police Minutes, 14 May 1890–12 Aug. 1890.
MAG. 1/38, Police Minutes, 5 March 1891–26 May 1891.
MAG. 1/39, Police Minutes, 27 May 1891–14 October 1891.
MAG. 1/68, Police Complaints Book, 20 Nov. 1878–30 Dec. 1881.
MAG. 2/4, Evidence, 9 Aug. 1881–Dec. 1881.
MAG. 7/23, Criminal Minutes, 27 Jan. 1920–20 June 1910.
MAG. 7/48, Criminal Minutes, 14 March 1921–9 June 1921.

General Court:
SC. 1/53, General Court Minutes, 15 April 1879–20 Jan. 1881.
SC. 1/54, General Court Minutes, 21 Jan. 1881–18 Oct. 1882.
SC. 1/56, General Court Minutes, 19 Oct. 1882–26 April 1884.
SC. 1/62, General Court Minutes, 15 July 1890–1 Feb. 1895.
SC. 1/63, General Court Minutes, 21 Oct. 1891–29 Oct. 1892.
SC. 1/64, General Court Minutes, 3 Jan. 1893–17 Jan. 1894.
SC. 20/1, Criminal Minutes, 15 July 1890–21 Oct. 1891.
SC. 20/10, Criminal Minutes, 20 July 1900–4 Feb. 1903.
SC. 20/11, Criminal Minutes, 25 July 1900–25 April 1901.
SC. 20/13, Criminal Minutes, 2 Aug. 1901–22 Jan. 1902.
SC. 20/14, Criminal Minutes, 23 Jan. 1902–4 June 1902.
SC. 20/54, Criminal Minutes, 15 Jan., 1919–22 April, 1920.

SC. 20/56, Criminal Minutes, 26 Jan., 1921–19 July, 1923.

Nassau Guardian. 5 February1887. https://dloc.com/AA00076890/02995/zoom/0.

———. 21 January 1922. Accessed 18 September 2022. https://dloc.com/AA00076890/06516/images/3.

Nassau Times. 7 May 1887. https://dloc.com/AA00079430/01468/zoom/1.

SECONDARY SOURCES

Brereton, Bridget. 2010. "The Historical Background to the Culture of Violence in Trinidad and Tobago." *Caribbean Review of Gender Studies: A Journal of Caribbean Perspectives on Gender and Feminism* no. 4: 1–16.

Craton, Michael, and Gail Saunders. 1998. *Islanders in the Stream: A History of the Bahamian People, Vol. II – From the Ending of Slavery to the Twenty-First Century*. Athens, GA: University of Georgia Press.

Damousi, Joy. 1995. "'Depravity and Disorder': The Sexuality of Convict Women." *Labour History* no. 68: 30–45.

———. 1997. *Depraved and Disorderly: Female Convicts, Sexuality and Gender in Colonial Australia*. Cambridge: Cambridge University Press.

Fryar, Christienna D. 2016. "Imperfect Models: The Kingston Lunatic Asylum Scandal and the Problem of Postemancipation Imperialism." *Journal of British Studies* 55 (4): 709–27.

———. 2018. "The Narrative of Ann Pratt: Life-Writing, Genre, and Bureaucracy in a Postemancipation Scandal." *History Workshop Journal* no. 85 (Spring): 265–79.

Fuentes, Marisa J. 2016. *Dispossessed Lives: Enslaved Women, Violence, and the Archive*. Philadelphia: University of Pennsylvania Press.

Green, Cecilia A. 2011. "'The Abandoned Lower Class of Females': Class, Gender, and Penal Discipline in Barbados, 1875–1929." *Comparative Studies in Society and History* 53 (1): 144–79.

———. 2012. "Local Geographies of Crime and Punishment in a Plantation Colony: Gender and Incarceration in Barbados, 1878–1928." *NWIG: New West Indian Guide / Nieuwe West-Indische Gids* 86 (3/4): 263–90.

Harris, Dawn P. 2017. *Punishing the Black Body: Marking Social and Racial Structures in Barbados and Jamaica*. Athens, GA: University of Georgia Press.

Hartman, Saidiya. 2008. "Venus in Two Acts." *Small Axe* 12 (2): 1–14.

Johnson, Howard. 1986. "'A Modified Form of Slavery': The Credit and Truck Systems in the Bahamas in the Nineteenth and Early Twentieth Centuries." *Comparative Studies in Society and History* 28 (4): 729–53.

———. 1988. "Labour Systems in Postemancipation Bahamas." *Social and Economic Studies* 37 (1/2): 181–201.

———. 1996. *The Bahamas from Slavery to Servitude, 1783–1933*. Gainesville: University Press of Florida.

Johnson, Whittington B. 2006. *Post-Emancipation Race Relations in The Bahamas*. Gainesville: University Press of Florida.

Jones, Margaret. 2008. "The Most Cruel and Revolting Crimes: The Treatment of the Mentally Ill in Mid-Nineteenth-Century Jamaica." *Journal of Caribbean History* 42 (2): 290–309.

Loomba, Ania. 2015. *Colonialism/Postcolonialism*. London and New York: Routledge.

McClintock, Anne. 1995. *Imperial Leather: Race, Gender, and Sexuality in the Colonial Contest*. New York: Routledge.

Mercier Allain, Jacqueline. 2020. "'They are Quiet Women Now': Hair Cropping, British Imperial Governance, and the Gendered Body in the Archive." *Slavery & Abolition: A Journal of Slave and Post-Slave Studies* 41 (4): 772–94.

Paton, Diana. 2004. *No Bond but the Law: Punishment, Race, and Gender in Jamaican State Formation, 1780–1870*. Durham, NC: Duke University Press.

Pleck, Elizabeth. 1989. "Criminal Approaches to Family Violence, 1640–1980." *Crime and Justice* vol. 11: 19–57.

Powles, Lewis D. 1996. *The Land of the Pink Pearl: Recollections of Life in the Bahamas*. Nassau: Media Publishing.

Robertson, Stephen. 2005. "What's Law Got to Do with It? Legal Records and Sexual Histories." *Journal of the History of Sexuality* 14 (1/2): 161–85.

Saunders, Gail. *Race and Class in the Colonial Bahamas, 1880–1960*. Gainesville: University Press of Florida, 2016.

Smith, Faith, ed. 2011. *Sex and the Citizen: Interrogating the Caribbean*. Charlottesville: University of Virginia Press.

Smith, Leonard. 2014. *Insanity, Race and Colonialism: Managing Mental Disorder in the Post-Emancipation British Caribbean, 1838–1914*. Basingstoke: Palgrave Macmillan.

Stoler, Ann Laura. 2002. "Colonial Archives and the Arts of Governance: On the Content in the Form." In *Refiguring the Archive*, edited by Carolyn Hamilton, Verne Harris, Jane Taylor, Michele Pickover, Graeme Reid, and Razia Saleh, 83–100. Dordrecht: Kluwer Academic Publishers.

Suárez Findlay, Eileen. 1999. *Imposing Decency: The Politics of Sexuality and Race in Puerto Rico, 1870–1920*. Durham, NC: Duke University Press.

Swartz, Sally. 1999. "Lost Lives: Gender, History and Mental Illness in the Cape, 1891–1910." *Feminism and Psychology* 9 (2): 152–58.

———. 2010. "The Regulation of British Colonial Lunatic Asylums and the Origins of Colonial Psychiatry." *History of Psychology* 13 (2): 160–77.

Themistocleous, Rosalyn. 1997. "L.D. Powles, Stipendiary Magistrate." *Journal of the Bahamas Historical Society* vol. 19 (October): 19–29.

Trotman, David Vincent. 1984. "Women and Crime in Late Nineteenth Century Trinidad." *Caribbean Quarterly* 30 (3/4): 60–72.

———. 1986. *Crime in Trinidad: Conflict and Control in a Plantation Society, 1838–1900*. Knoxville: University of Tennessee Press.

Ulentin, Anne. 2022. "'She Has Not Been Seen or Heard of Since': Gender, Incarceration, and Punishment in The Bahamas, 1860s–1920s." *New West Indian Guide / Nieuwe West-Indische Gids* 96 (3/4): 233–65.

Wiener, Martin J. 2001. "Alice Arden to Bill Sikes: Changing Nightmares of Intimate Violence in England, 1558–1869." *Journal of British Studies* 40 (2): 184–212.

Wilmot, Swithin R. 1980. "Race and Justice in the Bahamas: The Case of Lewis Powles." *College Forum* vol. 1: 15–18.

chapter 6

"The Brutal Passions of the Licentious"[1]

The Prosecution of Rape and Sexual Abuse in Nineteenth-Century Jamaica

JONATHAN DALBY

CONTEMPORARY DEFINITIONS OF GENDER-BASED VIOLENCE (GBV) encompass a wide range of abuses, ranging from femicide, physical violence and rape at one end of the scale, through female genital mutilation, sexual harassment, homophobia[2] and child marriage, to its more commonplace manifestations like psychological and verbal abuse. This chapter will be concerned only with those cases of sexual abuse of women and girls that were sufficiently violent to reach the courts.[3] While GBV has a centuries-old history, the term itself dates only from the late twentieth century. In this respect, any investigation of its manifestations in the past runs the risk of accusations of 'presentism' – "the willful or inadvertent misunderstanding of the past by applying standards or interpretations from outside the immediate era, context, or milieu under study"[4] – an approach which, historians are warned, should be avoided. For nineteenth-century Jamaica was a radically different society from that of today. Patriarchy was far more deeply rooted. As in Trinidad, men believed that they had "indisputable rights over the bodies and lives of women, and men used corporal punishment to enforce domestic law and order. It was taken for granted that men were entitled to punish women for real or imagined transgressions against their domestic sovereignty or to avenge real or imagined slights against their ego."[5] What today would be classed as abuse was in the nineteenth century viewed as tolerable, even normal. It was in these circumstances that the imperial power sought to impose – with very varied degrees of success – the increasingly Victorian middle-class values of the mother-country – like the nuclear family, legal Christian marriage and monogamy – on both the creole elite and the recently emancipated masses. And patriarchy remained, also, at the heart of this ideal. "Women were physically weaker, intellectually inferior and, therefore, ordained by nature to a subordinate and dependent position."[6] Wife beating – a contemporaneous umbrella term for all kinds of physical marital abuse – was generally tolerated as long as it was not too brutal, and minimal protection for wives against violent husbands was not voted in the imperial parliament until 1853.[7] The first Married Women's Property Act, granting wives some financial autonomy, was passed only in 1870. And the vote for women had to wait until after World War I. Women were first admitted to the Jamaica Constabulary Force only in 1949. In the courts, offenders were judged exclusively by male judges, prosecuted and defended by male lawyers, and convicted or acquitted by male jurors. It is in this context of a pervasive and authoritarian patriarchy, then, that a productive and meaningful exploration of GBV in post-emancipation Jamaica might be made.

Court records represent the only means of estimating the incidence and nature of different offences, including GBV, in nineteenth-century Jamaica. Records of the assize courts – principally the registers which recorded bills of indictment – have survived in large numbers. For the period 1770 to 1856, roughly 70 per cent of indictment registers have survived in the Jamaica Archives in Spanish Town.[8] For the second half of the nineteenth century, the proportion is rather more, rising to perhaps 80 per cent.[9] Overall, then, the survival of such a large proportion of court records enables us to gain a reasonably accurate picture of the patterns of criminal prosecution in nineteenth-century Jamaica. Indictment registers for the different assize courts listed all those who were indicted before that court.[10] Although their standardized and formulaic character make bills of indictment ideal for quantification, they reveal little or nothing of the nature and circumstances of the offence. They include only the name of the accused, the offence, the date of the offence, the name of the plaintiff or victim, the verdicts of the grand jury and of the trial jury, and, where appropriate, the sentence. Most of the remaining archival sources for an investigation of Jamaican criminality in the past are to be found in Colonial Office correspondence relating to capital cases.[11] Depositions and witnesses' testimonies – generally the most rewarding and detailed sources about individual cases – are rare. No more than a few hundred individual depositions have apparently survived in the Jamaica Archives for the period between 1834 and the end of the nineteenth century.[12] Of these, only a few dozen concerned cases of GBV. Complementing these various court records – and the most valuable source for details on crimes – are newspapers, which regularly reported on trials at the assizes and quarter sessions. Unfortunately, however, reports on the trials of sex offenders were invariably lacking in any details of the offence, which were routinely suppressed "for obvious reasons", or were "unfit for publication". In its report on the trial of Samuel Reeve for rape at the Trelawny quarter sessions, for example, the *Falmouth Post* merely observed, "His attack on this female was of the most brutal and filthy character, and we are therefore prevented from giving even a brief summary of the evidence."[13]

Those cases of gender-based violence that reached the courts were inevitably among the most serious: femicide, rape, and the most serious instances of assault. While it is fair to assume that the vast majority of cases of homicide were prosecuted, and that, therefore, there was little difference between the number of actual and recorded homicides, the prosecution rate for other offences, including sexual assault, was much lower. Estimates of the 'dark figure' (instances of an offence that remained undetected and unprosecuted) for homicide will inevitably be more accurate than those for sexual offences, a category for which a notoriously high degree of under-reporting has been evident worldwide since such statistics have been available.[14] Thus, while the actual incidence of femicide was likely little different from its recorded incidence,[15] the actual incidence of sexual offences against women and girls in nineteenth-century Jamaica certainly vastly exceeded the recorded incidence.

Rape and sexual assault in the early modern period appear to have been broadly understood in terms of uncontrollable male lust and female promiscuity. The early modern European rapist was sometimes viewed as a monster, but was more often seen as, in some sense, 'everyman' – the individual momentarily led astray by a loss of self-control.[16] By the nineteenth century, although aristocratic and middle-class sexual predators continued to be treated with a degree of sympathy by the courts in England, rapists from among the subaltern classes began to be viewed as increasingly aberrant and deviant – as fundamentally different from ordinary men. The image of the deviant 'monster-rapist' was definitively undermined, however, by the publication in 1975 of Susan Brownmiller's seminal and revolutionary *Against Our Will*. "I knew what rape was, and what it wasn't. Rape was a sex crime, a product of a diseased, deranged mind. Rape wasn't a feminist issue," she reminisced in her foreword; but, "I wrote this book because I am a woman who changed her mind about rape."[17] For the feminist Brownmiller, far from being the exclusive domain of the sexually deviant male, rape lay at the heart of modern Western patriarchy: not all men were rapists, but all men were potential rapists. The Brownmiller thesis did not, of course, go unchallenged,[18] but the figure of the 'everyman-rapist' was henceforth indelibly inscribed in the feminist handbook: "It turned out that he was, for the most part, an unextraordinary, violence-prone fellow."[19]

In pre-emancipation Jamaica, out of nearly forty-two hundred extant cases in the slave courts, only twelve (or 0.3 per cent) were prosecuted for sexual assault. In the assize courts, only fifteen out of 2,643 (0.6 per cent). Yet, in the two decades following emancipation – after the slave courts had been abolished and all Jamaicans were prosecuted for felony in the assizes – the figures rose sharply to two hundred and fifty (10 per cent) out of a total of 2,503 extant prosecutions. Between 1835 and 1854, nearly one in ten assize court cases were for rape or carnal abuse, and in the peak year of 1853, more than one in five. Before 1834, of course, the mass of the population, being enslaved, was subject to the 'justice' meted out by slave courts; prosecutions were instigated for the most part by slave owners, who made up the majority of justices in these courts, and it seems likely that if very few cases of sexual assault were heard, it is because they were not inclined to prosecute – rather than that such offences were rarely committed. These offences were evidently not considered criminal by the slave owner, since they represented little or no threat to his authority or to the stability of the plantation economy. That there were few cases of sexual assault prosecuted in the assize courts before 1834, moreover, should come as no surprise. Members of the white elite were in a position to ensure that such cases were hushed up and never reached the courts. The few cases that were prosecuted concerned the lower levels of the free population – mariners, soldiers, artisans and free blacks. The virtual absence of prosecution in any court in the pre-emancipation years, then, has the effect of rendering post-emancipation prosecution statistics that much more striking.

In this context, the prosecution of Thomas Simpson before the Cornwall assize court in 1822 represents a revealing exception to the norm in several respects, not least by virtue of the volume of evidence and detail that has survived for it. Simpson was an elderly St Elizabeth planter accused of brutally raping Charlotte, a little "negro girl slave" of no more than nine years old whom he owned. Simpson's former housekeeper, a free coloured woman, testified that she went over to Fyfe's Pen with a friend, having received a message that he had fallen from his horse and injured himself. Even before reaching the house, she heard a girl scream out,

> "Do massa stop, I will try to put it in with my fingers," that the said Thomas Simpson cried out "Put it in you bitch, hold up your foot"; that the child again cried out "Massa, it can't go in"; that the said Thomas Simpson again said, "If you do not take your hand and put it in, I will soak you with the supple jack, and if you do not stand, you bitch, I will tear you to pieces," and the more shocking expressions . . . The witness and her friend then entered the house, opened the bedroom door, and found Simpson, his breeches being down, his shirt, his breeches, and other parts of his dress being all covered and imbued with blood. The little girl was lying in a pool of blood on the floor, her foot chained to a weight called a "fifty-six". Her subsequent medical examination revealed a ruptured hymen, lacerations round the groin, and a "highly diseased and suppurating vagina."[20]

Even by the dismal standards of Jamaican slave society, this was a shocking case. The sixty-four-year-old Simpson was sent before the Cornwall Assizes, convicted of rape, and sentenced to death, in spite of a highly questionable recommendation for mercy on the grounds of "suspicion of mental derangement".[21] The notoriety of Simpson case, however, was ultimately associated less with the shocking nature of the crime than with the subsequent legal wranglings surrounding it. Following the assize court verdict in July 1822, the defence counsel applied for an arrest of judgment on the grounds of doubts whether the Elizabethan statute under which the offence had been tried was in force in the island, and whether this statute was applicable in cases where the enslaved were the victims.[22] By the time the whole dossier had been sent to London for the Colonial Office to sort out, Simpson had died in Montego Bay jail.[23]

Although the precise route by which the Simpson case reached court is not clear, the young age of the victim, the degree of violence involved, the gruesome detail contained in the depositions, and the fact that this offence occurred during the period of 'amelioration' evidently explain why it was prosecuted. But the 'dark figure' for such offences before 1834 remains unknown and unknowable, even if the fragmentary evidence which has survived, notably in the Thistlewood diaries,[24] suggests that sexual coercion of the enslaved by slave owners was, at the least, not uncommon. But what of the sexual coercion of enslaved women by their peers? Did the trajectory of incidence of sexual assault after 1834, as seems likely, broadly follow that under slavery? In a recent conference paper, Diana Paton has unearthed hints that drivers and boatswains, at least – those at the apex of the enslaved hierarchy – engaged in the sexual coercion of enslaved women.[25] But how representative was their behaviour of the mass of enslaved men? To what extent was sexual coercion the norm within the enslaved community and what impact did emancipation have on these relationships? In view of the paucity of evidence, only tentative answers to some of these questions can be suggested, based on informed guesswork.

I have argued elsewhere that the massive increase in sex offence prosecution as a whole (also including sodomy and bestiality) during the immediate post-emancipation years can be explained principally by a 'moral panic'; that this apparent epidemic of sexual deviance was largely manufactured; that it was less about sex, or crime, or law-breaking, and more about elite fears about the failure of emancipation.[26] Diana Paton, however, has suggested "that the rise in prosecutions for rape, carnal abuse, and indecent assault should be understood as primarily the product of women's actions, rather than the result of the concerns of Jamaican elites".[27] Separating and isolating sexual assault on women from the broad category of 'sexual deviance', as defined by mid-nineteenth century Jamaican elites, indeed, while implying a misguided conflation of offences on my part, certainly opens up new lines of inquiry. The key, of course, is evidence. The most fruitful sources for this evidence, which is wholly lacking in the indictment registers, and very rare in newspaper reports, are judge's notes and depositions. Fortunately, a few of these have survived. The first case, and perhaps the most revealing – albeit not a prosecution for sexual assault – came before the Middlesex grand jury in October 1834, when Dr Robert Bruce, a medical attendant at Moreland estate in Vere, was charged with exposing "to the view of persons so present part of the body and person, that is to say the thighs of one Jane Robertson . . . naked and uncovered for a long period of time . . ."[28] On 1 September 1834, according to the complaint she submitted to the stipendiary magistrate, Jane Robertson, a Moreland estate apprentice and married woman, was in the hothouse, following a fainting fit. When she came to, she was told that Dr Bruce had called two men to "make use of her" and he would "pay them half a dollar". Her story was corroborated by several witnesses. Bruce, supported predictably by the estate's bookkeepers, alleged that he had been joking, that he believed she was feigning sickness, and that no harm had been done. On the contrary, responded Jane Robertson, "Everybody had seen her nakedness and . . . her feelings were hurt; it was the doctor's duty to take her into a room and examine her privately and not to turn up her petticoats before everybody . . . she is a married woman."[29] Notwithstanding the stilted style of the transcribed testimony, these were the words of a free woman who knew she was free (albeit as an apprentice) and was determined to claim the benefits of freedom only weeks after the emancipation proclamation. Doubtless such scenarios, or worse, had been played out regularly at Moreland estate – and indeed throughout the island – under slavery. In this respect, Bruce's indictment might be regarded as a test case. Stipendiary magistrate Charles Brown, viewing the matter as one "of great importance to society", referred it to the governor, and although the doctor was soon to be dismissed as a magistrate, his case was predictably ruled *ignoramus* by the grand jury. If Jane Robertson was in any way representative of her peers under apprenticeship, then her case suggests that women's agency was indeed a powerful contributory factor in the sudden increase in rape prosecutions in the 1830s.

At least fifty-nine cases of rape and carnal abuse (and assault with intent) were tried between 1835 and 1839, and from 1835 to the end of the nineteenth century, a total of more than twelve hundred such cases were prosecuted. Twenty to thirty rape and carnal abuse cases came before the assize and circuit courts each year. Rape remained a capital offence until 1842,[30] but it continued to be difficult to prove in court. Several conditions had to be met if a rape charge was to lead to conviction in the early years. The most fundamental of these was penetration. Until 1837, moreover, when it was enacted that in cases of rape, carnal abuse and sodomy, "it shall not be necessary . . . to prove the actual emission of seed, but that the carnal knowledge be complete upon proof of penetration only",[31] ejaculation also had to be proved. The prospect of the protracted discussion in court of such details would have been sufficient to deter many would-be prosecutors. Even more intimidating, however, was the prospect of the woman's sexual history and moral character being subjected to minute scrutiny, for in many rape cases it was inevitable that the trial became as much that of the victim as of the defendant. The merest hint of consent on her part would lead inevitably to acquittal, and it was the task of the defence counsel to investigate her sexual history and to bring her lifestyle and reputation into question. In 1839, for example, Mary Beloma, "a very decent young woman from the parish of St David" and the alleged victim of rape by William McCulloch, a former policeman, was subjected to rigorous cross-examination by the defence counsel at the Surrey Assizes in January 1839, "but her evidence was consistent throughout". Another witness testified, however, that the two had previously cohabited, that "she does not bear a very good character in the parish", and that "she has a child by a black man – she herself is a mulatto." The case against McCulloch then collapsed (*Falmouth Post*, 6 February 1839). In another case, a few years earlier, Thomas Downer was charged with assault with intent to rape on Frances Bryan. Both were apprentices on Tom's Hope estate in Portland. The two were working together, digging cane holes, when he assaulted her and carried her into the bush. "She did all in her power to prevent him, but ineffectually, as he chonked her." She informed her master and mistress, and the authorities were contacted. At the trial, she resisted cross-examination "until being closely pressed – she admitted she stood on a bank on the roadside awaiting his approach". Such flimsy evidence was sufficient to persuade the attorney-general to abandon the case and the prisoner was acquitted.[32]

All these factors, when taken together, must inevitably have dissuaded many women from reporting such assaults. Yet, many did so. Moreover, that as many as 70 per cent of defendants in cases of sexual assault between 1835 and 1899 were convicted (albeit frequently of a reduced charge) of offences that were notoriously difficult to prove, suggests that these prosecutions might well be "only the tip of a broader and deeper iceberg;"[33] that women and girls in nineteenth-century Jamaica all too often faced threats of sexual coercion and violence.

Those cases most likely to reach court, to lead to indictment by the grand jury and to the conviction of the defendant, particularly in the decade after emancipation, tended to be those involving serious violence and those in which the victims were children. Visible evidence of injury to the victim would be more likely to convince her friends and family to report a case, even if the victim herself were reluctant, and would certainly be more likely to convince a jury of the guilt of the defendant. With a few notable exceptions,[34] the vast majority of both defendants and victims were listed as labourers – the term universally applied to denote the former enlaved and apprentices, "the class of persons among whom this crime prevails here".[35] Between 1835 and 1842, at least nine men were sentenced to death for rape, and at least three of them were, in fact, hanged. One was William Wallace, an apprentice at Shawfield estate in St Ann, who was convicted of a vicious assault on Ann Johnson, a fellow apprentice and mother of nine children. According to the victim, Wallace persuaded her to come with him on the pretext of helping him with something. Not far from the house, he threw her to the ground in a deep gully, knocked out two of her teeth, and had his way with her. "He said I will sleep with you this day. He did sleep with me. I have now no sweetheart. He entered me and did according to his power. I am sure he had connexion with me . . ." She told Louisa Piper, the 'doctor woman', who testified that "her mouth was bleeding and she was so hoarse she could hardly speak". Wallace was arrested in Dry Harbour two days later. "I never knew him to be rude to any woman," said Louisa Piper.[36] He was hanged on 31 October 1835 (*Falmouth Post*, 4 November 1835). Richard Johnson, also an apprentice, of Hyde estate in St Thomas-in-the-Vale, was more fortunate. Having been acquitted on rape charges at the same assizes in Spanish Town, he was then tried for attempted rape. The victim was a girl under ten years of age called Louisa Edwards, who lived on the same estate. Johnson had come to her house to ask her mother whether her daughter could help him carry goods to his hut, to which she agreed. In his hut, however, according to the victim's testimony, he forced her back on to his bed, stuffed a handkerchief into her mouth to prevent her screaming, and threatened her. "He pulled down his breeches," she said, "he poked his thing into me." She later found blood on her frock. Johnson only stopped when Sarah Francis, a neighbour, passed by. The latter later testified that "she saw him lying on Louisa Edwards. His trousers were down. He was criminally connecting himself . . ." Dr Charles McDermott, called to examine the victim, found traces of inflammation around the vagina. "Otherwise, there was nothing particularly remarkable," he concluded, "except the absence of the hymen, which is not always considered a test of virginity."[37] Johnson was found guilty of assault with intent and sentenced to six months in prison.[38]

Molly White was only eight when she was attacked in December 1835 by an apprentice named Simon Dixon from Water Valley estate in Trelawny. The testimony of the victim was – not surprisingly – somewhat confused and contradictory. ". . . The blood came from before me," she told the authorities, "He put nothing into me but bruised me all round. I felt something in me. Felt something hot come from the prisoner . . ." Dr Tuthill's medical report, however, was less vague. The little girl was shaken and bruised; there was an unpleasant discharge from her private parts; and he was sure that "sufficient penetration had been made to enable the man to have an emission of semen". Dixon was formally identified, arrested, tried, convicted and hanged.[39] In April 1851, when nine-year-old Elizabeth Glasson came home in Spanish Town with blood on her clothes, her mother was about to flog her. A neighbour persuaded her against this and managed to coax the truth out of the little girl. She had gone out to pick tamarinds and, on returning, she was followed by a labourer called Richard Hart. He "threw me to the ground and pulled up my clothes," she said. "He also unbuttoned his pantaloon and laid upon me. During the whole time I was bawling . . . He hurt me with his 'pepe'. He hurt me into my 'pepe'." The subsequent medical report, while noting bruising and laceration of the arms, concluded that "the vagina was not injured" and that "no penetration was effected". Hart was, therefore, convicted only of attempted rape and sentenced to twelve months in the General Penitentiary.[40]

The above cases constitute just a few of the many scores of sexual assault cases in nineteenth-century Jamaica. Young – sometimes very young – girls, made up an alarmingly large proportion of the victims, even if this number is certainly inflated by the fact that instances of violent assault on children were both more likely to be reported and more likely to be prosecuted. In cases of rape and carnal abuse where the victim was a minor, her age was routinely recorded in the indictment, and the records show that nearly half the victims were eight or younger, more than 15 per cent were six or under, while more than 38 per cent were nine or ten.[41] Only a handful of transcripts or depositions have survived for carnal abuse prosecutions, but the few scraps of detail available suggest scenarios very similar to the following. In July 1849, William Hedge, a private in the First West India Regiment, was put on trial for carnally abusing a ten-year-old girl called Frances Ann Cunningham. Victim and defendant apparently lived at the same premises in Montego Bay. According to the girl, Hedge persuaded her into his room, took off his trousers "and lay down upon me and wanted to play with me. He wanted to put it in but he did not. He did not hurt me. I did not want to play with him. The time I was going to bawl out he stopped my mouth . . . " Hedge was interrupted by a neighbour, who burst into the room when she heard shouting. The subsequent medical examination revealed no marks of violence, except traces of a recent flogging, and Hedge was convicted of attempted carnal abuse.[42] Thirty years later, a particularly horrendous case of sexual assault was tried in the St Catherine circuit court. The offence came to light only three weeks after the assault. On 28 November 1881, Dr James Tompsett, medical officer for the eastern district of St Catherine, was sent for to examine a seriously ill ten-year-old girl named Charlotte Davis in the Spanish Town suburbs. Her symptoms appeared to be those of peritonitis and he "found her external genital organs much swollen and inflamed and a persistent discharge issuing from her vagina". Further examination revealed evidence that the girl had been assaulted by someone who had gonorrhoea. Her mother had initially called the local doctor several days before, after the girl had complained of a pain in the bowels, but she (the mother) allegedly had no suspicion that her daughter had been assaulted. It was not until early January 1882 that the girl had recovered sufficiently to testify. She finally admitted that it was Henry Blackwell, who lived with her mother (it is not clear whether or not he was her partner), who had assaulted her and she said she was too ashamed to tell her mother. In early November, according to

Charlotte Davis, Blackwell had asked her to "play". She did not understand, but "he put me on the edge of the bed . . . put his finger into me and then lay on me and put his tongue in my mouth . . . and he put his long thing into me . . . He did this to me once before. I do not know exactly how long."[43] Blackwell escaped with a sentence of only eighteen months in the penitentiary.

Several of these cases of assault on young girls, as we have seen, reached court almost by accident. Most victims were reluctant to reveal the truth, either because they were ashamed, or because they feared violence from their aggressor, or perhaps also because they believed that such behaviour was normal (some of the victims were as young as three). Louisa Edwards testified that her attacker – whose offence was only discovered because a neighbour chanced to witness it – said "if she told her mother he would beat her".[44] Elizabeth Glasson's mother only reported the assault on her daughter when a neighbour insisted upon it. Charlotte Davis admitted that Blackwell "did this to me once before". Such evidence suggests that the sexual abuse of young girls was likely far more widespread than the prosecution figures would indicate. In most of these cases, moreover, the aggressor was known to the victim – a friend of the family, a relation, a neighbour, a stepfather, and (in at least five cases) the father – a fact which further reduced the reporting rate, and a pattern which conforms very much to that reported in the early twenty-first century.[45] Of the more than twelve hundred extant sexual assaults tried between 1835 and 1899, no more than a dozen or so might be classified – on the basis of the number of defendants charged – as gang rapes. Nor is there much trace in our court records of the 'stranger/monster' rapist, the sexually deviant Jack the Ripper figure who preys upon vulnerable women. Most often, the Jamaican rapist and child molester appears in the guise of Brownmiller's "unextraordinary, violence-prone fellow".

Given the very high levels of under-reporting, sexual assault rates over the long term are impossible to determine with any degree of accuracy. In so far as they are meaningful, assize court statistics in the post-emancipation nineteenth century show that cases of rape, carnal abuse, and indecent assault represented, on average, 7.6 per cent of total prosecutions, with a high of 15 per cent (1845–1849) and a low of 4.2 per cent (1865–1869). Equivalent twentieth-century (1900–1959) figures show an almost identical rate of 7.7 per cent, with a high of 12.6 per cent (1900–1904) and a low of 5.6 per cent

(1945–1949).[46] But it is doubtful whether these statistics tell us much about the real rate of incidence. Figures for the later twentieth century are no more precise. The Jamaica Constabulary Force indicated a rise of more than 110 per cent of offences reported in this category between 1980 and 1997,[47] though much of this rise may be explained by an increase in reporting, while an Amnesty International report simply noted in 2006, "The rate of sexual violence against women is very high."[48] In short, the real incidence of sexual assault in the late twentieth and early twenty-first centuries is no more easy to determine than that for the nineteenth century.

While there are clear signs of continuity in the nature and incidence of male violence against women between the post-emancipation nineteenth century and the early twenty-first century in Jamaica, there is little sense that such violence in the earlier period possessed a particular distinctiveness. It seems likely, however, that the culture of violence so characteristic of slave societies contributed to – if it does not wholly explain – the elevated levels of post-emancipation male violence against women, and of violence in general. For, as Trevor Burnard argues, "Brutality, violence, and death were not mere by-products of the extremely lucrative early modern plantation system but were the *sine qua non* of that plantation world."[49] Little comparative data exists for the wider Caribbean and the Americas, but recent research into intimate partner homicide by ethnic and racial group in late nineteenth and early twentieth-century Chicago, for example, shows that although issues of patriarchal authority, male control and poverty were central to domestic violence across the board, the homicide rate for black Americans was much higher than for Italian and German immigrants; reached a peak in the 1920s;[50] and persisted into the late twentieth century. In the 1990s, African-American women were nearly four times more likely to be killed by their partners than white women.[51] The figures for contemporary Jamaica are even more alarming. The UN Office on Drugs and Crime (UNODC) recently reported that the island currently has the second highest rate of femicide in the world, exceeded only by that of El Salvador.[52] The particular circumstances of the black community in a North American industrial city were, of course, very different from those of Afro-Jamaicans, but the legacy of violence left by slavery, and the challenges and disappointments of emancipation were common to both. As a consequence, largely of the massive demographic imbalance, however – the enslaved population of Jamaica outnumbered the white population by ten to one at the time of Tacky's Rebellion in 1760 and by fifteen to one on the eve of emancipation – planters in Jamaica were particularly reliant on violence and coercion to defend and maintain the plantation system. "White Jamaicans learned from their near-death experience in 1760 that if they were sufficiently resolute against any sign of slave rebellion and were prepared to use extreme violence to defend planter prerogatives, their safety would be secured."[53] In 1760–61, dozens of rebel leaders were tortured and put to death by slow fire or starved to death on gibbets. In 1831, the defeat of the Christmas Rebellion, in which fourteen whites died, was followed by the summary execution of more than three hundred alleged rebels, many of whom had little or nothing to do with the revolt. On a more mundane level, daily floggings were administered routinely on most Jamaican plantations, often for the most trivial offences. This culture of violence, which permeated the slave regime in Jamaica, inevitably affected the enslaved, who "responded to constant violence by being violent themselves",[54] and it is clear that emancipation did not simply sweep away such attitudes, as the events of 1865 were to demonstrate. We cannot attempt to quantify the violent legacy of nearly two centuries of slavery on the Jamaican people. But the conclusion seems inescapable that this legacy was substantial; that the mindset of men who assaulted, raped and murdered their women in nineteenth-century Jamaica was inextricably bound up with their enslaved past.

NOTES

1. Address of Chief Justice Joshua Rowe to the Surrey grand jury (*Falmouth Post*, 6 August 1844).
2. Homophobic gender-based violence in Jamaica merits a study on its own. Sodomy remained a capital offence in Jamaica until 1864. At least eight British army privates were convicted and hanged for sodomy in Jamaica in four separate cases in the early nineteenth century, and dozens more consenting adult males were convicted and imprisoned for this essentially victimless crime during the course of the nineteenth and twentieth centuries. This legislation has, in effect, represented over three centuries of state gender-based violence and has

underpinned and justified much of the homophobic violence which has carried through into twenty-first century Jamaica and other former British colonies. As one legal academic has argued, "The very existence of sodomy laws creates a criminal class of gay men and lesbians, who are consequently targeted for violence, harassment, and discrimination because of their criminal status" (Christopher R. Leslie, "Creating Criminals: The Injuries Inflicted by Unenforced Sodomy Laws," *Harvard Civil Rights-Civil Liberties Law Review* 35 (1): 103–82). This archaic British colonial 'buggery law' dealing with 'unnatural offences' (articles 76–79 of the Offences against the Person Act of 2009, handed down verbatim from the original 1864 law), which populist politicians are reluctant to repeal and which fundamentalist Christian lobbies defend, remains on the statute books in Jamaica in 2025.

3. Specifically, the following offences: rape and assault with intent; carnal abuse and assault with intent; and indecent assault.
4. David Arnold, "In Defense of Presentism," 4 (the pre-publication online version of the text available at: https://scholar.harvard.edu/files/armitage/files/in_defence_of_presentism.pdf). Arnold argues that presentism's bad name owes much to an absence of consensus among historians as to precisely how it should be defined, and that "the range of possible presentisms includes some that are compatible with writing good history and even conducive to human flourishing".
5. David V. Trotman, "Women and Crime in Late Nineteenth-Century Trinidad," *Caribbean Quarterly* 30 nos. 3&4 (September-December 1984): 64.
6. Moore, Brian L., and Michele A. Johnson, *Neither Led nor Driven: Contesting British Cultural Imperialism in Jamaica, 1865–1920* (Kingston: University of the West Indies Press, 2004), 138.
7. An Act for the Better Prevention and Punishment of Aggravated Assaults upon Women and Children, and for Preventing Delay and Expense in the Administration of Certain Parts of the Criminal Law.' (https://www.legislation.gov.uk/ukpga/Vict/16-17/30/enacted).
8. Jamaica Archives (JA) 1A/7. Bills of indictment were formal charges against the prisoner read out in court when he was arraigned.
9. JA 1A/5/1-29. Only the quarter sessions records for the parishes of St James,1793–1841 (JA 1A/2/8), St Andrew, 1821–1850s (JA 1A/2/2), and St George, 1799–1834 (JA 2/18/7) are sufficiently complete to be useable; surviving slave court records are even rarer.
10. Since grand juries rejected a proportion of these bills (up to 25 per cent in the pre-emancipation years, only 2 per cent between 1834 and 1871, when grand

juries were finally abolished), not all those who were indicted were actually tried before the court. For a fuller treatment of the prosecution system and the mode of assize court trial, see Jonathan Dalby, *Crime and Punishment in Jamaica, 1756–1856* (Kingston: Department of History, University of the West Indies, 2000), 1–2.

11. CO 137/137-591 (1813–1898). Files for all capital cases in which the prisoner was found guilty and faced the death penalty were sent to London for scrutiny.
12. JA 1A/1.
13. *Falmouth Post*, 22 February 1843.
14. In 2006, for example, Amnesty International reported that "one of the main problems in Jamaica, as elsewhere in the world, is that no-one wants to report sexual assault...the sexual assault investigation units in Jamaica estimate that only 25 per cent of sexual violence is reported" (*Sexual Violence Against Women and Girls in Jamaica: 'Just a Little Sex'*, London, 2006, 4. https://www.amnesty.org/en/wp-content/uploads/2021/08/amr380022006en.pdf.
15. Of the more than nine hundred homicides tried in Jamaican courts between 1835 and the end of the nineteenth century, women were the victims in at least 183 cases. Of these, roughly one-third can be positively identified as intimate partner femicides.
16. Garthine Walker, "Everyman or a Monster? The Rapist in Early Modern England, c. 1600–1750," *History Workshop Journal* no. 76 (Autumn 2013): 5–31; also, Shani D'Cruze, "Approaching the History of Rape and Sexual Violence: Notes Towards Research," *Women's History Review* 1, no. 3 (1993): 377–97.
17. Susan Brownmiller, *Against Our Will: Men, Women and Rape* (New York: Simon and Schuster, 1975), 8–9.
18. See, for example, Edward Shorter, "On Writing the History of Rape," *Signs* 3, no. 2 (1977): 471–82. Shorter argued that rape in early modern Europe was largely the consequence of male sexual frustration associated with the late age of first marriage.
19. Brownmiller, *Against Our Will*, 209.
20. Depositions enclosed in CO 137/153, Conran to Bathurst #31, 5 August 1822. The trial was also reported in the *Royal Gazette*, 6 July 1822.
21. JA 1A/7/1/4 (Cornwall Assizes indictment register, 1811–30); *Royal Gazette*, 6 July 1822.
22. Attorney General Burge to Conran, 30 July 1822, enclosed in CO 137/153 # 31.
23. Simpson died on 17 February 1825 (CO 137/160, Manchester to Bathurst #144, 24 February 1825).

24. See Douglas Hall, *In Miserable Slavery: Thomas Thistlewood in Jamaica, 1750–86* (Kingston, University of the West Indies Press, 1999); Trevor Burnard, *Mastery, Tyranny, and Desire: Thomas Thistlewood and His Slaves in the Anglo-Jamaican World* (Chapel Hill: University of North Carolina Press, 2004).
25. Diana Paton, "Sexual Crime and Sexual Violence in Jamaica Before and After Emancipation" (Association of Caribbean Historians Conference, Nassau, The Bahamas, May 2015), 5–11. I am grateful to Diana Paton for her perceptive comments on an earlier version of this chapter, even if I fear her queries have not been satisfactorily answered.
26. Jonathan R. Dalby, "'Such a Mass of Disgusting and Revolting Cases': Moral Panic and the 'Discovery' of Sexual Deviance in Post-Emancipation Jamaica (1835–1855)," *Slavery and Abolition* 36, no. 1 (2015): 136–59.
27. Paton, "Sexual Crime," 12.
28. CO 137/201, Sligo to Glenelg #77, 7 August 1835, enclosing the indictment.
29. CO 137/193, Sligo to Spring Rice # 57, 1 November 1834, enclosing judge's notes and depositions. I am indebted to Jenny Jemmott for the details of this case, which she discusses herself in a rather different context in *Ties that Bind: The Black Family in Post-Slavery Jamaica, 1834–1882* (Kingston, University of the West Indies Press, 2015), 41–42.
30. 6 Vict c 14, "For taking away the punishment of death in certain cases."
31. Clause 14 of 7 Will IV c 41, "For Consolidating and Amending the Laws in this Island Relative to Offences against the Person".
32. JA 1A/7/3/4 (Surrey indictment register, 1828–36); *Kingston Chronicle*, 15 January 1836.
33. Paton, "Sexual Crime," 18.
34. *Regina vs William Griffiths*, a lieutenant in the 37th Regiment of Foot, for the rape of the sixteen-year-old daughter of stipendiary magistrate Edward Baynes; both defendant and plaintiff were white and British (reported at length in the *Falmouth Post*, 6 and 13 March 1839); Griffiths was acquitted. *Regina vs John Gaggin Cox*, a lieutenant in the 2nd West India Regiment, for the rape of Cecelia Ogle, "a young woman of colour", at the Cornwall Assizes in 1843 (JA 1A/7/1/5; *Falmouth Post*, 19 and 26 July, 9 August 1843); Cox was also acquitted; this case was discussed by Diana Paton ("Sexual Crime," 14–15). *Regina vs William Baillie*, "practitioner in physic and surgery", for the rape of his servant in 1851 (JA 1/A/7/1/6; JA 1A/1/1006 [depositions]); this case was ruled *ignoramus* by the grand jury. "Respectability", that archetypal Victorian quality, ensured that "very few men of any status were convicted of rape" in nineteenth-century

England (Carolyn A. Conley, "Rape and Justice in Victorian England," *Victorian Studies* 29, no. 4 (1986): 530).

35. Address of the Chief Justice to the Surrey grand jury (*Falmouth Post*, 17 August 1842).
36. Judge's notes on the trial enclosed in Sligo to Glenelg, 1 November 1835, #178, CO 137/204. See also *Kingston Chronicle*, 23 October 1835; *Royal Gazette*, 24 October 1835; and *Falmouth Post*, 28 October 1835, for reports on the trial.
37. JA 1A/1/7217 (depositions). See also *Royal Gazette*, 17 October; *Kingston Chronicle*, 21 October; and *Falmouth Post*, 28 October 1835, for reports on the trial.
38. JA 1A/7/4/4 (Middlesex indictment register, 1835–36).
39. Judge's notes on the trial enclosed in Sligo to Glenelg, 30 July 1836, CO 137/212; *Falmouth Post*,13 July 1836.
40. JA 1A/1/1005 (depositions); JA 1A/7/2/7 (Middlesex indictment register, 1850–56); *Colonial Standard*, 18 June 1851.
41. A 1837 law distinguished between the abuse of a girl aged under nine, which was a felony, and of a girl aged nine to eleven, which was a misdemeanour (7 Will IV c 41, clause 13), the former being punishable by transportation from fifteen years to life or prison for up to three years (6 Vict c 14 [1].
42. JA 1A/1/2079 (depositions); also, JA 1A/7/1/6 (Cornwall indictment register, 1847–54); *Falmouth Post*, 13 July 1849. Hedge was sentenced to 6 months at hard labour in the penitentiary.
43. JA 1A/1/7301 (depositions).
44. JA 1A/1/7217.
45. "The Jamaica Injury Surveillance system has shown that 86 per cent of sexual assault cases reported in 2002 and 2003 were committed by a relative, a friend, an acquaintance or an intimate partner." Amnesty International, *Sexual Violence Against Women and Girls in Jamaica*, 6.
46. These twentieth-century figures are very rough estimates, since they are based only on circuit court reports published in *The Daily Gleaner*.
47. Marlyn J. Jones, "From the Footnotes and Into the Text," in *Understanding Crime in Jamaica*, ed. Anthony Harriott (Kingston: University of the West Indies Press, 2003), 124.
48. Amnesty International, *Sexual Violence Against Women and Girls in Jamaica*, 3.
49. Trevor Burnard, "Atlantic Slave Systems and Violence," in *A Global History of Early Modern Violence*, eds. Erica Charters, Marie Houllemare, and Peter H. Wilson (Manchester: Manchester University Press, 2020), 202. https://www.

manchesteropenhive.com/display/9781526140616/9781526140616.00020.xml.

50. Jeffrey S. Adler, "'We've Got a Right to Fight; We're Married": Domestic Homicide in Chicago, 1875–1920," *Journal of Interdisciplinary History* xxxiv, no. 1 (Summer 2003): 27–48.
51. Cynthia Grant Bowman and Ben Altman, "Wife Murder in Chicago: 1910–1930," *Journal of Criminal Law and Criminology* 92, nos. 3–4 (Spring-Summer 2002): 769.
52. "UNFPA in Jamaica collaborates with Government and CSOs to address GBV and Family Violence, Scale up HFLE," 19 January 2022. https://caribbean.unfpa.org/en/news/unfpa-jamaica-collaborates-government-and-csos-address-gbv-and-family-violence-scale-hfle-00.
53. Burnard, "Atlantic Slave Systems and Violence," 205.
54. ibid., 207.

REFERENCES

Adler, Jeffrey S. 2003. "'We've Got a Right to Fight; We're Married': Domestic Homicide in Chicago, 1875–1920." *Journal of Interdisciplinary History* 34 (1): 27–48.

Arnold, David. 2020. "In Defense of Presentism." https://scholar.harvard.edu/files/armitage/files/in_defence_of_presentism.pdf.

Bahadur, Gaiutra. 2014. *Coolie Woman: The Odyssey of Indenture.* Chicago: University of Chicago Press.

Brownmiller, Susan. 1975. *Against Our Will: Men, Women and Rape.* New York: Ballantine Books.

Burnard, Trevor. 2004. *Mastery, Tyranny, and Desire: Thomas Thistlewood and His Slaves in the Anglo-Jamaican World.* Chapel Hill: University of North Carolina Press.

———. 2020. "Atlantic slave systems and violence." In *A Global History of Early Modern Violence*, edited by Erica Charters, Marie Houllemare, and Peter H. Wilson, 201–17 Manchester: Manchester University Press. https://www.manchesteropenhive.com/display/9781526140616/9781526140616.00020.xml.

Conley, Carolyn A. 1986. "Rape and Justice in Victorian England." *Victorian Studies* 29 (4): 519–36.

Dalby, Jonathan. 2000. *Crime and Punishment in Jamaica, 1756–1856.* Kingston: Department of History, University of the West Indies.

———. 2015a. "Race or Place? Investigating East Indian Violence in Nineteenth-Century Jamaica." University of the West Indies, Mona, Department of History and Archaeology Staff/Graduate Seminar Paper.

———. 2015b. "'Such a Mass of Disgusting and Revolting Cases': Moral Panic and the 'Discovery' of Sexual Deviance in Post-Emancipation Jamaica (1835–1855)." *Slavery and Abolition* 36 (1): 136–59.

D'Cruze, Shani. 1993. "Approaching the History of Rape and Sexual Violence: Notes Towards Research." *Women's History Review* 1 (3): 377–97.

Grant Bowman, Cynthia, and Ben Altman. 2002. "Wife Murder in Chicago: 1910–1930." *Journal of Criminal Law and Criminology* 92 (3–4): 739–90.

Grzyb, Magdalena, Marceline Naudi, and Chaime Marcuello-Servós. 2018. "Femicide Definitions." In *Femicide Across Europe: Theory, Research and Prevention*, edited by Shalva Weil, Consuelo Corradi, and Marceline Naudi, 17–32. Bristol: Bristol University Press.

Hall, Douglas. 1999. *In Miserable Slavery: Thomas Thistlewood in Jamaica, 1750–86*. Kingston: University of the West Indies Press.

Higman, B.W., ed. 1980. *The Jamaican Censuses of 1844 and 1861*. Kingston: Department of History, University of the West Indies.

Jones, Marlyn J. 2003. "From the Footnotes and Into the Text." In *Understanding Crime in Jamaica*, edited by Anthony Harriott, 120–21. Kingston: University of the West Indies Press.

Mangru, Basdeo. 1987. "The Sex-Ratio Disparity and Its Consequences under the Indenture in British Guiana." In *India in the Caribbean*, edited by Brinsley Samaroo and David Dabydeen. London: Hansib Publications.

Mohapatra, Prabhu P. 1995. "'Restoring the Family': Wife Murders and the Making of a Sexual Contract for Indian Immigrant Labour in the British Caribbean Colonies, 1860–1920." *Studies in History* 11 (2): 227–60.

Moore, Brian L., and Michele A. Johnson. 2004. *Neither Led nor Driven: Contesting British Cultural Imperialism in Jamaica, 1865–1920*. Kingston: University of the West Indies Press.

Paton, Diana. 2015. "Sexual Crime and Sexual Violence in Jamaica before and after Emancipation." Association of Caribbean Historians Conference, Nassau, The Bahamas.

Roberts, G.W. 1957. *The Population of Jamaica*. London: Cambridge University Press.

Shepherd, Verene A. 1995. "Gender, Migration and Settlement: The Indentureship and Post-Indentureship Experience of Indian Females in Jamaica, 1845–1943." In *Engendering History: Caribbean Women in Historical Perspective*, edited by Verene Shepherd et al. Kingston: Ian Randle Publishers.

Shorter, Edward. 1977. "On Writing the History of Rape." *Signs* 3 (2): 471–82.
Trotman, David V. 1984. "Women and Crime in Late Nineteenth-Century Trinidad." *Caribbean Quarterly* 30 (3–4): 60–72.
Walker, Garthine. 2013. "Everyman or a Monster?" *History Workshop Journal* 76: 5–31.

chapter 7

Indo-Trinidadian Narratives of Violence

Histories, Trauma and Representations

Victoria V. Chang

THIS CHAPTER SEEKS TO ELUCIDATE GENDERED INEQUITIES AS well as gendered realities relating to indenture, and further considers specific ideologies and worldviews relevant to women's experience both during and after the indentureship period. The examination and insertion of gender into these historical contexts is not done with difficulty, since gender was very much implicated in these processes and played a powerful role in the choices of planters, the factors for emigrating and the lived experiences on the plantations. This chapter considers fictional narratives surrounding rape and highlights the imposed silence and as such, additional violence, imposed upon victims through the communal pressures to avoid shame, preserve images of female chastity and, additionally, uphold ideals of sacred womanhood as demanded by gendered ideologies. The novels reveal the further unravelling of selfhood and the tragic costs of generational violence caused by the imposed silence and blame surrounding victims of violence. As such, they can be considered cautionary tales with powerful lessons regarding the violent legacies of trauma that women must bear and, in turn, seek to reveal in order to heal.

BACKGROUND TO INDENTURESHIP

The year 1845 ushered in significant and irreversible changes to the social, economic and cultural landscape of Trinidad and Tobago. Slavery had been abolished in 1834 and apprenticeship ended in 1838. The formerly enslaved were now free to leave the sugar cane plantations and pursue alternative forms of employment, and this they did to a large degree, creating a "labour shortage which threatened the imminent collapse of the sugar industry, already in decline and now suffering from a shortage of capital and from foreign colonial cane sugar and European beet sugar competition" (Dookhan 1988, 9). Huge profits had been made from these plantations in the eighteenth century and now, in order to address the labour shortage and avoid ruin, planters looked to the "Eastern Caribbean, Africa, Madeira, the U.S. and China" (Brereton 2013, 21). In reality, and due to the competition mentioned before, the sugar colonies were in no state to take on extra labour, but the mindset of the planters "was so conditioned by slavery, that they assumed the remedy for every difficulty was to take on cheap labour and work them to death" (Tinker 1993, 66). The Indian subcontinent would provide a convenient response to this dilemma, proving a cheap, abundant and ready supply of workers. Thus begins the story of the Indian diaspora in the Caribbean.

Bridget Brereton explains that since India had a huge population, where millions lived in abject poverty, this increased the likelihood of emigration. Most of India was also under British rule, making the movement of peoples much easier: "It would be an emigration of British subjects from one British colony to another, under the supervision throughout of the British Government, and with no need to deal with foreign powers" (Brereton 2013, 21). Added to this, she notes, was the similarity of climate between the West Indies and India, and the fact that inhabitants of the latter were used to agricultural work. Although the costs of importation were high, it "was not prohibitive as it was in the case of China".

Rhoda Reddock further examines the plight facing those in India who were suffering under the oppressive schemes of the British. She explains how, in the eighteenth century, India had supplied cotton goods to Europe on a large scale, but was now losing this function as a manufacturing country, having become a purchaser of British consumables. She notes that the "textile industries were the first to collapse before competition" and that "weavers and other workers were left without employment and had no alternative but to fall back on the land. The land, however, did not welcome them" (Reddock 2008, 41–42). She quotes J.C. Jha, who explains that British land policy in India had "sought to create and perpetuate a class of large landowners to the detriment of the small peasant proprietors", which "destroyed the land tenure rights of small holders while increasing the powers of landlords or *zamindars* over the tenants or *iyots*". To make matters more difficult, recurrent famines in north India during the nineteenth century had detrimental effects on peasants and rural artisans, "whose conditions were worsened by the annexation of Oudh to the British Empire in 1856" (Reddock 2008, 41–42).

Despite the appearance of a well-monitored process, it did not work as it should have in preventing abuses. The office of "Protector of Immigrants", meant to serve the interests of the labourers, failed to meet its intended purpose. According to Tinker (1993, 67), "The protectors were pressured into becoming protectors of the planters, and squeezed into restricting the meagre rights of the indentured people until their status was, as nearly as possible, equal to that of slaves." The local authorities, "anxious to prevent any questioning of the system, consistently tried to convey the impression that all was smooth sailing. If there was any trouble it was because, as everybody knew, the workers were both indolent and grasping" (Haraksingh 1987, 73). Although this monitoring would allow for changes to be made to the system over time, especially due to the humanitarian efforts of those determined not to see a repeat of slavery, many times the administrators sought to justify the wrongdoings perpetuated rather than ameliorate them. So, although in a legal sense the indentured labourer was allowed to bring complaints against their employer before the Protector of Immigrants, whose office was located in Port of Spain, he had to "firstly obtain his employer's permission to leave the estate in order to make the complaint at all". Additionally, "The magistrates who were empowered to investigate charges of maltreatment or violations of contractual obligations generally shared the class interests of the plantocracy. Frequently while making their rounds in the countryside, they would be entertained or even hosted for the night by a manager who had a case to answer in court the following morning" (Haraksingh 1987, 67). Therefore, despite well-intentioned regulations, workers were subjected to punishments such as "floggings and beatings on some estates, arbitrary fines, and court sanctioned imprisonment which had the effect of lengthening the time under indenture, for periods spent in jail were not discounted" (Haraksingh 1987, 67).

Brereton paints a bleak picture of the physical conditions in the barrack ranges where most of the indentured labourers lived. Within each range were several rooms, one of which would serve to accommodate either a married couple and their children, or two to four single adults. Since the room partitions did not extend up to the roof, the inhabitants had "absolutely no privacy". The "kitchen" was on the front steps and no latrines were present until the twentieth century. Add to that a poor water supply and it is no wonder that there was a high incidence of diseases. In 1911, when the indentured population stood at approximately ten thousand persons, "no less than 24,000 cases of illness among Indians were treated". Many of these health issues were simply a result of the barrack-housing scheme with its "appallingly bad sanitation and water supply". While the plantations did have hospitals, they ranged in quality, some being good and others a "total disgrace". The example of the hospital at River Estate in Diego Martin is given, which was a "single-roomed, leaky wooden shack, with seven broken stretchers and two torn mattresses; the overseer, who knew nothing of pharmacy, dispensed the drugs". The conditions at some hospitals were so bad that Indians frequently sought to run away from them, prompting the passing of a law that those who did so would be imprisoned for three months (Brereton 2013, 25).

WOMEN'S PERSPECTIVES IN INDENTURESHIP

While much of the above history is fairly well-known or easily sourced, hidden within this narrative are the unique perspectives of female Indian emigrants. These stories are often subsumed within the wider history of indenture and hence not always presented with the nuances of a gendered perspective.[1] Since records show that the earliest female emigrants were single women, some of whom were accompanied by their children, as opposed to the monolithic portrait of the Indian family moving as a unit from India to the Caribbean, the story of female autonomy is one that cannot be avoided if the facts are examined impartially. Failure to do so strips these women of the agency and courage that were required to leave their homeland and independently seek a better life for themselves and, in some instances, their offspring. Indeed, for authors seeking to write about female experiences of indentureship, these characters cannot be realistically and faithfully created without the presence of authentic voices, but these voices must first be excavated from the official records.

Alison Donnell declares that the "absence of Caribbean women as historical subjects, as feminist theorists and as early writers" is a "serious deficiency", and adds that in order for Caribbean women's writing to be appreciated, they must be "restored, not only as writers but in all their historical dimensions – as slaves, as rebels, as mothers, as workers" (Donnell 2006, 142). She notes a previous disconnect between literary critics and feminist historiographers until very recently, which created a situation that, up until then, seemed to "underwrite the neglect of Caribbean women in the accounts of history that these studies present in their turn to the US or Britain for an historical context". Donnell further asserts that a "sense of the past as a vital resource for an understanding of the present and a productive engagement with the conditions of the future has been pivotal to many interventions in Caribbean feminist historiography" (Donnell 2006, 142–43). Brereton details such interventions as follows:

> . . . there has been a movement from the 'women's history' approach to that of 'gender history' . . . In the earlier phase, in the Caribbean as elsewhere, the focus was on recovering/retrieving information about women in past societies. The women's history approach concentrates on women's special historical experiences and insists on their centrality to the research: from women without a history to women in history, as Jean Stubbs puts it. The gender history approach, of course, tries to analyse significant differences in the historical experiences of men and women in a given society and chronological period; it concentrates on gender roles and ideologies, how they develop and are transformed over time, and how they help to shape historical change. (Brereton 2013, 1)

Feminist historiography, therefore, adds another dimension to the history of indentureship as presented earlier. For instance, aside from the general reasons for emigrating, there were gender-specific push factors as well. Historian Verene Shepherd (2002) notes, regarding the specific plight of the female Indian emigrant, that many were encouraged to leave both as a result of the recognition of "women's productive labour" and also because the sexual needs of the male workers had to be met. She breaks down the variations among the typical group of women who would have migrated, including "a mixture of single, independent women who emigrated voluntarily to be involved in commodity production on Caribbean plantations", as well as "those who had been kidnapped or otherwise forced into emigration by depressed financial circumstances linked to the impact of British economic policies on the textile industry in India". Others had been abandoned by their spouses and were in search of a new beginning in another country, while there were some "who had previously been indentured in Natal, Mauritius, Fiji or the Caribbean, and who had opted for return and reindentureship". Wives and dependents also made up the grouping, accompanying husbands or other relatives; there were even those who were simply seeking newness and adventure.

Shepherd further quotes Charles Doorly, the Protector of Emigrants at the Madras agency, who added as factors of emigration "domestic unhappiness caused by quarrels with their husband's relatives or with the other wives; widowhood and all its attendant miseries" (Shepherd 2002, 15–16). Gender issues, therefore, played a significant role in the choice for women to emigrate, since many of the circumstances from which they fled were specific to their sex. Shepherd also relates that the journey to the respective colonies was in itself different for the women than the men, the former being "preyed upon by males of various ethnicities, many of whom waylaid them in the area of the water closet (toilet)" (p. xxii). Even on the long voyage to the Caribbean, where the false promise was made of equal pay for equal work, they were reminded of their inferior position and treated as a commodity. Shepherd further notes, "This exploitation was related clearly to their gender, race, class and caste, and, of course, to their status as bonded labourers."

A HISTORY OF VIOLENCE

In "The Historical Background to the Culture of Violence in Trinidad and Tobago", Bridget Brereton details incidents of violence among the indentured workers. According to Brereton, Trinidadian Indians quickly gained a reputation for violence, including murder, against others from their ethnic community. In the 1880s, she notes that "they committed sixty percent of all murders in the colony, while constituting only about thirty per cent of the total population; in the 1890s the figure was seventy per cent. The great majority of their victims were fellow Indians, and most were women." It is important to note the gendered nature of the violence that Brereton describes: violence exacted to keep women in check and which continued long after indentureship, fuelled by similar motivations. Brereton (2010, 7) elaborates further: "Between 1872 and 1880, twenty-two Indians were murdered by Indians, and all the victims were women; between 1901 and 1910, sixty-two Indians were murdered by Indians, with twenty of the victims being women. Between 1872 and 1900, there were eighty-seven murders of Indian women, of which sixty-five were wife-murders." Patricia Mohammed (2002, 168–69) indicates that the "stories of female duplicity suggest that the Indian male felt threatened about his capacity to control his wife's libidinous instincts". She adds that the violent behaviour displayed hints to "a male concern with his increased powerlessness in the sphere of sexual relations". This further led many men to self-harm, including suicide and alcohol addiction.

Despite a system destructive to both men and women, the plantocracy was far more concerned with productivity and profits to consider "the Indian character" or conditions in India. These authorities ignored the "serious sex-ratio imbalance among those introduced" and the fact that they had "uprooted them from the stability and security of a communal village life" (Mangru 1987, 227–28). Instead of blaming a deeply flawed and inhumane system of labour, the colonial authorities instead blamed the low moral state of the female indentee for the violence present on the plantation, as mentioned earlier. They even went as far as to officially suggest ways in which a higher, more respectable caste of women could be induced into indenture and so have a moralizing influence (Mangru 1987, 224–25). In spite of their efforts and appeals to the Indian government, the scheme never materialized. However, the planters' reasoning was also shared by Indian men, who saw a natural correlation between the breakdown of community life and women's failure to fulfil their duties as good wives and mothers. The strength of the community, to them, lay in women who "adhere to a more rigorous morality while meekly accepting their spouses' transgressions or criticisms" (Nair 2013, 59). Thus, in the reconfiguration of community life post-indentureship, patriarchal control of women was to play a central role in the move towards a better future for "all". While men would be encouraged to take their place as leaders and providers, their sexual morality was not similarly viewed as being central to the well-being of the community.

In *Jahajin*, the narrative is centred around three women: the unnamed, first-person narrator; Deeda, a friend of the family who is a former indentee; and Sunnariya, the narrator's great-great-grandmother, who came to Trinidad on the same voyage as Deeda. Only the protagonist and Deeda are present in the "real-time" of the novel. However, their stories are all intertwined, showing the importance of other women's stories – especially those of female ancestors – in providing wisdom for creating one's own. The protagonist learns about the cost of a choice and the dangers of delayed happiness, particularly with respect to communal conformity. Portrayals of Indian womanhood in *Jahajin* are complex and they convey the real consequences of refusing to take control of one's destiny and allowing the ship of selfhood to be guided by the storms of life. Sunnariya, when first mentioned in the novel, is insistent on covering her hair and feet, keeping "her sari long, with the bottom reaching the ground, almost dragging as she walked" (Mohan 2008, 25). The novel clarifies what this would mean in the Indian context through Deeda, who remarks, "Only a woman from a good family would cover up like that."

Sunnariya, therefore, initially appears to fit the stereotypical pattern of the exotic, modest and submissive Indian woman. Yet, the image of her hiding under her clothing is not the only one presented; her father explains later that this behaviour is due to her mother's untimely death. As a result, she has taken on the burden of womanhood at a young age and this outward over-insistence on modesty is a consequence of her newfound, strict sense of responsibility of caring for herself and her father. In Trinidad, friendships formed with other indentees seem to replace this loss in her life temporarily, leading her to adapt a more carefree personality; when attacked by an overseer, she resumes "building back the walls around herself, saving whatever was left" (Mohan 2008, 152). The details of the traumatic event are uncertain as Sunnariya seems to be confused in this regard, stating eventually that he was too drunk to do any real harm. Deeda also asserts, "I could not see any blood. It did not look as if the overseer had managed to rape her". However, in an interview with Alison Klein, the author presents another perspective that is hinted at in the text.

Peggy Mohan states,

> I felt that the way it had been put to me, what happened to Sunnariya, it had been completely sanitized . . . my family . . . simply couldn't understand that she could have been abused. She managed to blip it out of her mind, she moved on, covered her head even more. I think what's interesting to me is the way people keep editing the memories, as I said, that we aren't the kind of people to whom such things could happen. Sunnariya is just too classy a lady to have been abused or assaulted. And her honor somehow never vanished. (Klein 2016, 69)

It should be considered, however, that Sunnariya's modified memory, her body more covered than before and her reticent disposition may have been the reason that her honour "never vanished". By her self-silencing – insisting and acting as though the rape never happened – others came to disregard the incident as well. As such, what is assumed to be simply giving in to external codes of conduct may also have been a cunning navigation of the very real societal standards of chastity for women that were transplanted from India. Sunnariya explains to Deeda, "The people in the barracks *still think I am a good girl,* even after all the trouble I caused. I don't want that to change" (Mohan 2008, 173; *my emphasis*). The choice of words is telling – despite her victim status, Sunnariya nevertheless implies that she is the one at fault, having been socialized into adopting sexist attitudes such as victim-blaming. An extension of this is the idea that somehow sexual violence leads to a "loss of honour/integrity" for the female victim and not the male perpetrator. As a result, Sunnariya chooses the path that leaves her with her dignity intact in the community's eyes. What she sacrifices, however, is her own happiness and the consequences are far-reaching. Sunnariya's father avenges her attack, but also declares that "She needs a husband to protect her" (Mohan 2008, 155), a decision that proves to be a turning point in his daughter's life. Her response is to obey unquestioningly, and her faith is placed, not in her ability to choose and insist upon a better life, but in obeying the strictures of tradition and culture – honouring her father, practising modesty and performing the roles of wife, mother and daughter-in-law well. Instead of fighting for happiness, she naively trusts that "if you were a good girl, you would find happiness in the end"; you "wouldn't have to do anything, it would happen by itself" (Mohan 2008, 174).

This distinction between shame and guilt arises frequently in the theorization of shame; the most straightforward way of understanding the distinction is that guilt concerns *something you have done*, while shame concerns "not your actions but *who you are*, that is, your deficiencies and inadequacies as a person as these are revealed to the shaming gaze of the other". Sandra Bartky offers a fuller analysis in her explanation that "[s]hame is called forth by the apprehension of some serious flaw in the self, guilt by the consciousness that one has committed a transgression. The widely held notion that shame is a response to external and guilt to internal sanctions is incorrect: Shame and guilt are alike in that each involves a condemnation of the self by itself for some failure to measure up."

The marriage turns out to be an unhappy one; Sunnariya's husband is an alcoholic and she later dies giving birth to her fifth child. *Jahajin*'s Sunnariya can be considered in light of a type of martyrdom brought about by sexual violence and cemented by the sincere desire to obey her father, and to remain honourable in the eyes of the community. Marriage is the means by which she accomplishes both, but to the detriment of her own happiness.

JOUVERT

As with *Jahajin*, *Jouvert* continues in the trend of historical excavation that yields details of violence, which continues to impact present generations. The protagonist, Annaise, learns her Aunt Laura's dark secret. Laura, sister of Annaise's father, Larry, is like Sunnariya, and serves as a cautionary tale of another victim of sexual violence. Laura is the 'after' portrait of one who lives in the shadow of a secret past and has suffered due to her father's quest to protect his family's reputation from scandal and disrepute. Yet, in response, Laura further inflicts unnecessary suffering upon others.

THE SEEDS OF RESENTMENT

Laura is initially painted as a greedy and self-serving "Toronto relative" eager to reclaim land that she co-owns with Larry. When she and other Canadian relatives learn that Larry has generously allowed a very distant relative of his wife – Black Maharajin – to live on this land free of charge, they become angry, despite having no use for the property while living comfortably in Canada. He reminds them of Trinidad's early kinship patterns brought about by both slavery and indentureship: "But this is how we grow up thinking. So many families in Trinidad have relatives and old people living with them and they not related by blood, but they still related." He further reminds them that Laura lived with Black Maharajin's family for three years and they treated her "like their own child". In response to this, Laura is described as being "angry" that Larry "had ventured into this piece of family history". Her words bring about a definite "shift in mood", ending with defeat on the part of Annaise's father, who agrees to repay Laura for the land in instalments (Mahabir 2006, 82–83). When Larry later dies, his wife sells their beloved family beach house in order to complete the payments (Mahabir 2006, 117). This is recalled bitterly by Annaise, who emphasizes that not only was the land unused and insubstantial, but that unlike her own family, Laura is financially secure and motivated by vindictiveness.

Yet, only later is this "shift in mood" and vindictiveness explained – as further into the novel Annaise's mother reveals a secret from Laura's past. Like Mona, Laura is a victim of her father's misplaced sense of what constitutes shameful behaviour in a 'girl child' and the fear of its impact on patriarchal respectability. When a cousin comes to work as a yard boy, Laura is discovered talking to him "in a flirtatious way, normal for a ten-year-old girl" (Mahabir 2006, 99). This behaviour enrages her father, Grandpa James, who beats Laura violently, putting "welts on her legs" and even tearing her skirt. As with Da-Da, the punishment is not accompanied by an explanation. Purportedly in angry defiance, Laura goes for a walk with this same cousin alone one evening. There, she is raped and later found semi-conscious and bleeding by villagers. Grandpa James does not thank these villagers, but dismisses them, being "shamed . . . in front of the entire village because his daughter had committed incest with her cousin" (Mahabir 2006, 99). As "the most respected man in the village" – he could not bear "the scandal of incest and rape", and thus sends Laura away to live with their maid, Black Maharajin's mother.

BLAMING THE VICTIM

It is interesting to note that Laura is punished for her cousin's crime, of which she is the victim. This punishment of the victim can be explained by notions of female respectability and honour, and the potential of rape to sully the "purity", and by extension, the "value" of a woman. It is, of course, ironic that it is the victim and not the perpetrator who loses that respectability and honour in the eyes of the community. Laura becomes an emblem of shame to her father, who felt "that he had too much to lose" as the principal of a primary school, lay preacher and, ironically, chairman of the recently formed East Indian Association for Justice (Mahabir 2006, 100). However, by physically removing her from the family home, Grandpa James is able to save face for the family and Laura is eventually welcomed back after three years, now as "the protected victim" who "could do no wrong". Yet, Laura is not unaffected; the bitterness of these years as the family pariah stays with her. Furthermore, since her experience has been "slipped into the stone repository of family secrets, never to be addressed or discussed", she is not offered healing through openness and words of restitution. Instead, she is given "everything she wanted", even much of the family land later on. Thus, a sense of entitlement extends deeply into the woman who was greatly wronged by her father. Laura develops the defensive barrier of a manipulator who knows best how to protect herself from the unsavoury truths that threaten to relegate her to outcast status once again.

Mahabir is keen to show creatively how family secrets, seemingly locked away, can still seep into the present. Secrets of violence are revealed and traumas are confronted, suggesting that when shameful realities are hidden, they reappear with a vengeance to later generations, who may be unaware of their implications. Ignorance, then, is not bliss, but a state of vulnerability, as retribution for past hurts are sought even on those who are innocent of former crimes but incriminated by association. Annaise's mother relates how the young Larry would visit the exiled Laura every Saturday, bringing her a picnic basket from their mother containing her favourite food (Mahabir 2006, 100). It was their mother's way of recompensing for her own powerlessness, and maintaining a relationship with Laura. Yet Annaise connects these weekend meetings to Laura's bitterness towards Larry, realizing "that she must have always resented my father . . . since that meeting probably intensified her feelings of abandonment and exile" (p. 115). Larry was a tangible reminder to Laura of the home she was being kept from, particularly since she was not sure of ever being welcomed back. Laura's revenge is exacted when Larry agrees to repay her for the land on behalf of Black Maharajin.

A LEGACY OF CRUELTY

In some ways, Laura possesses several elements of what might have been a sympathetic character – a true victim, subjected to violence through rape as well as at the hands of her father, and to gross unfairness through her banishment from home. However, she is difficult to empathize with, since the victim later becomes the perpetrator. Aside from punishing Larry, Annaise later learns from her cousin Kathy (Laura's daughter) that Kathy's brother, Mikey, once tried to sexually assault her while sleeping. Despite Kathy's screams, Laura never left her room to go to her daughter's aid. The next day, in the same spirit of victim-blaming displayed by Grandpa James, Laura pretends the incident did not happen and refuses to speak to Kathy for two weeks. Annaise notes, "It seemed that she wanted to maintain a certain image of her immediate family" – an image threatened by Kathy's experience of attempted incest (Mahabir 2006, 118). Instead of occupying the compassionate role of fellow victim to her daughter, she chooses the patriarchal role of "protector of the family image" – one into which power is engrained. Thus, by Laura's choosing of "secrecy and silence" (p. 117), what could have been an incident leading to empathy between mother and daughter is instead relegated to a cementing of power and a fortifying of barriers. Laura's childhood trauma has led her "to create the protective stone wall against the outside world the way she could not when she was a child" (p. 118).

As alluded to previously, Laura is a warning to the protagonist as one who has passively inherited her father's conceptions of "acceptable/respectable" behaviour and who in turn inflicts this upon Kathy. By refusing to speak about her traumatic past, this legacy of violence and victim-blaming continues, branching out into the extended family and contaminating all with whom it comes into contact.

THE VICIOUS CYCLE

Yet, Annaise does not exclude herself from judgement or blame, noting that her own indifference to this "inheritance of violence" meant that she "had not escaped it either" (Mahabir 2006, 130). Later on, Annaise places much of the ugliness within her family in the context of Trinidad and Tobago's past of plantation labour, stating, "I saw that left-handed elements of slavery and indentureship that I thought belonged only to working-class villagers were part of every Trinidadian's inheritance." In "The Historical Background to the Culture of Violence in Trinidad and Tobago", Bridget Brereton explains some of this historical violence. She notes:

> . . . physical violence against indentureds on the Trinidad plantations enjoyed customary, if not legal, sanction; and Indian workers, including some who had served out their contracts, were routinely beaten, cuffed and kicked by managers, overseers, *sirdars* (Indian foremen, the successors to the slave drivers) and, at times, African labourers or policemen. In the towns, the few Indians who lived or worked there (usually as porters, gardeners or domestics) during the period of immigration were often the victims of casual brutality from Africans or others, including policemen. (Brereton 2010, 6)

Annaise connects this historical brutality with her extended family's proclivity to inflict psychic violence and betrayal on "those in the family they considered lesser" – people like her and her father. No longer executed by physical force or relegated solely from male to female, it remains deeply damaging. Yet, the protagonist discovers that the harshest consequence of this is the potential damage to selfhood. She is wary of becoming a person who internalizes this inherited trauma and, thus contaminated, proceeds to infect others. This sympathetic understanding of what is, in many ways, a shameful past means that the shame therein is robbed of its haunting, insidious power. Liz Constable refers to psychologist Silvan Tomkins' work, in which he notes that "the experience of shame discloses to us the openness of the self to change within an affective and intersubjective context" and the possibility for "the past to be attenuated through the initiation of new perceptual experiences" (Sedgwick 1995, 175). Tomkins further notes that the internalization of the other's perspective offers "the beginning of leverage in changing [an individual's] ideology and feelings".

ENDING THE CYCLE

This newfound perception arms Annaise with the desire to fight back, and this, metaphorically speaking, requires surgery no less serious than amputation. It is the advice of Black Maharajin which gives her courage to separate herself from Laura's tribe and to choose those whom she calls family, defying "narrow trajectories of blood" (Mahabir 2006, 132). Furthermore, while discovering that she cannot rely on many of her relatives, Annaise finds healing and transformation in the story of her great-grandmother, Indira. Indira is described as having had a brutal life in India, but when she arrived in Trinidad, "refused to have her labour exploited by indentureship" and thus courageously helped to organize an estate strike. She was violently murdered by the men hired to break up the strike, yet her acts of courage, rebellion and rejection of the status quo inspire the protagonist. After her mother relates the story, Annaise hears the sound of *Matikor* drums and joins the celebration. What she experiences is similar to what Renu Juneja describes as an "energizing moment" in relation to the protagonist from George Lamming's *Season of Adventure.* In Lamming's novel, this comes "through a religious ceremony of the people". The *Matikor* celebration, with its cultural significance and spiritual ties to Hinduism, is similar to Lamming's ceremony, associated with "Vodun and surviving African elements in the culture". Juneja notes that the experience Lamming describes has seemingly "little connection to knowledge of history", but "nevertheless provides an access to the past and thus eases the burden of historylessness" (Juneja 1996, 14).

In contrast to Lamming, however, Mahabir positions the release of Annaise's burden as preceded by detailed, previously suppressed information, now related to her by her mother. Annaise learns of maternal ancestors such as Mama, Paramin Nani, Papillon, Nani Sumintra and, of course, Indira. Armed with this historical knowledge, she enters the *Matikor* ceremony – a specifically gendered space – as an insider, aware that she now has the knowledge of courage and strength that form her chosen inheritance. Her participation in the dance represents an embrace of this legacy and there, Annaise describes a sensation of renewal. She now feels "rooted to the whole" of her history, "the courageous and the left-handed parts, the fierce and vulnerable edges" (Mahabir 2006, 144). With this newfound perspective, increased self-knowledge and intentional acceptance, she returns with fresh vitality to her artistic work. For her, the balm of history begins to restore what has been lost by historical amnesia, and to heal the wounds of trauma. Like *Jahajin*'s protagonist, the past is appropriated by present generations to attain new heights of female courage and agency that combat the pervasive power of violent legacies.

NOTE

1. The past twenty years have seen a welcome focus on this perspective through the publication of important works, such as Verene Shepherd's *Maharani's Misery*; Gaiutra Bahadur's *Coolie Woman; Engendering History* (edited by Verene Shepherd, Bridget Brereton, and Barbara Bailey); *Women in the Indian* Diaspora (edited by Amba Pande); and the important work done by Rhoda Reddock, presented in her paper, "Freedom Denied: Indian Women and Indentureship in Trinidad and Tobago, 1845–1917".

REFERENCES

Bahadur, Gaiutra. 2013. *Coolie Woman: The Odyssey of Indenture.* Chicago: University of Chicago Press.

Bartky, Sandra. 1990. *Femininity and Domination: Studies in the Phenomenology of Oppression.* New York: Routledge.

Brereton, Bridget. 1985. "The Experience of Indentureship: 1845–1917." In *Calcutta to Caroni*, edited by John La Guerre, 21–31. St Augustine: University of the West Indies, Extra Mural Studies Unit.

———. 2010. "The Historical Background to the Culture of Violence in Trinidad and Tobago." *Caribbean Review of Gender Studies* no. 4: 1–16. sta.uwi.edu/crgs/february2010/journals/BridgetBrereton.pdf.

———. 2013. "Women and Gender in Caribbean (English-Speaking) Historiography: Sources and Methods." *Caribbean Review of Gender Studies* 7: 1–18. sta.uwi.edu/crgs/december2013/journals/CRGS_7_Brereton.pdf.

Donnell, Alison. 2006. *Twentieth-Century Caribbean Literature: Critical Moments in Anglophone Literary History.* London and New York: Routledge.

Dookhan, Isaac. 1988. *A Post-emancipation History of the West Indies*. San Juan: Longman Caribbean.

Haraksingh, Kusha. 1987. "Control and Resistance among Indian Workers: A Study of Labour on the Sugar Plantations of Trinidad 1875–1917." In *India in the Caribbean*, edited by David Dabydeen and Brinsley Samaroo, 61–79. London: Hansib Publications and University of Warwick, Centre for Caribbean Studies in cooperation with the London Strategic Policy Unit.

Juneja, Renu. 1996. *Caribbean Transactions: West Indian Culture in Literature*. Basingstoke: Macmillan Caribbean.

Klein, Alison. 2016."'Seeing Greater Distances': An Interview with Peggy Mohan on the Voyages of Indo-Caribbean Women." *Indo-Caribbean Feminist Thought – Genealogies, Theories, Enactments*, edited by Gabrielle Hosein and Lisa Outar, 63–72. New York: Palgrave Macmillan.

Lamming, George. 2000. *Season of Adventure*. Ann Arbor: University of Michigan Press.

Mahabir, Joy. 2006. *Jouvert*. Milton Keynes and Bloomington, IN: AuthorHouse.

Mangru, Basdeo. 1987. "The Sex-Ratio Disparity and its Consequences Under the Indenture in British Guiana." *India in the Caribbean*, edited by David Dabydeen and Brinsley Samaroo. London: Hansib Publications.

Mohammed, Patricia. 2002. *Gender Negotiations among Indians in Trinidad, 1917–1947*. New York: Palgrave.

Mohan, Peggy. 2008. *Jahajin*. New Delhi: HarperCollins.

Nair, Supriya M., et al. 2013. "Domestic Altars, Female Avatars: Hindu Wives and Widows in Lakshmi Persaud's *Raise the Lanterns High*." In *Critical Perspectives on Indo-Caribbean Women's Literature (Routledge Research in Postcolonial Literatures)*, edited by Joy Mahabir and Mariam Pirbhai, 48–69. New York: Routledge.

Pande, Amba. 2018. *Women in the Indian Diaspora: Historical Narratives and Contemporary Challenges*. Singapore: Springer.

Reddock, Rhoda. 2008. "Indian Women and Indentureship in Trinidad and Tobago 1845–1917: Freedom Denied." *Caribbean Quarterly* 54 (4): 41–68. doi:10.1080/00086495.2008.11829735.

Sedgwick, Eve K., Adam Frank, and Irving E. Alexander. 1995. *Shame and Its Sisters: A Silvan Tomkins Reader*. Durham, NC: Duke University Press.

Shepherd, Verene. 2002. *Maharani's Misery: Narratives of a Passage from India to the Caribbean*. Kingston: University of the West Indies Press.

Tinker, Hugh. 1993. *A New System of Slavery: The Export of Indian Labour Overseas 1830–1920*. London: Hansib Publications.

SECTION 3

PRIVATE VIOLENCE, PUBLIC SECRETS

chapter 8

At the Intersection of Noise and Silence

Intimate Partner Violence in Jamaica, 1900–1938

DALEA BEAN

GENDERED VIOLENCE WAS CENTRAL TO THE MYRIAD COLONIAL strategies of violence employed by Europeans in the West Indies. Gender-based violence (GBV), and intimate partner violence (IPV) served the plantation economy by exploiting enslaved men and women for the pleasure of the ruling class. The black woman was at the centre of a complex matrix of abuse from white men, white women and black men; all while being the backbone of plantations and reproducers of the status of enslavement (Bush 1990; Mair 2006; Shepherd 2007; 2011; Morrissey 2021).

European-styled laws were also defined by masculinity, shaped by male perspectives and were decidedly male-centred (Biholar 2022, 46). English common law, which heavily influenced Jamaican legal codes, enshrined family violence as part of the fabric of society. It was opined that "husbands had the right to chastise his wife though he emphasized that such correction was confined within reasonable bounds". In 1857, with the establishment of the English Divorce Court, women were allowed to divorce physically violent men, and she could only do so if she could prove adultery as well as cruelty (Aitken 2007, 110). It was not until almost a century later, in 1937, that the British Divorce Act made cruelty a separate ground for divorce.[1]

But twentieth-century Jamaican society was still firmly gripped by hegemonic (white) male dominance, with laws designed to favour men. As Maxwell (2007, 182) indicates, "ideologies of male dominance and control and the subordination of women were a part of the social order, and made it acceptable, in the minds of some, to use violent actions against women, particularly if women challenged male authority, or were perceived to infringe upon male superiority."

Colonial men of every race, creed and class seemed to accept a universal right to private chastisement of women. As African ancestry was pathologized by the colonial state, the prevailing view was that black men were uncivilized, brutish, lazy and vulgar to their women. Afro-Jamaican men did engage in wife-beating and assault. Acculturated by African[2] and European patriarchal values, Afro-Jamaican men often assuaged their powerlessness in society by exalting power over their female lovers. Brown and white men were also charged with abusing and killing their wives in the late nineteenth and early twentieth centuries, while scholars such as Trotman (1986) and Shepherd (1998) have excavated the ways in which Indian men abused Indian women. The historiography is clear: intimate relationships were often seasoned with assault.

This chapter focuses on reports of approximately seventy cases of abuse of women by male intimate partners in heterosexual relationships from the turn of the century to 1938, as reported in *The Daily Gleaner*, and will address the ways in which IPV was reported and views on the nature of abuse from both victims and perpetrators in their own words. Of particular interest is that IPV hid in plain sight; being publicly revealed through *The Daily Gleaner*, Jamaica's leading newspaper and colonial mouthpiece of the day, while being largely ignored by social activists. Violence against women sat at the intersection of noise and silence, and this is proffered as one of the antecedents to contemporary lukewarm public attitudes towards the seriousness of GBV.

SILENCES: THE LEGITIMACY OF VIOLENCE AGAINST WOMEN

Gender relations in colonial Jamaica were characterized by patriarchal values. While Jamaican women refused to fit neatly into any of the gender norm boxes provided by African, Indian and European cultural influences, male dominance and authority were pervasive, and these norms were still patriarchal and maintained that men were heads of households. Women of their race and class were not their social equals (Bryan 1991; Moore and Johnson 2004; Altink 2007).

In order to create a 'civilized' colonial state, gendered hierarchies were supported by Victorian visions of morality. Legal marriage and nuclear families were sites where sex and children were legitimatized (Moore and Johnson 2004, 96). The ideals were evidenced in the Moyne Commission's recommendations that poor women should be trained to accept 'proper families': nuclear, male-headed, and included a non-working housewife and children (French 1988, 40). Afro-Jamaicans did enter into legal marriages, but far more common was what Bryan (1991, 92) dubbed "the pragmatic, functional marriage often referred to as a 'faithful concubinage'." To legitimize these ad hoc unions, mass weddings were organized from 1939 onwards by the Women's Liberal Club and Mary Morris Knibb.

Whether these were consistently attainable is debatable, but they did serve to normalize male superiority over women of his class or race, and render wife-beating as natural. So normalized was the phenomenon that most, if not all, social commentators of the day – from the near white elite to the radical black middle class to the feminist ground-breakers to the Pan Africanists and leaders of new religious sects[3] – were curiously silent on wife beating. An opinion piece by Rev. Theodore Stephens in the *Negro*

Table 8.1: Examples of Essentialist Gendered Binaries

Ideal Men	Ideal Women
Intellectually superior	Intellectually inferior
Authoritative	Subordinate
Independent	Dependent
Leader	Obedient to male authority
Provider	Pious
Noble	Righteous
Powerful	Powerless
Active in Public Sphere	Homemaker/Domesticated

Source: Compiled by Dalea Bean

World in 1924 cited disregard of the sanctity of marriage through adultery as the main cause of divorce. Nowhere in the article "Divorce and its Causes" is there mention of ill-treatment of women by men (*Negro World,* 26 July 1924, 12.) Cases of wife-beating almost never appeared in the journals of the women's movement, despite frequent attention to such cases by the newspapers of the time.

Silences may also be explained by the "rule of thumb", as enshrined in English legal codes, which held "that a man may beat his wife with any weapon not thicker than his thumb" (Amussen 1994, 71). This rule was publicized by *The Daily Gleaner*'s editor extraordinaire, H.G. DeLisser. DeLisser's text wavered between satirical commentary to belittle men who worried about elite women's rising political power while being firmly rooted in his own belief in men's superiority:

> I have just read that the legal code (which must be applicable to Jamaica) enacts that a man may not beat his wife with any weapon not thicker than his thumb." I do not think this is generally known, so I hasten to give the fact the widest possible publicity. I am fain to admit that many men have not waited for this knowledge before proceeding to action. Following a pure and primitive instinct of right and righteousness, they have frequently beaten their female connections and with weapons considerable thicker than their thumbs. I now implore them to abide by the letter of the law . . . One can imagine in the future, a lady legislator, returning to her home after having voted contrary to her husband's views, being corrected with a weapon of prescribed dimensions. Unfortunately, this might lead to a law for abolishing all connubial punishment of women for permitting women to chastise their husbands. It would be a law brought in by a woman. The gentler sex is so unreasonable! (*Daily Gleaner,* 3 April 1924, 8)

His text reflected the socio-cultural cues related to family violence, which accepted the inevitability of men's castigation of women, particularly since the law emanated from England, of which he was a cheerleader. At the same time, DeLisser's piece, one of the few to give even a passing glance at wife beating, was instructive as to what would be necessary to change wife punishment laws and customs – female political leadership. Subtext in the piece alludes to the notion that the presence of female lawmakers would be simply incompatible with customs of wife beating.

The period under study was rife with commentary on topical gender issues of the day, including mass weddings, (il)legitimacy, birth control, child murder, and women's place in politics, to name a few. Several middle-class, educated and professional black men and women used various platforms to reflect on the condition of Afro-Jamaican women. From as early as the 1890s, men such as Robert Love, an Anglican minister and political radical who did much race advocacy in Jamaica, proved to be an advocate for women's rights. He included women at the highest levels of his organizations and activities, and was one of the few to speak on 'private issues' of issues, such as sexual harassment of working-class women in the island (Ford Smith 1988; Francis 2003, 119). As is well known, Marcus Garvey's Universal Negro Improvement Association (UNIA) was keen on uplifting black women across the African diaspora. The organization was grounded in a philosophy of a strong black manhood, with images of men as responsible fathers and strong husbands who respected strong black women (Bair quoted in Reddock 2004, 61).[4]

With a keen focus on the intersections of class, colour and gender discriminations, black women leaders, such as Eulalie Domingo, Una Marson, Amy Bailey, Amy Ashwood Garvey, Amy Jacques Garvey and Mary Morris Knibb, were never shy about voicing opinions on the existing state and future prospects of Jamaican women. Amy Jacques Garvey, whom Reddock (2004, 59) rightly describes as unapologetically feminist, invited black women to solidify their status as thinkers as much as doers by contributing to the *Negro World* (Taylor 2000, 109). The Women's Liberal Club (WLC), founded in 1936 by Amy Bailey, Eulalie Domingo and Mary Morris-Knibb focused on uplifting black women through a range of practical interventions, including offering classes in "Negro History", staging boycotts of stores that refused to employ black women, and critiqued regulations that limited women's economic and political opportunities based on gender (Altink 2006, Lindsay 2020). The political campaign launched by the WLC, which resulted in Mary Morris Knibb being the first Jamaican woman to be elected to public office, was certainly a gendered campaign (Bean 2018). The Save the Children's Fund, cofounded by Bailey and Marson in 1938, focused on providing supplies to destitute children, while the Birth Control League captained, by Bailey and May Farquarson, championed family planning, providing birth control advice, contraceptives and maternal advice. So topical was the issue, that 262 birth control-related pieces were published by *The Daily Gleaner* between June 1938 and March 1939 (Bourbonnais 2012, 40). Black Jamaican feminists also shared views on sexual behaviour and motherhood with working-class women; adopting the concept of the personal being political long before this was formally coined by the global feminist movement in the 1970s.

Black feminists of the early twentieth century changed the trajectory of women's and men's lives. However, lacking from their discourse was a unified position on the beating and abuse of women in intimate relationships. As Altink (2006, n.p.) alludes, black feminists unwittingly upheld gendered status quo by:

> omitting certain forms of gender discrimination, most notably the physical and sexual abuse that black women suffered at the hands of their employers, partners, fathers, and brothers . . . They did not ask . . . for legislation to protect women against domestic abuse or for other legislation that would improve their position within the private sphere. This can largely be explained by the fact that they had been socialized in a society that expected women to pay extreme deference to the men in their family. (Altink 2006, n.p.)

Black feminists' stance was as nuanced as the colonial system in which they existed and in which their race, feminist and class consciousness was formed. However, the voices of those involved in the cycles of abuse and violence would not be silenced for long, and can now be heard through the transcripts of court proceedings of divorce and assault cases.[5]

NOISES: VIOLENCE AGAINST WOMEN BY INTIMATE PARTNERS, 1900–1938

Cases of intimate partner violence, as reported in *The Daily Gleaner,* ranged from assaults of persons in a visiting relationship to those occurring in legal marriage or long-term relationships. Wife-beating in particular, was usually published as part of divorce proceedings and told tales of cruelty, desertion and adultery on the part of one or both parties. These cases were carried almost daily and were reported with a sordid mix of drama, humour and misery. Acts of violence included beating with hands, belts, sticks, iron and other objects, kicking, head butting, chopping with cutlass, starvation and biting. Of all the atrocities, biting seemed to be less accepted by society as it received some attention in 1928, as cases became more prevalent. As H.G. DeLisser emphatically commented, "This craze for biting women must be stopped. Whatever may be the purposes for which women were created, to be bitten is certainly not one of them. We must draw the line at the dangerous dentals" (*Daily Gleaner*, 26 April 1928, 10).

In many cases men not only beat the women, but took in other women, or deserted their wives to live with other women. In the case of Lillian Bartlett vs Frederic Bartlett of the 1st West Indies Regiment, it was alleged that Lillian was beaten (and lost three teeth) when she caught Frederick living with another woman. No less than four similar cases were carried in one day in October 1919, where tales of cruelty, chopping, starvation of wives and desertion for other women were heard (*Daily Gleaner*, 2 October 1919, 6). Witnesses frequently appeared in support of women, while far fewer were present for the accused party. In one such instance, a Mr Simon Moore noted, "From I born I never see a man treat a woman like he treats Melita." On one occasion, he intervened when he saw him throw her on the ground, kneel on her body and beat her savagely with both hands (*Daily Gleaner*, 6 December 1938, 27).

Despite the relative silence on intimate partner violence by social commentators of the day, Altink (2011), supported by Brodber's work on the second generation of freedmen in Jamaica, suggests that working-class Jamaicans had a very strong disapproval of wife beating. As she explains, "One second-generation freeman mentioned that it was impossible for a man who have beaten his wife to walk quite free along the road." Neighbours tended to abhor physical violence in marriage and ostracize men who routinely beat women (Altink 2011, 52).

However, assault of women was a common public spectacle. In 1923, John Malcolm was charged with assaulting his wife, Geraldine, at a shop on Kings Street. Geraldine, who was accompanied by their daughter, found herself being assaulted by John with a piece of leather without explanation. John was fined 20/ or fourteen days' imprisonment. In 1932, it was reported that Obadiah McLean of St Catherine assaulted his female friend, Annetta Heron, at a picnic after she refused to leave when he indicated he was ready to go home. Mclean took a piece of iron and hit the woman several times over her body, fracturing her right arm and landing her in hospital. In 1938, in a case of habitual abuse inflicted on Melia Whyte by her husband, Adanijah, he chased her down the street with a cutlass to a neighbour's house, where they had to protect her from Whyte (*Daily Gleaner*, 6 December 1938, 27).

Men not only landed blows on current girlfriends and wives, but on women from whom they were legally separated. In one such case in 1919, Hubert Munroe assaulted Olga Cruikshank, occasioning bodily harm. Munroe was reported to have beaten Olga at least three times; the final time he threatened to end her life. As Olga ran, he followed her, thumped her down, and burned her and her mother (who ran to her aid) with a burning stick. Munroe's sentence was a £5 fine or sixty days imprisonment (*Daily Gleaner*, 24 September 1919, 3). While suicide by perpetrators was not prevalent in the period under investigation, one notable case, a decorated British West Indies Regiment (BWIR) ex-serviceman in 1926, was linked to wife beating. James Edward of St Mary gave his wife a severe beating and she reported it to a justice of the peace and the police, who sought him for arrest. It was also reported that he was depressed, owing to financial difficulties (*Daily Gleaner*, 13 January 1926, 9).

And what of the women's own actions and voices? From testimonies, it can be gleaned that women tended to accept some chastisement as a normal part of marriage – until it became unbearable. However, many women did not take the beatings lying down and many altercations ended in fights, where women physically defended themselves from the assaults. In a significant case from Westmorland in 1931, Emma Eldemire was charged with manslaughter for killing her husband, Herbert, by striking him with a mortar pestle after an argument, which included his verbal and physical abuse. According to testimony, Herbert said to Emma, "Go home and fix my dinner for you gave me no breakfast this morning and go and look after the kids." When she refused, he took a tamarind switch and hit her. A fight ensued and Emma hit him in the face and head with a mortar stick, inflicting blows from which he later died. For her own brief defence, Emma said, "my husband and I were fighting in the kitchen. He held me in a corner. He bit me, butt me in my face and was beating me. To help myself I took a mortar stick and hit him but I do not know where the blow caught him."

The matter was referred to the Circuit Court on a charge of manslaughter (*Daily Gleaner*, 10 April 1931, 15).

When asked by judges why they chose to remain in bad marriages, women cited ignorance of the law as a rationale, as well as the need to get assistance to support young children (*Daily Gleaner*, 6 December 1938, 27). It should also come as no surprise that many women opted to stay with abusive men for economic reasons. The average working-class woman was in a dire state in the mid-twentieth century, leading to many being economically dependent on male partners. There was dramatic decline in the participation of women in the labour force between 1921 and 1943. During this period, while male employment rates increased, the entire female labour force declined from two hundred and nineteen thousand to one hundred and sixty-three thousand. In agriculture, female employment declined from one hundred and twenty-five thousand in 1921 to forty-five thousand, six hundred in 1943 (French 1988, 39). As Altink (2011, 63) explained: "a woman who stayed with an abusive or unfaithful husband was often better to feed and clothe her children than one who divorced him not just because maintenance support was in most instances less than a husband's weekly allowance, but also because by divorcing her husband a woman had to buy more foodstuffs as she no longer received part of his produce to feed the family."

The 1916 case of Miller vs Miller exemplifies this well. Etheline Miller petitioned for divorce from Edward Alexander Miller in 1916, ten years after his first physical abuse in 1910, after they were married in Panama.[6] He frequently boxed her, flogged her with belts, and courted other women. In 1911, he sent her back to Jamaica and she outlined in detail how little money was sent to her, still holding on to the male as provider trope, even in the face of miscellaneous cruelties (*Daily Gleaner*, 11 May 1916, 13). Some women also wavered between seeking redress and being lenient towards their abusers. In 1915, Thomas Dowie was sentenced to thirty days' imprisonment for 'disorderly conduct', after beating his pregnant wife to a bloody state in their Kingston temperance bar (*Daily Gleaner*, 13 October 1915, 6). "Wife and Children would be Disgraced by Man's Imprisonment" was the title of the follow-up article, where the abused wife spoke on his behalf to say the influence of liquor was the reason for the behaviour. The mother of his five children was "not willing that the whole family should suffer the disgrace of the husband's imprisonment". He was subsequently fined 40/ and sent off with a stern warning. In a St Mary case, in which a Melita Whyte was beaten "like a donkey in a pasture" by husband, Adanijah White, she was said to have repeatedly "interceded on his behalf" to stop him from going to prison (*Daily Gleaner,* 6 December 1938, 27). Eventually she was granted judicial separation from her husband and custody of the youngest child from the union.

Divorce proceedings were brought by both men and women. However, the motive for divorce was decidedly gendered, with men tending to bring cases involving adultery or misconduct of wives, while women brought cases of cruelty and neglect, signifying that more women were throwing off the shackles of ideals of obedience and total self-sacrifice for lives free of violence. A case of male petitioning for divorce in which spousal abuse was included was heard in the Supreme Court in 1923. Herbert Percival Headlam, a cabinet-maker from Kingston, petitioned to divorce his wife, Evelyn, on the ground of adultery. Norman Washington Manley represented the petitioner, while H.M. Radcliffe appeared for the respondent and raised two defences on Evelyn's behalf – denial of adultery and violent assault on the part of Herbert. The case was eventually dismissed for lack of sufficient evidence of adultery on the part of Evelyn, and not much fuss was made about the reports of his jealousy, violent assault and kicks inflicted on his wife. In fact, at the conclusion of the case, Justice Anthony DeFreitas addressed both parties and engaged in a counselling session towards reconciliation (*Daily Gleaner,* 10 December 1923, 15).

In another case of a male petitioning in 1931, E.E. Bucknell took his estranged wife to court on the grounds of adultery. Isolene A. Bucknell (nee Thomas) painted a picture of habitual abuse and neglect by her husband, which drove her into the home of another man, Harold Ricketts. She carried him to court in 1927 and 1928 on assault charges and two additional charges of non-support. She was said to have left the home three times since marriage in 1922, and accused her husband of being with another woman, one Hilda Clarke. The union, which bore no children, was rocky at best and E.E. Bucknell admitted to striking his wife, but only after being provoked by her use of "filthy language" or causing a public scene in their yard (*Daily Gleaner,* 9 April 1931, 9).

Indeed, provocation had an important part to play in decision-making around wife beating cases and in other cases where men assaulted women. In 1907, Resident Magistrate A.V. Kingdon's questions to an abused wife, Mabel Francis, suggested his view that women could provoke men to wrath:

> RM: "You do not want a beating?"
>
> Wife: No, sir.
>
> RM: Sometimes your tongue goes a little bit too much and he chastises you?
>
> Wife: No, sir . . . . (*Daily Gleaner*, 27 July 1907, 9)

In 1910, *The Daily Gleaner* carried details about a landmark case in New York in which Justice Crane of the Supreme Court of the state, refused a separation agreement brought by one Edith Robinson, the wife of a prominent Brooklyn lawyer. According to the text of the ruling, "A wife who teases her husband into a temper cannot justify an application for separation on the ground that he in the temper she herself provoked used violent language and struck her, since such an outburst is not necessarily cruel or inhuman (*Daily Gleaner*, 1 December 1910, 14.). H.A.L. Simpson, defence lawyer for a Cuban national, Angel Seriano, who was charged with kicking and head-butting Mrs Edith Brown, used a similar line of reasoning. Simpson submitted to the court that his client was "sorely provoked by the complainant who used provoking and insulting language to him" (*Daily Gleaner*, 11 April 1916, 8). Provocation was also cited by Vernal Glenn, charged with manslaughter of his common-law wife, Violet May Evans, in 1937 in the home circuit court. "I was provoked by her, Your Honour, through the words she used and what she did me," Glenn said as judgment of seven years' penal servitude was handed down to him by Justice Seton. In testimony given by various witnesses, the picture is painted of Glenn as a violent man, who threw Violet May down on the loose stones in the yard and kicked her repeatedly. He grabbed her by the throat, beat her in the face, and hit her in the head with a kerosene box. She eventually died at hospital. This incident stemmed from the accusation of infidelity, which the deceased denied, and the fact that she used dirty clothes to hit him. However, in cross-examination, Glenn wavered between denying the incident (saying he would not do such a thing to any woman, least of all a woman he loved) and only admitting to "thumping", without any intention of hurting her. The jury of his male peers, apparently swayed by his claim of lack of intent, found him guilty of manslaughter (*Daily Gleaner*, 15 January 1937, 21).

Men had opportunities to cross-examine women in divorce cases, giving an inkling into the views of men about women's respectability and worth. Catherine Mason petitioned for dissolution of her marriage to Thomas Mason on the grounds of cruelty and adultery in 1906. At the time of the petition, Thomas was in prison for wounding his wife. Married in 1894, the couple lived in Kingston and Catherine separated from him on many occasions, due to ill-treatment. He was alleged to have beaten her regularly and, in 1904, he stabbed her with a knife at the courthouse, for which he was charged, and serving a five-year sentence (*Daily Gleaner*, 27 April 1906, 1). Mason in cross-examining his wife accused her of attempting to poison him, sleeping with another man:

> Mason: "Haven't I given you ever penny I earned?"
>
> Catherine: "No, you never did any work."
>
> Mason: "How you lived then, my good woman?"
>
> Catherine: "I lived by my own hands. I did dressmaking."
>
> "Dress-making?" asked Mason scornfully. "The old rusty machine you brought from Westmoreland with you!"

After some testimony, the decree nisi was granted. On leaving the courthouse, Mason ran back to Catherine and threw her violently against the wall, assaulting her one final time, before he was taken away by police (*Daily Gleaner*, 28 April 1906, 12).

These cases were carried with much frequency. However, petitioners of the working class were surely outdone in terms of high drama and intense media coverage when compared to cases of prominent Jamaicans. *The Daily Gleaner* devoted all of five days of ongoing and lengthy coverage, between 5 June and 27 June 1935, to the case of Christiana hoteliers Steers v Steers, in which the petitioner, David Phillip Steers, filed for divorce from Ida Louise Steers on the grounds of adultery with medical doctor Horace Bramwell, co-respondent. In response, Ida Steers cross-petitioned for judicial separation because of cruelty by her husband. Justice Seton presided, with heavy hitters N.W. Manley representing David, and S.W.P. Foster Sutton for Ida and Hon J.A.G. Smith for Dr Bramwell. The case had the courtroom packed with the public, "many people being unable to secure places" (*Daily Gleaner*, 18 June 1935, 8), eager to experience the soap opera-like events. The Jamaican co-owners of the Savoy Hotel in Christiana were married in the United States, and returned to Jamaica to run the hotel in 1927. David Steers alleged that when Dr Bramwell started visiting the hotel in 1933, his wife was no longer only his. Ida Louise denied the charges and instead focused on the abuse she suffered from her husband. She recounted that on one occasion in 1934 "he assaulted her, pushed her backwards and seized her by the throat and threatened to crack every bone in her body" (*Daily Gleaner*, 5 June 1935, 5). David countered that charge by saying that any abuse she suffered was at her own hand; when he confronted her about the infidelity, she "jumped at him and tore his shirt . . . and took hold of a stick to hit him" (*Daily Gleaner*, 5 June 1935, 7). Norman Washington Manley painted Mrs Steers as the aggressor in the incidents, a point which the judge and jurors seemed to find favourable, as they did not award in her favour with regard to cruelty since she was the alleged aggressor in the physical altercations between the two. The case ended in favour of David Steers and a divorce was granted.

Class was, therefore, not a significant determining factor variable in incidents of spousal abuse, as also evidenced by the case of Captain Harry Donald, prominent Motor Vehicle Inspector of the Transport Board, who was charged with assaulting his wife, Kathleen Donald, and Annie Douglas, MBE, her aunt, a decorated Boer War Red Cross Nurse and the leading recruiter of Jamaican men for the British West Indies Regiment in World War I. Presided over by J. Leslie Cundall, the case against the captain was one of drunkenness and brutality. He was "a source of anxiety and menace", who frequently verbally and physically abused her in their home, and manhandled Annie Douglas when she intervened to help her niece (*Daily Gleaner*, 18 March 1938, 7.) Initially sentenced to serve a six-week prison sentence, his "good character . . . of quiet and kindhearted disposition . . . except when he had been under the influence of drink" absolved him of the sentence in the appeal court – though not of the conviction. His wife was granted judicial separation and the court "ordered the appellant to be bound over in his own recognizance to be of good behaviour and to come up for judgement if and when called upon" (*Daily Gleaner*, 12 April 1938, 12). The supreme court's claim of 'good character' was certainly related to his class and Donald's standing in government, but it did not absolve him from judgement or contempt on the part of the judge.

From the cases assessed, judges seemed sympathetic to female parties on most occasions, granting divorce nisi[7] without much effort in cases of physical assault, though some judges were known for encouraging couples to amicably work through differences. In 1907, *The Daily Gleaner* carried an article titled "Restore Peace", in which Joseph Francis and his wife, Mabel, were brought before Resident Magistrate A.V. Kingdon after Joseph unlawfully wounded Mabel in a domestic dispute. Joseph expressed regret at his actions and Mabel promised to try to make a life with him once more after RM Kingdon suggested they "see their minister and he might help them in the matter" (*Daily Gleaner*, 27 July 1907, 9). Judges tended to advise whom they considered to be 'respectable couples' (those legally married and with children) to "make it up" and keep the family unit together ("Justice Beard Tries to Reconcile Parties", *Daily Gleaner*, 11 May 1916, 13; and RM Court Judge T.D.H Bruce, *Daily Gleaner*, 17 October 1923, 14). It was not uncommon to see families being encouraged to work on mending bonds as heterosexual unions were important in the society. Una Marson, herself unmarried throughout her life, reminded young women through *The Cosmopolitan* magazine[37] that they were "created to be a companion" and should choose a husband based on virtues such as his loyalty (Altink 2011, 44). Vera, a contributor to Jacques Garvey's column "Our Women and What They Think", also painted a picture of the ideal wife as one who 'winds' herself into the rugged recesses of a husband's nature, and duly supports his dropping head and binding up his broken heart (*Negro World*, 5 April 1924, 10).

In questioning witnesses, judges also asked questions that probed for excuses for the beatings given to women. In the 1913 divorce case of Beene vs Beene, Justice Beard heard testimony from petitioner Dororthy Beene of frequent beatings from her husband:

> His Honour: How did he beat you?
>
> Witness: He put me on the ground, sir, and beat me in my face with his fist.
>
> His Honour: Why did he beat you – was he jealous?
>
> Witness: No, sir, he had no cause to be jealous. My husband flogged me three times after that and turned me away. He subsequently returned and asked me to come back and live with him.

His Honour: Did you go back?

Witness: Yes.

His Honour: And when you went back, did he beat you again?

Witness: Yes, sir, several times.

His Honour: Then why did he beat you – was he a drunken man?

Witness: No, sir – but he had another woman. (*Daily Gleaner,* 8 May 1913, 6)

At the same time, judges were not shy in voicing their views on men whom they considered to be less than respectable. As H.G. DeLisser reminded "savage beasts" who not only beat, but took to frequently biting women that "the judges and magistrates here are not prepared to tolerate that . . . or allow the heavy-handed brother to do good to women by administering sundry blows and bites" (*Daily Gleaner,* 26 April 1928, 10). In the case of Thomas Mason, Justice Lumb verbally agreed with his soon-to-be ex-wife, Catherine, that the money he earned as an obeah man was "very disrespectful" (*Daily Gleaner,* 28 April 1906, 12). In 1909, C.H.Y. Slader, acting stipendiary magistrate, admonished Alexander Parris that "your wife is not a slave" when Parris complained that he wanted Melvina to "be subject to my order" after she moved to Panama (*Daily Gleaner,* 27 Nov 1909, 18). The RM for Clarendon, Justice Kenneth Brandon, lost his temper at Walter Reid, accused of beating and biting a woman, saying he would have liked to "sentence Mr Reid to a good lashing". Instead, he initially sentenced Mr Reid to four months imprisonment without the option of a fine, but eventually "tempered justice with mercy" and allowed him to pay a fine of £12 and costs for the trial (*Daily Gleaner,* 26 April 1928, 10). If men were labelled as general troublemakers, this influenced the judgment on assault charges. In a case in 1915, where Luther Lewis violently assaulted his female friend, the presiding judge said that, for two years, he had tried to reform the accused and keep him out of prison, but he had failed. Lewis was, therefore, sentenced to three months imprisonment for the assault charge and, ostensibly, his general disregard for law and order (*Daily Gleaner,* 2 November 1915, 11).

CONCLUSION

Records from the era 1900–1938 are replete with cases of wife beating and intimate partner violence. On the surface, catalysts of violence included depression, drunkenness, jealousy, threats to self-esteem, and provocation by women. Deeper readings into the cases reveal that gender codes of conduct crafted the material and emotional realities of colonial people as much as race (Bean 2022). Patriarchy allowed the head of the household to discipline all under his charge. Abuse of women was made common by colonialities of violence and maintenance of patriarchal norms, which gave men ultimate rights to women's bodies. These bodies became sites of rage, frustration and carnage under the veneer of love, marriage and civilized family unions.

As the cases indicate, legal and socio-economic power remained with masculinity in this era and women were outnumbered in courtrooms as they sought to secure some modicum of human rights. Even men brought to court for crimes had the power to cross-examine their spouses, giving an insight into the views of men about women's respectability and worth. Deeply embedded in these questions were impressions of women's inferiority and inability to function without male protection and provision. Quips made by some judges reminded women of their place as second-class citizens and as known provocateurs of men's violent nature. These judges reflected the socio-cultural cues related to family violence, which accepted the inevitability of men's castigation of women, as well as the culpability of women in their own abuse. In fact, cruelty was not considered merely beating, but excessive beating and other heinous acts. However, many should also be credited with evolving away from the assumption that men should have rights to beat their wives as they saw fit. Regardless of the race or class of abuser, spousal beating became less legally acceptable in relationships, as evidenced by fines and prison sentences being imposed by the 1930s in the majority of cases explored.

In the final analysis, it remains a difficult task to reconcile the noise of such reports with the silence from the social commentators of the day. Very rarely was wife beating mentioned by black feminists or social commentators, who otherwise spoke truth to power. Incidents took place in the full view of neighbours, community members and passers-by. It often involved family members of the women, who were themselves harmed in the process of parting fights. Yet, Jamaican commentators mirrored a global silence in activism to wife beating, and violence against women resided in a curious, complicated space of visible invisibility. While black feminists were firmly rooted in empowerment discourses and interventions for black womanhood, they avoided the issue of interpersonal violence, or what Lindsay (2020, 129) terms as "a contradictory reading of racial, gendered and class-based inequalities." This incongruity unfortunately normalized violence through collective social agreement.

Perhaps the most poignant takeaway is that where the social leaders refused to act, women survivors of this violence took matters into their own hands to free themselves from the worst types of abuse. For these women, the personal was long-time political. Some fought back with their words, fists, bodies or objects. Others used legal recourse to make perpetrators accountable for their actions. While spousal abuse was accepted as part of the norm of unions, the testimonies of many survivors suggest that, eventually, they opted to take action to defend themselves from individual men and from a socio-political machinery that ignored the seriousness of the violence they faced. Their voices rang noisily: Enough was more than enough! And many successfully challenged established codes of respectability, which lauded marriage over singledom for adult women, and opted to provide for themselves rather than remaining in violent situations till death did them part.

NOTES

1. In Jamaica, legal protection of women included the Married Women's Property Act, passed in 1870, which granted wives some financial autonomy. Divorce was legally available after 1879, and by 1919, elite women received the right to vote. In 1938, the Legislative Council debated a divorce bill similar to the British Act of 1937 and black members also proposed further amendments to make it easier for women to seek divorce on the basis of cruelty only (Altink 2011, 52).
2. Altink (2011, 52) suggests that many societies in West Africa did allow wife beating, but generally regarded it as undignified.
3. However, as Dunkley's work indicates, in the Rastafari community of Pinnacle,

wife beating was not allowed and this provided a safe haven for women seeking to flee from domestic brutality. D.A. Dunkley, *Women and Resistance in the Early Rastafari Movement* (Baton Rouge: Louisiana State University Press, 2021), 20.

4. Veteran black journalist, and later editor of the *Negro World,* T. Thomas Fortune wrote, "In a large way, the question is the pivot upon which revolves the destiny of the race, as respect and protection of womanhood and childhood constitute albeit wholly the elements which make for a strong mental and physical race or a weak and decadent race (*Negro World,* 16 August 1924, 16; and 23 August 1924, 16).
5. Though a rich source of data, as Altink (2007) cautions, the paper's reporting was not without problems. Journalists did not always hear full testimony because of their placements in court rooms, sometimes leading to partial reporting of testimony.
6. It was not uncommon to see cases of Jamaican abuse stories from Panama; in one from 1927, James Davis was convicted of assault and battery of his wife, who lived with him in Cristobal. As the report went, "humour was deeply mixed with pathos" as the husband blamed a household cat for the assault; he admitted being drunk, enraged by the cat and hit his wife with the board intended for the animal (*Daily Gleaner,* 4 October 1927, 11).
7. It is a provisional decree of divorce that is given by the court when the legal and procedural requirements for divorce are met by a person. Following this, the marriage still continues and further action must be taken to become fully divorced. The decree nisi is the first goal in the divorce procedure and will likely lead to success for those who began the divorce process. Once a decree nisi has been successfully achieved, the person seeking the divorce must then wait at least six weeks and one day before making their application for the decree absolute – the deciding decree of the divorce which will dissolve the marriage. Once this has been granted you are divorced (jmw.co.uk).
8. *The Cosmopolitan* was the first publication in Jamaica with a female head catering for a female readership. Founded by Una Marson in 1928, it was the official organ of the Jamaica Stenographers Association.

REFERENCES

Adler, Karen S. 1992. "'Always Leading Our Men in Service and Sacrifice': Amy Jacques Garvey, Feminist Black Nationalist." *Gender and Society* 6 (3): 346–75.

Altink, Henrice. 2011. *Destined for a Life of Service: Defining African-Jamaican Womanhood, 1865–1938*. Manchester: Manchester University Press.

———. 2007. "'I Did Not Want to Face the Shame of Exposure': Gender Ideologies and Child Murder in Post-Emancipation Jamaica." *Journal of Social History* 41 (2): 355–87.

———. 2006. "'The misfortune of being black and female': Black feminist thought in interwar Jamaica." *Thirdspace* 5 (2). https://journals.lib.sfu.ca/index.php/thirdspace/article/view/altink/3177.

Amussen, Susan. 1994. "'Being stirred to much unquietness': Violence and Domestic Violence in Early Modern England." *Journal of Women's History* 6 (2): 70–89.

Bair, Barbara. 1992. "True Women, Real Men: Gender Ideology and Social Roles in the Garvey Movement." In *Gendered Domains: Rethinking Public and Private in Women's History*, edited by Dorothy O. Helly and Susan M. Reverby. Ithaca: Cornell University Press.

Bean, Dalea. 2022. "Looking Back to Move Forward: A Historical Reflection of Gender Based Violence and Intimate Partner Violence in Jamaica During Slavery." In *Critical Caribbean Perspectives on Preventing Gender Based Violence*, edited by Ramona Biholar and Dacia L. Leslie, 10–26. London: Routledge.

Beckles, Hilary. 2000. "Property Rights in Pleasure: The Marketing of Enslaved Women's Sexuality." In *Caribbean Slavery in the Atlantic World*, edited by Hilary Beckles and Verene Shepherd, 692–701. Kingston: Ian Randle Publishers.

Biholar, Ramona. 2022. "Discriminatory Laws: The Normalisation of Sexual Violence in Anglophone Caribbean Sexual Violence Laws." In *Critical Caribbean Perspectives on Preventing Gender Based Violence*, edited by Ramona Biholar and Dacia L. Leslie, 44–64. London: Routledge.

Bourbonnais, Nicole. 2012. "Class, Colour and Contraception: The Politics of Birth Control in Jamaica, 1938–1967." *Social and Economic Studies* 61 (3): 7–37.

Bryan, Patrick. 1991. *The Jamaican People, 1880–1902*. London: Macmillan Caribbean.

Bush, Barbara. 1990. *Slave Women in Caribbean Society, 1650–1838*. Bloomington, IN: Indiana University Press.

Dunkley, D.A. 2021. *Women and Resistance in the Early Rastafari Movement*. Baton Rouge: Louisiana State University Press.

Ford-Smith, Honor. 1988. "Women and the Garvey Movement in Jamaica." In *Garvey:*

His Work and Impact, edited by R. Lewis and P. Bryan. Kingston: Institute of Social and Economic Research, University of the West Indies.

———. 1988. "Una Marson: Black Nationalist and Feminist Writer." *Caribbean Quarterly* 34 (3/4): 22–37.

Francis, Wigmoore. 2003. "Nineteenth and Early Twentieth Century Perspectives on Women in the Discourses of Radical Black Caribbean Men." *Small Axe* 13: 116–39.

French, Joan. 1988. "Colonial Policy Towards Women after the 1938 Uprising: The Case of Jamaica." *Caribbean Quarterly* 34 (3–4): 38–61.

Gregg, Veronica. 2007. "'How with this rage shall beauty hold a plea': The Writings of Miss Amy Beckford Bailey as Moral Education in the Era of Jamaican Nation Building." *Small Axe* 23: 16–33.

Lindsay, Keisha. 2020. "Amy Bailey, Black Ladyhood and 1950s Jamaica." *Small Axe* 24 (3): 128–42.

Mathurin Mair, Lucille. 2006. *Historical Study of Women in Jamaica, 1655–1844*. Edited by Hilary Beckles and Verene Shepherd. Kingston: University of the West Indies Press.

Maxwell, Shakira. 2017. "Defiling the Feminine? Women who kill: Female Criminality in Jamaica and the Turn of the Twentieth Century." *Journal of Eastern Caribbean Studies* 42 (3): 122–51.

Moore, Brian, and Michele Johnson. 2004. *Neither Led nor Driven: Contesting British Cultural Imperialism in Jamaica, 1865–1920*. Kingston: University of the West Indies Press.

Morrissey, Marietta. 2021. "Sex, Punishment and Protest." In *Slave Women in the New World: Gender Stratification in The Caribbean*. Lawrence, KS: University of Kansas.

Reddock, Rhoda. 2004. "The first Mrs Garvey and Others: Pan-Africanism and Feminism in the early Twentieth-Century British Colonial Caribbean. *Feminist Africa: Pan Africanism and Feminism* 19: 58–77.

———. 2022. "CEDAW and Violence Against Women: Reflections After 40 Years." *Violence Against Women* 28 (8): 1723–27.

Robinson, Tracy. 2020. "Mass Weddings in Jamaica and the Production of Academic Folk Knowledge." *Small Axe* 63: 65–80.

Shepherd, Verene, ed. 2011. *Engendering Caribbean History: Cross-Cultural Perspectives*. Kingston: Ian Randle Publishers.

———. 2007. "Sex in the Tropics: Women, Gender and Sexuality in the Discourses of Asian Labour Migration to the British Colonised Caribbean." In *I want to*

Disturb My Neighbour: Lectures on Slavery, Emancipation and Postcolonial Jamaica, 30–43. Kingston: Ian Randle Publishers.

———. 1998. "Indian Migrant Women and Plantation Labour in Nineteenth- and Twentieth-Century Jamaica: Gender Perspectives." In *Women Plantation Workers: International Experiences,* edited by Shobhita Jain and Rhoda Reddock. Oxford and New York: Berg Publishers.

———. 1994. *Transient to Settlers: The Experience of Indians in Jamaica, 1845–1950.* Leeds: Peepal Tree Press.

Taylor, Ula Y. 2000. "'Negro Women are Great Thinkers as well as Doers': Amy Jacques Garvey and Community Feminism in the United States, 1924–1927." *Journal of Women's History* 12 (2): 104–26.

———. 2002. *The Veiled Garvey: The Life and Times of Amy Jacques Garvey.* Chapel Hill and London: University of North Carolina Press.

Trotman, David. 1986. *Crime in Trinidad: Conflict and Control in a Plantation Society 1838–1900.* Knoxville: University of Tennessee Press.

c h a p t e r 9

Mock Trials and Effigy Hangings as a Community Response to Sexual Violence Against Girls in Vincentian Communities

HALIMAH A.F. DESHONG

ON 20 FEBRUARY 1998, TWO WEEKLY NEWSPAPERS PUBLISHED in St Vincent and the Grenadines, *The Vincentian* and *Searchlight*, carried stories on egregious acts of sexual violence against girls by family members. *The Vincentian* headline read "Stop Incest Now" and the following details were provided:

> Incest and child abuse continue with unabated frequency in St. Vincent and the Grenadines despite ongoing public education by the Social Welfare Department and various non-governmental Organizations. Only two months ago an eighteen-month-old infant was hospitalized after being allegedly abused by her sixteen-year-old uncle in whose care she was left [name of village removed]. What is more shameful is that the child's mother is fourteen years old and is alleged to have borne the child for her father. Unconfirmed reports claim that this utterly despicable situation began in 1992 when the child's mother, then nine years old, was seen by a brother being sexually abused by their father. That incident, almost six years ago, resulted in a boisterous dispute in the home between the girl's mother and father. (cited in Adams 1999, 1)

The *Searchlight* article, which was headlined "It's Mock Hanging Time Again", stated:

> The practice of carrying out mock hangings on persons who have committed devious crimes, such as incest, is slowly cementing its way into the cultural psyche of the people of [name of Grenadine island removed]. The last hanging was held in 1994 and the next one is very certain to be staged this year. The reason for the hanging was the same then as it would be now and, incidentally, involves the same man. The nature of the crime is incest. It is strongly rumoured that a man who is originally from St Vincent [the mainland], was caught in the act with his 14-year-old daughter, a student of one of the three schools on the [Grenadine] island. It is also reported that the matter has been referred to the police. This followed a visit to the doctor by the girl and her mother. It is believed that the father has committed similar offences in the past. (cited in Adams 1999, 2)

Both articles chronicle public alarm at the rising reports of sexual violence against girls throughout the decade of the 1990s; reports which continued with an unrelenting frequency well into the twenty-first century. Increased reports of child sexual abuse to law enforcement followed a key dimension of 1980s and 1990s Caribbean feminist organizing focused on ending violence against women and girls. In fact, feminist activism in the region provided both the catalyst and expertise required for the emergence of CARICOM Model Legislation on Issues Affecting Women, out of which laws to address gendered violence emerged within the region (Reddock 1998; Pargass and Clarke 2002; DeShong 2022).

In the first excerpt, sexual violence against girls is cited as a form of gendered, intergenerational trauma, which marks the flesh of children, babies, girls and women, with long-term deleterious effects. The ongoing rape of a nine-year-old girl, which resulted in her becoming pregnant a few years later, was met with outrage by her mother, the community and her brother, who disclosed what he witnessed. It is important to appreciate the multiple and often contradictory responses to sexual violence against children by family members. Moreover, contemporary manifestations of sexual violence against children and the responses to such harms must be understood in the context of a history of racialized and gendered violence against women and girls (Spillars 1987; Hartman 1997; Mair 2006; Brereton 2010; Shepherd 2017; Bean 2022).

The second excerpt functions as my thematic point of departure for this chapter as it provides insights into a specific community response to sexual violence against girls that exists outside of formal state accountability mechanisms. Mock hangings, a practice for which there exists little official documentation, appears to have occurred between the decades of the 1940s and 1990s across various Vincentian communities (Abrahams and Bauman 1971; Rubenstein 1974; Abrahams 1982; Adams 1999). They consisted of two distinct yet interrelated activities – a stylized jury trial, which replicated an official high court hearing in terms of form and procedures, and a ritual hanging of full-scale, life-like images constructed by carpenters to resemble the actual guilty parties. The events occurred after it was established, to the satisfaction of the majority of villagers, that an incestuous act had occurred (Rubenstein 1974, 772).Using the retrospective accounts of seven Vincentians,[1] who witnessed these mock trials and their related effigy hangings in rural communities, and with reference to two major published works on the practice – one from the scholarly literature and a second from the popular literature (Rubenstein 1974 and Adams 1999 respectively) – I assess their meanings as not only a feature of the Vincentian cultural imaginary, but also as a means through which communities addressed child sexual abuse. I examine the tensions to have emerged from the interviews conducted and within the works of Hymie Rubenstein (1974) and Edgar Adams (1999), in which these events were framed as both a reflection of community outrage against sexual violence and as a form of community spectacle designed for the amusement of Vincentians from all across the country. I further suggest that the paradox of framing the practice as designed to censure, to entertain or to do both in these published works, and at some points in the interviews, masks the deeper and complex ways in which Caribbean communities and individuals have had to confront the trauma of violence.

Dr Edgar Adams was an Afro-descended optometrist by training, who was well known to be part of the development of the cultural landscape (including carnival, dance and theatre) in St Vincent and the Grenadines. In the latter decades of his life, Adams devoted much of his time to writing about various aspects of Vincentian history and, in the process, produced and published nine popular texts, including *Mock Hangings: A Cultural Tradition in St Vincent and the Grenadines.* Rubenstein is a retired white American male professor of anthropology, who spent his career at the University of

Manitoba in Canada. His essay, "Incest, Effigy Hanging, and Biculturation in a West Indian Village", was published in the third volume of the academic journal *American Ethnologist*, which is now in its forty-ninth edition. Both publications document the practice of mock trials and their associated effigy hangings, and while there are some parallels in how the issues are described, clear ideological divergences exist.

In brief, as a white American, Rubenstein conducted research on the practice in a particular village in St Vincent and the Grenadines to which he assigned the fictitious name Texier, a family name that can be traced back to the United States, the United Kingdom and Canada between 1880 and 1920. From the act of assigning a pseudonym of Euro-American extraction to the village, to his reading of the meanings of these events as part of a process of 'biculturation', Rubenstein's anthropology bears the markings of much of the racist, pathologizing, masculinist, disconnected research produced by white American and British (mostly male) researchers of the mid- to late twentieth century about the Caribbean. Several scholars have demonstrated the contradictions, tensions, voyeuristic gaze and racism inherent in much of the anthropological and sociological research *on* black and Indigenous communities in different parts of the world (Smith 2012; Tuck and McKenzie 2015; Bolles 2021; Navarro 2021; Ulysse 2021).[2]

In contrast, as an Afro-descended Vincentian, Adams occupies the liminal space of both inside observer with a keen interest in documenting local history and culture, but also working on several aspects of the experiences of the working class, while positioned as a middle-class professional.[3] Prior to writing this particular text, Adams had spent several decades in entertainment, had established himself a businessman outside of the medical field, and played a key role in the development of the annual carnival celebrations. In other words, he was well-anchored as an engaged and prominent Vincentian. I cite these works as they represent two of the few written descriptions of the now defunct practice of mock trials and effigy hangings.

Community response to sexual and gendered violence remains a key dimension of regional feminist organizing. In the Anglophone Caribbean, from the 1970s onwards, organizations like Sistren Theatre Collective in Jamaica, Red Thread in Guyana, the Committee for the Development of Women (CDW) in St Vincent and the Grenadines, the campaign led by women and women's organizations against violence also in St Vincent and the Grenadines (1985–1986), and community interventions in Trinidad and Tobago have functioned as important sites for feminist action and knowledge to reduce, eliminate and prevent sexual violence.

In 1985, a march was led by the then principal of an all-girls secondary school in St Vincent and the Grenadines in response to the rape and murder of a student, and the general rising incidence of violence against girls. Similarly, in the following year, the Business and Professional Women's Club of Barbados (BPW Barbados) and the island's National Organisation of Women (NOW) organized a march that included more than three hundred women expressing outrage at the incidence of rape and sexual violence in the country. These are but a few examples of Caribbean women's public organizing to address the enduring violence to which women and girls continue to be exposed.

Civil society and community responses to sexual violence against women and girls are by no means monolithic. Even as we name feminist and women's organizing in the region to end violence as part of larger political efforts to secure gender equity and justice, these actions have been pursued in diverse ways. Mock trials and effigy hangings operated outside Caribbean feminist action to end sexual and gendered violence. The contradictory, messy and even harm-producing effects of the tradition, as a community response to sexual violence, are examined in this chapter.

SEXUAL OFFENCES LEGISLATION: A FOCUS ON INCEST

Legal redress against sexual violence has both a racialized and a gendered history in the Caribbean. Dalea Bean (2022) and Lucille Mathurin Mair (2006) demonstrate the quotidian programme of sexual violence meted out against enslaved women and girls, in particular. Not only was this violence sanctioned by law, Caribbean political economy in plantation society and under colonialism created, maintained and sanctioned sexual and gendered harms against women, men and children. Existing laws, legal practice, law enforcement and community response to sexual violence against girls remain embedded in these histories (DeShong 2024).

Chapter VIII of the *Criminal Code* of St Vincent and the Grenadines outlines the laws pertaining to rape and other sexual offences, including offences against children (sections 122–48). In particular, sections 124–30 make specific reference to the following as offences punishable by law: "intercourse with a girl under the age of thirteen", "intercourse with a girl under the age of fifteen", "indecent assault", "indecency with a child", "permitting a girl under the age of 15 to use premises for sexual intercourse" and "causing or encouraging prostitution, etc., of a girl under the age of fifteen" Furthermore, reference is made to section 142 – "incest by a man", section 143 – "divesting of authority."[4] section 144 – "incest by a woman" and section 145 – "test of relationship in incest". Rape and other manifestations of sexual violence against girls are euphemized in law and in popular discourse as "intercourse", "sex" and "indecency". Elsewhere, Tonya Haynes and I have argued that in media and in law "there is also a tendency to reproduce accounts of sexual violence against girls as instances of shared responsibility, thus erasing asymmetrical relations of power" (Haynes and DeShong 2017, 118).

A number of details about the language of the laws against incest are of particular import when considering the observance of mock trials and effigy hangings. Framing these harms against girls as shared responsibility feature in both the law criminalizing incest and in some mock trials described by participants. Incest by a woman is defined in Chapter VII, section 144 of the sexual offences legislation as "Any woman of the age of fifteen or over who permits a man who she knows to be her grandfather, father, brother or son to have sexual intercourse with her is guilty of an offence and liable to imprisonment for seven years." Incest by a man is defined in section 142 as "Any man who has sexual intercourse with a woman whom he knows to be his granddaughter, daughter, sister or mother is guilty of an offence and liable to imprisonment for fourteen years." While the law appears to account for a presumed differential in age between the perpetrator (usually a man) and the person victimized (usually a girl) in terms of sentencing, the presumption of responsibility by girls fifteen years and older for creating the sexual violence she experiences is troubling.

The arrangement of power informed by age, gender, familial bonds, proximity, residential status, financial dependency on fathers, grandfathers or other familial guardians are not sufficiently accounted for under legislation related to incest. Remarking on the role of the Caribbean women's movement in connecting gendered violence to the "imperatives of the political economy whose logic was underwritten by heteropatriarchy itself", M. Jacqui Alexander (2005, 32) maps familial incestuous violence in the region as betraying a pattern of very young girls experiencing sexual violence perpetrated by much older adult relatives. In other words, the heteropatriarchal organization of families, and the wider society, creates the context in which such violence is simultaneously abhorred and maintained.

These tensions in law, particularly in its implication of shared responsibility, were also reflected in the design and staging of some mock trials and effigy hangings. Several of the proceedings, described in both the literature and the interviews, referenced instances where both fathers and daughters were tried in mock courts as culpable for engaging in socially censured sexual activities in ways that did not always acknowledge the violence to which girls were exposed. For example, in the interviews, several participants referenced events in which women and girls were tried alongside the perpetrator, which reflected harm-producing notions of shared responsibility inherent in the criminal law on incest.

BRIEF NOTE ON INTERVIEWS AND ANALYSIS

The analysis moves between a focus on interviews conducted with seven Vincentians, whose profiles are included below, and reference to two works outlining the Vincentian practice of mock trials and effigy hangings. I assess the meaning of the latter as a community response to sexual violence against girls. Contextual and qualitative interview data for this chapter were collected between May and October 2022. Although the practice was associated with communities in the Leeward and Windward areas of mainland St Vincent, and has been reported to have occurred on at least one of the Grenadine islands, the names of communities, as well as the actual names of interview participants will not be used as identifiers in this chapter.

MOCK TRIALS AND EFFIGY HANGINGS

There is a need to clarify the difference between effigy hangings and mock trials with their associated effigy hangings. The latter is often simply referred

Table 9.1: Participants' Profiles

Pseudonym	Gender Identity	Age	Educational Achievement	Occupation
Burt	Man	56	Primary education/ skills training	Artisan/Tradesman
Lester	Man	50	Primary complete	Mechanic
Max	Man	54	Primary incomplete	Artisan/Tradesman
Frank	Man	68	Technical College Complete	Retired graphic artist, plumber and performing artist
Kamara	Woman	65	Tertiary complete	Retired senior civil servant and teacher
Kyron	Man	Over 40*	Tertiary complete	Civil servant
Maxine	Woman	42	Tertiary complete	Aesthetician

*Kyron chose not to give his precise age.

to as mock hangings or hangings. Used on its own, effigy hangings was a practice engaged by community members mostly to shame politicians who had lost spectacularly at the polls following a general election.

Burt describes effigy hangings as follows:

> If you have a campaign and like you have an election and a politician lose badly in a constituency, they will organize a hanging. They will get a banana body. They would put it in a box and they would bury it and call that the person who lost. They would say the person dead. And it could go to anybody. It could be a fight. It could be two people fight and the one that get the most licks, they would say, "My boy kill him" and then they just decide to bury him in the same style. You get a banana body and you get a cardboard box, bury it and say that person dead . . . I started to learn about it in the 1970s, particularly when the Labour Party and the PPP [People's Political Party] were vying for political office.

Later in the interview, Burt stated: "Sexual abuse is something that has been going on for quite some time. It is not something you would get stopped, but when people find it out, they would hang the man, in a mock way, not necessarily hang the man himself, but they would find something like a tree or something they could use to stand up like a man and hang it and bury it and say that is the man."

According to Adams, "'Effigy Hanging' is not an alternative name for 'Mock Hanging'." The term mock hangings was only applied when the ritual of hanging the effigy was preceded by mock trials, whereas effigy hangings on its own was "used to express community reactions to certain activities such as identifying losers in a political election, or 'Hanging Mr. Harding' at Crop Over time in Barbados or Guy Fawkes in England" (Adams 1999, 25).

He also notes that an average of four or five mock trials and effigy hangings occurred annually and were spread across several villages and towns. Rubenstein (1974) estimated the frequency at two to three per year. Adams (1999) further suggests that these events emerged in response to rising levels of sexual violence in communities. The early hangings disguised the identity of the alleged offenders, but they soon dispensed with this practice and the rituals involved using pseudonyms, features of the effigy and information that would lead to positive identification of the alleged offender.

Writing against the backdrop of a plethora of sexual offence cases reported in local newspapers, Adams remarked at the alarming frequency with which sexual violence against children was being recorded, which itself did not reflect the true incidence. Increased reporting coincided with the heightened women's and feminist activism against gendered violence that emerged in St Vincent and the Grenadines and the region in the decades leading up to the 1990s, as well as the related shifts in the socio-legal response to both intimate partner and non-partner sexual violence against women and girls (Reddock 1998; DeShong 2022). These, coupled with several international treaties, conventions and agreements to which Caribbean governments became signatory in the latter decades of the twentieth century, provide further context for the increased frequency with which sexual violence against girls was being reported to the authorities.

Mock trials were organized in close connection to actual court procedures, court settings and the roles undertaken by various participants in the court process. Organizers selected from among the most articulate members of communities to assume the roles of judges, prosecuting and defence attorneys, defendants, members of the jury, witnesses, police constables, family members of the accused, bailiffs, doctors, prison wardens, and so on. The villager chosen to be the judge, according to Rubenstein (1974) was required to be exceptionally eloquent. Organizers were mainly men who selected pseudonyms to invoke humour and to point to the identity of the accused.

Names assigned contributed to the theatre-like atmosphere of these events. For example, Frank reported that names included "Mother Upholder" and "Father Whiner *something*" for mothers and fathers on trial respectively. The names were indicative of how the organizers felt about those suspected of being involved. Max and Lester remember the name "Father Habit" in reference to a prominent member of a community from the Leeward side of the island. "Father Habit" was a name designed to signal the repeated acts of sexual violence by a father against his daughter. Notions of women's and girls' culpability are evident in the names assigned and in some of the themes created for the events. Max and Lester also reported that one of the themes for a trial and hanging was "Daughter Love It, Mother Love It". The operation of gender and age in girls' experience of sexual violence is clearly effaced in this last example.

Before proceeding to trial in suspected cases of child sexual abuse in the family,[5] there was a period of investigation by a special committee, the result of which would feature at the trial. This is confirmed by Maxine, who remarked, "They used to dig all in your house, so if anything going wrong in there, they go talk." Adams (1999) also makes mention of the creation of a calypso, the slogan of which would be used to publicize and drum up interest for the event.

The length of a trial varied from a few nights in one week to a few nights per week over several weeks. Once the party (or parties) was found guilty, the related effigy hanging followed on the first full moon night after the trial. Skilled craftsmen were recruited between the period of the trial and the hanging to construct life-size effigies of the man accused and, sometimes, the girl who was victimized. In many ways this resonates with sections 142 and 144 (referenced earlier in the chapter) in which notions of shared culpability for men's violence against women and girls is embedded in law. The design of the effigy of the alleged perpetrator was constructed to ensure that the head was certain to be severed once hanged. If an error in design prevented this from happening, the accused was declared innocent. The effigies were designed to resemble real individuals in terms of their facial features and dress. They were displayed publicly in the days leading up to the hanging. Gallows were also constructed at the intended site of the hanging after the trial was completed.

Hangings were attended by hundreds of villagers, as well as residents of nearby villages. Participants also reported that others would come from villages that were considered far away, including persons from the Grenadines who sailed to mainland St Vincent to witness the event. Entrance fees were often charged for both the trial and hangings, and refreshments were sold at the latter event. There was entertainment, including the calypsos created for the event. It was at this stage that the hangings assumed a carnival-like atmosphere (Rubenstein 1974; Adams 1999). This tension between addressing sexual violence against girls and creating a series of events for pleasure is addressed in the next section.

'TO ENTERTAIN OR TO CENSURE': A CRITICAL READING OF MOCK HANGINGS

> "He ga pickney wid he daughta
> Heng um
> Ah wey we ah go do um?
> Heng um
> We go heng um down ah ball ground [community hard court where sports are played]
> Heng um
> Ah wey we ah go do um?
> Heng um."[6]

Two competing accounts of the purpose and function of these events emerge. Architects were respected men within communities: "A number of village men of outgoing personality, administrative abilities and good reputation organize and sponsor the events for personal amusement, to punish the guilty parties to publicly humiliate them in dramatic fashion, to enhance their own prestige and community standing and for personal financial benefit" (Rubenstein 1974, 774).

Rubenstein's reading sets up a paradox of competing and contradictory motives informing the practice: hangings as public spectacle and as censure for incest. Natasha Barnes (2010, 16) argues that "As members of the black working-class have been denied state-sponsored outlets for self-determination, their articulations of religiosity, choice about work and play, patterns of consumption, and struggles for personal dignity and respect have coalesced into a shifting, but ideologically discrete, subaltern political worldview." Situating the source of working-class Caribbean people's ways of being within a history of refusal against a violent colonialism and as a political worldview runs counter to Rubenstein's notion of biculturation as a framework for explaining hangings.

Though operating from the premise that these events represent "the Black, lower-class Vincentian response to exclusion from full access to and equal participation in the cultural traditions and socio-cultural institutions characteristic of the total society", the biculturation model defines this as a consequence of a cultural duality in which the reality of social class and the specificity of black culture in plural societies coalesce to produce various traditions (Rubenstein 1974, 766). Although Rubenstein briefly references a history of slavery and colonialism, their precise role in the emergence of these traditions, and an approach which centres the knowledges of Afro-Vincentians in defining our own experience, are muted in his conceptualization. Furthermore, as Barnes (2010) also reminds us of Caribbean cultural traditions such as carnival and calypso, the convergence of art and politics anchored in our history occurs in ways that provide a particular worldview of the Caribbean, drawing on perspectives of citizens most often circumscribed by race, class and geography.

It is, however, critical to read these traditions beyond acts of resistance. Vincentian and Caribbean people, particularly those made most vulnerable under race, class and gender systems, have always demonstrated a capacity to make life on terms outside of those which were imagined for us. This capacity cannot be reduced to 'resisting' or 'living in response to', even as we account for an enduring coloniality. In other words, our ontological and epistemological starting point must be explored beyond the limits of colonialism, neo-colonialism, imperialism and the current manifestation of neoliberal globalization.

This philosophical approach informs the analysis of the practice of mock trials and effigy hangings, away from the binary logic that it can be read as derived for entertainment value or as censure for child sexual abuse. It provides context for the calypso, excerpted above, that was created to accompany a hanging. The song tells of the collective outrage that sexual violence evokes among members of a community. Calypso emerged as a space in which mainly Afro-Caribbean working-class men told their stories and that of their communities from their own perspective (Reddock 2014; Lewis 2014). It is saturated with dominant representations of gender, class and sexuality (Lewis 2014). The repetition of the question "Ah wey we go do um?" is a call for a collective community response. Call-and-response is a popular device in the calypso genre designed to generate maximum crowd engagement. These songs were devised specifically for the night of the hanging, following a guilty verdict at the mock trial.

Maxine reports that:

> When the man going up in the black and white suit, everybody laughing and mekking a mock of it. Some people even firing spit – *twa* – and they laughing and gallivanting, drinking rum and then they would put up the girl going up now and if you see they dancing there, their babies and they dancing going up there, they dancing going up until they reach up to the gallows and then they will have fun, ring games and do all kind of activities, until the point in time to get the hanging where they say if you cut the throat.

Like Maxine, other participants describe a festive atmosphere on the night of the hanging, with musicians and calypsonians performing, games and activities, and children accompanying their parents. People attended from nearby villages. Food and drinks were on sale. In some villages, the event commenced between 6 p.m. and 8 p.m. and culminated with the hanging at the stroke of midnight. However, the activities also involved a show of disdain for perpetrators of violence with people 'firing spit'. The audience became part of the theatrical display at both the trials and the hangings.

Kamara explains the complex meanings of these events from her own perspective:

> My experience was that it was having sex with your own child or your sister, so incest. And we now say that it was a response to sexual abuse because we have

> now termed incest a form of sexual abuse, but my recollection was anything that persons think that was, for example, rape. If a man rapes a woman, they would hang him because the community took things of sexual nature that was illicit into their own hands. They didn't wait for a judge to pass judgement. They would pass judgement and by shaming you, they expect that there might be some reform or they expect that there is a reaction because that is not something that people look forward to. That was a very embarrassing and outrageous thing in a community. The community took action for resolution, as a way of resolving. So, I wouldn't, they wouldn't institute for their daughter. If it happen in the community, anybody could institute, instigate that. It was a communal thing.

For Kamara, naming the event a response to sexual violence against children has its resonance in a collective shift in consciousness; a shift which begins to occur with feminist organizing in the region. As someone who once headed the state gender machinery, Kamara is very aware of this history. She is also clear that the community identified such acts of sexual violence as illicit, and that the trials and hangings were designed to shame the perpetrator and end the violence. From Kyron's perspective:

> They were used as a deterrent to bring out the shame to prevent other persons from doing it, from committing such crimes and also to expose men who indulged in these activities. I think that was a way as it's not like today where you can put it out on social media or if a young lady cries rape, you might have redress because things are going through the court system at a faster rate. So it might appear as though people are turning a blind eye but there are now agencies and avenues that people can go to and let their voices be heard. So those things used to act as a deterrent.

He refers to generational, technological and ideological differences in how sexual violence is confronted and understood. For Kyron, these events emerged out of a sheer need to address gendered harms against girls, in the absence of official state action. He believes that with the introduction of laws, activism and state agencies, these mock trials and hangings have become obsolete. Globally, attrition rates for crimes involving sexual violence are high, and a significant proportion of events involving sexual violence go unreported. Kyron's reference to social media is not at all unfounded, especially when we consider the impact of #lifeinleggings and the on- and off-line activism of Tambourine Army as major Caribbean feminist activist efforts in recent times.

This putative tension to have emerged about the meanings of mock hangings (that is, to entertain or to censure) can be considered beyond a search for a rapprochement. In fact, it was while reviewing insights provided by Frank that a much clearer way of conceptualizing the events emerged. Rather than thinking about them as occurring with two opposing motives, Frank recalls how we have always navigated violent harms in our Caribbean:

> But like I say it's connected to the same thing – the money. It's connected to the entertainment because as one thing, what I notice about black people is that we love to entertain, and even though sometimes we have more serious issues, we take a more humorous way. That, too, used to alleviate some of the problems like stress, people getting crazy and all that kinda thing. Because even it's a serious issue with rape, because they put a lot of humorous stuff between it, they highlighting the problem, yes, but at the same time they highlighting it in such a way that you kinda free up people. People feel like, ok boy, at least you get that off your chest rather than it bundle up there and you want to talk about it and you can't talk about it. But when it come out like that, it kinda ease up a lot of the stress in terms of the events.

There are tensions in Frank's narratives. Talking about rape in ways that are meant to illicit humour trivializes the severity of these harms. From Frank we learn about communities' attempt to engage in collective catharsis, therapy and healing as they navigate sexual violence. The fact that this was sometimes done in ways that created more harm for the girls who were victimized should neither be missed nor minimized. He suggests that we confront some of the worst effects of violence through humour and other devices. As a veteran calypsonian, he draws parallels to how, in calypso and traditional carnival, a similar kind of catharsis unfolds. This approach to thinking about these events forces us to turn to the very tools, institutions and practices of a collective Caribbean imaginary. In so doing, it centres the knowledge base of communities and its members.

CONCLUSION

As we continue to theorize and search for answers in the face of these enduring, interconnected systems of inequality, out of which sexual violence against girls is maintained, community responses require greater attention. Mock trials and effigy hangings, as a specific Vincentian tradition and community response to sexual violence against girls, should not be confused with Vincentian and Caribbean feminist and women's rights activism against these gendered harms.

The late 1970s into the 1990s was indeed a period of heightened national, regional and global activism. Even though the practice of mock trials and effigy hangings preceded the emergence of an explicit feminist movement in the region – and even though the tradition cannot be named as feminist political action – it continued alongside feminist activism in Vincentian and Caribbean communities until the mid- to late 1990s. What can be said, however, is that the tradition emerged as part of the myriad, complex and often contradictory ways in which communities navigate violent harms. Very different from the feminist, anti-racist and anti-colonialist community works of Sistren Theatre Collective, and existing in stark contrast to the activism of Vincentian women's rights and feminist organizing of groups like the Committee for the Development of Women (CDW), these events were key instantiations of community action in response to sexual violence against children.

It is of significant concern that a tendency to attribute blame to girls for their own victimization was a feature of some of these events. More work is required to pursue any connections between a history of labour and sexual exploitation of children and the continuities of sexual violence against girls in the Caribbean; and a tradition of women rejecting both colonial and gendered violence. Several questions for future exploration arise in this regard. For instance, what is at stake if we do not confront a tendency to blame Caribbean girls for their own experiences of sexual violence? How might we more clearly demonstrate the continuities of race, gender, class and sexuality in the experience of sexual violence against girls in the region? A return to M. Jacqui Alexander's (2005) theorizing of the heteropatriarchal neo-colonial state and how it reaches into the lives of women, girls and gender-expansive people, as well as its connection to the Caribbean political economy, remains urgent.

Conceptually, my purpose with this chapter was to assess the meanings still in circulation about mock trials and effigy hangings. What emerged was the shared, contradictory and multiple ways in which the practice was defined, understood and expressed. All participants pointed to a tendency to use these events to discipline perpetrators and restore order within communities as well as a means through which to create public spectacle. Drawing on the theorizing of participants, rather than viewing these as purely contradictory motives, there is indeed room to consider also how they, in fact, coalesce. They coalesce, according to Frank, to reflect one of the ways in which we have always navigated harms and trauma in the region. Invoking play, humour, wit and other elements of performance provide a space in which to address some of the worst harms we have had to confront. As a response to sexual violence, however, these events expose the very contradictions inherent in law, policies and community actions. They, unfortunately, re/produce and perpetuate further harms against women and girls in their attempts at remediation and prevention.

NOTES

1. A portion of the analysis for this chapter is based on interviews with a small sample of Vincentians who witnessed mock hangings while growing up in their respective communities. There were challenges in securing participants who were involved in the planning of these events since it was reported that several practitioners had passed away. Notwithstanding the small sample size, the interviews conducted provided an important basis upon which to engage in interpretive qualitative analysis of the meanings of these events in Vincentian communities. These accounts provide explanations of the events from the perspective of community members. Even as Rubenstein (1974) conducted ethnographic research on the practice in the 1970s, much of his focus was not on how community members framed these experiences, but instead on how these experiences fit into a framework referred to as biculturalism (more on this later in the chapter). In contrast, this chapter situates participants at the centre of the knowledge generation exercise.

2. Another significant example of the mid-twentieth-century racist anthropological and sociological studies was those produced about Caribbean families, conducted by mainly white researchers from the Global North, in which Afro-Caribbean families were pathologized as dysfunctional; men derelict in their familial obligations; and in which mothers and other women heads of households were accused of emasculating men. See the works by Christine Barrow, Keisha Lindsay and several other Caribbean feminist scholars for a more in-depth critique of these studies.
3. Class is a rather complex, and often misapplied category in the Caribbean. Like gender, it can never be discussed away from race, given our history. To describe an African-descended person born in the early to mid-twentieth-century as middle class by dint of their education or occupation misses what Rex Nettleford said about most of us being only one generation (by now, a few) removed from the cane-piece.
4. Section 143 reads: "On the conviction before any court of any person for an offence under section 142, or of an attempt to commit such offence, against a female under the age of eighteen, it shall be in the power of the court to divest the offender of all authority over such female and, if the offender is the guardian of such woman, to remove the offender from such guardianship and in any such case to appoint any person to be the guardian of such woman during her minority period." (See full document at: https://www.oas.org/en/sla/dlc/mesicic/docs/mesicic5_svg_annex8.pdf)
5. Mock trials and effigy hangings were mainly held in cases of child sexual abuse against girls, but there is evidence from the interviews and the two studies reviewed that a smaller number of events were organized in response to men accused of what is legally defined as bestiality. There was also one case reported in which a woman was featured because her potential spouse did not turn up on their wedding day. It was alleged that she was pregnant for someone that was not the man she was supposed to marry.
6. An excerpt of a calypso created for a mock hanging (Adams 1999, 35).

REFERENCES

Adams, Edgar. 1999. *Mock Hangings: A Cultural Tradition in St. Vincent and the Grenadines*. Kingstown: Edgar Adams.

Abrahams, Roger D. 1982. "Storytelling: Wake Amusements and the Structure of Nonsense on St. Vincent." *Journal of American Folklore* 95 (378): 389–414.

Abrahams, Roger D., and Richard Bauman. 1971. "Sense and Nonsense in St. Vincent: Speech Behavior and Decorum in a Caribbean Community." *American Anthropologist* 73 (3): 762–72.

Alexander, M. Jacqui. 2005. *Pedagogies of Crossing: Meditations on Feminism, Sexual Politics, Memory, and the Sacred*. Durham, NC: Duke University Press.

Barnes, Natasha. 2010. *Cultural Conundrums: Gender, Race, Nation, and the Making of Caribbean Cultural Politics*. Ann Arbor: University of Michigan Press.

Bolles, Lynne. 2021. "Anthropological Research Methods for the Study of Black Women in the Caribbean." In *Methodologies in Caribbean Research on Gender and Sexuality*, edited by Kamala Kempadoo and Halimah A.F. DeShong, 397–406. Kingston: Ian Randle Publishers.

Brereton, Bridget. 2010. "The Historical Background to the Culture of Violence in Trinidad and Tobago." *Caribbean Review of Gender Studies* no. 4: 1–15.

Daly, Kathleen, and Brigitte Bouhours. 2010. "Rape and Attrition in the Legal process: A Comparative Analysis of Five Countries." *Crime and Justice* 39 (1): 565–650.

DeShong, Halimah A.F. 2022. "CARICOM Model Legislation on Domestic Violence: Negotiating Love, Intimacy and Abuse in Caribbean Law." In *Caribbean Integration: Uncertainty in a Time of Global Fragmentation*. Edited by Patsy Lewis, Terri-Ann Gilbert, and Jessica Byron, 224–38. Kingston: University of the West Indies Press.

———. 2024. "Gendered Violence and Gender as a Site of Violence: Reflections from the Caribbean." *Frontiers: A Journal of Women's Studies* 45 (2): 79–101.

Epstein, Rebecca, Jamilia Blake, and Thalia González. 2017. *Girlhood Interrupted: The Erasure of Black Girls' Childhood*. Washington, DC: Georgetown Law Centre on Poverty and Inequality.

Gilmore, Amir A., and Pamela J. Bettis. 2021. "Antiblackness and the Adultification of Black Children in a U.S. Prison Nation." *Oxford Research Encyclopedia of Education*. https://oxfordre.com/education/display/10.1093/acrefore/9780190264093.001.0001/acrefore-9780190264093-e-1293.

Hardaway, Ayana Tyler, LaWanda W.M. Ward, and Diamond Howell. 2019. "Black Girls and Womyn Matter: Using Black Feminist Thought to Examine Violence and Erasure in Education." *Urban Education Research and Policy Annuals* 6 (1): 31–46.

Hartman, Saidya. 1997. *Scenes of Subjection: Terror, Slavery and Self-Making in Nineteenth Century America.* New York: Oxford University Press.

Haynes, Tonya, and Halimah A.F. DeShong. 2017. "Queering Feminist Approaches to Gender-Based Violence in the Anglophone Caribbean." *Social and Economic Studies* 66 (1&2): 105–31.

Jones, Adele, and Ena Trotman-Jemmott. 2010. *Child Sexual Abuse in the Eastern Caribbean: Perceptions of, Attitudes to and Opinions on Child Sexual Abuse in the Eastern Caribbean.* UNICEF Unite for Children and University of Huddersfield. https://www.comminit.com/unicef/content/child-sexual-abuse-eastern-caribbean.

Lewis Linden. 2014. "Gender and Performativity: Calypso and the Culture of Masculinity." *Caribbean Review of Gender Studies* (Special Issue on 'Fragility and Persistence of Dominant Masculinities', Guest Editors: Wesley Crichlow, Halimah A.F. DeShong and Linden Lewis) no. 8: 15–42.

Mair, Lucille Mathurin. 2006. *A Historical Study of Women in Jamaica, 1655–1844.* Edited by Hilary Beckles and Verene Shepherd. Kingston: University of the West Indies Press.

Morris, Monique W. 2019. "Countering the Adultification of Black Girls." *Educational Leadership* 76 (7): 44–48.

Navarro, Tami. 2021. "'You Is One of We': Positionality in the Field." In *Methodologies in Caribbean Research on Gender and Sexuality,* edited by Kamala Kempadoo and Halimah A.F. DeShong, 441–50. Kingston: Ian Randle Publishers.

Pargass, G., and R. Clarke. 2003. "Violence Against Women: A Human Rights Issue Post Beijing Five Year Review." In *Gender Equality in the Caribbean: Illusion or Reality,* edited by G. Tang Nain and B. Bailey, 39–72. Kingston: Ian Randle Publishers.

Reddock, Rhoda. 1998. "Women's Organizations and Movements in the Commonwealth Caribbean: The Response to Global Economic Crisis in the 1980s." *Feminist Review* 59 (1): 57–73.

Robinson, Tracy. 2018. "What Do We Mean by Politics? Feminist Political Engagement: A Case Study." Presentation at Politics for Social and Environmental Justice in the Caribbean: A Regional Meeting. 24–25 March, Barbados.

Rubenstein, Hymie. 1976. "Incest, Effigy Hanging, and Biculturation in a West Indian Village." *American Ethnologist* 3 (4): 765–81.

Shepherd, Verene. 2017. "The History of Gender-Based Violence in the Caribbean." *diGJamaica,* 19 December. https://www.facebook.com/diGJamaica.

Smith, Linda Tuhiwai. 2012. *Decolonizing Methodologies: Research and Indigenous People*. London: Zed Books.

Spillers, Hortense J. 1987. "Mama's Baby, Papa's Maybe: An American Grammar Book." In *The Transgender Studies Reader Remix*, 93–104. New York and London: Routledge.

Tuck, Eve, and Marcia McKenzie. 2015. *Place in Research: Theory, Methodology and Methods*. London: Routledge.

Ulysse, Gina. 2021. "Downtown Ladies: Informal Commercial Importers, a Haitian Anthropologist and Self-Making in Jamaica." In *Methodologies in Caribbean Research on Gender and Sexuality*, edited by Kamala Kempadoo and Halimah A.F. DeShong, 408–24. Kingston: Ian Randle Publishers.

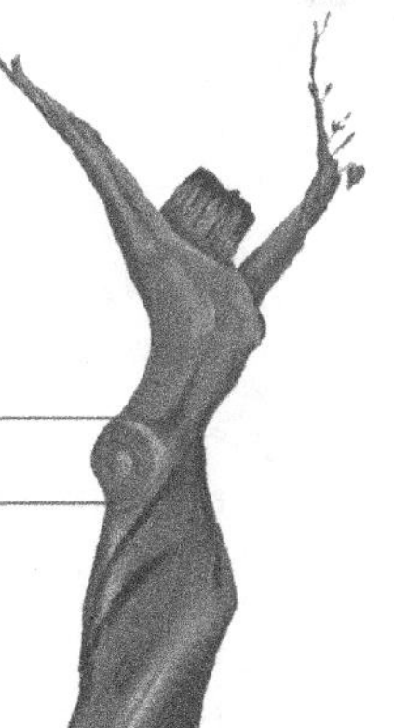

chapter 10

Rage and Regret

Narratives of Violence and Resolve Among Couples in Trinidad and Tobago, 1940–1960

O'Neil Joseph

FOR MRS KING, CHRISTMAS DAY OF 1958 BEGAN IN SORROW. On Christmas Eve she worked tirelessly to clean her home. She went to bed at two in the morning.[1] The sun had not yet risen when Mrs King was awakened by a blow to the head. In her words, "It was the worst set of licks I ever got in my life. All because I was sleeping, and breakfast was not ready. It was my mother-in-law who rescued me."[2] While replaying the events of that fateful Christmas morning, Mrs King pointed to her veranda and whispered, "You see that man sitting out there? He was not easy to deal with at all, but we made it. Is over forty years now we married. Praise be to God! We encourage young people to hold on to the marriage despite the trials."[3] Mrs King's account of surviving intimate partner violence and her simultaneous celebration of a long-lasting marriage, despite many years of gruesome physical abuse, is reflective of the fact that during the early to mid-twentieth century, it was common for many women who suffered abuse at the hands of their husbands to remain married well into old age. This chapter centres the oral testimonies of two couples from Trinidad and Tobago whose marriages were characterized by intimate partner violence.[4] Through the rich testimonies offered by these couples, we acquire insight into the causes of violence within their homes, the coping mechanisms employed by wives, and the resolutions made by the couples which ultimately led to the survival of their marriages. More broadly, an interrogation of these testimonies reveals how ordinary people navigated the complex gender ideologies of the early to mid-twentieth century. Taken together, this work contends that financial issues, infidelity, drunkenness and destructive ideas entrenched in traditional masculine practices transformed many households into sites of violence. However, religious beliefs and social pressures prompted many women to stay and work towards finding a solution to the violence that characterized their home lives. This knowledge enriches our understanding of intimate partner violence in the Caribbean from a historical perspective, and more significantly, offers rare mid-twentieth-century oral testimonies from both perpetrators and victims of IPV.

AFRICANS, INDIANS AND VIOLENCE: A HISTORICAL SNAPSHOT

In the Caribbean, intimate partner relationships have long been characterized by violence. Plantation records make mention of numerous acts of violence by enslaved men towards women and their wives. For instance, on the punishment records of the Eliza and Mary plantation in Berbice, an entry made on 9 July 1827 indicated that, Carl, an enslaved man, was given twenty-one lashes for "beating his wife in a brutal and merciless manner", and on Best Coffee Land, also in Berbice, an enslaved man called Joe was punished for "having a cutlass in his hand and threatening to kill his wife" (Browne 2017, 121). Patricia Mohammed (2004, 61) argued that one of the effects of chattel slavery was a tradition of fierce conflict between African-descended men and women. Moreover, Hilary Beckles (2004, 229) contended that while enslaved men were "kept down" on the plantation and their status as fathers was ignored, they shared white elite masculine ideas about domestic dominance. Beckles (2004, 238) opined, "Enslaved black men shared some basic patriarchal values with white men, expressed in terms of an assertion of masculine authority and power over women." This patriarchal value system persisted in the post-emancipation era. During the early twentieth century, the family life of African-descended Caribbean people became an area of major concern for colonial authorities and religious groups. For these entities, the idea of Christian marriage and the acceptance of the principles of Victorian femininity were essential for the progress of the region (Moore and Johnson 2004, 97).[5] However, marriage rates remained low, especially among the labouring classes (De Barros 2014). Intimate partner violence was common; many persons opted to marry later in life; and many black men did not deem it a problem to father children from multiple sexual conquests (Putnam 2014, 505).

From 1845, Trinidad's population was supplemented with approximately 143,900 Indian indentured labourers (Ali 1993, 5). The violence that characterized the intimate relationships between Indian men and their wives in Trinidad, during and after indentureship, is well documented.[6] Due to their lower numbers during the early days of indentureship, Indian women had acquired a freedom to choose or get rid of a man if he did not meet their desires sexually and economically. This scarcity of Indian women and the challenge to dominant patriarchal order in India led to conflict (Mohammed 2004, 60). During the period 1872 to 1900, sixty-five wives were murdered by their Indian husbands (Brereton 2010, 7). Thus, among both major ethnic groups in Trinidad and Tobago, IPV was prevalent.

Historians have long used oral histories/life histories to understand the past. Mary Chamberlain (2006), Rhoda Reddock (1994) and Susan Craig-James (2008) utilized oral histories to write about women and men's historical experiences in the Caribbean. Thus, the oral history/life history method employed in this chapter is in community with the work of these scholars. The life history approach provides "a voice to the experienced life of individuals, especially those voices that may be unheard, suppressed, or purposefully ignored" (Cole and Knowles 2016, 262). While oral histories/ life histories have been regarded as subjective and a narrow way to view the past, it is critical to note that "the individual voice may be representative of the collective voice, and provide evidence of broader attitudes, values and patterns of behaviour. [Indeed, as it relates to intimate partner violence], the voices can confirm cultural practices" (Chamberlain 2021, 43).

In this chapter, the testimonies of two couples are examined. Mr and Mrs King, and Mr and Mrs Brathwaite were all in their eighties at the time of the interviews. These couples self-identified as belonging to the labouring classes and were of African descent. Interviews took place at their homes and were completed in one sitting, which spanned two to four hours.

Some scholars suggest that researchers should evaluate their own position and experiences because it can influence "how research is conducted, its outcomes and results" (Holmes 2020, 2). Between the couples, each of the men requested to be interviewed separately.[7] As a male researcher, I observed that my conversations with husbands adopted a tone of 'men talk', where, through their accounts of violent behaviours, male interviewees appealed to my understanding and cultural knowledge as a man. Such appeals were usually communicated via sentences such as, "Well, brother, as a man, you know how it is" or "Young fellow, yuh know what we men does have to deal with."[8] However, husbands typically provided fewer details than wives and generally attempted to trivialize, deny or mitigate the consequences of their violent actions. Pseudonyms are used to protect the identity of participants. The oral testimonies are also supported by archival and newspaper sources, which help to establish the broader socio-cultural conditions that participants alluded to in their testimonies.

MR AND MRS KING

Mr and Mrs King married in 1956. Both were twenty-two and had known each other since childhood. Reflecting on his decision to marry Mrs King, Mr King noted, "At some time, a man must look for a wife. A woman who would take good care of me and my children while I out here working hard. A woman who could cook, clean, wash white clothes and was respectable. She was a good woman. We went to church and school together and I never one day hear her name call in no sort of thing where anybody had to question her."[9]

Mrs King also offered her reasons for accepting Mr King's proposal and how she viewed her role as a wife. She explained, "I always wanted to get married, and we started talking. He would come by the house and talk. So, I was happy when he decided to talk to my papa and say he wanted to marry me. I was ready, I was accustomed cooking and cleaning and washing and seeing about baby."[10]

Their testimonies indicated that they both shared a similar belief about marriage and gender roles, whereby emphasis was placed on a woman's ability to effectively execute tasks associated with child rearing and home-making. For Mr King, a woman's ability to clean and cook were early indicators of whether she would make a good wife. Mrs King also echoed her husband's sentiments by highlighting her years of experience conducting household tasks as evidence of her readiness for marriage. Thus, at the core of their marriage was a clear division of responsibility within the domestic sphere. Mrs King was expected to manage the home and children, while Mr King, as he put it, "out here working hard". Such a domestic arrangement was not rare. Scholars of the Afro-Caribbean family often noted that "men's familial roles were structurally marginal in the complex of domestic relations . . . [and men were] on the fringe of the effective ties which bind the group together" (Coppin 2000, 66). Women, on the other hand, were expected to have and care for children as part of the value system based on respectability (Wilson 2001, 344).

One of the first instances of conflict between Mr and Mrs King occurred only a few months into their marriage when Mrs King was informed by a friend that Mr King was expecting a child with another villager. According to Mr King, the child was conceived before he got married and, therefore, the community chatter about the pregnancy did not reflect poorly on his character. For Mrs King, however, it was an act of betrayal because according to her, "We were talking long before we get married, and he should have said something. People had it like I know about the baby and marry him before the baby come."[11] Deeply troubled by this information, Mrs King approached her husband. She explained, "He started to cuss and carry on in the house. If you hear noise in the house. He started to throw down things. All kinds of things he did say that morning. By the time I turn my back is one solid hand he give me. I was in shock. It shocked me because I never see him like that before."[12]

When asked about his recollection of this violent episode, Mr King admitted that an argument escalated, only because Mrs King was "cantankerous and carrying on because of some old talk from ah maco. She let Jean [the friend who informed Mrs King] nearly mash up we living."[13] Mr King disregarded any conversations regarding his physical violence. While he owned the argument, he shifted blame onto his wife, whom he believed had behaved in an ill-tempered manner. Blame was also placed on another woman, Jean, to whom he attached the label "maco", suggesting that she overstepped her boundaries and was involved in sharing his personal business. Mrs King also explained that this revelation about Mr King's "outside child" represented a turning point in their relationship. She noted,

> All these years I never know he was so ignorant and hoggish. Every little disagreement we had in the house was some big noise, all the neighbours in we business. Everything was lash for him. All on my head he used to hit me. He burst my lip many times. I couldn't open my mouth home here. Even when he knows he was wrong he never used to admit. That same woman that they say was making baby before we get married made a next child for him. Yes! She was one ah he concubines. So, after our first three children, he has a daughter with May [the outside woman] and then we had one more child after that. All when this happening I couldn't open my mouth home here is cussing, and kick and cuff.[14]

Mrs King's revelation that her husband fathered another child outside of their marriage revealed that the violence and tension within their household was often triggered by acts of infidelity. Mr King was allegedly unfaithful throughout the marriage, and even with very public egregious breaches of his marital vows, his rage and violent demeanour at home made it virtually impossible for his wife to voice her frustration or disappointment. Should she have questioned him, he would have enacted a litany of cruelties against her. Mr King's unabashed defilement of the marital bed was not out of the ordinary. Keith Otterbein argued that, in the region, it was expected for men to be unfaithful (Otterbein 1965, 67). Similarly, Herwald Davies, an Anglican minister who lived in Tobago during the early twentieth century, noted that men brazenly participated in all sorts of immorality and extramarital relations (Pemberton 1998, 3–4). In my work on family life in Tobago, I also highlighted several cases of men who fathered children outside of their marriage. I argued that while religion was central to the lifestyle of people in this territory, "men defied their vows of sexual fidelity so frequently that extra-marital affairs became expected and tolerated . . . some wives showed no obvious impartiality to illegitimate children who became members of their own household" (Joseph 2021, xx). Mrs King, however, was not one of those wives who appeared unbothered by her husband's adulterous acts. In fact, she noted, "I was hurt. Especially when he had that next child. I tell his mother. He was in a rage because I tell she. I had to run for my life. He had a stick in he hands."[15]

Commenting on the atmosphere of violence that permeated his home, Mr King reasoned, "Well, brother, as a man, you know how it is . . . sometimes yuh does have a little thing outside. Man cannot feed on one thing alone. But that woman used to nag me. Is you I marry, What the hell you talking about girl up the road about? Yes, we used to have we little fighting but it wasn't no beat-up thing. Sometimes I used to have to discipline she because this is my house. I in charge here."[16]

Mr King framed his successive extra-marital relationships as a normal masculine prerogative that was expected of all men during the early to mid-twentieth century. His use of the phrase "man cannot feed on one thing alone" pulled from a broader set of cultural ideas, which suggest that a man, even while married, must satisfy his sexual appetite with variety. Given that these ideas about men should have been widely understood, Mr King failed to understand why his wife was bothered by his extramarital affairs, especially since he had given her the title of wife. In the calypso arena, similar ideas were communicated as the general viewpoint of men. For instance, during the mid-twentieth century, Garfield Blackman, better known as Lord Shorty, outlined his rules for women in his hit calypso, "Sixteen Commandments". At the end of the first stanza, Lord Shorty warned his love interest, "If thou see me and a next young lady in a conversation, pass me straight like you ent see me, let me run my woman."[17] For the calypsonian, it was utterly inappropriate and out of place for a woman to intrude on their spouse's pursuit of other women. To oppose this masculine prerogative was to challenge the established gender norms. Therefore, in the case of the Kings, Mr King felt compelled to re-establish his masculine authority and domestic dominance by acting violently towards his wife whenever she argued about his outside woman.

He attempted to trivialize his behaviour by stating that they only had "little fighting", which should not be categorized as him beating up his wife. He then went on to establish a distinction between discipline and abuse. He sought to make it clear that he never abused his wife but only "disciplined" her in response to her constant nagging about his extramarital affairs. In so doing, he hoped to remind her that "This is my house. I in charge here."[18] In conversations with several Trinbagonian men born during the early twentieth century, "a box [slap in the face]" or "one quick clout" was considered appropriate when "disciplining a wife" and "keeping her in check".[19] However, using objects or excessive force to the point of bloodshed was beating.[20] According to these men, most men in Trinidad and Tobago during the early to mid-twentieth century "disciplined" wives and is only a few "who beat them up".

Given that physical and verbal abuse was customary in the King household, one wonders about the events of that fateful Christmas morning in 1958, which Mrs King described as "the worst set ah licks I ever get in my life".[21] In explaining why this particular beating was etched in her memory, Mrs King noted, "I think is because I was between sleep and wake and my hand did break and is because his mother and them run over to save me. They say they never hear me bawl so yet. All my legs did bruise up long after."[22] The broken arm, marks of violence on her body, her piercing screams and the physical intervention of her in-laws made this episode of violence one that Mrs King would always remember. She noted, however, that her mother-in-law and her own biological mother continually offered her advice on how to "keep the peace". Her acceptance and application of their advice is what made her cope with her husband over the decades. She explained, "Well, they remind me that this is how man is . . . just rough and ignorant, and I had to keep my tongue. Just leave him let he do whatever he wants, and not take him on. Once I stopped fussing, things kind of calm down."[23]

Mrs King further explained that her mother told her that "I need to behave myself and not aggravate the man . . . because my biggest sister was going through the same thing. She ran away and they [her mother] carried she back by her husband."[24] The advice offered by these older women to Mrs King reinforced Victorian gender ideologies that were propagated through the church and other social institutions. By accepting this Victorian gender ideology, Mrs King's household would reflect "an authoritarian male breadwinner in charge of his home . . . [a docile wife] who grooms daughters to be good housewives . . . girls [who would] dwell in quiet homes . . . submissive and retiring . . . [only] to be seen and not heard" (Bloomestein 2011, 1–2). Mrs King's testimony made it clear that in order for there to be peace in her home, she had to lose her voice, give her husband absolute freedom, subdue her desire to speak about matters that bothered her and adopt a more passive persona. Moreover, she certainly did not receive any empathy from her mother, whom she believed was annoyed that she refused to behave herself, and that she and her sister were causing stress to their husbands.

Speaking on resolutions that contributed to their marriage standing the test of time, Mr King noted that, in his late forties, he was diagnosed with diabetes, and it was through his battle with illness that Mrs King, "stop nag me and start to care me properly and I kind of soften up as well. She really cared me good over the years."[25] Thus, sickness on the part of Mr King, and advice from older women to keep the peace were the major factors that led to the couple staying together over the years. Indeed, the details that they offered centres the reality that infidelity can be considered a form of abuse that left wives deeply emotionally wounded and frustrated. Coercive measures, such as older women forcefully taking young wives back to their marital homes, also indicate that during the mid-twentieth century, several entities worked together to ensure women remained in abusive marriages. Husbandly control and violence was a cultural practice and par for the course in marriage.

MR AND MRS BRATHWAITE

Mr and Mrs Brathwaite married on 1 January 1959. He was twenty-one, a general labourer with a construction company in Port of Spain. It was at this company that he met Mrs Brathwaite, who worked as an accountant. As she remembered it, a fierce disagreement took place in the household as early as one month after the wedding. She noted, "He wanted me to stop working and [said] that married women should stay home with their children. Now, I was already carrying the first child. I didn't agree at all because I liked working. I went to school, and I really liked my job. We didn't have a house and I felt like we would have gotten things faster if both of us were bringing home pay."[26]

Mr Brathwaite also offered his reasoning behind asking his wife to stop working. He noted, "Well, growing up, when a woman married, they would stop working and take care of the children. My mother was a teacher and when she got married, she stopped work. So, she [Mrs Braithwaite] working still was like I can't take care of my family."[27] Scholars have noted that as the twentieth century progressed, even men of the labouring classes started requesting that wives remain at home (Joseph 2021, 12). Among men there was social status to be accrued from the ability to provide for a wife. For instance, in Tobago, the 1921 census indicated that roughly fifteen hundred or 24 per cent of adult women were engaged in unwaged domestic work. However, by 1946, the census estimated that around 4,264 or 64 per cent of adult women reported that they did not work outside the home.[28] When we look at Trinidad, in 1921, more than eighty-five thousand or 62 per cent of women were gainfully occupied, compared to fifty-two thousand or 26 per cent by 1946.[29] While demographers offer many explanations for this trend, it was also clear that masculinity had become associated with the breadwinner role. The idea that men should bear sole economic responsibility for their families was also reflected in the work of Edith Clarke, who noted that in Jamaica during the mid-twentieth century, a man was expected to be able to take care of a wife and children before proposing marriage. To have a wife at home was cause for great boasting (Clarke 1958, 78). Thus, it was an insult to Mr Brathwaite's manhood and reputation for his wife to continue working.

Mr Brathwaite's remembrances of his mother's departure from the workforce after getting married during the early twentieth century was also accurate. Indeed, women teachers were often asked to resign from their duties after marrying or getting pregnant.[30] Ann-Marie Bissessar (1999), in her assessment of policies within the public service in Trinidad and Tobago, noted that "Before 1921, women who married were mandated to retire; a policy that was only amended in 1956, but still afforded the governor the right to force women to resign after marriage." Thus, Mr Brathwaite's request for his wife to remain at home was supported by the institutional practices of the day. However, such ideologies placed many women in an economically dependent and, therefore, vulnerable position.

According to Mrs Brathwaite, her husband's demonstrations of violence stemmed from financial struggles. She explained,

> Any time we didn't have money he used to be on edge. You can't talk to him. He used to fuss about everything. He used to be cussing in front the children and all of that. He used to drink and be drunk too. So, I used to answer him back and that used to escalate the situation. Yes, he hit me many times, but I used

> to fight back. We fight in the yard already. One time he choke me in the yard. Is the men out the road had to shout on him to stop. So, it was on both ends.[31]

For them, domestic conflict was primarily triggered by money issues. Certainly, scholars have long established the critical link between masculinity and the provision of economic resources. For instance, Otterbein (1965, 70) noted that many men believed that a woman's fidelity could only be ensured when her husband took care of her material needs. Similarly, Rosalind Miles contended that inadequate income or a shortage of money to meet the needs of his household made a man less sexually appealing to his spouse, and in turn, he deals with feelings of low self-worth, loneliness and "reduced sexual potency" (Miles 1992, 98). It was this frustration with oneself and one's financial circumstances that triggered acts of verbal and physical violence. However, Mrs Brathwaite made it clear that she was no passive victim. She responded to her husband's aggression by "fighting, cussing him back, pelting thing and one time, I run him down with boiling water".[32] Her decision to respond with violence was not unique. Danns and Parsad noted that more than 80 per cent of the Afro-Guyanese women in their study reacted to acts of IPV with physical violence (Danns and Parsard 1989). In her own analysis of their research, DeShong (2010, 32) noted that one of the clear findings was that "Black women find solace in their own strength through verbal and physical counteractions, telling their partners to leave the home or threatening to leave him."

Mrs Brathwaite suggested that her husband's rage was also fuelled by intoxication, which made him take on another character; one that she was not familiar with.[33] Other Trinbagonian women who experienced violence at the hands of their husbands also blamed excessive alcohol consumption and drunkenness as the main cause of violence in their homes.[34] One woman even explained why she became resigned to her husband's abuse when he came home drunk. She rationalized, "He used to drink and turn stupid. Rum is a spirit, you know. When they drunk, they take on a spirit. So, I know it wasn't he acting so. It was the spirit."[35] This decision to blame her husband's violence on spirit possession may have been a coping strategy due to her belief that, in his right mind, her husband would not treat her in such a violent manner.

When asked to reflect on his violent actions towards his wife, Mr Brathwaite expounded,

> She used to stress me out. I used to work very hard every day and that woman never contented. The money was never enough. It was pressure. She was a trouble woman. She used to want to argue with me, all the neighbours hearing she mouth like I is some little pickney. You have to put down your foot as a man. She used to want to disrespect me. All of them men did know how she hasty and how she used to carry on. They used to give me talks. Any time I don't have money I can't touch she when night-time come. That is my right! So, we used to real get away in them early days.[36]

He labelled his wife "a trouble woman", suggesting that she was problematic and, therefore, difficult to deal with. Mrs Brathwaite's alleged dissatisfaction with her husband's attempts to provide for the household was a bitter pill for him to swallow. Indeed, her expressions of discontent with what he was able to provide eroded his sense of worth and the foundation upon which his masculinity was built. According to him, much of his stress and anger stemmed from the fact that his wife was unappreciative. Her tendency to argue, especially so that neighbours could hear, was also deemed as a gross disrespect and an attempt to emasculate him. He, therefore, felt like he had no choice but to assert his masculinity through violence. Thus, "putting his foot down as a man" meant engaging in verbal and physical acts that triggered fear and, in some instances, inflicted injury on his wife. Fear of a man's rage was one of the common strategies used to assert control within the home and "secure men's status over women" (Yodanis 2004, 658).

Indeed, throughout the Caribbean, "violence [was/is] justified as a means of preserving and restoring masculine identity" (DeShong 2011, 80). Mr Brathwaite also pointed to the fact that other men knew of his wife's violent conduct and "disrespect" at home. This knowledge would have elicited jeers and constant statements such as, "Yuh wife wearing the pants in the house" or "Brathwaite, go home before yuh wife beat yuh".[37] In spaces of male socialization, such as the rum shop or 'block', Caribbean men seek the support and respect of other men in their peer group. Keith Nurse (2004) has also suggested that men live in "fear of being viewed as wimps" or being called a "soft man". Therefore, Mr Brathwaite's violent actions can also be viewed as an attempt to regain the respect and support of other men who had knowledge of his wife's fierce opposition to him within the household.

Moreover, he also indicated that his wife withheld intimacy from him although, according to him, "That is my right!". He pulled out biblical and cultural principles that, as a wife, Mrs Brathwaite was obligated to satisfy his sexual needs. He explained, "That is biblical law! A woman not supposed to refuse she husband."[38] Historically, women have been framed as being in service to their husbands and their property. As such, sexual services are also framed as marital duty. Therefore, according to Mr Brathwaite, he was justified in being angry with his wife when she refused to have sex with him. No consideration was given to his wife's own desires or emotions. Mrs Brathwaite, however, felt like she had a right to decide whether she wanted to engage in sexual activity. She explained, "After this man done cuss me whole day, he wants thing in the night. That man will harass yuh whole night and start to fuss and cuss and toss and turn and vex. Yuh can't say no to he and sleep. Sometimes when ah couldn't take it anymore, I just used to let him fix up."[39] Her testimony made it clear that she indeed withheld intimacy from her husband because of the verbal abuse she encountered throughout the day. For her, it was extremely insensitive and unfathomable that her husband could disrespect her in the crudest possible ways during the day, but expect love and affection at night. However, Mr Brathwaite was often intent on making sleep impossible for his wife, until she gave in. Thus, for this couple, acts of intimacy were often the result of harassment and coercion, and she felt robbed of her bodily autonomy.

In reflecting on how she coped with living in such a volatile home environment, she explained,

> A Pentecostal church opened in the area, and I started going. One time we fight, and I complained to the pastor, and he counselled me because I was ready to leave and go back to work . . . he told me I cannot divorce because it was not right in the eyes of God and that I shouldn't be cussing with him and that as a Christian, peace begins with me. So, I started to hold my mouth. I stop answer him back and sometime just ignore him. The pastor knew my husband and he said he not a hasty man so that I should try to do the right thing and we wouldn't have so many problems at home.[40]

The church community and a relationship with God were credited as the tools employed by Mrs Brathwaite to cope with her unpleasant experiences in the home. While she was ready to put an end to her marriage, her spiritual leader discouraged her from such an act that, according to him, was displeasing to God. In fact, in a broader social context, divorce was frowned upon during the early to mid-twentieth century. For many people, such a final step represented an unacceptable response to even the horrific physical, sexual and verbal abuse that many women experienced in their marriages. According to Mrs Brathwaite, "Pastor showed me scripture on how God is vexed by divorce. I couldn't bring that damnation on myself."[41] Divorce was framed as an indefensible act that would contradict her decision to identify as a Christian. Biblical verses were used to instil fear and her pastor failed to speak to her husband about his abusive ways. Rather, he counselled her into acceptance and silent suffering. He pulled out the biblical trope that, within her household, peace should begin with her. Thus, it should be her obligation to respond and act in ways that would maintain a sense of calm within her home. The responsibility was hers and not her husband's.

In reality, this meant not responding aggressively to verbal, sexual or physical abuse. In terms of encouraging Mrs Brathwaite to "do the right thing", the pastor instructed her to behave herself because, given his relationship with her husband, she had to be provoking him and stressing him out for him to respond in these violent ways. While divorce legislation was introduced in Trinidad and Tobago in 1931, very few couples had the material resources to engage in the process of getting a divorce. If we look at Tobago, for instance, at the 1960 census, only thirteen women were reported as divorced.[42]

When asked about resolutions he made that contributed to the survival of his marriage, Mr Brathwaite sat in quiet reflection for a long time. He then explained,

> I was around fifty-two when I started to go to church. That is when I get baptized and really change my life around. When I really think back on my younger days, I really shake my head when I remember how I used to carry on sometime. Yes, she was a trouble woman, but I regret the things I used to do. When I baptized, I ask she [Mrs Brathwaite] to forgive me and let we move forward. She said, okay, and I really start to try to control myself. You know, with age come reason and we had smooth sailing since that time.[43]

While he maintained that his wife was a 'trouble woman', he expressed regret about the way he had treated her in the past. Given that he only got baptized and decided to change his violent tendencies at fifty-two, Mrs Brathwaite would have endured about thirty-one years of violence. While she took ownership of her own violent behaviour, she admitted that she, like many women of her time, lived in darkness for many years and could not fathom that a better life – one free of violence – was possible. The fear of social consequences and the wrath of God resulted in her and other women being forced to contort themselves into unassertive, meekly obedient beings in the name of keeping the peace within their homes.

CONCLUSION

The uncensored testimonies of intense traumatic violence endured and perpetrated by women and men during their marriages expands our understanding of the painful circumstances that many suffered within their homes. Among wives, the testimonies highlighted brutal episodes of physical and verbal abuse, and coercive sexual encounters. Among men, however, the testimonies indicated an unshakable belief in their power over women, and their need to establish and re-establish their dominance within the domestic sphere through violence. Wives were labelled as cantankerous, disobedient, irrational and hasty. Thus, husbands needed to discipline them for their constant provocation and to restore traditional authority within the household. The discussions that these testimonies provoked also revealed that patriarchal gender ideologies embedded in the psyche of men and women, and supported by the social institutions of the day, normalized and justified violence against women. Taken together, these findings bear much similarity to the contemporary discourses regarding causes and justifications of violence in the Caribbean. Indeed, history helps us to better understand that today's complex gender relations, characterized by violence against women, has roots in our past. Many of the causes and justifications for violence against women today were also common in the early to mid-twentieth century. As such, men in Trinidad and Tobago and the wider Caribbean must be called upon to reconsider their conflict resolution strategies and reject violence as a means to express anger or maintain control.

NOTES

1. Mrs King, in discussion with the author, 18 January 2018.
2. ibid.
3. ibid.
4. The experiences of only two couples are discussed in this chapter due to word constraints. These testimonies were gathered as part of a broader doctoral thesis conducted by the author. Several couples whose marriages were characterized by violence were interviewed during the period 2016–2019. The experiences of the two couples in this chapter are representative of some of the general experiences of couples and, therefore, they provide a lens through which we can understand the causes of family violence and coping strategies employed by wives.
5. Also, see Karen Fog Olwig, "The Struggle for Respectability: Methodism and Afro-Caribbean Culture on Nineteenth Century Nevis," *Nieuwe West-Indische Gids/New West Indian Guide* 64, nos. 3–4 (1990).
6. See, for instance, Patricia Mohammed, *Gender Negotiations Among Indians in Trinidad, 1917–1947* (Hampshire: Palgrave Macmillan, 2002); Jeremy Poynting, "East Indian Women in The Caribbean: Experience, Image, and Voice," *Journal of South Asian Literature* 21, no. 1 (1986): 133–80. https://www.jstor.org/stable/40872844; Lomarsh Roopnarine, "Interview with Patricia Mohammed: The Status of Indo-Caribbean Women: From Indenture to the Contemporary Period," *Journal of International Women's Studies* 17, no. 3 (June 2016): 4–16. https://core.ac.uk/download/pdf/48836338.pdf; Sumita Chatterjee, "Indian Women's Lives and Labor: The Indentureship Experience in Trinidad and Guyana: 1845–1917" (PhD diss., University of Massachusetts Amherst, 1997); Harinder Singh Sohal, *The East Indian Indentureship System in Jamaica, 1845–1917,* (Ottawa: National Library of Canada, 1979); Lakshmi Mansingh and Ajai, "Indian Heritage in Jamaica," *Jamaica Journal* 10, nos. 2–4 (1976): 10–19; Verene Shepherd, "Transients to Citizens: The Development of Settled East Indian Community in Jamaica," *Jamaica Journal* 18, no. 3 (1985): 17–26.
7. Mr Brathwaite, in discussion with the author, 4 May 2019; Mr King, in discussion with the author, 18 January 2018.
8. ibid.
9. Mr King, in discussion with the author, 18 January 2018.
10. Mrs King, in discussion with the author, 18 January 2018.
11. ibid.
12. ibid.

13. Mr King, in discussion with the author, 18 January 2018.
14. Mrs King, in discussion with the author, 18 January 2018.
15. ibid.
16. Mr King, in discussion with the author, 18 January 2018.
17. Lord Shorty, "Sixteen Commandments," YouTube video, 3:55, https://www.youtube.com/watch?v=dg-SKQeuTrI.
18. Mr King, in discussion with the author, 18 January 2018.
19. Albert Paul and Kenneth James, in discussion with the author, 10 August 2019.
20. Albert Paul, in discussion with the author, 10 August 2019.
21. Mrs King, in discussion with the author, 18 January 2018.
22. ibid.
23. ibid.
24. ibid.
25. Mr King, in discussion with the author, 18 January 2018.
26. ibid.
27. Mr Brathwaite, in discussion with the author, 4 May 2019.
28. *Census of Trinidad and Tobago 1921*, 65; *Census of Trinidad and Tobago 1946* (West Indiana and Special Collections Division, Alma Jordan Library, University of the West Indies, St Augustine).
29. *Census of Trinidad and Tobago 1946*, Table 53.
30. Parthenope Nicholson, in discussion with the author, 19 August 2017.
31. Mrs Brathwaite, in discussion with the author, 4 May 2019.
32. ibid.
33. ibid.
34. Martha Edwards, in discussion with the author, 2 February 2018; Monica Campbell, in discussion with the author, 12 May 2018.
35. Monica Campbell, in discussion with the author, 12 May 2018.
36. Mr Brathwaite, in discussion with the author, 4 May 2019.
37. ibid.
38. ibid.
39. Mrs Brathwaite, in discussion with the author, 4 May 2019.
40. ibid.
41. ibid.
42. *1970 Population Census of the Commonwealth Caribbean – Volume 7: Race and Religion* (Kingston: University of the West Indies, Census Research Programme), 14; *Census of Trinidad and Tobago 1931* (Port of Spain: Registrar-General's Office, 1932), 10.

43. Mr Brathwaite, in discussion with the author, 4 May 2019.

REFERENCES

INTERVIEWS

Mrs King, in discussion with the author, 18 January 2018.
Mr King, in discussion with the author, 18 January 2018.
Albert Paul, in discussion with the author, 10 August 2019.
Kenneth James, in discussion with the author, 10 August 2019.
Parthenope Nicholson, in discussion with the author, 19 August 2017.
Martha Edwards, in discussion with the author, 2 February 2018.
Monica Campbell, in discussion with the author, 12 May 2018.

SECONDARY SOURCES

Ali, Shameen. 1993. "Social History of East Indian Women in Trinidad since 1870." MPhil diss., University of the West Indies, St Augustine.

Beckles, Hilary. 2004. "Black Masculinity in Caribbean Slavery." In *Interrogating Caribbean Masculinities: Theoretical and Empirical Analyses*, edited by Rhoda Reddock, 225–43. Kingston: University of the West Indies Press.

Bissessar, Ann-Marie. 1999. "Determinants of Gender Mobility in the Public Service of Trinidad and Tobago." *Public Personnel Management* 28 (3): 409–23.

Bloomstein, Muriel. 2011. "The Victorian Gender Ideology and Women in the British Caribbean in the Post-Emancipation Era." *History in Action* 2 (1): 1–6. https://journals.sta.uwi.edu/hia/index.asp?action=viewPastArticle&issueId=164&articleId=1118&galleyId=994.

British Government. 1923. *Census of the Colony of Trinidad and Tobago 1921*. Port of Spain: Government Printing Office. West Indiana and Special Collections Division, Alma Jordan Library, University of the West Indies, St Augustine.

———. 1947. *Census of the Colony of Trinidad and Tobago 1946*. Port of Spain: Government Printing Office. West Indiana and Special Collections Division, Alma Jordan Library, University of the West Indies, St Augustine.

Browne, Randy. 2017. *Surviving Slavery in the British Caribbean*. Philadelphia: University of Pennsylvania Press.

Chamberlain, Mary. 2002. "Small Worlds: Childhood and Empire." *Journal of Family*

History 27 (2): 186–200. doi:10.1177/036319900202700207.

———. 2006. *Family Love in the Diaspora: Migration and the Anglo-Caribbean Experience.* Kingston: Ian Randle Publishers.

———. 2021. "Gender and Memory: Oral History and Women's History." In *Methodologies in Caribbean Research on Gender and* Sexuality, edited by Kamala Kempadoo and Halimah DeShong, 41–59. Kingston: Ian Randle Publishers.

Chatterjee, Sumita. 1997. "Indian Women's Lives and Labor: The Indentureship Experience in Trinidad and Guyana: 1845–1917." PhD diss., University of Massachusetts Amherst. https://ezproxy.sastudents.uwi.tt/login?url=https://www.proquest.com/dissertations-theses/indian-womens-lives-labor-indentureship/docview/304357034/se-2.

Clarke, Edith. 1957. *My Mother who Fathered Me.* London: Allen and Unwin.

Cole, A.L., and J.G. Knowles. 2016. *Lives in Context: The Art of Life History Research.* Oxford and Lanham: AltaMira/Rowman and Littlefield.

Coppin, Addington. 2000. "Insights into the Work and Family Lives of Afro-Caribbean Men." *Review of Black Political Economy* 27 (4): 65–86.

Craig-James, Susan. 2008. *The Changing Society of Tobago, 1838–1938: A Fractured Whole, Vols. I and II.* Arima: Cornerstone Press.

Danns, George K., and Basmat Shiw Parsad. 1989. *Domestic Violence and Marital Relationships in the Caribbean: A Guyana Case Study.* Georgetown:University of Guyana.

De Barros, Juanita. 2014. *Reproducing the British Caribbean: Sex, Gender, and Population Politics after Slavery.* Chapel Hill: University of North Carolina Press.

DeShong, Halimah. 2011. "Gender, Sexuality and Sexual Violence: A Feminist Analysis of Vincentian Women's Experiences in Violent Heterosexual Relationships." *Journal of Eastern Caribbean Studies* 36 (2): 63–96.

———. 2010. "Gendered Negotiations: Interrogating Discourses of Intimate Partner Violence." PhD diss., University of Manchester.

Holmes, Andrew Gary Darwin. 2020. "Researcher Positionality– A Consideration of Its Influence and Place in Qualitative Research: A New Researcher Guide." *Shanlax International Journal of Education* 8 (4): 1–10.

Joseph, O'Neil. 2021. "Surviving Home: Womanhood, Contentious Intimacy and the Trauma of Home in Tobago, 1900–1960." *Women's History Review* 31 (5): 805–25.doi: 10.1080/09612025.2021.1999567.

Miles, Rosalind. 1992. *The Rites of Man.* London: Paladin.

Mohammed, Patricia. 2002. *Gender Negotiations Among Indians in Trinidad, 1917–1947.* Hampshire: Palgrave Macmillan.

———. 2004. "Unmasking Masculinity and Deconstructing Patriarchy: Problems and Possibilities within Feminist Epistemology." In *Interrogating Caribbean Masculinities: Theoretical and Empirical Analyses*, edited by Rhoda Reddock, 38–67. Kingston: University of the West Indies Press.

Moore, Brian, and Michele Johnson. 2004. *Neither Led nor Driven: Contesting British Cultural Imperialism in Jamaica, 1865–1920*. Kingston: University of the West Indies Press.

Nurse, Keith. 2004. "Masculinities in Transition: Gender and the Global Problematique." In *Interrogation Caribbean Masculinities: Theoretical and Empirical Analyses*, edited by Rhoda Reddock, 3–37. Kingston: University of the West Indies Press.

Olwig, Karen Fog. 1990. "The Struggle for Respectability: Methodism and Afro-Caribbean Culture on Nineteenth Century Nevis." *Nieuwe West-Indische Gids/New West Indian Guide* 64 (3–4): 93–114. https://www.jstor.org/stable/24027219?seq=1.

Otterbein, Keith F. 1965. "Caribbean Family Organization: A Comparative Analysis." *American Anthropologist* 67 (1): 66–79. www.jstor.org/stable/668656.

———. 1966. *The Andros Islanders*. Lawrence: University of Kansas Press.

Pemberton, Rita. 1998. "In the Eyes of a Missionary: Tobago, 1909–1940." Paper presented at Tobago and Trinidad: One Hundred Years Together conference, University of the West Indies, St Augustine, 16–18 October.

Poynting, Jeremy. 1875. "East Indian Women in The Caribbean: Experience, Image, and Voice." *Journal of South Asian Literature* 21 (1): 133–80. https://www.jstor.org/stable/40872844.

Putnam, Lara. 2014. "Global Child-saving, Transatlantic Maternalism, and the Pathologization of Caribbean Childhood, 1930s–1940s." *Atlantic Studies* 11 (4): 491–514.http://dscholarship-dev.lib.

Reddock, Rhoda. 1994. *Women, Labour and Politics in Trinidad and Tobago*. London: Zed Books.

Roopnarine, Lomarsh. 2016. "Interview with Patricia Mohammed: The Status of Indo-Caribbean Women: From Indenture to the Contemporary Period." *Journal of International Women's Studies* 17 (3): 4–16. https://core.ac.uk/download/pdf/48836338.pdf.

Wilson, Peter. 2001. "Reputation and Respectability: A Suggestion for Caribbean Ethnology." In *Caribbean Sociology-Introductory Readings*, edited by Christine Barrow and Rhoda Reddock, 338–49. Kingston: Ian Randle Publishers.

Yodanis, Carrie L. 2004. "Gender Inequality, Violence Against Women, and Fear: A Cross-National Test of the Feminist Theory of Violence Against Women."

Journal of Interpersonal Violence 19 (6): 655–75.

University of the West Indies. 1973. *1970 Population Census of the Commonwealth Caribbean, Volume 7: Race and Religion*. Kingston: University of the West Indies, Census Research Programme.

chapter 11

Paying It Forward

Discrimination and Stigma as a Causal Factor of IPV in LBTQ Relationships in the Caribbean

Jennan Paige Andrew

Like many other regions whose histories are riddled with colonization, genocide, forced labour and the fight for independence, the Caribbean's backstory is a tale of violence. Consequently, Caribbean people – regardless of their biological sex, gender identity or sexual orientation – are products of a society which, despite all its multilingual and multicultural beauty, was built on and fortified with all manner of institutional and interpersonal violence. Brereton details this well in a 2010 article, sharing how the recorded history of the Caribbean is one of sustained systemic violence, coerced labour and social control, and makes the argument that "by the end of the nineteenth century a culture of violence certainly had been established in the Caribbean colonies" (Brereton 2010, 2). In contemporary Caribbean society, violence has been accepted as a means of establishing and keeping power, and a way to control behaviour, and to express frustration or discontent. In many cases, as seen historically in the Caribbean, violence has been used by the powerful to enforce and exercise control over the powerless; conversely, it has also been used by the powerless as a means of resistance (Bernard and O'Neill 2020, 701).

One such marginalized group in Caribbean society is the lesbian, gay, bisexual, transgender and queer (LGBTQ+) community (Human Rights

Watch 2014, 10–26; 2017, 28–37). While the members are not homogeneous, and their lived realities differ, based on the laws and social norms of the various Caribbean territories, much of the documented history of LBTQ+ people in the region has been one of violence. This has taken the form of discrimination and stigma, which they face in public and private spheres, and are often the result of homophobia, transphobia or queerphobia, which has historically impacted their rights to safety, employment, healthcare and happiness (Outright International 2022).

While much has been written about the high levels of violence meted out to members of the LGBTQ+ community in the Caribbean, little research has been done on violence perpetrated *within* the community, especially intimate partner violence. IPV is defined as any type of physical or sexual violence, controlling behaviour, or emotional and psychological abuse between a couple (World Health Organization 2012). While it can affect anyone, regardless of their sexual orientation or gender identity, it is still seen by many as an issue exclusive to heterosexual relationships (Rollè et al. 2018, 1). This lack of knowledge about IPV in LGBTQ+ relationships globally has implications for members of the community being able to recognize it, and the creation of effective prevention and interventions for both survivors and perpetrators. Knowledge of the impact that contextual factors such as homophobic and transphobic violence may have on the occurrence of IPV in LGBTQ+ relationships is important, as this informs the work of state agencies and other organizations working toward effective and sustainable prevention and intervention (Hatcher et al. 2013, 10; Ogum et al. 2018, 13–14).

In recent years, research around the topic has grown, indicating that the incidence of IPV among LGBTQ+ couples is comparable to that of heterosexuals (Lewis, Milletich, Kelley, and Woody 2012, 247–56), and prevalence rates among lesbian and bisexual women are higher than among gay and bisexual men (Walters, Chen, and Breiding 2013, 17–27). LBT women have been traditionally doubly marginalized by virtue of their status as women, and silenced within the wider LGBTQ+ community (Wilton 2002), which has been dominated by gay men. Additionally, few studies have examined IPV among queer,[1] trans, gender non-conforming (GNC)[2] and gender non-binary[3] people (Shields 2018, 3). In an effort to amplify the voices of these silenced groups, this chapter focuses on the experiences of lesbian, bisexual, trans and queer (LBTQ) people with IPV.

This chapter expands completed research on IPV in LBTQ relationships in Jamaica (Andrew 2020). In order to gain further insight into the ways that LBTQ people in the Caribbean[4] perceive and experience IPV, I interviewed twelve members of the community[5] from two Caribbean countries – Jamaica, and Trinidad and Tobago – to unearth a clearer understanding of IPV in their relationships, and the factors that led to it from the 1980s to the present day. Based on the interviews, a major factor that seems to impact IPV perpetration within LBTQ relationships is homophobic and transphobic violence, which presents as high levels of societal discrimination and stigma against LBTQ people in the Caribbean. For them, this violence – that is, discrimination and stigma – is perpetrated by institutions, such as the state and religious bodies, as well as individuals. Across territories this violence has taken the form of anti-LBTQ legislation; a lack of legal protections; homophobic and transphobic statements by religious and political leaders; and physical, mental, verbal and emotional abuse towards them in public and private spaces. During the interviews, many participants explained that violence towards LBTQ people in the Caribbean results in deep, unresolved trauma, extreme frustration and altered perceptions of self, which have significant impacts on their intimate relationships. The interviews also shed light on how this violence contributes significantly to internalized homophobia, as LBTQ people internalize negative messages perpetuated in society about the community and are likely to subsequently displace these feelings on to fellow members, including intimate partners.

Additionally, participants disclosed that the external pressure placed on LBTQ people, who are forced to hide their sexual orientation or gender identity for protection in a heteronormative society, leads to intimate spaces that are invisible and secretive, creating a solid barrier against help-seeking for both victims and perpetrators of IPV. Participant interviews clearly show how the high levels of violence perpetrated towards LBTQ people in the Caribbean breed unhealthy spaces where IPV thrives. In this way, the violence meted out to them by institutions and individuals within the Caribbean context is 'paid forward' through an expression of violence within their relationships.

The data that frames and grounds this chapter was collected using a qualitative methodological approach through semi-structured interviews[6] with nine Jamaicans in July and August 2019, and three Trinidadians in June 2022. This chapter centres the voices of Caribbean LBTQ people to discuss how the historical normalization of violence within Jamaica and Trinidad and Tobago grounds and intersects with the violence meted out to members of the LBTQ community in these territories, and contributes significantly to the perpetration of violence in their intimate relationships. This is seen primarily through the ways that minority stress and disempowerment, as well as internalized homophobia, increase the likelihood of IPV perpetration in LBTQ relationships. This chapter also explores the ways that violence, in the form of discrimination and stigma, acts as a significant barrier to help-seeking for LBTQ survivors of IPV.

SETTING THE CONTEXT: THE LBTQ LIVED EXPERIENCE IN THE CARIBBEAN

In most countries in the Anglophone Caribbean region, same-sex intimacy between men is criminalized. Whether through buggery or gross indecency laws, most countries prohibit same-sex relations between consenting persons (Outright International 2022). While in most territories the criminalized act is anal intercourse and not homosexuality, the general public perception is that any form of intimacy among LGBTQ+ people is illegal and immoral (J-FLAG 2013, 1). In some cases, these sentiments are upheld on a moralistic basis by the church, which plays an important role in social welfare and community building in most territories (Human Rights Watch 2017, 34).

Despite the fact that most of these laws are not enforced, by singling out one marginalized group, they legitimize and pave the way for social and legal discrimination, and stigma against members of the population (Human Rights Watch 2017, 1). In most Caribbean territories, no laws explicitly protect LBTQ+ citizens from hate crimes or discrimination (Outright International 2022). As a result, high levels of homophobia and transphobia persist, impacting the lives of LBTQ+ people (Boxill et al. 2011, 6; Human Rights Watch 2017, 3).

In recent years, countries like Barbados and Belize have overturned colonial age laws and the community has experienced greater social acceptance

(Outright International 2022). In Jamaica, there has also been progress with several incident-free stagings of Pride celebrations (Faber 2018). Nevertheless, the public perception of LBTQ people, combined with the lack of protection by the state, facilitates high levels of discrimination and stigma perpetrated toward the community.

THE CARIBBEAN'S CULTURE OF VIOLENCE

In order to better understand the lived experiences of LBTQ+ folks with IPV, I interviewed participants from Jamaica and Trinidad and Tobago on what their experiences with the phenomenon had been. In order to understand the historical underpinnings of their experiences, I spoke with participants who were actively involved[7] in their respective LBTQ communities in the 1980s, as well as younger participants who were active members of their communities in 2019 at the time of the interviews. A common thread throughout the accounts of those who had been involved in the community in the 1980s was the normalization and acceptance of violence in the Caribbean at the time, and the connections between this and IPV perpetration in relationships. That this narrative was not mentioned by the younger participants may not be indicative of a change in the normalization or acceptance of violence in contemporary Caribbean society, but more so an indication of progress in how violence, especially domestic abuse and IPV, is understood today. This inference is reflected in research completed by Pierotti (2013, 260).

Research by the Centers for Disease Control and Prevention (2018) asserts that one of the strongest predictors of IPV perpetration is an individual's past experiences with physical and psychological abuse and violence. In a 2021 article, Professor Andrea Allen, reflecting on her work on IPV in Brazil's LGBTQ community, remarks that while we typically think of violence as a product of masculinity, it is more a human enterprise shaped by the histories of people and places. In this way, histories influence how people think about violence. Sania, a LBTQ+ rights advocate who was born in Trinidad and Tobago in the 1960s, shares:

> I think who we are in this country is grounded in violence and trauma, coming out of colonial days and this whole notion that you had to hit your children for discipline and that women were property and if you're in a relationship it's

> okay to hit. As women got more progressive in the Seventies, Eighties, I think women maybe became more abusive, maybe verbally abusive, and well, women had been abusive to their children with licks [spanking], but I think it was historically normal to hit, that was a way a man showed he loved his woman.[8]

Sania's sentiments explain how, for many who lived in the Caribbean in the 1980s, violence was a part of daily life and ever-present in the relationships around them. This pervasive violence was, of course, historical and ancestral. Whipping of enslaved people and indentured workers was used as a means of control throughout the systems of enslavement and indentureship (Brereton 2010, 3–8). Even after these systems had been abolished, colonialism remained, and official violence, perpetrated by the state on individuals through policemen and troops, was not a rare occurrence. As many Caribbean territories became independent in the 1960s and 1970s, violence continued to be heavily ingrained as a way of life. Violence was present in romantic, familial and platonic relationships, as well as between individuals and the state as a means of punishment and control (Brereton 2010, 8).

Many participants shared that, in the 1980s, people were a lot less critical of violence between each other. Frances shares the following:

> In Caribbean countries, in families and communities, back in the Eighties, children saw and experienced violence through "licks". Discipline and trying to correct any sort of behaviour or any sort of attitude was with what we term today violence. In the Eighties, that's what we knew and the world was going through a very turbulent time. In the Seventies we had [the] Black Power [Movement][9] here . . . we remember the gunshots . . . and then 1990 [the coup][10] . . . more gunshots and there is a recognition there, even if it may be unconscious, that the way to get what you want sometimes is with violence. Mediation wasn't something used in the family or community setting. Violence was how we learned to deal with things.

Frances' quote explains the pervasive nature of physical and psychological violence in Trinidadian society in the 1980s and the attitude people may have developed toward using violence as a means of control. Similarly, Brereton (2010, 8) discusses the acceptance of violence in different types of relationships, including intimate ones. Wife beating, as she refers to it, happened in public spaces in an almost performative way and was a norm that went unchallenged (p.11). Most instances of IPV were not seen as a space for intervention, but rather a private issue. The article echoes much of the sentiment mentioned by interview participants. Ava, a media professional who was born in Trinidad in the late 1960s, shares that occurrences of IPV at that time were seen as "married people's business,"[11] and Sania shares that, though at the time she did not have the language to describe it, IPV was a normalized part of life: "We would have grown up in these violent households [with] a lot of verbal abuse and then you might have seen hitting in your family with your parents and you would have gotten licks like there was no tomorrow.[12] We used to get serious licks and your parents would tell you they beating you cause they love you. My mother used to say she was beating the devil out of me."

For most people growing up in Caribbean society in the 1960s, violence was a normal part of relationships, including romantic ones. As members of society, LBTQ people would have, therefore, been very likely to also normalize violence within their relationships. Sania shares: "In Trinidad, regardless of your orientation, you were still a microcosm of, you were still raised in [the same society] so unless there was a conscious effort or decision, or tools and mechanisms provided, you will just continue the same cycle of your parents regardless of your orientation. It didn't make no difference . . . if you don't know what a healthy relationship looks like, how do you model and fashion that?"

As shared by Sania, like other citizens, LBTQ people born and socialized in the region would have also undoubtedly adopted this acceptance and normalization of violence. Further research has shown the connection between this normalization of violence as a part of life and the acceptance of IPV in romantic relationships (Lacey, Jeremiah, and West 2019, 3). This was also seen in the interviews, as participants spoke openly about the clear connection between experiencing violence while growing up and the acceptance of IPV as a norm within LBTQ intimate relationships. Aforementioned research on the predictors of IPV perpetration asserts that past experiences with abuse and violence increase the likelihood of IPV perpetration (CDC 2018). For LBTQ people in the Caribbean in the 1960s, it is highly likely that IPV was seen as a normal part of a relationship. This, in turn, would have significant implications for the prevalence of IPV, the recognition of it as something unhealthy within a relationship, and consequently, for help-seeking behaviour among survivors and perpetrators.

IPV IN THE LBTQ COMMUNITY IN THE CARIBBEAN

With the rise of women's groups globally and in the Caribbean in the mid-twentieth century, discourse around gender-based violence (GBV), Violence Against Women and Girls (VAWG) and violence within relationships increased (Gibbons 2015, 5). Research on the prevalence of IPV in relationships – and later, educational material aimed at helping survivors identify IPV within their relationships – also increased (Gibbons 2015, 6). However, the educational campaigns developed in the Caribbean region have mirrored those globally which have primarily targeted cisgender, heterosexual people, as IPV has been thought of as a heterosexual issue (Rollé et. al 2018, 2). In doing so, much of the discourse around GBV and VAWG have ignored, invisibilized and silenced LBTQ folks who continue to experience IPV in their relationships (Rollé et al. 2018, 3). It is within this historical 'culture of violence' and contemporary culture of invisibility that many LBTQ people may have continued experiencing and perpetrating IPV within their relationships.

Apart from increasing the acceptance and perpetration of violence in intimate relationships in the Caribbean, the historical normalization of violence may have also created space for the acceptance of it towards the marginalized, such as LBTQ people. While violence within Caribbean territories was in some cases gendered, Brereton (2010, 5–9) writes about it being perpetrated by men towards women, by men towards other men, by women towards children, and by the state towards individuals. In this way, violence was often used as a means of controlling individuals with less power, and is best explained by hooks (2000, 585) as an occurrence within "which a person uses coercive measures to control a less powerful individual". Much of the discrimination, stigma and violence perpetrated on LBTQ people globally is carried out and condoned as a means of control of a group that does not conform (Jackman 2017, 92; European Institute for Gender Equality 2006). The lack of legal protection by the state and the existence of discriminatory laws across Caribbean territories, along with countless instances of verbal, physical and emotional abuse that LBTQ people face in public and private spaces, can all be seen as violence being used as a means of control. These interactions have had significant negative impacts on the lives of LBTQ people in the region (Outright International 2022; Human Rights Watch 2017, 3), contributing greatly to experiences of minority stress, disempowerment and internalized homophobia, all recorded factors that increase the likelihood of IPV in their relationships (Rollé et Al. 2018, 4–5).

The following sections within this chapter will use participant interviews and existing literature to explore the ways that violence, through high levels of discrimination and stigma perpetrated on LBTQ people in the Caribbean, is *paid forward* through the perpetration of IPV in their relationships.

MINORITY STRESS

Research shows that when compared to their heterosexual counterparts, LBTQ people face unique stressors (Perales and Todd 2018, 190). In some cases, the source of these stressors may be violence, harassment or abuse due to their sexual orientation or gender identity, or the concealment of such in spaces deemed unsafe to 'come out'[13] (Balsam and Szymanski 2002, 258–59). Research posits that these stressors, known as minority stress, increase the likelihood of IPV perpetration within LBTQ relationships (Rollé et al. 2018, 4–5). LBTQ people in the Caribbean region undoubtedly face external and internal stressors due to high levels of well-documented cases of discrimination and stigma (Human Rights Watch 2014, 21–26; 2017, 3). This connection between minority stress and IPV perpetration was apparent during interviews with participants.

Jackie, a Jamaican university graduate who identified as bisexual, explained the effect that experiencing daily discrimination has on navigating relationships: "It can impact how you see yourself, how you receive love, how you perceive relationships, especially if you have been victim to violence and harassment within the communities where you live. I imagine that can impact how you value yourself and how you want others to value you."[14]

Alicia, a mental health advocate from Jamaica, agreed with Jackie and shared the following:

> Because of all of the things you have to deal with, with identifying as LGBT, some of it stems from childhood trauma, some from being outed[15] by friends

> and family members. And as simple as those things are, that's an invasion of trust and care, it's almost like being segregated in a sense and really because our general society isn't socialized to be understanding and appreciative of people that come out as LGBT . . . when someone has had those feelings infringed on and it's not resolved properly...we get to a place where we have a large space filled with a lot of hurting people, and a lot of hurting people will continue to hurt each other.[16]

Alicia explained how high levels of stress due to discrimination may not only affect how LBTQ people navigate relationships, but also increase the likelihood that they enter relationships carrying personal trauma. As discussed in the literature, this high level of stress and trauma experienced by LBTQ people may increase the occurrence of IPV in their relationships.

Frances, a human rights activist from Trinidad and Tobago who was born in the 1960s, echoes a similar sentiment to Alicia, explaining that members of the community are often hurt, traumatized and have unresolved issues: "Things are not healthy around people and sadly and unfortunately, that unhealthiness manifests in a particular way, which is violence of some type. Hurt people hurt people." She explained that when this intersects with growing up in a society where it is normal to use violence when one feels challenged, it could lead to IPV: "The stressors outside of the relationship impact the relationship and since all they know of how to deal with the discord in the relationship is violence, it is going to happen."

Sania, a LGBT rights advocate from Trinidad and Tobago, who was born in the 1960s, explains:

> When you feel powerless or disempowered and you go to a job where you can't be yourself, or you get heckled in the road, who yuh go take it out on?[17] And if your relationship is already not healthy and you don't have the communication skills, you take it out on them. Because you have to deal with all the shit that comes with being gay in Trinidad and Tobago, and even not being able to be [openly gay] . . . when they make the "bullerman"[18] jokes and the *zami*[19] jokes around you, especially if people know or suspect and they say these things and you can't do anything because you don't want to lose your job. Or you sit in a taxi and have to listen to that. Who are you going to take it out on? The person you live with.

Sania's thoughts illustrate how experiencing daily discrimination and stigma in public spaces, such as the workplace, rids LBTQ people of their autonomy or power outside of their relationships. In some cases, this may result in some people exerting excessive dominance in the form of violence within their intimate relationships. Tracy, a young bisexual woman from Jamaica, shares similar sentiments: "If, for example, you don't feel like you are in control of other things in your life, it may trickle down into you wanting to control your partner. So, people who don't have power in other spaces exert their power in intimate spaces because it's easier." Frances suggests that this was a feeling that many LBTQ people struggle with: "In our community we don't feel okay. We want to have power to feel okay and this often leads to [people] trying to gain power through violence."

The feelings described by Frances, Tracy and Sania can be explained by exploring the disempowerment theory (McKenry et al. 2006, 239), which examines IPV from the perspective of the perpetrator. The theory suggests that people who feel inadequate are likely to use alternative means of assertion, including violence, in order to reclaim power. In contexts such as the Caribbean, where LBTQ people are likely to be disempowered due to widespread daily discrimination and stress, this disempowerment may increase the likelihood of IPV perpetration within intimate relationships (Archer 1994).

While many participants spoke of the impact that minority stress and feelings of disempowerment may have on their intimate relationships, the impact was especially noticeable in discussions about IPV within the trans community. Sonia, a trans woman and Jamaican makeup artist who, at time of interview, was in an abusive relationship, felt that trans people, "[have] been under a shadow for so long, so the very moment that we get upset we belch it out and we don't business[20] what the outcome may be".[21] For her, trans women were more likely to experience the effects of minority stress due to their marginal status within an already marginalized community, and may also be more likely to experience IPV in their relationships than their cisgender counterparts.

Research conducted by the Canadian National Centre for Suicide Prevention (2018) supports Sonia's argument. It explains that when compared to cisgender lesbian and bisexual women, trans women often experience differing stress levels due to gender dysphoria.[22] For many trans people, the daily stress of hiding their gender identity to avoid discrimination within private and public spaces can cause severe, suppressed individual frustrations, which may increase the likelihood of IPV occurrence in their intimate relationships.

A clear connection between minority stress and IPV perpetration within LBTQ relationships is evident in the literature and supported by the experiences of participants. This connection has significant implications within the Caribbean context as discrimination and stigmatization of the LBTQ community remain prevalent (Outright International 2022), thereby increasing the likelihood of high levels of minority stress among members, which, in turn, increases the possibility of IPV in intimate relationships.

NEGATIVE PERCEPTIONS OF LBTQ PEOPLE AS A BARRIER TO HELP SEEKING

Discrimination and stigmatization of LBTQ people in the Caribbean often make their way out of homes and churches and into public and private institutions. In many cases this creates hostile spaces within which LBTQ people fear being 'outed' or treated differently on the basis of their sexual orientation or gender identity. Sania and Ava, both part of the LBTQ community in Trinidad and Tobago, reflect on how this impacted their fellow members in the 1980s. Telling the story of the many stressors they faced, especially those who were closeted, Sania explained that back then, "There were no mechanisms for support. Everyone is in therapy nowadays but what therapy was available back in the 80s for queer folk?" Ava agreed and mentioned that not only was there a lack of LBTQ-friendly psychologists then, but many could not afford it. There was no protection if someone disclosed their sexual orientation at work, or if they were experiencing violence at the hands of a partner, they could not seek help through an employee assistance programme. Not only would this have impacted survivors and victims of IPV, but also perpetrators, who could not easily seek emotional and mental support through therapy.

For LBTQ individuals today who may be experiencing IPV, attempting to access support remains a challenge. As A.J., a gender non-binary Jamaican who works with the LGBTQ+ community, explained: "We don't think that we have the power to access services to report or talk about these things [. . .] we already have that shame of being queer, to access services it's like, What's the point? This person is gonna see me as gay or trans and this is what they're going to see anyway."[23]

While some of these feelings may be just perception, they are not unfounded. Many LBTQ people in the Caribbean have experienced discrimination and stigma when seeking services from mental health facilities, reporting instances of abuse at police stations, and asking family and friends for help (Andrew 2020, 112; Human Rights Watch 2014, 26–37). Frances, a longtime Caribbean human rights advocate, shared that during the 2022 Pride celebrations in Trinidad and Tobago, there was a lot of homophobic abuse online toward the LGBTQ+ community from the general public, and lamented that if one of them was in an abusive relationship and saw these comments about the community, many would think that there was no safe space for support. Some participants spoke specifically about their hesitation around reporting IPV to the police. Tia, a lesbian and women's rights advocate in Jamaica, explained: "I don't know if women are willing to seek help from the constabulary force or security forces in these situations. [It is] highly unlikely, next thing you go and them a look you.[24] I'm being abused in one area and trying to seek help, and being re-victimized."[25]

Research has shown that the prevalence of IPV in LBTQ relationships is just as high as heterosexual relationships (Rollè et al. 2018, 1). However, in the Caribbean, as IPV has been traditionally understood as the perpetration of violence towards women by men, policies, education and sensitization training have followed this narrative, and have thus invisibilized IPV in LBTQ relationships (McLaughlin and Rozee 2001). IPV service providers, such as members of the medical and justice system, may, therefore, in many cases, not be trained to respond to IPV in LBTQ relationships. This is evidenced by many documented cases of the police and medical service providers responding negatively to LBTQ IPV victims and survivors when they seek help (Calton, Cattaneo, and Gebhard 2016, 585–600; Human Rights Watch 2014, 26–37). A lack of trained, informed service providers is a major barrier to help-seeking for LBTQ people (Calton, Cattaneo, and Gebhard 2016, 585–600). As many LBTQ people may not be able to seek help from family and friends due to homophobia or transphobia, they may rely on public and private medical or judicial systems to support them.

It is important to note that experiencing discrimination and stigmatization at the hands of IPV service providers may not only impact LBTQ victims and survivors' willingness to report instances of abuse to the police or seek psychosocial help, but also may act as a barrier to leaving abusive relationships. Jackie, who has experience working with the LBTQ community in Jamaica, explained that:

> Reporting isn't something that we feel that we can do because we feel that if we go to the authorities, if you're a woman or part of the LGBT community, reporting violence is not taken seriously, reporting any sort of abuse is not taken seriously. You're automatically blamed for it, or it just goes nowhere, and I think sometimes having that knowledge, you almost don't feel like fighting it again, and that can cause you to stay [in the relationship]. You feel like you have no other out, so [you] might as well stay.

Jackie's story gives insight into the impact that negative experiences with police officers may have on LBTQ people's willingness to leave abusive relationships. Participant interviews show that LBTQ victims of IPV face fear and hesitancy when seeking support services due to expectant and experienced discrimination that members of the community face from service providers who have negative perceptions of them.

Through data from participant interviews and a review of the relevant literature, this chapter has explored the ways that violence towards the LBTQ community is *paid forward* by significantly increasing the likelihood of partner violence within their intimate relationships.

Both participant interviews and the literature illustrate the ways that this systemic discrimination and stigmatization negatively impacts LBTQ people in the Caribbean, leading to high levels of stress, internalized homophobia and disempowerment, which not only increase the likelihood of IPV in their relationships, but enable the ignorance and acceptance of it. The chapter has also examined the ways that discrimination and stigma create significant barriers to help-seeking for LBTQ people impacted by IPV.

LBTQ citizens are entitled to safety and protection. Without adequate legal protection from societal discrimination and stigma, and investment in initiatives that will facilitate socio-cultural shifts in public narratives about LBTQ people, high levels of discrimination and stigma will remain a norm in the region (McFee and Galbraith 2016). So, too, will high levels of minority stress and internalized homophobia, which further complicate a public health issue that significantly affects the LBTQ community.

There can be no one-size-fits-all approach to curbing IPV within the region. Preventative and intervention efforts towards curbing rates of IPV within the LBTQ community must consider the direct effects that navigating a discriminatory society may have on IPV perpetration within LBTQ relationships. With this in mind, aside from necessary legal and cultural shifts, organizations working with and for LBTQ people can consider providing mental health services through free or low-cost support groups facilitated by trained professionals to tackle issues such as minority stress and internalized homophobia within the LBTQ community. As mental health services tend to be expensive, organizations can also explore the creation of spaces where LBTQ people may also access free or low-cost alternative/non-traditional methods of healing to recover from high levels of stress and disempowerment that arise from navigating homophobic and transphobic societies. While the history of many Caribbean countries is a tale of violence, control and a lack of protection for those most vulnerable, it is in the interest of all Caribbean citizens to ensure that our future narrative is a different story.

NOTES

1. People who identify as queer often challenge heteronormative social norms concerning gender and sexuality (Human Rights Campaign 2020). For the purposes of this chapter, the term queer will be used when referring to and relating experiences of participants who identify as gender non-binary, gender non-conforming (GNC) or queer.
2. People who do not follow normalized ideas or stereotypes about how they should look or act based on the sex they were assigned at birth (Human Rights Campaign 2020).
3. The word non-binary describes a wide array of different identities which fall outside of the gender binary, and can be related to, or completely separate from male and female gender identities (Human Rights Campaign 2020).

4. While the word Caribbean is used throughout this chapter, the data collected only reflects experiences of LBTQ people from two English-speaking Caribbean territories – Jamaica, and Trinidad and Tobago. Additionally, all of the historical and legal narratives focus on those countries in the English-speaking Caribbean.
5. All names referenced within this chapter have been changed to protect participants' identity. The pseudonyms used have no association with the participants.
6. Participants interviewed in 2022 granted permission for the data collected to be used for publication. Participants interviewed in 2019 granted permission for use in a research publication rather than one sold for profit. All participants were compensated financially for their time and all identifying data has been destroyed.
7. Actively involved was defined by active participation in community events, such as parties, and active engagement of other members of the community in platonic and romantic relationships.
8. Interview with Sania, 30 June 2022.
9. The Black Power Revolution of 1970 was a movement by individuals and organizations in Trinidad and Tobago to effect social and political change.
10. The coup was an attempt by the Jamaat al Muslimeen to overthrow the government of Trinidad and Tobago in July 1990.
11. Interview with Ava, 27 June 2022.
12. Trinidadian dialect for being spanked excessively.
13. 'Coming out' refers to the process of sharing one's sexual orientation or gender identity with others.
14. Interview with Jackie, 25 July 2019.
15. The disclosure of someone's sexual orientation or identity to others without their consent.
16. Interview with Alicia, 25 July 2019.
17. Trinidadian dialect for "Who will receive the brunt of your frustration?"
18. Trinidadian slur for gay men and men who have sex with men.
19. Caribbean slang for lesbians and women who have sex with women.
20. Jamaican patois for "We don't care."
21. Interview with Sonia, 8 August 2019.
22. Clinically significant distress caused when a person's assigned birth sex is not the same as the one with which they identify (Human Rights Campaign 2020).
23. Interview with A.J., 26 July 2019.
24. Jamaican dialect for "They approach you in a sexual or flirtatious manner."
25. Interview with Tia, 30 July 2019.

REFERENCES

Almeida, Joanna, Renee M. Johnson, Heather L. Corliss, Beth E. Molnar, and Deborah Azrael. 2009. "Emotional Distress Among LGBT Youth: The Influence of Perceived Discrimination Based on Sexual Orientation." *Journal of Youth and Adolescence* 38 (7): 1001–14. https://doi.org/10.1007/s10964-009-9397-9.

Andrew, Jennan P. 2020. "Intimate Partner Violence in LBTQ Relationships in Jamaica." Master's thesis, Ohio University. https://etd.ohiolink.edu/acprod/odb_etd/etd/r/1501/10?clear=10&p10_accession_num=ohiou1585232198183695.

Archer, John. 1994. "Power and Male Violence." In *Male Violence*, edited by John Archer, 310–32. London: Routledge.

Badenes-Ribera, Laura, Julio Sánchez-Meca, and Claudio Longobardi. 2019. "The Relationship Between Internalized Homophobia and Intimate Partner Violence in Same-Sex Relationships: A Meta-Analysis." *Trauma, Violence & Abuse* 20 (3): 331–43. https://doi.org/10.1177/1524838017708781.

Balsam, Kimberly F., and Dawn M. Szymanski. 2005. "Relationship Quality and Domestic Violence in Women's Same-Sex Relationships: The Role of Minority Stress." *Psychology of Women Quarterly* 29 (3): 258–69. https://journals.sagepub.com/doi/10.1111/j.1471-6402.2005.00220.x.

Benjamin, Sherna. 2021. "Surviving Domestic and Intimate Partner Violence." In *Gender and Domestic Violence in the Caribbean*, edited by Ann Marie Bissessar and Camille Huggins, 239–55. London: Palgrave Macmillan.

Bernhard, Michael, and Daniel O'Neill. 2020. "The Uses of Violence." *Perspectives on Politics* 18 (3): 701–5. doi:10.1017/S1537592720002194.

Boxill, Ian, Joulene Martin, Roy Russell, Lloyd Waller, Racian Meikle, and Rashalee Mitchell. 2011. *National Survey on Attitudes and Perceptions of Jamaicans Towards Same-Sex Relationships*. Kingston: University of the West Indies, Department of Sociology, Psychology and Social Work. https://ufdc.ufl.edu/AA00003178/00001.

Brereton, Bridget. 2010. "The Historical Background to the Culture of Violence in Trinidad and Tobago." *Caribbean Review of Gender Studies* no. 4: 1–15. https://sta.uwi.edu/crgs/february2010/journals/BridgetBrereton.pdf.

Brown, Taylor, and Jody L. Herman. 2015. *Intimate Partner Violence and Sexual Abuse Among LGBT People: A review of existing research*. Los Angeles: University of California, Williams Institute.

Calton, Jenna M., Lauren Bennett Cattaneo, and Kris T. Gebhard. 2016. "Barriers to Help Seeking for Lesbian, Gay, Bisexual, Transgender, and Queer Survivors of Intimate Partner Violence." *Trauma, Violence & Abuse* 17 (5): 585–600. https://www.jstor.org/stable/26638153.

Carvalho, Amana F., Robin J. Lewis, Valerian J. Derlega, Barbara A. Winstead, and Claudia Viggiano. 2011. "Internalized Sexual Minority Stressors and Same-Sex Intimate Partner Violence." *Journal of Family Violence* 26 (7): 501–9. https://doi.org/10.1007/s10896-011-9384-2.

Centre for Suicide Prevention. 2019. "A suicide prevention kit: Transgender people and Suicide." Canadian Mental Health Association. https://www.suicideinfo.ca/resource/transgender-people-suicide/.

Centres for Disease Control and Prevention. 2020. "Prevention Strategies, Intimate Partner Violence: Violence Prevention." https://www.cdc.gov/violenceprevention/intimatepartnerviolence/prevention.html.

European Institute for Gender Equality. 2006. "What is patriarchal violence?" Daphne Programme of the European Union. https://eige.europa.eu/docs/28_HU.pdf.

Faber, Tom. 2018. "Welcome to Jamaica – No Longer 'the Most Homophobic Place on Earth'." *The Guardian*, 6 December. https://www.theguardian.com/global-development/2018/dec/06/jamaica-lgbt-rights-activists-pride-two-decades-of-progress-j-flag.

Gibbons, Allison Y. 2015. "Family Violence in the Caribbean." Presentation to Expert Group Meeting on Family Policy Development: Achievements and Challenges. United Nations, New York, 14–15 May.

Hatcher, Abigail M., Patrizia Romito, Merab Odero, Elizabeth A. Bukusi, Maricianah Onono, and Janet M. Turan. 2013. "Social Context and Drivers of Intimate Partner Violence in Rural Kenya: Implications for the Health of Pregnant Women." *Culture, Health and Sexuality* 15 (4): 404–19. https://doi.org/10.1080/13691058.2012.760205.

Herek, Gregory M. 2004. "Beyond 'Homophobia': Thinking about Sexual Prejudice and Stigma in the Twenty-First Century." *Sexuality Research & Social Policy* Vol. 1: 6–24. https://doi.org/10.1525/srsp.2004.1.2.6.

hooks, bell. 2015. *Feminism Is for Everybody: Passionate Politics*. New York and Abingdon: Routledge.

Human Rights Campaign. 2020. Glossary of terms. https://www.hrc.org/resources/glossary-of-terms.

Human Rights Watch. 2014. "Not Safe at Home: Violence and Discrimination against LGBT People in Jamaica." Human Rights Watch, 21 October. https://www.hrw.org/report/2014/10/21/not-safe-home/violence-and-discrimination-against-lgbt-people-jamaica.

———. 2018. *"I Have to Leave to Be Me": Discriminatory Laws against LGBT people in the Eastern Caribbean*. https://www.hrw.org/sites/default/files/report_pdf/easterncaribbean0318_web_0.pdf.

Jackman, Mahalia. 2017. "Protecting the fabric of society? Heterosexual views on the usefulness of the anti-gay laws in Barbados, Guyana and Trinidad and Tobago." *Culture, Health & Sexuality* 19 (1): 91–106. doi: 10.1080/13691058.2016.1207806.

Jamaica Forum for Lesbians, All Sexuals and Gays (J-FLAG). 2014. *Annual Report 2013: Promoting Respect for Diversity*. https://www.equalityjamaica.org/annual-reports/.

Lacey, Krim K., Rohan D. Jeremiah, and Carolyn M. West. 2019. "Domestic Violence Through a Caribbean Lens: Historical Context, Theories, Risks and Consequences." *Journal of Aggression, Maltreatment & Trauma* 30 (6): 761–80. https://www.tandfonline.com/doi/abs/10.1080/10926771.2019.1660442.

Lewis, Robin J., Robert J. Milletich, Michelle L. Kelley, and Alex Woody. 2012. "Minority Stress, Substance Use, and Intimate Partner Violence among Sexual Minority Women." *Aggression and Violent Behavior* 17 (3): 247–56. https://doi.org/10.1016/j.avb.2012.02.004.

MacDonald, Cynthia. 2021. "Exploring Passion, Violence and Religion Within Brazil's LGBTQ Community." Centre for Diaspora and Transnational Studies, Faculty of Arts and Sciences, University of Toronto. https://www.cdts.utoronto.ca/news/exploring-passion-violence-and-religion-within-brazil%E2%80%99s-lgbtq-community.

McKenry, Patrick C., Julianne M. Serovich, Tina Mason, and Katie Mosack. 2006. "Perpetration of Gay and Lesbian Partner Violence: A Disempowerment Perspective." *Journal of Family Violence* Vol. 21: 233–43. https://doi.org/10.1007/s10896-006-9020-8.

McLaughlin, Erin, and Patricia Rozee. 2008. "Knowledge About Heterosexual versus Lesbian Battering Among Lesbians." *Women & Therapy* 23 (3): 39–58. https://doi.org/10.1300/J015v23n03_04.

Merrill, G.S., and V.A. Wolfe. "Battered Gay Men: An Exploration of Abuse, Help Seeking, and Why They Stay." *Journal of Homosexuality* 39 (2): 1–30. https://doi.org/10.1300/J082v39n02_01.

Messinger, Adam M. 2011. "Invisible Victims: Same-Sex IPV in the National Violence Against Women Survey." *Journal of Interpersonal Violence* 26 (11): 2228–43. https://doi.org/10.1177/0886260510383023.

National Coalition of Anti-Violence Programs. 2017. *Lesbian, Gay, Bisexual, Transgender, Queer and HIV-Affected Hate and Intimate Partner Violence in 2017*. New York: NCAVP. https://avp.org/2017-hv-ipv-report/.

Ogum Alangea, Deda, Adolphina Addo-Lartey, Yandisa Sikweyiya, Esnat Chirwa, Dorcas Coker-Appiah, Rachel Jewkes, and Richard Adanu. 2018. "Prevalence and Risk Factors of Intimate Partner Violence among Women in Four Districts of the Central Region of Ghana: Baseline Findings from a Cluster Randomised Controlled Trial." *PLoS ONE* 13 (7): e0200874. https://doi.org/10.1371/journal.pone.0200874.

Outright International. 2022. *Discrimination at Every Turn: The Experience of Trans and Gender Diverse People in Eleven Caribbean Countries.* New York: UCTRANS and Outright International. https://outrightinternational.org/sites/default/files/2023-04/CarribeanTrans_Revised_OutrightInternational_1.pdf.

Perales, Francisco, and Abram Todd. 2018. "Structural stigma and the health and wellbeing of Australian LGB populations: Exploiting geographic variation in the results of the 2017 same-sex marriage plebiscite." *Social Science & Medicine* Vol. 208: 190–99. https://www.sciencedirect.com/science/article/abs/pii/S0277953618302508.

Pierotti, Rachael S. 2013. "Increasing Rejection of Intimate Partner Violence: Evidence of Global Cultural Diffusion." *American Sociological Review* 78 (2): 240–65. https://journals.sagepub.com/doi/full/10.1177/0003122413480363.

Rollè, Luca, Giulia Giardina, Angela M. Caldarera, Eva Gerino, and Piera Brustia. 2018. "When Intimate Partner Violence Meets Same Sex Couples: A Review of Same Sex Intimate Partner Violence." *Frontiers in Psychology* Vol. 9: Article 1506. https://doi.org/10.3389/fpsyg.2018.01506.

Russo, Ann. 1999. "Lesbians organizing lesbians against battering." In *Same-Sex Domestic Violence: Strategies for Change,* edited by Beth Leventhal and Sandra Lundy, 83–96. Thousand Oaks, London and New Delhi: Sage Publishing.

Shields, Leighann. 2018. "A Queer and Trans-Inclusive Response to Intimate Partner Violence." BA thesis, Portland State University. https://doi.org/10.15760/honors.574.

Stockman, Jamila K., Hitomi Hayashi, and Jacquelyn C. Campbell. 2015. "Intimate Partner Violence and Its Health Impact on Ethnic Minority Women." *Journal of Women's Health* 24 (1): 62–79. https://doi.org/10.1089/jwh.2014.4879.

Walters, Mikel L., Jieru Chen, and Matthew J. Breiding. 2013. *The National Intimate Partner and Sexual Violence Survey: 2010 Findings on Victimization by Sexual Orientation.* Atlanta, GA: National Center for Injury Prevention and Control, Centers for Disease Control and Prevention.

Wilton, Tamsin. 1995. *Lesbian Studies: Setting an Agenda.* London: Routledge.

World Health Organization. "WHO Multi-Country Study on Women's Health and Domestic Violence against Women." n.d., World Health Organization. Accessed May 14, 2020. http://www.who.int/reproductivehealth/publications/violence/24159358X/en/.

SECTION 4

VIOLENT FACT, VIOLENT FICTION

chapter 12

"Here Are the Stories Underneath"

Representing Gender-Based Violence in Contemporary Jamaican Poetry

Kelsi Delaney and Lucy Evans

GENDER-BASED VIOLENCE (GBV) IS A PRESSING ISSUE GLOBALLY, and in Jamaica levels of GBV are persistently high.[1] In March 2017, demonstrations took place across the region in protest against the high levels of GBV (Thakur 2018, 268). In Jamaica, these were led by the Tambourine Army, a radical social justice movement committed to ending sexual violence against women and girls. These recent protests extend a long history of anti-GBV activism in the Anglophone Caribbean, since this issue has, for several decades, been "one of the key issues around which women's and feminist organisations in the Caribbean organise" (Deshong and Haynes 2016, 2).

In this co-authored chapter, we argue that literary writing – and poetry specifically – can offer an important contribution to ongoing conversations around GBV. We focus our analysis on two recently published poetry collections by Kei Miller and Lorna Goodison. Paula Morgan and Valerie Youssef note how literary writing on violence is often "grounded in real-time events of personal or sociological significance or both" (2006, 4). This is true of Miller's *In Nearby Bushes* (2019) and Goodison's *Mother Muse* (2021); these poetry collections portray real scenarios of sexual violence and femicide in Jamaica. A sequence of poems within Miller's collection engages with a 2018 article in the *Jamaica Star* about the disappearance and death of a young woman. Part of Goodison's collection explores the murder of the dancer Anita Mahfood in 1965.

A key concern in our reading of these collections is the extent to which the poets' treatment of these real-life femicides overlaps with or differs from news media coverage of them. We ask: How does Miller and Goodison's poetry reference and reflect upon press reportage on GBV? What might these collections indicate about the potential of poetry to interrogate the limits of not only media representations of GBV but also the language of official data on GBV, and legal and policy frameworks? And what bearing might this have on discussions of GBV in the context of feminist scholarship and activism? We argue that these poetry collections counter the gender-normative framing of media discourse on this topic. In so doing, we suggest, they illustrate the power of imaginative writing to add depth and texture to narratives of GBV, and expose the "stories underneath" (Miller 2019, 8).[2]

GENDER-BASED VIOLENCE IN THE NEWS MEDIA

Feminist scholarship on GBV in Anglophone Caribbean countries has begun to address the question of how GBV is represented in the media and popular culture. Morgan and Youssef present "media and popular cultural expression" as a "causative factor" in rising rates of GBV in the region, arguing that these "largely support the culture of violence" (2006, 19). More recently, in a report conducted on behalf of UN Women, Hosein and her co-authors make a similar argument as it relates to the news media in Trinidad and Tobago, asserting that "beliefs about womanhood and manhood and love and family, reinforced by messages from religion and the media", have rendered women more vulnerable to intimate partner violence (IPV) (Hosein et al. 2018, 5). A United Nations Development Programme report also refers to the media, stating that the implementation of legislation and policy aimed at combatting GBV has been hindered by "the persistence of a patriarchal and discriminatory culture that subordinates women and that is still pervasive in many sectors of society, institutions (police, health services, legal system) and the media" (UNDP 2016, 63).

In their research on GBV in the Anglophone Caribbean, Haynes and Deshong have looked closely at media coverage of GBV. In a 2017 study, they analyse a sample of 108 online news articles published in 2013 and 2014 by media houses in various Anglophone Caribbean countries. These articles cover various forms of GBV, including "sexual violence, child sexual abuse, intimate partner violence, and violence against transgender, intersex, and gender non-conforming persons" (Haynes and Deshong 2017, 107). Haynes and Deshong find that media reporting on GBV in this context involves the use of "sensationalist, trivializing, and victim-blaming language which reinforces essentialisms about gender, sexuality and sexed bodies as well as hierarchies of gender, race and class", and which "serves to mark some bodies as [. . .] inherently violable, justifying the acts of violence committed against them" (2017, 125). Based on their findings, they argue that the "heteronormative and gender normative framing" of accounts of GBV in the Caribbean news media both reflects and reinforces attitudes which enable and justify GBV. They contend that, as a result, media reporting actively participates in the "reproduction of violence" (107).[3]

GBV is a prominent theme in contemporary Caribbean literary writing, including poetry. By focusing on the portrayal of GBV in contemporary Jamaican poetry, we seek in this chapter to extend interdisciplinary research on GBV in the region. Expanding on the important work already done by Morgan and Youssef on violence in Caribbean discourse, which incorporates analysis of both media and literary texts, we offer a contribution to scholarly work on GBV in the region which centres cultural production. Haynes and Deshong analyse online newspapers "as an important site in the production of commonsense knowledge about gender, sexuality and violence" (2017, 112). We are concerned here with how Miller's and Goodison's poetry contests the "commonsense" status of this knowledge, exposing its basis in gender normative assumptions. If, as Haynes and Deshong argue, media discourse on GBV enacts GBV, we argue that poetry can work against the violence of media representations.

POETIC EXPOSURE IN MILLER'S *IN NEARBY BUSHES*

Published in 2019, Kei Miller's poetry collection *In Nearby Bushes* takes its title from news media discourse. The collection's front cover contains excerpts from several online newspaper articles which include the phrase "in nearby bushes", taken from the *Jamaica Observer*, the *Jamaica Gleaner*, and *McKoy's News*. These excerpts describe scenarios in which a body is found, a crime is committed, or a perpetrator escapes "in nearby bushes". The repeated use of this phrase in the excerpts is visually highlighted on the cover image through the use of italics and bright yellow text which stands out against the surrounding white text and black background. The same bright yellow italicised text, slightly larger and in bold type, is used for the collection's title, linking it directly to the common use of this phrase in the newspaper excerpts. Therefore, even before readers open the book, the collection's critical engagement with media discourse – and specifically with news reporting on crime in Jamaica – is signalled.

Within the larger picture of high rates of homicide in Jamaica,[4] violence against women and femicide have been identified as particularly pressing issues.[5] This is registered in Miller's collection, which focuses in its third section, "In Nearby Bushes", on Petrice Porteous, a young woman whose body was found in 2018 after she had been missing for two weeks. Porteous's name is included in the unpaginated poem which precedes the collection's two main sections, "Here where once lay the bodies". Her name is later blocked out in the reproduction of the *Jamaica Star* article which is used as a source text for the sequence of poems in the collection's third section. The poem "Here where once lay the bodies" lists the names and ages of twenty-four people who have been killed in Jamaica between 2007 and 2019, along with the dates their bodies were discovered. As Lauren Alleyne notes, the repeated use of the verb "found" in the poem emphasises the process of "retrieval" of these bodies from the obscurity of the bushes (Alleyne 2021, para. 2). The poem invites a reading of the collection as an alternative archive to media discourse, one which recovers and preserves the names and identities of murder victims.

The collection's meditations on violence in twenty-first-century Jamaica emphasise GBV by foregrounding femicide, and by connecting acts of violence to assumptions and expectations around gender identity and gender roles.[6] In its inclusion and reworking of text lifted from online news articles, the collection draws attention to how the language of media reporting depersonalises victims of GBV and reinforces social norms which regulate women's bodies. At the same time, the poems resist and undermine media discourse on GBV. If continuous media reporting on this issue has had the effect of desensitising readers to the realities of GBV, Miller's poems – which invite an active reading practice – work to resensitise readers.

The concept of the "understory", associated with the vegetal "undergrowth" of a forested area (Miller 2019, 7), runs through the collection, and is the focus of the poem "The understory". In this poem the dense entanglement of plants, flowers and shrubs which make up the undergrowth, the "complication of roots" (8), serves as a metaphor for the intricate mesh of stories which, combined, make up the identity of the place and its people. In stanzas four and five, the poem's focus shifts from a more general concern with storytelling to the telling and writing of crime stories specifically. The speaker advises readers: "The original accounts / of witnesses are here, as well as a careful record / of all subsequent changes; you may compare" (8). Here the speaker refers to how media reporting can manipulate and distort the "original accounts" of witnesses at a crime scene. Using the second person in a direct address to readers, the speaker invites readers to "just listen", "compare" versions, "hear the long story", and look for "the stories underneath" (8). "The understory" comments on the violence that is done by media coverage of crime stories through the curtailment and repurposing of witnesses' original accounts. In the poetry sequence which makes up Part III of the collection, "In Nearby Bushes", Miller employs the form of the exposure poem to extend this critique. In this section, poems titled with roman numerals are interspersed with excerpts from news articles which all include the words "nearby bushes".

The section opens with a long excerpt from a 2019 online *Jamaica Star* article, which reports on the discovery of the body of Petrice Porteous, who had been missing for two weeks (Titus 2018). Following this excerpt, the same text appears on four subsequent pages, and again on the collection's penultimate page. However, on these pages, all of the text except certain words and letters is greyed out. Typically, erasure poems function through redaction, making parts of the original text illegible to highlight a new meaning ("Erasure", n.d.). Miller instead chooses to erase nothing, exposing selected words and letters by printing them in black, which stands out against the grey of the remaining text. His poems expose "the understory" latent within the online news story. If, as Capildeo proposes, the collection's front cover can be compared to a "photographic negative" (Capildeo 2019), we suggest that these pages of manipulated media text function as exposure poems. Just as in photography, exposure to varying amounts of light leads to varying levels of brightness and darkness in a photograph, in each of these poetic exposures different parts of the text are highlighted in black and washed out in grey.

In the first exposure, Miller highlights the following words:

> Mount Peace is in mourning she left to return on February 12 she did not arrive at her destination friends and loved ones pray for her safe return. However, a turn for the worst in nearby bushes. JAMAICA STAR, FEBRUARY 27, 2018 (Miller 2019, 44)

Next, on the facing page, Miller highlights these words:

> unPeace in Hanover after the decomposed body was found Reports are she did not arrive at her destination. Despite friends that pray for a turn. A group of dogs fight in JAMAICA (45)

The first exposure is closest to the original and offers a relatively straightforward account of what happened. In the second exposure, the play on the place name with the word "unPeace" locates violence and insecurity within the parish, hinting at how Porteous's death is not an isolated incident, but part of a pervasive and systemic problem facilitated by enduring structures of male domination and power. This is emphasised in the final sentence, "A group of dogs fight in JAMAICA". Abstracted from the context of the nearby bushes and Porteous's remains, this image of dogs fighting in Jamaica both extends the scope of the story geographically, and evokes a broader national and global culture of toxic masculinity. Whereas in the original text and the first exposure, "friends and loved ones pray for her safe return", in the second exposure "friends pray for a turn". Here, "a turn" alludes to the cultural shift necessary to end the ongoing waves of violence.

There is therefore a change in focus between exposures one and two: while the original text and the first exposure offer the story of an individual woman's experience of GBV and the community's concerns for her safety, the second exposure presents GBV as a broader societal problem which undermines the security and welfare of the parish and country. In doing so, it reflects how GBV, as "one of the most widespread forms of violence" in the Caribbean, "directly impact[s] citizen security and the stability and health of families and communities" (Hosein 2019, 94). The "understory" drawn out by the second exposure is the wider social and structural contexts in which GBV occurs, contexts which are beyond the scope of the first exposure and the original media text.

The fifth exposure poem is positioned adjacent to poem XIII.III, which we will quote in full:

> Cause woman is disposable as that,
> And this thing that has happened is common,
> common,
> common as stone and leaf and breadfruit tree.
> You should have known. You did always walk on this island aware
> of the nearby bushes
> the nearby bruises. (Miller 2019, 74)

This poem opens with a comment on the pervasiveness of GBV, so "common" that it seems to be embedded in the natural environment. The "nearby bushes", recast as the "nearby bruises", function in this poem as a signifier for the ever-present threat of GBV. If rape and femicide are common, an everyday occurrence, if women are perceived as "disposable", then GBV is normalised, and as inevitable as the existence of the stones, leaves and breadfruit trees. It is expected, and therefore tacitly accepted by families and communities.[7] With the words "You should have known", the speaker alludes to how in this context, the burden of responsibility is placed on women to avoid GBV and protect themselves from it.

In the exposure poem on the following page, all the text is greyed out except the following sentence:

> It is said that she left her sibling's home to return to her parish on February 12, but she did not arrive at her destination. (75)

The detail of Porteous's journey to and from her twin sister's home in Montego Bay, derived from sources within the community, is the only information the article supplies about Porteous other than the fact of her disappearance and death. While the article offers no explicit critique of Porteous's choice to travel alone between parishes, its inclusion of this information and exclusion of all other details of Porteous's identity and story quietly reinforce the victim-blaming mentality explored in poem XIII.III. The "stories underneath" illuminated by this exposure are the gendered assumptions implicit within the online news article.

The series of exposure poems is intertwined with a sequence of lyric poems written in the second person which also focus on Petrice Porteous. Poem I.I opens: "That this should be your death – walking so simple this last stretch that will stretch into eternity, thinking nothing more than the emptiness of your fridge, and the cupboards, and what feat of magic might produce this evening's meal" (48). Here, the speaker addresses Porteous, speculating how she might have been feeling moments before her death. At the same time, the speaker's second person address is directed towards readers, compelling them to align their perspective with that of the poem's subject.

The use of "you" in these poems distinguishes this version of Porteous's story from the version offered in the *Jamaica Star*. The *Jamaica Star* article conveys what seems to be a simple factual account of what occurred.[8] This is conveyed through the choice of third person narration over first or second person, the use of short sentences and of passive rather than active grammatical voice constructions, a focus on the events positioned in a logical order, and an absence of emotion. While Miller's poems both visually convey Porteous's decomposing corpse and imaginatively access her conscious and semi-conscious thoughts, in the news article Porteous's identity is stripped away as she is reduced to the role of a murder victim, a body discarded in "nearby bushes" (43).[9]

Whereas the style of the news article invites rapid consumption, both the series of exposures and the lyric poems in Miller's collection necessitate a slower reading process. First, as Neigh has argued, piecing together the exposed words and letters requires both time and concentration on the part of readers, necessitating they "slow down" to reconstruct Miller's meaning (2021, 32). Second, the temporality of the poetry sequence, which stretches over thirty-five pages, requires readers to invest significantly more time and attention than the two short paragraphs of the *Jamaica Star* article. As compared to the news article where Porteous's death is conveyed in the past tense, as an already completed event, the poems addressing Porteous are written in the present tense, and enact gradual shifts in time. This intensifies the presence of the poem's subject, with whom readers share the moments preceding and the hours and days following her death. In these poems, Miller enacts a technique similar to long exposure, or slow-shutter exposure, in photography, where the subject is captured over an extended period.

The lyric poems in Part III thus disrupt the easy consumption of violence as spectacle, requiring readers to stay with Porteous's presence across multiple poems. In this context, the "stories underneath" relate to the voice and perspective of Petrice Porteous, which Miller's poems imaginatively unearth from the obscurity of the "nearby bushes". By combining exposure poems and lyric poems in Part III of *In Nearby Bushes,* Miller unravels the complexity of this femicide case, freeing it from the formal and stylistic constraints of the *Jamaica Star* newspaper column. To return to the metaphor of the "understory" as "undergrowth" (7), Miller's collection emplots the narrative of Porteous's death within a "complication of roots" (8), illuminating its entanglement with entrenched cultural attitudes and values, gendered relations of power and structural inequality.

EXTENDING THE ARCHIVE IN LORNA GOODISON'S *MOTHER MUSE*

The first half of Goodison's 2021 poetry collection, *Mother Muse,* explores the biographies of two women, Sister Mary Ignatius and Anita "Margarita" Mahfood, who contributed to the Jamaican music scene in the 1960s. A point of connection between these two women is the famous trombonist Donald Drummond, Ignatius's mentee and Mahfood's lover. On July 27, 1966, Drummond was convicted for the murder of Mahfood on January 1, 1965 ("Drummond found guilty but insane" 1966). Media coverage of this incident and of Drummond's and Mahfood's relationship has mainly focused on Drummond, his music and his legacy.[10] In *Mother Muse* Goodison tilts the frame to centre the figure of Anita "Margarita" Mahfouz, an imagined version of Mahfood.[11] Mahfouz's story is presented from various perspectives, including that of Mahfouz herself. While the poems do tell the story of

Mahfood's untimely death, they also explore her life, her ambitions, her association with the Rastafari movement, and the role she played in developing Jamaican popular music.[12] In an interview Goodison has reflected on what she describes as the "misogyny and victim blaming" latent within how Mahfood's death has been, and continues to be, framed in the news media (Goodison and Lucien 2022). Writing against the dominant narrative of a tragic love story, in *Mother Muse* Goodison foregrounds Mahfood's status as a victim of IPV and femicide.

Mahfood's death precedes by several decades the criminalization of domestic violence in Caribbean countries which – in theory if not in practice – improved legal protection for victims of GBV.[13] For this reason, the violence Mahfood was subjected to by her husband Rudolph Bent and by Don Drummond would at the time have been considered a matter to be resolved privately, rather than a concern of the state. The historic invisibility of IPV in the eyes of the law coincided with its omission from official data on violence in Jamaica where "IPV has historically not been recorded separately from other types of violence but has been subsumed under the rubric of societal violence in general" (Smith 2018, 344). While there is now legislation against domestic violence, as yet, no Caribbean countries have "classified femicide, or feminicide, as a criminal offense" (ECLAC 2021). As a result, although the number of women murdered by an intimate partner is significantly higher than the number of men murdered by an intimate partner, femicide cases are treated as homicide cases.[14] Where IPV and femicide are collapsed into the broader societal phenomena of violent crime and homicide, their root causes, contributing factors and impact will not be properly understood. Through her retelling of Mahfood's story, Goodison counters the invisibility of femicide in both official data on violence and in legal discourse.

Coverage of Mahfood's death in Jamaica's newspapers ranges from 1965 to 2022; articles appear in the *Jamaica Star*, the *Daily Gleaner* and *Sunday Gleaner*, the *Jamaica Observer*, and the *Jamaica Daily News*. These overwhelmingly focus on Drummond. Of the forty-six articles we consulted, seventeen of the headlines mention Drummond by name. By contrast, not a single headline refers to Mahfood by name, although three refer to her by her nickname "Margarita". The headlines also draw attention to Drummond's musical talent, referring to him as the "instrumentalist", the "Don", the "immortal trombonist", the "legendary Don Drummond", the "dramatic Don Drummond", and the "Mad Genius". The one headline which refers to Mahfood's status as a dancer, "Rhumba dancer stabbed to death", emphasises her death rather than her talent. The few headlines which do reference Mahfood focus on her death rather than her life and creative identity. A glance at the headlines thus indicates how media discourse over the decades has celebrated Drummond's music and legacy, and sidelined Mahfood.

With references to either Drummond or his story as "tragic", Drummond repeatedly upstages Mahfood in the media coverage. For example, he is described as having "died tragically" (Selim 1976), and a later article in the same newspaper refers to the "tragic circumstances of his life", including his "crime of murdering his woman for being unfaithful" (Walters 1982). In other articles, Drummond's relationship with Mahfood is presented as "tragic" (Segree 1998) or a "tragedy" ("Rhumba dancer stabbed to death" 1965), a play by Kwame Dawes about Drummond is compared to a Greek tragedy (Reckford 2002), and Clive Thompson's dance production about Drummond's life, "Malungu", is described as a "romantic tragedy" ("NDTC's 51st set" 2013) and a "Romeo and Juliet type tale" (Reckford 2013). This framing of Drummond as a tragic hero and of his relationship with Mahfood as a tragic love story romanticises both Drummond himself as a troubled artist figure, and Mahfood's death at his hands. Since tragedy is normally associated with misfortune, presenting their story as tragic excises from it the context of GBV in which Mahfood's death occurred. This is illustrated in Thompson's dance production, where Mahfood is shown to die without being stabbed by Drummond.[15] Greek tragedy usually focuses on the downfall of a central male protagonist, a downfall which is at least in part due to circumstances which are out of that protagonist's control ("Greek Tragedy", n.d.). To cast Drummond as a tragic hero is therefore to position him as central to the story.

While Drummond is romanticised in the media coverage as a tragic victim of circumstance, Mahfood is often presented critically, in a way which implies that she is at least partially responsible for the crime which was committed against her. In one article she is described as an "exotic dancer", and as a "party girl" who was "wild" (Campbell 1996). Here, Mahfood is presented as sexually promiscuous and out of control. A similar kind of victim-blaming language can be found in other articles; the reference, already quoted, to Drummond's "crime of murdering his woman for being unfaithful" presents her supposed infidelity as a justification for her murder (Selim 1976). Elsewhere, the criticism of Mahfood is more overt: the reviewer of a play about Drummond blames Mahfood for Drummond's deterioration, exclaiming: "Couldn't he see that the foul-mouthed, erratic, promiscuous brown beauty Margarita wasn't good for him?" (Segree 1998). The media coverage of Mahfood's death thus offers a clear example of how, as Haynes and Deshong argue, media reporting on GBV not only trivialises GBV, but justifies it, marking some bodies as "inherently violable" (2017, 107).

In *Mother Muse,* Goodison shifts attention from Drummond to Mahfood, offering a more multi-faceted representation of Mahfood's identity and story than can be found in the media coverage of her death. The collection also reflects critically on this media coverage. Goodison's concern with media reporting on Mahfood can be seen in the poem "New Year's Morning, 1965":

> Out of the mesh mouth radio, the news strains at dawn:
> He'd killed her and surrendered to the Rockford police.
>
> Recall this: some said she was a wild woman; fair game
> for one straight blade to the heart. (Goodison 2021, 2)

In the first stanza, the news media is envisaged as a filter which sifts out information deemed irrelevant or unnecessary. The second stanza then illuminates the kind of narrative that emerges through this process, where victim-blaming either implicitly or overtly casts women as responsible for violence committed against them. As noted above, the word "wild" was used to describe Mahfood in a 1996 *Sunday Observer* article (Campbell 1996). Goodison's choice not to use quotation marks indicates how the language of the press seeps into common parlance, and vice versa. This is further emphasised with the words "some said".

The tendency in the press coverage to refer to Mahfood as "a rhumba dancer" or "a dancer" rather than use her name contrasts with the seventeen headlines that mention Drummond by name, consigning her to obscurity while celebrating Drummond's legacy. In the ironically titled poem "A Praise for Margarita Anita" Goodison draws attention to this, using Drummond's first name seven times with wording which is very close to the headlines we discussed earlier:

> His name itself was riddim; Don Drummond, don D
> Don man of mind split to hold his gift: don master
> of the eerily eloquent slide trombone.
>
> Don of sorrows born to catch and release one people's
> hurt from a horn's cup. Don Cosmic the astronomer
> who scored the sphere's music with indelible pencil stub. (Goodison 2021, 26)

These words to some extent contribute to and endorse the country's celebration of Drummond as a talented musician whose creative expression spoke to the descendants of enslaved peoples, releasing "one people's / hurt from a horn's cup". Yet the juxtaposition of these stanzas with the following account of Mahfood emphasises how his legend overshadows her memory:

> It is written how Margarita Anita was a dancer in the club
> and that she lost her children and home when doomed
> love set its seal upon her and her beloved. (26)

With the words "It is written how", Goodison alludes to the way that Mahfood's story has been widely circulated in the press. In the earlier two stanzas, Drummond's identity is directly identified with his music ("his name itself was riddim"). In this stanza, however, Mahfood's identity is tied to Drummond's and presented as part of their story of "doomed love". While Drummond is "master" of the trombone, whose mark on the world is "indelible", Mahfood is merely "a dancer". Here the use of an indefinite article presents her as non-specific and unremarkable, one of many dancers.

In "Woman a Come (1)" Goodison inverts this dynamic, retelling the story in a way which centres Mahfood. The poem references a song that Mahfood composed and performed for Drummond, "Woman a Come" (1964). It opens with these lines:

> Song of herself she composed herself from Rastafari
> chant, Hollywood musicals and ancestral memories
> of Bedouin airs keened as camel trains near oases. (31)

The double use of the word "herself" in the opening line, alongside the repetition of "Song of herself" in line four, emphasises Mahfood's identity rather than Drummond's. Although her song focuses entirely on Drummond to the point of self-erasure, it is nevertheless a moment of creative self-expression for her. Goodison's choice to engage with Mahfood's song enables her to bring Mahfood's voice into the poems. With its focus on the song as an act of self-construction, "Woman a Come (1)" counters the many tellings and retellings of Mahfood's story by others over the decades. There is an emphasis in this poem not only on the power and distinctiveness of her voice, as she "hits a high note and sings it slant" (31), but also on the specificity of her cultural identity and heritage, as an artist and performer who draws in her creative work on multiple cultural influences.[16] This emphasis on her voice and identity allows Mahfood – in these poems – to step out of Drummond's shadow.

We observed earlier how the framing of Drummond's story as tragic in media discourse has led to an erasure of the context of GBV in which Mahfood's death occurred. In "Woman a Come (1)" and "Woman a Come (2)", Goodison retells the story in a way which emphasises Mahfood's status as a victim of GBV. "Woman a Come (1)" is divided into three parts. The substance of Mahfood's song – that she loves Drummond and cannot envisage life without him – is conveyed in part I (Goodison 2021, 31). The song's "heart message" (31) is undercut in part II by a visual description of her "slashed and ribboned by a killing blade" (32). In Part III the poem explores Drummond's motives: 'He could not bear to see her arrange her limbs /in arabesques for hot-breath crowds' (32). In these lines, the speaker connects Drummond's act of femicide to the power dynamics of his relationship with Mahfood. The lines convey his struggle in seeing her perform for a large audience due to his need to control her sexuality, and restrict others' access to the spectacle of her moving body. The violence, it is implied, erupts out of the conflict between her ambitions as a dancer and his expectations of her as a lover. The poem thus hints at how GBV is rooted in heteropatriarchal gender ideals (see Hosein 2019, 95; Morgan and Youssef 2006, 9).

In "Woman a Come (2)", the speaker describes how Mahfood's 'fragrant body' was 'repurposed / as bleeding beating bag' (Goodison 2021, 33). Here the figure of Drummond blends into the figure of Mahfood's husband, heavyweight boxer Rudolph Bent. Since Bent is introduced in the poem's penultimate line about her children – "No, he took them" – it is not clear which of her abusive partners is being referenced in these lines. If the narrative of a "tragic love story" has singled out Drummond's relationship with Mahfood as one of particularly intense passion and drama, Goodison's retelling presents it as in no way unique; the overlap that the poem creates between Drummond and Bent points to the prevalence of GBV as an everyday reality in many relationships.

As we have shown, critical commentary on the way Mahfood's story has been conveyed through news media reporting runs through the collection, surfacing in several of the poems. The power of this media discourse to shape public opinion on the case is also highlighted; for example, in "A Praise for Margarita Anita" the speaker breaks off before describing Drummond's crime, ending with the words: "We know what happened next" (26). In such moments Goodison suggests that the story has been told so many times that it is accepted as fact, or as "common knowledge" (2). The collection questions both the "common knowledge" about Mahfood and Drummond, and the "commonsense knowledge about gender, sexuality and violence" which media reporting generates (Haynes and Deshong 2017, 112). In doing so, it creates space for retellings of Mahfood's story.

CONCLUSION

Our analysis of press coverage of the deaths of Mahfood and Porteous, coverage which spans nearly six decades, affirms the conclusions of scholarly research on media representations of GBV in the Caribbean – that media discourse tends to reinforce a heteropatriarchal value system which facilitates and normalises GBV. Miller and Goodison embed media discourse within their poetry in order to illuminate and comment on its inferences. We have argued that in addition to critiquing the "sensationalist, trivializing, and victim-blaming language" of the news, Miller and Goodison offer an alternative to this press archive, one that centres the figures of Porteous and Mahfood (Haynes and Deshong 2017, 125). Both collections explore stories of GBV from multiple vantage points. Both poets also imaginatively reconstruct the experiences of femicide victims. Through the construction of a "careful record" (Miller 2019, 8) of representations of GBV, Miller and

Goodison dislodge the dominance of the perspectives espoused in the news media, inviting the active participation of readers who are invited to "compare" accounts of victims' stories as they negotiate the collections (Miller 2019, 8).

Based on our findings in this chapter, we suggest that poetry can offer an alternative source of data on GBV that has the potential to transcend some of the limitations of press reportage. Through imaginative retelling, perspectives unavailable through witness reports, such as those of victims of femicide, can be explored. In contrast to the fast-paced temporality of news media discourse, poetry invites readers to pause and reflect on what they are reading. Poetry can also help readers to think in new ways, as is demonstrated in Miller's exposure poems, the form of which highlights the problematic shortcomings of the news media discourse more powerfully than might be possible in a prose account. Additionally, the sequential and episodic nature of most poetry collections enables poets to embed a range of accounts and perspectives within a larger text, and in doing so to resist oversimplification of narratives of victim and perpetrator; this can be seen in Goodison's exploration of the complex relationship between Mahfood and Drummond. Miller and Goodison are two of a growing number of poets who have addressed the issue of GBV in their work in recent years.[17] Through their contestation of harmful discourses on GBV and their emphasis upon the subjectivity of GBV victims, they demonstrate poetry's potential both to challenge and to constructively change the representation of gender-based violence.

ACKNOWLEDGEMENTS

This research was supported by the UK Arts and Humanities Research Council under grant number AH/T006951/1.

NOTES

1. Gender-based violence has been defined as "violence directed against a person because of their gender", and as violence (physical or psychological) which is "rooted in gender inequality" (EIGE 2025).

2. Research from this paper stems from the collaborative research project, "Representing Gender-based Violence: Literature, Performance and Activism in the Anglophone Caribbean". When looking for contemporary Anglophone Caribbean print poetry on the theme of GBV, co-author Delaney identified 126 poems across thirty-six collections and anthologies published from 2000. The project was funded by the UK Arts and Humanities Research Council, and was a collaboration between the University of Leicester and the University of the West Indies. Our project team, which included Gabrielle Hosein, Sonjah Stanley Niaah, Amílcar Sanatan, Zahra Warner and Dylan Kerrigan, explored representations of GBV in print literatures, spoken word and popular music. The co-authors of this chapter are both specialists in Caribbean literary studies who are located in the UK and employed by the University of Leicester. For more information about the co-authors and project, see https://le.ac.uk/anglophone-caribbean.
3. A recent Caribbean Policy Research Institute (CAPRI) report on the Jamaican news media and GBV further affirms these findings (2022).
4. The UNODC recorded a homicide rate of 44.95 per 100,000 population in 2020, one of the highest in the world (UN, n.d.).
5. For data on this covering the period 2016–19, see UN Women, *Caribbean Women Count: Ending Violence against Women and Girls Data Hub.*
6. We wish to acknowledge here that GBV is not the sole focus of Miller's reflections on violence in this collection. For a reading which locates Miller's representation of violence in relation to racial politics and hierarchies, see Neigh 2021.
7. The following sources further discuss the widespread cultural acceptance of GBV in the region at the levels of family, community and society: Morgan and Youssef 2006, 15; Spooner 2009, 385; Hosein 2019, 93–4).
8. Although the *Jamaica Star* is a tabloid paper with a focus on entertainment, this particular article of only 183 words conveys the events of the case briefly with little elaboration.
9. The title of the *Jamaica Star* newspaper article is 'Missing woman found in shallow grave'. Here, the use of the words 'missing woman' anonymises Porteous, de-emphasising her individual identity.
10. See the discussion below for examples of this.
11. Mahfouz is the ancestral name of the Jamaican Mahfood family. The Mahfood spelling originated when the family migrated to Kingston from Lebanon in the early 1900s, when a customs clerk misspelled their surname on their entry documents (Mahfood 2000).

12. Herbie Miller has drawn attention to Mahfood's role in "the fashioning of Jamaica's popular music and cultural identity" (2007, 49).
13. Domestic violence legislation was introduced in many Caribbean nation-states, including Jamaica, in the early 1990s (Spooner 2009, 377). There is a consensus in the scholarship that the introduction of this legislation did not, in practice, reduce incidences of IPV (see Spooner 2009; Robinson 2000; Morgan and Youssef 2006).
14. Smith (2018, 344) notes that "[a]ccording to the United Nations Office on Drugs and Crime (UNODC, 2014), globally, in 2012, almost half (47 percent) of the 93,000 female victims of homicide were murdered by their intimate partner, whereas less than 6 percent of male homicide victims were murdered by an intimate partner".
15. According to the mortuary report Mahfood was stabbed four times and went into critical haemorrhage (Augustyn 2013, 144).
16. Mahfood's association with the politics and spiritual beliefs of Rastafari, alluded to briefly in "Woman a Come (1)", is explored in more depth in "Testimony of her Rasta Brethren" (48), where the speaker describes how, at a time when Rasta performers were stigmatised by Jamaican music reportage and promotion, Mahfood used her platform as a popular musician to advocate for the Rasta community.
17. See footnote 2.

REFERENCES

Alleyne, Lauren K. 2021. '"This Sudden Abundance of Seeing." Review of *In Nearby Bushes*, by Kei Miller. *SX Salon*. http://smallaxe.net/sxsalon/reviews/sudden-abundance-seeing/.

Augustyn, Heather. 2013. *Don Drummond: The Genius and Tragedy of the World's Greatest Trombonist*. Jefferson: McFarland and Company.

Campbell, Howard. 1996. "The Legendary Don Drummond." *The Sunday Observer*, 25 August.

Capildeo, Vahni (Anthony Ezekiel). 2019. "Love is stronger than death." *Trinidad and Tobago Newsday*, 15 September. https://newsday.co.tt/2019/09/15/love-is-stronger-than-death/.

CAPRI (Caribbean Policy Research Institute). 2022. *Breaking News: Gender-Based Violence in Jamaican News Media*. Kingston: CAPRI. https://www.capricaribbean.org/documents/breaking-news-gender-based-violence-jamaican-news-media.

Collins English Dictionary. n.d. "Greek Tragedy." https://www.collinsdictionary.com/dictionary/english/greek-tragedy.

Deshong, Halimah A. F., and Tonya Haynes. 2016. "Intimate Partner Violence in the Caribbean: State, Activist and Media Responses." *Global Public Health* 11 (1–2): 82–94.

"Drummond found guilty but insane." 1966. *Daily Gleaner*, 27 July, 1966.

ECLAC (Economic Commission for Latin America and the Caribbean). 2021. "ECLAC: At Least 4,091 Women Were Victims of Femicide in 2020 in Latin America and the Caribbean, Despite Greater Visibility and Social Condemnation."

https://www.cepal.org/en/pressreleases/eclac-least-4091-women-were-victims-femicide-2020-latin-america-and-caribbean-despite.

EIGE (European Institute for Gender Equality). 2025. "What is gender-based violence?" https://eige.europa.eu/gender-based-violence/what-is-gender-based-violence.

Goodison, Lorna. 2021. *Mother Muse*. Manchester: Carcanet.

Goodison Lorna, and Vladimir Lucien. 2022. "The Path of Negative Growth." *SX Salon* 40. http://smallaxe.net/sxsalon/discussions/path-negative-growth.

Haynes, Tonya and Halimah A. F. Deshong. 2017. "Queering Feminist Approaches to Gender-based Violence in the Anglophone Caribbean." *Social and Economic Studies* 66 (1&2): 105–31.

Hosein, Gabrielle. 2019. "Masculinism, Male Marginalisation and Intimate Partner Backlash in Trinidad and Tobago." *Caribbean Journal of Criminology* 1 (4): 90–122.

Hosein, Gabrielle, Tricia Basdeo-Gobin, Colin Robinson, Sabrina Mowlah-Baksh, Simone Leid and Amílcar Sanatan. 2018. *Gender-Based Violence in Trinidad and Tobago*. Port of Spain: UN Women. https://caribbean.unwomen.org/en/materials/publications/2018/11/gender-based-violence-in-trinidad-and-tobago.

Human Rights Watch. 2014. *Not Safe at Home: Violence and Discrimination Against LGBT People in Jamaica*. New York: Human Rights Watch. https://www.hrw.org/report/2014/10/21/not-safe-home/violence-and-discrimination-against-lgbt-people-jamaica.

Mahfood, Emile Najeeb. 2000. "History." *Mahfood Family Tree*. https://www.mahfoodfamilytree.com/History.html.

Miller, Herbie. 2007. "Brown Girl in the Ring: Margarita and Malungu." *Caribbean Quarterly* 53 (4): 47–74.

Miller, Kei. 2019. *In Nearby Bushes*. Manchester: Carcanet.

Morgan, Paula and Valerie Youssef. 2006. *Writing Rage: Unmasking Violence through Caribbean Discourse*. Kingston: University of the West Indies Press.

"NDTC's 51st set for weekend start." 2013. *Daily Gleaner*, 23 July.

Neigh, Janet. 2021. "Reading Kei Miller's 'In Nearby Bushes' in the Wake of Dub Poetry." *Journal of West Indian Literature*. 30 (1): 18–43.

Poets.org. n.d. "Erasure." https://poets.org/glossary/erasure.

Reckford, Michael. 2002. "The Dramatic Don Drummond." *Daily Gleaner*, 1 February.

———. 2013. "Two new dances by NDTC veterans." *Daily Gleaner*, 26 July.

"Rhumba dancer stabbed to death". 1965. *Daily Gleaner*, 1 January.

Robinson, Tracy S. 2000. "Fictions of Citizenship, Bodies Without Sex: The Protection and Effacement of Gender in Law." *Small Axe* 7: 1–27.

Segree, Clifton. 1998. "Remembering great movies." *Daily Gleaner*, 4 May.

Selim. 1976. "The Instrumentalist." *Jamaica Daily News*, 20 September.

Smith, Delores E. 2016. "Prevalence of Intimate Partner Violence in Jamaica: Implications for Prevention and Intervention." *International Journal of Child, Youth and Family Studies* 7 (3/4): 343–63.

———. 2018. "Homophobic and Transphobic Violence against Youth: The Jamaican Context." *International Journal of Adolescence and Youth* 23 (2): 250–58.

Spooner, Mary. 2009. "Does Eligibility for Protection Orders Prevent Repeat Abuse of Domestic Abuse Victims in Caribbean States?" *Journal of Family Violence* 24 (6): 377–87.

Thakur, Dhanaraj. 2018. "How do ICTs mediate gender-based violence in Jamaica?" *Gender and Development* 26 (2): 267–82.

Titus, Mark. 2018. "Missing Woman Found in Shallow Grave." *The Jamaica Star*, 27 February, 2018. http://jamaica-star.com/article/news/20180227/missing-woman-found-shallow-grave.

UN (United Nations). n.d. "DataUNODC: Intentional Homicide." https://dataunodc.un.org/dp-intentional-homicide-victims.

UNDP (United Nations Development Programme). 2016. *Caribbean Human Development Report: Multidimensional Progress: Human Resilience Beyond Income*. New York: UNDP.

UNHCR (The UN Refugee Agency). n.d. "Gender Based Violence."
https://www.unhcr.org/gender-based-violence.html.

UN Women. n.d. *Caribbean Women Count: Ending Violence against Women and Girls Data Hub*. https://caribbeanwomencount.unwomen.org/about.html.

Walters, Basil. 1982. "The Immortal Trombonist." *Jamaica Daily News*, 30 April.

chapter 13

The White Woman's Burden

Empire, Embodiment and Trauma in Caribbean Fictions

Paula Morgan

The tumultuous history of the Caribbean peoples, as is the case for all histories of cataclysmic encounters between societies, exists vividly in the imaginaries of its interlocutors of diverse ethnicities and seasons. In the wake of debunking official narratives and authoritative voices comes the need to craft diverse imaginaries, each of which, by definition, is devoid of any potential claim to be the exclusive and entire truth. A primary agenda in the Caribbean has been exploring fictional evocations of the psychosocial outworking of empire's terrorist dynamic on black female bodies, given their location as productive, reproductive and sex labourers in the service of the capitalist machinery. Caribbean fictions have also inscribed – initially on its margins and recently more centrally – a paradoxical, psychosocial location for white women as beneficiaries of empire, as well as bearers of its lacerations and repositories of unresolved pain.

This chapter explores cross-gender, cross-ethnic and intra-ethnic constructions of white female embodiment during slavery and at a key transitional period between emancipation and independence. Through an exploration of Jean Rhys' *Wide Sargasso Sea* (1966), Monique Roffey's *The White Woman on the Green Bicycle* (2009), and Marlon James' *The Book of Night Women* (2009), this argument locates white women paradoxically as laden with culpability for the excessive abuses of empire and its legacies, and as abused, scapegoat figures in a sacrificial imperial economy that demands expiation of collective guilt. The aim of this chapter is to amplify insights articulated by a cross-section of the region's creative writers that the perilous out workings of deep-rooted, systemic abuses and societal injustices cannot be restricted to its victims. Perpetrators are not in hermetically sealed environments, locked away from the toxicities and contaminants that they release into the social order.[1] I argue that in the black vs white contestations over ascendancy, blame and belonging, white women's bodies also assume an excess of meaning, which correlates with the excesses of erasure, amnesia, silencing and dissociation that undergirded the enterprise of the Indies and its aftermath.

WOMANKIND: CULTURAL IDENTITIES IN MOTION

The novels speak to a complex range of issues which are of interest to feminist and post-colonial theorists. Adrienne Rich, in "Notes towards a Politics of Location" asks, ". . . where, when and under what conditions have women acted and been acted upon as women" (Rich 1986, 214) She points to the specific subjection of women through female embodiment. Arguably, the assertions of black feminists and the differential gendered effects of late capitalism's global relations have constrained Rich's acknowledgement of her own embodiment as Jewish, white, middle class, cared for, safe and privileged. Hence Rich confesses: "I need to understand how a place on the map is also a place in history within which as a woman, a Jew, a lesbian, a feminist I am created and trying to create. Begin though, not with a continent or a country or a house, but with the geography closest in – the body" (Rich 1986, 212). To facilitate our dive into these writerly disruptions of the rigid binaries – black-white, civilized-savage, good-evil, body-soul – which governed social relations in the plantation era and its aftermath, formulations that reject stasis and embrace fluidity will be instructive.

In "Moving Locations: The Politics of Identities in Motion", Aimee Carrillo Rowe and Adela Licona focus on "axes of power which constitute identity" (Rowe and Licona 2005, 11). They argue that relations and movement in space and time are pivotal to the construction of identity.

> To theorize identity categories as a set of practices that constitute and or discipline a community allows us to become more acutely aware of exclusionary or inclusionary relations that tell is who we are. To theorize agency/experience/ consciousness/ "woman" as collective processes, as movements that arise out of collective struggles and oppositional forms of being, is to reconfigure the face of feminist resistance. The term "location" may be more fully utilized if we reconfigure it in the spatial, temporal, corporeal and community bases out of which it emerges . . . as shifting over time and space". (Rowe and Licona 2005, 11–12)

This chapter will engage the applicability of these formulations to white and black women within Caribbean plantation societies, and burgeoning post-emancipation social orders and nation states. Even when the lifeblood of the plantation depended on race-based rigidly demarked and policed boundaries, the inexorable leakage of cultural identities occurred. Moreover, both the establishment of apparently watertight boundaries and the inevitable leakage – both of which were reflected in embodied materiality – depended upon discourses, narratives told to selves and to others about who we are and who we are becoming (Hall 1995, 224–25).

Like the enslaved and the indentured, Euro-Creole plantation women were constrained to grapple in creative ways with migrations, which have generated estranging relocations of the home and the world within the framework of violent and violating cultural confrontations. The resultant condition of "unhomeliness" as defined by Homi Bhabha as inherent to that "rite of extra-territorial and cross-cultural initiation" redefines comforting distinctions between private and public space: "The recesses of the domestic space become sites for history's most intricate invasions. In that displacement, the borders between home and world become confused; and, uncannily, the private and the public become part of each other, forcing upon us a vision that is as divided as it is disorienting" (Bhabha 1992, 141). The traumatic nature of this crisis is arguably evident in the work of successive generations of knowledge workers, including creative writers, who are enmeshed in uncanny repetition of its terms and compulsive grappling with its parameters (Morgan 2014). In the working through of cultural trauma, defined by Ron Eyerman as "trauma mediated through various forms of representation and linked to the reformation of collective identity and the reworking of cultural memory" (Eyerman 2001, 1), their fictional offerings become controversial sites of collective memory and memorialization. Far from demonstrating objectivity, they are valuable representations of the manner in which people groups and their interlocutors trace/mask/obscure trajectories, beg pardon, accept/shift culpability and entrench/disrupt gendered identity formations.

PARADOXES OF BEING WHITE, COLD AND SAD

It was the Dominica-born Euro-creole author Jean Rhys who initially figured the white woman of the planter class as simultaneously complicit with and traumatized by the imperial order.[2] Rhys' seminal post-emancipation novel, *Wide Sargasso Sea* (1966), charts the perilous journey of a white creole girl who is coming of age during the dismantling of empire. Meandering without moorings through a nightmarish fallen Eden, she is unable to lay hold of a secure ontological sense as she grapples with the horrific psychosocial dynamic which had been kept in place by planter class systemic terrorism and dehumanization of the raced other. The minority white hegemonic group is burdened by what Ramchand, after Fanon, terms "a terrified consciousness" characterized by personal and social disintegration, fragmentation and loss, with no way back "home" (Ramchand 1970; Morgan 2003).[3] Ironically, it is the quintessential fictional daughter of the planter class who first articulates the identity and displacement traumas that resonate throughout the entire corpus of Caribbean literature. Antoinette asks . . . "Who am I and where is my country and where do I belong and why was I ever born?" (Rhys 1966, 61).

Inexorable acculturation through generations of island living has produced creolized white women whose language, culture and world view reflect deep and profound interpenetrations with that of the enslaved Africans. Antoinette Cosway, traumatized by a weak and ineffectual maternal bond, and eventually mother loss due to insanity and death, is parented by the fierce, black nurse Christophine. The myriad complexities of imperial social relations, the paradoxical impact of black parenting and the tentacles created by contradictory allegiance to the colonial superpower is evident from the opening paragraph of the narrative: "They say when trouble comes close ranks. And so the white people did. But we were not in their ranks. The Jamaican ladies had never approved of my mother, 'because she pretty like pretty self' Christophine said" (Rhys 1966, 15). So, who are they? The ambiguous pronominal reference is the first indicator of floating identity markers. It speaks to the hostilities between the anglophone and francophone plantocracy, and the manner in which intra-ethnic, cross-national desires and prejudices play out on female bodies. The child, rejected by "Jamaican ladies", finds meaning and significance through the pronouncement of the black, enslaved, 'other' mother, Christophine.

Like the island body, Antoinette of French creole maternal lineage is pillaged for her fortune by a second son of British nobility, who has been disenfranchised by laws of primogeniture. She is unloved by her cold husband, sexually enslaved, and, in response to her growing mental instability, physically imprisoned. Antoinette ends her untenable imprisonment in a British mansion, by laying claim to the resistance modalities of the enslaved – setting fire to the house and leaping to a violent death. This final act parallels the ultimate act of resistance of the enslaved who leapt off the slave ships or opted for the self- destruction of their chained bodies so that their spirits might be free.

Rhys' powerful, unsettling fictional offering has created a rich symbolic and ideological repository, which has been mined by generations of writers seeking to capture the vantage point of Euro-creole women. Reaction has been eruptive because of the insidious ways in which the text plays with tropes of enslavement and belonging in ways that complicate and obscure white female complicity with Britain's genocidal project.[4] Rhys' evocation firmly lays in place a problematic symbolic location for white women, which resonates throughout the corpus of West Indian literature. In the psychosexual dynamic of the encounter between worlds, the white female body figures as an ethnic boundary marker for the supremacy of empire builders and for the 'othering' of the black and mulatto female bodies. The blacks are predominantly relegated to productive and reproductive labour, while the mulattos are perceived as built for sexual labour. Rhys' fictional intra-group fashioning demonstrates that symbolic boundaries are just as subject to leakage as actual boundaries. The result is that in her economy, it is the white woman's body which becomes a template for the narrative inscription of the traumatic encounter between worlds.

WHITE BUT LIKE MILK: THE ANGELIC AND THE DEMONIC

Marlon James' neo-slave narrative, *The Book of Night Women* (2009), set in 1803, deals with an extensive slave rebellion engineered by women from the Montpelier Estate in eastern Jamaica. Undermining common stereotypes in relation to divergent ethnic, gender and occupational roles and modes of being, James, in this revisionary construction, makes the chief architect of the rebellion, the highly influential head house slave Homer, supported by six mulatto daughters of the vicious, lascivious slave overseer, Jack Wilkins. Thus, he addresses the historical marginalization of female acts of resistance, and evokes a rebellion which is informed by the distinctives of enslaved women's psycho-sexual locations and embodied realities.

Of interest to this discussion is representations of the role of white women in the outworking of the murderous violence with which the enslaved had to contend daily; the strict ideological split between black and white womanhood as embodied most fulsomely in the characterization of Isobel Roget of Coulibre; the ginormous, debased sexual appetite which the archetypal plantation "lady", Isobel, develops despite her idealized psychosexual symbolic positioning as a pure flower of empire and boundary marker for white supremacy; the grim domestic intimacies, collusions and violations which bind female enslavers and the enslaved; and the thin edge between sanity and insanity which they walk together, as they negotiate the excesses of violence and play of shadows that constitute plantation life.

James treats penetratingly with the constructions of whiteness in plantation society, accentuating its dark underbelly, horrific brutalities, and deep insecurities. The sexualized, transgressive, boundary-crossing nature of plantation society is embodied in the French creole Isobel of Coulibre, who signifies on Rhys' Antoinette of Coulibre, as filtered through James' contemporary ideological stance and male gaze. Isobel, the violent, hypersexualized white creole gone native is represented as riddled with lust and as addicted to debased sexual encounters as the most degenerate of male slave masters. For all women in this economy, rape and the progeny of miscegenation looms large, begging the question of why the materiality of the flesh becomes such an apt slate for the inscription of oppressive, cross-ethnic power relations.

Opposing ideological notions of womanhood and womanness are played out in the interface of Isobel Roget with the green-eyed mulatto, Lilith. Isobel is schooled in Victorian notions of white womanhood, with its pillars of piety, purity, submissiveness and domesticity. She comes to adulthood announcing her identity as a good girl who demands to be treated in a respectable, courteous, and genteel manner (James 2009, 47). The façade swiftly wears thin under the overheated lasciviousness of plantation life, which find resonance in her proclivities. James' Lilith, on the other hand, under the thrall of Henry Fielding's *Joseph Andrews*, unsuccessfully tries to wrench out of the plantation systemic, a reality which mirrors her futile self-identification as a mulatto whose partially white bloodline singles her out for uplifting romantic attention from the dominant male – the plantation master. The two women function as cautionary portraits reflective of the outworking of flawed and dangerous ideologies of womanhood. The juxtapositions are foreshadowed in their naming. Isobel's name is of Hebraic origin and means God's promise or pledged to God; Lilith is named after the rebellious figure of Hebraic mythology, as the mother of Adam's demonic offspring. Isobel, who appropriates and disciplines Lilith for seeking to seduce her love interest, seeks to create a benighted foil, against which the trappings of white womanhood would shine all the brighter.

The construction of whiteness is strongly focused on facades and externalities. Isobel appears floating at the ball, angelically costumed in white: "It white but like milk, a deep colour that look like you could drink it. Right on her bosom wrap a cloth that hide and show at the same time. Look one way it white, look another way it clear to see through, look another way it shiny" (James 2009, 150–51). Isobel is mantled in this magnificent whiteness, which exemplifies enlightened thought and ideals. The masking, duplicities and play of shadows is revealed at the bosom/heart, which reveals alternative realities based on one's vantage point. Isobel regales Lilith, again based on externalities, race binaries, and biological determinism: ". . . Why are you here? You tried to use the mind, the brain, but you silly girl, those things are lost to the negro. What you have is a back that won't break, a skin that won't crack, legs like an ox and teeth like a horse. How fortunate that we have found each other, Lilith!"

Binary constructions of race embodiments are pivotal to self-definition. The figurative language Isobel deploys conveys a strange conglomeration of beasts of burden – an ox, which is domesticated to plough fields; a horse, which is domesticated to carry men. Moreover, like dumb animals, these labouring creatures must be seen as willingly yielding to domestication and biologically constructed to not show the lacerations of routine brutalization. James adds a facet to the ongoing discourse on how to define humanity and womanhood within the totalitarian regimes predicated on the inhumanity of the perpetrators and the non-humanity of its victims. If, as Zora Neale Hurston asserts in *Their Eyes Were Watching God*, persons are relegated to labouring conveniences: "tongueless, earless, eyeless conveniences all day long. Mules and other labouring brutes had occupied their skins" (Hurston 1937, 1), by what modality and in which space do they reclaim their humanity and femaleness?

Given the significance of enslaved female bodies for the reproduction of labour and for the disciplinary regimes of the plantation society, rape became practically endemic to the social order. As disciplinary mode, rape functions to cut down frisky, out-of-order women. The fear of black rape of white women triggered immense violence directed at enslaved men who so much as looked at a white woman. Black and white male sexual jealously also generated reductive myths of prodigious black male sexual endowment. Despite the ravages of Isobel's eventual drug and sex addictions, her ultimate humiliation – rape by two enslaved men during the Montpelier uprising – saves her life for a fate worse than death: the ignominy of possibly bearing mulatto offspring.

Lilith, in her resistance to systemic and systematic sexual violation, embraces instead a highly functional though dangerous, alternative construction of womanness, predicated on agency and resistance. Twice she murders her sexual abusers. In the latter case, to cover her tracks, she burns the plantation house, shedding the blood of her mistress, their young children and their enslaved, and creating reason for a spate of brutal and irrational revenge killings. Darkened conscience and vengeful spectral presences haunt her, driving her to affirm her murderous acts of self-defence, while threatening the loss of her sanity and humanity. Significantly in opposition to gender constructions of feminism's profuse articulations, this dark construction of womanness is rooted in silencing, inarticulateness, irrationality, erasure, submergence, masking, repression and hauntings.

In opposition to subject construction hinged on darkness, wildness and unspeakability is Lilith's tentative foray into the potential of love as connection and eros as power. Barriteau's theorizing in "Coming Home to the Erotic Power of Love and Desire" is instructive. Lilith grapples with a growing emotional connection with the Irish overseer Quinn who loves her and seeks to generate within the plantation, an enclave in which love, respect and sexual connection transcend exploitation and brutality. Even Lilith's receipt of careful instruction in the use of oral sex to increase her power over the white man yields to a state in which desire, sensuality and power topple over into what Barriteau, after Audre Lorde, terms: "a psychological and ontological dimension to assessment of the ideology of intimacy" (Barriteau 2012, 79) Drawing from Jónasdóttir, Barriteau redefines sexuality away "from being perceived only as an identity category to being understood as 'a set of relations, activities, needs, and desires, productive and reproductive powers and capacities and organizational and structural contexts'" (p.79). Both formulations feed into the concept of "a transformative, creative power at the centre of the love relationship" encapsulating both "care and erotic ecstasy" (pp. 83–84). These notions, applied to the burgeoning relationship between and Lilith and Quinn, opens up new counter-cultural potentialities of being and knowing for the interracial couple. Although the experiment ultimately fails, it nevertheless bears fruit in their child, Luvey Quinn, carrier of the seed of possibility planted by the union and narrator of the story, with its transformative potential and its ethical challenge. And it is this foil that reveals by juxtaposition, in all of its ugliness, sex as instrumentality, subjugation, oppression and escapism – a mindless, bottomless, indiscriminate, insatiable desire – which enslaves Isobel Roget, as surely as it threatened her fictional foremother, Antoinette Cosway. Ultimately, instrumental sex cannot meet the need for ontological security. Barriteau theorizes for many women, the "pursuit of what they define as erotic ecstasy" as located outside of themselves rather from within, is the eventual "source of their powerlessness" (p.84).

Stripping way of the hypocrisies of Enlightenment discourse, which undergirded the "civilizing" enterprise of the Indies, James constrains acknowledgement that the terrorist regime of plantation societies, which, in the absence of any credible moral authority, needed to be kept in place through ever-increasing excesses of violence, were a direct outgrowth of the dark underside of the Enlightenment. According to Forter, James suggests that the subjectivity of the white planter and managerial classes was indeed structured by . . . the disciplinary regimens of Enlightenment reason. Yet, this dispensation of modern power depended on the exercise of premodern power upon the slaves: "modes of physical coercion" which align with "the *feudal* order's dissemination of terror through the 'spectacle of the scaffold'– through public displays of bodily mutilation that indexed the master's absolute authority while subduing through terror those forced to witness it" (Forter 2016, 2). This ugly tale prefigures catastrophic outcomes should contemporary societies revert to brutalities of this nature, in the interest of protecting of their economic and political ascendancy. This cautionary tale points to the past, but even more so, it points to future potentialities and threats.

WHITE FEMALE BODIES IN MOTION

Would that we could relegate these tragic psychosocial locations of white women's bodies to the distant past. But not so. Monique Roffey's *The White Woman on the Green Bicycle* (2009) deals with the final wave of colonial migrants – low-level functionaries of Empire who arrived on the brink of independence in the mid-1950s to confront its legacies, emerging nationalisms and manifest anti-imperial hostility and sentiment. Roffey, a Trinidad-born author based in Britain, pens her fictional love letter to the island that invokes her parents' experience, to stake a conflicted claim for those colonials who remained, seduced by love of place, power, people and culture. The historical novel maps the interface of personal, familial and national histories; cross-ethnic, female-to-female power relations within the intimacies of the home; the challenge of building viable island societies out of the detritus of oppressive history; and the impact of systemic, race-based class relations.[5]

Deploying a bold strategy of naming and engaging key national, political, sporting and cultural personalities – both living and dead – as well as actual dates and events, Roffey blurs the boundaries between the fictional and the real to create strategic intervention into contemporary national discourses. Like Jean Rhys, Michelle Cliff and Barbara Lalla, this writerly female descendant of the planter class carries the post-colonial white/mulatto woman's burden – a problematic schizophrenic location of benefitting on an ongoing basis from the ignominies and legacies of empire, while adopting a more or less measured, anti-imperial stance.[6]

The young Britisher, George Harwood, and his French wife, Sabine, newlywed when they arrive on the island in 1956 for a short stint in a shipping company, share an intense love which withers under the dubious mores of the island culture. True to the pathways traversed by the first wave of conquistadors, George enters the island bent on conquest and dominance. Erasing/evading the essential evils of imperialism, he accesses the island even before he arrives through narratives of conquest and dreams of possession.[7] Neat classifications of the environment flow into disciplinary ways of knowing and modes of governing for profit, thus naturalizing the imperial process. George becomes a wealthy land developer, astutely preying on cycles of unrest unleashed in the aftermath of empire.

The novel is replete with intense ambivalences and paradoxes of love and hatred, belonging and non-belonging, beginning with evocations of the landscape. In the Rhysian tradition of inscribing the environment as excess, which overwhelms the sensibility, landscape is personified as a highly sexualized and restless green woman with intents and motives, with whom both George and Sabine converse. Constantly in motion, animal and vegetative worlds throb with rapacious and reproductive excess that dwarfs the human. The natural environment is represented as oppressive, stiflingly hot, overrun with predatory insects, yet, simultaneously as seductive, quivering with light, generative and combative. This contemporary novel leans in the direction of colonial myths of the heat, humidity and fecundity of tropical landscapes keeping sexual organs in constant excitation, and thus, so the rationale goes, makes lechery and miscegenation inevitable.

The expatriate woman enters into a far more relational love/hate interface with the island. The book cover images reality transfixed into fiction. Roffey indicates that her mother, Yvette Roffey, who, like Sabine, arrived in Trinidad with her husband in 1956, created a stir on the streets of Port of Spain by cycling through the city, becoming known as "the white woman on the green bicycle". The cover image extends the association graphically.[8] The white woman who does not have the desire to dominate the island body is entrapped in another conundrum. Sabine's desire is figured in the novel as a projection of the island's desire for a saviour and a father. Williams, to whom she writes repeatedly but never posts the correspondence, becomes her secret repository for dialogue about the traumas of the land. She carries, in a visceral manner, the woundedness of the island elicited by wrongs and injustices, which he presumably has the political and operational power to correct.[9]

Historical processes stacked to generate ruptures, discord and violence are kept in balance by spatial divides shored up by prejudice, stereotype, which keep all in their place. From the inception, Sabine refuses to retreat into the shady, incestuous enclaves reserved for whites on the island and characterized by the Country Club. So, into a society vested in stringent prescriptions of belonging and non-belonging, severing and segregating, rides a beautiful, young white woman with the courage to break spatial barriers which undergird the racially hierarchical social order – blond hair streaming, elegant legs bared in shorts, halter top and Dior sunglasses, the white woman on the green bicycle becomes a highly charged, sexualized, travelling symbol of the colonial spatial strictures, given shared assumption by the majority black and white alike of her non-belonging in that space. Oblivious to the tensions and hierarchies of the social order, she publicly flaunts her scantily clad body within the context that white womanhood was jealously guarded as the carrier of the genetic seed and the boundary marker of empire.

The willingness to dive into and learn the broader society bespeaks an openness and impulse towards connectivity and curiosity about the common people. She longs to claim a space of belonging and heart share within the nation and an affinity with its dispossessed and disempowered women. Since power attribution is kept in place by spatial boundary markers, offering visual access to the black man in the street is tantamount to inviting touch, invasion, violation. It makes her a lightning rod for the complex of desire mixed with ridicule, contempt, cynicism, hatred of the mass of people, which is barely contained by spatial division. Raw hatred overspills in the street when she is chased from Williams' pre-independence public education forum, the 'University of Woodford Square'. Corrosive verbal vitriol pierces her spirit when she is threatened by a Midnight Robber during her first

Carnival celebration in terms which echo the torture meted out to enslaved women: "Maybe you get a taste of you own treatment. Maybe we go bury you up to your neck near a red-ant nest! Paste your pretty mout wid honey . . . OR wossssss. Fill dat lovely ass of yours with gunpowder" (Roffey 2009, 256). Sabine's innocent appropriation of mobility and a broader place leaves her vulnerable to bear in her body the reproach of whiteness. This she willingly draws into her inner being as she assumes the role of scapegoat for the sins of empire.

In the present time of the novel, 2006, her decaying seventy-five-year-old physique signals that she has borne in her body the ills of the social order. Exemplary of an army of people who dare to possess a land for which they are physically unprotected, sun has stolen the youth, beauty and elasticity of her skin, placing her among a host of "white people, speckled with chocolate flecks of melanin, their skin like advancing leprosy" (p.124). Her retreat from the hostility of the street reflected in lack of mobility and exercise over the years leaves her entrapped in a fat, ageing body soused with anodynes of alcohol, Valium and nicotine, peering through the burglar bars of her mansion at a recalcitrant kingdom.

The novel culminates in flawed and evasive acts of atonement. Fifty years later, an act of vicious police violence against their housekeeper's son becomes the catalyst for George to enact a grandiose gesture of commitment to the well-being of the island. His doomed struggle against police violence is predicated as figuring the police as the root cause of the myriad wrongs which the island suffers – corruption, materialism, theft, abuse of authority, anomie, squandering of the national patrimony, neglect and impoverishment, violence and injustice meted out to the majority of the black population. And Sabine, characteristically visceral in her responses, reappropriates mobility, rides to the station, and in her own grand gesture, guns down the policemen. Both can be interpreted as limited and futile acts of atonement aimed at erasure of their own ancestral and personal culpability and complicity.

CONTINUITIES AND CONCLUSIONS

The complicities, vulnerability and unhomeliness of the white creole women are consistent across all three texts. The writers test the potential for female engagement across race and class lines specifically in relation to the hegemonic class and the Afro-Caribbean enslaved or impoverished urban and rural folk. Given the history of oppression and ongoing social inequities, is there potential for women across race and class lines to join hands in solidarity?[10] All of the texts explore the potential for black-white female collaboration and communality. In all instances, the prospects for solidarity heightened at times of social crises when the power dynamics were shifting off their axis and breakdown of established social order was borne, albeit inequitably by women of all racial groupings. Through furtive domesticities, Lilith, who, arguably in response to guilt at destroying the Roget family, becomes substitute family, supporter and enabler for Isobel, through her dissolution into addictions and her pregnancy of unclear paternity.

The sisterhood of Rhys' Antoinette and Tia has been hotly debated in Caribbean critical discourse. Jeremy Metz revisits the bitter debate which Braithwaite's indictment of Rhys' fiction triggered, in a manner which is both revealing and profoundly disturbing. While I value his conclusion, which recommends acknowledgement of the cultural traumas which impact Afro-Caribbean writers and critics, there are numerous issues with his reading of the climatic incident at the burning of Coulibri as exemplifying the interface between cultural trauma, and direct physical and psychological trauma.[11]

Reading this scene as the catalyst of traumatic wounding, elements of which are erased and repressed, Metz identifies it as the trigger for Antoinette's mental health decline and the catalyst for her suicidal leap. Metz argues:

> In this traumatic moment, Tia acts as perpetrator. Through her willed act of violence, she transforms Antoinette into a victim who thereafter bears the psychological scares of her traumatization. However, as a member of a community that has suffered profoundly from slavery, racism and economic exploitation, Tia is a victim of cultural trauma caused by the group to which Antoinette belongs. The moment in the narrative is precipitated by Antoinette's failed attempt to renounce membership in this group of victimizers to join Tia's community of victims. Tia and Antoinette's reciprocal and opposing positions in the traumatic moment conditions their response to each other and the reader's responses to the text. (Metz 2016, 48)

There are several flawed assumptions here. A major issue is the representation of the rabble of newly emancipated enslaved as victims of cultural – as opposed to direct – trauma. Many of those present would have borne scars of far more extreme markings of physical wounding though rapes, whippings, burning, amputations and myriad other spectacular abuses. The majority would have been living in abjection – poverty, dirt, squalor, hunger, diseases which characterize every day insidious trauma; the majority would carry the scars of psychological trauma – disorientation, displacement in time and space, identity confusion, destiny malaise, low self-esteem, silencing, lack of confidence, agency, and resolve. And all this, before cultural knowledge workers mobilize, decades and even generations later, in the interest of intergenerational transfer of cultural trauma.

Secondly, to lay responsibility for Antoinette's descent into mental disorder at Tia's feet as trauma perpetrator is to erase the mind-bending operations of plantation society – its abuses, deceptions, violations and irrationalities. It is to discount the wounding caused by maternal rejection and mother loss; it is to minimize the impact of the cold, soul-destroying husband. In other words, this reading demonstrated victim blaming and the same insensitive reading practices against which Metz warns.

All of the fictional female white creoles suffer from unhomeliness, but only Roffey's character rises above self-serving, convenient identification with the Afro-Caribbean folk and seeks to act, albeit in a futile manner, on behalf of the other and in the interest of the burgeoning social order. Trinidad, which she desperately longs to leave, infiltrates her soul and leaves her grappling with issues which are ultimately common to all – how to steer the nation out of the maw of its history into the fulfilment of its vast potentialities. Roffey boldly inserts her domestic family narrative into the nation's political farce. She claims a place of significance for those colonials who remained and, despite the considerable economic advantages they enjoyed, bore the brunt of shame and pain during the dismantling of Empire. Her narrative retraces the ground covered by Jean Rhys – of emigrants adrift in a dazzling, threatening landscape of excess; of feminization of sexually charged landscape laid open to patriarchal rites of possession; of nascent New World societies reeling under mayhem, crime, corruption, poor ineffective governance; unequal wealth distribution; neglect and impoverishment of disempowered segments of the African and Indian population; of sexual appropriation and abuse of women of all ethnicities; of cross-ethnic female-female collaboration to save the children of all ethnicities; of white children tenderly nursed by a black servant class in a system of other mothering; of black and white male complicity in self-enrichment and social oppression; of the saving grace of women's love and of grand self-sacrificial gestures, which, in the final analysis, may prove insufficient to alter disastrous trajectories, as the islands stumble along their perilous pathways, groping towards the clear light of day.

NOTES

1. It is this assertion which crystallized into the pivotal insight of George Lamming's *Natives of My Person* and William Faulkner's *The Sound and the Fury*.
2. This theme and similar characterizations of iconic "white" creole woman are picked up by numerous writers of Euro-creole descent, including Michelle Cliff (*No Telephone to Heaven*), Monique Roffey *(The White Woman on a Green Bicycle)*, Lawrence Scott ("The Wedding Photograph") and Olive Senior ("The Pain Tree"). Scott's and Senior's stories are the focus of my essay entitled "History's Intricate Invasions: Ageing and Traumatic Memory in Caribbean Literature" in *The Bloomsbury Handbook to Ageing in Contemporary Literature and Film*, edited by Heike Hartung, Sarah Falcus and Raquel Medina (London: Bloomsbury Publishing).
3. In *The Wretched of the Earth*, Frantz Fanon argues: "Decolonization is always a violent phenomenon . . . the need for this change exists in its crude state, impetuous and compelling, in the consciousness and in the lives of the men and women who are colonised. But the possibility of this change is equally experienced in the form of a terrifying future in the consciousness of another 'species' of men and women: the colonizers" (Fanon 1961, 29).
4. The early critique of Afrocentric scholars such as Edward Kamau Braithwaite, who then decried any real life potential for cordial black mother/sister relations on the plantation, finds an echo in contemporary feminist criticism. In *Contradictory Omens: Cultural Diversity and Integration in the Caribbean* (1974), Brathwaite delivered a controversial judgement of Rhys' work: "White creoles in the English and French West Indies have separated themselves by too wide a gulf and have contributed too little culturally, as a group, to give credence to the notion that they can, given the present structure, meaningfully identify

or be identified, with the spiritual world on this side of the Sargasso Sea" (Brathwaite 1974, 38).

5. Structured in four parts, beginning with the present time of the novel, Trinidad 2006; Trinidad 1956; Trinidad 1963; and Trinidad 1970, the domestic drama shows periods of socio-political significance: 1956 marks emergence and crystallizing of the nationalist movement, which was, by definition, an anti-imperial movement; 1963 is the year after the nation gains its independence from the British; 1970 the year of the Black Power uprising. The story is told in a series of flashbacks and flash forwards pivoting around birthing the nation and the loss of hope in the nationalist People's National Movement, and the present time. Disillusionment looms large in a series of interviews that George conducts with iconic figures, including the father of the nation, Eric Williams, with whom Sabine is obsessed.
6. Countless associations link Roffey's novel with *Wide Sargasso Sea*. Roffey borrows Rhys' opening lines to link marooned white women of post-emancipation and pre-independence seasons. Like Annette Cosway of Martinican ancestry, this French subject on British colonial territory is "pretty like pretty self. Both women encounter parrots whose cries echo their existential dilemmas. Both harbour intense relations with black servant women/sisters. Sabine finds a foil in Irit, who, after years, loves Trinidad passionately but retains her Hungarian accent and cultural habits, whereas Sabine internalizes/appropriates the sing-song Creole and loses her cultural moorings.
7. His mind and his dreams are filled with catalogues, classifications, semantic systems and filtering through Western epistemological frames which facilitate possession of a beauteous new world: "books of birds and butterflies, mammals, reptiles and insects of the Antilles marine life geology. Architecture, cricket. Rum distilling, cocoa . . . " (Roffey 2009, 192–93).
8. The white women coloured green on the book cover is conflated with the land, which she figures as the green woman she loves/hates. Her belonging is inscribed by the contradictory impulses of mobility afforded by the cycle and fixity imaged in the precise framing between the quintessential symbol of tropical exoticism and languor, two palms both leaning inwards as if to embrace.
9. The disempowered and neglected folk is represented by Granny Seraphina, the Afro-Caribbean grandmother, the avid supporter of the new political order and the one who suffers the brunt of its shortfalls, despite highly political vociferous in her support of the PNM, dies without receiving the pipe-borne water which becomes emblematic of a better life.

10. Aimee Carrillo Rowe, in "Be Longing: Towards a Feminist Politics of Relations", points to the infinitely shifting and contingent relations of belonging, argues: "The sites of our belonging constitute how we see the world, what we value, who we are (becoming)" (Rowe 2005, 16). Moving Adrienne Rich's notion from an individual to a collective basis, Rowe places the emphasis on craving for a connectivity which takes us to the end of ourselves and tips us towards others – in this instance the denigrated barely human colonized subject and sensibility which is also seeking to connect with other. According to Rowe, "who we love, the communities we that we live in, who we expend our emotional energies building ties with – these connections are all functions of power" (p.16).
11. The climatic incidence at the burning of Coulibri, as told through Antoinette's perspective reads:

    > Then, not so far off, I saw Tia, and her mother and I ran to her, for she was all that was left of my life as it had been. We had eaten the same food, slept side by side, bathed in the same river. As I ran, I thought, I will live with Tia and I will be like her. Not to leave Coulibri. Not to go. Not. When I was close, I saw the jagged stone in her hand but I did not see her throw it. I did not feel it either, only something wet running down my face. I looked at her and I saw her face crumple up as she began to cry. We stared at each other, blood on my face, tears on hers. It was as if I saw myself. Like in a looking glass (Rhys 1966, 38).

REFERENCES

Barriteau, V. Eudine. 2012. "Coming Home to the Erotic power of Love and Desire in Caribbean Heterosexual Unions." In *Love and Power: Caribbean Discourses on Gender*, edited by V. Eudine Barriteau. 72–105. Kingston: University of the West Indies Press.

Bhabha, Homi. 1992. "The World and the Home." *Social Text* nos. 31/32, *Third World and Post-Colonial Issues*: 141–53.

Braithwaite, Edward. 1974. *Contradictory Omens: Cultural Diversity and Integration in the Caribbean*. Kingston: Savacou Publications.

Burrows, Victoria. 2004. *Whiteness and Trauma*. New York: Palgrave Macmillan.

Cliff, Michelle. 1978. *No Telephone to Heaven*. New York: E.P. Dutton.

Eyerman, Ron. 2001. *Cultural Trauma: Slavery and the Formation of African-American Identity*. Cambridge: Cambridge University Press.

Fielding, Henry, 1707–1754. 1991. *Joseph Andrews; and, Shamela*. London: J.M. Dent and Rutland, VT: C.E. Tuttle.

Forter, Greg. 2016. "A Good Head and a Better Whip: Ireland, Enlightenment and the Body of Slavery in Marlon James's *The Book of Night Woman*." In *Slavery and Abolition* 37 (3): 521–40.

Hall, Stuart. 1995. "Cultural Identity and the Diaspora." In *Identity: Community, Culture, Difference*, edited by Jonathan Rutherford. 222–37. London: Lawrence and Wishart.

Hurston, Zora Neale. 1937. *Their Eyes Were Watching God*. New York: Harper and Row.

James, Marlon. 2009. *The Book of Night Women*. New York: Riverhead Books.

Lalla, Barbara. 1989. *Arch of Fire*. Kingston: Kingston Publishers.

Lamming, George. 1971. *Water with Berries*. London: Longman Caribbean.

———. 1994. *Natives of My Person*. London: Pan Books.

Metz, Jeremy. 2016. "The Trauma of the Caribbean Text: Ethics and Problems of Victimizer and Victims, Authors and Readers". PhD diss., University of Maryland.

Morgan, Paula. 2004. "Homecomings Without Home: An Intertextual Reading of *Wide Sargasso Sea* and *No Telephone to Heaven*." *Journal of Caribbean Literatures* 111 (3) (Special Issue on Jean Rhys, edited by Mary Lou Emory): 161–70.

———. 2005. "A Tall Far Island Floating in Cobalt Paint: Race and Displacement in Rhys's Fiction." Proceedings of the Jean Rhys Conference and Literary Festival, University of the West Indies, School of Continuing Studies, Dominica.

———. 2023. "History's Intricate Invasions: Ageing and Traumatic Memory in Caribbean Literature." *Bloomsbury Handbook to Ageing in Contemporary Literature and Film*. Edited by Heike Hartung, Sarah Falcus and Raquel Medina. Bloomsbury Publishing.

———. 2014. *Banal Violence and Trauma in Caribbean Discourse*. Kingston: University of the West Indies Press.

Morrison, Toni. 1970. *The Bluest Eye*. New York: Washington Square Press.

———. 1987. *Beloved*. New York: Vintage International.

Ramchand, Kenneth. 2004. *The West Indian Novel and Its Background*. Kingston: Ian Randle Publishers.

Redhead, Carol. 2012. "Madness and the 'Unspeakable Act' as Both Corrupt and Indispensable in Morrison's Texts." Presentation at the 'I Dream to Change the World': Literature and Social Transformation, 30th Annual Literature Conference, University of the West Indies, St Augustine. https://www.researchgate.net/publication/301359263.

Rich, Adrienne. 1986. "Notes Towards a Politics of Location." In *Blood, Bread, and Poetry: Selected prose, 1979–1985*. New York: Norton.

Rhys, Jean. 1934. *Voyage in the Dark*. Harmondsworth: Penguin.

———. 1968. *Wide Sargasso Sea.* Harmondsworth: Penguin.

Rowe, Aimee Carrillo, and Adela Licona. 2005. "Moving Locations: The Politics of Identities in Motion." *NWSA Journal* 17 (2):11–14. https://www.jstor.org/stable/i400039.

Senior, Olive. 2017. *The Pain Tree.* Leeds: Peepal Tree Press.

chapter 14

Violence, African Women and Slave Films

Revisiting Sankofa and 12 Years a Slave

Lisa Tomlinson

FILMS CENTRED AROUND ENSLAVED AFRICANS THAT ARE PRODUCED and directed by black male filmmakers often confront the terror of slavery and stress the sexual violence against African women's bodies as central tropes. These black filmmakers use the representation of sexual violence to contextualize a cinematic approach that exposes the brutal realities of slavery. To rewrite sanitized versions of the history of slavery, black male filmmakers also attempt to recast the representation of life on the plantation through the voices and narratives of enslaved Africans by employing sexual subjectivities. However, while black filmmakers are often applauded for their success in reimaging the history of slavery, I argue that black male filmmakers significantly reproduce the sexual violation against enslaved African women in cinematic presentations of their bondage experiences.[1] Accordingly, this reproduction of violence often excludes black women as active agents in the struggle for emancipation. My chapter critically analyses and revisits how black women's bodies are objectified in the films *Sankofa* (1992) and more recently, *12 Years A Slave* (2013), which amplify the history of white supremacist and patriarchal violence against black women. Unfortunately, they romanticize black women's dependence or reliance on male agency to overcome this sexualized subjugation.

HOLLYWOOD'S TREATMENT OF PLANTATION SLAVERY

Historically, Hollywood's version of plantation slavery has betrayed a fetish for sexual violence against black women. In the article "Dismantling Slavery-Master Narrative Through African Diaspora Cinema", Judylyn Ryan lists six ways to creatively unearth how films about African enslavement have misrepresented the realities of enslaved Africans. The six narratives proposed are all reflective of highlighting a white saviour trope that often centralizes whiteness or white people's role as positive figures in the lives of enslaved black people. These depictions of plantation society disable the agency and voice of enslaved Africans and locate them at the periphery. It also does not hold the system of slavery accountable for the dehumanization of African people. In Ryan's concept narrative of rescue for instance, Africans are presented as being rescued from the Dark Continent, Africa, and from "perpetual though benign servitude of white abolitionists" (2003, 130). Then she goes on to introduce the narrative of acquiescence, which reinforces the idea that Africans played little or no role in the collective liberation of themselves (131).

This representation holds despite historical evidence that shows that most runaway enslaved Africans were not assisted by benevolent whites. The narrative of indebtedness is another fictional notion that is used to preconfigure Africans as beneficiaries of European civilization or culture, and white people as the donor (Ryan 2003, 131). The narrative of tabula rasa and disconnection are interwoven because the former depicts Africans as people without culture and knowledge of self, literally as blank slates, while the latter reinforces the notion of Africans as without cultural connections, unlike other immigrants to the Americas (132). Therefore, Africans are portrayed as cultural orphans without ancestors or origins. The narrative of interracial romance points to the sexual attack on black women by underscoring how this narrative promotes and "redefines the systemic sexual exploitation of enslaved Black women by White men as an event where Black women were voluntary participants" (131). As Ryan explains, the most popular representation of this narrative is the revisionist account of the relationship between Sally Hemings, an enslaved African woman, and statesman Thomas Jefferson (132). A more contemporary portrayal of this romanticized relationship can be seen in Alex Haley's film, *Queen: The Story of an American Family* (1993), starring Halle Berry as the tragic mulatto character. Queen is the product of an interracial romance between Ester and James Jackson Jr., her slave master. Hence, popular narratives such as Hemings' and Jefferson's relationship supports the myth of the romantic involvement of the slave master and enslaved women, and like Hemings, they were "subjugated to slave law and vulnerable to sexual abuse and they bore their masters many children" (Tillet 2012, 44).

Although Ryan's proposed narrative choices are crucial in retelling the true history of enslaved Africans, and how black male filmmakers attempt to dismantle how these stories are told in movies, the interracial romance discourse has been the most complicated narrative to retell or revise. So, while films such as *Sankofa* have been successful in humanizing enslaved Africans and reaffirming their agency, it falls short in redressing the excessive depiction of sexual abuse against black women. Unfortunately, this failure might be because many slave-themed films, as Boyce Davies (2014) argues, fail to challenge the standard trope of violence and the dehumanizing of African bodies. As she further argues, "gratuitous display of the black woman's raped and flayed body is chosen to represent the horrors of slavery" ("12 Years a Slave Fails to Represent Black Resistance to Slavery," *The Guardian*, 10 January 2014). Frances Smith also makes a critical point that black women do not tend to focus on sexual abuse as the defining aspect of their existence. This approach contrasts with black male enslaved narrators, who often depict the sexualized violence against black women to address their own loss of masculinity (Smith 1994, XXXIII). In this way, 'slave' films have firmly constructed the image of "the Black male slave fighting for freedom" (Jackson 2014, 173–77). Therefore, this cinematic choice further problematizes how the brutal violence of slavery is represented on the big screen. Even when it is the expressed commitment of black male filmmakers to represent the authenticity of enslaved lives, the sexual aggression against black women remains the disturbing trope.

Sankofa Rewriting Hollywood Enslaved Cinematic Narratives

> "When Black bodies are on the stage, Black perspectives must be reflected. This is not simply a matter of 'artistic interpretation'; race and sex play a pivotal role in determining who holds the power to shape representation." —Tonya Pinkins

Sankofa, an independent film production, represents one of the first slave-themed movies to depart from Hollywood's slave-master narratives as characterized by Judylyn Ryan. So, while historians have long debunked these distorted narratives, Hollywood depictions, such as the helpless enslaved African or the white saviour trope, continue to prevail in their films. In this way, filmmaker Haile Gerima significantly rejects mainstream images that represent Africans as subordinates and voiceless. Gerima underscores the importance of recovering history or ancestral past as "an enabling metaphor", a "revisioning of cultural mythologies" (Holloway 1992, 2). Therefore, Gerima counteracts the narratives that enslaved Africans were without culture or knowledge of self and were merely dependent on good whites for their freedom. Essentially, the filmmaker addresses many of the misrepresented 'slave' narratives that Hollywood repeatedly perpetuates through its mythical depiction of slavery and presents the film as a site of memory. Yet, he still falls into the trap of re-enacting sexual violence against black women. Hence, the movie situates the story of Shola, the protagonist, in black history, thus giving a black woman a starring role. Gerima' centralization of Shola is worth commending because 'slave' narratives in film and literature often focus on the experience of enslaved African men, giving scant attention to the experiences of the women. Additionally, in Pamela Woolford's interview with Gerima, she cites the uniqueness of *Sankofa* compared to other films of the time because of how he [Gerima] "shows slave women with just as much power for rebellion and motivation for revolt as men" (Woolford 1994, 95).

Although Mona, an African-American model, is transported back to the plantation to relive the atrocities of slavery and to rediscover or retrieve her ancestral past, Gerima's female character, Nunu, does not experience the extreme sexual aggression as Mona, or at least the violence is not displayed on the screen. Instead, the viewers learn through stories that Nunu was raped on a slave trip by a white man. Nonetheless, she is portrayed as rebellious and the spiritual mother for the enslaved African community who draws on African spiritual powers to defy the oppressors. For example, she killed a white overseer just by staring at him. Nunu's character parallels with Nana Peazant in Julie Dash's film *Daughter of the Dust*, who represents the matriarch of the Peazant family and is the keeper of traditions on the island. While Nunu's multi-dimensional depiction troubles how some critics analyse *Sankofa*'s extreme violence against black women, we must not overlook how a close reading of gender-based violence is a useful approach in allowing the viewers to consider or apply a critical black feminist analysis that rewrites black women's existence into chattel slavery as (re)represented on screen or other visual forms.

Sankofa introduces Mona scantily dressed; in the background, a white man is taking her picture, which immediately signals the objectification and commodification of black bodies in the fashion industry. First, Mona's body in this scene is being objectified through the white male gaze. In this way, the camera lens serves as the male gaze, as the white fashion photographer instructs her: "Let the camera do it to you", nuancing the sexual nature of the photo shoot on the beach near the slave castle. The camera also figures Mona as the exotic or sexualized 'other'; the photographer directs: "Mona, more sex." Undoubtedly, the sexual overtones in the photographer's language can metaphorically describe the mainstream modelling space as one that oversexualizes black women's bodies. Gouldrine goes even deeper to frame this seductive space as rooted in the historical sexual violation against black women on the plantation. She states, "This figurative rape recalls the intersection between economic and sexual exploitation of Black women during slavery" (Gouldrine 2002, 19–20).

Successively, Mona is soon reprimanded by an elder for lacking self-knowledge and assimilating into white American culture as a fashion model. This scene also reveals how black women's bodies are policed in the US fashion industry, popular culture and even by black men themselves. Mona's punishment by the elder signifies that the ancestor is displeased with her choice in allowing herself to be sexually exploited for profit. The male drummer scolds her like a child, warning that, by exposing her body on the place that her ancestors had been captured, she shows no respect for them. Consequently, she is badly beaten and transported via filmic time to a nineteenth-century plantation. Now transformed into Shola, she is forced to live the life of her enslaved ancestors and to suffer her master's brutality. In this way, Shola is turned into the 'house slave' whose body becomes the sexual property of her master. This alternative narrative is in no way dramatized as the common interracial romance between enslaved African women and their enslaver. On the contrary, the viewers witness horrific scenes of Mona being raped repeatedly by her master. In describing the graphic sexual oppression that the female character endures, Z'etoile Imma asserts that such scenes "make visible and make known the impossible pain of sexual violence in his film" (Imma 1993, 23). However, the use of sexual violence as a trope to visualize black women's rape on screen uncovers more than the visibility of Mona's pain and suffering. Scholar Alexander Weheliye argues that the graphic images of Shola being raped by her master serves as the porno trope, "the cross-fertilization of violence and sexuality" (Weheliye 2014, 102). His use of the word porno to illustrate the violent scenes, therefore, implies a white male gaze, which dangerously evokes the perverse 'pleasure' that is engendered from this horrific site or scene of sexual aggression. Though Kelly Lawler (2016) contends that the choice to not show rape "would sanitize sexual violence" ("How 'Birth of a Nation' Mishandles Its Portrayal of Rape"), this again raises the concern of authenticity in representing the experiences of enslaved Africans. Unquestionably, the different critiques also speak to the complexities of depicting the authentic or uncensored experience of slavery through visual platforms.

Additionally, one must consider the question of the constant burden that is placed on the black woman's body to recuperate the past or to act as site of memory – a motif often used in popular black culture to demonstrate how black women are taken away from contemporary spaces and transported to the distance past to recover or retrieve history and cultural loss (Tomlinson 2017, 25). For example, in *Sankofa*, rape is treated as a site of memory that acts to confront the distortion or whitewashing of black history, which is 'explored' and 'interrogated' by the female character. As such, when a gang of white enslavers violently tear off Mona's clothes in the slave chambers, it is the threat of rape that initiates her entry into captivity and begin her ultimate journey to self-discovery. Consequently, Shola pays the price for her transition from the present to the past. While Woolfork shares Lawler's position on the film, she admits that Mona is indeed portrayed as "self-indulgent, inappropriate, and active opposition to the scared slave castle" (Woolfork 2010, 38). As Mona approaches the chamber, she protests, "You are making a mistake. I am American. I am not a slave."

Furthermore, despite the sexual aggression that Shola experiences at the hands of the enslaver, she remains an outsider in the enslaved community. Shango repeatedly questions Shola, "Why yu can't be like one o' we and crawl like a snake pon u belly?" to convince the viewers that she is not one of them and naive because she is ill-equipped to take on the "task of negotiating freedom within the context of oppression" (Woolfork 2010, 139). This idea is held of Shola because she is believed to have absorbed the master's belief system, echoing Mona's earlier rejection of her African heritage. Therefore, Shango's depiction of Shola's ambiguity to her sexual oppression and unreadiness to fight for freedom overlooks and reduces the role of female 'house slaves' to sexual victim, or as a supporter or proponent of existing power structures of patriarchy and white supremacy. In his revision of traditional assumptions of the domestically enslaved, historian Albert Bushnell Hart asserts that "house slaves were not the refined or well-kept slave" (quoted in Smith 2008, 128) as is often assumed in romanticized 'slave' narratives. Enslaved Africans who resided in the house were in fact also physically and sexually abused by their enslavers and life was just as traumatic for them as the 'field slaves'. The house slaves also engaged in rebellious acts and took part in revolts (Rushdy 1999, 109). Importantly, decades later, Tillet Salamishah, in *The New York Times*' review of the film *The Birth of a Nation,* expresses disapproval of how Gerima constructs black men's rebellion against the system as the catalytic response to seeing black women's sexual violation by white men, while silencing black women through victimization and "den[ying] the[m] their revolutionary gesture". In her initial assessment of the role of women in *Sankofa,* she overlooks Shola's silence to her oppression and naivety to her brutal conditions.

Finally, while Gerima defies the "preferred reading" of the interracial romance narrative or seduction, he over-emphasizes the sexual violation of the black female body through his "portrayal of the animalistic domination of anal rape" (Phillips et al. 2003, 142). As he defends in "Filming Slavery",

"I shot it [the rape scene] to show that white men's relationship to black women was like an outright treatment of an animal . . . " (Woolford 1994, 95). In this way, the viewers get a close shot of Shola's face and shoulder, and the master's face is hidden. We see his hand fiercely clutching Shola's hair with her painful facial expression and silent groans. Gerima also justifies the graphic representation of the rape scenes, explaining that he does not "see it [rape scenes] as graphic. Graphic, to me, is going into the elements of sex. For example, in that scene I don't even show him; I don't even care to show him. I only show the map of the idea of what I wanted to express" (Woolford 1994, 95). Gerima's comment reveals his effort to not only revise the narrative of interracial romance, but he also wants to reorient the viewers' attention to the terror of slavery through the uncompromised and gruesome act of rape. Unfortunately, to achieve this counternarrative, he relinquishes power from Shola, and makes her rely on Nunu and Shango for strength and spiritual reclamation.

PRIVILEGING WHITE MASCULINITY IN *12 YEARS A SLAVE*

The final section of my chapter turns to a close reading of *12 Years a Slave*. Dissimilar from *Sankofa*, *Twelve Years a Slave* follows the traditional narrative structure of 'slave' films, focusing on a male-centred narrative. In this way, the film depicts a historical narrative that stresses "Black men as national history while" denying "Black female historical agency and impact" (Charlery 2018, 1). This storyline contrasts with *Sankofa*'s female-centred plot, where women, such as Nunu, are empowered and play an active role in resisting the plantation system. Yet, like *Sankofa*, the black female body is recurrently violated to evoke the brutality of slavery. Even so, Tamara Winfrey Harris commends Steve McQueen for "a uniquely impressive job of illustrating female slave experiences through the women that Northup encounters during his years of bondage" (Harris 2013, 7), but she cautions that *12 Years a Slave* is still told through the eyes of Solomon Northup. Charlery also points out that "Patsey is denied narrative, agency, life and body" (Charlery 2018, 4). Equally, artist Kara Walker, whose artwork has also been criticized for reproducing black stereotypes, shares her alarm at the scenes portraying Patsey's abuse: "Staying on that scene and coming back to Patsey over and over, she is abused and deteriorating and wanting to die. We don't need to see that scene over and over again" (quoted in George 2013, 18). Indeed, decades later, the debate about the over-representation of violence against black women's bodies in slavery-themed films continues to resurface.

Although the film has a male protagonist, Steve McQueen, as noted by Winfrey Harris, tries to provide a close shot of the lives of enslaved African women: Eliza, Harriet Shaw and Patsey. While Harris' observation holds true (the privileging of female narratives), all the women's stories recast the horror of sexual and physical abuse. Eliza, for instance, is characteristically confined to the role of concubine. There is no resistance to rape on her part. Instead, she forcefully submits to the sexual demand of her enslaver to improve life for herself and her children. Eliza is later demoted from domestic to field worker status where she is further physically abused by the master's wife. Eliza is also separated from her children in one of the most dehumanizing scenes. She is kicked by the slave owner, Ford, who cruelly auctions off her young daughter and son. Sadly, Eliza never receives her freedom as promised by her white master, and she spends the remainder of her life heartbroken. Harriet Shaw also goes along with the master's infidelity to advance her social status. Formerly enslaved, Harriet marries her master because she believes it is worth being freed from the beatings and the inhumane treatment endured daily by enslaved Africans. God, Mistress Shaw says, will one day deal with these men who force their "love" on women, who, as property, cannot say no. For these sexual representations of black women confined to sexual abuse or concubine, *12 Years a Slave* receives similar criticism as Gerima's *Sankofa*. For instance, Stevenson's critique of *12 Years a Slave* is also concerned with how enslaved women are portrayed. She asserts that McQueen's imaging of Patsey, Eliza and Harriet Shaw "readily adopts this favourite Hollywood trope of Black women as sexually bound to powerful white men" (Stevenson 2014, 108).

She gives examples of other films that have the same plot or themes of caging black women within concubine relationships. Such films, she cites, include Steven Spielberg's *Lincoln* and Quentin Tarantino's box office blockbuster, *Django Unchained*. While Stevenson does not take issues with McQueen's inclusion of the excessive depiction of sexual violence against black women, she notes that he paints black women as one-dimensional, and that he overlooks how enslaved women were resistant to their own oppression. Taken further, Harris asserts, "The bargains that enslaved black women were forced to make with their bodies in order to survive are judged against racist and sexist views of chastity and womanhood and often viewed as a form of complicity" (Harris 2013). Therefore, I add that McQueen fails also to challenge the interracial romance narrative. Rather, Eliza and Harriet are merely depicted as willing agents and "by focusing on women as sex servant for white men" (Kay Siebler 2021, 195), a tragic role of agentless black enslaved women.

In contrast to Eliza and Harriet, Patsey's relationship with her enslaver is not the consensus, romanticized interracial romance that Ryan describes. Of course, it is Patsey, the prized cotton picker who suffers the most of the three women. She becomes the slave owner Edwin Epps' sex object and is regularly raped. Similar to Shola, the viewers witness the rape scenes at nights. Unlike *Sankofa*, the scenes are less graphic. They take place in the dark and close-up shots of Epps' and Patsey's faces are used. The images of naked bodies are not graphic, so while the scene is not overtly sexual, it is very violent, wherein Epps uses extreme force to get Patsey to take part in the sexual act by slapping and choking her. Additionally, Patsey is physically abused by her master and his jealous wife. During the dance scenes in the Epps home, the wife throws a bottle and hots Patsey. She also jabs her in the head with a sharp object at another social event. However, the most graphically violent scene is the severe beating of Patsey. She is whipped for sneaking to a nearby plantation for soap, a luxury that her master does not provide. When she returns, Epps violently confronts Patsey and forces her to tell him of her whereabouts. With a cracking voice, she explains that she left the plantation to purchase a bar of soap: "I stink so much, make myself gag," she cries. "Five hundred pounds of cotton. Day in Day out! And for that I will be clean." Her frank response angers Epps, and he orders that she is stripped of her clothes and tied to a tree. With the pressure from his jealous wife, he demands Northup to "Strike her until flesh is rent and meat and blood flow."

Like the representation of Eliza and Harriet, McQueen again fails to reimage the black cinematic trope and depicts Patsey within the one-dimensional stereotype as the abused enslaved black woman. In this regard,

McQueen's imaging does not disrupt the standard trope, but instead affirms it within the passivity of the non-resistant female other. Furthermore, the rape scenes in the film give the viewer the impression that Patsey is passive and, like Shola, she has no control over her body. McQueen faintly gives Patsey agency wherein she defiantly leaves the plantation without permission to get soap and expresses the desire to take her own life. "I ain't got no comfort in this life," she tells Northup. Taking one's life was a common form of rebellion against slavery and an act of heroism. McQueen's subtle representations of Patsey's rebellious behaviour is still not enough; however, it offers new ways of seeing and filming womanhood.

Seemingly, like Gerima, McQueen is also committed to the project of retelling black women's stories. McQueen has stated that one of the characteristics of Northup's autobiography that encouraged him to adapt this narrative to screen was because of the many images of enslaved women whom Northup detailed in his lengthy account. Assessing the scenes of enslaved women in the film, one can only conclude that Northup's narrative of enslaved African women is remembered mainly through the violent sexual assaults that they experienced and reads no differently from the filmmakers. At the same time, McQueen can be applauded for how he rejects romanticized accounts of the relationship between black and white women. In this way, he candidly implicates white women as perpetrators of violence against black women. In fictional work and revisionist histories about enslavement in America's South, white men are largely depicted as the sole perpetrators. This painfully vivid illustration is in stark contrast to the conventional kind-natured southern belle archetype, who often develops a nurturing relationship with the enslaved African women. The re-released film *Gone with the Wind* exemplifies this embellished relationship between the female enslaved African women and white women. In *Out of the House of Bondage,* Thavolia Glymph writes that the study of women and slavery in the United States has empathetically documented that planter women "suffered under the weight of the same patriarchal authority to which slaves were subjects" (Glymph 2008, xx) In *12 Years a Slave,* McQueen challenges and recontextualizes this narrative, making the relationship between Mistress Epps and Patsey totally opposite to the fairy tale one between Scarlett O'Hara and Prissy in *Gone With The Wind.* Although McQueen's revision attempts to capture the violent interaction between black females and plantation white women, one cannot ignore the anti-agency role that Eliza's and Patsey's characters are assigned. This representation is in juxtaposition to the white women who share some forms of power with their husband. And the enslaved women do not resist the abusive treatment from either the mistress or enslaver. As such, *12 Years A Slave* does not comprehensively question the white male status quo, but rather supports elements of the patriarchal system.

CONCLUSION

As part of a larger black feminist scholarship, historical stereotypes of violence against black women's bodies in slave-themed movies continue to reshape the discourse that is being challenged by film critics and academics. Therefore, the objective of this chapter is not to treat the sexual violence that black women experienced during enslavement as insignificant or reductive. However, my purpose is to analyse how using a feminist lens affords a more complex and fulsome reading of the representations of enslaved black women. Clearly, in repairing the distorted versions of 'slave stories', black male filmmakers see the need to depend on the sexual violence that most enslaved girls and women encountered – a reality that cannot be ignored. Harriet Shaw's story, for instance, parallels the real-life narrative of Harriet Jacobs (from *Incidents of a Slave Girl*), who was forced to marry a white lawyer to protect herself from the sexual harassment of her master.

Therefore, it is understood that violent oppression is important for black filmmakers to graphically portray the brutality of slavery because in Butler's words, it "get people to feel slavery" (quoted in Elia 2019, 21). However, violence against black women must not be the only cinematic trope used to define enslaved black women's existence. Slavery-themed films must offer different perspectives of black women, where they can also actively resist and play a role in their freedom and community. Hence, moving beyond the themes of subjugation and the horrors of sexual violence. To portray black women only "as disempowered sex slaves", Kelly maintains, "is to deny them the disunity of this history that inscribe active resistance, organised escapes, and communal acts of leadership" (*USA Today*, 7 October 2016). Characters such as *Sankofa*'s Nunu are, therefore, instructive in informing viewers of the diversity of enslaved black women's experiences and, importantly, a counter-narrative to traditional slavery-themed films that diminish the humanity of black women.

NOTE

1. Films by black male filmmakers that depict violence against enslaved women include: *Antebellum*, Gerard Bush, QC Entertainment and Lionsgate, 2020; *Birth of a Nation*, Nat Parker, Fox Searchlight Pictures, 2016; *The Book of Negroes* (six-part miniseries), Clement Virgo, CBC and BET, 2015; *Roots*, the miniseries, Marvin J. Chomsky, David Green, John Erman, and *Gilbert Moses, Wolper Productions, 1977. *Gilbert Moses is an African-American director, who directed some episodes of *Roots*. However, the principal directors of the film were David Green and John Erman.

REFERENCES

Abegunde, Maria. 2016. "Black Magic Woman and Narrative Film: Race, Sex, and Afro-Religiosity." *Black Camera* 8 (1): 247–49.

Boyce Davies, Carole. 2014. "12 Years a Slave Fails to Represent Black Resistance to Slavery." *The Guardian*, 10 January. https://www.theguardian.com/world/2014/jan/10/12-years-a-slave-fails-to-show-resistence.

Charlery, Hélène. 2018. "'Queen of the fields': Slavery's Graphic Violence and the Black Female Body in 12 Years a Slave (Steve McQueen, 2013)." *Transatlantica: American Studies Journal* 1 (1): 1–9.

Collins, Ronald K.L., and David M. Skover. 2013. *On Dissent: Its Meaning in America*. Cambridge: Cambridge University Press.

Elia, Adriano. 2019. "Old slavery seen through modern eyes: Octavia E. Butler's Kindred and Haile Gerima's Sankofa." *Altre Modernità: Rivista di studi letterari e culturali* 1: 20–30.

Foster, Frances Smith. 1994. *Witnessing Slavery: The Development of Ante-bellum Slave Narratives*. Madison: University of Wisconsin Press.

Glymph, Thavolia. 2008. *Out of the House of Bondage: The Transformation of the Plantation Household*. Cambridge: Cambridge University Press.

George, Nelson. 2013. "An Essentially American Narrative: A Discussion of Steve McQueen's Film '12 Years a Slave'." *New York Times*, 11 October, AR18.

Gourdine, Angeletta K.M. 2002. *The Difference Place Makes: Gender, Sexuality, and Diaspora Identity*. Columbus: Ohio State University Press.

Harris, Tamara Winfrey. 2013. "12 Years a Female Slave – Not Coming to a Theatre Near You." *American Prospect*, 6 November. http://prospect.org/article/12-years-female-slave%E2%80%94not-coming-theatre-near-you.

Horton, Dana Renee. 2018. "'You Will Sell the Negress!': Using the Post-Neo-Slave Narrative to Revise Representations of Women in Django Unchained and 12 Years a Slave." *Americana: The Journal of American Popular Culture, 1900 to Present; Hollywood* 17 (2).

hooks, bell. 2000. *Feminism Is for Everybody: Passionate Politics*. London: South End Press.

Jackson, Kellie Carter. 2014. "'Is Viola Davis in it?': Black Women Actors and the 'Single Stories' of Historical Film." *Transition* 114 (1): 173–84.

Lawler, Kelly. 2016. "How 'Birth of a Nation' Mishandles Its Portrayal of Rape." *USA Today*, 7 October. www.usatoday.com/story/life/movies/2016/10/07/birth-of-a-nation-nate-parker-rape-gabrielle-union/91694398.

Phillips, Kimberley Louise, et al., eds. 2003. *Critical Voicings of Black Liberation: Resistance and Representations in the Americas*. Münster: LIT Verlag.

Rushdy, Ashraf H.A. 1999. *Neo-Slave Narratives: Studies in the Social Logic of a Literary Form*. New York: Oxford University Press.

Ryan, Judylyn S. 2003. "Dismantling Slavery's Master-Narratives Through African Diaspora Cinema." In *Critical Voicings of Black Liberation: Resistance and Representations in the Americas*, edited by Kimberley Louise Phillips et al., 127–45. Münster: LIT Verlag.

Siebler, Kay. 2021. *Black Women Shattering Stereotypes: A Streaming Revolution*. Lanham, MD: Rowman and Littlefield.

Smith, John David. 2008. *An Old Creed for the New South: Proslavery Ideology and Historiography, 1865–1918*. Carbondale: Southern Illinois University Press.

Stevenson, Brenda E. 2014. "12 Years a Slave: Narrative, History, and Film." *Journal of African American History* 99 (1–2): 106–18.

Tillet, Salamishaha. 2016. "How *The Birth of a Nation* Silences Black Women." *New York Times*, 12 October. https://www.nytimes.com/2016/10/16/movies/how-the-birth-of-a-nation-silences-black-women.html#:~:text=First%2C%20they%20are%20silenced%20by,in%20the%20horror%20of%20slavery.

———. 2012. *Sites of Slavery: Citizenship and Racial Democracy in the Post–Civil Rights Imagination*. Durham, NC: Duke University Press.

Tomlinson, Lisa. 2017. *The African-Jamaican Aesthetic: Cultural Retention and Transformation Across Borders (Cross/Cultures Series, Volume 196)*. Leiden: Brill Publishers.

Turner, Diane D., and Muata Kamdibe. 2008. "Haile Gerima: In Search of an African Cinema." *Journal of Black Studies* 38 (6): 968–91.

Weheliye, Alexander, G. 2014. *Habeas Viscus: Racializing Assemblages, Biopolitics, and Black Feminist Theories of the Human*. Durham, NC: Duke University Press.

Woolfork, Lisa. 2010. *Embodying American Slavery in Contemporary Culture*. Champaign: University of Illinois Press.

Woolford, Pamela. 1994. "Filming slavery: A Conversation with Haile Gerima." *Transition* no. 64: 90–104.

chapter 15

Public 'Dis-chord'

Popular Music and Gender-Based Violence in Jamaica[1]

Sonjah Stanley Niaah and Nicole Plummer

THIS CHAPTER IS DIVIDED INTO TWO PARTS. Part 1 introduces the problem of gender-based violence (GBV) in Jamaica. The complex intersection of key variables that compound the way that GBV is experienced and finds support in the socio-cultural fabric of Jamaica is defined and explained. Part 1 outlines the scope of cultural studies analysis as well as key questions raised towards an understanding of Jamaica's culture of entitlement to the bodies of women and girls. In part 2, what is presented as the 'dis-chordant' underbelly of Jamaican music, in particular dancehall, is outlined using the following themes: The Ten Commandments of Man: Exacting Expectations; 'Hit You Let You Feel It': Power, Violence and Control in Relationships; 'Wreck A Pum Pum': The Dynamics of Sex and Violence; and 'Stop the Violence Against Women': Shifting Paradigms.

PART 1: PUBLIC SECRETS AND PRIVATE LIES

GBV is a very public secret that has plagued societies the world over and certainly Jamaica. Over the period 1 January–5 December 2022, there were 394 reported cases of rape in Jamaica compared to 443 for the corresponding period in 2021.[2] According to the Ministry of National Security, annual reported cases of domestic violence increased to eight thousand, representing a 100 per cent increase in the number of Jamaicans reporting the experience of domestic abuse or violence between 2017 and 2022 (Morris 2022).

Scholarly work on crime and violence, specifically sexual offences, has tended to focus on reported crimes of rape, incest, intimate partner violence, domestic abuse, and gender-based crime more broadly, arguably undergirded by a culture of rape which has been masked, but certainly resides securely in the popular cultural scripts of Caribbean societies. Through the lens of cultural studies, semiotic analysis that 'reads' cultural texts to uncover their meanings and narrative theory, which looks at the forms and patterns of stories such as those presented in songs, this chapter uses Jamaican popular music as a site to analyse representations of GBV.[3] We take a cultural studies theoretical perspective on popular music as a site of representation at the intersection with sexuality as a site of power/lessness. We use Jamaican popular music as a site to read GBV as a public 'dis-chord', deliberately referencing musical frequencies, pitches, notes and also songs in the representation of 'dis-chord' where it also denotes discordant values alongside disharmony, discontent and dis-ease. This public 'dis-chord' has been masked as a fetish culture of rape in music beyond the face value of crime statistics and against a historical trajectory which connects Thomas Thistlewood[4] to recent Jamaican musicians promoting a culture of rape and GBV.

Music, a cultural text, emits and reflects the norms, values, attitudes, and aspirations of a society. Music can, therefore, echo violent cultural patterns, systemic hegemonic masculinity and patriarchy, which are all linked to the prevalence of violence, particularly GBV in Jamaica. This chapter utilizes a sample of popular Jamaican music as well as relevant literature to unravel the treatment of and attitudes toward GBV in Jamaica. Specifically, using a combination of primary sources through lyrical analysis, analysis of secondary newspapers and other sources on the incidence of GBV in Jamaica, this chapter constructs a sort of historiography of violence in Jamaican popular music from the late twentieth century to present. Ultimately, this chapter explores the way in which popular music trends speak to a culture of entitlement, an 'aesthetic of rape' and public dis-chord.

Some of the questions that guided the evolution of this chapter were premised on more than twenty years of fieldwork and analysis of Jamaican dancehall music and culture, noting carefully literary studies analyses from scholars such as Carolyn Cooper, whose "lyrical gun" (1994) positions the violence as artistic and the explicitly sexual lyrical content/performance as "erotic play" (1993) and "fertility rituals" (2004). Taking a critical cultural studies approach, we ask the following: what social values, moral landscapes and even pathologies can musical content reveal? How are structures that enable consistent representation of violent lyrics maintained, and more importantly, dismantled? In a society dominated by female-headed households, how does socialization toward GBV flourish?

This chapter is not being written without awareness of the spectrum of pleasures experienced through and around sexual intercourse, including rough sex, sadomasochism and the variety of dominatrix options that see both men and women choosing experiences of subjugation, where various forms of pain are inflicted. Indeed, Cooper (2004) highlighted that "female fertility rituals" expressed in the dancehall space can be interpreted through lyrics and dance, which are performed in honour of the "holy vagina" – holy in the sense of being held in a place of honour and high esteem. Cooper explained the pleasure that women get from rough sex as expressed in song by dancehall artistes such as Lady Saw in "Stab Out the Meat". Here, Cooper explains that 'stab' is merely a metaphor being used in comparison to 'prick', which is what is done to season meat in the Caribbean.

However, this is not the context in which fetishism is being interrogated here. Fetishism is being used in reference to the degree of pathological displacement of erotic interest and satisfaction expressed in sexual encounters that are recorded in the lyrics of some dancehall artists. The fetish is with sex as a supernatural act, where the human is seemingly decentred, excised – a consistent expression which arguably borders on violation of the person. GBV, then, is being camouflaged or even naturalized/normalized in the lyrics of some popular Jamaican tunes as normative sexual intercourse – where men are expected to be aggressive with and possessive of female bodies during sex, and where women expect and cooperate with this assumed gender role. So, whether the sex is consensual or not on the woman's part, the intercourse or even its simulacra is at best violent and abusive (Stanley Niaah, 2010).

Finally, this chapter was not conceptualized without taking account of the songs that run counter to these dis-chordant tunes. These will be explored under the theme, Stop the Violence Against Women: Shifting Paradigms.

A CULTURE OF ENTITLEMENT

Popular music is a powerful tool that can operate as a weapon in some social contexts. There is a long history of anxiety over Jamaican popular music genres such as dancehall (Stanley Niaah 2006; 2021), which has characterized decades of incisive public commentary, journalism and scholarly critique. Music in Jamaica has been critiqued for echoing violent cultural patterns, systemic hegemonic masculinity and patriarchy, which are part and parcel of the complex cauldron that undergirds GBV. In a country that arguably boasts the most churches per square mile, the incidence of violence and propensity towards GBV, in particular, meet with some degree of contradiction when considering the overarching Christian moral codes on which all key socializing institutions function. This contradiction is nowhere more present than in the popular music trends that reveal explicit sexual and violent lyrics, a culture of entitlement, an 'aesthetic of rape' and public dis-chord.

The idea of the woman's body as property, subject to male domination, has been present in Jamaican music for some time, but academic studies have mostly argued for artistic licence in reading what has been considered benign lyrical dexterity. Music by artistes such as Prince Buster, Shabba Ranks, Vybz Kartel, Buju Banton, Mavado, Dexta Dapps, among others, reveal striking evidence of what is being referred to as a culture of entitlement in Jamaica. This culture of entitlement is reminiscent of and has links to the way in which black bodies were commodified by white plantation owners during enslavement, notably the black woman's vagina and uterus, which were subject to various levels of exploitation.

The issue which arises is that the fetish displaces female agency, desire and consent to one's body, which dancehall lyrics mobilize as an ever-present availability to sexual predators, manifested in the dancehall space as characters such as 'gyallis', 'stullas', 'di owner', and in the wider Jamaican society as the 'big man', 'di boss', 'di general' and 'sugar daddy'. What dancehall music displays is the assumption of consent from the woman, resulting in the music being complicit in forms of abuse and rape.

A Christian religious philosophy underpins the foundation of Jamaican society, which feeds dancehall philosophy around gender roles, stereotypes and status, and that also seems to inadvertently normalize the ideologies of male domination over female bodies and children. While not claiming that the bible supports or encourages rape, a dancehall masculinity, through patriarchy, has utilized biblical examples to justify male authority over female bodies and acts as a performative standard for virile masculinity. This Christian religious philosophy underpins the legal system in Jamaica and questions the act of rape in such cases as marriage. First Corinthians 7:3–4 (NRSV10) states that: "The husband should give to his wife her conjugal rights, and likewise the wife to her husband. For the wife does not have authority over her own body, but the husband does; likewise, the husband does not have authority over his own body, but the wife does."

The first half of the scripture is usually quoted in churches by men – that the wife has no authority over her body. However, close examination reveals that the intention of the verse is for mutual respect and consent as, "likewise, the husband does not have authority over his own body". Clearly, this scripture has been taken out of context to support patriarchal narratives.

It is patriarchy and virile masculinity, and specifically a "dancehall masculinity" (Hope 2010) that support the entitlement of powerful men to multiple female bodies, particularly young girls and even boys. A long line of feminist theorists and scholars, notably de Beauvior (1979), Brownmiller (1976), Chodorow (1989), and Green (2004) have identified patriarchy as involving alliances and hierarchies among men that enable and reinforce dominance over women, including through acts of rape. Furthermore, Muturi and Donald (2006, 85–86) explain in the Caribbean context the view that rape is a behaviour learned by men through interaction with others: one is socialized into masculinity, into a culture of entitlement and, thus, into rape. In the second half of this chapter, we detail some of the lyrics pertinent to making a case for a culture of entitlement to women's bodies in Jamaica.

PART 2: THE DANCEHALL DIS-CHORD[5]

A sample of popular Jamaican tunes over the last sixty years, starting with mento, ska and rocksteady and ending with dancehall, tell stories of a culture of male entitlement, deeply engrained divisions of power and male sexual bravado.[6]

"THE TEN COMMANDMENTS OF MAN": EXACTING EXPECTATIONS

"The Ten Commandments of Man" (1963), a ska tune by Prince Buster, explores the culture of male entitlement. A play on the biblical ten commandments, in this song, Prince Buster is a god-like figure to the subservient human woman in the relationship. While arguably satirical, it is deeply reflective of and derived from Jamaica's culture of male entitlement and is demonstrative of toxic masculinity, where the woman is under the thumb of her intimate partner.

The first and second commandments that the woman "shall have no other man but me" and "encourage no man to make love to you [but me]" exact faithfulness from her. The placement of the commandments illustrates the significance of the woman's fidelity. Violence is threatened against "any other man that may intrude in our love", while the ninth commandment, which winks at the complicity of the wider community, threatens femicide if the woman commits adultery.[7] "Men's fear of a partner's infidelity, real or perceived, arises out of the disrespect to his power, authority and threat to ego (virility) that this behavior engenders" (Priestley 2014, 162–163). Murder is used to restore this power and control. It is no wonder then that in 2019, Jamaica was second in the United Nations' ranking of domestic femicides ("Jamaican Women 2nd Most Vulnerable to Domestic Killing – UN report," *Loop Caribbean News*, 20 November 2019). Pottinger, Bailey, and Passard (2019, 1), in a review of archival data of intimate partner homicide-suicide in Jamaica between 2007 and 2017, concluded that "offender obsession, sexual jealousy, and fear of separation" were frequent factors that caused the violent outcomes. This illustrates the need to change cultural attitudes toward intimate relationships.

In "The Ten Commandments of Man" the woman is urged to accept her partner's infidelity, ignore rumours, and act with decorum and self-control at all times. In the sixth commandment, she is proscribed from searching the man's pockets or irritating him with gossip. The seventh orders her to protect his reputation by not publicly confronting him if he is with another woman. She should, instead, discuss the matter privately in their home since he despises "a scandal in public places". In "Sweetheart" (1975) by Bim and Clover, male infidelity is taken to the extreme where the man requests that his wife and his sweetheart should become friends to cure her jealousy. She rejects his offer and counters with an offer for him to befriend her lover, to which he vehemently retaliates: "Never use those words to me again." Though she said she was joking, he retorts: "That is one joke I don't run." A purportedly humorous song, like "Ten Commandments", it highlights the inequities of romantic relationships in Jamaica.

The culture of entitlement and the right to exact 'tribute' from the body of his partner are present in the third commandment, where the woman is required to kiss and caress the man, "honour and obey" him and cater to his sexual desires "seven days a week and twice on Sundays". It is redolent of the Christian patriarchal values to which many Jamaicans subscribe.[8] The woman's agency, autonomy and personhood are non-existent as Prince Buster continues to circumscribe her behaviour even further by ordering her to honour his name so that "every other woman may honour it also" in the fourth commandment. She is prohibited in the eighth from drinking, smoking and swearing.

It is clear from this series of exacting expectations that the woman exists to serve her partner and make his life easier, even as he does little to improve her existence. Instead, the tenth commandment instructs her to be satisfied with her lot and not desire anything that another woman has, or request that her partner buy her anything, since he "will not give thee anything but what/ You actually need for your purpose." In this uneven and one-sided relationship, there is no avenue for the fulfilment of the woman's needs. Indeed, there is little opportunity to express herself, her desires and exert her personhood. It is a classically abusive relationship.

In instances when the woman is provided with "everything"; those provisions serve as an indenture of sorts; a tacit arrangement to remain in the relationship. While Ken Lazarus' hit "Girl" (1971) was seen as a romantic tune, it, too, was replete with entitlement: "Gave you everything and/ Now you say/ Suddenly you want to go away." Echo Minott's 1986 dancehall tune, "What the Hell the Police Can Do" underscores the point that loyalty is the price a woman pays for receiving clothes, shopping trips, tuition, and so on. For transgressing the rules of the relationship, Minott will hit her in the eye, making it "black and blue". Vybz Kartel exacts sexual servitude for the items purchased for a woman in the tune "Tek Buddy"[9] (2003). For items such as money, furniture and electronic goods, the "gyal" must "tek buddy". Specific sexual positions are required for various items.

"HIT YOU LET YOU FEEL IT": POWER, VIOLENCE AND CONTROL IN RELATIONSHIPS

The culture of entitlement is evident in the use of violence to maintain power and control in relationships. This is rooted in patriarchy, which, as "a system produces and reproduces a set of personal, social and economic relationships that enable men to have power over women and the services they provide" (Hope 2006, 37). Jan Stets (1988), citing Walker (1979), provides a comprehensive breakdown of the characteristics of the victims of domestic abuse and the perpetrators. This is important in understanding the pathology of the dis-chordant tunes being examined. Often, a victim of domestic abuse has "low self-esteem, believes in traditional male-female sex roles, accepts responsibility for the batterer's actions, uses sex as a way to establish intimacy, and believes no one will be able to help her except herself" (Stets 1988). The perpetrator also "has a low self-esteem and believes in stereotypical sex roles. In addition, he blames others for his actions, is pathologically jealous, uses sex as an act of aggression to enhance self-esteem, and does not believe his violent behaviour should be viewed negatively" (Stets 1988). "Ten Commandments" reflects this pathology as it disempowers the woman in the relationship and elevates the man; absolves him of responsibility for murder; and underscores gender roles and expectations. In analysing intimate partner violence, scholars observe that the motivations for using violence against a party varies by gender. Men use violence "when they perceive themselves to be losing control of the relationship, or when they interpret their partner's words or behaviour as challenges to their authority" (Renzetti, Follingstad, and Coker 2017, 2). Women typically resort to violence in self-defence or "in retaliation for being attacked" (Renzetti, Follingstad, and Coker 2017, 2). The Jamaican tunes analysed certainly bear out these conclusions. In these songs, violence is used by men to restore power and maintain control, while the women primarily use violence in reaction to aggression.

In "Ten Commandments", Prince Buster uses violence to maintain control. The fifth commandment warns his partner not to make him angry, otherwise she will feel his "wrath . . . descend" on her heavily – a not-too-subtle reference to physical abuse. In the ska tune "Hit You Let You Feel It" by the Two Kings, physical violence is used to reassert control in the scenario where the woman tried to "make a fool" of the man. Hitting her so that she "feels it" is the way for the male protagonist to ensure that the woman knows that he "mean[s] it". In "Legal Rights", a 1983 dancehall tune, Papa San will beat his partner (Lady G) until her body "come dung"[10] if she cheats on him. To maintain a semblance of power in the relationship, and in line with the pathology of victims of IPV outlined above, Lady G responds to this by saying that she will get her cousin in the police force to shoot Papa San, who retorts that guns are not only in the hands of the police. In this toxic relationship in which both grapple for power and control, Papa San and Lady G trade lyrical and metaphorical blows. The dub tune "Fist to Fist Rub a Dub" (1979) by Kojak and Liza has a man and a woman trading blows while at the same time promising to stay with each other.

It is not uncommon for some victims of domestic violence to feel empowered because they hit the perpetrator. Sophia George's "Murder" (1994) outlines the frustrating life led by one victim of domestic violence. Directed by Leo "Big Daddy" O'Reggio, the music video in which the female protagonist, Lorraina, is cheated on and physically abused is superimposed against newspaper headlines referencing domestic violence in Jamaica. Lorraina now has murder on her mind in retaliation for the treatment she has endured. Violence is not the only means used to restore control. Disrespect, dishonour and power are themes in Papa San and Lady G's "Round Table Talk". The unemployed Papa San is given a list of household and parenting chores to do by Lady G. Feeling emasculated, he retorts that Lady G now "run[s] tings". To affirm his masculinity and hurt Lady G, Papa San reveals that numerous young women visit the house and complete the chores. In response, Lady G divulges her own affair and casts doubt on the paternity of their child. The relationship is destroyed by these confessions.

Echo Minott's "What the Hell the Police Can Do" underscores the futility of intervention by the authorities. While the song starts with him "accidentally" punching his woman in the face, it escalates to deliberately "thump[ing]" her in her eye for infidelity. In the music video, Minott is surrounded by community members who support him as he rhetorically asks: "What the hell the police can do?" The implicit, unspoken response is nothing. In societies where victims are often blamed for the actions of the perpetrators,[11] the music video and Minott's rhetorical question are fitting.

Patterning themselves off the violent patriarchal playbook, women who wish to keep their men in check also use violence. In her 1988 hit tune "Kuff", Shelly Thunder hits her partner with a frying pan (kuff) for cheating and doing so publicly by creeping home at 7:30 a.m. It is the idea of losing face in the neighbourhood that provokes Thunder's attack as respect and reputation are important and to be defended at all costs.

"WRECK A PUM PUM"[12]: THE DYNAMICS OF SEX AND VIOLENCE

This section explores lyrics which underpin and even promote aggressively violent sexual escapades and limited or inhibited consent by the victims, as well as language steeped in rape metaphors. In these lyrics, dominance – not pleasure – is the primary focus; the agency and pleasure of the female partner is of little importance. In some instances, she is alienated from her body, becoming a vagina, buttocks or breasts (or all combined). The woman's body becomes the de-personalized canvas or site on which hegemonic masculinity displayed.

While women are combatants on this battlefield, this chapter is primarily concerned with songs done by men, and so the pathology of women who sing of violent sex will not be explored.[13] As Tafari Ama (2017, 120) writes, the ska tune "Wreck A Pum Pum" (1969) by Prince Buster "was the first big time 'slackness' tune in Jamaica's modern music history". It is noteworthy that Jamaica's first very popular "slackness" tune was steeped in misogyny and violence, and alienated the woman from her own vagina.[14] The vagina is symbolic of the feminine; it becomes the site of conquest, that "must be conquered before it becomes too powerful and results in the subjugation and submission of men and the corruption or elimination of their masculinity"

(Hope 2006, 50). Exploring intimacy in Jamaica, Morgan (2017) suggests that distrust between men and women, resulting from their upbringing, is a factor that precludes intimacy and communication in relationships. This may be the root cause of these tense episodes, exacting expectations, and the struggle for power and dominance in romantic relationships. In this battle of the sexes, Prince Buster then chooses to "wreck" and "tear" the vagina to relieve his pent-up urges. Demonstrating little interest in the woman's agency or personality in his two songs, it is unsurprising that he uses the word tear – a traumatic word for most women – to describe the damage that his penis does to the vagina.[15]

Shabba Ranks, in "Caan Done" (1990), follows Prince Buster's trend of alienating the woman from her vagina.[16] The 1994 dancehall hit by Spragga Benz, "Jack It Up", describes violent sex that also isolates the woman from her vagina. In this song, men are advised to "cock up"[17] the vagina and "dig out" its redness. The labia, whose "redness...denotes a healthy, strong vagina" and, by extension, a healthy, strong, aggressive woman, who must be subjugated, is the target for forceful, painful removal and negation. Hence, Spragga Benz's exhortation to "dig out di red" (Hope 2006, 49) without relief. During the conquest, the woman may cry out in distress as expressed in "Agony" (1989) where Red Dragon "rides" her to break her in, as a jockey does a wild horse.[18] In these songs, sex is a violent battlefield for dominance, where the man must be the winner and takes no prisoners.

"Live Blanket" (1987), a song by Shabba Ranks, extols the virtues and pleasure of having someone in bed to provide mutual comfort. On the surface, it may appear innocuous. However, its wording becomes problematic as Shabba sings that women are "live" blankets – inanimate materials to provide warmth and softness, especially when it is cold or when the man needs tenderness. The song is reductionist and functional in its approach to intimacy, rather than romantic. By making her a live blanket – as opposed to a person – the song is very much in keeping with the legacy established by Prince Buster.

Separating the woman from her vagina and her body in general has implications when it comes to agency and consent. The use of date rape drugs is the theme in Little Twitch's "Send Fi Spanish Fly" (1988). He sings that women who are greedy may end up getting poisoned by "Spanish fly".[19]

The song is supposed to be a warning to young women not to take food or drink from anyone, and not to leave them unattended. No line in this song condemns the perpetrator who taints the drink or food. It blames the victim; and by so doing, rape is minimized and even condoned.

Inner Circle's "Sweat" (1992) is a catchy, upbeat tune about a man's sexual fantasy upon meeting a woman. In his fantasy, she is enjoying the intense sexual encounter and sweating. She cries out. On the one hand, crying out can be the cry that comes from ecstasy. Alternately, it can be a cry requesting an end to the sexual encounter. Whichever, the response is that if the woman cries out, the man will continue to "push it some more". Consent during the sexual act is important as one can give consent and during the act rescind it. Songs such as these, which have men pushing some more, feed into a culture in which consent is not always sought or respected. Spragga Benz, in "Could a Deal" (1994), obliterates consent when he sings that, regardless of the woman's input, she has to sample his ""long steel" or penis. "Afi Get Yu Body", by controversial dancehall and reggae artiste Buju Banton, evidences the violence that is prevalent towards women in dancehall lyrics, when he states, "Gyal, mi serious / Mi afi get yu tonight / Afi get yu body even by gun point."[20] These lyrics go beyond fetishizing to the idea of rape and also brings into play a weapon of assault, even a gun crime. These lyrics are engaged with the charge of grievous assault and bodily harm. Whether an extreme metaphor expressing desperation or addiction to the female body or not, the line can be read as a threat. It further conceptualizes the woman as an empty shell, an object for sexual pleasure. Songs with such suggestive lyrics provide evidence of societal norms that minimize the crime to the point of promoting a culture of rape.

The language of rape (and culture of rape) is omnipresent in Mavado's "Squeeze Har Breast" (2007) and "Force It Up" (2007). In the former, after an intense sexual session where her vagina starts to "burn", the woman flees the bedroom. He eventually catches up with her and she complains that she has suffered a vaginal tear and wants to end the session. His response is to throw her on the ground and put her foot in the air and continue the session. "Force It Up" addresses rough sex that is consensual, but the title of the song itself seems drawn from a rapist playbook, where the perpetrator "Force it up hard in her [vagina]". In this warzone, Mavado sings: "Mi cocky versus her punanny war".[21] "Bedroom Bully" (1992), by Shabba Ranks, outlines the intergenerational trajectory of combative sexual norms. Ranks indicates his father was a bedroom bully and his mother gave birth to a bedroom bully. This chapter, by using a sample of songs produced over several decades, provides evidence of this intergenerational perspective. In the lyrics explored, sex is encoded in the language of subjugation, punishment and war.

'STOP THE VIOLENCE AGAINST WOMEN': SHIFTING PARADIGMS

In the period 2017–2022, an increase in kidnappings, rapes, femicide and more largely, GBV,[22] precipitated responses in entertainment spaces such as the 2022 Reggae Sumfest festival, where the main stage was used as a site of activism by artistes Shaneil Muir and Christopher Martin, both of whom called on their audiences to reflect on the lives of female victims. Muir used placards while Christopher Martin called on patrons to say a recent victim's name, which was displayed in a hashtag that formed the backdrop to his performance. Similarly, Romain Virgo first performed "Dutty Man" at the 2019 Reggae Sumfest, following an increase in the outcry against GBV in Jamaica. While dancehall artistes have been criticized for being silent on social pathologies, such as GBV and femicide in particular, these form concrete examples of countervailing acts. This advocacy is imperative to altering attitudes towards GBV.

Performers such as Queen Ifrica, Tarrus Riley, Charly Black, Macka Diamond, Govana, Romain Virgo, Christopher Martin, Kiprich and others are singing out against GBV. This is a departure from musical content previously discussed in this chapter. These songs speak out against rape, femicide, domestic violence, and encourage reporting of violence against women, and protection of women. They advocate shifts in Jamaican culture and attitudes towards GBV. Dancehall artiste Kiprich, in an interview about his new single "Women Protests" (2022), lamented, "I'm tired of the headlines repeating themselves; always about another female gone missing or murdered at the hands of a lover . . . or men in general. Is like it a become a trend." Advocating a polemic shift that goes contrary to the trend laid out by Prince Buster, Kiprich stated: "The man dem need fi realise say dem nuh own no woman life . . . There is never no 'explainable' reason for a man to use his force or a weapon to take a woman's life and think him can justify it" (Lyew 2022). In this statement, Kiprich acknowledged and respected the boundaries and agency of women; a complete reversal and disavowal of more exacting, possessive and hegemonic ideas. Though some may view a number of the songs previously discussed as satirical, satire and humour are often based on reality, and a narrative, often repeated, engrains itself in the common psyche. It is for this reason that several artistes use their songs to counter prevailing narratives surrounding GBV. It is worth mentioning that prior to some of the more recent dancehall interventions, reggae artistes Queen Ifrica and Tarrus Riley advocated against domestic violence and incest respectively in their songs "Daddy" (2009) and "Start A New" (2009).

CONCLUSION

Jamaica has a violence problem. The island is among the top ten most murderous places on earth, nearing civil war proportions in some communities. Germane to this chapter is the fact that Jamaica has the second highest rate of femicide in the world and one of the highest rates of intimate partner violence. Numerous factors produce such statistics, not least of which is the socialization of men (and women) into a culture of violence, particularly GBV.[23] This chapter problematized the issue of GBV as a culture of GBV, notably rape, which music lyrics reflect and serve to underpin, if not socialize men and women into it. We analysed and historicized a sample of popular Jamaican music over at least six decades, moving through the culture of entitlement established in romantic relationships that are heavily weighted in favour of men, but draining to women. It explored the use of violence to maintain power and control in romantic relationships, which are articulated and represented in popular Jamaican music in a manner that borders on pathological. We utilized the same pathological lens to explore representations of sex in music; noting that the language is not only reflective of rape culture, but also rape enabling. We have demonstrated that there is a rape culture that lives in the aesthetic realm of music, but which comes from and is reinforced in the way life unfolds in Jamaica. Words such as 'force', 'tear', 'wreck' and 'bully', among others, cannot be categorized as romantic, but must be seen as a culturing of men to tear, wreck, bully and force sex from women's bodies. The songs alienated women from their bodies; they became pieces of forced, torn, wrecked meat to be stabbed and daggered into submission. And, certainly for further discussion and exploration, this sexual war zone has female artistes championing their ability to take the abuse.

This chapter ends by noting that more artistes are lending their voices as advocates against GBV and it is hoped that their voices will lead to positive changes and a reduction in the number of femicides and rapes in Jamaica. As the lines between performance and performativity remain blurred in music, the onus is on the citizenry to take ownership of the social transformation that must take place.

NOTES

1. Components of this chapter were first presented by Sonjah Stanley Niaah under the title "An 'Aesthetic of Rape': Exploring Dancehall, Music and the Dismantling of Dignity in Jamaica" at the Social Change & Gender-Based Violence: Representations in Caribbean Literature & Performance Cultures Symposium (Virtual), University of the West Indies and University of Leicester, 23 September 2022; and before that as "An Aesthetics of Rape or Culture of Rape?: Reflections on Jamaica", presented at the Institute of Caribbean Studies Staff/Postgraduate Seminar Series, 10 October 2019.
2. While the published figures for rape represent an 11.1 per cent decrease for the period, it is well known that this crime is under-reported and convictions in such cases are, therefore, low.
3. Representation is "the process by which members of a culture use language (broadly defined as any signifying system) to produce meaning" (Stuart Hall 1999, 61).
4. Owner and overseer of enslaved African people and notorious rapist who lived in Jamaica from 1751 to 1786.
5. We would like to thank Leo "Big Daddy" O'Reggio and Danielle Fuller for assisting us in compiling the list of songs analysed in this section.
6. While there is a corpus of songs from women that touch on such themes, including female dancehall artistes with explicit sexual lyrics, the number of such songs from men outstrip those by women.

7. This is likely drawn from Old Testament edicts about adultery: "If a man commits adultery with another man's wife, even with the wife of his neighbour, both the adulterer and adulteress must be put to death…" (Leviticus 20:10–12). While the bible condemns both, Jamaican patriarchal norms condemn primarily the women and make allowances for the men; in fact, the hegemonic male ideal is one who is unfaithful with "nuff gal inna bungle" (Beenie Man 1996; Chevannes 2001).
8. For example, Ephesians 5: 22–24: "Wives, submit yourselves to your own husbands as you do to the Lord./ For the husband is the head of the wife as Christ is the head of the church, his body, of which he is the Saviour./ Now as the church submits to Christ, so also wives should submit to their husbands in everything."
9. Buddy is a euphemism for penis.
10. Gives out.
11. See headlines pulled from popular media sites in Jamaica: Twila Wheelan, "Victim Blaming A Hindrance In Reporting Crimes," Jamaica Information Service, 7 September 2021, https://jis.gov.jm/victim-blaming-a-hindrance-in-reporting-crimes/;Twila Wheelan, "Jamaicans Encouraged To Avoid Victim Blaming," 6 September 2021, https://jis.gov.jm/jamaicans-encouraged-to-avoid-victim-blaming/; "Don't victim-blame! – justice ministry," *Jamaica Gleaner*, 3 September 2021, https://jamaica-gleaner.com/article/news/20210903/dont-victim-blame-justice-ministry; Opal Palmer Adisa, "Don't shame and blame victims of gender-based violence," *Jamaica Observer*, 5 April 2021, https://www.jamaicaobserver.com/all-woman/dont-shame-and-blame-victims-of-gender-based-violence/; "Stop victim-blaming women for crimes of passion – Grant", *Jamaica Gleaner*, 14 January 2020, https://jamaica-gleaner.com/article/lead-stories/20200114/stop-victim-blaming-women-crimes-passion-grant. These headlines point to a pervasive culture of blaming the victims for the violence perpetrated against them. It is not uncommon to see comments on social media pages rationalizing violent outcomes.
12. Pum pum is Jamaican slang for vagina.
13. Suffice to say that there are songs by women that address rough sex. Tanya Stephens, for example, uses language that demands a skilled sexual partner (Plummer 2020). Lady Saw, Spice, Shenseea and others offer songs that either indicate their ability to endure a rough ride, and request a long ride or a skilled rider. Earlier, the Soul Sisters sang "Wreck a Buddy" (1969), which plays on Prince Buster's "Wreck a Pum Pum".

14. Although, Jamaican music has always been sexually suggestive, with its double entendre. Mento, for example, was notorious for its suggestive content.
15. For women, the word tear does not connote anything pleasurable. Women experience vaginal tears during vigorous sex; and in rape and childbirth, both traumatic experiences for wholly different reasons.
16. Incidentally, General Echo, in "Cocky Nuh Beg No Fren" (1979), turns his penis into an instrument separate and apart from himself; though his instrument is one that affirms his masculinity and acts upon his agency.
17. Lift up.
18. Little Twitch's "Stallion" (1988) also has a horse-riding motif, though more recent dancehall tunes replace horses with motorbikes or cars.
19. Spanish fly is a centuries-old aphrodisiac made from beetles; though in Jamaica (and in this song) it refers to anything that makes a person more susceptible to the idea of a sexual encounter or any drug that removes full consciousness around consent.
20. "Girl, I am serious. I have to have you tonight. I have to get your body, even if I have to use a gun."
21. A war between his penis and her vagina.
22. Ainsworth Morris, "Near 100 per cent rise in domestic violence reports in five years," 20 July 2022, *The Gleaner*, https://jamaica-gleaner.com/article/news/20220720/near-100-cent-rise-domestic-violence-reports-five-years.
23. Violence has also led to quite a few artistes finding themselves before the courts on matters ranging from assault and rape to murder. "Local Reggae Acts and the Charges They Have Faced," *Jamaica Observer*, 7 October 2011, https://www.jamaicaobserver.com/entertainment/local-reggae-acts-and-the-charges-they-have-faced/.

DISCOGRAPHY

Beres Hammond, *Love from a Distance*, "Can't Stop a Man," VP Records, 1996, cassette.

Buju Banton, *Mr Mention*, "Have to Get You Tonight," Penthouse Label, 1992, vinyl.

Capleton, More Fire, "Hunt You," VP Records, 2000, cassette.

Capleton, *The Buzz Riddim Mix*, "I Love to See (Hot Girl)," Black Shadow Records, 2001, vinyl.

Charly Black, "Domestic Violence," Crawba Productions/Team Unstoppable, 2019.

Christopher Martin, "Stop the Violence Against Women," Seanizzle Records, 2017, digital download.

Echo Minott, *What the Hell . . .*, "What the Hell the Police Can Do?" Jammy's Records, 1987, vinyl.

Elephant Man, *Higher Level*, "Nuh Come Fast," Greensleeves Records, 2002, vinyl.

Elephant Man, "Di Anaconda," *Riddim Driven*, VP Records, 2003, CD.

Chuck Fender, "Gash Them," Juke Boxx Productions, 2006, vinyl.

General Echo (as Ranking Slackness), *Slackest LP in the World*, "Cockie Nuh Beg No Fren," Techniques, 1979, CD.

Govanna, *Convo: The Series*, "Convo," Emudio Records, 2020, digital download.

Tucker, Junior. 1990. "16 (Into the Night)," Ten Records, vinyl.

Keith and Tex, "Stop That Train," Island Records, 1967, vinyl.

Ken Lazarus, "Girl," FRM (Federal Records), 1971, vinyl.

Kojak and Liza, "Fist to Fist Rub a Dub," Belmont Records, 1979, vinyl.

Little Twitch, *Twin City Spin*, "Stallion," Two Friends Records, 1989, vinyl.

Little Twitch, "Send Fi Spanish Fly," Jammy's Records, 1989, vinyl.

Lovindeer, "Babylon Boops," The Sound of Jamaica (TSOJ), 1994, vinyl.

Macka Diamond, *New Money Riddim*, "Talk Up," Platinum Camp, 2020, digital download.

Mavado, *Gangsta for Life: The Symphony of David Brooks*, "Squeeze Har Breast," VP Records, 2007, CD.

Papa San and Lady G, "Legal Rights," Techniques, 1983, vinyl.

Papa San and Lady G, "Round Table Talk," Anchor Records, 1988, vinyl.

Potential Kidd, *Reggae Gold*, "Yah So Nice," VP Records, 2012, CD.

Prince and Princess Buster, "Ten Commandments from Woman to Man," RCA Victor, 1967, vinyl.

Prince Buster and the All Stars, *Welcome to Jamaica: Wreck a Pum Pum*, "Wreck A Pum Pum," Fab, 1969, vinyl.

Prince Buster, "Ten Commandments," Blue Beat, 1963, vinyl.

Red Dragon, *Best of Techniques Hits Vol. 1*, "Agony," Techniques, 1989, cassette.

Romain Virgo, "Dutty Man," Upsetta Records, 2020, digital download.

Shabba Ranks, "Live Blanket," Moodies Records, 1987, vinyl.

Shelly Thunder, "Kuff," Witty, 1988, vinyl.

Sophia George featuring Lloyd Lovindeer, "Murder Johnny Be Good," SPV Recordings, 1995, vinyl.

Spragga Benz, *Jack it Up*, "Could a Deal," VP Records, 1994, LP.

Spragga Benz, *Jack it Up*, "Jack it Up," VP Records, 1994, LP.

The Soul Sisters, "Wreck A Buddy," Amalgamated Records, 1969, vinyl.
Two Kings, "Hit You Let You Feel It," Island Records, 1965, vinyl.
Vybz Kartel, "One Box," Vybz Kartel Muzik, 2018, digital download.

REFERENCES

Augustyn, Heather. 2020. *Women in Jamaican Music.* Jefferson, NC: McFarland and Company.

Brownmiller, S. 1976. *Against Our Will: Men Women and Rape.* Harmondsworth: Penguin.

Burt, Martha. 1980. "Cultural Myths and Supports for Rape." *Journal of Personality and Social Psychology* 38 (2): 217–30.

Caribbean Policy Research Institute. 2022. *Breaking News: Gender-Based Violence in Jamaican News Media.* Kingston: CAPRI.https://www.capricaribbean.org/sites/default/files/documents/breakingnewsgender-basedviolenceinjamaican-newsmedia.pdf.

Chevannes, Barry. 2001. *Learning to be a Man: Culture, Socialization and Gender identity in Five Caribbean Communities.* Kingston: University of the West Indies Press.

Chenoweth, Michael, and Thomas Thistlewood. 2003. "The 18th Century Climate of Jamaica: Derived from the Journals of Thomas Thistlewood, 1750–1786." *Transactions of the American Philosophical Society* 93 (2): i–153.

Chodorow, Nancy J. 1989. *Feminism and Psychoanalytic Theory.* New Haven, CT: Yale University Press.

Constable, Ayesha. 2016. "Dancehall: Dream or Nightmare?" *Words in the Bucket.* 20 June. www.wordsinthebucket.com/dancehall-dream-or-nightmare.

Cooper, Carolyn. 1993. "Slackness Hiding from Culture: Erotic Play in the Dancehall." In *Noises in the Blood: Orality, Gender and the 'Vulgar' Body of Jamaican Popular Culture,* edited by Carolyn Cooper, 136–73. Warwick University Caribbean Studies Series, London: Macmillan (Caribbean).

———.1994. "'Lyrical Gun': Metaphor and Role Play in Jamaican Culture." *Massachusetts Review* xxxv (3&4): 429–47.

———. 2004. *Sound Clash: Jamaican Dancehall Culture at Large.* London: Palgrave Macmillan.

Davis, Adranna. 2017. "Rape Culture in Jamaica – The International Clarion." *Medium,* 13 October. http://www.medium.com/@theinternationalclarion/rape-culture-in-jamaica-c92b32cf0668.

de Beauvior, Simone. 1974. *The Second Sex.* New York: Vintage Books.

Dunkley-Willis, Alicia. 2021. "Over 700 Cases Referred to Domestic Violence Centres." *Jamaica Observer,* 8 October. https://www.jamaicaobserver.com/news/over-700-cases-referred-to-domestic-violence-centres/.

Feldman, David. 2018. "Why Do People Blame the Victim?" *Psychology Today,* 2 March. www.psychologytoday.com/us/blog/supersurvivors/201803/why-do-people-blame-the-victim.

Frank, Kevin. 2007. "Female Agency and Oppression in Caribbean Bacchanalian Culture: Soca, Carnival, and Dancehall." *Women's Studies Quarterly* 35 (1/2): 172–90.

Green, J.L. 2004. "Uncovering Collective Rape: A Comparative Study of Political Sexual Violence." *International Journal of Sociology* 34 (1): 97–116.

Gunst, Laurie. 1995. *Born Fi Dead: A Journey Through the Jamaican Posse Underworld.* London and Edinburgh: Payback Press.

Hall, Douglas. 1989. *In Miserable Slavery: Thomas Thistlewood in Jamaica, 1750–1786.*

London: Macmillan.Hall, Stuart. 1999. "The Work of Representation." In *Representation: Cultural Representations and Signifying Practices,* edited by Stuart Hall, 13–74. London: Sage Publications.

Harriott, Anthony. 2000. *Police and Crime Control in Jamaica: Problems of Reforming Ex-colonial Constabularies.* Kingston: University of the West Indies Press.

Hope, Donna P. 2010. *Man Vibes: Masculinities in the Jamaican Dancehall,* Kingston: Ian Randle Publishers.

———. 2006. *Inna di Dancehall: Popular Culture and the Politics of Identity in Jamaica.* Kingston: University of the West Indies Press.

Jamaica Constabulary Force. 2022. Crime Statistics – Serious Crimes Report for 1 January to 1 October 2022 and comparative period for 2021. https://jcf.gov.jm/stats/.

Knight, Dawn. 2005. "The Reggae Star Rapist." *The Guardian,* 8 April.https://www.theguardian.com/music/2005/apr/08/popandrock.gender

Lonsway, K.A., and L.F. Fitzgerald. 1994. "Rape Myths: In Review." *Psychology of Women Quarterly* 18 (2): 133–64.

———. 1995. "Attitudinal Antecedents of Rape Myth Acceptance: A Theoretical and Empirical Reexamination." *Journal of Personality and Social Psychology* 68 (4): 704–11.

Lyew, Stephanie. 2022. "Kiprich Pens Tribute to Female Victims of Violence." *The Gleaner,* 31 October. https://jamaica-gleaner.com/article/entertainment/20221031/kiprich-pens-tribute-female-victims-violence?utm_source=newsletter&utm_medium=email&utm_campaign=am_newsletter.

Mitchell, Damion. 2017. "UPDATED: Moravian Minister Charged with Sex Crime, Booked for Court Wednesday." *The Gleaner*, 3 January. jamaica-gleaner.com/article/news/20170103/update-moravian-minister-charged-rape-booked-court-wednesday.

Mohammed, Farahnaz. 2014. "Trouble in Paradise: Jamaica's Culture of Misogyny." *Girls' Globe*, 9 February. www.girlsglobe.org/2014/02/09/trouble-in-paradise-jamaicas-culture-of-misogyny/.

Morgan, Kai A.D. 2017. "'Into-Me-See': Breaking Down Intimacy for the Jamaican Landscape." In *Interweaving Tapestries of Culture and Sexuality in the Caribbean*, edited by Karen Carpenter, 165–89. Cham: Springer Nature/Palgrave Macmillan.

Morris, Ainsworth. 2022. "Near 100 Percent Rise in Domestic Violence Reports in Five Years." *The Gleaner*, 20 July. https://jamaica-gleaner.com/article/news/20220720/near-100-cent-rise-domestic-violence-reports-five-years.

Muturi, Nancy, and Patricia Donald. 2006. "Violence against Women and Girls in the Caribbean: An Intervention and Lessons Learned from Jamaica." *Caribbean Quarterly* 52 (2/3): 83–103.

Patterson, Orlando. 1969. *The Sociology of Slavery: An Analysis of the Origins, Development, and Structure of Negro Slave Society in Jamaica*. New York: Humanities Press.

———. 1982. *Slavery and Social Death: A Comparative Study*, 1st ed. Cambridge: Harvard University Press.

Planning Institute of Jamaica. 2017. "Economic and Social Survey of Jamaica: 2017 Overview." https://www.pioj.gov.jm/product/the-economic-social-survey-jamaica-essj-2017-overview/.

Plummer, Nicole. 2020. "The Call to Resistance: The Weaponization of Language in the Music of Tanya Stephens." In *Rough Riding: Tanya Stephens and the Power of Music to Transform Society*, edited by Adwoa Onuora, Anna Kasafi Perkins, and Ajamu Nangwaya, 127–52. Kingston: University of the West Indies Press.

Pottinger, Audrey, Althea Bailey, and Nickiesha Passard. 2019. "Archival Data Review of Intimate Partner Homicide-suicide in Jamaica, 2007–2017: Focus on Mental Health and Community Response." *Rev Panam Salud Publica* 43 (e99): doi: 10.26633/RPSP.2019.99. PMID: 31819747.

Priestley, Sharon. 2014. "The Prevalence and Correlates of Intimate Partner Violence in Jamaica." *Social and Economic Studies* 63 (1): 15396, 232–33, 235. https://www.proquest.com/scholarly-journals/prevalence-correlates-intimate-partner-violence/docview/1614082214/se-2.

Renzetti, Claire M., Diane R. Follingstad, and Ann L. Coker. 2017. "Preventing Intimate Partner Violence: An Introduction." In *Preventing Intimate Partner*

Violence: Interdisciplinary Perspectives, edited by Claire Renzetti, Diane Follinstad, and Ann Coker, 1–14. Bristol: Policy Press, University of Bristol.

Shields, Emily. 2018. "33 Children Murdered in Jamaica in the First 8 Mths of the Yr; 152 Raped. #RJRnews This Is a National Emergency." Twitter, 31 August. twitter.com/emilymshields/status/1035503241730187264?s=21.

Stanley Niaah, Sonjah. 2006. "'Slackness Personified', Historicized and Delegitimized." *Small Axe: A Caribbean Journal of Criticism* 11 (1): 174–85.

———. 2021. "'Sounding' the System: Noise, In/Security and the Politics of Citizenship." *Journal of World Popular Music* 8 (1): 51–73.

Stets, Jan E. 1988. *Domestic Violence and Control.* New York: Springer Publishing.

Tafari Ama, Imani. 2017. *Blood, Bullets and Bodies: Sexual Politics Below Jamaica's Poverty Line.* Lancashire: Beaten Track Publishing.

Thomas, Christopher. 2022. "Police Commissioner Concerned about Multiple Murders Trend."

The Gleaner, 4 October. https://jamaica-gleaner.com/article/news/20221004/police-commissioner-concerned-about-multiple-murders-trend.

Turner, Rasbert. 2022. "History of Violence Against Victim." *The Gleaner*, 29 August. https://jamaica-gleaner.com/article/lead-stories/20220829/history-violence-against-victim.

United Nations Development Programme. 2012. *Caribbean Human Development Report 2012: Human Development and the Shift to Better Citizen Security.* https://www.undp.org/sites/g/files/zskgke326/files/migration/jm/2012-HDR-EN.pdf.

UN Women. 2020. *Bridging the Gap: Sexual Exploitation, Abuse and Harassment.* https://www.unwomen.org/sites/default/files/Headquarters/Attachments/Sections/Library/Publications/2020/Discussion-paper-Sexual-exploitation-abuse-and-harassment-SEAH-en.pdf.

Wilson-Harris, Nadine. 2016. "SHAME! Twenty-four Women Killed in 2016; Former Victim of Domestic Violence Urges Women to Protect Themselves." *The Gleaner*, 17 December. https://jamaica-gleaner.com/article/lead-stories/20161218/shame-twenty-four-women-killed-2016-former-victim-domestic-violence.

World Health Organization. 2021. "Violence Against Women." https://www.who.int/news-room/fact-sheets/detail/violence-against-women.

chapter 16

Gender-Based Violence in Calypso

Grappling with Shifting Paradigms[1]

PATRICIA MOHAMMED

CALYPSO, SOCA AND INCREASINGLY *PITCHAKAREE*[2] ARE CULTURAL FORMS of communication, homegrown in Trinidad and Tobago, that allow for a range of taboo subjects to be ventilated, either with humour or with impunity, and generally without reprisal. Gender is a term that for better, rather than worse, has resisted facile explanations. Those of us involved daily in gender work understand the complexity that is inherent once you attach the analytical category of gender. Gender-based violence (GBV) comes in many different forms, including domestic violence, rape, incest, sexual harassment, emotional and psychological violence, financial abuse, forced prostitution and even arranged marriages. GBV is not experienced only by women. Men and boys are increasingly being empowered to speak up about how they have and continue to experience GBV, although as far as we know, women and girls still dominate in the majority as victims.

Let us imagine the calypsonian Mighty Spoiler[3] coming back from the grave and singing a calypso about the origins of GBV on earth. In his scenario, in the bible, Eve, as the proverbial temptress, would be blamed for sexually harassing Adam, for cajoling him with an apple, no doubt so that she could claim part of his inheritance, when what she was really lusting after was the virgin garden property with a view of the hills. Then Spoiler would, in these days, have to include the Hindu scriptures in this postmodern gender analysis and pick on Sita's ordeal by fire in the Ramleela[4] story of the Ramayana. Sita was made to walk over burning coal under her feet, feeling "hot hot hot", as the singer Arrow would say, and come through unscathed to prove her chastity before the crowd of people before Rama could accept her back as his queen.

This testing of Sita's fidelity happened after Rama was banished for fourteen years in the jungle, during which time she was abducted by the demon Rawan. Both these religious narratives reflect some hardcore emotional and psychological violence. So it was from the beginning. I started with this probe, some might consider a travesty – not to diminish the importance of GBV but to underscore its long history in society, even while we must consistently work at its eradication. The human capacity to carry out GBV has been with us for millennia, although harmful acts directed at a person based on their gender were not always recognized as criminal or heinous offences. Ideas about GBV keep changing, along with our thinking about gender itself. While we use the term 'victims of violence', we are also consciously working through means of empowerment to prevent victimhood setting in, and thus reducing the propensity for GBV to occur. The construct of GBV is also not viewed as a problem experienced by only women, but has expanded to accommodate and to reflect the ways in which men and boys may suffer from it.

The relations between men and women have occupied us as a subject in every scriptural and art form. Gender and GBV are ironically, or understandably, two of the main themes that can be elicited from early calypso written and sung by men up to the present. Maude Dikobe (2008), a lecturer in Tanzania who has written on calypso and violence, points to the pervasive ways in which abuse has entered our idioms of culture without missing a beat. Reading this paper, I am reminded that a perfect example of how traditional calypso lyrics can obscure the painful nature of sexual abuse is found in the Mighty Sparrow's song "Mabel". Sparrow[5] presents a situation in which the singer himself abusing a minor – thirteen-year-old Mabel – but he narrates it without the slightest irony or self-awareness. In his calypso, Mabel is a seductive teenager who will not listen to her grandmother and entices the older male calypsonian. When virginal Mabel gets pregnant, it is her fault, not Sparrow's:

Granny was furious
But Sparrow was curious
While grandmother talking
This time Sparrow attacking
At length and at last, ah bust the tape . . .

Sparrow, among others, was a master at double entendre and euphemism in calypso. "Ah bust the tape" is the colloquial expression he applied for relieving a young thirteen-year-old of her virginity, but it also references two other metaphors: that of breaking and entering a guarded entrance, and winning a race, any kind of race that involves reaching the finish line first. This is a race between men. This is not to dismiss all male calypsonians, or even Sparrow, as completely misogynistic. Rather it is to point out that violence against women in calypso has a long and culturally accepted tradition that passes for humour and lightweight entertainment. Some have recognized and used the calypso against this tendency though. For instance, in "Rocket In Yuh Pocket", the Mighty Duke[6] appeals to his fellow men, that if a woman says no, the man should leave her alone:

Women should be protected
Women shouldn't fear to walk any street
Any time they choose
Without you appear like a bull in heat
When yuh drink yuh booze
Let she dress how she feel to dress
And not subjected to abuse
To be so molested or disrespected
. . .
Let her be who she wants to be
That's a woman's prerogative
You can't force yourself down on she
Let her give what she choose to give ("Rocket In Yuh Pocket", Mighty Duke 1993)

The Mighty Duke joins peers such as David Rudder, who celebrates women's sexual confidence in "Bahia Girl" and "Bacchanal Woman", and Scrunter, who urges women to be on their guard when taking public transportation, reminding them to note the licence plate number of the taxis they take. Still others, like Lord Nelson in "Ah Goin and Party Tonight, understands that the times they are a-changing. In this calypso the female protagonist tells her partner, "I is a young woman and I eh ready to shelf / You does forget I have feeling, so tonight I going to do meh thing / Doh vex if you see me wining, I going and party tonight." By the 1980s, the tables had turned once more. Calypsos emerged about the long-suffering male, who now has to concede more freedoms to women because they hold, according to them, the upper hand. More women were employed in waged or salaried positions; they had greater economic freedoms, and could, therefore, challenge partners who tried to exert control.

Calypsos sung by men can be read against those sung by women, many of which were also written by women and were targeted responses to the abuses to which they had been subjected for years. Calypso Rose's "Fire in Your Wire" is viewed primarily as a song about female sexuality, in particular, celebrating the sexual libido of older women. Born in Tobago to the family of a Spiritual Baptist preacher, Linda McCartha Sandy-Lewis "grew up with relatives in Trinidad where she had access to a better education and the bustling cultural scene of the capital, Port-of-Spain. As she revealed only recently, she was raped in her teenage years and as a survivor ceased all sexual relations with men," writes Hanna Klein-Thomas (2020). "Fire in Your Wire" was first released in 1967 on a 45 RPM vinyl record in Trinidad and Tobago. Although her song predated the second wave movement in the country, numerous examples exist of first wave women's challenges to prevailing ideas of women's inequality, which had already stimulated a slow and steady activism from different vantage points in these islands. For example, Leonora Pujadas-McShine, born in 1910, was a women's rights activist and community worker. When citizens (over twenty-one years) in Trinidad and Tobago were granted universal suffrage in 1945, she established the first League of Women Voters in the 1950s to educate them about their civic roles. She was also an advocate of equal pay and labour practices.

Rose's calypso, picking up on these incremental nuances of different kinds of freedoms, tells of an old woman who runs out to her neighbour, Ram, singing, "Fire fire, in meh wire, *dame mucha agua*, heat for so." I don't think I appreciated this song fully until I was being interviewed alongside

Calypso Rose in 2009 for the film titled *Calypso Rose: The Lioness of the Jungle*. She confided about the competitiveness with the male calypsonians at the time, including with Sparrow, Kitchener and others, and her fight to find a place on stage as an equal. In its fuller interpretation, "Fire in Your Wire" is about the smouldering passions of women, not a sexual passion waiting to be kindled by any neighbouring male, but a creative one that was being stifled.

By 1979, Singing Francine had become one of the earliest female calypsonians to speak out directly against violence against women, urging them to leave the situation of abuse in the unforgettable lines from "Run Away" – "Dog does run away / Cat does run away / Woman put two wheels on your heels / You can run away too." This is a radical break from the conventional notion of womanhood and the established conjugal tradition, where women in marital and other married-like relations are expected to suffer the slings and arrows, and gun butts of outrageous misfortune, and put up with abuse, until miraculously, they find their reward in their longevity beyond male life expectation – or when the man is no longer capable of inflicting violence because of infirmity. By 1996 others had taken up the themes with a vengeance; signally important among them was Singing Sandra (Sandra Des Vignes). The titles of her songs tell their own story: "Raperman" (1984), "Sexy Employers" (or "Die with My Dignity", 1987), the latter which has now become a feminist mantra in Trinidad and Tobago, and "Equaliser" (1994). In "Equaliser" (written by Christopher Grant), Singing Sandra makes no attempt to hide her anger at, and hatred for, the brutal purveyors of sexual violence. On the contrary, she describes herself as the "Equaliser" – the only one capable of punishing the perpetrators.

The nuances of how gender-based violence is confronted yet again changes in the calypsos of the 1990s and into the twenty-first century, where we find the new younger singers – soca divas – as they have been described by Kai Barratt (2008): Sanell Dempster, TC, Alison Hinds, Destra, Michelle Xavier and Fay Ann Lyons. Renelle White[7] dubs this group and genre of calypsonian and singers "soca feminism". These women use language and lyrics to take back the female body, take back power, take back control; to take back what was once violently taken away from them – but not directly, through male violence. They use the power of the spoken word to claim rights.

In "Who De Hell is Kim", TC addresses the issue of infidelity as she asks her partner, "Who de hell is Kim / What foolishness you talkin? / Yuh better check yuhself and go and check yuh health" after he calls her by a wrong name. "Call for a ride to pick up yuh tings outside," she shouts at his departing back, underscoring that infidelity and betrayal are violent acts that women will not tolerate, the same way men have felt cuckolded by women over the years, so have women felt the burden of male infidelity. Sanell Dempster uses violent lyrics in her answer back and response, exemplified in her 2009 song "Punish Yuh". Here she uses her body against the male, giving it power over his assumed dominance. She can be seen as metaphorically fighting violence with violence: "Ah go punish yuh, ah go finish yuh" is part of the chorus. The violent words 'punish' and 'finish' are not meant to physically inflict harm but to demonstrate that she can outdo him in the Caribbean art form of wining. Fay Ann Lyons, another strong, independent soca artiste, takes a stab at gender relations in "Heavy T Bumper". The line "No man cya mash up meh structure" is repeated over and over in the chorus, making a direct reference to men not being able to mash up or abuse her "structure" (body).

Soca ambassador Machael Montano, a seemingly progressive and modern young man, sings in "Bend Over", "Gyal bend over wine to the ground / Me love how you do your thing" on stage, his female performer twists and bends, gyrates and jiggles, wines and grinds as Montano stands and walks around her, singing and addressing the crowd. The female body is objectified and made to do all kinds of different stunts for both male and female pleasure and views. Many see this as female sexual and Caribbean empowerment, but there are elements of abuse in terms of how the female body is treated as compared to the males. This can be seen as a form of female exploitation, which indeed falls into the realm of violence, and in the not so old-fashioned terminology, smacks of the continued objectification of woman.

What now can media figures, such as calypsonians, and male and female soca artistes, do to sensitize the listening public to issues of gender-based violence? There are no facile answers.

GBV continues to mutate in ways that do not allow us to easily understand or grasp the problems that are already surfacing – perhaps the expressive messages that women now signal outweigh those held on to by masculinity. But there is a downside to each time period and form that surfaces. Have we really appreciated the impact of internet communication and digital technologies? When a young woman's explicitly sexual staged performance in a private club is flashed on thousands of screens, gender-based violence has occurred. When someone can put revealing photos from any scene on Facebook within seconds of it taking place – without the permission of the person or persons – this is an invasion of privacy and is abuse. When a well-meaning media host features a rape scene via a televised digital phone recording, another kind of GBV has occurred. While the host thought his intentions were good, it brings to light the other fundamental ingredient in the relationship between GBV and calypso – that the media is an interlocutor and has an uncomfortable relationship in the middle. The media also sell sexuality and scandal (among its other very honourable duties), and as consumers, we collude equally as we delight in the prurient entertainment that it provides. And for those who write calypsos and other musical genres, love, sex and gender relations remain some of the eternal themes. There is no genre of song that has not been consumed with the themes of man, woman, love, romance, sex and heartbreak.

Another, more drastic gender paradigm shift is needed for violence to end than has already surfaced with the women's movement and the efforts of global human rights advocates. If music has been used as an instrument of protest and resistance on various platforms, then it can equally be used to send messages about gender-based violence. Until we are proved otherwise about the influencing power of music and media, we cannot relieve the song-makers and the media of their responsibility for the messages that they may send to old and young about the wellbeing of a society, and of the relations between the sexes. A survey of musical genres in a range of societies globally, as for instance in the United States with rap and hip hop,[8] in India through Bollywood singers and songs,[9] have made a direct link between music and its promotion of sexual violence. Increasingly, however, many societies have imposed bans or are deploying music for advocacy and activism against GBV – in fact, violence of all kinds.[10]

To end on a more optimistic note, however, an idea of what this shifting paradigm might resemble is revealed in the implicit message in Michelle Xavier's 2007 song "Do You Like It?", which suggests the basis for a levelling of the playing field, both on and off the stage. She sings:

I've seen your type around before and I know it very well
The kind of man that spins me round and sends me straight to hell
I'm not wasting time with you
Let's do what we wanna do
Cause you've got the get and I've got the go
So, grab my car keys
I got my money
I got your number
I know exactly where I am going to
Tonight's about me and you . . .

I leave you to keep thinking about the possibilities inherent in this shift.

NOTES

1. This chapter was originally presented at a breakfast seminar in Commemoration of the International Day for the Elimination of Violence Against Women in 2011 for the Ministry of Gender, Youth and Child Development, Trinidad and Tobago.
2. Pichakaree (or pichakaaree) is an indigenous Indo-Trinidadian musical form named after the long syringe-like tubes used to spray abeer (powdered dye and water) during Phagwah celebrations. Pichakaree songs are generally social commentary that use a mixture of Hindi, English and Bhojpuri words.
3. Theophilus Philip (23 March 1926–24 December 1960), better known as Mighty Spoiler, was a Trinidadian calypsonian whose career began in 1946.
4. Ramleela or Ramlila, literally "Rama's play", is a performance of the Ramayana epic in a series of scenes that include songs, narration, recitals and dialogue. It was carried over by East Indians who migrated from India as one of the ritual events held annually.
5. The Mighty Sparrow is the pseudonym for Slinger Francisco, a Trinidadian calypso vocalist, songwriter and guitarist active since 1949.
6. Kelvin Pope, better known as The Mighty Duke (1932–14 January 2009), a Trinidadian calypsonian who was born in Point Fortin.
7. Renelle White is a past post-graduate student of the Institute for Gender and Development Studies, University of the West Indies, St Augustine, and is outspoken on the different contemporary forms of feminism that have emerged, including cyberfeminism in the Caribbean.

8. https://www.latimes.com/archives/la-xpm-2000-jul-01-ca-46613-story.htm.
9. https://feminisminindia.com/2015/12/02/mis-representation-of-gender-based-violence-in-music/
10. See, for example, https://www.jamaicaobserver.com/columns/gender-based-violence-in-jamaica/ and https://www.auxsons.com/en/breves/sounds-of-the-world-music-against-gender-based-violence-in-south-africa/

DISCOGRAPHY

Calypso Rose, "Fire in Your Wire", National Record Company, 1967, vinyl.
David Rudder, "Bahia Girl", London Records, 1993, vinyl.
David Rudder, "Bacchanal Lady," Lypsoland, 1997, vinyl.
Fay Ann Lyons, "Heavy T Bumper", 2009. https://www.youtube.com/watch?v=dsRP5Iw7w5M
Lord Nelson, *Family*, "Ah Goin and Party Tonight", B's Records, 1982, vinyl.
Machael Montano, *The Return*, "Bend Over," Mad Bull Music, 2011, CD.
Michelle Xavier, "Do You Like It?", 2007.
Mighty Sparrow, *More of Sparrow's Greatest Hits*, "Thirteen-Year-Old Mabel," Tropico, 1960, vinyl.
Sanell Dempster, "Punish Yuh," 2009.
Singing Francine, "Run-A-Way/Look What You Doing," Charlie's Records, 1978, vinyl.
Singing Sandra, "The Raperman Coming," 1984.
Singing Sandra, *Rising Stars '87*, "Die with My Dignity," Charlie's Records, 1987, vinyl.
Singing Sandra, *The Soca Switch: The Stars of Soca 3*, "Equalizer," JW Records, 1999, CD.
TC, *Colour Me Soca*, "Who De Hell is Kim," Starchild, 2001, CD.
The Mighty Duke, *The Phung-Uh-Nung Sweet*, "Rocket in Yuh Pocket," Straker's Records, 1992, vinyl.

REFERENCES

Barratt, Kai. 2008. "I Found My East Indian Beauty: Locating the Indo-Trinidadian Women in Trinidadian Soca Music." *Man in India* 88 (1): 101–11.

Dikobe, Maude. 2008. "'Treat 'Em Rough': Gender and Heterosexual Violence in Calypso." http://genderlinks.org.za/wp-content/uploads/imported/articles/attachments/historical_culture_of_gender_hetersexual_violence_maude_dikobe.pdf.

Klein-Thomas, Hanna. 2020. "#LeaveSheAlone: Feminist Hashtag Activism and Carnival popular Culture in the Caribbean." *Participations Journal of Audience and Reception Studies* 17 (2): 335–53.

SECTION 5

CONTEMPORARY CONTINUITIES: BREAKING THE CHAINS

chapter 17

Heteropatriarchy, Intersectional Structural Violence and Adolescent Girls' Sexualities in Trinidad and Tobago

GABRIELLE JAMELA HOSEIN

SPEAKING WITH STAFF OF THE MINISTRY OF HEALTH IN TRINIDAD AND TOBAGO, I asked about the protocols when an adolescent girl, say sixteen years old, comes to a community health centre for medical services. Once such a girl discloses that she is sexually active, medical providers believe that the Child Protection Unit of the Trinidad and Tobago Police Service (TTPS) and the Children's Authority of Trinidad and Tobago (CATT) must become involved. Since the age of adulthood and consent were harmonized at eighteen years old in the Children Act (2012), all sexual activity disclosed by minors is considered to require mandatory reporting and investigation.[1]

District Medical Officers often also believe that it is illegal for children to have sex under the age of eighteen. This is incorrect as consensual heterosexual adolescent sex among those within two to three years of age has been decriminalized, but health care providers are often not willing to take any risks in providing services when they believe parental consent to health services for minors is mandatory. As well, they fear potential "threats, violence and physical harm" to them and adolescents (Ministry of Health 2020, 12).

Indeed, the 2020 National Sexual and Reproductive Health Policy (NSRHP) acknowledges health providers' reluctance as well as "unwillingness of adolescents to access SRH services for fear of being reported which may result in more non-medicalized termination of pregnancy and greater incidence of unwanted pregnancies, HIV and other STIs among young people" (Ministry of Health 2020, 13). This explains advocacy efforts for a legal amendment to enable provision of sexual and reproductive health services to adolescents sixteen to seventeen years old without parental consent (UNFPA 2021).

Such services were provided to heterosexual adolescents when the age of sexual consent was sixteen. With the change to eighteen, those services became a risk for providers who are now unsure whether they are mandated to report all cases to the police, and to require parental consent for counselling and provision of contraceptives. Non-reporting, even for those cases where sex was between mutually (or within two years) aged minors and was consensual, became considered a potential criminal offence, restricting services that were once provided.

Currently, when girls visit public clinics, they are advised to return with a parent or guardian. Doctors (and pharmacies) believe that it is also illegal to give contraception to a minor under eighteen without parental consent. A girl can leave without advice, contraception, diagnosis of STIs or pregnancy, or assessment of intimate partner violence or risk, her name and contact unrecorded – for a file cannot even be started without parental permission. There is no follow-up unless they come back. Most girls will not seek SRH services in the first place, and after encountering such a protocol, they may not return. Such denial of access to SRH services is a form of state harm.

This example highlights the realities of sexually active adolescent girls in Trinidad and Tobago. A sixteen-year-old who can only access SRHR (sexual and reproductive health and rights) services with parental consent may be having consensual sex with another minor, or may be in an inter-generational or transactional relationship with someone much older. She may also have experienced multiple forms of interpersonal gender-based and sexual violence, from child sexual abuse to forced sexual initiation. Even where sex is consensual and decriminalized, there is a higher risk of unplanned pregnancy and IPV, particularly without confidential minor access to SRHR information and services (Ministry of Health 2020, 6).

While heterosexual sex between minors was decriminalized[2] in the Children Act of 2012, same-sex sexual activity between minors was further criminalized, with penalties increased to life imprisonment.[3] There are limited studies on adolescent same-sex praxes, LBGTQI-identifying adolescents or seeking of SRHR services by this group in Trinidad and Tobago (Mohammed et al. 2020; Noreiga and Burkholder 2022). However, legislative exclusion from protection means same-sex-desiring adolescents are denied the right to consent to sexual activity, making them less likely to seek services and to report sexual violence or sexual risk (UNFPA 2021).

Trinidad and Tobago has a law which allows for heterosexual adolescent sexual desire, a national sexual and reproductive health policy (NSRHP) that recognizes and advocates for much-needed adolescent access to services, and a nation-wide school-based Health and Family Life Education (HFLE) curriculum. Yet, these reproduce a reality where girls seeking health education and services leave without necessary information or care. State take-up of feminist goals regarding public health therefore highlights both recognition and denial of the realities of adolescent girls' sexualities, illustrating how Caribbean states enact heteropatriarchal structural violence. Attention to legislation, policy, and curricula sheds light on these intersections of vulnerability, violence, desire, and denial in adolescent girls' lives.

STRUCTURAL VIOLENCE

Girls' vulnerability to interpersonal and gendered violence is connected to structural violence, which can be understood as historical and social arrangements "embedded in the social, political and economic organization of our social world", and marked by unequal access to determinants of health, such as housing, good-quality health care, unemployment, and education (Montesanti 2015, 2). This creates inequitable life opportunities, reduced quality of life and diminished human potential, particularly for girls and women. They are disproportionately harmed because "gender is inescapably embedded in social systems and institutions" (p.2) reproducing subordination and knowledge deprivation. "Institutionalized relations of power which are supported by, and support, gendered social hierarchies in the form of social relations, customs, and norms" (Alexander 2018, 35) comprise and enact what Mazurana and McKay describe as patriarchal structural violence (2001). Yet, gendered subordination of women and compulsory heterosexuality are embedded in institutional and ideological practice in mutually constitutive ways, and structural violence must be further understood as heteropatriarchal. Catignani and Basham (2021, 101) define heteropatriarchy as "that assemblage of practices and processes through which binary gender relations, masculinity and heterosexuality become normalized and privileged within society".

These are reproduced and legitimized through socio-cultural, economic and political ideologies and institutions that normalize injury, disempowerment, impoverishment, risk, exclusion, and human rights violation of girls and women. Such normalization is an example of symbolic violence which makes interpersonal and structural forms invisible or unrecognizable as violence. More specifically, heteropatriarchal structural violence includes denial of girls and women's control over their bodies and sexualities through laws, policies and institutional processes.

Such denial is supported by gender "as a symbolic institution which . . . shapes the kind and extent of individual and social support that women receive if they do not act in the roles expected of them" (Montesanti and Thurston 2015, 6). Yet, this is insufficiently recognized as state failure to protect girls' rights through overlapping legislative, policy and educational practices that shape their life trajectories and place them in harm's way (Santhya and Jejeebhoy 2015). Similarly, for Everett et al., the term "structural heteropatriarchy" articulates how oppression based on gender and sexuality are interconnected, including in "laws, policies, and our educational and professional systems" (Everett et al. 2022, 91).

It is useful to think about such systemic overlap in terms of "structural intersectionality". As Williams et al. write, "intersectionality is not just an analysis of the convergence of identities but is also an analysis of convergences of structural and institutional oppression . . . that subjects people who are located in intersecting vectors of oppression to multiplicative experiences of domination, exclusion, and harm in social and institutional spaces" (Williams et al. 2023, 12). Age, sex, sexuality and gender, along with legislative exclusion, policy invisibility and curricula silence highlight how state harm is managed through such structural intersectionality.

Feminist scholars have long characterized structural violence as a technology of masculinist, postcolonial Caribbean statehood (Hosein and Parpart 2016). As Eudine Barriteau has argued, political relations between women (and girls) and the state are also relations of gender, and they reproduce both material and ideological asymmetries of power. For Caribbean girls and women, the state is an ensemble of power relations continually shifting between macro and micro levels, not a "monolithic, homogenous, single entity" (Barriteau 2001, 43).

This calls for attention to how such an assemblage works and, therefore, how the structural intersectionality of state response maintains unjust gender systems (Barriteau 2001, 44), which continuously reinforce inequities. Framed this way, Trinidad and Tobago's structures and practices (p.31) cannot be described as gender neutral or as "benign neglect" (p.33) when they exclude, invisibilize and deny the realities of adolescent girls' needs and lives. Rather, what is being administered is intersectional structural violence.

Michelle Rowley (2011) has argued for seeing gender mainstreaming as "inclusion as containment" of feminist visions of women's rights and sexual citizenship. As Rhoda Reddock (2008) highlights in relation to child marriages, sexuality and its regulation remain symbolically significant to ethnic/religious boundary-marking; and as Jacqui Alexander (1991; 1994) and other scholars have theorized (Atluri 2001; Tambiah 2009; Wahab 2012), we need to remain critical of the ways that sex outside of patriarchal conjugality constitutes desiring adolescent girls engaging in informal unions, sexual-economic exchange, and same-sex intimacies as sexual outlaws, outside the boundaries of citizenship and state protection.

The "brutality" of heteropatriarchal state power is, therefore, wielded through regulation of both gender and sexuality (Robinson 2007, 120). As Kamala Kempadoo outlines, "Sexual identities, practices and desires are thus firmly etched into Caribbean society as semi-autonomous from gender, constituted through, and fully embedded in, national state laws, discourses and everyday social practices", creating "conceptual and legal distinctions between sexuality and gender" (Kempadoo 2003, 63), and state practices that discipline and punish targeted sexual behaviours.

Caribbean feminist scholarship has thus long pointed to "the perverse legislative practice of using statutes ostensibly designed to keep women safer as a site for retrenching the erotic autonomy of sexual dissidents" (Robinson 2007, 119). This is the case for sexually active adolescents, especially with same-sex praxes, who would benefit from sexual and reproductive health services and sexual health information as part of national school curricula.

Intersectional structural violence is thus supported by heteropatriarchal social norms. Adolescent girls are expected to fulfil stereotypes of docility and obedience through virginity and sexual abstinence before marriage. As Curtis (2009, 57) points out in relation to girls in Nevis, "the 'moral' body is the disciplined body, the closely controlled and restricted body". Christine Barrow has thus described how an "ABC" formula, "prescribed sexual regulation as urgent and, although presented in neutral public health language, was imbued with conservative morality – Abstinence for young persons followed by Being faithful in marriage, and Condoms for "sexual dissidents who insisted on having sex otherwise" (Barrow et al. 2009, xxxi).

Law is also used to discipline adolescents for contravening moralistic codes of heterosexuality. As Charmaine Crawford (2012), writing about lesbophobia in Barbados, notes, "Patriarchal religiosity is invoked to scare teenage girls into compliance." Policy on youth has additionally left "the structural vulnerabilities and sexual cultures that under-gird social arrangements that dispose youth to risk" both understudied and untransformed (Rogers 2017, 150). This continues as, "Across the Caribbean, new waves of reactionary faith threaten to derail gains in sexual and reproductive rights and impede further progress" (Barrow 2019, 42), particularly for adolescent girls and those adolescents with same-sex praxes.

REALITIES OF ADOLESCENT GIRLS IN TRINIDAD AND TOBAGO

The Caribbean context is marked by early sexual debut, multiple partnering, adolescent pregnancy, and disproportionately high rates of HIV and STI infection among adolescents (Allen 2013; WHO/GSHS 2017a and b), some of which are closely linked to high rates of family violence. Adolescents in the Caribbean continue to be sexually active, despite parental, school, religious/community-based and governmental abstinence messages. However, compared to heterosexual sex among adolescents in Trinidad and Tobago, there is no comparative data for adolescent same-sex sexual praxes.

According to the Global School-Based Student Health Survey,[4] reported in 2017 for Trinidad and Tobago, one in three adolescents between thirteen and seventeen already had sexual intercourse (28.8 per cent), with more than half of this group (55.9 per cent) having first had sexual intercourse before the age of fourteen (61.8 per cent of boys and 43.2 per cent of girls). More boys between thirteen and seventeen were sexually active (39.5 per cent) than girls (19.4 per cent). In 2011, 25.1 per cent of women aged 20–49 years with none/pre-school/primary level schooling were married/in union before the age of eighteen compared to 10.2 per cent of women with secondary education. Similarly, 23.4 per cent of women 20–49 years old from the poorest wealth index quintile were married/in a union before the age of eighteen, compared to 6 per cent from the richest quintile (Ministry of Social Development 2011, 114).

These realities are underscored by low educational attainment, the experience and witnessing of family and sexual violence, and economic insecurity (Allen 2013, 24; Parliament 2020). Low socio-economic status is also linked to the development of intimate relationships between teenage girls and multiple (usually older) men, resulting in teenage pregnancies (Rawlins et al. 2013), and higher risk of gender-based violence and HIV (Hawkins et al. 2007). What are the gendered implications of Trinidad and Tobago's approach for this group?

Girls aged nineteen or younger accounted for 9 per cent of all births between 2017 and 2019 (Parliament 2020).

In terms of violence, in the 2018 Women's Health Survey, one in five women reported experiencing sexual abuse before the age of eighteen. This was also the ratio for fifteen- to nineteen-year-olds in the survey (18 per cent). Furthermore, "one in four women (25%) who were first married or cohabiting with a male partner by the age of 18 or younger also experienced sexual abuse before they were 18" (Pemberton and Joseph 2018, 64).[5] This finding confirms age at first union as an associated factor for all forms of partner violence. Child sexual abuse and early unions are also correlated. Women whose first sexual experience occurred before age fifteen were also more likely to report being forced into this act than women whose first sexual experience was at fifteen years or older.[6]

Additionally, in a study of 651 secondary school students in Trinidad and Tobago, 10 per cent of all students reported "forced performance of sexual acts" (Ghisyawan 2017, 25). Importantly, one hundred students "reported having been molested or being unsure of their experience . . . and 51 students were raped or were unsure of whether what happened to them would be considered rape" (p.40). Of the total group, 11.6 per cent identified that "they liked people of the same sex, both sexes or that sex does not matter to them" (p.17). However, in terms of adolescent girls with same-sex praxes, there is little data on sexual practices, experiences or violence.

This data illuminates unequal power relations in girls' lives. It also speaks to the gendered social norms which idealize religious respectability and promote moral panics, state masculinism and public health failure. As highlighted by the head of the Family Planning Association of Trinidad and Tobago (FPATT) to a parliamentary Joint Select Committee, girls' engagement in sexual activity is linked to "vulnerabilities born out of gender inequality and disempowerment" (Antoine 2020).

Caribbean development models that reproduce persistent socio-economic inequalities and poverty also administer heteropatriarchal structural violence with consequences for girls. For example, Rhoda Reddock (2021, 61) describes states "increasingly unable to adequately address the social, psychological and even the family and parental support needs of the young . . ." System-related drivers of adolescent pregnancy in the Caribbean also include limited access to health services, limited use of contraception methods, and stigma and discrimination towards sexually active adolescents (Ministry of Health 2016).

I now turn to the public health response, looking at legislation, policy and educational curricula regarding adolescent sexuality. Regarding legislation, I show how amendments intended to protect girls exacerbated their risk as desiring subjects and as survivors of violence by limiting their access to SRHR services without parental consent until eighteen years old. Such legislative change excluded teenagers with same-sex praxes from child protection and expanded their experience of heteropatriarchal, intersectional structural violence.

Regarding policy, I read the 2016 draft and 2020 approved NSRHPs to show how they efface adolescent girls, again both as a vulnerable group and as one with sexual desires and agency. Their gender-neutral and heteronormative approach to data on youth on the one hand, and emphasis on addressing the needs of heterosexual male youth on another, further invisibilize the extent to which adolescent girls' sexual and reproductive health and rights remain inadequately affirmed and addressed.

Finally, regarding educational curricula, I show how girls' legislative exclusion is the foundation on which curricula invisibility rests. In addition to social norms which are hostile to and fearful of adolescent desire, and particularly adolescent girls' and same-sex sexualities, such exclusion results in silences that reproduce the position that adolescents cannot consent. I provide some examples from recent revisions of HFLE curricula in Trinidad and Tobago.

LEGISLATIVE EXCLUSION

In the Sexual Offences Act, 1986, same-sex sexual activity between minors was established as an offence and required mandatory reporting from medical practitioners (Section 16, 12–13). In the Sexual Offences (Amendment) Act, 2000, a minor under eighteen years old was defined as unable to consent to sexual penetration and a minor under sixteen years old could not consent to sexual touching, unless in both instances the partners were close in age (excluding same-sex acts). All sexual intercourse with a minor under sixteen was thus considered to require mandatory reporting and investigation. The Children Act (2012) (which came into force on 18 May 2015) harmonized the age of adulthood and consent at eighteen.[7] For all minors under eighteen, even consensual sex had to be reported to the police for investigation regarding a) the age difference between the minor and their sexual partner; b) whether there was a familial relationship or position of trust; c) whether they were not of the same sex; and d) whether the "circumstances do not reveal any element of exploitation, coercion, threat, deception, grooming or manipulation in the relationship" (Children Act, 138–39). The exception was married minors. The outlawing of child marriages was finally achieved on 9 June 2018, after extensive feminist advocacy, public debate and religious resistance (Miscellaneous Provisions (Marriage) Act 2017; Children Act Chapter 46:01). This established a single age of consent and marriage in harmony with global norms and with the Children Act.

Medical health care providers pointed out that the Children Act restricted provision of sexual and reproductive health services to persons over eighteen or those minors with parental consent. Sixteen- and seventeen-year-olds who were previously able to independently access such services were now excluded, and those health care providers who provided services without reporting minors' sexual activity to the police were at risk of committing an offence. Legislative power consolidated girls' limited agency in sexual decision-making, despite feminist calls for the adoption of Gillick and Fraser guidelines, which direct tests of reasonableness and maturity to assess a child's suitability, say at sixteen and seventeen years old, for sexual health education without parental consent (Antoine 2020).

Laws meant to protect minors exacerbated denial of their capacity to consent as, even if such capacity was acknowledged in relation to heterosexual sex in the legislation (through 'Romeo and Juliet' clauses), it became foreclosed in medical health practice through expanded exclusion from SRHR services. Given what I have described about ages of sexual initiation, forced sex and informal unions, such foreclosure amounts to a form of structural harm. This is particularly so for those adolescents with same-sex praxes for whom, under the Children Act, sexual touching and penetration of another minor is liable to increased penalties, ranging from imprisonment for ten years to life. Therefore, mandatory reporting is required of this legally defined offence – a brutal act of heteropatriarchal state criminalization of adolescence.

POLICY INVISIBILITY

Trinidad and Tobago's National Sexual and Reproductive Health Policy (NSRHP) is aligned with the United Nations' Sustainable Development Goal 3 (to ensure healthy lives and promote healthy wellbeing for all at all ages) and SDG 5 (to achieve gender equality and empower all women and girls). This includes universal access to sexual and reproductive health and reproductive rights (Ministry of Health 2020, 2).

Specific to adolescents, the policy aims to "reduce adolescent pregnancy through the provision of comprehensive Adolescent SRH information and services" including "comprehensive age-appropriate sexuality education information and services for in and out of school adolescents and youths (including adolescents and youths in institutions)" and the Ministry of

Education's Health and Family Life Education (HFLE) programme (Ministry of Education 2020, 16).

The policy recognizes the problem of sexual offences and sexual abuse, and seeks to prevent gender and sexual violence. It doesn't specify that these crimes are predominantly by men against women and girls (though it notes that one-third of women report intimate partner violence and seeks to strengthen legal protection systems to prevent sexual violence against women and girls). There is no data on adolescent sexual activity. There is no HIV data on adolescents in the 2020 policy. In the 2016 draft, the HIV rate among youths aged 15–24 (which is 1.8 per cent) is not sex-disaggregated, either in terms of risk factors or rates (NSRHP 2016, 47). As Eudine Barriteau has pointed out, gender neutrality invisibilizes the need to confront gender hierarchies (Barriteau 1998, 192).

Tracy Robinson (2003, 256) long highlighted the difficulty of maintaining "the legitimacy of women as the subject of analysis", and the inversion of a feminist narrative of gender as fundamentally implicated in (analysis of) life and law in the region (p.244). Observing this in relation to HIV/AIDS, Peggy Antrobus (2005) also called for sex-disaggregated data as key to assessing public health services' approach to addressing gender inequalities. It should be noted that sex-disaggregated data, while giving visibility to the effect of inequality, also fixes "'gender' as a binary, and by extension, an exclusionary concept" (Rowley 2017, 118).

Given the legislative foreclosing of SRHR services for adolescents described earlier, and its specific impact on girls, the NSRHP is a crucial step in ensuring recognition of girls' sexuality. Yet, even here there is significant invisibility. The policy identifies as key populations/vulnerable groups those "specific groups who are specifically targeted in this policy as they may not or infrequently access SRH services" (Ministry of Health 2020, iii).

This includes "persons with disabilities; the elderly; sex workers; men; persons diagnosed with infertility; persons living with HIV and AIDS; migrant populations; adolescents and youths; the poor; the illiterate; substance users; and persons in their post-fertility years" (Ministry of Health 2020, iv).

Adolescents here are an ungendered category. Women and girls are invisible as a key population, despite the policy's acknowledgment of high rates of adolescent pregnancy – and, therefore, sexual activity. The 2016 draft policy noted that, between 2011 and 2013, "In one county 17% of all births were for young women ages 19 and under, and only 17% had attended their first antenatal clinic during the first trimester" (NSRHP 2016, 21). This data is not in the 2020 policy. One can argue that girls are repeatedly included under the category of "safe motherhood", though critiques of reducing female sexuality to reproduction and heteronormative state disciplining of the maternal body have long been made (Rowley 2003). Beyond reproduction is an invisibilizing of adolescent girls as sexual(ly desiring) citizens (Barrow 2009). Indeed, sexually active (non-pregnant) girls seeking SRH services are likely to experience greater stigma than boys. This is a masculinist framing of gender, sexuality and power, and exclusion of a group that experiences significant "reproductive discrimination" (Rowley 2017, 129).

The NSRHP excludes the LGBTI+ population's need for SRHR services through targeted outcomes (Rambarran and Simpson 2016). Indeed, while the 2016 draft acknowledges "men who have sex with men and other members of the lesbian, gay, bi-sexual, transgender (LBGT) community" (NSRHP 2016, 11) as a vulnerable group, they have been entirely *excised* from the 2020 version (NSRHP 2020, iv). This means that patriarchal conjugality and compulsory heterosexuality as norms are reinforced rather than problematized. Indeed, the NSRHP is specific in its reference to women, men, girls, and boys, thus excluding non-binary and transgender persons. In deference to gender stereotypes, "a 'Pink Room' for Women's Health and Breast Services and a 'Blue Room' for Men's Health including SRH" (NSRHP 2020, 41) are recommended. Thus, "broader societal pressures to maintain the gendered status quo" remain powerful and continue to "undermine efforts to transform gender relations and gendered structural inequalities" (Parpart 2013, 390).

One final observation about girls' disappearance within the gender-neutral category of youth is its contrast with the highlighting of young men. Here, the policy plans a "Military-Led Academic Training Academy (MILAT) programme for at-risk young men aged 16–20 years" (Ministry of Health 2020, 44). This continues take-up of 'gender' as 'including men', often as categories of victims, and often to the exclusion of women (Barriteau 2003, Haynes 2016).

CURRICULA SILENCE

The Ministry of Education is responsible for implementation of age-appropriate Health and Family Life Education (HFLE) curricula in all primary, secondary, vocational and tertiary institutions or programmes in Trinidad and Tobago. It is responsible for training educators and sensitizing parents "to support the process of maturation of their children, so that their children can achieve their full potential, particularly in the areas of sexual behaviour and reproductive health". The goal is to "delay early sexual initiation, prevent and address sexual and gender-based violence and adolescent pregnancy" (Ministry of Health 2020, 44).

The provision of HLFE to secondary school students is part of the NSRHP's approach to adolescent pregnancy prevention. For example, at the Form 2 level, one of the curriculum's objectives is for students to understand "the pitfalls associated with teenage pregnancy" by encouraging "the idea of sexual abstinence whilst a student" (Ministry of Education 2009, 106). As Theodore et al. (2010, 28–29) observed, cultural values expect girls "to have restricted knowledge and practical experience about sex and therefore femininity is equated with female abstinence". By promoting abstinence instead of educating school-aged children about safe sexual practices, the curriculum fails to consider gendered power relations in girls' lives.

Religious leaders and moral conservatives have long been opposed to HFLE. As the draft policy itself notes, "While multiple partners and sexual activities are glorified in popular music, there are also strong religious influences that perceive the provision of SRH information or services to adolescents is a 'licence to have sex'" (Ministry of Health 2020, 26). Adolescent sexuality is also a battleground between the Ministry of Education and religious organizations controlling denominational schools (Lindo 2023, Ramdeo 2023).

Moral panic about sexually active girls and LBGTQI adolescents (and growing transphobia) has made public education about adolescent sexual and reproductive rights a site for disciplining desiring subjects and minor citizens.[8] Adolescents know this. While 64.4 per cent of 2,284 secondary students reported it would help them to "feel prepared for sexual situations" (Ghisyawan, Kissoon, and Khan 2019, 18), in a study of fifty-two adolescents, "the law" and "church" were identified as the most significant barriers to SRH information (UNFPA 2021, 2), particularly for girls, LBGTQI youth, and those living with HIV.

In 2021, the Spotlight Initiative Programme to end all forms of gender-based violence, funded by the European Union and administered through the United Nations, undertook a revision of HFLE curricula in partnership with the Institute for Gender and Development Studies and the School of Education at The University of the West Indies (UWI), St Augustine Campus. The goal was to address discriminatory norms that perpetuate GBV. The Ministry of Education, in reviewing curricula recommendations aimed to ensure that they reflected relevant issues and concerns regarding family violence, included the SDGs, were supported by national policy and law, and were "developmentally age appropriate and culturally relevant to the culture of Trinidad and Tobago".

Ministry feedback on The UWI's secondary school curriculum recommendations emphasized that the national policy did not support concepts such as "diverse sexual orientation" and "gender identity" because national "recognition is only given to heterosexual persons" (Ministry of Education 2021, 5), and that "consent" in relation to identity, desires, practices and behaviour was not considered "developmentally age appropriate and culturally relevant" (pp. 2–3). Regarding consent, denial of both sexually active and LBGTQI adolescents can be seen in the response that discussion of sexual choice "creates opportunities for discussion on sexual orientation", which are antithetical to state policy.[9] The ministry thus mobilized denial and silence as a biopolitical strategy.

Consent was recommended for inclusion to address peer pressure, unwanted sexual attention, privacy about one's body, and safe access to water and toilets for girls. However, the ministry responded that consent is considered problematic for some parents as it "suggests an acknowledgment that young persons are sexually active" (Ministry of Education 2021, 5). Intimate partner violence was rejected as a form of GBV to be discussed, while approved foci were "bullying, sexual harassment, psychological violence, and domestic violence" (p.10). This was because of a concern that the discussion of IPV might include same-sex relationships (p.4). Bullying was treated as if it was unrelated to sexual orientation and gender identity, despite data to the contrary (Ghisyawan 2017). Showing contradictions in state assemblages, HIV prevention topics related to sharing of fluids during sex, blood transfusions and sharing of needles were approved.

In later national consultations with faith-based organizations (FBOs) and civil society stakeholders, FBOs further insisted on "exclusion of gender ideology that differentiates between sex and sexuality"; replacement of "young persons" with "boys and girls"; and retention of the gender stereotype that "women are created to be nurturing and caregivers". A petition emerged that, among other demands, stated that no HFLE programme should teach "unscientific and ideological gender identity theories (i.e. that gender is different to sex, that sexes exist other than male or female or that sex is fluid and can be changed) or that gender is a social construct and is different to sex".[10] In mid-2023, the Ministry of Education issued a press release confirming it had approved no revisions proposing GBV prevention education in schools (Phagoo 2023). Such enforced curricula silence denies the vulnerabilities and agency of girls and adolescents with queer practices and identities.

CONCLUSION

Legal exclusion, policy invisibility and curriculum silence are intersectional technologies of heteropatriarchal state surveillance and discipline. They enact structural violence. As Jamaican legal scholar Tracy Robinson wrote twenty years ago, "Liberated femininity is always in the neighbourhood of transgressive citizenship and that is key to understanding the politics of gender in the Caribbean today" (Robinson 2003, 352). Added to this is displacement of those who already constitute the queer nation-state (Rowley 2017, 133).

We return to the teenage girl seeking services. Having been taught abstinence in school and having been turned away from health care, to whom will she reach out? Who will reach out to her? In Debra Curtis' (2009) study of adolescent sexuality in Nevis, it was adult men who spoke most to girls about sex, often conveying misinformation. In Trinidad and Tobago, adolescents reach out to peers, older siblings, the internet and older partners. As one said, "A young person who is sexually active can feel very alone when trying to access information" (UNFPA 2021, 23). Reproductive, sexual and gender justice, therefore, remain urgent as long as state sovereignty and domination are defined and deployed through disavowal of desires and sexualities associated with girls and adolescents with same-sex praxes.

NOTES

1. Reporting is mandatory if an offence is considered to have been committed, but health care providers may not want responsibility for such an assessment and may opt to interpret the law as expecting all sexual activity to be reported.
2. See Sections 18–21: https://www.ttparliament.org/publication/the-children-act-2012/.
3. According to Tracy Robinson, legal amendments to sexual offences laws to protect women and "increase penalties for sexual violence . . . also heighten the criminalisation of same-sex sex" (Matthews and Robinson 2019, 137; Robinson 2009). This occurred with the Children Act precisely because of this precedent.
4. The 2017 Trinidad and Tobago (Trinidad) GSHS was a school-based survey of 2,836 students from Forms 1 to 6 (on average between thirteen and seventeen years).
5. Women who entered their first union aged nineteen or older had a lower prevalence of childhood sexual abuse (18 per cent).
6. Approximately 12 per cent of women indicated that the age of their first sexual experience was younger than fifteen. Of this group, almost 25 per cent of East Indian women said their first sexual experience was violent, compared to 29 per cent of mixed, 35 per cent of 'other', and 36 per cent of African women (Pemberton and Joseph 2018, 63–66).
7. This occurred because legislators argued that adolescents couldn't be allowed to legally engage in same-sex relations which would then become criminalized when they reached eighteen.
8. For example, https://catholictt.org/gender-conversation/
9. As of 2025, Trinidad and Tobago still does not have an approved National Policy on Gender and Development. A Green Paper states that the policy "does not provide measures for dealing with or relating to the issues of termination of pregnancy, same-sex unions, homosexuality or sexual orientation" (Office of the Prime Minister 2018, 15).
10. https://www.comprehensivesexualityeducation.org/international-map/trinidadandtobago/

REFERENCES

Alexander, Jacqui. 1991. "Redrafting Morality: The Postcolonial State and the Sexual Offences Bill of Trinidad and Tobago." In *Third World Women and the Politics of Feminism*, edited by Chandra Talpade Mohanty, Ann Russo, and Lourdes Torres, 133–52. Bloomington and Indianapolis: Indiana University Press.

———. 1994. "Not Just (Any) Body Can Be a Citizen: The Politics of Law, Sexuality and Postcoloniality in Trinidad and Tobago and the Bahamas." *Feminist Review* no. 48: 5–23. https://doi.org/10.2307/1395166.

Alexander, Ronni. 2018. "Gender, Structural Violence and Peace." In *The Routledge Handbook on Gender and Security*, edited by Caron Gentry, Laura Shepherd, and Laura Sjoberg, 27–36. London: Routledge

Allen, Caroline. 2013. *Situation Analysis of Adolescent Sexual and Reproductive Health and HIV in the Caribbean: Executive Summary*. Washington, DC: Pan American Health Organization.

Antoine, Rose-Marie Belle. 2020. "Family Planning Association of Trinidad and Tobago – Report to the Nation 2020 – Sexual and Reproductive Health Rights – An Essential Element to Universal Health Coverage." Family Planning Association of Trinidad and Tobago, 19 August. http://www.ttfpa.org/family-planning-association-of-trinidad-and-tobgao-report-to-the-nation-2020-sexual-and-reproductive-health-rights-an-essential-element-to-universal-health-coverage/.

Antrobus, Peggy. 2005. "Critiquing the MDGs from a Caribbean perspective." *Gender and Development* 13 (1): 94–104. https://www.jstor.org/stable/20053139.

Atluri, Tara. 2001. "When the Closet Is a Region: Homophobia, Heterosexism, and Nationalism in the Commonwealth Caribbean." Working Paper Series No. 5 Cave Hill, Barbados: Centre for Gender and Development Studies, University of the West Indies.

Barriteau, Eudine. 1998. "Theorizing Gender Systems and the Project of Modernity in the Twentieth-Century Caribbean." *Feminist Review* 59 (1): 186–210. https://doi.org/10.1080/014177898339523.

———. 2001. *The Political Economy of Gender in the Twentieth-Century Caribbean*. New York: Palgrave Macmillan.

———. 2003. "Confronting Power and Politics: A Feminist Theorizing of Gender in Commonwealth Caribbean Societies." *Meridians* 3 (2): 57–92. https://www.jstor.org/stable/40338575.

Barrow, Christine. 2009. "Contradictory Sexualities: From Vulnerability to Empowerment for Adolescent Girls in Barbados." In *Sexuality, Social Exclusion and Human Rights: Vulnerability in the Caribbean Context of HIV*, edited by

Christine Barrow, Marjan De Bruin, and Robert Carr, 215–38. Kingston: Ian Randle Publishers.

———. 2019. "Sexuality Research, Sexual Politics and Sexual Rights in the Anglophone Caribbean." In *SexPolitics: Trends and Tensions in the 21st Century – Contextual Undercurrents, Volume 2*, edited by Sonia Correa and Richard Parker, 41–71. Rio de Janeiro: Sexuality Policy Watch.

Barrow, Christine, Marjan de Bruin, and Robert Carr. 2009. Introduction to *Sexuality, Social Exclusion and Human Rights: Vulnerability in the Caribbean Context of HIV*, edited by Christine Barrow, Marjan de Bruin, and Robert Carr, xvii–xxxxii. Kingston: Ian Randle Publishers.

Catignani, Sergio, and Victoria Basham. 2021. "Reproducing the Military and Heteropatriarchal Normal: Army Reserve Service as Serious Leisure." *Security Dialogue* 52, (2): 99–117. doi: 10.1177/0967010620923969.

Crawford, Charmaine. 2012. "'It's a Girl Thing': Problematizing Female Sexuality, Gender and Lesbophobia in Caribbean Culture." In *Theorizing Homophobias in the Caribbean: Complexities of Place, Desire and Belonging*, edited by Angelique V. Nixon and Rosamond S. King. http://www.caribbeanhomophobias.org/.

Curtis, Debra. 2009. *Pleasures, and Perils: Girls' Sexuality in a Caribbean Consumer Culture*. New Brunswick, NJ: Rutgers University Press.

Everett, Bethany, Aubrey Limburg, Patricia Homan, and Morgan M. Philbin. 2022. "Structural Heteropatriarchy and Birth Outcomes in the United States." *Demography* 59 (1): 89–110. doi:10.1215/00703370-9606030.

Ghisyawan, Krystal. 2018. *2016 Trinidad and Tobago School Climate Report: Bullying and Gender-Based Violence in Secondary Schools*. Port of Spain: The Silver Lining Foundation/UNESCO ASPnet Trinidad and Tobago. https://silverliningtt.com/2016-school-climate-report/.

Ghisyawan, Krystal, Yasphal Kissoon, and Katija Khan. 2019. *Trinidad and Tobago National School Climate Survey Report 2019: Bullying and Gender-Based Violence in Secondary Schools*. Port of Spain: The Silver Lining Foundation. https://silverliningtt.com/wp-content/uploads/2021/08/TTNSCS_2019_Final.pdf.

Hawkins, Kirstan, Joel Joseph, Kim Longfield, and Tiffany Best. 2007. "Money Make the Nookie Go 'Round': Young Women and Sexual Relationships in Two Locations in Trinidad." Port of Spain: Options Consultancy Services Ltd and Population Services International.

Haynes, Tonya. 2016. "Sylvia Wynter's Theory of the Human and the Crisis School of Caribbean Heteromasculinity Studies." *Small Axe* 49: 92–112. https://doi.org/10.1215/07990537-3481570.

Hosein, Gabrielle, and Jane Parpart, eds.2016. *Negotiating Gender, Policy, and Politics in the Caribbean: Feminist Strategies, Masculinist Resistance and Transformational Possibilities*. London: Rowman and Littlefield Publishers.

Kempadoo, Kamala. 2003. "Sexuality in the Caribbean: Theory and Research (with an Emphasis on the Anglophone Caribbean)." *Social and Economic Studies* 52 (3): 59–88. https://www.jstor.org/stable/27865341.

Lazarus, Latoya. 2019. "Debating Sex Education: The Politics and Discursive Framing of Comprehensive Sexuality Education in Barbados." *Journal of Eastern Caribbean Studies* 44 (2): 12–37.

Lindo, Paula. 2023. "RC Archbishop: Government Needs our Consent for Sex Education in Denominational Schools." *Trinidad and Tobago Newsday*, Saturday 24 June. https://newsday.co.tt/2023/06/24/rc-archbishop-government-needs-our-consent-for-sex-education-in-denominational-schools/#:~:text=RC%20Archbishop%3A%20Government%20needs%20our%20consent%20for%20sex%20education%20in%20denominational%20schools,-Paula%20Lindo%203&text=RC%20Archbishop%20Jason%20Gordon%20has,the%20consent%20of%20the%20denomination.

Matthews, Janeille Zorina, and Tracy Robinson. 2019. "Modern Vagrancy in the Anglophone Caribbean." *Caribbean Journal of Criminology* 1 (4): 123–54. https://ssrn.com/abstract=3210831.

Mazurana, Dyan, and Susan McKay. 2001. "Women, Girls, and Structural Violence: A Global Analysis." In *Peace, Conflict, and Violence: Peace Psychology for the 21st Century*, edited by Daniel Christie, Richard Wagner, and Deborah Winter, 1–15. Englewood Cliffs, NJ: Prentice-Hall. https://u.osu.edu/christie/about/peace-conflict-and-violence-peace-psychology-for-the-21st-century/.

Ministry of Education (Curriculum Planning and Development Division). 2021. Spotlight Initiative – Comments of the Ministry of Education on the Gap Assessment of the Health and Family Life Secondary Curriculum, 2 December.

Ministry of Health. 2020. *National Sexual and Reproductive Health Policy*. https://www.health.gov.tt/sites/default/filewomenshealth/National%20Sexual%20and%20Reproductive%20Health%20Policy.pdf

Ministry of Social Development and Family Services, Central Statistical Office and UNICEF. 2011. *Trinidad and Tobago Multiple Indicator Cluster Survey 2011, Key Findings and Tables*. Port of Spain: Ministry of Social Development and Family Services, Central Statistical Office, and UNICEF. https://cso.gov.tt/stat_publications/multiple-indicator-cluster-survey-mics-2011/

Mohammed, R.A., L. Theron, K. Carrillo, and N. Rambarran. 2020. *From Fringes to Focus: A Deep Dive into the Lived Realities of Lesbian, Bisexual and Queer*

Women and Trans Masculine Persons in 8 Caribbean Countries. Amsterdam: COC Netherlands. https://ufdc.ufl.edu/AA00083427/00001.

Montesanti, Stephanie, and Wilfreda Thurston. 2015. "Mapping the Role of Structural and Interpersonal Violence in the Lives of Women: Implications for Public Health Interventions and Policy." *BMC Women's Health* 15, 100. DOI 10.1186/s12905-015-0256-4.

Montesanti, Stephanie Rose. 2015. "The Role of Structural and Interpersonal Violence in the Lives of Women: A Conceptual Shift in Prevention of Gender-based Violence." *BMC Women's Health* 15, 93: 1–3. https://doi.org/10.1186/s12905-015-0247-5.

Noreiga, Alicia, and Casey Burkholder. 2022. "Forging Queer Solidarities in Trinidad and Tobago and New Brunswick, Canada through Cellphilm Method." In *Annual Review of Comparative and International Education 2021 (International Perspectives on Education and Society, Vol. 42B)*, edited by A. Wiseman, 119–37. Leeds: Emerald Publishing. https://doi.org/10.1108/S1479-367920220000042B007.

Parliament of Trinidad and Tobago. 2000. Sexual Offences (Amendment) Act, 2000. Assented to on 25 September 2000. https://www.ttparliament.org/publication/the-sexual-offences-amendment-act-2000/.

———. 2015. Children Act, 2012. Proclaimed on 18 May 2015. https://rgd.legalaffairs.gov.tt/Laws2/Alphabetical_List/lawspdfs/46.01.pdf.

———. 2017. "Miscellaneous Provisions (Marriage) Act 2017." Assented to on 22 June 2017. https://www.ttparliament.org/publication/the-miscellaneous-provisions-marriage-act-2017/.

———. 2020. *13th Report of the Joint Select Committee on Social Services and Public Administration: Inquiry into the Prevalence of Teenage Pregnancy and the State's Capacity to Minimise the Occurrence of Teenage Pregnancy and Provide Services and Assistance to Teenage Parents*. Laid in the House of Representative on 6 March. Laid in the Senate on 10 March. https://www.ttparliament.org/wp-content/uploads/2021/11/p11-s5-J-20200306-SSPA-R13.pdf.

Parpart, Jane. 2013. "Exploring the Transformative Potential of Gender Mainstreaming in International Development Institutions." *Journal of International Development* 26 (3): 382–95. https://doi.org/10.1002/jid.2948.

Pemberton, Cecile, and Joel Joseph. 2018. *National Women's Health Survey for Trinidad and Tobago: Final Report*. Washington, DC: Inter-American Development Bank (IDB). https://publications.iadb.org/en/national-womens-health-survey-trinidad-and-tobago-final-report.

Phagoo, Vishanna. 2023. "Education Ministry: No change to health, family life education curriculum." *Trinidad and Tobago Newsday*, 17 June. https://

newsday.co.tt/2023/06/17/education-ministry-no-change-to-health-family-life-education-curriculum/.

Rambarran, Natassia, and Joel Simpson. 2016. "An Exploration of the Health Care Experiences Encountered by Lesbian and Sexual Minority Women in Guyana." *International Journal of Sexual Health* 28 (4): 332–42. http://dx.doi.org/10.1080/19317611.2016.1223254

Ramdeo, Jesse. 2023. "Archbishop reaffirms no LGBTQI+ material in schools: Concordat protecting our children." *Trinidad and Tobago Guardian*, 23 June. https://www.guardian.co.tt/news/archbishop-reaffirms-no-lgbtqi-material-in-schools-6.2.1737672.830020b89a.

Rawlins, Joan, Isaac Dialsingh, Tazhmoye V. Crawford, Samantha G. Rawlins, and Donovan A. McGrowder. 2013. "The rate of pregnancy in Trinidad and Tobago: A comparison Between Pregnant Teenagers and Pregnant Adults Registered at Three Health Centers." *International Journal of Medicine and Public Health* 3 (3): 129–33. DOI: 10.4103/2230-8598.118942.

Reddock, Rhoda. 2008. "Gender, Nation and the Dilemmas of Citizenship: The Case of the Marriage Acts of Trinidad and Tobago." In *Global Empowerment for Women: Responses to Globalization and Politicized Religions*, edited by Carolyn Elliot. New York: Routledge. https://doi.org/10.4324/9780203933756.

———. 2021. "Welcome to Paradise: Neoliberalism, Violence and the Social and Gender Crisis of the Caribbean." In *Decolonial Perspectives on Entangled Inequalities: Europe and The Caribbean*, edited by Encarnación Gutiérrez Rodríguez and Rhoda Reddock, 55–76. London and New York: Anthem Press. https://doi.org/10.2307/j.ctv22d4tmb.

Robinson, Tracy. 2003. "Beyond the Bill of Rights: Sexing the Citizen." In *Confronting Power, Theorizing Gender: Interdisciplinary Perspectives in the Caribbean*, edited by Eudine Barriteau, 231–61. Kingston: University of the West Indies Press.

———. 2007. "A Loving Freedom: A Caribbean Feminist Ethic." *Small Axe* 24: 118–29. https://doi.org/10.1215/-11-3-118.

———. 2009. "Authorised Sex: Same-Sex Sexuality and the Law in the Caribbean." In *From Risk to Vulnerability: Power, Culture and Gender in the Spread of HIV and AIDS in the Caribbean*, edited by Christine Barrow, Marjan de Bruin, and Robert Carr, 3–22. Kingston: Ian Randle Publishers.

Rogers, Tracie. 2017. "Silence, Invisibility and Social Policy: Putting the Pieces Together with HIV Positive Youth." *Caribbean Review of Gender Studies* 11: 141–80.

Rowley, Michelle. 2003. "Crafting Maternal Citizens? Public Discourses of the 'Maternal Scourge' in Social Welfare Polices and Services in Trinidad." *Social and Economic Studies* 52 (3): 31–58. https://www.jstor.org/stable/27865340.

———. 2011. *Feminist Advocacy and Gender Equity in the Anglophone Caribbean: Envisioning a Politics of Coalition*. New York: Routledge.

———. 2017. "Should We Still Hope? Gender Policy, Social Justice, and Affect in the Caribbean." *Caribbean Review of Gender Studies* 11: 111–40.

Santhya, K.G., and S.J. Jejeebhoy. 2015. "Sexual and Reproductive Health and Rights of Adolescent Girls: Evidence from Low- and Middle-income Countries." *Global Public Health* 10 (2): 189–221. doi: 10.1080/17441692.2014.986169.

Senate of Trinidad and Tobago. 2017. "Miscellaneous Provisions (Marriage) 2017.01.17 Bill 2016." 7th Sitting of the Senate – 2nd Session of the 11th Republican Parliament. Hon. F. Al-Rawi. Unofficial Hansard. Tuesday, 17 January. https://www.labour.gov.tt/mediaroom/parliamentary-contributions?download=148:tuesday-17-january-2017-the-senate-miscellaneous-provisions-marriage-bill-2016.

Tambiah, Yasmin. 2009. "Creating (Im)moral Citizens: Gender, Sexuality, and Lawmaking in Trinidad and Tobago, 1986." *Caribbean Review of Gender Studies* 3: 1–19.

Theodore, Karl, Althea La Foucade, Kimberly-Ann Gittens-Baynes, Patricia Edwards-Wescott, Roger Mc Lean, and Christine Laptiste. 2010. *Situation Analysis of Children and Women in Trinidad and Tobago*. UNICEF Office for the Eastern Caribbean Area.

United Nations Population Fund. 2021. *Legal Barriers that Affect Adolescent Access to Sexual and Reproductive Health Services in Trinidad and Tobago: A Qualitative Study*. Kingston: UNFPA Caribbean. https://caribbean.unfpa.org/sites/default/files/pub-pdf/legal_barriers_that_affect_adolescent_access_to_sexual_and_reproductive_health_services_in_trinidad_and_tobago.pdf.

Wahab, Amar. 2012. "Homophobia as the State of Reason: The Case of Postcolonial Trinidad and Tobago." *GLQ: A Journal of Lesbian and Gay Studies* 18 (4): 481–505. https://doi.org/10.1215/10642684-1600707.

Williams, Charmaine, Margaret F. Gibson, Emily Mooney, Joellean R. Forbes, Deone Curling, Datejie Cheko Green, and Lori E. Ross. 2023. "A Structural Analysis of Gender-Based Violence and Depression in the Lives of Sexual Minority Women and Trans People." *Affilia: Feminist Inquiry in Social Work* 38 (3): 350–66. doi: 10.1177/08861099231155887.

World Health Organization. 2017. "Global School-based Student Health Survey Trinidad and Tobago (Trinidad) 2017 Fact Sheet." https://cdn.who.int/media/docs/default-source/ncds/ncd-surveillance/data-reporting/trinidad-and-tobago/gshs/trinidad_and_tobago__trinidad_2017_gshs_fs.pdf?sfvrsn=5e5f4895_5&download=true.

chapter 18

"Smile for Me, Sweetie!"

An Analysis of Contemporary Gender-Based Violence and Discrimination in The Bahamas

JENNIFER MUNNINGS

CATCALLING IS AN ALMOST INESCAPABLE PHENOMENON FOR WOMEN in The Bahamas. Men jeer at women as they go about their daily activities, giving unwanted comments about their appearance. "Smile for me, sweetie!" is a common catcall, one that asserts control over the ways in which women express themselves. While catcalls may appear to be compliments, they are a form of sexual harassment, indicative of the normalization of patriarchal attitudes within the country (Walton and Pederson 2022).

In The Bahamas, there is a disconnect between public perception and the actual state of gender relations. The absence of a definitive caste system and the relatively higher graduation rates of girls and women from high school and college (Fieldinling 2015) paint a picture of equality. However, progress made towards gender equality is often short-lived or overemphasized. Government intervention in issues surrounding gender-based violence (GBV) and discrimination ignores the ways in which sexism is embedded in social institutions and operates as a macro-level structure. The government's individualistic approach that focuses on behaviours and attitudes to gender inequality mirrors the broader conceptualization of sexism in The Bahamas.

GBV and gender discrimination are prevalent throughout Bahamian social, cultural and political institutions. Constitutional discrimination, low female political participation, and high rates of rape are indicators of persistent gender inequality throughout the country. The Bahamian government and the public have yet to critically address the role of women within the country and analyse the impact of socio-political structures in promoting a culture that normalizes violence and discrimination against them. Patriarchy is embedded in the foundations of The Bahamas wherein legacies of colonialism and gendered aspects of nation-building established women as second-class citizens. Social institutions similarly work to promote traditional gender roles that establish women as inferior to men.

Efforts to eliminate gender inequality must attend to the ways in which sexism operates at the structural level of society; is embedded in major social institutions; and shapes gender identities and ideologies, and interactions between women and men. I highlight the activist perspective to examine gender inequality and their proposed solutions to eliminate sexism in the country. This chapter benefits from the wealth of knowledge that the activists have on gender relations in The Bahamas to critically assess, in particular, the impact that the nation's colonial legacy and the institutions of religion and politics have on gender relations.

CONTEXTUALIZING BAHAMIAN GENDER RELATIONS

Women in The Bahamas have made notable achievements throughout the country and are graduating from high school and college at higher rates than men (CEDAW 2017), and have more public visibility than ever before in Bahamian history. However, women are highly represented in middle-management positions but earn less than men do for the same work (CEDAW 2017). The increase in women's visibility in low-wage jobs has led to the perception that women are overtaking men economically (Benjamin and LeGrand 2012). The perception, however, differs from reality; a study found that men were represented in the labour force at higher rates than women at 80.5 per cent and 71.9 per cent respectively (CEDAW 2017). Different aspects of gender inequality, including gender roles and expectations, sexual objectification and infantilization, and unequal access to power have worked to legitimize and perpetuate violence against women (Russo and Pirlott 2006).

Gender-based violence is an indicator of persistent and pervasive gender inequality in society (Russo and Pirlott 2006). One form of such violence that is prevalent in The Bahamas is intimate partner violence. IPV has been normalized in Bahamian society through institutions of socialization, as many children grow up in homes with recurrent domestic violence. In 2009, a survey of nearly six hundred college students in Nassau found that around 21 per cent of students reported experiencing or witnessing domestic violence at home (Plumridge and Fielding 2009). Between 2010 and 2016, almost one hundred women were killed as a result of IPV, accounting for 10 per cent of all murders during that time (United Nations Human Rights Council 2018).

Rates of rape and sexual assault are significantly high in The Bahamas. While the worldwide average for rape in 2007 was fifteen per one hundred thousand persons, The Bahamas had an average of one hundred and thirty-three – which, at the time, was the highest in the world (UNHRC 2018). The rampant rates of sexual abuse have made it so that the first sexual experience of many sexually active girls was "forced" or "somewhat forced" (UNHRC 2018). The Royal Bahamas Police Force found that more than sixty-two hundred cases of sexual offences were reported over a ten-year period (2003–2013) (UNHRC 2018). However, consistent with the trend around the world, incidents of sexual violence are systematically underreported. Emergency room data found that cases of rape treated at the Princess Margaret Hospital alone were nearly 1.6 times higher than those recorded by the Bahamian police department (UNHRC 2018).

The normalization of violence against women extends into the political sphere as well. Gender inequality manifests at the micro, meso and macro levels of society, which intersect to perpetuate and reproduce inequality. Traditional gender roles in the home and at work instil gendered differences in people's perceived entitlements, and place different values and meanings on the resources that women and men provide in relationships (Russo and Pirlott 2006). These traditional gender roles are reinforced by various social institutions that encourage women to be submissive to their partners, thus normalizing sexist conceptions of women as inferior to men (Nicolls 2014). Meso- and macro-level analyses of institutions are necessary to understand the different ways in which gender discrimination and violence against women are reinforced through social institutions.

For example, gender inequality in the government and marriage are mutually reinforcing to legitimize GBV in society broadly. In particular, the failure of the Bahamian government to outlaw marital rape exemplifies how the institution of marriage legitimizes men's sexual and physical violence against their wives (Russo and Pirlott 2006). The issue of marital rape has long been a point of contention in Bahamian society, as religious leaders and women's rights groups continue to argue over its legitimacy. The marital rape exception, which exempts spouses from the constitutional definition of rape, can be traced back to as early as 1736 and is tied to the colonial view of women as chattel or property (Benjamin and LeGrand 2012). In 2009, the Bahamian government tabled a bill to criminalize marital rape and again in 2017, following a statement from the Special Rapporteur, citing the spousal exception as the most pressing issue to women. The government, however, has refrained from moving forward with the bill because of public objection and the powerful influence of the lobbyist group, the Christian Council (Benjamin and LeGrand 2012).

The rhetoric surrounding the marital rape exception is reflective of the view that intersecting institutions such as politics and religion reinforce sexism. Myths about rape permeate the national conversation on addressing sexual violence. Some have expressed fear that wives would use rape as a "weapon" against their husbands, undergirded by the more general fear that women are spiteful and liars. The 2017 bill also failed to gain support from women who, in line with conservative religious views, felt that it is a wife's duty to submit to her husband (Benjamin and LeGrand 2012). The lack of female support for the bill highlights the significant impact of institutions of socialization like the church in maintaining patriarchy. Marital rape is also frequently framed by the media, politicians and religious officials as a privacy issue. Bahamians felt that what happens between spouses is a private matter and that the government should not have the authority to interfere, undertaking an individualistic understanding of violence against women (Benjamin and LeGrand 2012). In this way, marriage works to silence victims and normalize violence against women. Inequality in different contexts has a compounding effect when they intersect to reinforce the structural nature of GBV and sexual violence (Reskin 2012).

NATION-BUILDING, RACE AND MISOGYNY

Attitudes towards women today are largely the result of the making of the Bahamian nation-state, which was entrenched in a battle for racial equality that sacrificed the constitutional status of women to achieve independence. The move towards independence saw the overthrow of a white colonial power that had been ruling since the mid-1600s by a black-majority government. The making of the Bahamian nation could begin only after racial empowerment was achieved; as a result, Bahamian independence was more about racial justice than nation-building (Bethel 2003). The construction of Bahamian citizenship and nation-building are entrenched in racial politics and the control over women's bodies and reproductive choices.

To preserve a clear racial binary, women of the newly independent Bahamas were made second-class citizens in the constitution, despite their instrumental efforts that led to independence in 1973 because of fear that they would have mixed children with white men (Bethel 2003). The unequal conferral of citizenship is representative of colonial-era, sexist attitudes towards women that persist today. In the Bahamian constitution, the wives of Bahamian men are automatically entitled to Bahamian citizenship; however, the husbands of Bahamian women have to apply for citizenship like any other immigrant. Similarly, the children of Bahamian men, whether born in The Bahamas or elsewhere, are Bahamians at birth, whereas the children of Bahamian women have a more complex journey towards citizenship (Bethel 2003). The limited ability of women to confer citizenship is the result of a political move by the new black government to ensure that the population and the government remained majority black (Bethel 2003). The new government placed emphasis on women, who were seen as a way in which a white majority could regain control over the government – even though men presented the same challenge as they could have biracial children with white wives. The double standard discriminates against women and places limitations on women's reproductive rights.

The failure of the 2016 referendum to eliminate constitutional gender discrimination highlights the ways in which macro-level structures and micro-level behaviours and beliefs mutually reinforce gender discrimination. The referendum proposed four bills that would neutralize discrepancies in the transference of citizenship and add sex as a ground of discrimination under the constitution. The bills proposed in the referendum were overshadowed by a contentious political climate and fear that the inclusion of the word "sex" would open the door to same-sex marriage, which Bahamians overwhelmingly opposed (Wallace 2017). Thus, the rampant homophobia in The Bahamas played a large role in the country's vote against the gender equality referendum. Many Bahamian women, in particular, felt that there was no need for the changes because of fundamentalist beliefs that women are meant to be submissive to men, not equal, and that the referendum was actually anti-men.

THE ACTIVIST PERSPECTIVE

Gender discrimination and gender-based violence are pervasive in all aspects of Bahamian society; however, scholarship about Bahamian gender relations is limited in its exploration of the relevance of the nation's history to contemporary gender relations. Interviewing activists provides a new perspective on the current state of gender relations. Scholars have acknowledged the importance of non-governmental organizations (NGOs), as they have influenced politics and private institutions, and play an important role in good governance and economic development (Teegan and Doh, 2004; Johnson and Prakash 2007). Bahamian NGOs and activists similarly play a significant role in persuading the government and the public to more seriously analyse the status of women in society.

The seven activists interviewed have worked to champion women's rights in The Bahamas and challenge the government and the public to reimagine women's role in society. As gender rights activists, they have significant experience in combatting gender-based violence and discrimination, and their work to dismantle unequal institutions, educate the public, and support victims provides a unique perspective on the issues. These activists are acutely aware of the challenges that fighting for gender equality in the Bahamian context poses. The names and background of activists interviewed are listed in table 18.1.

Table 18.1: Profiles of Bahamian Activist Interviewees (*N*=7)

Interviewee	Affiliation	Background
Ternielle Burrows	Rise Bahamas!	Ternielle Burrows is the founder of Rise Bahamas! An organisation dedicated to raising awareness about women's rights in The Bahamas. Rise Bahamas is a grassroots organisation that advocates for increased government accountability in regard to gender relations. It is an expansion of The Bahamas Sexual Violence & Child Abuse Prevention group that was founded in 2009.
LaToya Johnson	Zonta	LaToya Johnson is the current president of the Zonta Club of Nassau. Zonta is an international activism club dedicated to empowering women and girls through education and raising awareness to gender inequality. Johnson also works as a management consultant.
Alicia Wallace	Equality Bahamas	Alicia Wallace launched Equality Bahamas in 2014 which is an organisation that works to promote women's rights as human rights and advocates for equality through public education, community engagement, and empowerment of women, girls, and LGBT+ people in The Bahamas.
Allicia Rolle	The Department of Gender and Family Affairs	Allicia Rolle is a gender equality and human rights advocate. Rolle works for The Department of Gender and Family Affairs as a Gender Specialist conducting data collection and reporting and assists government representatives in preparation for international conventions like CEDAW.
Erin Greene	Independent queer rights activist	Erin Greene is a women's rights and queer rights activist who has been partnered with various advocacy groups throughout the years. Most recently Greene was involved in educating the public about queer rights in regards to the gender equality referendum.

Table 18.1 continues

Table 18.1: *(cont'd)*

Interviewee	Affiliation	Background
Dr. Sandra Dean Patterson	Crisis Centre	Dr. Sandra Dean Patterson is a psychotherapist and founded The Bahamas Crisis Center in 1982 to provide services for people who are the victims of physical, sexual, and emotional abuse. The Center has received many accolades for its efforts to address gender-based violence. Patterson continues to be at the forefront of women's rights advocacy in The Bahamas through the development of educational campaigns and organising talks to promote gender equality.
Marion Bethel	CEDAW	Marion Bethel is an attorney, poet, essayist, filmmaker, human and gender rights activist, and writer. In 2012 she directed the documentary "Womanish Ways" on the Bahamian suffrage movement. Bethel currently holds a position on the United Nations Committee on the Elimination of all Forms of Discrimination Against Women (CEDAW).

DETERMINANTS OF GENDER INEQUALITY

The seven interviewees identified three social forces that work together to maintain a patriarchal system and high rates of GBV and SV in The Bahamas. First, they spoke about the influence of religion, specifically the role that this social institution plays in shaping the Bahamian understanding of gender and perpetuating gender inequality. Religion influences gender socialization and gender roles, including the perception of familial roles, extra-familial roles, and gender stereotypes (Mikołajczak and Pietrzak 2014). Most Bahamians identify strongly with Christianity, with the church representing one of the few shared experiences in the nation. According to the CIA World Factbook, 70 per cent of Bahamians identify as Protestant, 12 per cent as Roman Catholic, and 13 per cent as "other Christian" (including 1.1 per cent Jehovah's Witness). Erin Greene – an independent women's and queer rights activist, once affiliated with the Rainbow Alliance – said, "Bahamians don't have any cultural rites of passage and so the greatest collective experience is the church and then family and then Junkanoo." The centrality of religion is reflected in the large role that Christianity plays in gender socialization and defining the nation's understanding of gender roles. Bethel said: "The Christian cultural notions are one of the root causes of discrimination against women and the continuing and persistent and prevalent discrimination against women. I don't think [Bahamians] see women as worthy of any other way of life than what Christianity prescribes." Ternielle Burrows, founder of Rise Up Bahamas!, indicated that fundamentalist Christianity teaches women to be submissive.

It is noteworthy, however, that the seven activists disagreed over the extent of the impact of religion on GBV, SV and GD. Specifically, some of the interviewees cited religion as the *primary* source of sexist discrimination, while others felt that the role of religion in perpetuating gender inequality was more indirect. For example, Greene said: "I think that for many churches, they're not focusing on messages that promote misogyny or the subjugation of women. But I think that they are also not challenging these norms in their church environments, and they are not encouraging their parishioners to challenge these norms in their family lives." Bethel disagreed, arguing: "Embedded in Christianity is a notion of patriarchy and women's subordination to men. I think this is a very strong part of our culture." The disagreement is based on differences in the perceived power of the church in shaping the national conception of gender. However, the interviewees agreed that strong fundamentalist Christian beliefs played a role – whether primarily or more indirectly – in producing and maintaining the Bahamian patriarchy. Scholars agree that the conservative culture of The Bahamas, often bolstered by religion, reinforces sexist gender roles and stereotypes (Nicolls 2014).

The second determinant of gender inequality cited by the interviewees was the legacy of colonization on Bahamian gender relations. According to the interviewees, the colonial legacy of The Bahamas functions in similar ways as the role of religion in normalizing colonial-era notions about gender. Speaking about the lingering effects of colonization, Bethel said, "[t]he law has a normative effect and impact, so growing up as a colonial subject and moving into independence with colonial laws that are not changed still permeates the social understanding of norms." Sexist stereotypes and patriarchal institutions rooted in the colonial understanding of women still inform Bahamian society today. Notions of submissive women, or even women as men's property, are directly linked to colonization. Patterson articulated this in the following quote: "If you look at [the perception of women] historically, the attitude was that women need to know their place [in society]. As long as the instrument with which you beat your woman is 'no thicker than your thumb', it's okay to do it. That was in British law, that's where the 'rule of thumb' comes from."

Despite more than forty-five years of independence, the colonial legacy of the nation informs Bahamian laws and social norms that continue to impact the status of women today (Elvy 2016). The interviewees identified the citizenship laws and the marital rape exception as sexist legislation left behind by colonialism. Sandra Dean Patterson, a psychotherapist and the founder of The Bahamas Crisis Centre, said, "Our constitution makes it very clear that if you are a woman and you marry a foreigner, you can't come back here [to The Bahamas]. That was a part of the colonial mentality." The Bahamian constitution includes unequal conferral of citizenship to the spouses and children of Bahamian men and women. Regarding the marital rape exception, Allicia Rolle, a gender specialist at the Department of Gender and Family Affairs, said, "Bahamians are still under the impression that you cannot rape your wife because she belongs to you." The interviewees argued that the colonial-era mentality that women were not full, valued citizens persists today.

The final determinant of GBV and GD identified in the interviews is the idea that Bahamians are taught to romanticize unhealthy and abusive relationships because they have been normalized in society. For example, Patterson remarked, "The messages that we've given boys about what the definition of a man is and what the definition of what a woman is, and the exposure to domestic violence, is creating the problems in our country that we're seeing today." In a study of Bahamian high schoolers, Nicolls (2014) found that 16 per cent of boys and 6.6 per cent of girls thought that a woman who dresses too sexy deserves to get hit by her male partner. The interviewees argued that such normalization of relationship violence instils in the public a sense of impunity towards men who perpetuate violence against women.

Rolle reflected on these seemingly normal dynamics of traditional gender roles and violence against women who deviate from those roles: "A lot of women and children don't know that they're being abused. A lot of high school kids are in abusive relationships and their boyfriends slap them, verbally abuse them and they just think that's what's supposed to happen in a relationship."

In addition, Bethel said, "There is a tolerance clearly of violence against women. That in some ways [women] are deserving of it – this is our lot." Some of the interviewees linked this tolerance and acceptance of GBV back to agents of socialization that objectify women like religious institutions, schools and the family.

The activists also identified patterns of objectification and infantilization of women as sources of inequality that can also lead to GBV, SV and GD. They argued that Bahamian society does not view women as autonomous beings with agency over their own bodies. Patterson said: "This idea that men are supposed to be in charge and women are supposed to follow instructions creates this environment where if women do not follow instructions or if they make mistakes they are to be punished."

Alicia Wallace, founder of Equality Bahamas, added: "There's also this infantilization of women – this idea that women are akin to children under patriarchy, where the father gives them away to a husband and that husband becomes the new owner, the new parent almost. So, you have this idea of disciplining another adult added into the equation." Scholars agree that the infantilization of women in The Bahamas is used under patriarchy as a tool to reinforce the subordination of women and is correlated with acts of GBV and SV (Namy 2017). The socialization of Bahamians through institutions like religion, politics and culture, according to the interviewees, acts as a significant determinant of gender inequality and frames contemporary gender relations. These institutions work together to reproduce patriarchy and the subordination of women and normalize GBV, SV and GD within Bahamian society.

BARRIERS TO ADDRESSING GENDER-BASED VIOLENCE AND DISCRIMINATION

The second major theme that emerged from the interviews is barriers to effectively addressing GBV, SV and discrimination in The Bahamas. The interviewees identified various socio-political barriers that prevent The Bahamas from achieving gender equality, including the colonial legacy, the political landscape and the role of religion. The activists argued that the determinants and barriers to addressing GBV and GD are all interconnected, and so, some of the social forces mentioned in the preceding section are also mentioned below.

The interviewees argued that the legacy of colonization acts as a barrier to achieving gender equality because the beliefs and values about women from the colonial era remain engrained in Bahamian society today. Indeed, the nation is only just beginning to grapple with the extent of colonialism and the way it affects Bahamian women today. For example, Bethel said, "The colonial legacy is one that says that what we have is superior to anything we could possibly re-enact." Part of the colonial mentality is an understanding of the political system implemented by the British as superior to anything native Bahamians could create. Greene argued that these remnants of the nation's colonial history are difficult to change: "It goes well beyond just colonialism. It's the laws around sexuality, the laws about men and women, the way that we relate to each other and the paradigms of relationship and living together." She argued that the way that Bahamians understand relationships, sexuality and gender are deeply rooted in the enslaved and colonial experience; consequently, it proves difficult to redefine contemporary norms regarding gender and sexuality.

The activists suggested legislative reform as one way to address the colonial legacy of patriarchy. However, they expressed concern that attempts to change laws have proven to be challenging because of the state of the Bahamian political arena. In particular, the interviewees identified a general lack of political will to combat GBV and GD as a second barrier to achieving gender equality. Bethel said: "There's a direct link between gender inequality and violence against women, and the government doesn't understand that. It doesn't have a political will to address it. There's no political currency for them to address it. The government gets the vote of women regardless."

The interviewees surmised that gender inequality in The Bahamas is not considered a pressing issue – neither by the people nor the government. Despite numerous studies by the UN, governmental agencies and local NGOs that highlight the need for structural change, the Bahamian government has done little to enact them. Specifically, three of the seven interviewees identified different times between 2014 and 2015 when their respective organizations made attempts to reach out to the government to provide data or assistance – only to be met with silence. Wallace said the following:

> In 2014, when we first started doing this work, following the non-joke that Leslie Miller [former member of parliament] made about domestic violence, Equality Bahamas presented to the government a proposal that included a very wide public education campaign about domestic violence to talk about the statistics and resources that are available for women, talking about the signs, how to get help, that kind of thing . . . We sent it to the Prime Minister. We sent it to what was then the Gender Bureau. They didn't respond.

Although the entire population would benefit from reform as indicated by the interviewees, the lack of political currency around gender equality prevents progress towards challenging the status quo.

Whereas Bahamian politicians, who are overwhelmingly men, refuse to recognize gender inequality as a pressing political issue, the interviewees stressed the importance of increasing the number of women at the decision-making level in the government. Latoya Johnson, current president of Zonta, an activism club dedicated to education on gender equality, said, "Women are not in places and spaces to be able to speak for women. And that is one of the biggest challenges that we have right now. Is not having someone to advocate at the top level." Indeed, at the time of interview, Johnson reported, "There's only one female in the Cabinet. That means things are only being seen from one woman's perspective in a Cabinet of thirty-four." They argued that there is a pressing need for more women in positions of power because they would advocate for legislation that recognizes men and women as equal, and shift public perception about women. Prior scholarship confirms that increased female participation in government has far-reaching benefits, even beyond gender issues, including a reduction in corruption (Dollar 2001).

However, the activists cited deterrents to women taking office and the subsequent lack of representation of women in public office in The Bahamas as another barrier to promoting gender equality. The structure of the parliamentary system and the political violence that women candidates face limit their presence in office. Johnson said, "It's not even the country because the country can only choose from who goes on the ballots. But the party chooses who goes on the ballot." In the Bahamian parliamentary system, political parties choose who they think can get elected, which, given the current state of gender relations, is generally not women.

Rolle argued that "[a]nother reason why [The Bahamas] has a lack of women even interested in running for politics is because of the way that women are treated when they run. They are torn apart by the media, torn apart by the general public." Women face harsher scrutiny by the party and the public, limiting their ability to attain decision-making positions in government. Women entering the political sphere are more likely to experience this type of violence than men (Bardall 2013; Kammerud, 2011). In fact, Bardall conceptualized these character assaults as a form of political violence – any harm or threat of harm towards any person or property involved in a political race during the election period. Owing to their fear of widespread backlash, it is unsurprising that only 21.2 per cent of parliamentarians worldwide are women (Bardall 2013).

While the interviewees cited religion as a powerful determinant of GBV, SV and GD, they also characterized it as a hindrance to advocating effectively for gender equality in The Bahamas. Specifically, the activists remarked that notions of male superiority and female subjugation are embedded in Christianity, which, in turn, informs the response of the public and the government to gender inequality. Bethel said, "A part of [Bahamian] culture is a very strong affiliation that we are a Christian nation. That, for me, really frames a part of [the country's] response to issues of gender-based violence." The interviewees highlighted the issue of the marital rape exemption as a prime example of how religion poses a challenge in dealing with GBV.

Reflecting on the debates regarding the marital rape bill, Wallace said, "Women's rights organizations and advocates were calling for [the bill] to be more progressive. The Christian Council was calling for it to be lighter and framing it as something that was a threat to the family." The Bahamas

Christian Council (BCC) is a major lobbyist group that advocates for traditionalist values (Benjamin and LeGrand 2012). The church and the BCC work to reify in legislation the sexism they teach to the public. Wallace said:

> Typically, the government is open to making changes in law and policy to address gender issues and to the benefit of women and girls, but it is often impeded by religious bodies that have a significant amount of power and which they, political parties, government administrations, depend on to move their constituents in a particular direction. So, they're not inclined to go against them because the church is the largest constituency in the country.

Religious institutions, as a result, have a lot of power in The Bahamas and act as both determinants of gender inequality, GBV and SV, and barriers to preventing them.

PROPOSED SOLUTIONS

The final theme that emerged from the interviews with Bahamian gender rights activists is proposed solutions to effectively combat GBV and GD. The interviewees introduced various methods to promote gender equity, including legislative reform, economic investment and educational campaigns. According to the interviewees, because gender inequality, GBV and SV have structural explanations they, in turn, require macro-level solutions. For example, Bethel said, "There needs to be a holistic approach to gender-based violence against many structural qualms. It can't be seen in isolation from other social structures."

First, the interviewees highlighted education as a potential site for transformation. Arguing that the government alone cannot solve gender inequality and GBV, they noted that successfully promoting gender equity required participation from all sectors of society. In particular, they called for increased collaboration with NGOs to combat gender inequality. Bethel said, "The State has a responsibility for public education around gender equality. The other responsibility lies with civil society." In addition, each interviewee argued that both civil society and the government need to reach a broader scope of women in educational programmes about gender inequality and GBV. Greene remarked, "Feminism is seen in the Caribbean as classist – it's something that the educated have the privilege of enjoying. But it should be for the woman who works two, three jobs, and has five kids. She should understand that she is entitled to her rights just as much as the college graduate or CEO."

The interviewees called for an intersectional approach to gender rights that supports all women, including migrant and queer populations. The activists opined that the government and women's rights organizations needed to engage in widespread education about gender, consent and healthy relationships – a sentiment echoed by researchers who argue for an increase in education around gender relations (Nicolls 2014). Wallace called for widespread compulsory education: "We need to have anti-sexual harassment training for all government departments, in schools, and we need to have it in corporate Bahamas. We need to have gender sensitivity training in all those same places."

The interviewees also proposed the creation of more spaces for Bahamians to critically engage gender inequality besides the University of The Bahamas, the country's main institution of higher learning. Greene said, "I think we need to invest seriously and substantively at the national level and at a social level in creating infrastructure mechanisms to engage issues to provide spaces for people to learn and to get help, to access services, information, and assistance." Greene also argued that rather than attempting to challenge a person's religion as biased, it is best to help people understand their relationship with the church to allow for more substantive engagement and examination of the role of religion in gender relations. These types of proposed solutions were offered to address the lack of understanding by the public and government on gender relations by providing spaces where Bahamians would feel safe to ask questions and analyse their environments.

The activists concluded that a lot of work needs to be done in the political sphere to address gender discrimination and GBV, including applying a gendered perspective to policy. For example, Bethel said, "At a very basic level, you would have to have a national policy that recognizes gender as a part of every aspect of national political culture." Some of the interviewees advocated changing the current gendered perspective from one that privileges men and disadvantages women to a perspective that grants equal benefits. Wallace said, "We need to talk about gender mainstreaming and how we can do the same work that we're doing now, but with a gender perspective." Gender mainstreaming is an institutional approach to addressing inequality that embeds gender-sensitive practices and norms in the structures and policies of all political institutions (Daly 2005).

To further address inequality within the government, some of the interviewees introduced the idea of temporary special measures in government, specifically quotas. These activists argued that gender quotas were necessary because it requires intentionality on the part of the government, which, as highlighted above, is lacking. Indeed, scholars argue that quotas tend to be implemented when NGOs see no other way to put women in government and are effective measures to disrupt the status quo (Davidson-Schmich 2016). Rolle said:

> Implement legislation that says if you have this many men at the table, you should have this many women at the table. You give men this much land, you need to give women this much land. Instead of leaving it up to happenstance because what happens is, we say well, it was open to everyone, but only men qualify or sign up, which usually is not true.

Some of the activists disagreed, suggesting that quotas would not effectively address gender inequality at all. For example, Patterson said: "I'm not sure [quotas] are the way to go because I think that it can't just be any women, just to say we have women just for the sake of being women. It has to be women who are aware, conscientious and wanting to ensure gender equality and the acceptance of men and women as equals." Those who disagreed with the implementation of gender quotas were fearful of public backlash and candidates being framed as incapable by the media and public (Franceschet and Piscopo 2008). In addition, they were concerned about possible political violence as a response to the increased presence of women in government.

Another potential avenue for reform identified by the interviewees was systematic data collection regarding gender. The activists argued that there is currently little data about gender differences in The Bahamas, which makes their work to promote gender equality challenging. Wallace said: "People request data and they know that we don't have statistics on a lot of things and that is used to invalidate what [activists] are saying is happening and what is needed." Some highlighted poor technological infrastructure as the reason behind the lack of data. Wallace continued, "I think we need data, we need statistics, we need individual stories to be able to connect to individuals and understand where they are and how they may have struggled or the opportunities they may have missed because of gender." Public opinion impacts political will; therefore, data collection, according to the interviewees, is important because it provides evidence of problems that they know exist.

Several activists identified promoting women's economic independence as a way to curb GBV and SV. Bethel said: "One of the ways I think we might begin to address this at the national level is economic empowerment of women. I think that the more women are economically empowered and have their own sense of wage-earning and autonomy from the so-called male head of the household, that is one way to address the issue of gender-based violence." Prior research suggests that women's economic independence empowers them and allows them to contribute meaningfully to expenses or start small businesses (Al-Mamun 2014). Furthermore, women's economic independence has been proven to reduce violence against them (Borraz and Munyo 2020). Initiatives, such as conditional cash transfer programmes aimed at women and designed to end the cycle of poverty, address structural economic inequality, with positive effects on both women and children. Once women gain economic autonomy, household dynamics improve, as they can then contribute to economic burdens; children have increased access to healthcare; and the quality of life for women and children improve in general. These programmes can be developed through government agencies or independently to address gender-based violence and inequality.

THE PATH FORWARD

The interviewees identified aspects of Bahamian society that act as *interrelated* determinants of gender-based violence and discrimination. In particular, they spoke of the ways in which gender inequalities perpetuated by religion, colonialism, gender socialization and the Bahamian political system compound and mutually reinforce each another. These social institutions converge to justify and legitimize violence against women and create a culture that is forgiving of men who commit violence against them.

The activists highlighted the fact that gender inequality is perpetuated and reinforced through institutions of socialization that have not been critically addressed. As a result, Bahamian women are subjected to extreme rates of GBV and discrimination. The solutions proposed require intervention throughout all strata of society to tackle issues of gender inequality. It requires an intersectional approach that addresses challenges unique to migrant and disabled populations. Particular attention must also be paid to gender non-conforming, intersex and LGBTQ populations. Interventions in one institution will ultimately fail if it is not also addressed in others (Reskin 2012).

REFERENCES

Acker, J. 1992. "Gendering organizational theory." *Classics of Organizational Theory* 6: 450–59.

Al-Mamun, A., S.A. Wahab, M.N.H. Mazumder, and Z. Su. 2014. "Empirical Investigation on the Impact of Microcredit on Women Empowerment in Urban Peninsular Malaysia. *Journal of Developing Areas* 48 (2): 287–306.

Bahamas Department of Statistics. 2016. *The Bahamas 2013 Household Expenditure Survey*. Nassau: Ministry of Finance.

Bardall, G. 2013. "Gender-Specific Election Violence: The Role of Information and Communication Technologies." *Stability: International Journal of Security and Development* 2 (3): 1–11.

Bethel, N. 2003. "Engendering the Bahamas: A Gendered Examination of Bahamian Nation Making, or National Identity and Gender in the Bahamian Context. *International Journal of Bahamian Studies* 12: 72–84.

Borraz, F., and I. Munyo. 2020. "Conditional Cash Transfers, Women's Income and Domestic Violence. *International Review of Applied Economics* 34 (1): 115–25.

Charmaz, K., and L.L. Belgrave. 2007. "Grounded Theory." In *The Blackwell Encyclopedia of Sociology*, edited by George Ritzer, 2023–27. Oxford, Victoria and Malden, MA: Blackwell Publishing.

Convention on the Elimination of All Forms of Discrimination Against Women (CEDAW). 2017. *Consideration of reports submitted by States parties under article 18 of the Convention – Bahamas*. New York: United Nations.

Davidson-Schmich, L.K. 2016. *Gender Quotas and Democratic Participation: Recruiting*

Candidates for Elective Offices in Germany. Ann Arbor: University of Michigan Press.

Dollar, D., R. Fisman, and R. Gatti. 2001. "Are women really the 'fairer' sex? Corruption and women in government. *Journal of Economic Behavior & Organization* 46 (4): 423–29.

Ellis, A., C. Manuel, and M. Blackden. 2005. *Gender and Economic Growth in Uganda: Unleashing the Power of Women*. Washington, DC: World Bank.

Elvy, S.A. 2015. "A Postcolonial Theory of Spousal Rape: The Caribbean and Beyond." *Michigan Journal of Gender and Law* 22 (1): 89–167.

Equality Bahamas. 2018. *CEDAW Shadow Report on The Bahamas for the 71st Session*. Nassau: Equality Bahamas.

Franceschet, S., and J.M. Piscopo. 2008. "Gender Quotas and Women's Substantive Representation: Lessons from Argentina." *Politics & Gender* 4 (3): 393–425.

Htun, M., and J. Piscopo. 2014. *Women in Politics and Policy in Latin America and the Caribbean*. CPPF Working Papers on Women in Politics: No. 2. New York: Conflict Prevention and Peace Forum, Social Science Research Council.

Johnson, E., and A. Prakash. 2007. "NGO Research Program: A Collective Action Perspective." *Policy Sciences* 40 (3): 221–40.

Merry, S. 1991. "Law and Colonialism." *Law & Society Review* 25 (4): 889–922.

Mikołajczak, M., and J. Pietrzak. 2014. "Ambivalent Sexism and Religion: Connected Through Values. *Sex Roles* 70 (9–10): 387–99.

Namy, S., C. Carlson, K. O'Hara, J. Nakuti, P. Bukuluki, J. Lwanyaaga, and L. Michau. 2017. "Towards a feminist understanding of intersecting violence against women and children in the family." *Social Science & Medicine* 184: 40–48.

National Task Force for Gender-Based Violence. 2015. *Strategic Plan to Address Gender-Based Violence in The Bahamas*. Nassau: Commonwealth of the Bahamas, Ministry of Social Services and Community Development.

Nicolls, D., C. Russell-Smith, S. Dean-Patterson, L.D. Deveaux-Stuart, I. Gibson-Mobley, E.J. Williams, and W.J. Fielding. 2014. "Attitudes of High School Students Regarding Intimate Relationships and Gender Norms in New Providence, The Bahamas." *International Journal of Bahamian Studies* 20 (1): 38–51.

Plumridge, S.J., and W.J. Fielding. 2009. "Domestic violence in the homes of college students, New Providence, The Bahamas." *International Journal of Bahamian Studies* 15: 45–55.

Reskin, B. 2012. "The Race Discrimination System. *Annual Review of Sociology* 38 (1): 17–35.

Ridgeway, C.L. 2009. "Framed Before We Know It: How Gender Shapes Social Relations. *Gender & Society* 23 (2): 145–60.

Risman, B. 1998. "Gender as Structure." In *Gender Vertigo: American Families in Transition*, 13–44. New Haven and London: Yale University Press.

Russo, N.F., and A. Pirlott. 2006. "Gender-Based Violence: Concepts, Methods, and Findings." *Annals of the New York Academy of Sciences* 1087 (1): 178–205.

Sen, A. 2001. "The Many Faces of Gender Inequality." *New Republic* 226 (22): 35–39.

Šimonović, Dubravka. 2018. *Report of the Special Rapporteur on violence against women, its causes and consequences, on her mission to the Bahamas*. A/A/HRC/38/47/. New York: United Nations Human Rights Council.

Teegen, H., J.P. Doh, and S. Vachani. 2004. "The importance of nongovernmental organizations (NGOs) in global governance and value creation: An international business research agenda." *Journal of International Business Studies* 35 (6): 463–83.

Wallace, Alicia. 2017. "Policymaking in a 'Christian nation': Women's and LGBT+ rights in The Bahamas' 2016 referendum." *Gender and Development* 25 (1): 69–83.

Walton, K.A., and C.L. Pedersen. 2022. "Motivations Behind Catcalling: Exploring Men's Engagement in Street Harassment Behaviour." *Psychology & Sexuality* 13 (3): 689–703.

Williams-Pulfer, K. 2016. "'When Bain Town Woman Catch A Fire, Even the Devil Run': The Bahamian Suffrage Movement as National and Cultural Development. *VOLUNTAS: International Journal of Voluntary and Nonprofit Organizations* 27 (3): 1472–93.

Yodanis, C.L. 2004. "Gender inequality, violence against women, and fear: A cross-national test of the feminist theory of violence against women." *Journal of Interpersonal Violence* 19 (6): 655–75.

chapter 19

Intersecting Vulnerabilities and GBV

Voices and Experiences of Jamaican Women

Natasha Mortley and Carol Watson Williams

GENDER-BASED VIOLENCE (GBV) IS AN UMBRELLA TERM THAT refers to harmful acts directed at an individual or group of individuals based on their gender. O'Toole and Schiffman (1997, xii) offer a broad definition to include "any interpersonal, organisational or politically orientated violation perpetrated against people due to their gender identity, sexual orientation, or location in the hierarchy of male-dominated social systems such as family, military, organisations, or the labour force". Studies indicate that while men and boys can also be victims of GBV, women and girls suffer disproportionately from this phenomenon. The most prevalent form of GBV, violence against women and girls, manifests historically unequal power relations between men and women (Shepherd 2017). Furthermore, the term GBV is typically used to underscore the fact that structural and gender-based power differentials place women and girls at risk of multiple forms of violence, which constrain their enjoyment of human rights everywhere. It is both a manifestation of power and control, and a tool to maintain gender inequalities, affecting the health, survival, safety and freedom of women and their families. Contemporary feminists, for instance, argue that violence by men against women is seen as a tactic of coercive control to maintain male power (Wiltshire et al. 2012).

This problem affects women of all ages, socio-economic status and educational backgrounds, making it widespread across all communities. In Jamaica, the Women's Health Survey of 2016, commissioned by the Statistical Institute of Jamaica (STATIN), the Inter-American Development Bank (IDB) and UN Women, indicated a GBV prevalence rate of 27.8 per cent (Watson Williams 2018). In 2016 also, the Centre for the Investigation of Sexual Offences and Child Abuse reported that 97.3 per cent of the 1,094 child abuse incidents in Jamaica affected girls; demonstrating their high vulnerability to abuse. The term gender-based violence is also used to describe targeted violence against Lesbian, Gay, Bisexual, Transgender, Queer, Intersex (LGBTQI+) populations when referencing violence related to norms of masculinity, femininity and gender norms.

Haynes and DeShong (2017:107) argue that Caribbean discourse around GBV often fails to recognize GBV outside of intimate heterosexual relationships. They assert that this representation and understanding of GBV excludes experiences of transgender, intersex and gender non-conforming people, for whom gender is central to their experience of violence. The authors argue that the possibility exists that these frameworks reproduce heteronormative theorizing and do not account for the multiple ways in which gender and sexuality are implicated in violence experienced by diverse groups. In light of this, the understanding of gender used in gender-based violence should extend to mean "relations of power which have ideological and material dimensions; gender and sexuality as fundamentally imbricated; gender as identity, embodiment and performance; and gender as intersecting with, and giving meaning to, other relations of power" (Haynes and DeShong 2017).

While this paper is focused on violence against women and girls, it proposes an interrogation of the gendered dimensions of abuse and violence. We examine gender constructions, and how power and gender inequalities interface with other social factors, thus contributing to multiple forms of risk. The chapter focuses on the intersection of gender with other social factors, such as socio-economic status, sexuality, age and disabilities, which increase the levels of risk to violence by focusing on women who are most vulnerable, including those who are pregnant, disabled, living with HIV, and LBTQ. Given this focus on vulnerable and at-risk groups of women, the chapter uses the term GBV rather than violence against women and girls (VAWG), where the former allows for the exploration of multiple forms of discrimination and the multiple ways in which gender is implicated in violence among diverse groups of women and girls. Additionally, we also recognize that to end VAWG, we must ensure their full empowerment, which requires understanding various forms of discrimination and oppression that they face in all aspects of their lives.

Based on qualitative research, this paper provides a deep understanding of violence through the lived experiences of Jamaican women, especially the most vulnerable groups, who face multiple forms of oppression and thus, increased risks of violence. The research engaged these diverse groups of women to understand better how they comprehend GBV; their experiences of violence; and the ways in which it impacted their lives. The research fills a gap by centring the experiences of those traditionally ignored groups of women, thus providing evidenced-based research to inform mechanisms that provide support, and interventions that meet their differential needs, including the promotion and protection of women's rights and empowerment. The findings contribute to understanding patterns of gender norms, behaviours and practices, which have been normalized and institutionalized over time to the detriment of all women and girls.

GENDER-BASED VIOLENCE IN JAMAICA

Jamaica, the largest of the English-speaking Caribbean countries, has a population of approximately 2.9 million, with an average age of 30.7 (UNDP 2020). At the end of 2019, women made up 50.5 per cent of the total population, with a higher life expectancy rate than males (Planning Institute of Jamaica 2019). Although women in Jamaica have higher levels of achievement in the areas of education and training, the labour market continues to show high levels of sex segregation, with lower levels of labour force participation and higher rates of unemployment for women. In terms of the gender pay gap, although the gap has narrowed, Jamaican women on average earn 62 per cent of the salary of their male counterparts (World Economic Forum 2019). In recent years, Jamaica has performed commendably on the Gender Development Index (GDI), which sex disaggregates performance on the Human Development Index (HDI) by looking at gender inequalities in achievement in three basic areas of human development:

health, education and command over economic resources. Despite these areas of progress, the year 2016 recorded the highest homicide rates for women and girls in Jamaica's history. Anecdotal evidence suggests that during the COVID-19 pandemic, Jamaica witnessed a spike in those rates. As such, the matter of VAWG has become the main gender-related human rights concern of the government of Jamaica and its stakeholders.

In Jamaica, GBV is characterized not only by physical violence, but also emotional, sexual and physical assault, verbal abuse, humiliation, stalking and sexual harassment. This violence occurs within both private and public domains, and not only is it debilitating for women and their families, but it also has ripple effects on society. For instance, research has shown that direct and indirect economic costs of interpersonal violence and aggression can reduce a country's GDP growth. Fearon and Hoeffler (2014) have reported the astonishing cost of domestic violence at 11.1 per cent of world GDP. In Jamaica, to understand the severity and the extent of VAWG, UN Women commissioned a study to estimate the economic cost of violence against women and girls (UN Women 2020). Furthermore, GBV is intertwined with larger development issues; it undermines women's basic freedoms and rights, their sexual and reproductive health, education and level of productivity. Fundamentally, women's experiences of violence nullify their realization and participation as full citizens; reinforce and support discriminatory gender norms, and maintain systematic inequalities (Manjoo 2016). Since women represent more than half of the Jamaican population, this greatly impacts sustainable development efforts.

As it relates to at-risk groups of women who experience violence in Jamaica, it has been noted that women and girls at the intersection of gender and disability have distinct experiences of disadvantage and discrimination, making them highly vulnerable to GBV.[1] Women and girls with disabilities are two to four times more likely to experience domestic violence than women without disabilities (Taylor 2019). LGBTQI persons are also at high risk of GBV,[2] often because they represent a direct challenge to traditional gender norms, stereotypes and expectations embraced by society. This recognition at the national level underscores the need to explore further these multiple ways in which gender is implicated in violence among diverse groups of women and girls.

INTERSECTIONAL ANALYSIS OF GBV

Intersectionality, a critical theoretical framework in feminist research, focuses on the qualitative differences in women's experiences based on their different, yet intersecting social identities[3] (Crenshaw 1991; Shields 2008). Developed out of the black feminist movement, this framework foregrounds the complex dynamics and processes through which gender identity is constructed, insisting on the need to examine "multiple grounds of identity when considering how the social world is constructed" (Crenshaw 1991, 1245). It is predicated on the idea that gender is relational and, therefore, qualified by other defining social characteristics. Within this framework, the ways in which social positions and identities overlap and determine differential experiences, including gendered experiences, are explicitly interrogated to understand how they shape women's lives. Hence, intersectionality enables understanding of how gender is experienced based on social identities, such as age, sexuality, ableness, health status and class, inter alia (Shields 2008). In doing so, it upholds inclusivity as a central tenet in feminist research and is an effective tool to inform theory and explicate the social construction of women's lives. Intersectionality is used as a theoretical tool in this chapter to understand how groups of women have different experiences of discrimination and oppression.

Intersectionality captures the interplay and symbiosis among social identities, as well as the power relations embedded in them (Collins 1990; Crenshaw 1991). As such, it examines the structural and political domains that conflate to create the location of women's experiences, and the extent to which the power dynamics rooted in these domains can define and constrain the interests of entire groups. Without intersectional framing, one or more of women's identities may be denied, resulting in some groups being silenced, relegated to the margins, or wholly excluded from our understanding of how women experience GBV, reinforcing or replicating the oppression and subordination of those groups.

Intersectionality is built into this research as both a theoretical framework and an analytical tool. The chapter examines how different groups of women experience GBV, but moves beyond the identification of 'difference' to explain the processes through which intersecting identities define and shape each other, and determine the materiality of women's lives. The qualitative approach used in this study also reflects the intersectional grounding of the research. Qualitative methods are considered "more compatible with the theoretical language and intent of intersectionality" (Shields 2008, 306) as they are flexible, providing more opportunities to explore linkages and to understand the processes through which these intersections are created. Specifically, the approach is in keeping with fluid social constructions of gendered realities of female research participants.

CENTRING WOMEN'S EXPERIENCES THROUGH FOCUS GROUP DISCUSSIONS

This chapter is based on a phenomenological study of the lived experiences of Jamaican women. Phenomenology falls within the qualitative research approach and is premised on the belief that a true understanding of a phenomenon must be found through an understanding of how persons experience and describe it. A critical element of phenomenology is that the phenomena are presented from the perspective of the research participants, and that meaning is constructed from how they interact and interpret the world (Mortley 2017). This methodology, combined with intersectionality, centred on subjective and situated knowledge and experiences of GBV among diverse groups of women, including those who are "multiple burdened" (Crenshaw 1989), bringing them fully into the frame of GBV prevention and response efforts in Jamaica.

Employing focus group discussions, women were given a safe, empowering space for stimulated discussions on their experiences of GBV. This method is suited to gender research where the focus is on marginalized persons within a specific social context. Gender researchers operate on the premise that the marginalized, the excluded and the voiceless need to be heard and that their lived experiences and the meanings that they give to these experiences are most valuable to knowledge creation. The focus group within qualitative research represents a powerful tool for bringing visibility and giving a voice to the voiceless. Seven focus group discussions (FGDs) were conducted with a cross-section of Jamaican women, including from rural areas, with disabilities, living with HIV, LBTQI and professionals. Participants were asked to describe meanings, understanding and experiences of violence. It was also important to ensure that participation in the FGD did not cause harm to these women. It was made clear to them that their participation was completely voluntary, and that they were not required to discuss details of any uncomfortable or traumatic experiences. The findings from FGDs represent not only descriptions of their lived experiences, but also meanings they gave to their experiences. Narratives from FGDs are used to illustrate women's differential experiences of GBV more clearly. The use of narratives is in keeping with the epistemological approach adopted in this study, where voices and first-hand experiences of the phenomenon are amplified and given a privileged position in terms of knowledge creation.

WOMEN'S EXPERIENCES AND UNDERSTANDING GBV

Underpinned by an intersectional approach to ensure a nuanced understanding of how different communities of women experience and are affected by GBV, this chapter places specific focus on women who are often isolated and most vulnerable. Those living with HIV, with disabilities, in rural areas and who were LBTQ represented some of the most marginalized and at-risk women and girls in Jamaica. Since under-aged girls were not included in the research, female participants reflected and shared their personal experiences at different stages of their lives, including childhood. Although participants were told that they were not obligated to share personal experiences that were particularly traumatic for them, the women saw the sessions as a space of shared experiences and mutual respect, which allowed for their authentic stories to be told. According to one female with disabilities, "I have some experiences and I am not afraid to talk about them, because every time I talk about them, it make me feel stronger within me." She went on to say at the end of the session, "I wish we had more time because I could go on for some more hours."

Most of the women who participated in the FGDs admitted experiencing some form of violence within their intimate relationships, their families or public spaces. Within the focus groups with women living with HIV and with disabilities, all participants indicated that they had experienced some form of GBV. Within the groups of rural and LBTQ women, most had experienced some form of violence. The discussions with university and professional women centred more on the broader knowledge that they had on women and girls who had experienced violence within the communities that they lived or worked. Among those women who shared personal stories, some had experiences in multiple relationships and some had near-death encounters. In the case of the latter, the women saw themselves as survivors, who had become stronger and were determined to share their stories, and in some cases, to contribute to making a change for other women.

It was also important to assess whether women from different social backgrounds and contexts give different meanings to violence or have a common understanding of the characteristics and scope of GBV in Jamaica. Understanding what constitutes GBV and how it manifests is the first step in tackling the problem. Furthermore, a comparative analysis of how women and how institutional actors who represent and provide support to women and girls understand GBV is important to our assessment of whether these institutions have a good grasp of Jamaican women's realities and are effectively serving the interests and needs of victims.

Physical and sexual abuse were the most popular definitions of GBV given by women, with physical abuse occurring mainly within intimate partner relationships (including same-sex relationships) and within the family. Within three of the focus groups – women living with HIV, professionals and rural residents – it was revealed some women in their communities did not view beatings and physical abuse as GBV. Among those women, beatings were either viewed as normal behaviour within relationships, seen as a form of love or a form of discipline. Women also explained that these sentiments were prevalent within the inner-city communities, remote rural areas or among women with lower educational attainment. Within these communities, there appeared to be a high level of acceptance of gendered behaviours that normalize the abuse from men. According to one woman living with HIV, "Some like the beatings – they say it makes them feel alive. You see them downtown with dem eye black and blue and dem proud." She went on to explain, "But when it reach to death now, that's when people open up them eye and talk out and speak out and talk out, saying 'Him should not lick har' and they knew he was beating her for years."

Within the focus group with rural women, one participant, referring to the community that she grew up, explained, "Growing up, I would see a lot of couples fighting. There would be blood, but I didn't know that it wasn't normal."

Within the group of professional women, it was stated, "The communities within which I work, I don't think on a large scale it is even considered. When myself and other practitioners observe it, hear the stories and can classify it as GBV, the persons involved don't see it as such, it isn't even a thought. They see it as an act of love, or keeping me in my place, which is where I need to be, or seen as managing the relationship."

Within all the FGDs, women expressed the view that GBV takes place across all socio-economic spectrums in Jamaica. Generally, the women acknowledged that verbal, emotional and financial abuse also constituted GBV. University graduates and professionals explained that broader definitions and understandings of GBV came with higher levels of education. For rural women a broader understanding of the phenomenon came with increased exposure to other communities and spaces.

In the sessions with women from the LBTQ community, the broadest definition/understanding of GBV was expressed. These women, who were within the 21–30 age range, said it included street harassment, bullying in public spaces, family violence, neglect from parents and other relatives, having religion forced upon them, being forced to suppress their sexuality and being forced into heterosexual relationships to appease their family. One participant said, "I know of physical violence from the parents, especially the father, when you are suspected of being queer." These women also explained that, due to their sexuality, they felt they were at greater risk of GBV in public spaces. One participant explained, "Queer women are at risk of being sexually violated as a way of correcting their sexual orientation . . . you can't go out with your partner and hold hands. At taxi stands, on the streets, at restaurants, you are attacked and you can't present who you are."

The experiences described during the FGDs are in keeping with studies that show that people who identify as LGBTQI suffer greatly from familial violence. D'Augelli et al. (1998) found that lesbian, gay and bisexual individuals, aged 14–21 years, living at home, who disclosed their sexual orientation to at least one parent, reported verbal and physical abuse by family members. Familial response to individuals 'coming out' include beatings; eviction from the family home; severe punishment with the aim to 'change' the individual; arranging for them to meet or have sex with someone of the opposite sex; or engaging a religious leader to have the demon removed or devil beaten out of them (Naidu and Mkhize 2005). The women in the discussions identified GBV in their community as manifesting within intimate partner relations, the family and the community. The adoption and presentation of a masculine or dominant personality by women self-identified as queer, and the fact that they represent a challenge to traditional gender norms, place them at significant risk of violence and hate crimes. The women identified verbal abuse, sexual harassment and physical assault as examples of GBV that they faced from the wider Jamaican society.

MARGINALIZED AND AT-RISK WOMEN EXPERIENCE GBV

During the FGDs, women were also asked if marginalized and at-risk women, such as pregnant women, the elderly or those with disabilities in their communities experienced GBV to the same extent or were at greater risk. The overwhelming view was that those groups faced multiple forms of oppression and thus were more vulnerable to various forms of violence, including physical, verbal and financial abuse from intimate partners and family members. Women with disabilities, in their FGD, indicated that they faced additional risks for GBV. They explained that their unemployment status, lack of financial independence and physical isolation made them more vulnerable than abled women. This was especially the case for physically disabled women, they explained. A visually impaired woman described her experience, "The boy, he beat me, kick me, bite me for no reason. He say, 'You can't leave me because no one will want you.'"

Another with a physical disability explained that being wheelchair bound and pregnant put her at greater risk. When her partner (and abuser) learned of her pregnancy, it caused him to be more aggressive and abusive towards her. She explained,

> He raped me and I got pregnant. He didn't want to accept he was the one I was pregnant for and treated me even worse. His mother put me out on the road. I had to sleep on cold concrete while he sleep in his bed. Someone told her to take me back in because her son raped me. She said no, I am handicapped.

> They said no, you cannot discriminate the lady. Didn't your son know she was disabled before he went there?

The results of the FGDs with women living with disabilities are in keeping with previous studies and related literature. Women with disabilities experience an intersecting confluence of violence that is reflective of gender-based and disability-based violence. The intersection of gender and disability create a distinct experience of disadvantage and discrimination, which makes them highly vulnerable to GBV. Studies (Cepko 1993) reveal that women with disabilities are substantially more susceptible to violence than their non-disabled counterparts. The World Health Organization (WHO) reports that women with disabilities experience intimate partner violence twice as often than non-disabled women. The marginalization of people living with disabilities often forces them to reside on the fringes of society. Poverty and gender further exacerbate the marginalization of this population and make women living with disabilities in poverty some the most vulnerable, isolated and forgotten people in society. This sentiment was expressed within the FGDs, with women speaking about the lack of financial resources and fear of being targeted in public spaces as the main reasons why they remain isolated.

In the FGD with women living with HIV, these participants explained that their HIV status and poverty levels made them more vulnerable to violence. They had all experienced various forms of GBV and described the ways in which their intimate partners used their HIV status to torment and threaten them. Threats to divulge their status were mainly used to keep them in abusive situations. One participant explained, "If it's a financial relationship and he is the sole responsible person you depend on then you have to go back to him to feed your pickney. And some people in the community tell him too, Don't feed her, when you try speak out or report." According to another participant, "We don't want people know we status. The man threaten me all the time, saying he will let everyone know."

Much of the literature focuses on the ways in which GBV undermines women's sexual and reproductive health. Studies (Dunkle et al. 2004; Garcia-Morene and Watts 2000) found a strong association between GBV and HIV and other negative reproductive health outcomes, such as mortality, poor outcomes of pregnancies and births (Curry et al. 1998), gynaecological morbidity, non-use of contraceptives and unwanted pregnancies. GBV has the potential to contribute to HIV infection through rape, and indirectly through increased vulnerability due to risky sexual practices. During the discussions, women focused on how their HIV status made them more vulnerable in their intimate relationships and thus put them at greater risk of being abused by partners. All the women within this group explained that their HIV status contributed to lowering their self-esteem, their self-confidence, and increased feelings of insecurity in public spaces. These factors affected their motivation to seek employment, which left them economically dependent on partners and reinforced existing gender power inequalities that made them more at risk of intimate partner violence.

GBV NORMALIZED AND REINFORCED

Heise et al. (2002) put forward an ecological model to explain causes of GBV against women. Although the model was first introduced as a framework for understanding some of the key factors contributing to women's and girls' risk of intimate partner violence, it has been adapted to examine other types of violence to which women are exposed. According to the model: "Violence is a result of factors operating at four levels: individual, relationship, community and societal" (WHO 2012). The model promotes the understanding that VAWG is multifaceted in nature and rarely the result of one single factor. The ecological model is also a preferred frame of analysis because it underscores the connection between family, community and society. Furthermore, this framework is seen as the best approach to achieving the transformation envisaged to break the normalization and acceptance of violence, which starts very early in life and continues throughout adulthood.

Women identified the main risk factors for GBV at the relationship/family level as jealousy and insecurity within intimate partner relationships; economic dependency; control over women's bodies; relations of power; men feeling threatened when women advance at the educational level; and relationship conflict brought on by women provoking men through cheating and hitting first. One participant in the group of university women described a scenario, "I remember once the violence was because this woman was using words that were too big and the man didn't understand her because she was more educated than him. This is just how she spoke, but her making him feel inferior in that way led to the violence, because he was not on a level where he thought he could compete with her in any other way than physically, and I see that happening a lot in relationships." Within the focus group with self-identified LBTQ women, factors at the family level were discussed, including feelings of shame brought on the family, violence as a form of discipline or beating girls/young women to make them 'straight'.

In the FGDs, women identified factors at the individual level as the second main causes of VAWG. These included normalizing behaviours from childhood, men who witnessed their fathers abusing their mothers, substance abuse, poor anger management and mental illness on the part of male perpetrators. Societal and cultural factors identified included patriarchy and men being socialized to feel superior to women, masculinity, which was linked to aggression and the need for respect, and the culture of homophobia. According to a professional, "Respect is a big thing in our culture, so once a man feels disrespected, he uses force."

In a study on masculinities and crime in Jamaica, Mortley (2018) reported similar findings, where some key and related concepts of masculinities included aggression, survival, protection, retaliation, respect, ownership and control, and boastfulness. In addition, the need for respect and a culture of retaliation by any means necessary drive violence within some communities, including GBV.[4] In the FGD with women self-identified as LBTQ, the issue of homophobia was discussed as a societal level risk factor that leads to violence against women:

> There is a lot of verbal abuse and physical abuse. If I am out with my partner and a man calls out to me, and I say, "This is my girlfriend, I am not interested in men," it becomes an issue. They insult the person, sometimes they do become physical, "Leggo off her hand" and will literally put hands on you and drag you away from her. It has happened. I've seen it and it has happened to me . . . he started shouting, "Old sodomite!" and yanked her out of my hand.

Finally, factors at the community level identified included peer pressure from other men, living in a hostile environment, and the inability by women to access resources or help. One woman living with HIV explained, "For example, let's take my son. His baby mother was unfaithful and is not the unfaithful make him beat her – it's what his friends were saying. So, to save face they will do it. They called him soft."

The ecological model, as well as evidence from the FGDs, reveal that GBV is a multifaceted phenomenon, which is often grounded in an interplay among several factors that reinforce each other at the various levels. These factors often link back to gender ideologies that prescribe what it means to be a man and to be in or take charge of your woman. Even within same-sex relationships, the women from the LBTQ community explained that often one partner mimics the masculine traits, which manifest in control and abuse. As one woman explained, "Not because we are not socialized in the same way men are doesn't mean we don't uphold this same power dynamic. It still happens where the relationship is still mimicking 'man and woman' relationship, where one person is more dominant, one is more assertive, one is more submissive." The pervasiveness of patriarchal norms and gender ideologies that normalize violence against women and girls tells us that to have transformative change, much more is needed than provision of services for survivors and victims. A holistic and coordinated approach to resocialization and behavioural change at all levels is urgently required.

IMPACTS OF GBV ON JAMAICAN WOMEN

The discussions revealed that many victims of abuse and violence experience several of those impacts simultaneously, which have a detrimental effect on their ability to function daily and be productive in the workplace. In some instances, the feelings of shame and fear caused them to isolate themselves further from friends and colleagues. The evidence indicates that GBV causes harm and suffering on many levels, which deprives women and girls of their liberty and ability to achieve their full human rights. Not only are their human rights denied, but the impacts are intertwined with other developmental issues, including a range of sexual, reproductive and mental health issues, productivity, education and decent work life.

It was noted in three of the FGDs that economic dependency was both an underlying cause and an impact of GBV. In two of the groups, women explained that by either leaving the abusive relationship or staying away from work due to physical bruises and shame, their economic livelihoods were affected. In one case, the woman had to shut down her business and leave the country to escape her abusive partner. In the LBTQI community, it was noted that lack of acceptance within the family and the consequent abuse from relatives resulted in women self-identified as queer having to find their own accommodations at an earlier age. Some were forced to live with partners, which placed them in dependent relationships and thus at risk of IPV. Self-identified queer women also had to spend more to navigate public spaces in Jamaica due to harassment and violent acts against them, at a greater financial toll. For instance,

> A straight person would take the route taxi or bus for a hundred dollars. As a queer person, you wonder, Do you want to face the harassment, or do you spend the extra to charter a taxi? If I want to live in a space, I don't have the option of going into a shared space for housing. I have to pay a little extra, so it's a studio because I don't want to have to explain to a roommate why I am bringing over a woman. There is a financial toll also trying to navigate these spaces and avoid the violence. A lot of us could be living at home, but that is not an option for queer people, because you cannot live freely at home because you cannot bring a partner home or you cannot dress as you would if you are a more masculine-presenting person. So yeah, it is taxing.

By using the ecological frame of analysis for assessing impacts of GBV, the link between family and society is evident. There is a ripple effect from impacts of violence occurring with relationships and families on communities and the broader society. When viewed within the model, the data also reveals that gender norms and the culture of silence at the relationship/family level is reinforced at the community level, thus perpetuating the cycle of violence against women. When the women were asked how persons within the community treated those who were victims of GBV, one explained the situation of further victimization of victims:

> The victims are always treated like they are at fault or they are guilty. "You're lying" is always the first response – especially if the person is prominent, well-dressed, well-spoken, eloquent, and the victim is from another social class. Also, if it is from a child, the story is not seen as believable. I don't know why. The story is not as readily believed. It also depends on the support system. If there are enough people who believe the story and are ready to support the report. Otherwise, the victim is victimized further.

IMPACTS ON MARGINALIZED AND AT-RISK WOMEN

Women with disabilities and those living with HIV reported some of the most violent forms of violence during their focus group sessions. These were the only two FGDs where women spoke of experiences and cases of stabbing, killings and being burned by intimate partners. They also described feelings of trauma and experiencing suicidal thoughts. Trauma was experienced by both the victims and their children, who witnessed the domestic violence. Furthermore, the women experienced severe health risks because of the abuse. These were compounded by their social isolation and conditions of poverty. Several studies found that women with disabilities that experience intimate partner violence have more health problems (Plichta 2004; Rivara et al. 2007) and higher health costs (Jones et al. 2006). They reported several health problems, including headaches, vaginal infections, back pains, abdominal pains and sexual transmitted diseases more often than other ailments (Campbell et al. 2002). They were also found to have twice the need for mental health treatment, but seldom receive it (Lipsky and Caetano 2007). The women with disabilities who participated in the study did not report adverse impacts on their mental health. On the contrary, despite all they had been through, they viewed themselves as survivors who had gained strength and a sense of purpose from their experiences. They spoke of being motivated to becoming financially independent and inspired to become stronger and more empowered women for their children's sake. They attributed their strength to the support that they received from the Combined Disabilities Association. One participant explained, "My determination is my daughter. From she was born I realise she can't walk. But in spite of her father not minding her, me alone, I struggle with her. I never give up on my daughter. I realised I had to fight for her. I gave her her education and she pass all her subjects."

LBTQI women who focused predominantly on family violence, and violence in public spaces, described how it impacted their rights to express themselves freely, their freedoms to exist within society and the financial burdens created by GBV. They explained how Jamaica's heteronormative conceptualization of gender-based violence, and conservative assumptions of sexual expression and binary oppositionality regarding sexual and other forms of violence, resulted in a lack of legislation and policy to protect members of their community, who experience GBV due to gender/sexual identity. This placed them at further risk of violence because in the absence of state protection, coupled with Jamaica's homophobic culture, their only support sometimes were their partners, who were also their abusers.

CONCLUSION

Combining intersectionality and the phenomenological research approach, this chapter explores GBV against women and girls in Jamaica. Through the lived experiences of women survivors, we discuss important insights into how GBV manifests, its root causes and its impacts on the lives of women and girls in Jamaica. An important aspect of this chapter is a focus on marginalized and at-risk groups of women, including those with disabilities, living with HIV, from the LBTQ community and socially isolated due to socio-economic conditions, such as extreme poverty. By bringing these groups of women into focus and giving them a voice, the chapter explores under-researched and traditionally left-behind groups. The focus on these groups of women also demonstrated the multiple ways in which they are disadvantaged, discriminated against and oppressed, thus increasing levels of vulnerability and risks to GBV in Jamaica.

The participants also recommended ways to help address GBV: primarily through legislative and policy changes, public awareness campaigns and gender training within the relevant organizations, including those that provide services to women who experience GBV. Women are generally not aware of the support services that exist; and when they are aware, they are of the view that the services are not fast, long-term or responsive enough, and do not give them the level of empowerment needed for a complete break from their abusers.

We contend that the research participants generally have a comprehensive understanding of GBV and the many ways in which it manifests. Violence is inherently linked to power, and arguably, no act of violence does not intersect with gender (Shaw 2017). A theory of violence which is gender-blind or does not adopt a feminist lens thus fails to provide a deeper understanding of violence by analysing how it is connected to, and embedded in, patriarchal structures of power (Cockburn 2004). Using the ecological model as a frame of analysis, the chapter demonstrates that GBV manifests at four distinct but interconnected levels: individual, family, community and societal. The gender lens adopted goes further to demonstrate how gender norms shape – and are shaped by – power dynamics at these various levels. Furthermore, patriarchal and gender ideologies operating at all four levels serve to normalize behaviours that facilitate violence against women and girls. This shows that the problem is more pervasive and entrenched within our society in terms of root causes and impacts. Through stories of women, we understand how violence has been detrimental to their bodies and minds, and has also had ripple effects on economic livelihoods, education, health and social interactions in Jamaica. These stories also give insights into possible sites for intervention, and the kind of support and services women consider valuable for the prevention and response to GBV.

NOTES

1. The National Strategic Action Plan to Eliminate Gender-Based Violence, Jamaica.
2. See also Human Rights Watch (2014). "Not Safe at Home: Violence and Discrimination Against LGBT People in Jamaica." https://www.hrw.org/news/2014/10/21/jamaica-unchecked-homophobic-violence.
3. The social categories in which women claim membership as well as the personal and social meanings given to these categories (Shields 2008, 301).
4. This study, *Males, Community and Crime in Jamaica: Final Report*, was conducted by the Institute for Gender and Development Studies (IGDS), Regional Coordinating Office, and funded by the Jamaica National Commission for UNESCO and the Ministry of Culture, Gender, Entertainment and Sport.

REFERENCES

Barrett, K.A., B. O'Day, A. Roche, and B.L. Carlson. 2009. "Intimate partner violence, health status, and health care access among women with disabilities." *Women's Health Issues* 19 (2): 94–100.

Buvinic, M., A. Morrison, and M. Shifter. 1999. *Violence in Latin America and the Caribbean: A Framework for Action*. Washington, DC: Inter-American Development Bank. http://dx.doi.org/10.18235/0008938.

Campbell, J.C. 2002. "Health consequences of intimate partner violence." *The Lancet* 359 (9314): 1331–36.

Chege, J. 2005. "Interventions linking gender relations and violence with reproductive health and HIV: Rationale, effectiveness and gaps." *Agenda: Special Focus on Gender, Culture and Rights* (special issue): 114–23.

Cooper, B., and C. Crockett. 2015. Gender-based violence and HIV across the life course: Adopting a sexual rights framework to include older women. *Reproductive Health Matters* 23 (46): 56–61.

Creswell, J.W., and C.N. Poth. 2018. *Qualitative Inquiry & Research Design*, 4th ed. Thousand Oaks: SAGE Publications.

Curry, M.A., D. Hassouneh-Phillips, and A. Johnston-Silverberg. 2001. "Abuse of women with disabilities: An ecological model and review." *Violence Against Women* 7 (1): 60–79.

Curry, M.A.1998. "The interrelationships between abuse, substance use, and psychosocial stress during pregnancy." *Journal of Obstetrics, Gynecology, and Neonatal Nursing* 27 (6): 692–99.

Dammeyer, J., and M. Chapman. 2018. "A national survey on violence and discrimination among people with disabilities." *BMC Public Health* 18 (1): article 355.

D'Augelli, A.R., S.L. Hershberger, and N.W. Pilkington. 1998. "Lesbian, gay, and bisexual youth and their families: Disclosure of sexual orientation and its consequences." *American Journal of Orthopsychiatry* 68 (3): 361–71.

DeShong, H. 2018. *Women's Health and Life Experiences: A Qualitative Research Report on Violence Against Women in Grenada 2018*. Bridgetown: UN Women Caribbean. https://caribbean.unwomen.org/en/materials/publications/2020/8/womens-health-and-life-experiences-a-qualitative-research-report-on-vaw-in-grenada-2018.

Duvvury, N., A. Callan, P. Carney, and S. Raghavendra. 2013. *Intimate Partner Violence: Economic Costs and Implications for Growth and Development*, Women's Voice, Agency and Participation Research Series, no. 3. Washington, DC: World Bank.

Dunkle, K.L., R.K. Jewkes, H.C. Brown, G.E. Gray, J.A. McIntyre, and S.D Harlow. 2004. "Gender-based violence, relationship power, and risk of HIV infection in women attending antenatal clinics in South Africa." *The Lancet* 363 (9419): 1415–21.

Ellsberg, M., and M. Gottemoeller. 1999. "Ending violence against women." *Population Reports* 27 (4): 1–44.

Hoeffler, Anke, and James Fearon. 2014. *Benefits and Costs of the Conflict and Violence Targets for the Post-2015 Development Agenda.* Conflict and Violence Assessment Paper. Copenhagen Consensus Centre.

Haarr, R. 2020. *Intimate Partner Violence in Five CARICOM Countries: Findings from National Prevalence Surveys on Violence Against Women.* Bridgetown: UN Women Caribbean. https://caribbean.unwomen.org/en/materials/publications/2021/7/research-brief---intimate-partner-violence-in-five-caricom-countries.

Haynes, T., and DeShong, H.A. 2017. "Queering feminist approaches to gender-based violence in the Anglophone Caribbean." *Social and Economic Studies* 66 (1&2): 105–31.

Hosein, G., T. Basdeo-Gobin, C. Robinson, S. Mowlah- Baksh, S. Leia, and A. Sanatan. 2018. *Gender-Based Violence in Trinidad and Tobago: A Qualitative Study.* Bridgetown: UN Women Caribbean. https://www.undp.org/content/dam/unct/caribbean/docs/20181011%20AF%20Trinidad%20and%20Tobago%20Health%20for%20digital.pdf.

Manjoo, R. 2016. Special Guest Contribution: "Violence against women as a barrier to the realisation of human rights and the effective exercise of citizenship." *Feminist Review* 112 (1): 11–26.

Mansingh, A., and P. Ramphal. 1993. "The Nature of Interpersonal Violence in Jamaica." *West Indian Medical Journal* 42 (2): 53–56.

Morrison, A., and M.B. Orlando. 2004. *The costs and impacts of gender-based violence in developing countries: Methodological considerations and new evidence.* Washington, DC: World Bank.

Mortley, N. 2018. *Males, Community and Crime in Jamaica: Final Report.* Kingston: Institute for Gender and Development Studies, Regional Coordinating Office, University of the West Indies.

O'Toole, L.L., and J.R. Schiffman, ed. 1997. *Gender Violence: Interdisciplinary Perspectives,* 2nd ed. New York and London: New York University Press.

Shepherd, Verene. 2019. "Historicizing Gender-Based Violence in the Caribbean." In *New Daughters of Africa: An International Anthology of Writing by Women of African Descent,* edited by Margaret Busby, 259–63. Oxford: Myriad Editions.

Teti, M., M. Chilton, L. Lloyd, and S. Rubinstein. 2006. "Identifying the links between violence against women and HIV/AIDS: Ecosocial and human rights frameworks offer insight into US prevention policies." *Health and Human Rights* 9 (2): 40–61.

UN Women. 2024. "FAQs: Types of violence against women and girls." UN Women, 27 June. https://www.unwomen.org/en/articles/faqs/faqs-types-of-violence-against-women-and-girls.

van Manen, M. 1990. *Researching Lived Experience: Human Science for an Action Sensitive Pedagogy*. Albany: State University of New York Press.

Violence Prevention Alliance. 2018. *Overview of 2017 Findings from Residents' Feedback on Women and Children's Safety and Security in 13 Volatile Communities*. Kingston: Citizen Security and Justice Programme (CSJP), Ministry of National Security.

Walby, S. 2016. *Ensuring data collection and research on violence against women and domestic violence: Article 11 of the Istanbul Convention*. Strasbourg: Council of Europe.

Watson Williams, Carol. 2018. *Women's Health Survey 2016 – Jamaica*. Kingston: Statistical Institution of Jamaica, UN Women and Inter-American Development Bank.

World Health Organization. 2012. *Understanding and Addressing Violence Against Women: Intimate Partner Violence*. Geneva: WHO. http://apps.who.int/iris/bitstream/handle/10665/77432/WHO_RHR_12.36_eng.pdf;jsessionid=92AA92E7E653936248B57ADCEF16E9DD?sequence=1.

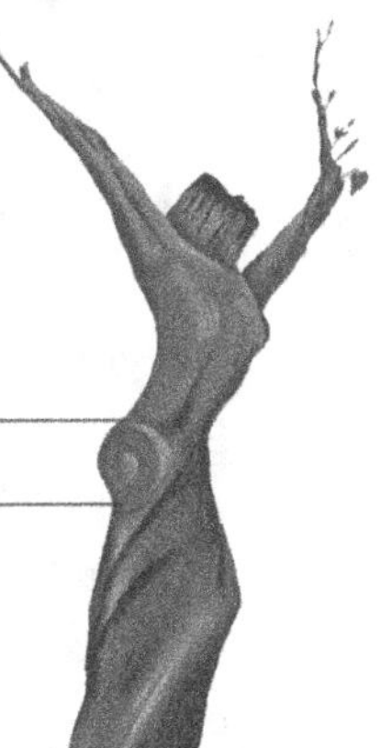

chapter 20

Reflections on Men's Organizing to End Gender-Based Violence in the Anglophone Caribbean

Amílcar Peter Sanatan

IN MAY 2022, AT THE TWELFTH PUBLIC MEETING of the Joint Select Committee of the Parliament of Trinidad and Tobago that inquired into "the State's capacity to provide support for victims of Domestic Violence and Family Conflicts (with specific focus on the availability of support mechanisms during the COVID-19 pandemic), it was revealed that between March 2020 and May 2022, 4,857 reports of domestic violence were received by the Trinidad and Tobago Police Service (Parliament of Trinidad and Tobago 2022). Domestic violence is one dimension of gender-based violence (GBV). However, the data illustrates the depth of the problem in Trinidad and Tobago. Similarly, states throughout the Anglophone Caribbean are seeking to redress the longstanding challenge to end GBV and develop a post-COVID-19 public infrastructure to safeguard the vulnerable.

Gender-based violence (GBV) influences everyday decisions in life, such as mobility, communication, financial choices, and physical and mental health. Gravely, it also leads to death. Social movements continue to organize via collective public actions and summon the names and memories of victims and survivors to construct a society free from violence, where all people, especially women and girls, can explore their full human potential.

For more than ten years, I have co-organized and co-created spaces and programmes for gender transformation in the tertiary educational spaces, civil society and public sectors. My primary area of activism has been engaging boys and men to end GBV. There are a range of male figures and 'experts' who have come to the fore in the national and regional landscape on men engaging men and boys to eliminate GBV. In my context, I occupy a minority position, as I am part of a small cadre of men who organize within and alongside the feminist and women's rights movements. While there are no specific Caribbean-based feminist men's institutions to advance this politics and form of social organizing, individual voices and strategically positioned men in the public, civil society and private sectors promote public actions for gender transformation.

Few explorations have been undertaken of men's involvement in collective and public actions to eliminate GBV in the Anglophone Caribbean. It is important to account for the personal transformation that men undergo, their entanglements in feminist and women's rights projects, understandings of privilege, and experiences of disempowerment in varying settings to appreciate the complexities of their navigations with different social groups and institutions. Michael Flood's (2013, 35) assertion that "men's anti-violence activism is a clear instance of counter hegemonic practice" attempts to illustrate the ethos and ethics of feminist and gender-transformative inspired actions by men to end violence against women, and address wider issues of GBV. However, in practice, men's organizing in this area is dynamic, diffuse and multi-faceted, with varying masculinity politics.

In the context of the Anglophone Caribbean, the most visible and status-generating male organizers against GBV have done so on socially conservative, at times, religious fundamentalist, ethno-nationalist and paternalistic pretexts. This is so largely because male organizers are challenged to be perceived as "real men" and figures who assert masculine standards of leadership in a public space with entrenched masculinist political cultures. Still, work to end GBV continues to be the primary issue of social organizing for men in the field of gender because it is a fundamental development problem of Caribbean societies that interrupts the socio-economic well-being of families, communities and the nation.

As a young, university-educated, childless, heterosexual, Afro-Caribbean, brown-skinned male, I have received, for the most part, a positive public reception for mobilizing men to end GBV throughout the region. Since boys and men, especially adolescent males of African descent, are widely perceived as "in crisis" and there are high levels of male disengagement in the social and education sectors, public actions to enhance the standing of boys and men generate high regard, and attract material and social resources as a male organizer. Yet, I often feel isolated as there are few male organizers with a feminist political orientation, and educational and activist training, who are committed to community-based actions. Very few male organizers sustain work with trade unions, public agencies, national security services, faith-based groups and institutions, and youth, especially those who are not in employment, education and training. Campaigns and social organizing often take place at donor-funded workshops, university organized fora, international days of commemoration and social advocacy, when public concern escalates on a specific issue related to GBV. This gap in the field leaves significant room for male organizers, who disavow feminist politics and gender equality and are perceived as better connected to the everyday experiences of the majority of the population (which strengthens their political networks), to occupy the gender equality and anti-violence landscape. For this reason, in the absence of a critical mass and bold, autonomous institutions of feminist men who promote collective actions, and change social and spatial environments, men's rights organizations that advance paternalistic and sexist positions gain the largest socio-political constituency, and posture as effective agents to delegitimize feminist men, feminist politics and the larger struggle for women's rights and gender equality.

PUBLIC ANXIETY AND THE PRIORITIZATION OF MALES AND THEIR DISENGAGEMENT

The twenty-first century marks a significant shift in the ways that men are framed as instrumental to the advancement of gender transformation and the elimination of gender inequalities. This builds on the framework promoted in the Beijing Platform for Action and Declaration.[1] The current political climate is also informed by the perception that women have gained greater prominence in the public sphere at the expense of men. In the wider political context, concern about the status of men has been advanced by the members of the two main political parties. For example, Shamfa Cudjoe, Member of Parliament and Minister of Sport and Community Development, at the launch of the Male Empowerment Programme, cautioned attendees about the "sense of duty", possibly by the state or women, to "nurture" men who have been left behind due to the advances that women have made:

> Sometimes we ask, How did we get here? Where the women seem so far ahead and the men seem to be stumbling and struggling. I like to consider myself a feminist and I think that everything about my socialization [has] cultured me to be a feminist . . . What is interesting in women's socialization is that there are different strategies and programmes to come back to check on women to make sure that we are doing okay. Yes? Whether it is in sport or science, there are these little clusters for women. And, we continue to make these advancements forgetting about the men. Then, we expect men to be socially sound, morally sound, financially sound . . . The systems that have cultured us [have done so] in such a way to leave the men behind. [This was] not on purpose but it just happened that way. So, we have a sense of duty to correct it, to nurture our men and give them that necessary support [for] an equal and level playing field. (Cudjoe 2022)

In a more direct message published on Father's Day, which cites the contemporary "fourth wave feminist movement" as responsible for "attacking" men, Kamla Persad-Bissessar, then leader of the opposition and political leader of the United National Congress, who was also the first elected female prime minister of Trinidad and Tobago, stated:

> The majority of men are good and the majority of fathers are good men. The ideology of the battle of the sexes must be rejected when it comes to raising children . . . Unfortunately, in today's world, fathers and fatherhood have wrongly come under attack by some radical fourth-wave feminists in their war against 'the patriarchy, masculinity and what they view as 'problematic behaviour'. (Persad-Bissessar 2022)

Both statements were met with little resistance by activist and academic women and men in the public sphere. This might be so because sparse attention is given to the business of government and the contents of speeches that offer insight into the ideological orientation of a particular administration, instead of abstracted conceptualizations of the state. Furthermore, the political affiliations of activists and academics in the national community and even fear of political vindictiveness significantly reduce gendered critiques of the positions of political leaders. It is not uncommon for women and men alike to espouse anti-feminist and ahistorical analyses of gendered power relations.

"Where are the men?" is the popular, but deeply problematic question, which either charges critiques for women's exclusion of men in the policies, programmes and discourses on gender equality or explores a more profound concern about men's responsibility and political commitments for gender transformation. Lewis (2007, 11) provokes, "Could it be then that the current concern about [male] under-achievement has less to do with the fact that girls are out-performing boys educationally, and more to do with the fact that the latter are defying tradition and acting out of character? Is there a fear of what it might be if women began to occupy all of the major decision-making positions in society?" Whether expressed as concern for the "social alienation of men" (CARICOM 2009), imagining the development challenge of responding to crime through the *Executive Report of the Committee on Young Males and Crime in Trinidad and Tobago* (Ryant et al. 2013), or the widely ambitious "One Thousand Men Programme" in Guyana set up to develop male models of community-based leadership, organizing men as a specialized group in development is a dominant feature of the Caribbean's socio-political landscape. Decades since Errol Miller's *Men at Risk* (1991) and Eudine's Barriteau's counter-response in "Requiem for the Male Marginalization Thesis in the Caribbean: Death of a Non-Theory" (2003), redressing male disengagement occupies the popular political imagination of wide sections of Caribbean society and the leadership class.

Men play an instrumental role in the transformation of gender inequalities because they, too, are embedded in complex structures of interactive social relationships. Connell (2003, 3) argues that men are also important in advancing gender equality and the work to prevent GBV because "the existing pattern of gender inequality – men's predominant control of economic assets, political power, cultural authority, and armed forces means that men (often, specific groups of men) control most of the resource required to implement women's claims for justice."

Globally, pro-feminist organizations that followed the second-wave feminism of the 1970s emerged to redress men's roles as perpetrators of violence against women. Organizations such as Men Against Patriarchy (MAP), Men Opposing Patriarchy (MOP) and contemporary movements such as the White Ribbon Campaign, MenEngage, Equimundo and Sonké for Gender Justice advocate for feminist and women's rights-inspired transformations of gender inequalities. In the Anglophone Caribbean, the Caribbean Male Action Network (CariMAN), through a process of growth and increasing alignment with global pro-feminist men's networks, has embraced an organizing politics that applies feminist and women's rights-inspired praxis in some of their campaigns and organizational structure. Younger voices on podcasts and social media community pages have created spaces for feminist-inspired analyses of Caribbean gendered power relations and development. This takes place on digital platforms created by youth-led feminist organizations, such as Intersect in Antigua and Barbuda, Life in Leggings in Barbados, and FeminiTT and IGDS Ignite! in Trinidad and Tobago. Notably, a growing number of men – albeit small – are now in gender bureaux throughout the Anglophone Caribbean. This justifies the ongoing need for the Caribbean Institute for Gender and Development – facilitated by the Institute for Gender and Development Studies – to provide the specialized knowledge and skills for gender practitioners in the state.

At the height of the COVID-19 pandemic in 2021, MenEngage organized a seven-month virtual MenEngage global symposium (referred to as the MenEngage Ubuntu Symposium). The symposium, its third, clearly pointed out the rights of fundamentalist and anti-democratic political movements as a backlash to feminism. This backlash did not only signal a shift in the language of political leaders, it also extended to a withdrawal of public sector spending in the social sector, delegitimization of women's rights and feminist movements, and an increase in GBV. Countries such as Brazil, under the leadership of Jair Bolsonaro, and the United States of America, led by Donald Trump, were put into sharp focus. For activists in the global community, gender-based violence and conflicts were "rooted in conservative groups in various parts of the world – including white supremacists – propagating the idea of a 'pure' and 'perfect' tradition and culture" (MenEngage Alliance 2021, 36). As Linden Lewis emphatically stated, "Gender does not stand outside of social relations" (Lewis 2007,

12). Programmes must be conscious of global and regional trends and their impact on local conceptualizations of masculinity, meanings of violence and geo-political shifts that imbue conflict.

SIMPLISTIC PROGRAMMES FOR MEN TO END GBV

Programmes that target men to end GBV have been reductive and sloganeering for the most part in the Anglophone Caribbean. 'Men's suffering' in health and education sectors are of great concern for governments invested in redressing these issues (Flood 2015a, 5). The human, financial and political resources for gender-transformative, male-focused programmes are few and far apart and are usually executed by international development agencies. Regarding support for gay, bisexual and queer men, it has been received with disproportionately externally sourced resources, with little to no assistance from public agencies.

Furthermore, community-based and public institutions often lack the required technical expertise in gender analysis to address harmful gender beliefs effectively; manage group dynamics, trauma, conflict and power imbalances; and provide the relevant knowledge and psycho-social resources to programme beneficiaries. Programmes tend to raise awareness of their social responsibility, which is not always framed as a challenge to patriarchy, but a call to notions of men as protectors and paternal figures. This is prevalent among youth, student and 'grassroots' community mobilizations for working-class and socially excluded men. On the contrary, the "men as gender equality champions" have traditionally targeted high-status men, such as private sector leaders, politicians and national athletes, who possess the symbolic and material trappings of male hegemony to speak out and use their influence in political, economic, cultural and social sectors to challenge men to end GBV. This simplistic approach, undergirded by classist conceptions of social programming for specific social groups, render the political terrain for men's organizing against GBV as narrow. Lack of sensitivity to the complexities of ethnicity, class and geography (namely, urban and rural divisions) limit the effectiveness of interventions. Moreover, boys and men may bring forward different viewpoints based on their subject positions regarding the issue of GBV, sharing experiences as perpetrators, survivors and bystanders, and therefore, the single narrative of men's violence against women falls short of engaging men and the complexity of their experiences.

Though feminist scholarship, and more broadly the social sciences, has embraced intersectional approaches[2] to theorizing; it is significantly difficult to do so in programme implementation. The complexities of racial self-identification; the dynamism of masculine construction in a multi-ethnic and religiously diverse postcolonial society; violence associated with homophobias and working across diverse age groups for generational interventions complicate organizing men for the eradication of GBV. There is also a pattern of embracing models to engage boys and men from the Global North. In cheap imitation, many efforts to transform the local understanding of a group are not done so effectively. Intersecting identities means that there are intersecting social divisions. Flood (2015b, 7) contends: "Although there is little systematic knowledge of how to address intersecting forms of gender, class and race in working with boys and men, there is at least recognition among the leaders of women's anti-violence organisations of the challenge of intersectionality."

THERE ARE NO SHORTCUTS TO SOCIAL CHANGE: THE IMPORTANCE OF SOPHISTICATED PROGRAMMES

There are fears, by some activists, that resourcing men's organizing around gender-based violence puts feminist and women's rights organizations in competition for the small pool of public and available funding for gender transformational projects. In the Caribbean, there is no empirical evidence to suggest that male-focused program syphoned off a significant level of resources from women-focused programmes and projects. While this may be so, the legitimacy, status and political prioritization of 'supporting' and 'nurturing' boys and men by both women and men is who are decision-makers, reinforce male privilege, rather than challenge it for a more gender equal framework for social, political and material resource distribution. In an environment where there is high public insecurity, crime and community conflicts, the political desire to manage the crisis has taken the form of re-masculinization of the state securitization to enforce discipline and control, and simultaneously specially include boys and men in the social sector, which have generally undergone a process of feminization. For this reason, engaging boys and men, not necessarily for gender equality but involving them in greater social and economic participation, shapes the interest of Caribbean governments and men's organizations.

Rhondall Feeles, CEO of the Single Fathers Association of Trinidad and Tobago, posited that GBV and domestic violence are misnomers for experiences of intimate partner violence:

> I've said it for years. We won't fix our problem until we remove 'gender' out of this whole intimate partner issue. I don't say 'domestic violence' and 'domestic issue' because the domestic goes beyond the spouse. We are dealing with an intimate partner violence issue and to treat with intimate partner violence we need to address issues that both men and women have via communication, the way they relate . . .
>
> We cannot say we want to end violence towards women because we have seen women violent towards women. We have also seen men violent towards men. Once it is the same sex, nobody cares. We cannot say we want to end violence towards women and we also see that we have the problem where women are taking the lives of women also. Is a woman who is murdered by a woman less significant than a woman who is murdered by a man? The two responses are different. If we have different responses where a woman dies by her murderous gender, then we are all foolish! . . . We might need gender to look at the nitty gritty part to finding solutions for taking down violence toward any particular person, we don't need to use that as the rhetoric when we [are] advocating. Sometimes [gender advocacy] is more divisive than it brings us to coming to a solution. (Feeles 2021)

The trope that outrage is selective and often biased against men, is meant to discredit the substance of women's rights and feminist organizing. For Feeles, gender is only relevant to a small "nitty gritty" concern and not fundamental to the analysis for which scholars and activists alike can explain violence against women, in addition to women's violence against men, men's violence against other men and women's violence against other women.

The development challenge that governments must confront in the twenty-first century is to establish policies and programmes that are gendered and informed by robust gender analyses to address power differentials between and among women and men, while promoting the meaningful inclusion and participation of all. Without this sophistication of policy and programme development, as well as men's organizing, trust and confidence in the process of gender transformation and social change will be wanting.

THE RIVER WE ARE YET TO CROSS: HOMOPHOBIAS AS BARRIERS TO TRANSFORMATION

Homophobias are pervasive in Caribbean societies and profoundly impact programme design and implementation. Men's organizing in the region fundamentally engages a male heterosexual constituency. Solidarity between men's organizing and LGBT organization is limited, but even when the leadership of organizations establish a rapport and formal working relationship, public mobilizations which acknowledge the diversity of sexualities and gender identities are met with high levels of resistance, rejection and, at times, sustained discrimination. Thus, performing masculinity becomes crucial to the facilitation of interventions. The popular understanding of GBV as a problem and solution have been done so largely within the confines of heterosexist discourses. This has even reproduced knowledge gaps in Caribbean feminist scholarship. Haynes and DeShong (2017, 106) note, "Feminist approaches to GBV in the Caribbean typically assume a heterosexual, non-transgender, gender conforming subject."

As an organizer who has had professional experiences with public institutions, namely, national security services, youth workers, and community and faith-based institutions, event organizers and participants openly establish their resistance to "LGBT ting" and "gender nonsense". In preparation for an International Men's Day Symposium in 2018 at an institution of the national security services, the chair of the event informed me, "Mr Sanatan, we look forward to your presentation because we heard you were very controversial. All I am asking is that you don't do a presentation that tells the officers to wear their uniform like a man in the day and go home to put on a dress in the night." The comfort with which the organizer openly discriminated against non-heterosexual men and the enforcement of the terms of discourse at the event represent the ways in which heterosexist practices impact men's organizing and experiences of workers in the field.

Religious settings also provide large, affordable venues for community mobilizations. It is not uncommon for a religious leader to enforce "ground rules"' that openly discriminate against LGBT people and uphold gender inequalities. I consciously work in these spaces because I believe that heterosexual men should manage this complexity. But when is it that we undermine this privilege and advance a subversive message to promote gender equality and progressive visions on the eradication of GBV? Further studies should explore the experiences of organizers challenging homophobias and also examine the experience of men, across diverse sexualities, and their negotiations as organizers among men. Due to entrenched homophobias, male-focused programmes often do not address the diversity of sexualities and masculine performers; instead, they focus on 'nurturing' and 'developing' men who are less violent and socially responsible for the well-being of women. These programmes are more invested in engaging men and not the meanings and identities associated with masculinities.

MEN'S ORGANIZING AND CRITICAL SELF-REFLECTION

Men involved in men's organizing, including those who have received training in feminism and women's rights, sometimes perceive the relationship with women academics and practitioners in the field as acrimonious. On several occasions, women have challenged men – publicly and privately – about their standpoints, positions of privilege and sense of entitlement. All criticisms charged against some male allies are not justified, but it is important for male organizers to not see critique as an attack. How do actors in the movement for gender transformation manage processes and challenges for accountability? Do we critique with care? Can those who fall short, listen, learn and have further opportunities to grow? I am the beneficiary of years of critique by women and men in the movement who provided several teachable moments and opportunities for growth.

Ethically, men must consider that challenges to their social advantage, privilege and entitlements will be called into question. Feminist social leader Roberta Clarke (2012) made a call for reliable male allies in a reflective blog. She said, "I sometimes pessimistically think of women working with men on gender equality as a high-risk endeavour, akin to walking on the verge of a precipice or a high-tension wire. . . . We know that to make change in our personal and public lives, both men and women have to reject patriarchy, to reject rigid gender roles, harmful stereotypes and inequality. For women this is hard too."

This vulnerable and brave reasoning is applied feminist principles of care, which is important for self-development and movement building. These conversations are especially important as some male organizers prefer to create distinction and division between men's organizing and the women's and feminist movements. There were once proclamations of 'male sovereignty' by some male activists who sought to disavow the critique of women's rights and feminist activists of all-male panels when discussing the status of men. Exclusive spaces are not the answer. Yet, I recognize the importance of men guiding a process among themselves for self-reflection, accountability and growth. In 2018, I formed an informal network, Feminist Bredren, of male organizers to achieve this. The fifteen members are activists, educators and public workers in gender bureaux from Trinidad and Tobago, Antigua and Barbuda, Guyana, Jamaica and Canada.

Like Colin Robinson, I do not position myself as an ally. I am an ethical worker, a comrade in solidarity, a citizen invested in national liberation, freedom, equality and fairness. While I acknowledge the positionality and politics of the subject position ally, the term ally defines one specific relation to a movement. There is a wider movement for gender transformation and Caribbean freedom, of which I am a member. For this reason, solidarity with women's rights, feminist, LGBTQ and people living with disabilities, and more, are fundamental to such actions and engagement. Pioneering regional LGBTQ activist Colin Robinson observed, "I don't see myself as an ally; I see myself as a part, a partner in a gender justice movement, working with women's issues with women who work on mine . . . Overall in the Caribbean we have problems confronting privilege and cultivating empathy; perhaps the solution is not gender specific. We men engage in gender advocacy all the time – for ourselves. The lack of confidence that we can engage in joint advocacy that yields justice is the problem" (Sanatan 2019).

Though the process of critical self-reflection can be uncomfortable, the experience allows for profound introspection on practice, motivations and an individual's approach to decision making. It also serves men's interest to consistently learn through reinforcement about male dominance, patriarchal practices and accountability for personal and professional development. Men and women organizers must create a space for bold conversations about feelings and experiences. Social organizing is a deeply human process, therefore social psychology, behaviour, attitudes and group identity formation influence the experiences of people in the space. Personality conflicts are as much a part of social organizations as there are political conflicts externally. This is especially true in small geographic places where family relations, intimate partners, perceived rivals and political opponents are in close proximity and constant contact.

CONCLUSION: A DEPATRIACHAL MOVEMENT

It is important to take stock of the critical interventions to engage men to eliminate GBV as well as assess the politics of men's organizing in the Anglophone Caribbean. For all the national and international agreements to end GBV, public anti-violence campaigns and development of the field of Caribbean masculinities studies, led by regional feminist scholars, little discussion illustrates the experiences of men's organizing, the gaps between rhetoric and practices and complexities of engaging men and boys. In a highly politicized field, the necessary ethnographic insights and 'bacchanal' that provide the context for activist work and social movement building share understandings, which allow for deeper reflection and enhancement of the efforts to achieve gender transformation.

For now, men's organizing to end GBV will turn to 'strong men' and men who embody the trappings of hegemonic manhood as Caribbean societies grapple with increasing levels of public insecurity, crime and violence. States have re-militarized and re-masculinized communal space in the interest of maintaining law and order. Structurally and spatially, violence is normative and it requires a deeper, more far-reaching project than awareness building and behaviour change to confront them. An organized depatriarchal movement of men, women and gender nonconforming people are fundamental to the prospect of transformative Caribbean development and freedom. The system of oppression and socio-economic inequalities are deeply rooted in racial, classed, gendered and sexualized histories. Indeed, the historical oppression of women's bodies and resistance to their autonomy founded the social and economic order of the society, with all its interlocking exclusions. Depatriachalization, inspired by Latin American feminist and women's movements, namely in Bolivia, seeks to end patriarchal power relations in everyday life that perpetuate conflict, constructs division between women and men, and the structural and spatial contexts that exclude people from equal participation. This structural and spatial project takes time, human and financial resources, public leadership, collective action, care and commitment to long-term change.

NOTES

1. At the Fourth World Conference on Women, at Beijing in 1995, the Beijing Declaration expressed governments' determination to "Encourage men to participate fully in all actions towards equality" (Item 25).
2. Intersectionality is "an analytical tool for studying, understanding and responding to the ways in which gender intersects with other identities and how these intersections contribute to unique experiences of oppression and privilege" (Association for Women's Rights in Development 2004, 1).

REFERENCES

Association for Women's Rights in Development (AWID). 2004. "Intersectionality: A Tool for Gender and Economic Justice." *Women's Rights and Economic Change* (9): 1–8.

Barriteau, Eudine. 2003. "Requiem for the Male Marginalization Thesis in the Caribbean: Death of a Non-Theory." In *Confronting Power, Theorizing Gender: Interdisciplinary Perspectives in the Caribbean*, edited by Eudine Barriteau, 324–55. Kingston: University of the West Indies Press.

Caribbean Community. 2009. "CARICOM Assistant Secretary-General Appeals to Women's Bureau to Address Social Alienation of Men." CARICOM, 8 October. https://caricom.org/caricom-assistant-secretary-general-appeals-to-womens-bureau-to-address-social-alienation-of-men/.

Clarke, Roberta. 2012. "In Need of Reliable Allies." *Roots and Rights* blog, 25 November. https://rootsandrights.wordpress.com/2012/11/25/in-need-of-reliable-allies/.

Connell, R.W. 2003. "The Role of Men and Boys in Achieving Gender Equality."

Presentation at Expert Group Meeting, Division for the Advancement of Women in collaboration with International Labour Organization, Joint UN Programmes on HIV/AIDS, UNDP, Brasilia, 7 October. https://www.un.org/womenwatch/daw/egm/men-boys2003/Connell-bp.pdf.

Cudjoe, Shamfa. 2022. "MPower TT 2022 Launch Event." Speech delivered at MPower TT Launch Event, Hilton Trinidad, Port of Spain, Facebook Live, 8 August 2022. https://www.facebook.com/watch/live/?ref=watch_permalink&v=3387183198227901.

Feeles, Rhondall. 2021. "Domestic Violence Policies – Rhondall Feeles." Posted on 28 July 2021 by TTT Live Online. YouTube, 11:58. https://www.youtube.com/watch?v=hYpdLbsFFL4.

Flood, Michael. 2014. "Men's Antiviolence Activism and the Construction of Gender-Equitable Masculinities." In *Alternative Masculinities for a Changing World*, edited by Àngels Carabí and Josep M. Armengol, 35–50. New York: Palgrave Macmillan.

———. 2015a. "Men and Gender Equality." In *Engaging Men in Building Gender Equality*, edited by Michael Flood with Richard Howson, 1–33. Newcastle upon Tyne: Cambridge Scholars Publishing.

———. 2015b. "Work with Men to End Violence Against Women: A Critical Stocktake." *Culture, Health and Sexuality* 17 (S2): 159–76.

Haynes, Tonya and Halimah A. F. DeShong. 2017. "Queering Feminist Approaches to Gender-based Violence in the Anglophone Caribbean." *Social and Economic Studies* 66 (1&2): 105–31.

Jain, Rimjhim. 2021. "Engaging Men and Boys in Ending Gender-based violence, including Violence against Women and Girls." In *MenEngage Ubuntu Symposium: I am Because You Are – A summary report of discussions at the 3rd MenEngage Global Symposium*. Washington, DC: MenEngage Alliance. https://menengage.org/wp-content/uploads/2022/02/MenEngage-Ubuntu-Symposium-Discussion-Papers-Ebook-EN.pdf.

Lewis, Linden. 2007. "Man Talk, Masculinity, and a Changing Social Environment." *Caribbean Review of Gender Studies* 1: 1–20.

Miller, Errol. 1991. *Men at Risk*. Kingston: Jamaica Publishing House.

Parliament of Trinidad and Tobago. 2022. "12th Virtual Meeting – JSC Social Services and Public Administration – 25 May 2022 – Domestic Violence." Virtual meeting, posted 25 May 2022 by ParlView [the Parliament Channel]. YouTube, 2:05:31. https://www.youtube.com/watch?v=V5kob9b8pQk.

Persad-Bissessar, Kamla. 2022. "Opposition Leader Father's Day Message. United National Congress." United National Congress blog, 19 June. https://unctt.org/opposition-leader-fathers-day-message/.

Ryan, Selwyn, Indira Rampersad, Lennox Bernard, Patricia Mohammed, and Marjorie Thorpe. 2013. *No Time to Quit: Engaging Youth at Risk – Executive Report of the Committee on Young Males and Crime in Trinidad and Tobago.* St Augustine: University of the West Indies, Faculty of Humanities and Education. https://www.ttparliament.org/wp-content/uploads/2021/10/No-Time-to-Quit-Engaging-Youth-At-Risk-Executive-Report-of-the-Committee-on-Young-Males-and-Crime-in-Trinidad-and-Tobago.pdf.

Sanatan, Amílcar. 2019. "Writing is an Arsenal: An Interview with Colin Robinson." *Sx Salon* 32. https://smallaxe.net/sxsalon/discussions/writing-arsenal-interview-colin-robinson.

chapter 21

Historicizing 'The Domestic' in Domestic Violence

Solidarity and Struggle in the Domestic Violence Lobby in Trinidad and Tobago[1]

KENDRA-ANN PITT

> "The domestic violence act was [a] struggle and what was good with all the struggles is that you [had . . .] solidarity [. . .] You know, that was really very important for the success of [. . .] things."

THE QUOTE ABOVE IS FROM AN INTERVIEW WITH MAY, a self-identified feminist from Trinidad and Tobago, who was actively involved in the country's domestic violence lobby from the late 1970s until the implementation of the Domestic Violence Act in 1991. May was reflecting on the tensions that existed among women's groups involved in the lobby – tensions, in part, rooted in the diverse values and frameworks mobilized to understand domestic violence across these groups. Her comments are indicative of the complexities within the movement and the range of ideological and material preoccupations that drove the women involved to respond to this social problem. What is clear from her statement is that alongside these tensions was a solidarity that enabled some success in the movement.

In Trinidad and Tobago, as elsewhere, the naming of domestic violence and the introduction of legal sanctions in response to violence against women were significant as moments of publicly delegitimizing these acts. They also represented a shift in women's status, a challenge to the assumed separation of public and private spheres, and the beginning of public awareness of domestic violence as an urgent issue. Fuelled by an active women's movement, domestic violence activism in Trinidad and Tobago in the late 1970s and 1980s led to the passing of the first domestic violence legislation in the Anglophone Caribbean. What is of note is that the concerns of the stakeholders across this movement, while all geared towards alleviating the violence experienced by women in the community, were not uniformly articulated.

This chapter explores the divergence in perspectives on domestic violence in the women's movement in the 1970s and 1980s in Trinidad and Tobago.[2] I suggest that one of the central points of this divergence is embedded in the very notion of 'the domestic', given the historical trajectory of the domestic sphere in the colonial context of the region. Following the abolition of the slave trade, concerted efforts were made to establish and promote heteropatriarchal families, defined by marriage, among colonized peoples. The heteropatriarchal family became a means of securing labour and regulating gendered, sexualized, classed and racialized subjects. It also functioned as an indicator of civility, morality and respectability among the colonized, who had been dominantly represented as incapable of civility in colonial discourse. When Caribbean kinship patterns failed to reflect this ideal, it created enduring anxieties about the deficiencies of the domestic sphere.

I argue that these anxieties were invoked during the domestic violence lobby through commitments to idealized notions of family and their concomitant gendered roles. As such, although constituents of this lobby were all committed to enacting legislation to redress domestic violence, there was no singular approach to understanding this issue. While there were stakeholders invested in maintaining heteropatriarchal domestic relations, I suggest that, simultaneously, a Caribbean feminist perspective on domestic violence emerged that considered this violence beyond the confines of the domestic sphere. These feminists mobilized an understanding of domestic violence that not only aimed to destabilize heteropatriarchal familial relations and gender roles, but also situated the issue as structural and enmeshed in the region's colonial history. I highlight and explore these tensions in the domestic violence lobby and their implications for contemporary domestic violence frameworks in the region. I aim to make visible how the domestic sphere became a site of struggle in framing and articulating desired responses to domestic violence within the movement. I do this by first historicizing the domestic sphere in the Caribbean, illustrating its centrality in constructing colonized women and men as civilized and respectable subjects. Second, following an overview of the domestic violence lobby in Trinidad and Tobago, I explore how diverse perspectives on the issue during the lobby expose preoccupations with producing respectable subjects through the family.

HISTORICIZING THE DOMESTIC SPHERE IN THE CARIBBEAN

The history of the domestic sphere in the Caribbean is critical to understanding domestic violence in the contemporary period. In the years leading up to the abolition of the slave trade in 1807, the heteropatriarchal family emerged as central to the regulation of colonized women and men. At the height of the slave system, marriage was not prioritized for the enslaved; the 'private' family served as a site of racialized, gendered and classed distinction (see Beckles 1999). For enslaved families, kinship existed squarely in the 'public domain';[3] families could be separated and sold at the whim of owners to support the operationalization of the slave system (Reddock 1994). Heteropatriarchal marriage unions among the enslaved were fostered only when the abolition of the slave trade was on the horizon (see Chamberlain 2014; Reddock 1994).[4]

This turn to the heteropatriarchal family and legal marriage created a series of possibilities. First, a domestic sphere that mirrored ideal European family forms facilitated attempts to govern the colonized to support the colonial order. Governmentality scholars purport that the family serves to direct the conduct of social subjects, while maintaining the veneer of the separation between the public and private spheres (Rose 1999; Rose and Miller 2010). The family could facilitate regulation from afar – something not required during enslavement because the conduct of the enslaved was managed through sanctioned direct violence (see Egerton 2003; Thomas 2011). Family, then, served as an entry point for cultivating appropriate gendered, classed, sexualized and racialized conduct (see Hall 1995; Sheller 2012; Trotz 2009), governing colonized women and men in freedom to support the colonial order (see Lazarus-Black 1994).[5] 'Stable' familial unions secured labour in a context where the enslaved were no longer commodities that could be traded at will (see Mohapatra 1995; Morrissey 1991), keeping labour in place.

This regulation exemplified through the conditions of indentureship. The large-scale migration of Indian migrants through indentureship schemes began in 1845. A series of murders of Indian women by Indian men on plantations in Trinidad and British Guiana in the 1860s – dubbed 'wife murders'– began to draw the attention of colonial officials. Mohapatra (1995) argues that the women killed during this period were not all wives or even in long-term relationships, but were often casual sexual partners,[6] and that constructing a narrative of 'wife murder' was important to the official response. By invoking marriage, colonial officials linked violence to women transgressing the boundaries of normalized gendered and sexualized domestic relations. Legislative responses to this violence more solidly defined domestic parameters, formally regulated the legalization and dissolution of marriage, and prioritized the constitution and primacy of heteropatriarchal domestic relations.

While Hindu and Muslim marriages were not recognized upon the introduction of indentureship, by the 1860s civil marriage was made possible in both Trinidad and British Guiana (Robinson 2006).[7] Regulations governing responses to women at risk of violence from men changed. Initially, either she or the (potential) abuser could be moved to another plantation. If this violence was deemed a response to the woman's relationships with multiple partners, however, amendments allowed for the removal of 'the seducer', leaving the woman on the same plantation as the man threatening the violence (Mohapatra 1995).[8] Officials remained preoccupied with limiting instances of polyandry and adultery. With legal marriage now more easily attained by Indian women and men, familial units were protected from behaviours viewed as compromising them. These interventions secured access to labour while facilitating the normalization of the heteropatriarchal family (Trotz 2003).

Prioritizing heteropatriarchal marriage and family was also widely perceived as a pathway to constructing colonized women and men as moral, respectable, civilized and rights-bearing social subjects capable of enacting freedom. This is relevant given that the subjugation of the colonized had been justified by their incivility and savagery. Stable domestic relations that reflected idealized European family forms were considered the foundation of good citizenship (Chamberlain 2006) and civility (Hall 1995). Robinson (2006) notes that in the post-emancipation period, black people's moral and social development was linked to their capacity to take up 'proper' familial roles. For women, wifedom, dependency and domesticity, or what Reddock (1994) refers to as the "housewifization" (32) of women. Tropes of domesticity had previously been reserved for white women, who represented the ideals of sexual purity, social benevolence and morality (Beckles 1999). This was a major departure from Indian and black women's lives as labourers in fields alongside men. Colonial education incorporated training "to instill into young minds the colonial European middle-class ideal of 'womanhood' and 'manhood'" (Reddock 1994, 54).[9] Despite this, marriage did not hold the hoped-for appeal for many black women and men and was not a requirement for establishing families (Chamberlain 2006). While Indian women and men in the post-indentureship period did marry, many did not register these marriages for legitimate acknowledgement by the state (Robinson 2006). Concubinage and the multiple partnerships associated with black women and men remained ongoing concerns, both for colonial governments and the emerging black and Indian middle classes (Reddock 1994).

With heteropatriarchal family installed as a touchstone of modern civilized life, other kinds of domestic relations were framed as indicative of moral decay. The colonial state cements this perspective with the *Report of the West India Royal Commission* of 1945, the result of Great Britain's investigation into the social and economic state of the colonies in the region. Illegitimacy, single mothers and absent fathers were blamed for a series of social ills, including poor health and delinquency. T.S. Simey (1946), the architect of the welfare machinery that emerged based on this investigation, asserted that the West Indian family was an unreliable institution, and that its loose structure produced weak social organization from which disorganized social life emerged. What is exposed here is the privileging of the heteronormative European ideal as a mark of respectability and morality, and the pathologization of non-conforming regional kinship patterns, narratives that endured beyond the official end of colonization in the region. The notion of the heteropatriarchal family as ideal has been central to post-independence nation building (Barriteau 2001), with the idea of non-heteropatriarchal families as problematic entrenched in approaches to policy and within social science and anthropological discourse (Trotz 2009).

These narratives of the domestic sphere and the notion of an idealized private family as a hallmark of civility were critical to later debates about the meanings of domestic violence during the lobby against it in Trinidad. In the following sections, I provide an overview of the lobby, followed by an examination of the divergent perspectives and their link to preoccupations with the domestic sphere.

FROM 'THE DOMESTIC SPHERE' TO DOMESTIC VIOLENCE: THE DOMESTIC VIOLENCE LOBBY IN TRINIDAD AND TOBAGO, 1975–1991

Many credit the United Nations Decade for Women (1975–1985) as pivotal to sparking collective action to eliminate violence against women in Trinidad and Tobago in the 1970s (Baksh-Soodeen 1998; Lazarus-Black 2007; Rowley 2011). This period marked the development of a dynamic discourse on the issue that culminated in the passing of the Domestic Violence Act in 1991. The first UN World Conference on Women, held in Mexico City in 1975, placed violence against women on its agenda (Gopaul and Cain 1996) and instigated initiatives focused specifically on women's equity in Trinidad and Tobago (Mohammed 1991). One such initiative was the National Commission on the Status of Women, which launched an investigation into their standing in a range of fields. Recommendations were forwarded to the government in 1978, and in 1980 they hosted a conference on domestic violence (Bishop and Rahamut 1996, as cited in Lazarus-Black 2003). These state-sponsored inquiries into women's status legitimized their issues in public discourse, and further authorized and promoted the perceived validity of women's claims (Mohammed 1991).

NGOs played a key role in raising public awareness about domestic violence. Some groups dealt with violence as part of their mandate; others were instrumental to the movement through their focus on women's equity, even if violence was not their primary focus. For instance, the Housewives

Association of Trinidad and Tobago (HATT), formed in 1975, focused on organizing around the regulation of prices of consumer goods, and raised the profile of women activists who were not affiliated with 'legitimate' political organizations (Henderson 1988), while also creating interest in challenging women's subordinate status (Nicholas 1990). Groups such as Concerned Women for Progress (CWP), formed in 1980, addressed a range of concerns related to women including their rights to abortion, economic issues (from a socialist framework), and all forms of violence against women.

Women's groups facilitated a series of public forums and discussions, drawing attention to domestic violence and sexual violence in the 1980s, leading to the emergence of transformative institutions, including the Rape Crisis Society in 1984. In 1989, the organization identified the need to deter potential domestic violence offenders and ensure that women and children were protected (Daly 1982). Collectives such as the Caribbean Association for Feminist Research and Action (CAFRA), founded in 1985 and based in Trinidad, were heavily active in organizing to address violence against women across the region. They were consultants on the development of CARICOM's model domestic violence legislation and conducted the Women and the Law Project between 1987 and 1988. The first shelters, established in 1986 and 1987, were run by civil society organizations, with the government providing the property for one of these sites (Mohammed 1991), illustrating that concerns about domestic violence were being afforded some credence by the state.

By 1986, the Sexual Offences Bill was being debated in parliament and several women's organizations were involved in public debates regarding the inclusion of marital rape as an offence. Initially included in the bill, the marital rape clause was ultimately removed. An action committee comprising various women's organizations and union representatives was formed to respond to its omission (Nicholas 1990). The Sexual Offences Act was passed in 1986 and although the marital rape clause was eventually included, the act stipulated that marital rape could only occur if a couple had been separated for at least two years. The debate on this issue intensified women's organizations' efforts at public education, advocacy campaigns, and ongoing lobbying for legal reforms (Babb 1997).

In January 1991, the parliamentary debate on the Domestic Violence Bill began. Dr Emmanuel Hosein – the Minister of Social Development and Family Services – introduced the bill as part of a commitment to "social justice and equal rights for men and women" (as cited in Lazarus-Black 2007, 29). He cautioned that the bill was not the state's attempt to intervene in the private lives of citizens, but to create a means for individuals to protect themselves from violence and abuse, illustrating a commitment to asserting the family as private. A debate ensued among a male-dominated parliament, exposing the precarious meanings of these equal rights.

There were protests against the idea that a man could be removed from his property for being abusive; against police officers being allowed to enter a home without a warrant if they suspected abuse was occurring; and about who qualified as a spouse or de facto spouse, eliciting questions about the boundaries of the domestic sphere. Given the range of family patterns in the Caribbean, the latter debates centred on whether common-law and visiting heterosexual relationships would be included as legitimate domestic relationships, illustrating the discursive weight of the legislation. Parliamentarians stated that the bill did not take into consideration the cultural attitudes that men had toward women and their property, and a range of amendments were proposed to reflect these concerns.

Women's groups organized in response to these attempts to weaken the act's provisions. Twenty-one groups – including CAFRA, the Coalition Against Domestic Violence (CADV), Working Women for Social Progress (Working Women) and the Rape Crisis Society – banded together to sign petitions, write letters to legislators and participate in newspaper interviews (Lazarus-Black 2007; Nicholas 1990). They also staged a silent protest, sitting in parliament, dressed in all black. These women succeeded in having some provisions kept in the act. While officers did require a warrant, a definition of spouse that included heterosexual common-law partners was included, and magistrates were given the power to order abusers to vacate the home. The act was passed in April 1991.

STRUGGLE AND SOLIDARITY IN THE DOMESTIC VIOLENCE MOVEMENT

INVOKING 'THE DOMESTIC' IN DOMESTIC VIOLENCE

While working in solidarity, contingents in the domestic violence lobby conceptualized domestic violence in divergent ways. Preoccupations with traditional notions of the domestic sphere were central to these divergent views. One interview with a participant, May, she referred to the significance of these traditional perspectives and their role in the lobby. She noted: ". . . when we began, we weren't so close to [the] older women [. . .]. We hadn't heard much feminist talk coming from them . . . they were middle-class, most of them, but the thing is we knew nothing of their history [. . .]. Many of those groups had aligned themselves with nationalist political parties – the [People's National Movement in Trinidad and Tobago], the [People's National Party in Jamaica], or even the [People's Progressive Party] in Guyana [. . .] – so they had lost some of their original concern with women."

May frames a divergence in perspectives as rooted in differences in the class status and values of women across generations. This affiliation of women's groups with political parties that May references occurred alongside bids for independence in Caribbean nation states (Alexander 1994; Patrick 1988; Reddock 1998), as women of the pre-established "middle-strata women's movement" (Reddock 1998, 59) were often recruited to consolidate political parties' activities. Traditional and middle-strata women's groups were also involved in work to address sexual and domestic violence (Mohammed 1991). For instance, business and professional women were involved in establishing the country's first battered women's shelter.

However, less traditional interventions in the domestic violence lobby challenged the politics of many older women's groups, as many newer organizations moved beyond focusing on women's inclusion and equal rights (Gopaul, Morgan, and Reddock 1994; Reddock 1988). The 'traditional' framework, however, had been meaningful for women's groups in the early post-colonial era with Caribbean nation states eager to achieve 'modernity'. Such liberal discourses were congruent with dominant nationalist perspectives that saw colonized men leading the nation and taking up their rightful position as head of the heteropatriarchal family – what Barriteau (1998; 2001) calls the "Enlightenment promise". Middle-strata women's groups active during this period were also invested in this promise (see Alexander 1994; Barriteau 1998; 2001; Robinson 2000) and women representing these ideals were viewed as operating within the boundaries of a respectable femininity.

Reddock (1988) notes that the women's movement in Trinidad was reinvigorated in the late 1970s with a more radical character. Tensions existed between traditional and radical pperspectives often associated with feminism. For instance, Henderson (1988, 373) notes that the women's arm of the Transport and Industrial Workers' Union, which in part focused on "the organizing of women for the complete understanding and recognition of their position in political, social and economic spheres", lost significant membership over debates about women's rights to control their bodies, and their involvement in politics, abortion and religion. Such demands to reorganize hegemonic gender and sexual relations undermined the desire to establish colonially informed norms of gendered respectability rooted in the heteropatriarchal family.

While some were committed to traditional social mores, for others, feminism was understood as exclusionary and as an inappropriate entry point for responding to domestic violence. 'Feminist' had been framed by many not only as foreign and irrelevant to Caribbean women, but also as an expression of women's sexual deviance and a disruption to the domestic sphere (see also Alexander 1994). The desire to criminalize domestic violence was not necessarily accompanied by a reflection on issues of gender and power, and domestic violence was not always perceived as a feminist issue, but rather as a crime. As such, responses did not require attention to gender relations, but rather, a focus on punishing perpetrators for violent behaviours.

A participant who defined herself as feminist reflected on her engagement with social workers involved in domestic violence work. She shared the view that perceptions of this violence deviated from one to another, noting that she perceived a "line between what [social workers] saw as [. . .] supporting [the] issue but not seeing it as a feminist issue. That's an interesting contradiction there . . . they didn't see it as feminist necessarily – they saw it as an act of abuse . . . and a crime . . . because it was a crime." She also mentioned that such groups brought a different "consciousness" to thinking about domestic violence, while still being invested in ending it. One participant, Frida, a social worker, who had been heavily involved in the lobby, noted that she did not view herself as a feminist, as she did not want to destroy men. Acknowledging domestic violence as a crime that requires a punitive state response does not necessarily query dominant gendered relations enshrined in traditional notions of the family. Furthermore, the notion that a feminist response would destroy men is indicative of how hegemonic masculinity is predicated on these traditional perspectives.

This divergence is further articulated in a 1991 presentation addressing legal responses to sexual and domestic violence in Trinidad and Tobago. The commentator states, "The feminist movement, for all its break with tradition, has not taken women out of the home, but it has heightened her awareness of other options. The home is no longer her circumference but it remains her centre" (Barnes 1991, 5). While the significance of feminism is acknowledged, women's ongoing belonging within and responsibility to the domestic sphere is re-articulated. From this perspective, allowing women to be better positioned to respond to violence in their lives is not to be at the expense of the domestic being "their centre". Criminalization was acknowledged as an apt response to domestic violence, and interventions were not expected to disrupt women's traditional place.

The address further suggests that "the marital/spousal relationship [is something] which the Domestic Violence Bill saw the need to preserve" (Barnes 1991, 6). In 1991, while the Domestic Violence Bill was under discussion in parliament, the attached explanatory note made it clear that "the object of the Bill [was] to strike a balance between the need to preserve an existing marital or spousal or parental relationship on the one hand [and] the need to protect these persons from exposure to violence on the other" (as cited in Barnes 1991, 2). The focus on preservation of the conjugal relationship despite violence replicates the logic of the ordinances responding to violence against Indian immigrant women on plantations close to a century earlier as they centred the (re)production of the heteropatriarchal family. Maintaining the family became a justification for the bill. The commitment to criminalization, while seen as a pragmatic response to domestic violence, was used to preserve traditional notions of the domestic sphere.[10]

The colonial framing of 'the domestic' in domestic violence is captured elsewhere. In 1991, months following the passing of the Domestic Violence Act, the head of National Family Services in Trinidad commented on issues and challenges relevant to working with domestic violence and other forms of abuse in the Caribbean. The "vulnerability of the Caribbean family" (Bishop 1991, 2) is cited as a prime issue. In addition, 'the status of men' is identified as an issue with their "high rates of unemployment and attendant male marginalization from psychological and economic participation in family life are seen as underlying forces which are adversely affecting the fabric of society". While issues such as migration and unemployment are cited as relevant, the language and sentiment of the *Report of the West India Royal Commission* (1945) is invoked, centring the 'loose and unreliable' structure of the Caribbean family and its innate fallibility as the problem. The Caribbean family continued to be portrayed as problematic, while structural factors creating challenges for families were less relevant. This issue was addressed by Caribbean feminist approaches to framing domestic violence.

CARIBBEAN FEMINIST CONCEPTUALIZATIONS OF DOMESTIC VIOLENCE

While commitments to the traditional domestic sphere emerged throughout the domestic violence lobby, the campaign was also informed by a Caribbean feminist perspective on the issue. This perspective centred challenges to heteropatriarchal social relations and undermined the confinement of domestic violence to the interpersonal relations of the domestic sphere, instead framing it as a structural problem. This regional reading of violence was concerned with sexism and the patriarchal conditions that produced domestic violence, while also situating it in relation to the co-constitution of oppressions experienced by women. Pansy, who during our interview described herself as coming "from the bowels of the women's movement . . .", described her interconnected activism in the domestic violence movement as also challenging women's experiences of economic injustice and addressing reproductive rights.

Pansy's integrated framing reflects perspectives of the women's movement in Trinidad and Tobago and the wider Caribbean during this period. Reddock (1996) writes:

> A small but vocal band of women locally have argued, along with colleagues and sisters internationally, that the subordination of women which is characterised by . . . [factors such as domestic violence] cannot be seen separately from the overall inequality, violence, discrimination, and general unfairness characteristic of the present socio-economic system – that women's subordination is only the most fundamental aspect of a generally unfair and violent system based on racism, classism and of course sexism. (87)

Reddock notes that feminists working on domestic violence in Trinidad and Tobago were making links among class, race, socio-political and economic systems as well as inequitable gender relations as they aimed to address violence.

This approach was informed by a range of struggles and social movements. By the time of the 1970s, feminist anti-violence protests race, class and colonialism were already well-rehearsed fields for challenges to the state in Trinidad and Tobago. Contingents involved in organizing during the 1930s riots were heavily informed by anti-colonial, Pan-African and Marxist ideologies (see Reddock 1994). Working-class women were active in organizations and protests in response to poor social and economic conditions – and by extension, colonial policies – during these riots. Meanwhile, middle-class women were involved in social welfare activities challenging colonial-era racism against women and were invested in uplifting them through education (Reddock 2010), while also supporting independence efforts in the 1950s. While not wholly reflective of the radical discourse that characterized the Caribbean feminists to follow, these activities were founding aspects of later feminist action and were variably grounded in class, anti-racist and anticolonial movements. Likewise, Trinidad and Tobago's Black Power movement of the 1970s built race and class consciousness as well as cross-racial alliances (Samaroo 2014). While these perspectives did not necessarily challenge dominant masculinities or women's secondary status, they did permeate feminist discourses (Pasley 1997; 2001).

The economic downturn of the 1980s, and the imposition of neoliberal economic policies in the form of structural adjustment programmes, were also significant to how feminists framed domestic violence. Women's groups, such as Concerned Women for Progress, Working Women for Social Progress, The Group, and CAFRA, exemplified multifocal approaches that were concerned with both the patriarchal power relations associated with gendered violence, and the challenges faced by working-class women in this moment of economic struggle (Nicholas 1990). Critiques linked precarious economic conditions to violence within and outside the home (Reddock 1996), and for many activists the goal was to "remove male dominance, which [. . .] oppresse[d] men as well as women, [along with] the overall social and economic system of which it is a part" (Reddock 1996, 87–88). This structural framing of violence exemplified by Caribbean feminists was evidenced in a press release issued by Working Women for Social Progress, which stated "structural adjustment policies imposed from abroad are seen as a major contributor to domestic violence in that they increase poverty, thus fuelling tension in families" (Working Women for Social Progress 1995). The development of these arguments in Trinidad and Tobago was consolidated by the connections made with other feminist activists of the Global South who were coping with the global economic crisis and had similar post/colonial experiences (Antrobus 1988; Gopaul, Morgan, and Reddock 1996; Reddock 1998; 2008). Working to critically address issues of gender and development, women worked across borders, reinforcing their conceptualizations of the connections among colonial histories, race, the economy, gender and violence. Organizations such as Development Alternatives with Women for a New Era (DAWN) – co-founded by Caribbean feminist activists Peggy Antrobus and Lucille Mair, along with others – provided a forum for feminist research, analyses and advocacy on global issues affecting the livelihoods, living standards and development prospects of women, especially marginalized women in the Global South. Combatting violence against women was connected to struggles for economic justice, national liberation and emancipatory development strategies (Sen and Grown 1987). Such perspectives shifted debates about domestic violence from simplistic notions of patriarchy to globalized relationships of power, justice and equity.

These approaches to domestic violence were concerned with addressing women's equity in a holistic manner. They considered the multiple sources of oppression that women were experiencing and troubled easy distinctions between 'the private' and 'the public'. This perspective centred addressing male dominance and heteropatriarchal values, while also aiming to undermine related forms of marginalization. Domestic violence was not seen solely as an issue of the family, but was understood as linked to structural conditions of the neocolonial context.

CONCLUSION

While feminists aimed to challenge the separation of the public and the domestic spheres in a context where domestic violence was enmeshed in persistent (neo)colonial and economic violence, interests more aligned with traditional notions of family permeated official domestic violence discourses. Tensions between these approaches were informed by colonially rooted anxieties about the family, respectability and the morality of (post)colonial subjects in the Caribbean. Historical responses to these anxieties emerged before and after emancipation, and were exemplified by family-building efforts that privileged hegemonic perspectives of family. These interventions were an important strategy of biopolitical restructuring and management, which prioritized the needs of the labour market and the colonial order. Despite such attempts to address the Caribbean family's 'innate dysfunction', these concerns persisted, eventually punctuating the domestic violence lobby in Trinidad and Tobago and the resulting legislation.

As Lazarus-Black (2003) suggests, re-gendering state practices – bringing previously unacknowledged acts of harm to women to public and legal attention – does not always guarantee or even centre women's equity (see also Alexander 1994; Robinson 2000). Tracking the evolution of Trinidad and Tobago's Domestic Violence Act illustrates the effects of such failures and their relationship to conceptualizations of the domestic sphere. For instance, definitions of family were overtly negotiated in initial debates about the Domestic Violence Bill. The first iteration of the legislation allowed individuals of the opposite sex in common-law relationships to access the act's provisions, but precluded those in visiting relationships. This was rectified in 1999. The 2020 amendments were accompanied by fierce disputes about whether individuals in same-sex relationships should be granted access to the legislation's provisions. This would have countered the existing language, which meticulously described varying expressions of conjugality and domestic living arrangements that could constitute domestic violence but excluded same-sex unions (see Pitt 2017). The proposed changes were not passed, leaving queer women and those in same-sex relationships without access to the act's remedies and further putting them in harm's way. Such decisions illuminate how the persistent hierarchization of family forms undergirds the exclusion of women who fall outside of the boundaries of normative domestic relations. They are also a reminder of how the state is implicated in the family's discursive production, the regulation of sexed and gendered subjects, and the inaction that exacts further violence on the women it is charged to protect.

NOTES

1. This research was supported by the Social Science and Humanities Research Council of Canada and the International Development Research Centre.
2. Interview data is drawn from a larger qualitative study exploring the provision of domestic violence support services in Trinidad and Tobago. The data, collected between 2012 and 2016, was generated from interviews with thirty-three social support workers and key informants, document analysis and observation. Pseudonyms have been used to protect respondents' identities.
3. This does not imply that the enslaved did not develop complex kinship networks. Familial ties, both blood and fictive, were important to navigating slave life and enacting resistance (Chamberlain 2006). The parameters of kinship could be and were overtly and violently manipulated, and enslaved women and men were excluded from possessing the status and rights associated with parenthood (see Patterson 1982; Rowley 2011).
4. Chamberlain (2014) notes that marriages among the enslaved were not encouraged or acknowledged by civil and church institutions before the late eighteenth century. Writing of Trinidad, Reddock (1994) illustrates how in the years following the abolition of the slave trade, regulations were introduced to prohibit the division of enslaved biological families through sale, and there was a concerted effort to encourage marriage among the enslaved.
5. In making this suggestion, I am not simply situating the family as a sphere of producing conformity, as women and men constantly negotiated and resisted these idealized family forms. Rather, I wish to highlight the colonial logic and liberal doctrines mobilized to inform the 'ideal' family.

6. Colonial commentators dominantly viewed these murders as Indian men's 'natural' response to being greatly outnumbered by Indian women during this period of indentureship, and as a result of the innate character of Indians – fiercely jealous, uncontrollable and violent men responding to women's immoral and loose behaviours.
7. British Guiana's Heathen Marriage Ordinance of 1860 allowed Hindus and Muslims access to husband-and-wife status (Robinson 2006). Trinidad made legal provisions in 1863 to allow for Indian immigrants to have civil marriages performed by wardens, and in 1881 a law was introduced that allowed for the recognition of 'heathen' marriages, once registered within six months of the religious ceremony. The need for the subsequent registration of marriages was only repealed in the 1900s when laws allowed for the registration of Hindu and Muslims marriage officers.
8. This intervention was first approved in British Guiana in 1873 and was later adopted by other colonial territories.
9. While colonial domestic ideals were being shaped through legal and educational interventions as pathways to civility, the realities for many women and men contradicted these ideals. In Trinidad, "housewifization" did not proceed as expected and women's participation remained significant in agriculture, manual labour and petty production and trade until the 1930s (Reddock 1994).
10. Even after the 1999 amendments, the theme of protecting the family persisted, with guidance noting that the court, when deliberating on domestic violence cases, must have regard for "the need to preserve and protect the institution of marriage . . . affording protection and assistance to the family as a unit" (Domestic Violence Act 1999, 13).

REFERENCES

Alexander, M. Jacqui. 1994. "Not Just (Any) Body Can Be a Citizen: The Politics of Law, Sexuality and Postcoloniality in Trinidad and Tobago and the Bahamas." *Feminist Review* 48: 5–23.

Antrobus, Peggy. 1988. "Women in Development Programmes: The Caribbean Experience (1975–1985)." In *Gender in Caribbean Development*, edited by Patricia Mohammed and Cathy Shepherd, 35–52. Kingston: University of the West Indies.

Babb, Cecilia. 1997. "Taking Action against Violence: A Case Study of Trinidad and Tobago." In *Violence Against Women: Breaking the Silence*, edited by Ann Marie Brasiliero, 100–14. New York: United Nations Development Fund for UNIFEM.

Baksh-Soodeen, R. 1998. "Issues of Difference in Contemporary Caribbean Feminism." *Feminist Review* 59 (1): 74–85.

Barnes, Monica. 1991. "Responses to Violence Against Women." Paper prepared for the Regional Meeting on Women, Violence and the Law. Sponsored by CAFRA; Rape Crisis Society of Trinidad and Tobago; UNECLAC. Port of Spain, Trinidad and Tobago.

Barriteau, Eudine. 1998. "Theorizing Gender Systems and the Project of Modernity in the Twentieth-Century Caribbean." *Feminist Review* 59 (1): 186–210.

———. 2001. *The Political Economy of Gender in the Twentieth-Century Caribbean.* London: Palgrave Macmillan.

Beckles, Hilary. 1999. *Centering Woman: Gender Discourses in Caribbean Slave Society.* Kingston: Ian Randle Publishers.

Bishop, Joan. October, 1991. "*Out of The Abyss: Opening Doors and Minds.*" Paper prepared for the Caribbean Regional Conference on Community-Based Response to Violence, Child Abuse and Sexual Abuse, St Thomas, Virgin Islands.

Chamberlain, Mary. 2006. *Family Love in the Diaspora: Migration and the Anglo-Caribbean Experience.* New Brunswick, NJ: Transaction Publishers.

———. 2014. "Legacy and Lineage: Family Histories in the Caribbean." In *Emancipation and the Remaking of the British Imperial World*, edited by Keith McClelland, Nicholas Draper, and Catherine Hall. Manchester: Manchester University Press.

Daly, Stephanie. 1982. *The Developing Legal Status of Women in Trinidad and Tobago.* Port of Spain: National Commission on the Status of Women.

Domestic Violence Act. 1999. "Chapter 45:56." Port of Spain: Parliament of Trinidad and Tobago.

Egerton, Douglas R. 2003. "A Peculiar Mark of Infamy: Dismemberment, Burial, and Rebelliousness in Slave Societies." In *Mortal Remains: Death in Early America*, edited by Nancy Isenberg and Andrew Burstein, 149–60. Philadelphia: University of Pennsylvania Press.

Gopaul, Roanna, and Maureen Cain. 1996. "Violence Between Spouses in Trinidad and Tobago: A Research Note." *Caribbean Quarterly* 42 (2/3): 28–40.

Gopaul, Roanna, Paula Morgan, and Rhoda Reddock. 1994. *Women, Family and Family Violence in the Caribbean: The Historical and Contemporary Experience with Special Reference to Trinidad and Tobago.* Prepared for the Caricom Secretariat. St Augustine: Centre for Gender and Development Studies, University of the West Indies.

Hall, Catherine. 1995. "Gender Politics and Imperial Politics." In *Engendering History:*

Caribbean Women in Historical Perspective, edited by Verene Shepherd, Bridget Brereton, and Barbara Bailey, 48–59. New York: Palgrave Macmillan.

Henderson, Thelma. 1988. "The Contemporary Women's Movement in Trinidad and Tobago". In *Gender in Caribbean Development*, edited by Patricia Mohammed and CathyShepherd, 363–72. Kingston: University of the West Indies.

Lazarus-Black, Mindie. 2003. "The (Heterosexual) Regendering of a Modern State: Criminalizing and Implementing Domestic Violence Law in Trinidad." *Law & Social Inquiry* 28 (4): 979–1008. https://doi.org/10.1111/j.1747-4469.2003.tb00829.x.

———. 2007. *Everyday Harm: Domestic Violence, Court Rites, and Cultures of Reconciliation*. Chicago: University of Illinois Press.

Lewis, Gail. 2000. *'Race', Gender, Social Welfare: Encounters in a Postcolonial Society*. Cambridge: Polity Press.

Mohammed, Patricia. 1991. "Reflections on the Women's Movement in Trinidad: Calypsos, Changes and Sexual Violence." *Feminist Review* 38 (1): 33–47. https://doi.org/10.1057/fr.1991.18.

Mohapatra, Prabhu. 1995. "'Restoring the Family': Wife Murders and the Making of a Sexual Contract for Indian Immigrant Labour in the British Caribbean Colonies, 1860–1920." *Studies in History* 11 (2): 227–60.

Nicholas, Elizabeth. 1990. "Patriarchal Power and Women's Resistance in Trinidad." Master's thesis, Institute of Social Studies, The Hague.

Pasley, Victoria. 1997. "Black Power, Gender Ideology, Cultural Change and the Beginning of Feminist Discourse in Urban Trinidad in the 1970s." Working Paper No. 2. St Augustine: Centre for Gender and Development Studies. University of the West Indies.

———. 2001. "The Black Power Movement in Trinidad: An Exploration of Gender and Cultural Changes and the Development of a Feminist Consciousness." *Journal of International Women's Studies* 3 (1): 25–42.

Patrick, Nesta. 1988. "My Views on Women's Involvement in Organizations in Trinidad andTobago and the Caribbean." In *Gender in Caribbean Development*, edited by PatriciaMohammed and Cathy Shepherd, 357–62. Kingston: University of the West Indies.

Patterson, Orlando. 1982. *Slavery and Social Death: A Comparative Study*. Cambridge, MA: Harvard University Press.

Pitt, Kendra-Ann. 2017. "Exploring Domestic Violence Social Support Work in PostcolonialTrinidad and Tobago: Old Talk, New Conversations." Unpublished PhD diss., University of Toronto.

Reddock, Rhoda. 1987. "The Women in Revolt." In *The Trinidad Labour Riots of 1937:Perspectives 50 Years Later,* edited by Roy Thomas, 233–64. St Augustine: University of the West Indies.

———. 1988. "The Quality of Life: A Commentary." In *Trinidad and Tobago : The Independence Experience, 1962–1987,* edited by Selwyn D. Ryan and Gloria Gordon, 495–503. St Augustine: University of the West Indies, Institute of Social and Economic Research.

———. 1994. *Women, Labour and Politics in Trinidad and Tobago: A History.* London: Zed Books.

———. 1996. "Women and Poverty in Trinidad and Tobago." *Beyond Law* 5 (14): 87–95.

———. 1998. "Women's Organizations and Movements in the Commonwealth Caribbean: The Response to Global Economic Crisis in the 1980s." *Feminist Review* 59 (1): 57–73.

———. 2008. "Global Feminist Networks on Domestic Violence." In *Women, Crime and Social Harm: Towards a Criminology for the Global Age,* edited by Maureen Cain and Adrian Howe, 179–200. Oxford: Hart Publishing.

———. 2010. "The Early Women's Movement in Trinidad and Tobago, 1900–1937." In*Selected Essays of Rhoda Reddock,* edited by Rhoda Reddock, 103–20. Alexandria,VA: Alexander Street Press.

Robinson, Tracy. 2000. "Fictions of Citizenship, Bodies without Sex: The Production and Effacement of Gender in Law." *Small Axe* 4 (7): 1–27.

———. 2006. *Taxonomies of Conjugality.* Hauser Global Law School Program, New York University School of Law.

———. 2013. "The Properties of Citizens: A Caribbean Grammar of Conjugal Categories." *Du Bois Review* 10 (2): 425–46. https://doi.org/10.1017/S1742058X13000209.

Rose, Nikolas. 1999. *Governing the Soul: The Shaping of the Private Self,* 2nd ed. London: Free Association Books.

Rose, Nikolas, and Peter Miller. 2010. "Political Power beyond the State: Problematics of Government." *British Journal of Sociology* 61 (S1): 271–303. https://doi.org/10.1111/j.1468-4446.2009.01247.x.

Rowley, Michelle. 2011. *Feminist Advocacy and Gender Equity in the Anglophone Caribbean: Envisioning a Politics of Coalition.* New York: Routledge.

Samaroo, Brinsley. 2014. "The February Revolution (1970) as a Catalyst for Change in Trinidad and Tobago." In *Black Power in the Caribbean,* edited by Kate Quinn, 97–116. Gainesville: University Press of Florida. https://doi.org/10.2307/j.ctvx074ws.7.

Sen, Gita, and Caren Grown. 1987. *Development, Crises, and Alternative Visions: Third World Women's Perspectives.* New Feminist Library. New York: Monthly Review Press.

Sheller, Mimi. 2012. *Citizenship from Below: Erotic Agency and Caribbean Freedom.* Durham, NC: Duke University Press.

Simey, Thomas Spensley. 1946. *Welfare and Planning in the West Indies.* Oxford: Clarendon Press.

Thomas, Deborah A. 2009. "The Violence of Diaspora: Governmentality, Class Cultures, and Circulations." *Radical History Review* 103: 83–104.

———. 2011. *Exceptional Violence: Embodied Citizenship in Transnational Jamaica.* Durham, NC: Duke University Press.

Trotz, D. Alissa. 2003. "Behind the Banner of Culture? Gender, Race, and the Family in Guyana." *Nieuwe West-Indische Gids* 77 (1): 5–29.

———. 2009. "The Caribbean Family?" In *A Companion to Gender Studies,* edited by Audrey Lynn Kobayashi, Philomena Essed, and David Theo Goldberg, 370–80. Oxford: Wiley-Blackwell.

West India Royal Commission. 1945. *Report of the West India Royal Commission.* ParliamentaryPaper by Command 6607. London: His Majesty's Stationery Office.

Working Women for Social Progress. 1995. "Working Women for Social Progress Has Launched a Round of Workshops to Campaign Against Increasing Domestic Violence." Press release.

SECTION 6

ACTIVISM FOR CHANGE: REFLECTIONS AND PERSPECTIVES

chapter 22

Everybody's Business

Reflecting on Red Thread's Anti-Violence Advocacy in Guyana

Susan Collymore, Karen de Souza, Halima Khan, Joy Marcus, Vanessa Ross and Wintress White, with Alissa Trotz

ESTABLISHED IN 1986, RED THREAD IS AN INDEPENDENT, multiracial women's organization that focuses on grassroots women's lives across differences. We do not ask and have never been interested in political party loyalties. Our work is carefully structured with this principle in mind, focusing instead on how issues like the cost of living, defending the rights of low-wage workers, and reproductive rights and health provide spaces for grassroots women to break silences, see and learn from each other, building relations of trust in the process of transformation. Red Thread's work can be grouped into three overlapping areas of concern: political voice, with a particular focus on enabling grassroots women to advocate for themselves and their communities; living income; and domestic, gender-based, economic, state and other forms of violence.

Writing about the Caribbean, Red Thread co-founder Andaiye notes, "In all our territories there is a great deal of violence, and all of that violence is turned inwards" (Andaiye 2020, 35). We understand her to be referring to how we have been unable to move past histories of violence – indigenous dispossession, slavery, indentureship – and the ways in which they turn us against each other. Guyana today is a country with some of the most advanced legislation, but recent statistics show that more than 50 per cent of women (55 per cent) who have been in a relationship have experienced intimate partner violence, compared with figures of 33 per cent for women globally (Rodney and Bobbili 2018).[1] In this chapter we reflect on Red Thread's engagement with gender-based violence, focusing on domestic violence against women and girls.[2] This is not a comprehensive account, but a discussion of some key themes and activities that have defined our approach over three decades of organizing.

"VIOLENCE IS ALL AROUND US"

Everyday violence is a key part of the story of how some women got involved with Red Thread. We share three stories (names have been changed); they may not be easy to read but they are ours and we believe it is important to name violence in order to challenge it.

Edith's story:

> I was living in a rural area and was in a very abusive relationship, and a person said Red Thread was coming into our community and would be sharing out money. At that time, I was hungry for days and thinking about what could happen if I had a little money of my own. I was not allowed to go anywhere other than the backdam, so I change off into backdam clothes, walk through the backdam and change back when I got to the meeting place.[3] I was the first one present. When Red Thread said they came to do a workshop, I was vexed. They said the workshop was on domestic violence and it still didn't register but when they started, I began to recognise myself in it. I said, this is worth more than money, and right then I said I will stay because I knew I might get some help and support. They came around the room with a microphone for people to talk, but I didn't, because everybody is interconnected in my community and it would have gotten back to my partner and I would get more blows. The community knew I was getting blows, and if the littlest child complained to my husband was blows, everything for me was blows. People were laughing and saying, "Edith, you does get licks – you should talk." One of the Red Thread women said, "If the girl don't want talk, y'all don't force her."
>
> After more workshops I was still in an abusive situation, but it was different because I recognized it was wrong and that people out there would support you. But he never eased up. Red Thread had given me some money to create

a business. I bought some green bananas and stashed them away to ripen. Then my father died and I had to leave for a bit, and my sister told me that the bananas began to ripen and smell. My husband found them and began to destroy them, and I lost my money. The last licking I get was a lash with a drink bottle in my head. That night all I heard in my head was "tick, tick, tick". When I wiped my nose, there was blood. When I touched my ears, there was blood. And even with that, the man ran in to beat me some more. I ran upstairs to his mother, and he came after me with his son in his hand and a cutlass, trying to force his way in. Eventually I ran down the back step and through the cow pen. That was the last time.

I was the one who had to move. I went to his family but after the man of the house [who was his family] said I couldn't stay, I came to Georgetown. In Red Thread I found support. They made me see that nobody should go through what I went through. I was intolerable, there was so much going on in my head. I had drunk poison and was found on the brink of death. I was not a nice person back then – I would lash out at everything. I had a lot of paranoia. It took years, and a lot of patience from Red Thread, to get me to where I am now. I especially remember the health team.[4] There was a time I could not eat, and I remember they would take food and put it in my mouth and tell me when to swallow, and encourage me to eat.

Sharmini's story:

I was always in the house, yard, look after cows, go in the rice field. I thought I needed a break, but my husband didn't see it that way. Red Thread formed a group in this area, and when they invited persons to a meeting, I seized the opportunity and went, and after that I kept going to meetings until I was afforded an opportunity to come to town for training. It wasn't easy. When I got home, I never told the team members, but sometimes I was barely able to get an hour sleep. He was verbally abusive. When we travelled for workshops, that was a next issue, because at the car park you had to wait until the minibus was full before it would leave to take you home. But I endured it because I had wanted to let him see the other side of me. When I started receiving the little stipend from Red Thread, I would not discuss it with him. But I used to discuss it with my big son, and one day he put his father to sit down and said, "Daddy, it is high time you come off this stupidness. What Mommy doing is to benefit everybody." Then he started to loose his grip a little. He changed but not a whole lot. It was really terrible.

Jean's story: Jean had been raped but the police were not doing anything about her case. She was frustrated and afraid because the rapist was moving about freely. In her frustration, she attempted to kill herself. The police were about to charge her with attempted suicide (they charges were later dropped). Upon learning about this incident in the news, we decided to stage a protest in solidarity outside the police station, and we also made representations to the Director of Public Prosecution in relation to the threat to charge Jean. Jean's sister saw the news and called her about it. Neither of them knew about us, but they looked us up in the telephone directory and called to express their gratitude, and Jean said she would like to join us on the picket line. She became a member of our network, Grassroots Women Across Race (GWAR), and since then she has been working in the drop-in centre and championing the court support work.

It is not easy to recover from years of abuse. Edith engaged in deeply self-destructive behaviour and vented her anger on the women in Red Thread; Sharmini was ashamed to share her husband's ongoing verbal attacks when she returned home from conducting workshops (including ones on domestic violence); faced with the lack of accountability, Jean attempted to take her life. For all three, the grassroots women of Red Thread offered the space to break ingrained patterns of violence. The importance of having structures in place that can support women materially, emotionally and psychologically cannot be underestimated.

We see how violence not only takes many forms – financial, physical, emotional and verbal – but is tangled up in many other issues. Making a change is often defined as the act of exiting an abusive relationship, but it becomes – and feels like – an individual action and is very difficult to accomplish when society is largely unsupportive, and where, as in the case of Sharmini, one has children to support. The exit journey is not a straight line. Edith made many attempts to leave her husband – in fact she had even returned at one point and got married to him – and it was not until she was nearly killed that she fled for good. Looking back, she cited "hardship and family pressure" as keeping her in place. Family pressure refers to the general expectation that what happens between a man and woman is their business, and this is reproduced in the community, where Edith's abuse was known, but no one intervened. In the absence of support – including in-laws who refused to house her – Edith had to leave her community. And it was Red Thread's public support that offered Jean a lifeline in a moment of complete despair, traumatized by the violence she faced from her rapist and the cruelty of the police who tried to charge her.

Hardship is a form of violence that makes women materially dependent on men. Edith and Sharmini were denied opportunities to earn their own incomes, although they were expected to contribute time and labour farming and looking after livestock. For Edith, access to an income was a matter of daily survival – literally finding food for herself – and the reason she attended her first Red Thread meeting, whereas Sharmini wanted a change from a highly restrictive routine that kept her firmly under her husband's control. Economic independence was key to enabling them to make key decisions about their relationships, but as these stories underline, it was the wider structure of support from Red Thread that allowed both women to reflect on their situations and confront their abusers.

VIOLENCE IS EVERYBODY'S BUSINESS

Red Thread's initial focus was on income-generation for grassroots women as a way of tackling economic violence. Domestic violence was not centrally on the agenda, but it kept coming up in community workshops on topics like water and sanitation and women's reproductive health.[5] You can't talk about the pressures of everyday life without encountering the question of violence. In 1988, members of the Sistren Theatre Collective from Jamaica came to Guyana for about six weeks to train Red Thread women "in the use of participatory methods of popular education, drama and skit development, and workshop technique" (Andaiye 2000, 65). In 1990, four women from Red Thread travelled to Jamaica to work with Sistren, and we also worked with the Women and Development Unit in Barbados on workshops titled "A Woman's Place". Some of the popular theatre methods we learned were put into practice in our community outreach as we began to focus on domestic violence. In the early 1990s, Red Thread was part of a regional campaign by the Caribbean Association for Feminist Research and Action (CAFRA) to raise awareness about domestic violence. We worked on a radio serial, covering a number of different and related issues: school dropouts; teenage pregnancy; domestic violence; single-parent households, and so on. We dealt with issues of poverty, discussing why people stay in certain situations and identifying where they could go to get help. The script drew on some of our own experiences. The programme director at the government radio station at the time was very supportive and we recorded it there for free. It was first aired in 1993 and subsequently rebroadcast.[6]

We decided to turn *Everybody's Business* into a play. Danuta Radzik (one of Red Thread's co-founders) transcribed the radio serial, and we worked with the neighbour of a Red Thread member in the mining town of Linden, a man who ran drama groups and who produced a script for us and directed it. We took it to several schools in 1994 (Linden on the Demerara coast, and Charity, St John's and Hackney on the Pomeroon River). Staging the plays made the issues come alive so that people could see and relate to them.

Focusing on domestic violence became a central part of our community outreach. We would go from house to house and invite people to come out. We would find an ice breaker that related to what we wanted to focus on, and we would act out a skit about violence to get the conversation going. Sometimes we encouraged participants to act out the parts themselves. That approach was successful in bringing a lot of people in; depending on the size of the audience, we would split participants up into smaller groups, which led to very lively discussions.

Help and Shelter, an NGO established in 1995 that works "against all types of violence, especially domestic and sexual violence and child abuse" and supports victims/survivors, and Red Thread were central to the development of Guyana's National Domestic Violence Policy, as well as ensuring the passage and implementation of the Domestic Violence Act (DVA) in 1996, and later, the Sexual Offences Act in 2010 (both Help and Shelter and Red Thread sat on the Task Force for the Prevention of Sexual Violence). With the DVA, there is no point in having legislation to protect survivors if those most affected could not understand it; "[b]y making the Act accessible to people, the household guide and accompanying workshops contribute to the task of making it work" (Andaiye 2000, 92). We spent a lot of time trying to understand the law, and then we prepared a simplified booklet, *The Household Guide to the Domestic Violence Act* (Red Thread 1996). We printed a few thousand copies, which were distributed to households, Help and Shelter, and Legal Aid, the Women's Affairs Bureau (WAB), and the police, and we conducted participatory workshops in several communities. We gave permission to the WAB and anyone else to reprint the booklet so that it could be made widely available. For another booklet, *Domestic Violence: A National Problem*, we extracted and repurposed information from women's health books, and distributed them to communities, organizations and the police – although, without the same kind of funding, we were unable to print as many copies. Our work has also entailed conducting research on domestic violence, and the knowledge that we gained has come to inform our advocacy (Red Thread and Peake 2000; see Kempadoo 2013 on method).[7]

Having laws in place is one thing – ensuring they are implemented properly requires constant oversight. The courts were very resistant to granting protection orders to survivors, and the attitudes of magistrates were deeply problematic. Help and Shelter and Red Thread were represented on the oversight committee set up by the government for the implementation of the National Domestic Violence Policy, and out of this work we started going into the courts to monitor what was going on and to support and advocate with survivors.

Domestic violence advocacy has taken the form of picketing exercises and letter-writing campaigns to raise public awareness and advocate for change. Some of this work has international and regional dimensions. For several years, Red Thread coordinated a national International Women's Day march and demonstration with the Global Women's Strike, and violence against women has been a regular focus. In 2017, we joined several Guyanese women's, children's and LGBTQ organizations for a regional march that focused on survivors of violence (Podur and Cummings 2017).[8]

SPACE

Questions of space are important to understanding Red Thread's advocacy, but this goes beyond a straightforward understanding of having our own space, which we did not have for several years. Thinking about space has to do with understanding that domestic violence is not something that takes place in a private domain. It is not a discrete event; it pervades everything – something we come back to in the final section of this chapter. Thinking about space is also important to how Red Thread has sought to do its organizing and advocacy across the communities we work with. Our work takes a decentralized approach through direct community engagement. People would talk about violence, or pull us aside after meetings, and sometimes we would quietly approach others who had been pointed out to us. People would ask us where they could go to get help, which organizations they could contact.

It has not been easy to find resources to put structures in place in communities so that they could advocate for themselves. When we were able to access modest resources, Red Thread worked with five communities on the coast and in the interior, holding workshops and identifying and training a few monitors who would become point persons for survivors. We established support groups which included men – businesspersons, regional democratic councillors, *toshaos* [Indigenous village leaders], religious and spiritual leaders, police, health workers, teachers and others who could intervene and help handle a situation. Local interventions are key as they return power to the community – as opposed to believing that problems must always be referred to a central location. It makes a difference when communities understand the law and the power and responsibility of the system and are prepared to insist on their right to have these systems work in their interests. Resources need to be put into expanding this across Guyana.

A big part of the work has to do with changing how women experience and move through different spaces as they navigate violent situations. So, for instance, when a survivor comes to Red Thread, that support entails accompanying them to the police station, attending hearings at the magistrate and High Court; and if someone has to go for a medical examination, we accompany them. In several cases, we have housed survivors in our homes and at the centre. But our work goes beyond this – advocacy is about self-emancipation. Survivors need to learn about the system so that they can represent themselves, especially in the event that they cannot reach us. For instance, we couldn't make it to a court appointment with a survivor, and she was able to use what she had learned from working with us to make her own case successfully before the magistrate. She called us afterwards all excited, saying "Y'all think I didn't learning!" She was able to stand up to the prosecutor and represent herself before the magistrate, drawing on her knowledge of the Domestic Violence Act.

In addition to court support and ensuring that survivors understand the legal process, we have trained police on domestic violence issues, and we have worked with magistrates – observing how they were handling issues in court and bringing our concerns forward. There was a case in which the father had been accused of molesting his daughter and the mother feared for her life. We were present in court and taking notes as we normally do when we are observing the proceedings, and the magistrate ordered the clerk to confiscate our jottings and instructed us to leave the court and not return. Red Thread ended up filing a formal complaint against this magistrate. The relationship is straightforward, but we have definitely gone from a situation where we were treated with great suspicion by the police and the judiciary to being recognized when we show up in court.

HALIMA'S STORY

There was an interior community where we had been doing workshops on domestic violence and training community monitors. A girl had been raped a few days before we returned to continue the work. As soon as we got off the plane, the women who we were training met us and told us about the case. They said that the girl was in the hospital and nothing was happening. We went straight from the plane to the hospital to meet with her, and it was our intervention that brought that case before the court – we just started moving and getting behind the police to act. At first, they told us that they had received the report but they had not arrested or questioned anyone; in fact, they had done nothing. Once we got busy, you should have seen the police start to buckle down! They decided to take a statement from the girl in our presence. We were also at the initial hearings. The magistrate was calling the survivor by her name, and I got so mad, I forgot that I was in a court. I stood up and interrupted the proceedings and said, "With due respect, Sir, you're not supposed to be calling the virtual complainant's name in court." But the magistrate kept insisting on doing this, and the girl was not answering him. Other Red Thread women were nudging me, telling me to calm down. The magistrate got mad and asked, "Who the hell is this woman and these people?" He hurled some insults at us and then he adjourned the court. After we had a meeting with the community monitors, it was clear that they were scared and seemed ready to back off. We discussed the situation and realized that the magistrate was wrong, but the manner in which we challenged him did not get the result we had hoped for, and we agreed that the best way forward was to set an example. So, we reached out to the prosecutor and the magistrate to apologize for interrupting his court and to give him the respect that was due. And actually, after we apologized, he also apologized and said we are supposed to be working together and not against each other. He decided to make that case the priority before we left, and ended up committing it to the High Court. He told us, "To err is human" and those four words stuck in my head. They stayed there all these years (also see Seales 2009). There are a few local lawyers whom we have turned to for legal advice, and Caribbean lawyers from the University of the West Indies' Rights Action Project have also conducted workshops and community legal training with Red Thread and Guyana Trans United on issues related to violence against women, girls and trans persons.

Before we acquired our own building, we got temporary space in Georgetown. Once we had an available office and an accessible place, people started to come to us. It was word of mouth as we don't advertise, and sometimes police and magistrates would refer survivors to us. Once we moved to our permanent building, this work continued.[9] We had written reports and letters to the newspapers and some of our work was being reported in the press, and people saw that and started coming to the centre. We formed the Domestic Violence Survivors Self-Help Support Group (DVSSHSG), which included the women we would have gone to court with. The main purpose was to draw strength from each other. The DVSSHSG was also a space for group therapy, for having discussions about how survivors felt, where they could vent their frustrations with their families, communities, the police, and more. We were also working with children through a literacy programme we had established, and through our engagement with their parents, we encountered all kinds of issues and we realized that some of the children were living in situations of violence.

Sometime after the formation of the DVSSHSG, we established a drop-in centre. We had been talking about it for a long time; sometimes conversations happen and you don't do anything about them and then an opportunity presents itself. We met churchwomen who were visiting Guyana from the World Day of Prayer, and we were invited to apply for funding. This allowed us to set up an accessible and child-friendly space in 2005–2006. For a while, we even had a safe space for supervised visitations – this came about because there was a woman we were supporting in court and the High Court judge asked what our role was and after that case they would occasionally refer families with custody matters to us for visitation and exchange. We've had a number of university students in violent situations who were referred to us. But most of the women who came in were grassroots. On the few occasions that middle-class professional women approach Red Thread, they always ask to speak directly to co-founder and co-ordinator Karen de Souza, and that is a class thing. They soon recognize or are advised that these matters are dealt with by grassroots women who deal with the authorities on a daily basis.

There needs to be as many people on the ground dealing with gender-based violence in our society as possible; everyone brings their strengths to the table. In Red Thread, the grassroots women are not trained social workers or counsellors. But we have a saying that we have used elsewhere in our work, "Who feels it knows it". We don't operate as if we're coming from a different place, as if the survivor has the problem and not us, or as if we are better than anyone else. The grassroots women understand domestic violence because we are survivors and we have learned not to be ashamed of that (others might also have experienced violence but they make it their business not to disclose this in the work they do). We will show up throughout the survivor's journey through the system. Grassroots women are coming from a place where we know that what is needed is change, not help. Our practice involves sharing our experience so that survivors can feel comfortable and know that they are not alone.

A WORLD WITHOUT VIOLENCE: NAMING THE CHALLENGES, MAKING THE CONNECTIONS

Addressing violence systematically requires sustained public investment. A lot of work has been done with the magistrates to expose them to understanding gender-based violence in relation to questions of power (several projects have brought in psychologists, judges and other professionals from the region and beyond), and you can see the difference in the way some of them approach cases. But much of this training is the result of one-off initiatives funded by international organizations. We need perpetrator programmes attached to courts, and support for survivors. The university could train counsellors for these positions. Ongoing public education is key, because family and community members – including faith leaders – are part of the problem; carrying news to perpetrators; putting pressure on the woman to stay; being abusers themselves.

We have to deal seriously with the police; we are still getting the same answers that we did years ago when we first started this work. The supervision and monitoring that takes place in the stations is not good enough. If there is a certain kind of violence, we call the police. For example, we once had to trap a man in the centre who came in looking for a woman he wanted to kill. But it is important to recognize that the police force is a reflection of the violent society that we live in. There is violence in their ranks; there are victims and perpetrators of violence in their homes; and they bring those responses to the people who go to them. Answers to violence do not come from an institution born out of violence.

The solution to violence "cannot be just at the level of the individual household", a point that Andaiye made in her discussion of an African-Guyanese woman, Sonia Hinds, whose partner maimed her for life, making it impossible to support her children on her previous precarious jobs as a part-time seamstress and security guard, leaving her dependent on public assistance. Andaiye concludes, "We have to build a movement not only against the injustices of sex or the injustices of race, but against the economic system that we increasingly treat as a given – immovable – and which exploits and oppresses Sonia Hinds via the unequal power relations of sex, race, class, age, dis/ability and nation. Nothing less can liberate her" (Andaiye 2020, 203, 204).

Guyana is now becoming a major oil producer; what we are seeing on the ground is increasing inequalities between rich and poor, and a skyrocketing cost of living. We need to ask questions about an economic system that makes it difficult for grassroots women to get access to a living income, which will enable us to make decisions about our own lives. Young mothers can't keep a job when they cannot afford daycare, and at any rate the hours are not flexible. One of the things we would love to establish is a 24-hour daycare facility, while at the same time advocating for better working conditions for all. We have been tracking household budgets, and the current minimum wage cannot keep up with the prices of the most basic commodities (Red Thread 2022c; 2022d). Our focus on a living income and our anti-violence work are deeply interrelated; today the Self-Help Drop-In Centre – renamed in 2013 after Red Thread member and domestic violence survivor Cora Belle and Clotil Walcott, Trinidadian founder of the National Union of Domestic Employees – provides support for and advocates with survivors of domestic violence, as well as low-wage workers. It's all well and good to tell people, We have strong laws, you should go to the police, make a report, leave the man, but then what? A number of the women whom we have supported to leave – including some of us – end up going back into those relationships or end up in another abusive situation.

We have been saying for a long time that there should be dedicated, safe, long-term social housing for survivors that is affordable or free and protected. A minority of women have access to shelters; we have ended up occasionally using our building to house women, but this is not sustainable. And the grassroots women we see have little income security – they are security guards, or domestic workers, or salespersons, or doing unpaid work as housewives, or pensioners – and this affects the choices they can make, regardless of what they really want.

Our experience over three decades of domestic violence work is that integrated social investment is not what governments are prepared to spend resources on – we have ministries with designated responsibility (in Guyana, it is the Ministry of Human Services and Social Security), even though this is an issue that touches employment, housing, judicial services and more. It is also our experience that the state continues to push the responsibility for addressing domestic violence on other groups. Those who are in positions of power may have the language of zero tolerance down; most recently, the government announced a Men on Mission initiative to address violence ("President Ali's Men on Mission initiative launched across Guyana," *Guyana Chronicle*, 20 November 2022), but that is it. And it starts from the top. There is a bad track record of holding powerful persons accountable for acts of violence, especially if they are part of or connected to whoever is in political office at the time. The laws protect the powerful. And disgracefully, female parliamentarians are part of the problem; they close ranks through silence or excuses or pointing fingers at the 'other side', instead of condemning violence, regardless of who the offender is.[10] As Andaiye has noted, this kind of backward position enables "leaders who abuse women to set the standard for the kind of Caribbean civilization we are building" (Andaiye 2020, 217).

In Guyana, our political system is polarized along racial lines, making it difficult to bring people together, even for an issue as important as this. While most of the violence that targets women is at the hands of someone they know, we have also challenged other forms of gender-based and inter-racial violence related to our politics– for instance, speaking out against violence meted out to Indian-Guyanese women during and immediately after elections, or the deadly targeting of African-Guyanese men by the state (see Trotz 2004; 2014; 2020). A lot ends up coming down to groups and individuals, like the advocacy of organizations such as Help and Shelter, and there are limits. For example, Red Thread receives no government subventions. Much of our work consists of our unwaged contributions. Finding resources has been a constant struggle (see Andaiye 2000). Funders – mainly international – have enabled important work. But it means spending time engaging potential donors, working on proposals, and this is not a sustainable response to an ongoing crisis of violence. Plus, it puts organizations under pressure to be accountable to the timelines and priorities of funders, rather than to communities we work with. This work continues, funding or no funding, because it is a political issue for us, but it is not easy. The survivor self-help group does not meet anymore, and the drop-in centre is not as structured, but people still come, and we are still writing letters to the newspapers. In a lot of our earlier work in riverain and interior communities, we could not go back or sustain the work and we do not have an active physical presence in many places like we did before. But people remember us; they came to a workshop and it captured their imagination. In communities where we have trained domestic violence monitors, the women have no project money to collect, but they are still going to court, to the police, and magistrates still approach them. A lecturer from the University of Guyana asked us to go into her class and students disclosed that they were survivors of violence and identified us as their counsellors. There was another project that we did with Help and Shelter on survivor assessments of service providers. One woman singled us out, saying that she was suicidal and that we had saved her life. So, something is working.

It sometimes feels, though, like a futile exercise. What we do is really no more than a drop in the bucket in terms of an integrated, sustained systematic response to the violence all around us. With a firm focus on grassroots women, we make connections between violence against women, children, LGBTQ persons and the wider violence of societies organized around forms of living and organization based on destructive, non-sustainable and deeply exploitative relationships. And we will keep speaking out.

NOTES

1. Between January and December 2022, twenty women were killed. We write their names here and dedicate this chapter to them and to all those lost to gender-based violence: Edith Rueben, 48; Loretta Simon, 24; Savitri Raj, 57; Shenese Walks, 19; Waynmattie Permaul, 53; Deissy Perdomo, 49; Omega Ault, 39; Miriam Edwards, 25; Agnes Dillon, 86; Donalesa Park, 29; Cindy Ramchandar, 25; Tasina Dazzle, 28; Hannah Boston, 25; Vanessa Rodrigues, 36; Nirmala Sukhai, 33; Analee Gonsalves, 20; Sharon Scott, 53; Oma Devi Virasamy, 30; Kelly Charlotte, 22; Asasha Ramzan-Charles, 31.
2. This work is not limited to just women and girls; boys and men have also come in and benefitted from Red Thread's advocacy and support. Red Thread's definition of women and girls is one that accounts for trans women and girls, and we have also worked with the Society Against all Forms of Sexual Orientation Discrimination (SASOD); Guyana Trans United (GTU); and Guyana Rainbow Foundation.
3. While most settlement is on a narrow strip of Guyana's coast, the backdam refers to the inland areas where farming takes place and livestock are reared.
4. The health team, organized by Nesha Haniff in 1989/1990, ran popular education workshops on community, women's and environmental health (Andaiye 2020, 70).
5. For a detailed account of the earlier, more vibrant phases of Red Thread's work, in various communities and across the overlapping group building, education,

health and research teams in the 1980s and 1990s, see Andaiye 2000; Peacocke 1995.

6. Margaret Lawrence was the programme director. Dion Abrams and Kidackie Amsterdam read the male parts in the scripts.
7. A research team was established, then trained by Professor Linda Peake of York University to carry out interviews on household survival strategies across two communities. In addition to conducting Red Thread research on domestic violence, reproductive health, sex work and trafficking of women, the team also received contracts from the University of Guyana and the government for research projects (Andaiye 2000, 73). Red Thread members also worked alongside the Global Women's Strike to carry out an extensive time-use survey among grassroots women in Guyana (Andaiye 2020b).
8. Organizations from six countries participated, including #LifeInLeggings (Barbados), #Tambourine Army (Jamaica), Hollaback! (the Bahamas), and Womantra (Trinidad and Tobago). In Guyana, the march, dedicated to girls and against all forms of gender-based violence, was coordinated by the University of Guyana's Students' Society Against Human Rights Violations, and featured speeches by domestic violence survivors and transgender activists.
9. At one point, in the absence of money to travel, meetings were held and women lived in and worked out of the home of one of the Red Thread members in Georgetown. Temporary office space in Georgetown was provided by co-founder Jocelyn Dow, who was hugely important in accessing financial and other resources for Red Thread in its early years. The permanent location at Princess and Adelaide Streets was purchased by Red Thread with funds made available by the research consultancy on domestic violence and reproductive health; Red Thread women contributed their stipends for a year, and resource member and Professor Linda Peake of York University contributed her consultancy fee. It was an initiative led by Cora Belle, Red Thread member, who died in 2012. See Andaiye (2013); tribute to Cora Belle on the Red Thread website (https://www.redthread.org.gy).
10. Recent events include the use of sexually abusive language by members of the Guyana Teachers Union against the Minister of Education, Priya Manickchand, in 2021, a verbal assault that was amplified by Member of Parliament for the opposition coalition, Sherod Duncan; the remark made in parliament in 2022 to a female MP by MP Nigel Dharamllal from the ruling People's Progressive Party that she needed a dildo; the sexually abusive insults hurled at an Indian national in 2022 by Charrandas Persaud, then Guyanese High Commissioner to

India. While Persaud was removed from his position following public outrage, none of the parliamentarians or party activists have condemned any of these actions taken by those associated with their political parties.

REFERENCES

Andaiye. 2000. "The Red Thread Story." In *Spitting in the Wind*, edited by Suzanne Francis-Brown, 51–98. Kingston: Ian Randle Publishers.

———. 2020a. *The Point is to Change the World: Selected Writings of Andaiye*. Edited by Alissa Trotz. London: Pluto Press.

———. 2020b. "Grassroots women learning to count their unwaged work: Summary report on a 2001–2002 trial." In *The Point is to Change the World: Selected Writings of Andaiye*, edited by Alissa Trotz, 117–20. London: Pluto Press.

Help & Shelter, Red Thread, et al. 2020. "Restorative justice in domestic violence settings here will put safety and well-being of survivors at serious risk." *Stabroek News*, 18 March.

Hereman, Alessandra. 2019. *A Phenomenological Qualitative Research on Intimate Partner Violence against Trans Women in Georgetown, Guyana*. Research report, University of Guyana.

Kempadoo, K. 2013. "Red Thread's research: An interview with Andaiye." *Caribbean Review of Gender Studies* no. 7: 1–17.

Kissoon, V. 20221. "Educating others, speaking out and holding hands to build just communities." *Stabroek News*, 12 September.

Peacocke, N. 1995. *Case Study of Red Thread Women's Development Organisation, Guyana*. Regional Rural Development Strategy and Programme. Georgetown: Caribbean Network for Integrated Rural Development and Inter-American Institute for Cooperation on Agriculture.

Podur, J., and J.G. Cummings. 2017. "Women rise up against gender violence in the Caribbean." *Stabroek News*, 27 March.

Radzik, D., and J. Whitehead for Help & Shelter, et al. 2020. "Restorative justice in domestic violence settings here will put safety and well-being of survivors at serious risk." *Stabroek News*, 18 March.

Red Thread and Linda Peake. 2000. *Women Researching Women: Red Thread Report on Surveys on Domestic Violence and Women's Reproductive and Sexual Health in Guyana*. Washington, DC: Inter-American Development Bank.

Red Thread. 1996. *The Household Guide to the Domestic Violence Act of 1996*. Georgetown: Red Thread.

——— 2022a. "Red Thread calls on police to act in Ossie Rodgers assault case." *Stabroek News,* 27 October.

———. 2022b. "We continue to see and witness actions which appear to contradict social harmony." *Stabroek News,* 5 April.

———. 2022c. "Who Feels it Knows it Guyana." Posted 28 August 2022, by Red Thread Women's Centre Guyana. YouTube, 19:33. https://www.youtube.com/watch?v=77_a4AQYWH4.

———. 2022d. "Who feels it knows it." *Stabroek News,* "In the Diaspora" column, 7 November.

———. 2003. "Guyanese Women Against Violence Everywhere." Statement and signatories, Georgetown.

Rodney, R., and S. Bobbili. 2019. *Women's Health and Life Experiences: A Qualitative Research Report on Violence Against Women in Guyana.* Bridgetown: UN Women Caribbean.

Seales, I. 2009. "Region Eight grassroots women working to stamp out domestic violence." *Stabroek News,* 27 October.

Surujnauth, N. 2022. "These women should not be known as numbers or another headline; we have to say their names." *Stabroek News,* 15 December.

Trotz, D.A. 2004. "Between despair and hope: Towards an analysis of women and violence in contemporary Guyana." *Small Axe* 15: 1–25.

———. 2014. "'Lest we forget': Terror and the politics of commemoration in Guyana." In *In a Far Country: Women of Colour and the War on Terror,* edited by S. Razack and S. Perera. Toronto: University of Toronto Press.

———. 2020. "Moving forward better Guyana." *Stabroek News,* 14 September.

chapter 23

Standing with Survivors

A Reflection on Disruption, Testimony, Performance and Ritual in Jamaica's Survivor Empowerment March

Taitu Heron

THIS CHAPTER IS A PERSONAL REFLECTION ON MY involvement as a women's rights activist with the now-defunct Tambourine Army, which organized the Survivor Empowerment March in March 2017. I claim no objectivity from the participants of the movement. I am a survivor of sexual assault, intimately acquainted with the inhumanity of gender-based violence; my experience is the lens through which I see violence against women and children, and the impetus behind my activist work. I carry no pretence about how the events unfolded that led to the dissolution of the Tambourine Army, but lessons and self-growth for the ongoing journeys of women who see the power in healing. My story is at once deeply personal, sisterly, collective, divisive, spiritual, disappointing, triumphant, painful and still healing. Mine is not a singular story as there are many more to be told by others. This is a singular interpretation.

At the end of 2016, Jamaica saw a spate of femicide, where more than twenty women died at the hands of their partners in December alone. Then in Barbados, Ronelle King and Allyson Benn started what blossomed into the #LifeInLeggings movement, an online campaign where survivors of violence against women shared their experiences. The stories shared were harrowing and numerous, highlighting the pervasive nature of sexual abuse and harassment throughout the Caribbean. Another watershed moment occurred in December 2016: Rupert Clarke, a minister of the Moravian Church of Nazareth in Maidstone, Manchester, was charged with statutory rape of a girl child (*Loop Jamaica News*, 2017).[1] This called for a radical shift in how, as human rights activists, a state and society, we respond to sexual violence. A Facebook callout from Donaree Muirhead, one of the Tambourine Army's founding members – "Ah feel like bombing a church. who waa go a Nazareth?"[2] – led to about fourteen of us[3] from Kingston and Montego Bay organizing, via WhatsApp, to stage a silent T-shirt protest at the Moravian Church of Nazareth. Unexpected events unfolded: the pastor leading the service that Sunday was a known paedophile to one woman among us, and there he was at the podium, delivering a sermon to a fractured congregation,[4] reeling from the news of their previous paedophilic pastor.[5] It was an emotionally charged day that ended in one of us slapping the Reverend Paul Gardner on his head with a tambourine and all of us being chased out of the church. On our return to Kingston, five of us met at Cable Hut Beach to process it all and shared our experiences of sexual violence, particularly the experience involving Reverend Paul Gardner, who was later arrested and charged with carnal abuse. In the midst of our sharing, we mused at the instrument of choice – a tambourine, which disrupts, with orchestrated noise in church and is mostly played by women, and we joked that Michelle Serieux, also a founding member, was going to make a movie about it called *Tambourine*. This gathering at the sea led to the formation of the Tambourine Army, centred on survivor empowerment of women and girls who were sexually violated.

The Tambourine Army, according to an internal concept note, is:

> a coalition of organisations, women, and Feminists that/who have become radically fed up with the culture of silence and inertia around sexual violence in Jamaica. It calls for bold action for change. It aims to provide safe alternative spaces that facilitate the healing and empowerment of survivors, targeted public education around sexual grooming and sexual abuse, and survivor-friendly legislative reform. . . .[We] are advocates in our own right, and work in various professional fields, namely human rights advocacy, youth development, gender, development planning and management, entertainment, film and photography, academia, spirit-centred healing, security, project management, education, social work, and cyber-activism. (Tambourine Army 2017)

Figure 23.1: Core members of the Tambourine Army. *L–R (back):* Abby Brooks, Taitu Heron, Donaree Muirhead, Latoya Nugent; *L–R (front):* Shawna Stewart, Nadeen Spence, Rochelle McFee, Michelle Serieux. Photo: WE-Change Jamaica.

The Survivor Empowerment March was one of the activities of the Tambourine Army. Held on 11 March 2017, at the close of International Women's Week, it was coordinated and held in solidarity with the #LifeInLeggings movement[6] and other marches taking place across the Caribbean that day.[7] That year's theme for International Women's Day was #BeBoldForChange, and the Survivor Empowerment March was executed intentionally to welcome and acknowledge the humanity of survivors and to encourage sharing experiences of sexual violence. This bold-facedness took many forms in terms of how the Tambourine Army unfolded and what it represented at that time (Tambourine Army 2017).

"NOT A BLOODKLAAT!" – DISRUPTION

"A revolution has never started with a hug – it is going to need some disruption. . . . some disturbance of what is considered normal" Jodi-Ann Brown (interview, 2020).

The first thing required was to disrupt the respectability of the English language, how it obfuscates honesty and its epistemological stamp as to what constitutes 'appropriate' behaviour and communication. If one is going to be bold in Jamaica, English is arguably not the language of choice. When the Tambourine Army declared "Not a Bloodklaat!" and "Fire pon rapists", it was a tipping point for many who were fed up with the violence against women and girls perpetrated by certain men, and equally fed up with the culture of silence around the aftermath for survivors. Declaring "Not a Bloodklaat!" represented a form of activism that aimed to emancipate itself from previous approaches to 'decolonial' activism in Jamaica that had become bureaucratized, neutralized and ineffective because of funding arrangements with select international development organizations. "Not a Bloodklaat!" was a point of departure, a hasty, organic historical moment that sought a path influenced by ancestral veneration, Ifa/Yoruba spirituality, and the 'divine feminine' embodied by kindred association with Jamaica's Nanny of the Maroons and the Orisha Oya. We did not have it all figured out at the time, nor were we all in agreement, but we knew we had to try something new. The movement was visceral. It captured collective rage. It came from the spiritual core of experiences of survivors and we were not asking permission. It could not be guided by the Englishness of things.

The use of the African-derived word *bloodklaat* and slapping a paedophile on the head with a tambourine ruffled the dominant, Christian, middle-class sensibilities of the women's movement (Riley 2017). Senior leadership of the women's movement was already being tested by a younger generation of activists, myself included, who operated in both spaces – the women's movement and the LGBTQ+ movement – and sought an inclusive and intersectional practice. Our tactics created rifts and tension in Jamaica's women's movement, particularly with those elders who felt it was "too violent" (Miller 2017). Some were more preoccupied with the pastor's tambourine-induced injury than fighting the prevailing rape culture. Others felt that we shouldn't incite violence by using expletives. The disruption had started, and the energy had begun to shift. But what if our use of *bloodklaat* was a liberating utterance? That word was gifted to us by our former enslaved African ancestors and it captured pain and rage and disrupted stagnant energy. According to Joan French: "The 'bad word' issue of Latoya Nugent was the elephant in the room . . . reducing potential older feminist participation . . . but leaving the focus 'clean and new' . . . The march moved beyond Latoya to the issues . . . which does not mean the bad-word dividing issue was not somewhere in the background (Interview, June 2020).

Upon examination, the offence we take to the word *bloodklaat* does not belong to us. It is an internalization of the fear that former British colonizers and enslavers had of a word they did not understand. The etymology of the word – as a woman's menstrual blood cloth – is further layered with misogynist condemnation and disgust because of where it sprang from: woman. Instead of paying homage to the life force and the womanbeing that brings it, *bloodklaat* occupies a space of profanity. It needed to be elevated from the profane back to the divine. The humanity of women deserved more than silence and complicity. We were wronged; our rage was valid, but we were misunderstood and chastised for expressing it. As Brittany Cooper says: "Whenever someone weaponizes anger against black women, it is designed to silence them . . . to discredit them and to say that they are overreacting, that they are being hypersensitive, that their reaction is outsized." The question for me was: Why were more people in government, civil society, among the international development community, especially women whom we also knew as activists, *not* angry or incensed enough about the violence against women and girls?

Latoya Nugent, former co-founder of the Tambourine Army and queer activist, asked:

> When a little girl tells you that a man has touched her inappropriately, or that he molested her . . . When a woman tells you that a man raped her . . . why do we first question the veracity of that experience that may have taken much bravery and vulnerability and nakedness for the little girl or the woman to share? Why do we then consider how damaging this must be to the man's character? When a little boy tells you that a man has touched him inappropriately, or that he molested him . . . what makes us first believe the boy, become enraged and begin to do everything in our power to get justice for that little boy? Why can't we first believe our girls and our women too, and do everything in our power to get justice for them? Why don't we at all times . . . shame the perpetrator and provide healing, care and support for survivors – all survivors? What is it about a man's reputation that becomes so critical when he is accused of perpetrating

> sexual violence against women and girls that we wilfully, and sometimes blindly, disregard the very humanity of our women and girls? What kind of society have we have created for ourselves? Where is the protection of the value and dignity of our women and girls?[8] (Nugent 2017)

If the protection of and value of the humanity of women and girls were not apparent, the march was the vehicle through which space had to claim and demonstrate that value and to facilitate the testimonies of Jamaican women who survived sexual violence. The purpose of disruption meant that the march itself could not be dominated by English in form or in spirit, and so the flyer and posters[9] were done in Jamaican Patwa, our mother tongue, to capture the rage and promote the seriousness of the march as well as to be linguistically inclusive.

The march began the night before because the selected route traversed five crossroads. The meaning of the crossroads was not lost on myself and Donaree Muirhead, in particular. For me, as an Orisha devotee, the crossroads hold deep symbolic and spiritual significance. The crossroads is often seen as a liminal space, a point of intersection between different realms, literally neither here nor there, betwixt and between. In African diasporic spiritual paths like Vodou, Lukumi/Santeria, and Candomblé, crossroads have a special meaning as places where spirits known as *Lwa* or Orishas are believed to dwell.

Join the #TambourineArmy for a
Survivor Empowerment March
Saturday, March 11, 2017 at 3:00PM
RSVP here: goo.gl/igtcHa
#March11March, Kingston JM
(WEAR PURPLE)
Wi fed up wid de sexual abuse! And wi naa mek dem win!
In solidarity with the #LifeInLeggings movement and with the kind support of
FiWi Jamaica | I'm Glad I'm A Girl Foundation | IGDS | JMMB | IrieFM | PRiDE JA Magazine | UN Women | Island Grill Eve For Life | Jamaica Teas | Equality For All Foundation Jamaica | Jamaica AIDS Support for Life | 360 Artists | WE-Change

Figure 23.2: The Flyer

In these traditions, the crossroads are seen as the domain of Eshu/Elegua/ Legba, the divine messenger between the human and spirit worlds. The gatekeeper who stands between the material and the spiritual, the visible and the invisible, between existence and oblivion had to be appeased the day before the march, and we left offerings at each crossroads so as not stir up chaos. That year, I was going through the Lukumi initiation of Regla de la Ocha and so I was forbidden from doing the fifth crossroads; in addition, the energy that I had absorbed feeding the previous ones was too intense for me to bend the corner to take on the largest crossroads in Half Way Tree. The white flag to cut and clear each crossroad became necessary and we agreed that someone else would take that one if spirit required it.

For Donaree, who is steeped in her Maroon heritage, the crossroads represented a testing ground where individuals are presented with challenges and opportunities for growth. Overcoming the challenges of an overarching rape culture in Jamaica and helping survivors through personal empowerment and spiritual advancement, coupled with the challenges that the Tambourine Army was facing from the mixed public response, was a crossroad that held deep resonance. We travelled to each one and invoked Eshu, other Orishas, and Nanny of the Maroons for protection and guidance, and offered water and rum to break the stagnant energy that collects at crossroads because of vehicular traffic and traffic lights. We asked the ancestors for protection on the road for all who planned to attend and to clear the way for change. This clearing of the way and paying our respects to the crossroads prior to the march was an important disruptive act as we felt the heavy energy of the crossroads and it was spiritually necessary to do so.

The route of the march was almost 3.7 kilometres (2.2 miles) and it purposefully began with disruption. Starting off with an African libation done by me at the Covenant Moravian Church on Molynes Road, we named and honoured all survivors of gender-based violence who came before us; we asked for strength and cool heads on the road. Survivors, friends and family members, and activists of all stripes – women, men, LGBTQ+ people and those with intersecting identities – as well as singers, poets and musicians, especially drummers and percussions, joined us.[10]

The march commenced at 3:05 p.m., going through the five different crossroads, cutting and clearing stagnant energy at each crossroads again, and ended at the clock in Half Way Tree, a major crossroads of transport, traffic and people, and a site for all forms of street harassment of girls, adult women and gender non-conforming people.

The march's emphasis on survivor empowerment and centralizing the testimonies of survivors drew parallels with the divine feminine, exemplified by Nanny of the Maroons, a powerful historical figure who defied colonial oppression and symbolized the strength of black womanhood. Similarly, the manifestations of the Orisha practice in the march represented a reclaiming of spiritual heritage. By centring African-derived spirituality in a Christian-dominant society with a male godhead, the march promoted a spiritual alternative, fostering resilience, liberation and unity.

What this disruptive form looked and felt like differed among the women who participated, but there were commonalities between their experiences. For Tanya Stephens, the march was:

> . . . so loud and inappropriate, [it] couldn't help but be disruptive . . . [I]f there was anything wrong with the volume, it was that it wasn't loud enough. It was just needed, like it made people stop and look and ask what's going on and listen, [join], [walk] along. Even if out of curiosity alone. I heard people in the crowd walking, talking about their experience and people they knew about . . . It was disruptive enough because it made the entire country stop and look. (interview, September 2020)

Nadeen Spence's examination of the disruption was personal with a twist of understanding the classism within the women's movement:

> We knew we were disrupting because we knew we had to, but we never prepared for the backlash. . . . After a while, we go, Rass, people nuh like what we doing. People nuh like what we a say. We were disruptive in respectability politics. Breaking the mould of heteronormativity. And we were doing it within institutions that were patriarchal. Because we were women who they would approve of. We speak English, we have education. They expected us to do better . . . You must do better and you have friends in parliament – if you upset, go tell them. Why you out a road talking so for? You should be ladylike. I think we threw away convention. . . . some of the older women in the [women's] movement . . . felt it was unnecessary because they had won the war so we're going on like we have more to fight for. But you cannot go to the next generation and warn them off. And so, the disruption we were causing [was] amongst them

> as well. It was too Christian with women who are choir leaders. We couldn't have been a part of it. . . . I see it as us necessarily disrupting the space but not being prepared for the backlash . . . I think the disruption was necessary . . . it allowed for the exploration of my own authenticity. . . . [E]ven when I was there trying to be authentic, there was so much I was burying and had buried from I was a youngster that I could not have voiced. It disrupted that . . . [and] on a personal level . . . it made me stand up for myself. (interview, August 2020)

Only survivors were allowed to play key roles in the march, and that was in itself a political act, arguably sidelining those with social and political power. This was not without risk, and we repeatedly had to explain why. This focus on survivors' voices was important because we had always been silenced before. In an interview with Madeline Green, I opined: "Having the march centred on an African-derived spiritual path was an important counter-narrative to Christianity. . . . There's a way in which a certain kind of Christian indoctrination oppresses the voice of women and represses the kind of confidence to speak out if things happen to us . . . [and] there's a way in which Christianity crushes our courage and promotes a certain kind of submissiveness to Jesus Christ as Lord and Saviour that inhibits personal liberation (interview, July 2020).

RITUAL AS RECLAMATION

The march's disruptive power was amplified through ritual, which transcended the mundane and created a sacred space for transformation. These rituals included a libation at the start and at the end of the march in honour of our ancestors, relying on Verene Shepherd's documented evidence of Phoebe, Cuba, Egypt, Minetta, Abba and other enslaved African Jamaican women, who paved the way through their resistance and activism during the eighteenth and nineteenth centuries. A survivor/advocate from the LGBTQ+ community, Madeline Green, took on the charge of fire burner/energy clearer and burned sage and incense throughout the length of the march. Another sister took responsibility for carrying all the spiritual tools in a backpack, such as flowers, rum, water, sage, honey, and protective herbs for use by myself and Shango priestess Afia Walking Tree to soothe the road and protect us from negative energies. I wore white and used a large white flag to cut and

Figure 23.3 Pouring libation

clear each crossroads, with the assistance and guidance of three Jamaican priestesses seated in African-derived spirituality: Okomfo Afofie (Carol Miller), Afia Walking Tree (Camille Thomas) and Iyalosha Omi Zaide (Dr Yanique Hume). We were guided by the Survivor Empowerment March's objectives and made room for the elevated survivors' voices, harnessing their stories as tools of empowerment.

The use of ritual was important to the Tambourine Army's praxis in order to ground us, dispel negative energies, soothe ancestral spirits, and ensure protection and harmony on our route. Our spirit had been lost in our violation and a spiritual response was required to awaken energy, to elevate the spirits among us and to connect us all. It was also important as an alternative to the usual "let us bow our heads and pray" to a male godhead. It was a deliberate effort to lean in on our African heritage to ground us on the day. Neila Ebanks, dancer/choreographer, led the vanguard of women who formed part of her dance company, eNKompan.E. In an interview, Neila said:

> Disruption through performance and ritual was pivotal to this kind of protest and declaration in ways that persons gathered might not have expected. These elements provided a sense of structure and transcendence inasmuch as they were also grounded in survivors' realities and so the kind of disruption that

> occurred was guarded by ritual. . . . [T]he insistence on ritual at the beginning, throughout the march as well as at the end also included stopping at points to hear from survivors and also the protest posters made by Simone Harris were key to that disruption. . . . The posters had a visual of open mouths evidencing the fact that the moment belonged to survivors – to speak; so the ritual of having that recurring visual throughout the march, with different people holding it as well at each crossroads, was critical. There is a sort of spiritual sewage that collects at our urban crossroads – so many people cross them for so many varying purposes that they also tend to harbour a certain maleficent darkness . . . underneath the surface and tends to prey on the vulnerable. **It was disruptive because we also felt safe – on that one day.**

Ritual in the march was received with mixed feelings. The activities of the Tambourine Army, which started in January 2017, unfolded swiftly, and on reflection, there was insufficient dialogue about the use of ritual on the march and how it would have been received by other activists, individuals and organizations we were working with. Some welcomed it, while others were less sure. Tanya Stephens said, "I was afraid that we would divert the focus. . . . Asking Jamaicans to accept us being very African felt like adding another fight to the fight. It felt like a distraction that could easily undermine some of the progress made by just getting this discussion into public space. Because you know Jamaicans are really hypocritical about so many things because we are all Afro-centric, but we don't like to admit it in public."

Joy Crawford felt that it would have been good "if somewhere in the communication . . . there was some kind of written brief about them, what they meant, and where they would fall in the process. Because we also had to try and explain to some of the women what was happening. [S]ome of those things . . . may have created curiosity or excitement but it may have also been a distraction" (interview, 2020).

In my interview with Madeline Green, she stated,

> You and the organizers were able to tap into the soul with the rituals and the type of movement of bodies and songs and words that were being used, plus the shaking of the tambourines. It was really as much a spiritual experience as it was a physical and emotional experience. That plays into the disruption because of the times when you hear about these marches, it's just a placard-carrying thing. A lot of people don't really think of the spiritual aspect of how

Figure 23.4: Shaking tambourines

> it affects people in terms of what you're marching about, and how it affects you spiritually. (interview, 2023)

Nadeen Spence shared:

> The core thing for me is how [the ritualistic aspect of the march] dislodged my religious centre, because I'm a Christian. I grew up in . . . the Moravian Church, which was more religious than spirituality. . . . The awareness of the Tambourine Army and the need for spirituality and where my spirituality was grounded was upended and destabilized. I was adrift. So, there was a need for me to find new rituals. So, I loved the rituals and because I'm Afrocentric, they meant a lot to me. It was like, I'm taking up pieces of myself and putting back together and I was like, Yes, this feels right.

Neila Ebanks, as a dancer, choreographer and a student of performance culture and African retention, understood the importance of ritual not just for priming connection to the ancestral, but also:

> for establishing our connection to the depth, strength and power in our own selves. Ritual can help to start us off on the best foot possible. Cleansing the energy of external space and personal mental space is very important in activism work when there are diverse groups of persons within one larger group. . . . Ritual helps to galvanize, centralize and firm up spirits and ready everyone for

"the fight". We have a way of saying that ritual is only spiritual gobbledygook, but no, ritual is the kind of recognized symbolic act that makes a moment fixed in the mind and transforms it into legend.

TESTIMONY: TRANSFORMATIVE VOICES

Andrea Dworkin (1989, 105–6) wrote about transformative value of the testimony of survivors:

> The anger of the survivor is murderous. It is more dangerous to her than to the one who hurt her. The clarity of the survivor is chilling. Once she breaks out of the prison of terror and violence in which she has been nearly destroyed, a process that takes years, it is very difficult to lie to her or to manipulate her. She sees through the social strategies that have controlled her as a woman, the sexual strategies that have reduced her to a shadow of her own native possibilities. She knows that her life depends on never being taken in by romantic illusions or sexual hallucinations.

As far as Madeline Green was concerned,

> It's commonplace for women and girls now to feel more bold and empowered to say the names of their abusers or to call out certain injustices that happening to them. . . . Post-Tambourine Army . . . [w]e can talk about this, we can express our feelings. . . . Tambourine Army really gave women and girls the voice that they didn't even know that they needed . . . Because it was just something in our culture to just be like . . . that's how it is. You get harassed on the street – that's how it is. If somebody touch you on your bottom uninvited, that's how it is. You get raped, so it go. . . . Ten years later, you're expected to carry on with your life and be normal. The Tambourine Army disrupted that to say that listen . . . This is not okay and . . . we won't be hushed. We will speak and you will listen to us.

Testimonies transformed personal pain into communal empowerment. Shango priestess and spirit drummer Afia Walking Tree of One Billion Rising said:

> What was beautiful about it was how many of the stories were similar. In that, are we still here? And also, the breadth and scope . . . it's not just heterosexual violence we are talking about. It's not just gender-based violence. The violence just goes on in all these various realms and we have so much work to do. That

> was the overall feeling of deep, deep compassion for all the folks who were both sharing their stories and just how deep this illness, the wound, goes.

Testimony was also important for Tanya Stephens, who said:

> [I] survived sexual violence myself on multiple occasions [and] I wanted to share my experience because I wanted to make it clear that there's no specific type of person who's living with that kind of . . . experience. . . . [On] that day I feel like I am one of the strongest people. I feel like I'm okay talking about me, but then I realized that previously I wasn't really. I skirted around it and I couldn't say the word rape. I would say I got shell down and I was like, What was that . . . Because I just couldn't stand in front of so many people and tell them I got raped. **But I did on that day.** Having that space and that kind of atmosphere helped me too and I can only imagine it helped a lot of other people just come to terms with the reality of our situation. (interview, 2020)

The act of testimony during the course of marching, for Neila Ebanks, was "critical to the Tambourine Army's strategy on that day. . . . it connected importantly with the real reasons behind the march – empowerment and survival stories and their ability to empower those on the margins and even give those who are the centre of their own personal dramas some courage."

Figure 23.5: Participants listening to the testimonies of survivors

Figure 23.6: Marchers with 360 Artists posters, and Tambourine Army posters

Survivors' voices shattered the silence about gender-based violence and provided a space for collective healing and catharsis. By sharing their stories, survivors disrupted the oppressive norms and ignited a potent conversation that reverberated.

PERFORMANCE

The march had a performative aspect. A line of mostly women served as a vanguard. This included me, the ancestral worker/Orisha devotee in white; the priestesses, Afia Walking Tree and Afua Okomfo Afofie; Kheon Brown, who carried our tools; the NKompanE Dance Company, led by Neila Ebanks; the 360 artists led by Simone Harris, carrying posters; master drummers Calvin MacKenzie and Afia Walking Tree; and percussionists Ouida Lewis and Jodi Brown. The vanguard served a protective role that symbolized the collective strength of the community of marchers, and tapped into the energy and wisdom of our ancestors, who had to fight for justice. We did our best to lead the march and had ongoing communication with members of the Tambourine Army on the music truck – Donaree, who was moderating

Figure 23.7: Cutting and clearing the crossroads

the testimonies and the audience in general, and Latoya, who managed the playlist.

The playing of instruments carried us through each of the five crossroads as we cut and cleared energy. This vanguard was instrumental in the interplay of performance, ritual and activation of a kind of visual and spiritual disruption. The front of the march was the space where ritual was sustained throughout and the line of demarcation that absorbed ancestral presence; we gave offerings as we charged through each crossroads and swept away grime that gathered there to clear the way for those behind us. The most crucial crossroads were the third one (the longest) and the one in Half Way Tree (the widest and most dangerous).

Once we cleared a crossroad, we stopped when Donaree asked us to so that the survivors, including Shaneka Hall, Julie Mansfield, Tanya Stephens, Jomaine McKenzie and Keisha Firmm (whose "Nah Mek Dem Win" was the theme song of the march), could share their testimonies. At the end of each testimony, motivating songs played to activate the crowd into singing and feeling encouraged. This was crucial in supporting the emotions on the road – we did not know how the audience would respond to the harrowing testimonies.

The percussionists and drummers in the vanguard were there to support

Figure 23.8: Some of the vanguard

the rituals and to carry the vibe and harness an energy of sisterhood of women and unity over all along the route. Jodi Ann Brown played percussion on the march and shared: "When I saw the set-up, I didn't exactly know what to expect but I got an instrument. I felt like I was telling my story through performing . . . so many layers of pain leave my body that day (interview, 2020).

Everything done on that day was performative inasmuch as it was also lived reality; marchers demonstrated feelings and took action. The march was also a performance of anger, of stories of triumph, of victory in the way that re-enacted a battle – not as falsehood or as pretence, but as a reminder of the strength of the warriors. Combining performance and ritual demonstrated how unity can be activated when an effort is made. There were other elements aligned with ritual performance at the various crossroads on the route, and throughout the march, drumming served as a galvanizing force. When we got to Half Way Tree, its energy as an unsafe site for women filled the air, but this was craftily dissipated by music at the major intersection. However, once we cleared the intersection, the music truck broke down and the sound system lost power. The musicians stepped up and joined the vanguard. As spirit would have it, Neila Ebanks danced and completed the last ritual to cut and clear the fifth and biggest crossroad.

Figure 23.9: Smack in the middle of Half-Way Tree

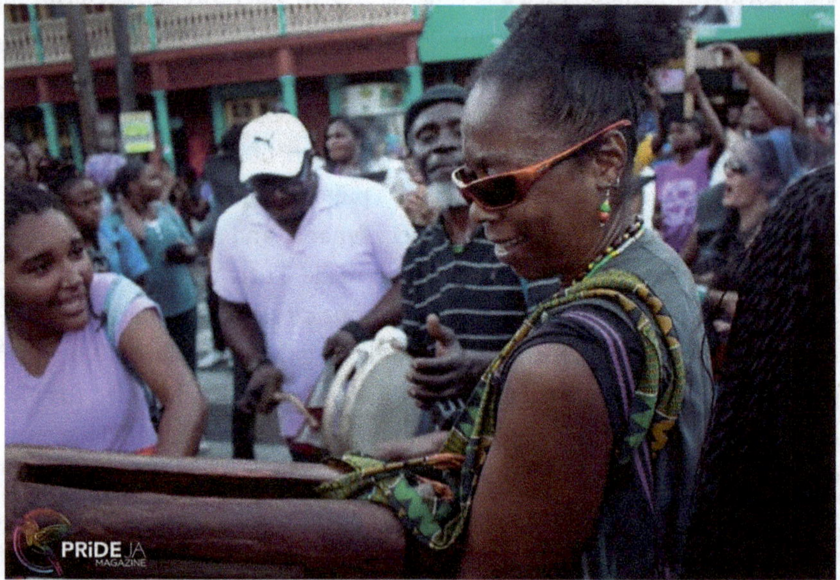

Figure 23.10: When the truck broke down, the power went and the artistes took over here

Figure 23.11: Neila Ebanks and the musicians clear the last crossroad

Wrapping up the march, Nadeen Spence shared the plans of the Tambourine Army at that time, then Jamaican singers Etana and Sugar sang, and it all ended with a libation by me.

CONCLUSION

The Survivor Empowerment March of 11 March 2017 stands as a testament to the power of collective anger, spirituality and disruption, encapsulating Audre Lorde's wisdom on using anger to fuel transformative change. The embodiment of the divine feminine, through Nanny and the Orisha practice, rekindled ancestral power and resistance. By weaving these threads together, the march became a triumphant moment of empowerment, reclamation and disruption – a testament to the strength of unity guided by the spirit of our ancestors in challenging gender-based violence that was achieved on that day. I learned what can happen when we trust spirit to take over, and that the battle to end violence against women and children is also a spiritual battle, which our ancestors can help us with. Freedom fighters across the Caribbean relied on African wisdom to fight against structural violence, and we in the twenty-first century must see the value in reclaiming these tools of protection, of spiritual submission and strength, knowing that the ancestors have our backs. The challenge we faced and failed at was to stay in execution mode and remain trusting of spirit and sisterhood when the backlash from the state unfolded. While some of us had support from colleagues and friends at the University of the West Indies, in the legal fraternity, and some women's rights and LGBTQ+ organizations and among family, the absence of support from key feminist elders was not lost on us. In moments of crisis, especially after Latoya Nugent's arrest, we were moving rapidly and making decisions. While I interviewed women who were willing and able to speak, there were others who were not because they had a different experience with the Tambourine Army, one that caused emotional discomfort, especially given the nature of how things got distorted and diverted from our original focus. There was need to establish space and distance from each other to heal. Even that provided lessons as to how difficult it is to maintain cohesion within a circle of women and femmes who all carry trauma and are at different stages on our healing journeys.

The experience was also a lesson in how much we underestimated the octopus-like nature of the state and how it enacted punishment on some members of the Tambourine Army. The lessons from the women's movement raised more questions than answers: To what extent does the Western epistemology of feminism that lies at the foundation of Caribbean women's activism and feminist intellectual discourse perpetuate binaries and hierarchies between mind, body and spirit? Does the false separation of mind, body and spirit subjected to feminist intellectualization prevent an engagement with our African spiritual heritage? Is feminism led by Western epistemology adequate for finding strategies to eliminate gender-based violence? Does the requirement of proving the agenda of feminism hinder broader ways of experiencing, interpreting and eliminating GBV? To what extent does the Englishness of things overshadow advocacy meetings and funding negotiations, causing us to lose sight of points for strategic agreement? How does the formality of communication between the generations in the women's movement prioritize status and hierarchy, and therefore overlook the humanity of other women? The Caribbean is a geographical space where people are still struggling to recognize and accept each other's humanity, and how many of us love ourselves enough to extend seeing and giving grace to the women and girls who are survivors of gender-based violence?

In the Tambourine Army, we attempted to emancipate ourselves from the vortex of patriarchy to reclaim and centre alternative ways (African and spiritual) of organizing and interpreting what happens to women and children who are violated. The march was about activating what this could mean. When the spirit of a woman or child is damaged, that spirit has to be accessed for healing, recovery and thriving. The march brought to light the weaknesses and intellectual dissonance created by submitting to a Judeo-Christian male godhead, while embarking on the gargantuan objective of ending gender-based violence. Engaging with an African-derived alternative rooted in the divine feminine discomfited many in Jamaica's women's movement.

By elevating the voices and experiences of survivors through performance, ritual and testimony, the march disrupted the conventional ways of addressing GBV. The use of Jamaican Patwa, the embrace of the African-derived spiritual path, and the influence of the Orisha tradition contributed to the march's potency and resonance. Additionally, some of the interviews provide insights into the emotional and transformative impact of the march, even though it was only one significant activity of the Tambourine Army. Shortly after the march, Latoya Nugent's arrest derailed other plans and led to a far too singular focus on her challenges, detracting from the larger objective of radically addressing gender-based violence and the realities of survivors. We were stretched thin and tired.

Additionally, undercover acts of strategic institutional violence were directed at some core members of the Tambourine Army, which negatively affected family life, employment, property and our relationships with each other. So many things got shattered in the backlash of the march that personal survival prevailed over sisterhood. Although some of us have healed from this fallout, there is still mending to do.

Regardless, the Survivor Empowerment March had an impact on the day and on the lives of those who participated. It showed how disruption, performance and testimony, guided by our African spiritual heritage and the divine feminine, collectively contributed to empowering survivors. The march sparked widespread and much-needed conversations about GBV and the humanity of women and girls. The actions of the Tambourine Army also expelled intergenerational and intragenerational toxic energy within the women's movement, which, mired by the ego-centred requirements of deference and formality, had not emerged authentically before. The urgent need to respect the humanity of women and children in Jamaican society remains; it arguably has gotten worse. Jesus Christ is still the Lord and saviour of many women and frames the heteronormative patriarchy. Throwing away our reliance on a male godhead and finding more wholesome spiritual paths along the continuum of the divine feminine and divine masculine, and uprooting Caribbean feminist dependency on Western epistemology are some of the remaining steps of the project of emancipation in the Caribbean. This is the project of the next generation of women and men, in all their diversity and those in between, who are a range of multifaceted activists, artists, healers, educators, entrepreneurs and queer folk. Thankfully, some of them are already exploring African, ancestral and Indigenous alternatives that can help them better navigate the world without shame and judgement, and work towards the discipline that freedom requires.

NOTES

1. "Pastor charged with rape after allegedly being caught 'moonlighting' with a 15-year-old girl," https://jamaica.loopnews.com/content/pastor-charged-rape-after-allegedly-being-caught-moonlighting-15-year-old-girl.
2. "I feel like bombing a church, who wants to go to Nazareth". Deliberate reference to Bob Marley's song, "Talking Blues" – "I feel like bombing a church, now, now that you know that the preacher is lying."
3. Activists and individuals representing themselves or women's rights NGOs, including WE-Change, I am Glad I am a Girl Foundation and Eve For Life Jamaica.
4. "Moravian clergymen charged with carnal abuse," https://jamaica-gleaner.com/article/news/20170123/update-two-more-moravian-clergymen-charged-carnal-abuse.
5. "Sunday protest at Manchester 'sex' pastor's church," https://jamaica.loopnews.com/content/sunday-protest-manchester-sex-pastors-church; *Jamaica Gleaner*, "Sex Scandal rocks Moravian Church,"; https://www.youtube.com/watch?v=wFlT7L6FfCM.

6. According to its website, Life In Leggings: Caribbean Alliance Against Gender-Based Violence is a grassroots organization in Barbados, founded to eradicate the rape culture and GBV in the Caribbean region. The movement began in 2016 with the hashtag #LifeInLeggings, was created as a safe space for women who had experienced sexual harassment and sexual assault. Women, encouraged by solidarity, were empowered to speak out on their social media platforms about their experiences. This hashtag went viral – making an appearance in countries all around the globe. However, it particularly championed the experiences of women and girls throughout the Caribbean region and its diaspora as this was the community it originated from and the community it wanted to challenge.
7. Marches were also held in The Bahamas, Barbados, Dominica, Guyana, and Trinidad and Tobago.
8. Facebook post by Latoya Nugent (aka Stella Gibson), 6 February 2017. Accessed 2 June 2019. https://www.facebook.com/stellatambourinegibson/posts/670628526474481.
9. The posters had these phrases: "Fire pon paedophiles", "Bun out rape culture", "Nah mek dem win".
10. An estimated one thousand people came to the march.

REFERENCES

Lewis, Emma. 2017. "'Tambourine Army' Gathers Recruits as Jamaicans' Anger Over Child Sexual Abuse Grows." *Global Voices*, 7 February. https://globalvoices.org/2017/02/07/tambourine-army-gathers-recruits-as-jamaicans-anger-over-child-sexual-abuse-grows/.

Mendes-Franco, Janine. 2017. Global voices, 18 March. "With Tambourines in Hand and Led by Survivors, a Powerful Movement Against Sexual Violence in Jamaica Rises." https://globalvoices.org/2017/03/18/with-tambourines-in-hand-and-led-by-survivors-a-powerful-movement-against-sexual-violence-in-jamaica-rises/#:~:text=They%20carried%20tambourines%20to%20break,longer%20prepared%20to%20stay%20silent.

Miller, Kei. 2017. "Why I Would Have Shaken A Tambourine." Under the Saltire Flag, 17 March. https://keimiller.wordpress.com/2017/03/15/why-i-would-have-shaken-a-tambourine/.

Parker, Rachel. 2022. "The 'Angry' Black Woman." *NineteenFifty-Six*, 11 April. https://1956magazine.ua.edu/the-angry-black-woman/.

Paul, Annie. 2017a. "'Nah mek dem win': The rise of the Tambourine Army." *Active Voice*, 18 March. https://anniepaul.net/2017/03/18/nah-mek-dem-win-the-rise-of-the-tambourine-army/.

———. 2017b. "See and blind, hear and deaf . . ." *Active Voice*, 22 March. https://anniepaul.net/2017/03/22/see-and-blind-hear-and-deaf/.

chapter 24

A Personal Reflection on the Influence of Gender-Based Violence on Activist Women

An Interview with Peggy Antrobus

PEGGY ANTROBUS WITH DALEA BEAN

IN THIS CHAPTER, CARIBBEAN FEMINIST ICON SCHOLAR AND activist Peggy Antrobus speaks to Dalea Bean about her work and its relevance to family violence. Antrobus, who identifies as a Caribbean resident, was born in Grenada, educated in St Lucia and St Vincent, and had her most significant work experiences in Jamaica and Barbados. Her book, *The Global Women's Movement: Origins, Issues and Strategies*, was published by Zed Books in 2004. Her doctoral work, "Macro-Micro Linkages in Caribbean Community Development: The Impact of Global Trends, State Policies and a Non-formal Education Project on Rural Women in St Vincent (1974–1994)", examines the linkages between internationally defined macroeconomic policies of structural adjustment and the policy framework adopted by CARICOM governments in 1984, and their impacts on Caribbean people, with a focus on the St Vincent and the Grenadines economy.

Dalea Bean: Peggy, this volume is dedicated to an exploration of the subject of gender-based violence (GBV), a phenomenon that has driven your activism. How would you define GBV?

Peggy Antrobus: I know that GBV commonly refers to violence against a person (most commonly women) because of their gender. In fact, GBV is almost synonymous with violence against women. However, on reflection, it seems to me that it would be useful to think of GBV as violence that is deeply embedded in (patriarchal) definitions of masculinity: the ways in which male children are socialized to be 'strong', 'tough/hard', 'controlling', 'dominant', 'takers'; while girls are expected to be the opposite – 'obedient/compliant', 'pleasing' (especially to men), 'gentle/soft', 'helpful', 'givers'. It would be useful because it would go to the roots – linking it to what is thought to be 'acceptable' male behaviour – as well as allow us to see the continuum between violence against women, the economic violence of imperialism and capitalism, and armed conflict/war.

I recall an experience when I was driving a couple of young children, a boy of around nine and his sister of five. They were sitting in the back of the car and misbehaving (I think the boy was teasing his sister) and I asked him to stop his bad behavior. His response was, "I'm a boy, I can mess up." Where did that come from? I'm sure it was not from anything his parents or anyone said to him directly. Male entitlement to do as they please in relation to females is a cultural issue, embedded in a gender ideology that's derived from notions of patriarchy. It crosses different cultures.

DB: Many of our readers will know of your impressive career in women and gender studies in the region. But for an audience that might not know you as well as they think they do, or who do not connect you with work on GBV, how does GBV connect with your work?

PA: In 1974, on the eve of taking up the post of Advisor on Women's Affairs for the government of Jamaica, my two younger sisters were killed by the boyfriend of the older – because she was trying to leave him. According to her close friends, there had been episodes of violence during their relationship of several years. She had never acknowledged it. Other family members, except possibly the sister who was killed, knew nothing about it. The immediate cause was probably related to the fact that she was trying to end the relationship and had been getting involved with someone else. I never connected this trauma to my work until years later when a friend observed that a work-related photo showed my sisters standing at my shoulder. My advocacy has always focused on issues of political economy, and yet, I had concluded years ago that in matters concerning women, all issues are related, and that the forces that lead to GBV also contribute to the marginalization and subordination of women. In retrospect, I realize that my life's work has been driven by that insight.

DB: I understand. That must have been a traumatic event for you and your family. Before this life-changing incident, what was your academic trajectory and how did your approaches change along the way?

PA: In 1953, I won a scholarship to attend the University of Bristol and chose to read for a degree in economics, thinking that it would enable me to contribute to Caribbean development, the other side of the coin of independence. From my first job in the Jamaica Ministry of Finance I realized that what I had learned about economics at a British university did not help me understand Caribbean economies. This job was as administrative cadet, which was the designation given to new graduates who were thought to be on track for further training for careers in the public service.

DB: So, what did help you, and what shaped your journey?

PA: What helped me was an understanding of unequal power relations between countries (specifically the Caribbean and former colonial powers), between classes, races, as well as the binary gender relations of male and female. Fundamental to understanding any economy is the 'invisibility' of the unwaged work of women in the household/social reproduction. I deepened my feminist consciousness, grounded in the lived experience of the women I encountered, and how these related to my own life – that has shaped my journey. More than anything else, feminism/feminist analysis gave me an understanding of structured power relations across all the categories.

Ironically, now, in this final stage of my life, I have come to understand that my life's work wasn't arrived at by chance. My work in community development and in the broad field of women's rights and development has enabled me to contribute to making life better for Caribbean people, rather than anything I could have done if I had achieved my earliest goal of working in public finance. Indeed, as I reflect on my work, I see a logical progression from working with government at a national level, with a regional institution, and finally, internationally, as part of a global movement for social justice.

DB: You have said that what was to become your life's work was arrived at by chance. Expand on that.

PA: Realizing that I could not make a career in public finance if I was going to be in and out of the labour force as a wife and mother, I took a job as an assistant registrar at UWI, the point person in the Registry for a major building programme financed by a Colonial Development and Welfare grant. The registrar needed someone dedicated to monitoring the programme to ensure that the funds were spent in a timely manner. Failure to spend the grant meant that unspent funds would have to be returned. This took me to the Mona campus, where I met Lucille Mathurin Mair, historian and at that time head of Mary Seacole Hall (the women's hall of residence).

Lucille saw me as someone who could get things done. When, ten years later, she was thinking of someone who could take her place as Adviser on Women's Affairs to the government of Jamaica, she chose me – not because I knew anything about the status of women, but as someone without an agenda, who would faithfully and determinedly follow a path laid out by others. In fact, she probably thought it an advantage that I had no personal, professional or political agenda, being neither a member of the People's National Party nor Jamaican, nor associated with women's organizations. For my part, I was looking for a part-time job as I had two young children – my priority.

DB: What did the new job entail? Did you remain in the post passed on by Lucille Mathurin Mair?

PA: The title of Advisor on Women's Affairs changed to Head of the Women's Desk at the Ministry of Social and Community Development within a short time. And shortly after that, thanks to the lobbying of Lucille and other influential women (like Beverley Manley) in the People's National Party, the 'Desk' was upgraded to a 'Women's Bureau' and moved to the Office of the Prime Minister.[1]

Taking advantage of the UN's designation of 1975 as International Women's Year and drawing on my experience working in community development in St Vincent and the Grenadines, the new programme conducted a series of parish-level, one-day workshops across Jamaica to introduce the bureau and to get a sense of issues of concern to women of every age and class. Because the bureau lacked a budget for such a programme, we worked closely with the field staff of the ministries of health, education and agriculture. For data, I drew heavily of the interests of individual faculty on the Mona campus of the University of the West Indies to prepare the position papers needed for Jamaica's participation in UN events.

Representing Jamaica at all the UN meetings organized in the context of International Women's Year (IWY), and the ensuing UN Decade for Women, provided an amazing opportunity to learn more about women's experiences across the globe. These spaces also provided a unique view of the relations between states and how these impacted the lives of women. There is no better place than UN meetings for this learning.

DB: What were the major achievements of the bureau during your time in terms of the advancement of women?

PA: In its first two years, the bureau recorded a number of advances in the status of women in Jamaica, almost entirely thanks to the work of the leadership of the Women's Auxiliary of the PNP. These include a Status of Children's Act, removing the stigma of birth outside wedlock; the inclusion of domestic workers in the [increased] minimum wage; the prioritizing of women in special employment programmes intended to improve the economic wellbeing of working-class women; support and a training programme for girls who dropped out of school because of pregnancy (the Women's Centre). A small group of self-identified feminists, led by Lucille Mair and others, worked behind the scenes to ensure that their vision for the participation and advancement of Jamaican women was reflected in the framework of democratic socialism. An important strategy for this work was the transformation of the Women's Auxiliary into a Women's Movement – not just a change of semantics, but of substance: the purpose of the women of the PNP was no longer to serve the male-dominated party, but to help shape the party's agenda and influence policy.

DB: Your work expanded beyond Jamaica though?

PA: Yes; I became involved in regional work. In 1977, before moving with my husband to Barbados, where he was to take up the post of Family Health

Advisor with the Pan American Health Organization, I worked with Sybil Francis at the Social Welfare Training Centre on the Mona campus to organize a regional conference on Caribbean Women in Development. The idea for such a meeting came out of my realization of the need for a regional approach to advancing the status of women in the Caribbean Community. Participating in meetings organized by the UN Economic Commission for Latin America (ECLA),[2] I realized how different the experience of women in the Commonwealth Caribbean was from that of women in Latin America[3] – and not just the language, but history, governance systems and culture – and that CARICOM would need its own voice, if our priorities were to be addressed.

The meeting made several recommendations, including the establishment of a women's programme within UWI's outreach, the Extra Mural Department.[4] As secretary of the steering committee set up to follow up the recommendations, I worked on developing a programme and sought funding and the support of the university for this purpose. In 1978, I was appointed by UWI to head the Women and Development Unit [WAND].

DB: What were WAND's objectives and how would you assess the unit's regional impact?

PA: WAND's objectives were deliberately general to allow for the specifics to emerge through our consultations and interactions across the region.

These included:

1. To build awareness of women and development issues;
2. To develop strategies/methodologies for the increased participation and integration of women in the development process;
3. To build in capacity of women's programmers for integration in development;
4. To promote non-sexist approaches to curriculum development;
5. To develop cohesive and coordinated WID programmes;
6. To increase financial/technical support to WID programmers.

We also implemented pilot projects to test transformative approaches to addressing issues of concern to women – one of these was a project that focused on the leadership of rural women (working with women at community level was always important to me). Space and time make it difficult to record the scope and richness of WAND's work over the years.[5] However, one of our chief contributions to the region was to serve as a catalyst for the establishment of several regional programmes, including Caribbean Association for Feminist Research and Action, Caribbean Policy Development Centre and, of course, the Women and Development Studies programmes within the teaching areas of The UWI.

DB: How did your work expand internationally?

PA: In 1984, on the eve of the final year of the UN Decade for Women, I was part of a small group of feminists from the Economic South meeting to prepare a Platform Document for the upcoming NGO Forum of the Third World Conference of Women to be held in Nairobi the following year.[6] Participants [from Latin America, Africa, Asia, the Pacific, and the Caribbean] spoke of the experiences of poor women in their countries over the decade. Out of this came the intersectional, interlinked analysis that has continued to characterize the analysis of the network of Southern feminists promoting Development Alternatives with Women for a New Era, that was to become known as DAWN.[7] This framework transformed my work thereafter.

DAWN was established following the conference in Nairobi, and from 1990 to '96, I served as General Coordinator of the network, continuing as tutor/coordinator of WAND. These were important formative years for DAWN, whose work focused on participating in most of the major UN conferences of the 1990s: environment (UNEC 1992) [United Nations Conference on Environment and Development, 'Earth Summit', Rio de Janeiro), population (ICPD 1994) [International Conference on Population and Development, Cairo], poverty (the Social Summit 1995) [World Summit for Social Development, Copenhagen], and women (the 1995 Beijing Conference). At all these conferences DAWN's intersectional, interlinked feminist analysis was fundamental to strengthening the voices and advocacy of women from the South and changing the terms of the debates on these issues.

DB: What concepts were most helpful in your work in the field of women and development over the past forty-seven years?

PA: I would name three concepts – power, structures and paradigms.[8] Understanding power in terms of the economy (colonialism/ imperialism/ capitalism) as well as in terms of the social relations between men and women (patriarchy) allowed me to see the connections between systems of production and social reproduction. Intersectional, feminist analysis exposes the ways in which capitalism, an economic system dedicated to extracting and maximizing profits, achieves this end by the exploitation of women's unwaged work in the household – the base of the economy.

This is the common understanding of power: hierarchical, dominating, controlling. But there are other, non-hierarchical, kinds of power. These include power within and the power of working in solidarity with others. In my work I spent a lot of time thinking about and applying the concepts of 'power with' (building solidarity, organizing, mobilizing) and 'power within' (spiritual practices, self-care) to counter dominating power.[9] In fact, when I discuss formal power structures I emphasize the importance of these other sources of power to counter, resist and challenge those structures. It's the only way forward.

Understanding structures allowed me to distinguish between broader structures (race, class, gender, and so on.) and individual agency within them. Understanding paradigms allowed me to see how the concept of 'world views' that encompass a particular set of ideologies, values and practices allow for the mutual reinforcement of intersecting power structures.

DB: A discussion of power is also critical to the issue of GBV. What did you learn about gender-based violence from your work up to 1985 when the UN Decade for Women ended? Also, which of these concepts best explains GBV?

PA: I think that all three concepts help explain GBV, and that GBV is an underlying factor in all. The concept of power is the most fundamental: in my view, violence is a consequence of imbalances of power – violence is used to dominate and control someone perceived as less powerful. Anyone working on countering violence against women must understand how power is constructed and maintained. This will help our understanding of how it might be countered. For instance, when we understand how women's compliance enables and strengthens GBV, we can develop programmes to build self-awareness in those engaged in socialization of the young, as well as in potential victims. In relation to violence against women, power within and power with are particularly important. Organizing protests is common practice; more attention needs to be paid to finding and strengthening the power within. Empowerment is fundamental to taking action. This concept has too often been taken to mean education/training and other 'external' factors. What I am getting at here is the process of finding one's inner strength and purpose through the practice of meditation or other practices of deep reflection and self-awareness. Personal change in order to be in control of one's own life is an essential part of being an agent of change.

Regarding structures, gender relations are constructed through socialization practices. They reflect a structure of power and cannot be viewed simply as relations between individual men and women: most men are not violent – many men are gentle, compassionate and supportive of women. Nevertheless, there is a structure that determines behaviours that are deemed acceptable to men and those recognized as appropriate for women. These gender 'norms' are reinforced by other structures, institutions of power – starting with the 'traditional' nuclear family, the church, education, governance structures, the media. The structure of gender relations leads to a culture of male superiority and entitlement (for example, "boys can mess up").

As a Caribbean woman, I understand that violence today is nurtured and reinforced by legacies of imperialism, colonialism and slavery. These institutions themselves reflect structures of power. Plantation society and slavery are vivid examples of how power structures based on economics, class, race and gender are linked and intertwine to make each more powerful. These structures all reflect a culture of male entitlement to dominate and control others, especially women and children, as well as the natural environment. The concept of paradigms helped me understand how these intersecting power structures can form a world view that is ideological and almost impossible to change.

DB: How did your community work benefit from all your experiences, especially your own consciousness about how to detect and educate women in the fight against GBV?

PA: There is no doubt that I applied what I learned. In fact, even before I embarked on this journey that opened my eyes to the interlocking structures of power, I worked with women at the community level in St Vincent and the Grenadines. In the 1960s, I worked at community level in two programmes. The first was with the Commonwealth Save the Children Fund in an applied nutrition programme, aimed at reducing infant mortality caused by malnutrition and gastroenteritis. My interaction with women focused on their role as 'mothers of malnourished children' (social reproduction). Later, I helped the government of St Vincent establish a community development programme. There my interaction with women focused on involving them in income-generating projects in handicrafts [production]. Then, I related to women either as mothers or as producers. If I had [had] the understanding I now have, I would have gone beyond these assigned roles to engage the women with whom I worked as autonomous agents in an exploration of the complexities of their lives to articulate for themselves how to address their needs – as WAND did in the 1980s working with rural women in St Vincent and The Grenadines, in some of these same communities.[10]

In an amazing coincidence, I also gained a profound insight in reflecting on this project. Although the project did not focus on ending violence against women, we discovered, years after the project ended, that a community known as a dangerous place for women had become one in which it was unthinkable for women to be abused. Might this have anything to do with the emergence of strong women leaders in the context of this project? I can't be sure, but it seems to me that it was the empowerment of women, through their leadership in the project, that generated the kind of respect for women throughout this small community that would change the culture and protect them from abuse. Solidarity among women and male colleagues in the community would also enable individuals to detect abuse and intervene to stop it.

I now see all forms of violence as gender-based, that is, as grounded in the gender relations embedded in different power structures – economic, political and cultural [race and gender] – all combining to reinforce each other, making it almost impossible to achieve the change needed to save humanity and avert the deepening climate crisis. With these insights, deepened over the years, I began to understand why all the strategies – legislation; education and training; parent and care giver support; sensitization of law enforcement;

counselling of victims and perpetrators; the creation of hot lines and safe spaces; economic security – strategies now woven into an innovative and impressive framework by UN agencies concerned about violence toward children and adolescents (INSPIRE), could be undermined by male privilege within various hierarchies of power. Despite years of policies and programmes to address the issue of violence, the pandemic shutdown was a sharp reminder of how vulnerable women and children continue to be when left isolated with people who exercise power over them.

Of all the strategies employed, the most difficult to implement are those attempting to change norms and values. And yet these are the most important: all the progressive policies, legislation and support services will be of limited effect if there is not a change in the norms and values that allow power and male privilege to prevail with impunity. To do this requires a comprehensive, multifaceted and long-term programme involving governments as well as civil society groups, men as well as women.

DB: How do you assess the current programmes, policies and activism to address GBV in the Caribbean? Are we doing enough?

PA: I'm impressed by the breadth and depth of the work being done, especially by the understanding that work against violence against women must be multifaceted, coordinated and involve men. It is understood that no one person or programme can be expected to deal with the complex web that traps women in vulnerability to psychological and physical violence. However, everyone whose goal is to end violence against women and children needs to see the connections between this and the gender ideology that is produced and reproduced by key institutions, such as the family (including female caregivers), the church, school, the legal system and the media.

Just as important, is recognizing the underlying violence of an economic system dedicated to extracting and maximizing profits by the exploitation of labour, including women's unwaged labour in the household, and the natural environment. Understanding these connections means that they must stand in solidarity with other projects, groups and movements for justice – gender, class, race, economic and ecological. As Audre Lorde says, ". . . the war is the same".[11]

DB: I know that we still talk in terms of women's vulnerability when we talk about GBV and, of course, that is still true: but can you say something about how women's changing economic circumstances, especially as they seek upward social and economic mobility through education at the tertiary level (in excess of men), contributes to GBV?

PA: Improvements in women's education, economic and social circumstances do not necessarily protect them from GBV. These improvements are lauded, and can, as in the case of the rural community referred to above, increase respect for women in general. The situation for some women may be the opposite. Women can be increasingly vulnerable to GBV when they challenge male privileges, for example, when they predominate or out-perform men in tertiary education; or when improved socioeconomic status challenges male control. It is known that women are most vulnerable when they try to leave an abusive relationship, as was the case with my sisters.

DB: What is your take on the enduring belief in the Caribbean that there is something called "male marginalization" and that women are responsible for that?

PA: I was head of the Jamaica Women's Bureau when Professor Errol Miller published his book, *Marginalization of the Black Male* – a good example of male entitlement! I do not accept the argument that the underperformance of boys in school is due to the predominance of female teachers, nor do I accept the broader thesis that Caribbean men are "marginalized". The underperformance of Caribbean men in education and in the economy have more to do with issues of race and class than of gender.

In relation to gender, it might be more useful to consider some of the same factors that I have referred to – the socialization of boys to be free to do as they wish, sex-role stereotyping, and so on – as well as the disconnect between education and the ability to get a job. It seems to me that the acceptance of this notion of "male marginalization" has helped undermine programmes to advance female empowerment and mask the reality of women's condition (including the disproportionate burden of responsibility for social reproduction, income disparities and the silencing of women) within our male-dominated (patriarchal) societies.

DB: Finally, as you look back on your life and work, what advice do you have for junior scholar activists who may feel daunted by the growing range of expressions of GBV they have to face and combat (such as violence against the LGBTQI community, GBV against men and boys, persons with disabilities, cybercrimes and street harassment)?

PA: I would say, try to understand the connections between GBV and a larger structure of domination and control (patriarchy and capitalism) intended to preserve the economic privileges of a small group of people, even as you focus on the specific issue you're trying to address. In this way, you can see yourself as part of a larger movement for justice.

NOTES

1. Antrobus reported to Senator Arnold Bertram, Minister of Local Government, Youth and Community Development.
2. At that time the word 'Caribbean' had not been added to ECLA.
3. The chief differences related to family structure (in Latin America the nuclear family was the norm, in contrast to the Caribbean's many extended families) and the level of female labour force participation (in Latin America, it was one of the lowest, 12 per cent; in the Caribbean, one of the highest, more than 40 per cent).
4. Later renamed the School of Continuing Studies, now the Open Campus.
5. See *The UWI Gender Journey: Recollections and Reflections*, ed. Joycelin Massiah, Elsa Leo-Rhynie, and Barbara Bailey (University of the West Indies Press, 2016) for a good account of WAND.
6. The book, *Development, Crises and Alternative Visions: Third World Women's Perspectives*, ed. Gita Sen and Caren Grown (Zed Books, 1986), is based on the Platform Document.
7. Many articles and books have been written about DAWN, including my chapter in *The Oxford Handbook of Transnational Feminist Movements*, ed. Rawwida Baksh and Wendy Harbourt (Oxford Academic, 2014). See also their website, https://dawnnet.org.
8. The books that I found most helpful are those by Selma James and Mariarosa Dalla Costa (1972), *The Power of Women and the Subversion of the Community;*

Zillah Eisenstein, ed., *Capitalist Patriarchy and the Case of Socialist Feminism* (1978); Maria Mies and Vandana Shiva, *Ecofeminism* (1993).

9. See pages 131–33 in my book, *The Global Women's Movement: Origins, Issues and Strategies* (2004).
10. In a pilot project on "The Integration of Women in Rural Development", WAND introduced a group of women to participatory action research (PAR) as a methodology for assessing their needs and taking action. One of their ensuing projects was a daycare centre. Years earlier, with Save the Children Fund, I had tried to establish such a centre, which ultimately closed for lack of material support (contributions of food) from the community. When women decided for themselves that daycare was a priority, they found the means to establish one. They had ownership, and WAND's role was to support them.
11. We have chosen each other and the edges of each other's battles
    the war is the same
    if we lose someday women's blood will congeal upon a dead planet
    if we win there is no telling
    we seek beyond history
    for a new and more possible meeting
    —Audre Lorde, excerpt from "Outlines" (1996).

REFERENCES

Antrobus, Peggy. 2004. *The Global Women's Movement: Origins, Issues and Strategies.* London: Bloomsbury Publishing.

Baksh, Rawwida, and Wendy Harcourt, eds. 2014. *The Oxford Handbook of Transnational Feminist Movements.* Oxford and New York: Oxford University Press.

Dalla Costa, Mariarosa, and Selma James. 1972. *The Power of Women and the Subversion of the Community.* Bristol: Falling Wall Press.

Eisenstein, Zillah, ed. 1978. *Capitalist Patriarchy and the Case of Socialist Feminism.* New York: Monthly Review Press.

Massiah, Joycelin, Elsa Leo-Rhynie, and Barbara Bailey. 2016. *The UWI Gender Journey: Recollections and Reflections.* Kingston: University of the West Indies Press.

Mies, Maria, and Vandana Shiva. 1993. *Ecofeminism and the Sacred.* Nova Scotia: Frenwood Publications.

Sen, Gita, and Caren Grown, eds. 1986. *Development Crises and Alternative Visions: Third World Women's Perspectives.* London: Zed Books.

chapter 25

Diligent, Enterprising and Painstaking

Reflections on a Life of Activism

LINNETTE VASSELL

I WAS BORN IN MARCH 1945 AT BURYHILL in Ramble district near Broadleaf, a few miles from Porus in Manchester. Buryhill maybe got its name from the many tombs and graves on the property. These included those of two wives of Michael Berry (Dada), and my grandmother, Sarah Pitter, whose tomb was also in the graveyard. My grandmother was connected to one of Dada's wives and she, as well as her daughter, Catherine, my mother, also grew up there at Buryhill. Way up at the top of this hill, we lived on a large compound with a two-roomed dwelling for sleep surrounded by other living spaces. In this multi-generational household, I was surrounded by a large network of women with one man, Dada, in charge. He was an influential man in the district and in my own life. I remember that it was he who decided that it was time for me to go to school, when, seated on his lap, I read the word 'O-X-O' from the *Gleaner*, which he regularly bought in Porus.[1]

I went along with the bigger girls in Ramble to Broadleaf Primary School, one of the oldest schools established by the Moravian Church in Manchester. I have vivid memories of that experience – playing in the yard with bigger girls, pampered by my aunt, Isabel Mowatt, shielded from bullies by my mother's first child, my older sister, Gloria Ellis, who lived with her paternal grandmother. My brother, Owen (OG), one of (my father) Godfrey Davis' many children, was part of the circle of memories from those early days. I remember as well the big excitement at the school when Queen Elizabeth was crowned in 1952, but this could not measure up to the return to Buryhill of my mother. She had left for some time to go and fend for herself, and she had come to take me back with her to May Pen, Clarendon.

My mother, Catherine Thomas (she would marry twice – first to Adolphus Boothe and then on his death, and much later, to John Smith), was definitely the earliest and most influential person in my life. She was a very spirited and industrious woman. After we settled in May Pen, she did domestic work, worked at the citrus factory and later at the May Pen Infirmary – the Alms House, as it was called then. Her influence was foundational – she never ceased talking to me about life. I understand fully when Delores Williams, the African-American womanist theologian, explained: "We black women raise our children with sermons."[2] In Mama's case, the sermons were on the lessons of her own life as a single woman raising a child alone in a tough environment, grieving that she could not have both her children with her. Her sermons were often delivered with great emotion, with firmness bordering on anger and with warnings: "Tek to yu book – mi nuh waan yuh come up and come out like how me have to wash white people dutty clothes"; ["Study hard – I don't want you to come out like me and have to wash white people's dirty clothes"]; "Don't forget where you coming from"; . . . Her maxim, "Memba, manners tek yu through the worl', don't forget where you coming from" [Remember, manners will take you through the world"], which I heard repeated by Walter Rodney years later – cautioning young people who came to university against forgetting their roots – is part of what has kept me anchored in the core values of the working people.

OTHER MOTHER – AUNT PET

My "other mother", as I regard her, was Miss Enid Petrona Miller. She had the greatest influence on me in terms of expanding my pathway through education and into what one could define as the base for professional life. Aunt Pet, as we called her, was from the influential community-building Miller family of Rock River in Clarendon. She was part of a whole generation of women, teachers in the main, who made personal sacrifices to support young people. Aunt Pet taught mathematics at May Pen Primary school, where I was enrolled in an experimental 'comprehensive' programme, in which primary-level students were taught subjects to prepare them for overage scholarships to secondary schools. Aunt Pet advised my mother to send me to Excelsior High School in Kingston. She did all the preparatory work – my application, found boarding for me a stone's throw from the Excelsior back gate with the Baileys, from a noted family of teachers and civil servants. From there I moved to the nearby Keane home, and lived with other Excelsior girls. A retired school principal, Thomas Keane, operated a small school in the home, providing lessons to primary-level students. His wife, also a teacher, was in charge of the boarders and created another kind of finishing school for us young girls from the country. We were exposed to certain so-called 'social graces' – setting the dining table, not speaking or playing the radio loudly, not standing 'idly' at the gate, engaging quiet time for reflection and Bible study, especially in preparation for church on Sundays! These were examples of the teachings that shaped the attitudes and behaviours of the black middle class, what Keisha Lindsay has identified as the construction of "black ladyhood" in 1950s Jamaica by women like Amy Bailey, the noted and most outstanding advocate for women and social change from the 1930s.[3]

Excelsior, owned by the Methodist Church, was on a similar mission to open a pathway through secondary education for children and young people of the poorer and upcoming middle class. Mr Aston Wesley Powell had started the school in 1931 and by the time of my enrolment there in 1960, starting in the fourth form, a big campus existed at Mountain View Avenue, with strong and diverse academic, cultural and sports programmes. Excelsior made a mark on my life. By the time I left in 1964, I was on the path to seek a scholarship to enter The University of the West Indies (UWI).

THE REST IS HERSTORY/HISTORY

In the trajectory of my life, history shaped my identity as a poor black girl from the country, and my obligations within family, at that time narrowly defined in terms of my mother and my sister.[4] In 1965, when I entered the University of the West Indies, I chose to do History Special – courses covering the wide span of countries and themes, including experiences of colonial and imperial exploitation, all coming together in Caribbean history and the experiences of the enslavement and exploitation of our African ancestors and the struggles for freedom. That brought visibility to forces and peoples who had been marginalized and silenced in history. It was a sense of history that propelled the progressive struggles, including the Rodney protests of 1968, in which I was involved with so many other women and men.

In studying history, one comes to locate oneself inside or outside of that history. Very quickly, the force of imperial domination and colonial subjugation is manifested. Alongside this, one sees the absence and marginalization of women in the historical narrative. This silencing of women derives from the force of patriarchal control of society in all aspects. Conventionally, history is presented mainly as the works and activities of men, and predominantly so-called "great men". Within this framework, men and women subjected to exploitation by empire have long been regarded as being on the margins of history.

Studying history at The UWI brought the lives and struggles of the women in Indigenous and plantation society into sharper focus and deeper understanding. Verene Shepherd's (2011) *Engendering Caribbean History* is an example of the progress that was made in earlier years in making visible issues of gender and women's place in history and transforming Caribbean historiography. My own experience in teaching and supporting initiatives to promote women's history, alongside academics such as Verene in the Department of History, and others in the Institute for Gender and Development Studies (IGDS), were strongly influenced by my activist engagement in the women's movement. This dynamic interaction between teaching, research and advocacy, revealed our varied social and political engagements and perspectives. For example, a compilation of various women's speeches and engagements gave some visibility to their varied interests and approach to activism in the nineteenth into the twentieth century (Vassell 1993a). My 1993 MPhil thesis (unpublished) – "Voluntary Women's Associations in Jamaica: The Jamaica Federation of Women, 1944–1962" – examined the work of some women leaders who shaped the organizational activities and ideological perspectives of broad groups of women up to the pre-independence period in Jamaica. These included church-affiliated, charitable and welfare organizations, many organized across the British empire and by white elite and black and brown women of the middle strata, and also including women of the working masses. Whether organized within their own ranks, or coming together in mass organizations, the race, class and gender divisions of colonial Jamaican society are laid bare. For example, the struggle for the vote for women, secured in 1918 on higher requirements than those for men, benefitted the minority of women with property (Vassell 1993b).

It was the Women's Liberal Club, formed in 1936, that carried the explicit political agenda for women to vote on equal terms with men, and supported the growing nationalist movement that advanced the call for Jamaica for Jamaicans. It fielded and won the first seat by women in local electoral politics through the successful candidacy of Mrs Mary Morris Knibb in 1939. Alongside these activists were women involved in building professional bodies among teachers, nurses, stenographers, businesswomen, including dressmakers, which defined the scope of their activism.

The Jamaica Federation of Women, formed in 1944 by women associated with the colonial elite, co-opted women of the black and brown middle strata, as well as large numbers of rural women, into an island-wide 'alliance' seeking to effect changes in their 'status' within a liberal conservative mode. It served to cement conformity to colonial gender ideology by promoting and stressing as policy and practice 'women's service' – not 'women's rights' – and drew women into affiliation with the growing political party divide, mainly in support of the Jamaica Labour Party.

From my observation, the Jamaica Women's Assembly (JWA), formed in 1953, plainly articulated the vision to promote the rights of women, particularly of the working masses. Daphne Campbell, a one-time cigar factory worker, was the leader of the organization (Vassell 2011). She had a background in social welfare organizations, and was active in grassroots organizing in urban Kingston communities, working with the Marxists who had been expelled from the People's National Party (PNP). The JWA was formed to "uplift the status of women, especially working-class women and to alert them to their rights", and was active in street meetings and workers' rallies related to political campaigning in 1954 and 1955 (Vassell 2011). Their demands included a minimum wage for domestic workers, a 'people's agenda' with maternity leave with full pay for at least fourteen weeks, and prohibition for the dismissal of pregnant women or nursing mothers. The spirit of the JWA resonated in the formation of the Committee of Women for Progress (CWP) in 1976, and of the Women's Resource and Outreach Centre (WROC), its offspring, which emerged in 1983.

I am located within this brief overview of women's organizational history in Jamaica from the nineteenth into the twentieth century. The ideological battle between promoting women's service as opposed to women's rights has been central in shaping organizational development and the impact by and among women. Rooted in plantation society, colonial gender policy has shaped and systematized biased gender social norms, which influence economic social and political power relations between men and women at all levels and in all spheres of life (Vassell 1998). Understanding the history has been a motivating force for my own activism, particularly against gender-based violence.

FIGHTING FOR AN END TO GBV

When the causes of GBV are explored among many women individually or collectively, most responses are in the vein of – "Him beat her because him was drunk" . . . or "Him jealous if she talk to anybody" or "He feels he is not getting respect as the head of the house". What is here cited as causes are really triggers for the action of the perpetrator. The root cause is patriarchy – a system that has established and continues to perpetuate power relations between men and women based on the ideological standpoint that men are naturally superior to women and, therefore, have the right and power to dominate women and to restrict our choices. Patriarchy, in practice, establishes that men must hold power as the head of the household and leaders in society, and that women are, in the main, to be responsible for care of the family and home, and respect the authority of the man. Because patriarchy shapes these values of our culture and their outworking in the economic, social and political systems within which we all live our lives, they are learnt from infancy by both girls and boys in the family, the media, our schools and religious institutions – in short, in the cradles of culture and cultural identity.

The 2016 *Women's Health Survey*, the first to examine the prevalence of gender-based violence in Jamaica, states, "The findings indicate that the norm is for men in Jamaican society to be seen as aggressive, powerful, unemotional and controlling, which contributes to a social acceptance of men as dominant. Similarly, expectations of females as passive, nurturing, submissive and emotional reinforce women's role as weak, powerless and dependent upon men. Though changing, some aspects of these stereotypes linger across the culture" (Watson Williams 2018). They linger because they are systemic, embedded into the economic, social and political structure through centuries of exploitation, first of the Indigenous Jamaicans, enslavement and genocide of our African ancestors, and discrimination also of East Indian indentured workers. Patriarchal control of the economy and society has influenced thinking at various levels.

My own work on colonial gender policy in Jamaica indicates how this thread of patriarchal control evolved and became systematized as part of the so-called 'civilizing mission' of the British Empire, and particularly after 1865, was directed towards promoting social stability. Deeply embedded in the policy was inherent and systemic violence against Jamaican womanhood. The policy was systematized especially from the period of 'modernization' in the post-1865 period and was interwoven into all aspects of economic, political and socio-cultural life in Jamaica (Vassell 1998). The mission was to conform the population to the values of the Victorian patriarchal order, to improve the "morals, manners, character and behaviour of the Jamaican people" (Moore and Johnson 2004). Consistent with these Victorian patriarchal values, women were to conform to the ideal of womanhood – domesticated, refined and restricted to the home, where her role was to ensure that the environment was conducive to the proper upbringing of children and the comfort of the husband, the breadwinner and head of the household. Men and women of the middle strata, many influenced by the Christian church, sought to conform to these values of the 'cultured and civilized' society, especially in their valuing of marriage and the nuclear family.

Colonialism also shaped gender relations in the economy. While the majority of women had no choice but to engage in subsistence-earning activities outside the home, in areas such as domestic service, trading and agriculture, more educated women in the emerging middle strata – as well as women of the privileged elite – were barred, well into the late nineteenth century, from work outside the home. Women were also barred from the legal profession and up to 1900, men made up the majority of teachers, even at the elementary level. When women were admitted into the teaching profession, they were paid less than men occupying the same positions and this could well be seen as a measure that, over time, influenced the lowering of renumerations within the profession, as men moved into alternative occupations.

In addition, women had to meet higher entry requirements than men for recruitment into the colonial civil service and a policy directive in 1942 stipulated that women were not to be promoted nor appointed to the position as first-class clerks. This was not only to preserve the preferential position of the male breadwinner, but to reinforce the norm that women should not have authority over men. Colonial gender policy in employment also directed that women in the civil service resign from their positions once they married. Quite ironically, this did not apply to postmistresses, who were expected to be unmarried but also paid maternity leave if they became pregnant. They were required "to leave the service if and when they protect themselves by the honourable estate of matrimony", to quote Iris Collins, the first woman elected to the House of Representatives in 1944. The gaps and distortions in the labour market continue to undermine the life chances of women and their families.

The impact of colonial gender policy as violence on women's lives is perhaps most unyielding around women's sexual and reproductive rights. The Offences Against the Person Act (OAPA), for example, adapted in Jamaica in 1864, carries the penalty of life imprisonment with or without hard labour to "every woman, being with child" who seeks or secures a termination of pregnancy. It also stipulates that anyone convicted of giving support to the woman towards this end also faces three years of imprisonment. Despite minor exemptions in its application, the law continues to criminalize abortion, despite evidence of widescale 'illegal' abortions affecting the health and life chances of mainly poor women and families. Women with economic means have access to abortion services safely and privately.

The OAPA also has the so-called 'buggery clause', which is enforceable mainly against homosexual men and also imposes the penalty of ten years with hard labour for persons convicted. Despite long-standing and persistent research and advocacy, the Jamaican state in independence has not liberated itself from the conceptions and practices embedded in colonial gender policy. Patriarchy is still alive and its underlying role in shaping the gendered power relations between women and men in all spheres is yet to be effectively unmasked.

ADVOCACY IS A WAY OF LIFE

The process of unmasking patriarchy has consumed much of my life in practical and tangible ways. As I delved deeper into academic research on the ways in which colonization and patriarchy worked together to stymie the futures of ordinary Jamaican folk, I had no choice but to work to dismantle such structures. The Committee of Women for Progress (CWP) was formed in October 1976. A progressive politically 'left' organization, our members were mainly young, middle-strata professional women, with a few from the working class. CWP aimed to provide a platform to expose the conditions of women, to lobby for reforms of those conditions and to mobilize women to seek changes in the economic, social and political conditions which the majority of women and the Jamaican people faced. What was on the ground was movement among the people – what Rupert Lewis (2019) has analysed as a "window of radicalization" that opened up in Jamaica and the Caribbean from the late 1960s into the 1970s.

The popular movement and the political opportunities created and expressed in that context showed itself in the coming to power in 1972 of Michael Manley and his regime, and its declaration in 1976 of a democratic socialist agenda. This provided the conditions that prompted the formation of the communist Workers Liberation League (WLL) in 1974 and of the Workers Party of Jamaica (WPJ) in 1978. The formation of the CWP was part of the establishing by the left forces of an organized presence among women.

What was also important on the ground was my own consciousness of my own journeying through political spaces. Joining the CWP and eventually also the WPJ was a kind of political coming of age and making up my mind to participate in politics on behalf of the working people as a whole and not within the partisan divide of a Jamaica Labour Party (JLP) or of the People's National Party (PNP). My "Sista Fren" E.T. – Elean Rosalyn Thomas (18 September 1947–27 May 2004), whom I had known for years, influenced my decision. She was a founding member and leader of the WLL/WPJ, a passionate advocate for women's rights and for the interests of grassroots people. She had a key role in discussions about the formation of the CWP. It was the kind of politics that met my mother's approval.

Research and discussions led by a number of women active in the formation of the CWP brought to light the economic and social challenges facing the working people, especially women. The first pamphlet *Women, Vote for Progress*, published shortly before the December 1976 general elections, spoke to high unemployment, low wages, high and spiralling prices of basic goods. Research also revealed that middle-class professional women, within a short space of weeks after giving birth, were forced to return to work for fear of losing their jobs. Voting for progress meant supporting a government sensitive to the needs of the people and not one alert to the influence of the capitalist class and their allies locally and internationally.

On the ground also women were mobilizing themselves for action according to their varied interests. For example, Sistren Theatre Collective, formed in 1977 with a core of grassroots women who had gained employment under a government street-cleaning programme, came to express concerns around poverty and employment, and conditions facing domestic workers. Middle-strata activists – Honor Ford Smith and Joan French – worked alongside as sistren to build the organization and the expansion of women's activism. This process made it possible to secure cooperation among different women and organizations to pursue shared goals. CWP's initiative to launch the observance in 1978 for the first time of International Women's Day, and following that, the struggle for maternity leave with pay in collaboration with the PNP Women's Movement, benefitted from that expanding landscape of women's activism. Partnerships and combined advocacy secured, despite powerful opposition, the historic Maternity Leave Act to benefit women and their families in 1979. An advocacy goal of the left-wing Jamaica Women's Assembly had been achieved.

By 1983, the window of radicalization was being shuttered by the storm from reactionary, pro-imperialist forces and their policies. A major aspect of this was the whole-scale adoption of structural adjustment policies dictated by the International Monetary Fund and embraced by the government of the Jamaica Labour Party, which came to power in October 1980. CWP's response was along two pathways – deep involvement in the consumer rights struggle with the formation in 1981 of the Voluntary Price Inspectors (VPIs) Organisation. This involved collaboration with the Prices Commission, a state entity, in monitoring consumer abuses, including taking supermarkets to court and winning cases against them. Widescale complaints of increases in rent and food were ignored. Mounting pressure on women and consumers came with the widescale removal of price controls and other former consumer protection measures.

This was the context that shaped the CWP's second broad response: the formation of the Women's Resource and Outreach Centre (WROC) on International Women's Day in 1983. It was founded to support women to address their practical welfare needs, while the CWP, shortly thereafter to be rebranded as the Organisation of Women for Progress (OWP), would remain strong in political advocacy to seek systemic changes. A one-room office space provided at the Social Action Centre (SAC), followed by securing its own home at Beechwood Avenue, Kingston, enabled a range of services in health, counselling, legal aid, education and training to be provided to women and their families through a cadre of volunteers and development support over the years.

WROC can record a dynamic history of community organizing to address issues such as natural hazards and climate change, agricultural development, education and training of children and youth, and support of the elderly. Currently, its work and partnership with the Women's Empowerment Group (WE Group) is directed towards supporting women in the local Lyndhurst/Greenwich community to build their capacity to sustain their families, including addressing the persistent gender-based and broad insecurity they experience living in vulnerable communities.

This has been hard and challenging work with many lessons – among them the fact that even if there were hundreds of WROCs all over Jamaica, they would not solve the problems of the people because these are systemic structural issues which are not solved by responses that may open new paths but are not sustainable. Within this consciousness, WROC has measured its success by the degree to which, standing in that social welfare space, it tried to plant seeds to influence people-centred development in practice. Visionary disaster management meant training communities to construct safe roofs to withstand the impact of hurricanes; in agriculture it involved ensuring that community members could agree and provide to women farmers special grants to provide them labour support; in environmental management it meant community mobilization, for example, in Somerset, St Thomas, to construct seven check dams to arrest massive soil erosion. The vision is not sustainable on the ground if the environment is not enabling for the community or for civil society organizations, such as WROC.

In WROC, from the early 2000s, we undertook research initiatives to influence a turn to advocacy and to secure policy change. This included building partnerships – resulting in the founding and nurturing of the Coalition for Community Participation in Governance (CCPG), which was focused on support of the local government reform process. Research, education and capacity-building in advocacy among middle- and working-class woman were anchored in the publication of *Rights a di plan, wid CEDAW in wi han* (2008); *Gender and Governance: Implications for the Participation of Women on Board and Commissions* (2008); *Women's Leadership: Wellspring for Transformation in Jamaica* (2011). In the last publication, a database of eighty-two professional and ten working-class community facilitators profiled women who had been trained and expressed willingness to participate on boards and commissions. Coming out of this, the 51 % Coalition was formed among thirteen women's organizations and individual women in November 2011 with an explicit feminist transformational mandate.[5] The implosion in 2017 of the 51% Coalition has been a signal of the growing vulnerability of women, and the growing instability and gaps in the institutional capacity of all our organizations.

A life of advocacy was not without its challenges. Over these many years, I have come to reflect more on these realities that I have experienced as a black woman from the grassroots, a country girl coming into one's own in a society like Jamaica, steeped in classism, colour prejudice and discrimination. This boiled down – despite the progressive outlook of the 1970s – to insecurity, linked to an implicit questioning of your suitability for leadership. And it came from different sources; from the ruling class, and it came from within the movement itself, as Maziki Thame (2024) has begun to explore in her recent essay. Another challenge came from "wounds I was given at the house of my friends", as Louis Lindsay, of blessed memory, quoted from Zechariah

13:6, as we contemplated my experience of being arrested, jailed and charged by the state in 1983 in connection with a bank robbery in which my car was used. The experience brought much pain – also for my husband, our child, and other family and friends. My health and professional life also suffered and although I was vindicated, the consequences do not go away easily; in fact, perhaps never do. Another challenge I recognize as troubling to me over the years has been coping with the complexities of interpersonal relations among women. I do not take myself out of the equation at all and I have come to recognize that conflict among women leaders has been a constant feature of our experience historically. I saw it in histories from the 1930s into the present, and I just hope that there could be a space for us to bravely talk about this. Of course, a right-wing, pro-imperialist government made the unfavourable socio-economic conditions facing the majority even worse.

You may ask what has kept me committed to the cause. I try to keep myself in context of the long struggle of black women in all spaces and places – against hardship of all kinds. Thinking on that trajectory, I have been blessed and highly favoured with lots of support along the way, especially from my family. We accept and respect that women will support their men who are in public life and hardly think of it otherwise as when a man has a partner who is the public eye. I tell people all the time that much of what I do and can give on a personal or private level is due to the generosity of spirit of Cyril Vassell, my spouse for fifty-four years, who died on 10 October 2023. His thanksgiving service on 1 November was a memorable testimony of a man who was progressive, caring and solid in his support in all aspects of our private family life together, as a friend and activist citizen in community.

Since his death, I am more so than ever connecting the dots in my life and am both challenged and supported to live from a place of commitment to the leading and purpose of God in my life. I am very much attuned and committed to struggle for the mandate of Jesus – for justice, righteousness and for the transformation of life in all aspects.

FUTURES

The legitimacy of civil society in governance is often questioned by some in the political class, and our civil society organizations are under intense pressure for resources – human and material – and have been floundering for many years. Because it has been so weakened over the past decade, in particular, there has been questioning of whether we can speak about a 'women's movement' at this stage, for example. Furthermore, in this epoch, within the neo-liberal 'development' paradigm, we have moved away from solidarity building towards emphasis on self-investment for self-development. The idea is that we can make progress more as individuals – whether entrepreneurs, innovators, social media influencers or otherwise – and make provisions for ourselves and our families. Then maybe we can set up foundation to respond to individual cases of need that grab our interest. In many aspects, this approach is commendable and the individual advancement paradigm linked to busy social media engagement does have the potential for mobilization for action. However, to achieve the changes we seek requires organizational interventions – the pressing of flesh in collective action to achieve the desired practical end of changing people's lives.

In terms of what we can do, building partnerships among entities in and across sectors of interest is a priority. But such partnerships among women and with men must be rooted in a perspective linked to some agreed undertakings, among them:

i. data and information gathering on the economic, social and political contribution of civil society organizations to national and regional development;
ii. specific realistic recommendations on state/government and civil society relations, interface and the financing implications based on findings;
iii. agreement on a shared perspective around the key agreed priorities towards addressing the pressing issues facing women.

In so doing we will be better able to tackle issues of GBV and build on insights and measures that have emerged from the national and regional Spotlight Project. This process would include:

i. broadening and strengthening the national response to GBV;
ii. addressing GBV as a human rights violation rooted in patriarchy. This means, inter alia, pushing for measures to transform the economic, socio-cultural and political context within which it is fed and perpetuated;
iii. systematizing the collection and management of data, including

administrative data related to violence against women and girls. Within the regional partnership approach, administrative data must inform legislation, policies and programmes as well as aid in monitoring and evaluation of existing initiatives;

iv. Celebration of individual stories of triumph over violence to break the silence surrounding this scourge. I think of the experience of Sister Monica Ferguson, one of the outstanding working-class women in CWP. Early in her association with the organization, she boldly left her abusive partner to make life on her own with her children. Her story, bound up with that of her children, is phenomenal and she narrates it with passion.

There are many potholes in the road to progress and for women realizing our empowerment, but this comes from our resisting and rising as ordinary everyday black women in relation to the daily struggles to survive – the legacy from our enslaved ancestors, summoning the will to survive from day to day in a system meant to kill them in body mind and spirit. For them, as for us today, claiming of rights to live in the system designed to destroy was and is resisting and rising.

So, I draw my lessons of rights and empowerment from women in my family, among my friends, including sisters of the Lyndhurst Greenwich community, whom I've known from they were young girls. Like my mother, their mothers struggled to keep them in school, to keep their heads above water, and on the straight and narrow path. Many came to the centre for services – in the homework programme, for example. Now, as adult women, they are positive about the economic and social progress that their sons and daughters have made.

What empowerment means, then, is not living as victims, but claiming our right to life and confronting the struggles along the way. My hope is that sooner, rather than later, we will commit to and pursue that transformative agenda, and that we will come to know and to act within a consciousness that this is the will of God, in whose likeness and for whose purpose we were and are created equally as women and men, girls and boys.

NOTES

1. OXO was a popular soup additive.
2. Delores Williams (1937–2022), an African-American theologian, noted for the development of womanist theology, was the author of *Sisters in the Wilderness: The Challenge of God-Talk.* See "Delores Williams's voice in the wilderness," Cheryl Townsend Gilkes, *The Christian Century,* 2 January 2023. Christiancentury.org /article/features/delores-williams-s-voice-wilderness.
3. Bailey herself had taken the practical step of founding the Housecraft Training Centre for women in 1945. See Keisha Lindsay, "Amy Bailey, Black Ladyhood and 1950s Jamaica," in *Small Axe* 24, no. 3 (2020): 128–42. https://smallaxe.net/sx/issues/63.
4. When Gloria left her grandmother's home to join Mama in May Pen, our lives took another turn. Mama decided to send her to Kingston to get an opportunity to establish herself as a dressmaker. Under her plan we rented a room, which was furnished with her own basic furniture transported from May Pen. My scholarship money helped to pay the rent; every fortnight, Mama sent food packages by bus, and my sister's meagre earnings as a dressmaker sustained us.
5. The specific mandate was to: Promote gender equality on boards and in decision making as a means of ensuring that Jamaica has her best chance at national development; lobby for quotas so that no board should have less than 40 per cent and no more than 60 per cent of either sex for both public and private sector boards; undertake training to support women's effective participation on boards and in all areas of development; monitor boards and build partnerships to improve accountability systems for them, and advocate for the consistent use by all public boards of the "Corporate Governance Framework for Public Bodies in Jamaica" (See 51% Coalition, *Women in Partnership for Development and Empowerment through Equity,* Advocacy Resource Kit).

REFERENCES

Lewis, Rupert. 2019. "The Jamaican Left: Dogmas, Theories and Politics, 1974–1980." *Small Axe: A Caribbean Journal of Criticism* 23 (1) (no. 58): 97–111.

Moore, Brian L., and Michelle A. Johnson. 2004. *Neither Led nor Driven- Contesting British Cultural Imperialism in Jamaica, 1865–1920.* Kingston: University of the West Indies Press.

Perkins, Anna Kasafi. 2022. "Christian Norms and Intimate Male Partner Violence: Lessons from a Jamaica Women's Health Survey." In *The Holy Spirit and Justice Interdisciplinary Perspectives: History, Race and Culture*, edited by Antipas L. Harris and Michael Palmer. Lanham, MD: Seymour Press.

Shepherd, Verene, ed. 2011. *Engendering Caribbean History: Cross-Cultural Perspectives*. Kingston: Ian Randle Publishers.

Thame, Maziki. 2023. "The Significance of 'Communists Wearing Panties' in the Jamaican Left Movement, 1974–1980." In *Black Women in Latin America and the Caribbean: Critical Research and Perspectives*, edited by Melanie Medeiros and Keisha Khan Perry, 56–74. New Brunswick, NJ: Rutgers University Press.

Vassell, Linnette. 1993a. *Voices of Women in Jamaica, 1898–1939*. Kingston: Department of History, University of the West Indies.

———. 1993b. "The Movement for the Vote for Women, 1918 to 1919." In *The Jamaican Historical Review*, vol. XVII: 40–54.

———. 1998. "Colonial Gender Policy in Jamaica, 1865–1944." In *Before and After 1865: Education, Politics and Regionalism in the Caribbean*, edited by Brian Moore and Swithin Wilmot. Kingston: Ian Randle Publishers.

———. 2011. "Women of the Masses: Daphne Campbell and 'Left' Politics in Jamaica in the 1950s." In *Engendering Caribbean History: Cross-Cultural Perspectives*, edited by Verene Shepherd. Kingston: Ian Randle Publishers.

Watson Williams, Carol. 2018. *Women's Health Survey 2016 Jamaica*. Kingston: Statistical Institute of Jamaica, Inter-American Development Bank, United Nations Entity for Gender Equality and the Empowerment of Women.

chapter 26

Silver Learnings of Judith Wedderburn

Reflections on Feminist Advocacy in Jamaica

JUDITH WEDDERBURN WITH HELEN ATKINS

JUDITH WEDDERBURN IS A JAMAICAN GENDER PRACTITIONER, CARIBBEAN feminist and lifelong activist. As a founding member of the women's rights organization Women's Media Watch (WMW) conceived in Jamaica in 1987, she has been at the forefront of advocating for the rights of women and girls for decades. This retrospective, facilitated by postgraduate researcher Helen Atkins, explores Wedderburn's silver learnings in her personal, professional and political lives, and offers a series of thematic snapshots that join the dots between gendered experience, human conviction and feminist activism.

EARLY DAYS

Helen Atkins: How did gender shape your childhood, education, and teenage years?

Judith Wedderburn: I grew up loved and protected in a cocoon of six strong, independent women. I had a single mother – my father died when I was three years old, and my mother was eight months' pregnant with my younger sister, Bunny. My mother sent us both to the country when Bunny was three months old to stay with an aunt, while she studied to be a secretary. She expressed later that she knew she had to provide for herself and two daughters. My interpretation of this is that she was an independent-minded woman, who sought to be financially independent rather than seek another husband to support her family.

We were surrounded by these strong women, including my mother and two godmothers; that was my village. I felt protected and nurtured and loved by that cocoon. These women were almost always around; they were all at my wedding, supporting me in many important ways. Fewer were married than single, with husbands who were around, but their impact on my life was minimal. I learned from these women that there was nothing that I could not do; the thought never crossed my mind. Two among them had their own businesses – one a famous dressmaker (who made my wedding dress), the other had her own bakery (who made my wedding cake).

During primary school, I experienced and demonstrated anger at favouritism shown towards boys in math class by a female teacher, who was also the principal. Instinctively, I knew it was wrong, not fair, but couldn't challenge the principal, who was a friend of my mother and my deceased father. I was so frustrated! In my early teenage years, my mother told me – in response to my question about getting married again – that she will raise two independent young women and no other man, except our father, was allowed to influence or shape us.

At St Andrew High School for Girls, I was by then conscious about the race/class divide and other differences, but did not feel challenged by the situation. I knew that I had to study hard and get good grades, was physically active in all sports, became a Queen's Guide, became a prefect, and also deputy Head Girl. By the time my sister Bunny became Head Girl, I had left high school.

As an undergraduate at the University of the West Indies on the Mona campus in Kingston, Jamaica, I acknowledged being a typical, middle-class, young black woman. I socialized easily, was confident with friends – both male and female students in my social class. I was primarily interested in the leftist politics of the day, which was dominated by male students. I had positive relationships with them in this political space and was deeply conscious of my untraditional tendencies from then, in resenting the typical domesticated role for women.

THE PARADOX OF THE FEMINIST WIFE

HA: How have your intimate relationships informed your feminist knowledge and practice?

JW: I ended up doing what was expected anyway: I did well at school and university, got married to a man who I met on campus. This made my mother very happy, and my in-laws – the two families "fitted very well" (to quote). I found myself in the United States, as the breadwinner while my husband went to school. I took work seriously and provided as expected. My husband and I planned for our son, and five years later, returned to Jamaica. Eventually I filed for divorce, deeply resentful of carrying the full responsibilities for childcare, provision of finances for the home and family, as well as multiple infidelities.

I worked in Cuba at the Jamaican embassy for a year and a half, instead of the intended three years, as the Manley government was defeated in the violent 1980 election. While I was in Cuba, my son needed an operation in Havana. I made sure it was done, and then I made my way home eventually. I didn't have any money, but I had a son to support, so I made my living typing, just like my mother did. I needed to earn for myself, and I trace that back to her.

Divorce was a wonderfully freeing, empowering experience and I would not marry again. Whenever the issue of power came up, for example, the refusal of a partner to accept my right to decide how I spent my time, to accept that I was actively involved in local politics or performed as a dancer in the National Dance Theatre Company of Jamaica or in community work, or spending time with my son and family. The issue of gendered power – which is at the core of an intimate relationship (in my view and experience), how power is, or is not shared, or used – informed my decisions.

HA: Which external relationships have made your life's work to end gender inequality more challenging?

JW: Relationships primarily with religious institutions, and schools governed by different churches, and governments grounded in the patriarchy.My mother, sister and I attended St Andrew Parish Church every Sunday morning, always sitting in a pew near the front because my mother was a pillar of the church – a high-brown, light-skinned woman, well-educated and employed. It was extremely important for her to walk down the aisle and sit at the front of the church with her two daughters. When I was about ten years old, I recall looking up at this huge stained-glass window with the face of 'Jesus', beyond the altar, a man with white skin, blue eyes, long blond straggly hair. I knew then he was not my "Lord and Master". But I was not about to displease my mother, so I went to church feeling that I didn't have anything to lose.

CARIBBEAN FEMINISMS: ORGANIZING AND UNBURDENING

HA: Who have been your greatest feminist influences over the years?

JW: My interest in gendered relations of power led me to explore the works first of feminists from North America, and then of Caribbean feminists – Peggy Antrobus, Joan French, Andaiye, Honor Ford-Smith, more recently, Eudine Barriteau and Professor Verene Shepherd. Her research increased my understanding of enslaved women's contribution to plantation society, to rebellions and resistance movements across Caribbean patriarchal slave societies, Jamaica included. This was critical to explaining how and why women's bodies were and are controlled, used, and abused – the foundation for gender-based violence – across generations. Shepherd's research established how deeply ingrained the patriarchy was in plantation society, dictating the role and presence of enslaved women in this framework in which they had little autonomy over their own bodies.

Sistren Theatre Collective was started in 1977 and because of my previous experiences with gender and power, I was attracted to this organization. It was founded by Honor Ford-Smith, Joan French and a number of grassroots women out of the experiences of these women who, for the first time, through the Manley programme, were able to earn an income for themselves – cleaning streets. This was historic! Many of the women will tell you it was the first time they had earned money by their own hand. I became a friend of Sistren and went to many meetings to help, sharing whatever research I could access.

There was resentment towards Sistren, all of "those 'black-black' women from downtown" – a perceived changing of their social status. They were invited on international tours, performing their plays in the Caribbean, in the UK, and they provided visibility about their *gendered* lives. They learned to think and do for themselves, which generated hostility among the middle and white upper classes.

HA: You worked for years at the highest level with the German foundation Friedrich Ebert Stiftung (FES) in Jamaica. How did you become involved with the organization and go on to lead it in Jamaica?

JW: I was appointed as Director of FES, a German social democratic foundation, during the mid-1980s. My relationship to FES and how it allowed me to do what I did coincides with a period during which I was active in the political education programme of the PNP, and their Women's Movement. I was employed by the Inter-American Institute for Cooperation on Agriculture. They were empowering women through rural programmes, using dried banana leaf on greeting cards. This was my day work, then in the evenings, it was political education. Michael Weichert, who was the first Director of FES in Jamaica was present at PNP activities. As a social democratic foundation, it saw Jamaica – through the PNP – as an ally. Michael was present at the training programmes, where we had many conversations. He observed how I worked, taking notes and writing reports, demonstrating a clear understanding of national politics. In 1985, I was invited to work as Programme Officer at FES, where I edited publications, used research in workshop design, organized training and sensitization for young women and men in leadership, for household workers, and the main trade unions in Jamaica and some CARICOM countries.

As Director of FES, I had authority on how to spend the budget under these pillars: human rights and justice, economic empowerment for women and youth, peace, and sustainability at the global level. FES provided the funds for training activities, research and editing publications under the FES pillars, which enabled the creation of partnerships.[1] In collaboration with the Caribbean Association for Feminist Research and Action's secretariat, FES provided training on violence against women, and women's leadership, which is where my work on gender and trade began. Because small island developing states (SIDS) are disadvantaged and had just begun to examine the gender implications of trade agreements, especially for women, this required attention. FES organized a training programme for public sector officials in Guyana in partnership with the Institute of International Relations of the UWI's St Augustine campus. During that time, I visited Red Thread and met with founders Karen de Souza, Andaiye, and other members. The time spent with Andaiye helped in shaping my own then-nascent understanding of Caribbean feminism.

Through CAFRA, my presence in the region became known to Peggy Antrobus. Peggy was a founding member of Development Alternatives with Women for a New era (DAWN) in 1984. At that time, DAWN had regional focal points in other parts of the world and suggested CAFRA as the focal point for the Caribbean, not wanting to start another regional organization. Initially, I had no official relationship with DAWN, but through Peggy, I was exposed to her research in the network, and through FES, collaborated around a number of activities in Jamaica, with CAFRA. This networking provided the opportunity to establish DAWN Caribbean with members in Jamaica, including Linnette Vassell, Taitu Heron, Joan French, Shakira Maxwell and myself. Using the DAWN Caribbean name, and with FES support, we collaborated with the UWI's Centre for Gender and Development Studies (now the Institute for Gender and Development Studies).

This network worked mostly with no money, but we used what we had, and learned to piggyback on other activities throughout the region. One year, DAWN Global had a retreat for members in East Africa, held in Kenya. FES supported me to go and represent DAWN Caribbean in that meeting and another one, a few years later, in South Africa. Several Caribbean women went to South Africa, and we were able to interact with some of the DAWN South African activists on the ground, but not really long enough to answer their many questions. We were coming from Jamaica, so apart from what we read, this was also an important fact-finding mission for us.

Because FES was born out of the German labour movement, it was very supportive of trade unions, which became strategic allies in countries where FES had a presence. The Jamaica Household Workers' Union developed a powerful relationship with FES Jamaica, through which support was provided for household workers island-wide, mostly women, to be trained about their rights as workers, and how to use various ILO (International Labour Organization) conventions to strengthen their advocacy for decent working conditions and wages. In the context of activities organized by FES Jamaica, I was able to partner with local and regional activists such as Linnette Vassell and Hilary Nicholson in Jamaica, Peggy Antrobus in Barbados, and Nelcia Robinson in Trinidad and Tobago, and in many OECS (Organization of Eastern Caribbean States). Our partnerships addressed subjects such as women's leadership and empowerment, women's rights and challenges to their rights, discrimination facing women, and gender-based violence.

WOMEN'S MEDIA WATCH JAMAICA

HA: As a founding member of WMW Jamaica and still a director, nearly forty years on, you have guided the organization from a loosely formed group to an official membership and, more recently, a full-time employer in advocacy for gender-based violence prevention. How was WMW Jamaica conceived? What have been the key successes?

JW: UNESCO invited a number of women's organizations to a meeting in Kingston. A concern was expressed about how women and violence were being portrayed in the media. UNESCO wanted to find out from active women's rights organizations (WROs) which aspects they found most disturbing, the way women and their bodies were treated in the media, and what links there were to violence. A number of committees were formed, including legal and education to develop strategies to prevent violence against women. WMW grew out of the education committee.

HA: There were seven founding members of the organization, originally known as Women's Media Watch: yourself, Hilary Nicholson, Patricia Donald Phillips, Michelle Golding Hylton, Samere Tansley . . . Evadney Crooks and Evelyn Scott have recently passed.

JW: Evelyn was one of the early presidents of the Jamaica Household Workers Union, and despite a disability, was a phenomenal activist. We, the seven original members, began working together. There were certain things to be done, to establish an organization, so we did them. We were mindful that the more work we did, the more reading we did. This just confirmed that there was a need for an organizational response – that's what drove us. For the first few months, the office was a car trunk! Then there was an old building associated with a church. Then we had our office on Patricia Donald's back veranda. It's where she lives now. We didn't have any money to pay rent and it was spacious enough. The business of volunteering was central to what we did. Gender-based violence was a big problem, a growing problem and we developed a sense of how vast it was. I remember our first grant – from a private business owner, known to members, who understood the issues and just donated.

THE CARE BARRIER

HA: What were the teething problems in developing WMW? How were they overcome?

JW: Some problems were associated with who the membership was – women. On some occasions, your family became the priority, your children needed you, but volunteering also required your time – it was the most important resource. You just couldn't be sure you were going to be available every weekend for a workshop – you had to be available for family. But I am quite sure it did not stop us doing the work; we worked around it. There was an Anglican property somewhere up in the hills – it was beautiful. We needed dormitory accommodation; WMW co-founder Patricia Donald Phillips got permission to use it. All members could bring their children, allowing us to focus on the work we needed to do without childcare concerns.

HA: What challenges have persisted over time for WMW Jamaica?

JW: If we go back to the original scheduling, we are supposed to have a retreat in the first three months of every year. We needed to engage members, especially new ones, to wrap their heads around the work. It costs money to volunteer, sometimes people forget that – either gas in the car, or time. If you spend five hours on an advocacy action, you could use that to earn money elsewhere, so we have had to be very realistic about engagement, encouraging volunteerism around the core values we hold dearly, as we have to find a way to make it happen. We knew to ask the membership – how do we best engage you? – demonstrating that we value volunteerism. This country functions on volunteering! Fast forward to 2022 and WMW is embarking on a national gender-based violence project with international support that has an entire outcome dedicated to alleviating women's care burden. How times have changed.

PARTY POLITICS

HA: You were a core supporter of the PNP Women's Movement in the 1990s and were recently quoted in an international newspaper as saying the following about the current administration: "What is happening inside of their party, especially the Government party, which has a majority of women? Why are they so silent? So one can assume that in that space of political leadership, women are not making any progress" (*Gleaner*, 7 March 2022).

Feminism can be divisive – what would it take to unite women in both parties to fight for political equality, irrespective of who is in power?

JW: The main purpose of the 51% Coalition was to bring together different groups of women from civil society, both political parties, and the private sector. In that space over a two-year period, the question of quotas was discussed, whether it was an appropriate way to allow women more access to political spaces. The dominant position was "yes", you need more women to be at the table. Research tells us generally you need 30 per cent to be heard, but numbers are never enough.

We were not advocating only for numbers because when the women get there, they need to decide to make a difference, that whatever is discussed will be evidence-based, then together come to a decision about what to do about it. This did not take place. So, my position is, the government knows that it has a whole host of women in parliament, and in the Senate, but have their numbers made a difference? It is hard to say yes when we consider the reports in the press, for example, the George Wright case.[2] In the public's memory, this had not happened before, but it was captured on video then circulated widely. The ruling party's decision was ludicrous. They could not press the case to ensure this man went to court to face justice.

HA: Do you believe there is fear about opening the floodgates? Can you identify any progress in cross-partisan efforts towards gender equality?

JW: Absolutely. There have been many allegations over the years about sexual harassment and "allegations" of abuse. I do believe, that going beyond "allegations" of abuse to securing evidence sufficient to make a case in court may just open the floodgates of reports of cases involving political figures. This may be so of political parties generally which are not progressive.

A leading party usually has an interest in retaining male dominance, of that kind of masculinity that says, "men have all the answers". In that sense, to me, as a woman in politics, if you accept the invitation to become a Member of Parliament and the party invests in you and you win your seat, who are you beholden to then? Regarding the presence of more female parliamentarians, (1) we have not had clear examples of how their presence makes a difference, and (2) has not facilitated bi-partisan conversations, for example, which can lead the women of the two parties to form a political caucus to examine issues facing women when the tribal politics doesn't allow for this.[3]

It is very disappointing because they are not serving the interests of Jamaican women. This is really different if you go back and look at documentation from the Committee of Women for Progress (CWP). The reason why the Maternity Leave Act of 1979 passed in the end was due to intense collaboration between the CWP, the PNP women, those women outside who were not PNP but were progressive, and a few elements of the private sector who went along with it. The mobilization was not partisan, it involved a cross-section of grassroots, socialist and middle-class women. Beverley Manley-Duncan, who led the PNP Women's Movement, is very clear that this is a women's issue which applies to every woman.

UNEQUAL FOUNDATIONS

HA: Recent years have brought unprecedented investment in responses to gender-based violence in Jamaica and globally. Do you see this as timely intervention or long overdue?

JW: It is very important to go back to where the gender norms started in our society, which means we have to go back to the plantation economy from 1655 to 1838. We know the plantation economy was based on free labour, relations of exploitation, and structures of inequality that were established as the way of life. The lived experiences and relationships of enslaved African women and men were shaped by these physical, social, financial, and spiritual interactions.

The plantation space is where enslaved men and women lived and fought. Professor Verene Shepherd has provided ground-breaking data on how this patriarchal economy impacted enslaved lives. It not only shaped gender relations, but how race, class and gender interact was established, through the dehumanization of bodies. I'm very grateful to her for that *real* data. Real work is now being done about intergenerational trauma, about the seriousness of the trauma experienced by women and men, for example, third-generation descendants of enslaved people. I am arguing that the unequalness of those relations persists. The interventions are long overdue.

"TIE THE HEIFER, LOOSE THE BULL"

HA: From "tie the heifer, loose the bull" to 'male marginalization theory' to 'toxic masculinity' to 'male vulnerabilities' – how has the narrative about men and violence changed over your lifetime in communities, in advocacy, and in politics?

JW: Tie the heifer, a young female cow – where? In the household! Gender norms were well established and entrenched. "Loose the bull" because they are meant to spread their seed wherever, with no constraints, no restrictions. Perhaps the modern meandering of men from woman to woman is connected to this forced removal from the only family they knew. To rebel against this, they would have been killed or brutalized. Likewise, the inability of an enslaved woman to exercise agency over her body was a permanent feature of her life, and of her vulnerability to the brutality of the system.

HA: It has been said that men suffered more during enslavement, in terms of sexual violence, because they were more likely to be penetrated with objects, whereas women were more likely to be violated by flesh. How do you relate to that school of thought?

JW: Were men more brutalized than women? Male marginalization theory came about through Errol Miller – as a pushback when women were beginning to make some progress, in terms of leadership. It helped his argument that he was in education and had access to data on women in emerging leadership roles in this sector.

HA: And yet Errol Miller's work is still being used by prominent public commentators . . .

JW: I say to my young male friends who are doing advocacy now: for years, men were complaining on the quiet about gender-based violence against them, but the evidence base was not there. Now they can refer to research being done to guide their advocacy activities on behalf of men. Parenting Partners are focusing on what it means to be a good father. I can't argue with that because children need good fathers. But I am also saying, now (men) you have to do the work – we can't do it for you. When you see fathers who are not good fathers, better you (men) call them out, than we (women) call them out.

For years, police would also laugh at women. It was only when enough women went and made a report, provided evidence – then reported cases appeared as data. Police still admit that these are only the reported cases; that many go unreported, if a woman's partner or the church threatens her, and she has no support. It is the lack of reporting by men. For me, if there's no data to support it, how do you know? Carry your "bredren" with a lawyer to the police station, and if physically abused, support him to report it.

Male vulnerabilities relate to a shifting of power on the part of some women to understand that if they earn more – which some of them do – it will cause a shift in the power that a man has over a woman. In that space, men say they are vulnerable as they are no longer totally in charge. Many young women are saying, "Well, you don't have to be in charge." This is toxic, especially in a space where a woman has a right to do what she is doing, such as earning more money. Using the phrase of 'toxic masculinity' upsets the man, as it challenges his traditional way of being masculine.

HA: Policy and practice places growing emphasis on men and boys as victims of gender-based violence, as well as prevention engagement through violence interruption, including couples' mediation. What are the potential benefits and pitfalls of the so-called 'victimization of perpetrators'?

JW: I must emphasize the importance of understanding the basic pieces of gender-based violence legislation, assuming they are relevant to how violence interrupters are used and do their work. The first question is, how do you choose such persons? The understanding is that most perpetrators are male, and to reach them you have to have an interrupter with whom they can have a conversation, without being victimized. What does the training of those interrupters involve? Are they sufficiently aware of gender norms? What is their understanding of why they are needed? Are they really expected to help bring down the level of community violence? Will that help the security forces bring down the level of widespread violence? What can they actually do if the community is overrun by gender-based violence? What then does the interrupter do, compared to the social worker? What authority does he or she have? These questions need to be addressed.

HA: What defines the male feminist advocates that you know?

JW: Fabian Thomas of the Caribbean Male Action Network (CariMAN) is far more in touch with the lived gendered realities of young men and women. He allows himself to be guided by what young people say. Young people often do not get the chance to really talk to parents, so they will find someone else to confide in. Fabian is present in many spaces and has his fabulous book, *Djembe,* about visibility, inclusion, tolerance and acceptance that helps to define him as an advocate. The way he presents the issues is evidence of how he thinks, and he expresses himself with credibility.

HA: How is that gap to be bridged for people who do not have the capacity or lived experience to understand these issues?

JW: You have a right to express how you feel. A lot of youngsters don't experience that in their home community because they don't have the space. On the male side, there is something systemically wrong with our educational system. I am very concerned – we have more women than men.[4]

I used to track the number of women with First Class honours – men were disadvantaged at the university then. There's a higher percentage of women graduating, and it's not showing up in their employment in higher paying jobs in key sectors. Barbara Bailey's ground-breaking work showed that our education system doesn't cater to boys – they mature slower, they learn differently, they not allowed to do art or to cook.

By the time a boy turns sixteen, he is seen as a man now – he needs money and status. Such a young man is an easy pick to be drafted into a gang, gain popularity, profiling, money – and with that status, he can get a woman. In all of these ways, I am conceding that young men are vulnerable to the system itself. I do believe some changes are happening. Once upon a time, you were allowed to see an advertisement for a principal stating, "Women need not apply." I still look at the careers that are being advertised, and thankfully I don't see that anymore.

THE FORECAST

HA: Recent years have brought unprecedented investment in gender-based violence response in Jamaica, and globally. Do you see this as timely intervention or long overdue?

JW: The global system has its own driving forces. For the last ten to fifteen years, the data – about how bad violence against women and girls is – has been collected and cannot be ignored anymore. Global religious institutions have a strong presence in Jamaica, demanding that traditional gender norms be strictly maintained. Funding partners have to put their money behind evidence-based reduction and prevention of violence against women and girls. At the community level, in this post-COVID time, there is a need for people to have personal interactions. A lot of the work we do – and did – is about relationships. This does not work so well with video conferencing. When you eyeball someone and you sit down and hash out things, it's different as a form of advocacy.

HA: The Caribbean preceded the global #MeToo movement with #LifeinLeggings in Barbados, followed by Jamaica's Tambourine Army. What's next for the local movement to end gender inequality?

JW: The UN-EU Spotlight Initiative brought significant investment in gender-based violence responses in Jamaica and countries across several continents. Through this initiative, WMW trained hundreds of pedagogical stakeholders, enhanced secondary curricular content, created a multi-use, gender-based violence prevention activity pack. Latest interventions have focused on particularly vulnerable groups, such as teenagers and people living with disabilities. Before this, there was very little funding for WROs generally, for gender-based violence, and VAW specifically. In 2018–19, the World Association of Christian Churches provided funds to implement public education workshops screening a short film titled *Where is Melissa?* about sex trafficking. There was less available funding – many WROs lost traction and either ceased to exist or hobbled along. In the last ten years, globally, gender-based violence is *so* bad, it is in people's faces. The UN Sustainable Development Goals 2015–2030 include ending poverty and gender equality – both are intrinsically linked.

There is gender machinery in regional countries, but many do not have a dedicated budget to fully implement national action plans to address gender-based violence. The government itself has to decide to provide adequate funding, otherwise the Bureau of Gender Affairs[5] cannot fulfil its obligations. I am concerned about a government structure in which the gender portfolio is not considered sufficiently serious to be provided with an adequate budget.

BELIEF AND SYSTEM: PLATFORMS FOR ACTIONS

HA: WMW's public education efforts have included rewriting discriminatory headlines, media training, awareness-raising in schools, churches and businesses, and social media content. Which prevention spaces need development going forward?

JW: We speak about parliamentary democracy. We have had fourteen elections since Independence in 1962 with peaceful transitions – no coups – despite political violence. Democracy can be taken for granted, and challenged because a sense of stability often covers weaknesses and deficits. There is no way of holding a public official accountable under the law for corruption, unless a formal report is made public. Deeper understanding of such matters, which are central to sustaining the democracy, is known as information literacy. It is important for citizens to be able to make informed decisions about all aspects of their personal, professional and political lives. Who do they vote for and why? Can they discern the difference between policy and propaganda? Who should people trust? Journalists have a stake in that, to challenge stereotypes, to challenge a certain type of masculinity and avoid misinformation. Amartyar Sen, in *Development as Freedom* (2000), argues for freedom to "make informed choices to promote collective consciousness to enlarge people's choices". If you're not presented with opportunities, you don't know they exist. We need good information about the country's leaders to promote discussions about leaders, and to acknowledge diverse needs of citizens, which takes us back to the plantation economy. This is related to the same deep social inequalities, and how gender needs intersect with race and class. When our citizens, especially younger people, become aware of the importance of making informed choices, it provides a 'platform for action' and a tool for sustaining democracy.

SPIRITUAL HEALTH

HA: A juggling act is required to balance the values of individual prayer, collective worship, and faith-based organizations in the feminist realm, with following an androcentric 'higher power'. What role does organized religion play in the gender-based violence sphere in Jamaica?

JW: WMW Jamaica has run programmes with churches, for example, through member Dawnette Hinds-Furzer having conversations about relationships, women and men in the church and in the home, and to build confidence. It would be going along very well, we would distribute care packages, then raise the question of power: who in the household makes the decisions, for example? At that moment, the curtain would drop, and we were at the end of the conversation about the business of power and shifting power to women, with the women feeling guilty and that they had let down the church. They would be very polite and say, "We think it's time to bring this conversation to an end." But if women were suffering abuse, at least now they could reach out to us for support.

In keeping women's meetings, this is what they were saying. They will increase their pressure at home, maybe gently, maybe not so gently. Some young women will walk away, or they don't say anything, but they help the mother who is working so hard to support and protect the family. It is very complicated! But I don't believe there is enough pushback from progressive organizations. If you look at the overarching, multi-denominational network of churches, which follow the traditional doctrines, many have affiliations with North America. In the abortion debate, as soon as the pro-choice group – the so-called "murderers' group" – would appear, the US fundamentalist right, represented here in Jamaica, would respond and resist.

The church as an institution is as patriarchal as it ever was, and for some denominations it is even more rigid. Historically, one role of the church is to provide safe spaces for women and children sometimes, for example, in a situation where household poverty is so bad or community engagement is so negative and the church is the only place to go, but it comes with a price: male autocratic leadership and sometimes it's abusive. Sometimes women don't quite know how to disengage from "Jesus Christ the Lord". They're worried about family, that they're going to embarrass them. This matters! The church sometimes promotes the culture of silence in which abusive and discriminatory practices against women, girls, young men, and boys take place.

TOWARDS EQUALITY

HA: Looking ahead, from present-day uncertainties to the imagined future, what opportunities, concerns or dreams do you envisage for yourself as a gender practitioner and for Jamaica as a nation?

JW: People in women's organizations are doing the work, but I do believe there is a space needed for "women in crisis" when the system often doesn't respond as it should. So, there is a network of women who are called upon to do just that – a woman needs to move tonight, she may be dead tomorrow. I support that as a concrete way to give women and their children hope. Since I am of another generation, and the women are usually younger, I really am committed to working with people "on the ground" to identify appropriate solutions.

For Jamaica as a nation, it's hard not to say it is looking bleak. The economic situation is looking very bad; growth is reported as 5.2 per cent, according to the Planning Institute of Jamaica's 2022 GDP growth rate per capita (World Bank 2022).[6] But which part of society is experiencing this? The rich are getting richer; the wealth gap is widening. I honestly believe the average Jamaican family wants to work – they want to earn for themselves. When people cannot survive, after a while, they give up hope. I am mortified by the rates at which qualified people are leaving Jamaica in search of a better life.

Don Anderson national polls are credible and indicate low levels of trust in the leadership of law enforcement. It's a very bad sign to lose public confidence in senior public and political leaders, critical to a democratic internal governance process. What is really happening? Young people are increasingly sensitive about this, and they start to examine their options: What am I likely to be earning? Where can I live? What healthcare can I access? When persons lose faith, they become vulnerable to all kinds of situations.

What gives me hope is that there are women working very hard, keeping their heads above water and getting through school, serving their communities very well – have been doing so for decades. They will not stop but encourage men to join them. I'm hopeful because volunteerism is alive and well. It is central to who we are as women. It is why tourists come, to benefit from our engagement, and natural hospitality. Important also is engaging our new generation of WMW members, asking them what would volunteering look like for you? When you have a group of like-minded women, sometimes of the same age, sometimes across generations, of women with shared values, they find a way to share the work. Organizations alongside WMW Jamaica, such as Eve for Life, Sistren, Women's Resource and Outreach Centre (WROC) and Woman Inc. are doing whatever they can in the moment – working, volunteering, and taking care of women and their children. So, there is hope but there is also deep despair.

CLOSING REMARKS

JW: On reflection, for most of my "activist history", I had the benefit of networking and building relationships of trust and common understandings of challenges facing women in Jamaica and the Caribbean. In the absence of adequate funding, or any funding at all, it was these relationships – organizational and individual – and the resources which came with them, that made it possible for myself and colleagues to do the work of understanding gender-based violence, and importantly, identifying the social/gender inequalities which must be addressed to reduce and prevent it.

Main lessons learned: the danger of continuing to work primarily on a volunteer basis with small project funds; getting the work done, which brought recognition to the organization, and provided important support for women facing gender-based violence, while not paying sufficient attention to the internal governance processes, and financial sustainability of the organization itself.

As the global political economy has fragmented, and well-funded conservative organizations with social media platforms have intensified their anti-democratic and gender-discriminatory campaigns, an environment now exists which is different and more hostile in several ways. Any assumptions I had during the last thirty years, that we – the global movement to end gender inequality – would have reduced VAW, are not holding.

A future free from violence – and the fear of violence – is the dream. It is important that we hold on to this dream, claim it as our reality and continue to work together towards the ultimate goal of a future without gender-based violence.

NOTES

1. For example, FES had a partnership with CAFRA, headquartered in Trinidad and Tobago, with members in most CARICOM countries.
2. The George Wright incident refers to clear footage of a sitting Member of Parliament beating his intimate partner, resulting in allegations in the press.
3. Since this interview was held in September 2022, a partnership with ParlAmericas has resulted in the formation of a Bipartisan Women's Political Caucus, involving women from both parties.
4. In recent years, averaging at about 70 per cent at The UWI, and 50 per cent at U-Tech.
5. The Bureau of Gender Affairs is "mandated to mobilize the Government to address the problems that confront women, given the impact of patriarchy

and sexism. These problems include high rates of unemployment, violence against women in various forms such as spousal abuse, rape, incest and sexual harassment. Its objective is to enable women to recognize their full potential as individuals and to create avenues for their full integration in National Development." The Bureau's three main functions are research and policy development, public education and training, and project planning and monitoring." Retrieved from: https://jis.gov.jm/government/agencies/bureau-gender-affairs/.

6. Retrieved from https://data.worldbank.org/indicator/NY.GDP.PCAP.KD.ZG?locations=JM.

REFERENCES

Andaiye. 2020. *The Point is to Change the World: Selected Writings of Andaiye*. Edited by Alissa Trotz. London: Pluto Press.

Antrobus, Peggy. 1995. "Women in the Caribbean: The Quadruple Burden of Gender, Race, Class and Imperialism." In *Connecting Across Cultures and Continents: Black Women Speak Out on Identity, Race and Development*, edited by A.O. Pala, 53–60. New York: UN Development Fund for Women (UNIFEM).

———. 2004. *The Global Women's Movement: Origins, Issues and Strategies*. London: Zed Books.

Barriteau, E., ed. 2003. *Confronting Power, Theorizing Gender: Interdisciplinary Perspectives in the Caribbean*. Kingston: University of the West Indies Press.

French, Joan. 1988. "Colonial Policy Towards Women After the 1938 Uprising: The Case of Jamaica." *Caribbean Quarterly: Women in West Indian Literature II* 34 (3/4): 38–61.

———. 1994. "Hitting Where It Hurts Most: Jamaican Women's Livelihood in Crisis." In *Mortgaging Women's Lives: Feminist Critiques of Structural Adjustment*, edited by Pamela Sparred, 165–73. London: Zed Books.

Heron, Taitu, and Shakira Maxwell. 2012. Introduction to Special Issue on Women's Reproductive Health and Rights in Select Caribbean Countries. *Social and Economic Studies* 61 (3): 1–5.

Heron, T., D. Toppin, and L. Finikin. 2009. "Sistren in Parliament: Addressing Abortion and Women's Rights through Popular Theatre." *MaComère* 11: 45–60.

Nicholson, H. 2002. "Gender as a Dynamic Concept in the Media." In *Gendered Realities: Essays in Caribbean Feminist Thought*, edited by Patricia Mohammed, 361–81. Kingston: University of the West Indies Press.

Planning Institute of Jamaica and Statistical Institute of Jamaica. 2017; 2019. *The Jamaica Survey of Living Conditions*. Kingston: PIOJ and STATIN.

Sen, A. 1999. *Development as Freedom*. Oxford: Oxford University Press.

Shepherd, Verene. 2012. *Engendering Caribbean History: Cross-Cultural Perspectives*. Kingston: Ian Randle Publishers.

Shepherd, V., B. Brereton, and B. Bailey. 1995. *Engendering History: Caribbean Women in Historical Perspective*. London: Palgrave Macmillan.

Sistren and H. Ford-Smith. 2005. *Lionheart Gal: Life Stories of Jamaica Women*. Kingston: University of the West Indies Press.

Sistren. 1983. *Sistren Theatre Collective: European Tour Programme*, August-October 1983.

Vassell, L. 1998. "Voices of Women in Jamaica, 1865–1945." In *Before and After 1865*, edited by B. Moore and S. Wilmot. Kingston: Ian Randle Publishers.

Wedderburn, J., and P. Phillips. 1988. *Crime and Violence in Jamaica: Causes and Solutions*. Kingston: Department of Government, University of the West Indies

Women's Media Watch Jamaica. 1995. "Articles and Memorandum of Association." Kingston: Women's Media Watch.

WMW Jamaica. 2012. "Certificate of Incorporation, Companies Act." Kingston: WMW Jamaica.

———. 2015. "Constitution." Kingston: WMW Jamaica.

———. 2018. "Ten-Year Strategic Plan." Kingston: WMW Jamaica.

Epilogue

THE HISTORY OF VIOLENCE IN THE CARIBBEAN is the history of gendered violence. There was no "non-gendered" violence since it was meted out to gendered persons by gendered persons under the umbrella of gendered systems of power and oppression. These systems are like a house that has sustained flood damage in sections. It is tempting to live our lives without addressing it, but it is always there, rotting and eating away at the foundation, spreading toxic mould and decay through the fabric of the dwelling; threatening our very lives. As Wilkerson (2020, 15) alludes, "Whatever is lurking will fester whether you choose to look or not. Ignorance is no protection from the consequences of inaction." Don't look away.

It has been the unified goal of contributors to this collection to address the rot and make evident the opaque; for gendered violence is neither modern, accidental nor unchallenged. The Caribbean region has endured a consistent diet of insidious gendered violence, which was (and still is) as much intentional as it has been beneficial to colonial, imperial and neoliberal structures. Such violence was at the same time private, public, personal, beneficial, harmful, transparent, muddy, institutional, interpersonal, past and very present. As DeShong (2024) observes: "What appears as 'contemporary' enactments of violence in the everyday are profoundly connected to prior and future moments; to systems of state formation; and to economic, social, cultural, and political arrangements."

The central tripartite question of inquiry guiding this collection is: how has gendered violence manifested in the Caribbean? What are its roots? And how do we occlude its continuation? It is an investigation as well as a celebration of those who have been advocating for themselves and others, and whose echoes are calling us to continued action. Even as the articles in this collection tackle broad areas of focus, Caribbean countries (primarily the Anglophone Caribbean, with a critical intervention from Suriname) and topics spanning various historic and contemporary time zones, it is a joint commitment to the ethos of violence erosion that acts as the tie that binds. The collection challenges any notion that contemporary schemas of violence are far removed from historic structures that fostered violent interpersonal relations. In the collection there is agreement with the importance of naming discrete yet interwoven manifestations of violence plaguing the region. These typologies include wife beating, spousal abuse, child sexual abuse, domestic violence, family violence and intimate partner violence. In addition to these representations, the collection goes further to address the intersections of identities, such as sex, youth, gender and sexual identity, femininities, masculinities, disabilities, marital status, race and popular culture. Importantly, archival silences, inadequate state responses and representations of violence in historic and contemporary media are also interrogated as sites of resistance and crucibles of violence.

Read together, the pieces in this collection offer critical perspectives on gendered violence as:

- Marred by archival silences and the politics of colonial knowledge (re) production (Shepherd, Ulentin, Neus, Bean and Chang);
- Culturally evolutionary and politically represented in not-so-fictional relics (Brereton, Delaney and Evans, Mohammed, Morgan);
- Critical to the materialization of Caribbean masculinities (Beckles, Sanatan and Joseph);
- Utilized by the powerless to resist attacks on personhood (Andrew, Bean, DeShong, Shepherd);
- Socially created and policed through codes of sexual morality (Hosein, Munnings, Andrew, Shepherd);
- Taken for granted by some men as part of the benefits of patriarchal primogeniture (Dalby, Bean, Sanatan, Beckles);
- Providing fuel to individuals' agitation and Caribbean grassroots organizations (Pitt, Sanatan, Heron, Wedderburn, Vassell, Antrobus, Collymore et al.);
- Especially dangerous when (mis)represented as a single rather than nuanced narrative in popular culture (Tomlinson, Mohammed, Niaah and Plummer);

- Eliciting contradictory responses from community members and formal state accountability (Shepherd, DeShong, Bean, Heron);
- Resulting in (and from) multiple forms of risk (Mortley and Williams, Hosein, Pitt, Munnings).

Critically, the work also reframes historical realities through the lens of gendered violence. It is revealed that the concept of race, invented to serve the plantation economy, did not merely *result* in violence; it *was* violence, and was a fundamental harbinger to the brutality of European modernity. Violence between and among social groupings is explored as more than a legacy of race relations and enslavement, but also a consequence of the malignant neoliberal cells. Much like social reproduction feminists, such as Tithi Bhattacharya (2017), the work locates the historical prevalence and acceptance of inter- and intra-racial gendered violence within the context of neoliberal pressures, capitalist violence, the ranking game (Shepherd 2002), and strain on marginalized people to eke out an existence in a system rigged against their ascent. In this way we develop on Nayak and Suchland's (2006) concept of gender as a site of violence, which is materially and institutionally maintained and produced through systems, beliefs and practices of surveillance, reward, punishment and in connection with other valences of power and difference.

As the collection's aim was to intentionally centre individuals' voices: from victim/survivors to researchers, to scholar/activists, the role of the 'everyday' and 'ordinary' are assessed as important to the maintenance and destabilization of gendered violence. As Deborah Thomas (2016) points out, recurring moments of exceptional violence are produced out of quotidian harms that betray wider patterns of structural violence. Similarly, moments of exceptional struggle in the Caribbean have long time been maintained by the daily agitation against injustice. So, we unapologetically conclude that one of the greatest antidotes to violence has been the agency of persons (mainly grassroots women and their organizations), who refused to accept its inevitability, regardless of its epistemic and haunting nature. These individuals have long understood the truth of gendered violence as being reproduced through interlocking relations of power. Decolonizing these bastions of a toxic colonial inheritance is everyone's business – even those who may benefit from established hierarches of difference.

Organizing around ending gendered violence in the region has been consistent, dynamic and at times contentious. While being free of violence is the aim for all, the paths are fraught with politics of respectability, inconvenient constructions of masculinities and femininities, minimal human and financial resources, and lack of political will to give state support to those who need it most. But the evidence is overwhelming; hard working women and men of the region have mounted the greatest fight against the scourge of gendered violence, and remain undefeated and unwavering in the battle. A handful are represented in this work. It is their legacy which is celebrated through these pages.

In the end, as any good scholar should know, an epilogue often serves to reveal the fates of the characters. After reading an epilogue, one should leave satisfied – never confused. However, rules are often broken by historiography, where satisfaction is relative, and dissatisfaction can be a new tool to dismantle the master's house (see Lorde 2018). Troubling discourses of centuries of gendered violence could hardly ever end in satisfaction. Until the wrongs of the past are met with justice, and structures of violence exist in zero-tolerance environments, which starve it of nutrients, causing it to wither and die, we remain dissatisfied. This is why this collection could not exclude the issue of reparations for colonial and post-colonial harm, which very much centres the experiences of women. The collection has demonstrated the historical roots of gender-based violence and the violence of chattel enslavement, which black women had to endure, although not uncomplainingly. Those experiences and their lingering legacies are central to the demand for reparatory justice. This collection will certainly be required reading for all those involved in the campaign.

REFERENCES

Bhattacharya, Tithi. 2017. *Social Reproduction Theory: Remapping Class, Recentering Oppression.* Edited by Tithi Bhattacharya. London: Pluto Press.

DeShong, Halimah. 2024a. "Violent Continuities: Revisiting Race, Gender and Sexuality in the Caribbean." Institute for Gender and Development Studies, University of the West Indies' 30th Annual Caribbean Women Catalyst for Change Lecture.

———. 2024b. "Gendered Violence and Gender as a Site of Violence Reflections from the Caribbean." *Frontiers* 45 (2): 79–101.

Lorde, Audre. 2018. *The Master's Tools Will Never Dismantle the Master's House.* London: Penguin Books.

Nayak, Meghana, and Jennifer Suchland. 2006. "Gender Violence and Hegemonic Projects." *International Feminist Journal of Politics* 8 (4): 467–85.

Shepherd, Verene. 2020. "The Ranking Game: Discourses of Belonging in Jamaican History." Inaugural professorial lecture, University of the West Indies, Mona.

Thomas, Deborah. 2016. "Time and the Otherwise: Plantations, Garrisons and Being Human in the Caribbean." *Anthropological Theory* 16 (2–3): 177–200.

Wilkerson, Isabel. 2020. *Caste: The Origin of Our Discontents.* New York: Random House.

Contributors

EDITORS

DALEA BEAN is the head of the Institute for Gender and Development Studies (IGDS) at The University of the West Indies, Mona Campus, Jamaica. She has researched extensively in the areas of women and gender in Caribbean history, including two books, and more than twenty book chapters and journal articles. Her first single-authored book, *Jamaican Women and the World Wars: On the Front Lines of Change,* was published in 2017 by Palgrave Macmillan. She was also commissioned by the RJR Gleaner Communications Group to write *Jamaican Women of Distinction: Holding up Half the Sky* in 2020.

VERENE A. SHEPHERD is Professor Emerita of History and Gender Studies at The University of the West Indies, Mona Campus. A social historian, she is also the immediate past director of the Centre for Reparation Research at The University of the West Indies, and a former chair of the United Nation's Committee on the Elimination of Racial Discrimination. She holds BA and MPhil degrees in history from The University of the West Indies, Mona Campus; and a PhD from the University of Cambridge. She researches Jamaican economic history, slavery, reparations and gender discourses in Caribbean history. She is the author of seven books, including *Livestock, Sugar and Slavery: Contested Terrain in Colonial Jamaica* and *I Want to Disturb My Neighbour: Lectures on Slavery, Emancipation and Post-Colonial Jamaica.* Among her awards are the Order of Distinction, Commander Class, from the government of Jamaica; the Africana Studies Distinguished Award from Florida International University and the 2017 UWI Vice Chancellor's Award for Excellence in Public Service.

CONTRIBUTORS

JENNAN PAIGE ANDREW is a queer Caribbean feminist from Trinidad and Tobago with deep interest in sustainable social change that is guided by intersectional and participatory practices. She is a Programs Co-Manager at FRIDA| The Young Feminist Fund, where she co-creates feminist realities and disrupts traditional philanthropy daily, and a co-founder of WE-Change, a LBQ women's rights organization based in Jamaica.

PEGGY ANTROBUS, third recipient of the CARICOM Triennial Award in 1990, has a true Caribbean cross-national identity. She was born in Grenada, acquired citizenship of St Vincent and the Grenadines, and now resides in Barbados. Her vast and much recognized work and contributions in the area of women's affairs has earned her respect, admiration and acclaim both regionally and internationally. She served as Chief Community Development Officer for St Vincent (1969–1970); Director, Women's Bureau, Office of the Prime Minister, Jamaica (1974–1977); Secretary, Caribbean Coordinating Committee on Women's Affairs (1977–78); Tutor-Coordinator, Women and Development Unit (WAND), UWI at Cave Hill, Barbados (1978–1995).

HELEN ATKINS is a graduate of the Institute for Gender and Development Studies, with an MSc in Gender and Development Studies and a law degree from the University of Cambridge. She has committed her life to women's rights and advocacy for numerous human rights issues. She focuses on applied intersectionality to sexual violence responses. Active in Jamaica and the United Kingdom, she advocates for a holistic or 'whole systems' approach to prevention.

HILARY McD. BECKLES is Professor of History and Vice-Chancellor of The University of the West Indies. He has published widely on a range of subjects, including Caribbean slavery, women and gender, and cricket. He has also co-edited, with Verene Shepherd, a series of history textbooks for secondary school students. His most recent works include *The First Black Slave Society: Britain's Barbarity Time in Barbados, 1636–1876, published in 2016 and How Britain Underdeveloped the Caribbean: A Reparation Response to Europe's Legacy of Plunder and Poverty*, published in 2021.

BRIDGET BRERETON is Professor Emerita of History at The University of the West Indies, St Augustine Campus, Trinidad. She is the author of several books on the history of the Caribbean and of Trinidad, including standard works such as *Race Relations in Colonial Trinidad, 1870–1900* and *A History of Modern Trinidad, 1783–1962*. She is the editor or co-editor of several more (including Volume V of the *UNESCO General History of the Caribbean*), and the author of many journal articles, book chapters and book reviews. She is a former head of the Department of History, Deputy Principal, and Interim Principal of the St Augustine Campus of The UWI.

VICTORIA V. CHANG holds a BA, MA and PhD in Literatures in English (2022) from The University of the West Indies, St Augustine Campus, Trinidad. Her core research interests pertain to issues of gender, identity, culture and ethnicity, as well as nationhood. She is a three-time scholarship recipient, having been awarded a national scholarship from the government of the Republic of Trinidad and Tobago, an Erasmus Plus scholarship (funded by the European Union), and was one of two Caribbean scholarship recipients of the "Other Universals" project, supported by the Andrew W. Mellon Foundation in the United States.

SUSAN COLLYMORE originally became involved with Red Thread through her children after they attended literacy classes in the afternoons. Through this introduction, Collymore began to cook for the literacy classes and to attend meetings. Today, her role has grown to include working with women and children who have experienced domestic violence. Additionally, she acts as a support for victims of domestic abuse in court proceedings.

JONATHAN DALBY is a historian and former head of the Department of History, UWI, Mona Campus. He has published principally on crime and criminality in the Caribbean, the history of France and the social history of the French countryside in the eighteenth and nineteenth centuries.

KELSI DELANEY is a postdoctoral research associate and teaching fellow at the University of Leicester. Her research areas are Caribbean literature and poetry. She co-edited *Caribbean Journeys* (University of Leicester Centre for New Writing, 2018), a collection of biographical travel narratives by Nottingham-based Caribbean elders. Her manuscript, *Form in Contemporary*

Anglophone Caribbean Poetry, is near completion, and a proposal has been requested by Cambridge University Press.

HALIMAH A.F. DESHONG is the University Director of the Institute for Gender and Development Studies (IGDS) and former head of the IGDS Nita Barrow Unit at The University of the West Indies, Cave Hill, Barbados. She is an experienced feminist researcher, published in the areas of gendered and gender-based violence, feminist methodologies, anti-colonial feminisms, qualitative interviewing and analysis. She is the co-editor (with Professor Kamala Kempadoo) of *Methodologies in Caribbean Research on Gender and Sexuality* (2020). Dr DeShong served as an ambassador and Second Deputy Permanent Representative at the Permanent Mission of the government of St Vincent and the Grenadines to the United Nations.

KAREN dE SOUZA is a women's and child's rights activist, primarily advocating and supporting victims of violence, and educating on issues such as poverty, trafficking and domestic violence. Beginning her career in political activism in the late 1970s, de Souza co-founded Red Thread alongside women in the Working People's Alliance (WPA). In 1993, she left the WPA and became a full-time coordinator for Red Thread. Since joining, she has made significant contributions, including drafting laws to protect against trafficking and violence, promoting self-advocacy, and establishing a domestic violence survivors' group.

LUCY EVANS is an Associate Professor in Postcolonial Literature at the University of Leicester. Her research specialty is contemporary Caribbean literature, with current research focusing on crime fiction and representations of crime in the Anglophone Caribbean, and on gender-based violence, arts activism, and Caribbean literary cultures. Dr Evans has published widely on contemporary Caribbean literature; this includes a number of journal articles and book chapters as well as her monograph, *Communities in Contemporary Anglophone Caribbean Short Stories* (Liverpool University Press, Postcolonialism Across the Disciplines Series, 2014; paperback 2021).

GABRIELLE JAMELA HOSEIN has a BA in Political Science from the University of Toronto, an MPhil in Gender and Development Studies from The University of the West Indies, and a PhD in Anthropology from University College London. She is a senior lecturer and former head of the Institute for Gender and Development Studies at The UWI, St Augustine Campus, and has been involved in Caribbean feminist movement-building for twenty-five years.

O'NEIL JOSEPH is a PhD candidate in history at The University of the West Indies, St Augustine Campus. His research and writing explore the social and cultural histories of Caribbean societies, issues of identity, and the intersections of gender and sexuality. His work has appeared in *Women's History Review* and *Tout Moun: Caribbean Journal of Cultural Studies.*

HALIMA KHAN has been with Red Thread since the beginning. In the early 1990s, Khan used Red Thread to escape her home at a time when she was a victim of verbal and physical abuse from family members. Khan saw Red Thread as a community centre and a safe space. Today, Khan looks to provide that same comfort for other women and children struggling with domestic violence.

JOY MARCUS has been a member of Red Thread since she was sixteen years old. Marcus' mother, a member of Red Thread, advised her to go to a meeting called "A Woman's Place". Though Marcus was reluctant at first, she was amazed at how women in the workshop were able to address the issues she had seen within her community. Marcus also finds it important to highlight the uniqueness of Red Thread as an organization that speaks for grassroots women, while addressing intersectional issues such as labour, violence and politics in Guyana.

PATRICIA MOHAMMED, Professor Emerita at The University of West Indies, is a key thinker in Caribbean feminist theory and has been involved in feminist activism in the region since 1979. Her scholarly contributions include more than a hundred publications in journals, edited books and media, including self-authored books *Imaging the Caribbean: Culture and Visual Translation* (Macmillan Education, 2010), and *Gender Negotiations Among Indians in Trinidad: 1917–1947* (Palgrave, 2001). Since 1986, Professor Mohammed has also been involved in the production of films and other media on gender and cultural issues. In 2019, she was awarded the Public Service Medal of Merit (gold) for outstanding and meritorious service to Trinidad and Tobago in the development of women by the president.

PAULA MORGAN is a retired professor from The University of the West Indies, who served in several capacities, including teaching, curriculum development, programme coordination, public service, research and university administration. In 2012, she became a Coordinator in Literatures in English until 2015, and thereafter headed the Institute for Gender and Development Studies at the St Augustine Campus from 2016 to 2017. Her publications span three decades and range from pedagogical approaches to Caribbean literature and culture, societal trauma and gender violence, and representations of disability in Caribbean discourse.

NATASHA KAY MORTLEY has a PhD in Migration and Diaspora Studies, an MPhil in Sociology of Development and BSc in Sociology. She is a Senior Research Fellow at the Institute for Gender and Development Studies, Regional Coordinating Office at The UWI in Jamaica. Her scholarship has focused on integrating a gender perspective in Caribbean social development and policy issues, and her areas of research work include migration and diaspora studies; diaspora tourism; sports tourism; gender and leadership; gender and entrepreneurship; gender and climate change; Caribbean masculinities and gender-based violence.

JENNIFER MUNNINGS is currently pursuing an LLM in International Law and Global Governance at the University of Leeds in the United Kingdom. Munnings is a social science researcher from The Bahamas with interests in sustainability, gender equality and race relations.

HILDE NEUS is a teacher of Literature and Gender, and women's history, currently employed by the Research Institute for Social Sciences (IMWO) at the Suriname Anton de Kom University. In 2003, her monograph, *Susanna du Plessis* – on a cruel plantation mistress – was published and she co-authored several other volumes. Currently, she is studying free women (white and coloured) in eighteenth-century Suriname.

KENDRA-ANN PITT is a lecturer in the Social Work Unit at The University of the West Indies, St Augustine. She holds a Master of Social Work degree and a PhD in Education and Women and Gender Studies. Her research and teaching focus on the overlaps between social work, transnational feminist, critical race, critical disability and Caribbean studies. She is currently engaged in research examining the experiences of women with disabilities facing gender-based violence in Guyana.

NICOLE PLUMMER is a lecturer and Undergraduate Coordinator with the Institute of Caribbean Studies at The University of the West Indies, Mona Campus. Her doctoral thesis examined the development of a business culture in early Jamaica. Other areas of research interest include: Caribbean stories, myths, folk philosophy and folklore, Caribbean business culture and economic development, Caribbean history and cultures of survival, and language and representation in popular Jamaican Music.

VANESSA ROSS has been a member of Red Thread for twenty-seven years, after she found herself wanting to upgrade her skills. Ross sees the importance of Red Thread as a place where one can go to find community – a place where anybody can feel welcome, no matter what race or social situation. Ross saw the benefits of Red Thread as a place that offers greater opportunities and support, both financially and otherwise. For the future of Red Thread, Ross hopes that members are able to have a larger involvement.

AMÍLCAR PETER SANATAN is Deputy Director of the Gender and Child Affairs Division in the Office of the Prime Minister of Trinidad and Tobago. An artist, academic and activist, he is a PhD candidate in cultural studies at The University of West Indies, St Augustine Campus. His research interests include men and masculinities in the Caribbean, youth and student development, and cultural geography.

SONJAH STANLEY NIAAH is a Jamaican Professor of cultural studies and music scholar, author and international speaker. Her work focuses on Jamaican popular culture and its consumption in a global context. She is the author of acclaimed books and edited collections on Jamaican dancehall, old and new black Atlantic performance geographies, as well as popular culture and the sacred. She is a former director of the Institute of Caribbean Studies at The University of the West Indies, Mona Campus, where she is based.

LISA TOMLINSON is the Head of the Department of Literatures in English and Senior Lecturer in Literary and Cultural Studies at the Institute of Caribbean Studies, The University of the West Indies, Mona Campus. She holds a PhD in Comparative Perspective and Culture from York University and she is the author of *The African-Jamaican Aesthetic: Cultural Retention and Transformation Across Borders.*

ALISSA TROTZ is a Professor of Caribbean Studies at New College and the Director of Women and Gender Studies at the University of Toronto. She is affiliate faculty at the Dame Nita Barrow Institute of Gender and Development Studies at The University of The West Indies, Cave Hill, Barbados. Her recent publications include: *The Point is to Change the World: Selected Writings by Andaiye* (2020), which was published in Portuguese by Edition Funilaria in Brazil (2022).

ANNE ULENTIN received her PhD in history from Louisiana State University. She is an Assistant Professor of History in the School of Social Sciences at the University of The Bahamas and teaches Atlantic World History and Caribbean History. Her current research examines incarceration and the intersectionality of race, ethnicity, class, and gender in The Bahamas. Her most recent publication is titled "'The Scale of Punishment has been Framed Specially for the Black Man:' Imprisonment, Race, and Punishment in the Colonial Bahamas," in *The Journal of Caribbean History* (June 2021).

LINNETTE VASSELL Historian, activist and women's rights champion, Vassell was a founding member of the Committee of Women for Progress (CWP) and the Women's Research and Outreach Centre (WROC), an organization that has served hundreds of women from inner-city Jamaica. Vassell is currently Advocacy Specialist of Maternal, Neonatal and Infant Health at the Women's Resource Outreach Centre. Recently, the Caribbean Community of Retired Persons (CCRP) honoured Vassell with the 2019 Living Legacy Award.

WINTRESS WHITE has been an active member of Red Thread since 1992. As a survivor of domestic abuse, White stumbled upon Red Thread when she mistakenly attended one of their workshops. This workshop not only brought to light her abusive relationship, but also provided her with a purpose that she had not found previously. After benefitting from the support provided by Red Thread, White decided to dedicate her life and time to the same organization that helped her. She provides training on domestic/sexual violence through workshops and community meetings across the country.

CAROL WATSON WILLIAMS is a gender specialist, social policy analyst and researcher, with special interest in applying rights-based approach to social policy issues. She has worked for more than two decades on a range of social policy issues, and has a special interest in how effective policies and programmes, grounded in data, can drive improvements the lives of citizens, particularly women. She authored the *Women's Health Survey 2016* Jamaica's first report on the prevalence of violence against women and girls.

JUDITH WEDDERBURN is the recently retired director of Friedrich Ebert Stiftung (FES) Jamaica and the Eastern Caribbean, and for more than 30 years, has been an advocate in the field of gender and development in Jamaica and the wider Caribbean. Her main research areas and related publications focus on the impact of the globalization process on Jamaica's foreign policy; gender, trade liberalization and the CARICOM Single Market and Economy (CSME); gender and the CARIFORUM-EU Economic Partnership Agreement; and gender and poverty.

Index

n after the page number indicates a note; *t* after the page number indicates a table

www.ingramcontent.com/pod-product-compliance
Lightning Source LLC
Chambersburg PA
CBHW050622280326
41932CB00015B/2488

* 9 7 8 9 7 6 6 5 8 0 2 8 5 *